Russian Autocrats from Ivan the Great to the Fall of the Romanov Dynasty:

An Annotated Bibliography of English Language Sources to 1985

by
DAVID R. EGAN
and
MELINDA A. EGAN

The Scarecrow Press, Inc.
Metuchen, N.J., & London
1987

Library of Congress Cataloging-in-Publication Data

Egan, David R., 1943–
    Russian autocrats from Ivan the Great to the
fall of the Romanov dynasty.

    Includes index.
    1. Soviet Union--History--1533-1613--Bibliography.
2. Soviet Union--History--1613-1689--Bibliography.
3. Soviet Union--History--1689-1800--Bibliography.
4. Soviet Union--History--19th century--Bibliography.
5. Soviet Union--Kings and rulers--Biography--
Bibliography. I. Egan, Melinda A. II. Title.
Z2506.E35 1987 ⌊DK100⌋ 016.947'00992   86-26003
ISBN 0-8108-1958-9

CONTENTS

v

INTRODUCTION

Purpose

The primary goal of this bibliography is to provide a comprehensive list of English language sources written about Russian monarchs and/or their policies. By aiming for comprehensiveness rather than restricting coverage to scholarly works, it has been necessary, naturally, to include a considerable number of popular and journalistic writings. While such sources are generally of limited value to scholars and tend to mislead non-specialists, they have been included because they have played a significant role in shaping Western opinion in regard to Russia and its rulers, and, in some instances, have been responsible for the creation and perpetuation of widely subscribed to generalizations, stereotypic images, and myths. In a sense, then, the fact that many of these sources contain inaccuracies, exaggerations, and oversimplifications, and are sometimes guilty of tendentiousness, does not lessen but rather constitutes their historical value.

Scope

The sources listed include monographs, broad studies, chapters from general works, essays, articles, reminiscences, memoirs, letters, and doctoral dissertations. Generally, these works are either centered upon or contain a titled section dealing with, at least in part, the life and/or reign of one of the rulers of Russia during the 1462-1917 period. However, in a number of instances, sources unique or particularly insightful but containing only scattered references to one or more monarchs have also been included.

A selection of reviews has been provided for recommended books (marked by asterisks) devoted to individual sovereigns.

The majority of sources listed are American and British in origin, but a significant number consists of translations from French, German, and, especially, Russian language works. Therefore, "English language sources" should not be construed as a geographic restriction but a linguistic one since this bibliography is very much an international one.

A number of sources published since 1984 have been included (without annotations), but no claim to comprehensiveness is made with regard to such recent publications.

Works of fiction have been excluded with the exception of those considered to be classics.

Format

The twenty-six Russian rulers listed have been arranged chronologically. Successive rulers not widely studied appear together in a single section, whereas more studied monarchs have been listed individually with entries grouped beneath broad subject headings. Throughout, individual entries have been listed by author when there is one and by title otherwise.

To assist the user in locating entries dealing with specific aspects of a ruler's life or reign, a detailed subject index (arranged alphabetically by monarch rather than chronologically) has been appended. However, works dealing with all or most of Russia's rulers as well as general histories of Russia have not been indexed but appear as a group in an introductory section. The more highly regarded works in this group have been marked with asterisks.

When more than three entries have been listed from an anthology or a general study other than a history of Russia or its sovereigns, publication information and editors' names have been omitted and the works' titles reduced to a simple abbreviation. For example, following the author and title of an entry taken from Marc Raeff's anthology, Catherine the Great: A Profile (New York: Hill and Wang, 1972), there would appear only CGP (anthology) and the page range of the essay. The abbreviated titles along with the names of editors and publication data appear in an introductory section.

For the user's convenience, Library of Congress call numbers have been provided whenever possible.

Annotations

The annotations are descriptive rather than critical and, therefore, merely indicate scope and emphasis for noninterpretive works and thesis and evidence for interpretive ones. Judgments on the accuracy or degree of validity of individual sources are beyond the scope of this bibliography, but asterisks have been provided for sources that focus upon one or more monarchs and are comprehensive, scholarly, or unique in some way.

The annotations are designed to be intelligible to the nonspecialist; hence, few assumptions have been made on the user's command
of Russian history.

Spelling

Authors' names have been spelled the same way as they appear
on the title pages of their respective publications; consequently, for
some entries, there are different spellings for the same name. Spell-
ing has been standardized in the annotations and author/subject
indexes. Some liberty has been taken with the Library of Congress'
transliteration system to render Russian names more palatable for
the nonspecialist, most notably with respect to soft signs and name
endings; for example, Novosiltsev rather than Novosil'tsev, Yurievsky
not Yurievskaya, and Kliuchevsky not Kliuchevskii.

AHSGR	American Historical Society of Germans from Russia (E184.R85.A53a)
ASEER	American Slavic and East European Review (D377.A1A5)
A Lit ASH	Acta Litteraria Academiae Scientiarum Hungaricae (PN1.A3)
Aberdeen Un R	Aberdeen University Review (LH5.A3)
Academy	Academy
Acta Balt-Slav	Acta Baltico-Slavica (DK511.B25A612)
Am Book Coll	American Book Collector (Z990.A5)
Am Cath Q	American Catholic Quarterly (Ap2.A332)
Am Eclectic	American Eclectic (AP2.M89)
Am Heritage	American Heritage (E171.A43)
Am Hist R	American Historical Review (E171.A57)
Am J Archeol	American Journal of Archeology (CC1.A6)
Am Merc	American Mercury (AP2.A37)
Am Pol Sci R	American Political Science Review (JA1.A6)
Am R	American Review (AP2.A426)
America	America (BX801.A5)
Americâs	Americâs (E11.A4)
Ang-Rus Lit Soc Proc	Anglo-Russian Literary Society Proceedings
Ann Am Acad	Annals of the American Academy of Political and Social Sciences (H1.A4)
Ann Med Hist	Annals of Medical History (R11.A85)
Ann Ord Souv Mil M	Annales de l'Ordre Souverain Militaire de Malte
Ann Ukr Soc Arts Sci	Annals of the Ukrainian Society of Arts and Sciences
Antiq Coll	Antique Collector (NK1125.A28)
Antiq J	Antiques Journal (NK1125.A143)

xi

Antiq W	Antiques World (NK1125.A314)
Apollo	Apollo (N1.A255)
Architect	Architect (NA1.A4)
Arena	Arena (AP2.A6)
Ariz Q	Arizona Quarterly (AP2.A7265)
Army Q Def J	Army Quarterly Defense Journal
Art N	Art News (N1.A6)
Artibus Asiae	Artibus Asiae (N8.A75)
Asiatic R	Asiatic Review (DS1.A7)
Athen	Atheneum (Ap4.A5)
Athen (Lon)	Athenaeum (London)
Atlan M	Atlantic Monthly (Ap2.A8)
Aus J Pol Hist	Australian Journal of Politics and History (DU80.A945)
Aust Hist Y	Austrian History Yearbook (DB1.A772)
Belgravia	Belgravia (AP4.B412)
Bellman	Bellman (AP2.B43)
Bentley's M	Bentley's Miscellany (AP4.B53)
Bks Abroad	Books Abroad (Z1007.B717)
Blackwood's M	Blackwood's Magazine (AP4.B6)
Bookman	Bookman (Z1007.B713)
Brit Q R	British Quarterly Review (AP4.B8B813)
Bull Br Mus	Bulletin of the British Museum of Natural History (QH15.B73)
Burlington M	Burlington Magazine (N1.B95)
Cahiers du monde	Cahiers du monde russe et soviétique (DK1.C2)
Calif Slav S	California Slavic Studies (DK4.C33)
Camb Hist J	Cambridge Historical Journal (D1.C25)
Can Am Slav S	Canadian-American Slavic Studies (DK1.C23)
Can F	Canadian Forum (AP2.C125)
Can Hist R	Canadian Historical Review (F1001.C27)
Can J Hist	Canadian Journal of History (D1.C27)
Can M	Canadian Magazine (AP5.C2)
Can Slav S	Canadian Slavic Studies (D377.A1C34)
Can Slavonic P	Canadian Slavonic Papers (PG6.C3)
Cassell's M	Cassell's Magazine (AP4.C26)
Cath Hist R	Catholic Historical Review (BX1404.C3)
Cath W	Catholic World (AP2.C3)
Cent Lit M	Central Literary Magazine
Century	Century (AP2.C387)

Chambers' Edinb J	Chambers' Edinburgh Journal (AP4.C45)
Chaut	Chautauquan (AP2.C48)
Choice	Choice (Z1035.C5)
Christ Cent	Christian Century (BR1.C45)
Church Hist	Church History (BR140.A45)
Church Q R	Church Quarterly Review (BR1.C685)
Cinema J	Cinema Journal (PN1993.C55)
Citizen	Citizen (PR3404.C52)
Colburn's	see New Mo M
Commonweal	Commonweal (AP2.C6897)
Comp Lit S	Comparative Literary Studies (PN851.C596)
Connois	Connoisseur (N1.C75)
Contemp R	Contemporary Review (AP4.C7)
Cornhill	Cornhill (AP2.C765)
Coronet	Coronet (AP2.C767)
Cosmopol	Cosmopolitan (AP2.C8)
Country Life	Country Life (Britain)
Cur Hist	Current History (D410.C82)
Cur Lit	Current Literature (AP2.C95)
Cur Opin	Current Opinion (HM261.C86)
Daedalus	Daedalus (Q11.B7)
Dial	Dial (AP2.D471)
Diplo Hist	Diplomatic History (E183.7.D48)
Dublin R	Dublin Review (AP4.D8)
Dublin U M	Dublin University Magazine (AP4.D83)
Durham Univ J	Durham University Journal (AS121.D8)
E Eur	East Europe (DR1.N363)
E Eur Q	East European Quarterly (D1.E33)
Eclectic M	Eclectic Magazine (AP2.E2)
Eclectic R	Eclectic Review (AP4.E17)
Economist	Economist (HG11.E2)
Edinb R	Edinburgh Review (AP4.E3)
Eng Hist R	English Historical Review (DA20.E58)
Eng Ill M	English Illustrated Magazine (AP4.E5)
Enl E	Enlightenment Essays (B802.E59)
Etudes Slav	Etudes slaves et est europeenes (DK1.E8)
Eur St R	European Studies R (D1.E76)
Everybody's M	Everybody's Magazine
Fate	Fate (BF1995.F2)

For Aff	Foreign Affairs (D410.F6)
Forsch Ost Ges	Forschungen zur Osteuropäischen Geschichte (DR1.B45)
Fortn R	Fortnightly Review (AP4.F7)
Fortune	Fortune (HF5001.F7)
Forum	Forum (AP2.F8)
Forum Mod Lang St	Forum for Modern Language Studies (PB1.F63)
Fr Hist S	French Historical Studies (DC1.F69)
Fraser's M	Fraser's Magazine (AP4.F8)

Gateway H	Gateway Heritage (F466.G34)
Gaz Beaux Arts	Gazette Beaux Arts (N2.G3)
Gent M	Gentleman's Magazine (AP4.G3)
Geog M	Geographical Magazine (G1.G34)
Germanic R	Germanic Review (PD1.G4)
Germano-Slavica	Germano-Slavica (PT123.S586647)
Good H	Good Housekeeping (TX1.G7)
Good Words	Good Words (AP4.G6)
Grps Use Psych Hist N	Groups for the Use of Psychology in History Newsletter
Gunton's M	Gunton's Magazine (H1.G9)

Harper's B	Harper's Bazaar (TT500.H3)
Harper's M	Harper's Magazine (AP2.H3)
Harper's W	Harper's Weekly (AP2.H32)
Harv M	Harvard Magazine (LH1.H3A5)
Harv Ukr S	Harvard Ukrainian Studies (DK508.A2H33)
Heritage R	Heritage Review (F645.R85N67)
Historian	Historian (D1.H22)
Hist Bull	Historical Bulletin (D1.H28)
Hist J	Historical Journal (D1.H33)
History	History (D1.H815)
Hist Ed Q	History of Education Quarterly (L11.H67)
Hist Today	History Today (D1.H818)
Horizon	Horizon (AP2.H788)
House W	Household Words (AP4.H9)

Il Pol	Il Politico (JA18.P65)
Independent	Independent (AP2.I53)
Indiana Soc S Q	Indiana Social Studies Quarterly
Inst Hist Res B	Institute of Historical Research Bulletin
Int Aff	International Affairs (JX1.I53)
Int J Slav Ling Poetics	International Journal of Slavic Linguistics and Poetics (PG1.I5)

Int R	International Review (AP2.I78)
Irish Hist S	Irish Historical Studies (DA900.I63)
Isis	Isis (JF847.I8)

Jahr Amer	Jahrbüch für Amerikastudien (E1691.J33)
Jahr Ges Ost	Jahrbücher für Geschichte Osteuropas (D1.J3)
James Joyce Q	James Joyce Quarterly (PR6019.09.Z64)
Jew Soc S	Jewish Social Studies (DS101.J555)
J Am Mus S	Journal of the American Musicological Society (ML27.U5.A8336)
J Baltic S	Journal of Baltic Studies (DK511.B25B78)
J Cent Eur Aff	Journal of Central European Affairs (D1.J57)
J Ch State	Journal of Church and State (BV630.A1A6)
J Eco Hist	Journal of Economic History (HC10.J64)
J Eur S	Journal of European Studies (D1.J58)
J Friends Hist S	Journal of Friends Historical Society (BX7676.A1F6)
J Hist Ideas	Journal of the History of Ideas (B1.J75)
J Hist Med Pub H	Journal of the History of Medicine and Public Health (R131.A1J6)
J Lib Hist	Journal of Library History (Z671.J67)
J Mod Hist	Journal of Modern History (D1.J6)
J Mos Patr	Journal of the Moscow Patriarchate
J Peasant S	Journal of Peasant Studies (HD1513.A3J68)
J Relig Hist	Journal of Religious History (BR140.J65)
J Soc Hist	Journal of Social History (HN1.J6)
J Urb Hist	Journal of Urban History (HT111.J68)
Judaism	Judaism (BM1.J8)

Kent For Lang Q	Kentucky Foreign Languages Quarterly (P1.K4)
Kritika	Kritika (Z2506.K7)

Ladies H J	Ladies Home Journal (AP2.L135)
Laurentian Univ R	Laurentian University Review (AS42.L38A28)
Leisure H	Leisure Hour (AP4.L4)

Lib J	Library Journal (Z671.L7)
Life	Life (AP101.L6)
Liguorian	Liguorian (BX4020.A1L5)
Lippin M	Lippincott's Magazine (AP2.L55)
Listener	Listener (AP4.L773)
Lit D	Literary Digest (AP2.L58)
Lit R	Literary Review (AP2.L6377)
Liv Age	Living Age (AP2.L65)
Lond M	London Magazine (AP4.L515)
Lond Q	London Quarterly (AP4.L53)

M Valley Hist R	Mississippi Valley Historical Review (F351.M69)
McClure's M	McClure's Magazine (AP2.M2)
Mankind	Mankind (D1.M3)
Mariner's M	Mariner's Mirror (VK1.M4)
Med Hist	Medical History (R131.A1M4)
Melbourne Slav S	Melbourne Slavic Studies (PG1.M43)
Mennon L	Mennonite Life (BX8101.M39)
Mentor	Mentor (AP2.M417)
Met Mus	Metropolitan Museum of Art Bulletin
Mich Acad	Michigan Academician (AS30.M478)
Mid-Am	Mid-America (BX1415.I3M5)
Mil Aff	Military Affairs (E181.M55)
Mod Age	Modern Age (AP2.M628)
Mod Lang S	Modern Language Studies (PB1.M66)
Mod Lang Q	Modern Language Quarterly PB1.M642)
Munsey's M	Munsey's Magazine (E701.M96)
Mus For Lit	Museum of Foreign Literature (AP2.M89)

N Z Slavonic J	New Zealand Slavonic Journal (PG1.N47)
Nat R	National Review (AP2.N3545)
Nation	Nation (AP2.N2)
New Eng M	New England Magazine (AP2.N4)
New Eur	New Europe (D410.N4)
New Mo M	New Monthly Magazine (AP4.N5)
New Quar R	New Quarterly Review (AP4.N6)
New R	New Review (AP4.N622)
New R E Eur Hist	New Review of East European History (DK508.A2N4)
New Rep	New Republic (AP2.N624)
New Soc	New Society (H1.N47)
New W R	New World Review (DK266.A2N46)
New Yorker	New Yorker (AP2.N6763)
Newsweek	Newsweek (AP2.N6772)
Nineteenth C	Nineteenth Century (AP4.N7)

See note on page xxv.

CCRC   Dumas, Alexandre. Celebrated Crimes of the Russian
         Court. Boston: L. C. Page and Company, 1905,
         321pp. DK37.6.D9

CG   Oliva, L. Jay, ed. Catherine the Great, Empress of
         Russia. Englewood-Cliffs, N.J.: Prentice-Hall,
         1971, 184pp. DK170.O38

CGP   *Raeff, Marc, ed. Catherine the Great: A Profile.
         New York: Hill and Wang, 1972, 231pp., bib.
         323-25. DK170.D35

CP   Tarsaidzé, Alexandre. Czars and Presidents. The
         Story of a Forgotten Friendship. New York:
         McDowell and Oblensky Inc., 1958, 383pp., bib.
         356-69. E183.R9T3

CRFP   *Jelavich, Barbara. A Century of Russian Foreign
         Policy 1814-1914. Philadelphia: J. B. Lippincott,
         1964, 308pp. DK189.J4

DAC   Treue, Wilhelm. Doctor at Court. Francis Fawcett,
         Trans. New York: Roy Publications, 1958,
         206pp. R133.T683

DRH   *Golder, Frank A., ed. Documents of Russian His-
         tory, 1914-1917. New York: Century Company,
         1927, 663pp. DK251.G6

DRLC   Wortman, Richard S. The Development of a Russian
         Legal Consciousness. Chicago: University of Chi-
         cago Press, 1976, 345pp., bib. 323-36. KR91.W6

EAR   Leary, Daniel Bell. Education and Autocracy in Russia

from the Origins to the Bolshevikii. Buffalo:
University of Buffalo Studies, 1919, 127pp., bib.
124-27. AS36.B95

ECR   *Garrard, J. G., ed. The Eighteenth Century in
             Russia. Oxford: The Clarendon Press, 1973,
             356pp. DK127.G33

FDRRT   *Howe, Sonia E., ed. The False Dmitri. A Russian
             Romance and Tragedy. Described by British Eye-
             Witnesses, 1604-1612. New York: Frederick A.
             Stokes Company, 1967, 289pp. DK112.H85

FEER   Papmehl, K. A. Freedom of Expression in Eighteenth
             Century Russia. The Hague: M. Nijhoff, 1971,
             166p., bib. 152-61. JC599.R9P36

FIR   Ransel, David L., ed. The Family in Imperial Russia.
             New Lines of Historical Research. Urbana: Uni-
             versity of Illinois Press, 1978, 342pp., bib. 305-
             32. HQ637.F35

GBR   *Cross, A. G., ed. Great Britain and Russia in the
             Eighteenth Century: Contacts and Comparisons.
             Newtonville, Mass.: Oriental Research Partners,
             1979, 323pp. DK67.5.G7G73

HECRL   Brown, William Edward. A History of 18th Century
             Russian Literature. Ann Arbor, Mich.: Ardis,
             1980, 659pp., bib. 621-40. PG3007.B7

HJRP   Dubnow, Simon. History of the Jews of Russia and
             Poland, 3 Vols. Philadelphia: Jewish Publication
             Society of America, 1916. DS135.R9D78 1975

HREP   *Hans, Nicholas. History of Russian Educational
             Policy (1701-1917). New York: Russell and Rus-
             sell, 1964, 255pp., bib. 244-52. LA831.H35

HRET   *Letiche, John M., ed. A History of Russian Eco-
             nomic Thought: Ninth Through the Eighteenth
             Century. Translated with the Collaboration of
             Basil Dmytryshyn and Richard A. Pierce. Berk-
             eley: University of California Press, 1964, 690pp.
             HB113.A2A43

HRSS   McCormick, Donald. A History of the Russian Secret
             Service. New York: Taplinger, 1972, 568pp.,
             bib. 555-58. HV8225.M23 1972b

HRSSP   Mitchell, Donald W. A History of Russian and Soviet
             Sea Power. New York: Macmillan, 1974, 657pp.,
             bib. 603-25.

IA   *Billington, James A. The Icon and the Axe. An
              Interpretive History of Russian Culture. New
              York: Random House, 1970, 786pp., bib. 599-625.
              DK32.7.B5

IEH   *Gooch, Brison D., ed. Interpreting European His-
              tory, Vol. I. Homewood, Ill.: Dorsey Press,
              1967, 422pp. D210.G6

JR   Greenberg, Louis. The Jews in Russia. The Strug-
              gle for Emancipation, 2 Vols. New Haven: Yale
              University Press, 1965. DS135.R9G68 1965

LUTS   Dunn, Edgar C. Lutheranism Under the Tsars and
              the Soviets, 2 Vols. Ann Arbor, Mich.: Xerox
              University Microfilms, 1975. BX8063.R9D84

LWTS   Whyte, Frederic. The Life of W. T. Stead, 2 Vols.
              Cynthia F. Behrman, intro. New York: Garland,
              1971 (reprint of 1925 edition). PN5123.S7W6 1971

MMR   *Kohn, Hans, ed. The Mind of Modern Russia.
              New Brunswick, N.J.: Rutgers University Press,
              1955, 298pp. DK268.3.K64

MRPC   *Dmytryshyn, Basil, ed. Modernization of Russia
              Under Peter I and Catherine II. New York:
              John Wiley and Sons, 1974, 157pp. DK133.D58

MRSB   Dmytryshyn, Basil, ed. Medieval Russia. A Source
              Book, 900-1700. New York: Holt, Rinehart and
              Winston, 1967, 312pp. DK3.D57 1973

MRTFE   *Wilson, Francesca. Muscovy. Russia Through Foreign
              Eyes 1553-1900. New York: Praeger, 1970,
              328pp., bib. 316-18. DK19.W53 1971

PAT   *Palmer, William. The Patriarch and the Tsar, 6 Vols.
              London: Trubner and Company, 1871-1876.
              BX597.N5P3

PG   *Olivia, L. Jay, ed. Peter the Great. Englewood
              Cliffs, N.J.: Prentice-Hall, 1970, 181pp., bib.
              178. DK131.039

PGCR   *Raeff, Marc, ed. Peter the Great Changes Russia.
              Lexington, Ky.: D. C. Heath and Company,
              1972, 199pp., bib. 195-99. DK131.R3

PIAR   *Ragsdale, Hugh, ed. Paul I. A Reassessment of
              His Life and Reign. Pittsburgh: University Center
              for International Studies, 1979, 188pp. DK186.P38

PPG   Bain, Robert Nisbet. The Pupils of Peter the Great.
               A History of the Russian Court and Empire from
               1697 to 1740. New York: New Amsterdam Book
               Company, 1899, 318pp. DK156.B16

PPR   Raeff, Marc, ed. Plans for Political Reform in
               Imperial Russia, 1730-1905. Englewood Cliffs,
               N.J.: Prentice-Hall, 1966, 159pp. DK61.R3

RD   Cowles, Virginia. The Russian Dagger. Cold War
               in the Days of the Tsars. London: Collins,
               1969, 351pp., bib. 327-36. DK189.C63

RFR   *Mazour, Anatole G. Rise and Fall of the Romanovs.
               Princeton, N.J.: D. Van Nostrand, 1960, 189pp.,
               bib. 184-85.

RIH   Raeff, Marc, ed. Russian Intellectual History. An
               Anthology. Isaiah Berlin, intro. New York:
               Harcourt, Brace and World, 1966, 404pp., bib.
               402-04. DK32.7.R3

RIRC   *Riha, Thomas, ed. Readings in Russian Civilization,
               3 Vols. Chicago: University of Chicago Press,
               1970. DK4.R52

RIRH   Walsh, Warren B., ed. Readings in Russian History.
               New York: Syracuse University Press, 1959,
               702pp. DK3.W3 1959

RJTS   Baron, Salo W. The Russian Jew Under Tsars and
               Soviets. New York: Macmillan, 1964, 427pp.
               DS135.R9B28

RM   Tompkins, Stuart Ramsay. The Russian Mind. From
               Peter the Great Through the Enlightenment. Nor-
               man: University of Oklahoma Press, 1953, 291pp.,
               bib. 251-77. DK32.7.T6

RMWW   Duffy, Charles. Russia's Military Way to the West.
               Origins and Nature of Russian Military Power 1700-
               1800. London: Routledge and Kegan Paul, 1981,
               256pp., bib. 243-50. DK525.D83

RRH   *Harcave, Sidney, ed. Readings in Russian History,
               Vol. I. New York: Thomas Y. Crowell, 1971,
               388pp. DK4.H3

RRPDH   *Senn, Alfred Erich, ed. Readings in Russian Politi-
               cal and Diplomatic History, Vol. I. Homewood,
               Ill.: Dorsey Press, 1966, 235pp. DK60.S45

RSH   *Rowney, Don Karl, and G. Edward Orchard, eds. Russian and Slavic History. Columbus, Ohio: Slavica Publishers, 1977, 300pp. DJK1.5.I57 1974

RUWE   *Cross, Anthony G., ed. Russia Under Western Eyes 1517-1825. New York: St. Martin's Press, 1971, 400pp. DK19.C76

RW   *Oliva, L. Jay, ed. Russia and the West from Peter to Khrushchev. Boston: D. C. Heath and Company, 1965, 289pp., bib. 285-89. DK61.04

SBIR   *Putnam, Peter, ed. Seven Britons in Imperial Russia 1689-1812. Princeton, N.J.: Princeton University Press, 1952, 424pp., bib. 414-16. DK23.P3

SRH   *Cherniavsky, Michael, ed. The Structure of Russian History. New York: Random House, 1970, 436pp. DK40.C54

TPRSD   Coxe, William. Travels into Poland, Russia, Sweden and Denmark, 2 Vols. London: T. Cadell, 1785. D965.C7

UIR   *Raeff, Marc. Understanding Imperial Russia. State and Society in the Old Regime. Arthur Goldhammer, trans. John Keep, foreword. New York: Columbia University Press, 1984, 248pp., bib. 231-39. DK113.R3413 1984

WITR   Wren, Melvin The Western Impact upon Tsarist Russia. Chicago: Holt, Rinehart and Winston, 1971, 254pp., bib. 231-48. DK32.W67

WT   Deriabin, Peter. Watchdogs of Terror. Russian Bodyguards from the Tsars to the Commissars. New Rochelle, N.Y.: Arlington House, 1972. 448pp., bib. 427-39. HV8224.D45

*   *   *

The preceding title abbreviations have been used for anthologies and general studies from which three or more selections or chapters have been extracted. Asterisks indicate works of special value for the study of Romanov rulers and/or their immediate royal predecessors.

REFERENCE SOURCES CONSULTED

Access; the Supplementary Index to Periodicals. Syracuse, N.Y.:
Gaylord Professional Publications, 1975-1985.

America: History and Life. A Guide to Periodical Literature.
Santa Barbara, Cal.: Clio Press, 1964-1985.

American Bibliography of Russian and East European Studies. Bloomington: Indiana University Press, 1956-1966. Continues as
American Bibliography of Slavic and East European Studies.

American Bibliography of Slavic and East European Studies. Various
publishers, 1967-1982.

American Historical Association. Recently Published Articles.
Washington, D.C.: American Historical Association, 1976-1985.

Besterman, Theodore. A World Bibliography of Bibliographies,
5 Vols. Lausanne: Societas Bibliographica, 1966.

Bibliographic Index. A Cumulative Bibliography of Bibliographies.
New York: H. W. Wilson, 1937-1985.

Biography Index. New York: H. W. Wilson, 1946-1985.

Book Review Digest. New York: H. W. Wilson, 1905-1985.

Book Review Index. Detroit: Gale Research, 1965-1985.

British Education Index. London: Library Association, 1954-1985.

British Humanities Index. London: Library Association, 1962-1985.

British Museum, Department of Printed Books. General Catalogue
of Printed Books, 263 Vols. London: Trustees of the British
Museum, 1959-1966. Covers pre-1956 publications; supplements
consulted, 1956-1985.

British National Bibliography. London: Council of British National
Bibliography, 1950-1984.

Canadian Essay and General Literature Index. Toronto: University
of Toronto Press, 1973-1985.

Canadian Index to Periodicals and Documentary Films, 1948-1959.
Ottawa: Canadian Library Association, 1962, 1180pp. Continues
as Canadian Periodical Index.

Canadian Periodical Index. Toronto: Ontario Department of Education, 1928-1947. Continues as Canadian Index to Periodicals and
Documentary Films.

Canadian Periodical Index. Ottawa: Canadian Library Association,
1964-1985.

Catholic Periodical Index. New York: Catholic Library Association,
1939-1967. Continues as Catholic Periodical and Literature Index.

Catholic Periodical and Literature Index. Haverford, Pa.: Catholic
Library Association, 1968-1985.

Clendenning, Philip, and Roger Bartlett. Eighteenth Century Russia.
A Select Bibliography of Works Published since 1955. Newtonville,
Mass.: Oriental Research Partners, 1981, 262pp.

Combined Retrospective Index to Book Reviews in Scholarly Journals,
1886-1974, 15 Vols. Arlington, Va.: Carrollton Press, 1981.

Combined Retrospective Index to Journals in History, 1838-1974,
11 Vols. Washington, D.C.: Carrollton Press, 1977.

Comprehensive Dissertation Index, 1861-1972, 37 Vols. Ann Arbor,
Mich.: Xerox University Microfilms, 1973. Annual supplements
consulted to 1985.

Crowther, Peter A. A Bibliography of Works in English on Early
Russian History to 1800. New York: Barnes and Noble, 1969,
236pp.

Cumulated Magazine Subject Index, 1907-1949. Boston: G. K. Hall,
1964. A cumulation of the Annual Magazine Subject Index.

Cumulative Book Index; A World List of Books in the English Language. New York: H. W. Wilson, 1928-1985.

Cumulated Subject Index to the Public Affairs Information Service
Bulletin, 1915-1974. Arlington, Va.: Carrollton Press, 1978.

Cumulative Index to Periodical Literature. Princeton, N.J.:
National Library Services Corporation, 1959-1970.

Dossick, Jesse J. Doctoral Research on Russia and the Soviet Union. New York: New York University Press, 1960. Updated for 1960-1975 in a supplementary volume; annual updates since 1976 in the December issue of the Slavic Review.

Education Index. New York: H. W. Wilson, 1932-1985.

English Catalogue of Books, 1801-1965. London: S. Low, 1864-1901; Publishers' Circular, 1906-1966.

Essay and General Literature Index. New York: H. W. Wilson, 1934-1985.

Foreign Affairs Bibliography. New York: Council on Foreign Relations, 1919-1962.

Historical Abstracts. Santa Barbara, Cal.: International Social Science Institute, 1955-1985.

Horecky, Paul. Russia and the Soviet Union. A Bibliographic Guide to Western Language Publications, 1964-1974. Littleton, Colo.: Libraries Unlimited, 1978.

Humanities Index. New York: H. W. Wilson, 1974-1985.

Index to Religious Periodical Literature. Chicago: American Theological Library Association, 1953-1985.

International Index to Periodicals. New York: H. W. Wilson, 1907-1965. Continues as Social Sciences and Humanities Index.

National Union Catalog, pre-1956 Imprints. London: Mansell, 1968-1975. Supplements consulted, 1956-1985.

Nerhood, Harry W. To Russia and Return. An Annotated Bibliography of Travelers' English Language Accounts of Russia from the Ninth Century to the Present. Columbus: Ohio State University Press, 1968, 367pp.

New York Public Library. Dictionary Catalog of the Research Libraries. New York: New York Public Library, 1972.

_____. Dictionary Catalog of the Slavonic Collection, 44 Vols. Boston: G. K. Hall, 1974.

Public Affairs Information Service Bulletin. New York: Public Affairs Information Service, 1917-1985.

Readers' Guide to Periodical Literature. New York: H. W. Wilson, 1905-1985.

Sader, Marion, ed. Comprehensive Index to English Language Little

Dukes, Paul. The Making of Russian Absolutism 1613-1801. London/
New York: Longman Group, 1982. DK113.2.D84

*Florinsky, Michael T. Russia. A History and an Interpretation,
2 Vols. New York: Macmillan and Company, 1966. DK40.F6

Fowler, G. Lives of the Sovereigns of Russia, 2 Vols. London:
S. Low, Sons and Company, 1858. DK41.F78

Gerhardi, William. The Romanovs. Evocation of the Past As a Mirror
of the Present. New York: G. P. Putnam's Sons, 1939.
DK113.G4

Grey, Ian. The Romanovs. The Rise and Fall of a Dynasty. Garden City, N.Y.: Doubleday and Company, 1970. DK37.8.R6G7

Harcave, Sidney. Russia. A History. Philadelphia and New York:
J. B. Lippincott, 1968. DK41.H3

*   . The Years of the Golden Cockerel: The Last Century of
the Romanov Tsars. New York: Macmillan and Company, 1968.
DK189.H34

Hingley, Ronald. The Tsars 1533-1917. New York: Macmillan and
Company, 1968. DK37.6.H54

*Kliuchevsky, V. O. A History of Russia, 5 Vols. C. J. Hogarth,
trans. New York: Russell and Russell, 1960. DK40.K613
Volumes three and four in this classic five-volume history of
Russia have been published separately under the titles The Rise
of the Romanovs (Liliana Archibald, trans. London and New
York: Macmillan and Company/St. Martin's Press, 1970) and
Peter the Great (Liliana Archibald, trans. New York: Random
House, 1958).

Lawrence, John. Russia in the Making. London: George Allen and
Unwin, 1957. DK41.L37

*Lincoln, W. Bruce. The Romanovs. Autocrats of All the Russias.
New York: Dial Press, 1981. DK113.L54

McCabe, Joseph. The Romance of the Romanoffs. London: George
Allen and Unwin, 1918. DK113.M2 1918

*Masaryk, Thomas. The Spirit of Russia, 2 Vols. Eden and Cedar
Paul, trans. London: George Allen and Unwin, 1919. DK32.M36

Mazour, Anatole G. Russia. Tsarist and Communist. Princeton,
N.J.: D. Van Nostrand Company, 1962. DK41.M39

*Miliukov, Paul. History of Russia, 3 Vols. Charles Lam Markmann, trans. New York: Funk and Wagnalls, 1969. DK40.M4613

Pares, Bernard. A History of Russia. New York: Random House, 1965. DK40.P3

*Pokorvskii, Mikhail N. Russian History from the Earliest Times. Jesse D. Clarkson, trans. London: Martin Lawrence, 1931. DK40.P6

Pushkarev, Sergei. The Emergence of Modern Russia, 1801-1917. New York: Holt, Rinehart and Winston, 1966. DK189.P813

*Raeff, Marc. Imperial Russia, 1682-1825. The Coming of Age of Modern Russia. New York: Alfred A. Knopf, 1971. DK127.R24

*Riasanovsky, Nicholas V. A History of Russia. New York: Oxford University Press, 1969. DK40.R5

Rice, Tamara. Czars and Czarinas of Russia. New York: Lothrop, Lee and Shepard, 1968. DK37.6.R5

Rogger, Hans. Russia in the Age of Modernization and Revolution, 1881-1917. London and New York: Longman Group, 1983. DK241.R63 1983

Saltus, Edgar. The Imperial Orgy. An Account of the Tsars from the First to the Last. New York: AMS Press, 1970 (reprint of 1920 edition). DK37.6.S3 1970

Seth, Ronald. Milestones in Russian History. Philadelphia: Chilton Book Company, 1968. DK41.S468

*Seton-Watson, Hugh. The Russian Empire 1801-1917. Oxford: Clarendon Press, 1967. DK189.S44

Spector, Ivar. An Introduction to Russian History and Culture. Princeton, N.J.: D. Van Nostrand Company, 1949. DK41.S72

Sumner, B. H. A Short History of Russia. New York: Harcourt, Brace and World, 1949. DK41.S8

*Vernadsky, George, and Michael Karpovich. History of Russia, 5 Vols. New Haven: Yale University Press, 1943. DK40.V44

Walsh, Warren B. Russia and the Soviet Union. Ann Arbor: University of Michigan Press, 1958. DK41.W33

CHRONOLOGY OF RUSSIAN RULERS

Ivan III, 1462-1505

Vasily III, 1505-1533

Ivan IV, 1533-1584

Feodor I, 1584-1598

Boris Godunov, 1598-1605

Feodor II, 1605

False Dimitry, 1605

Vasily Shuisky, 1606-1610

Michael Romanov, 1613-1645

Alexis I, 1645-1676

Feodor III, 1676-1682

Ivan V (Co-Tsar), 1682-1689

Peter I, 1682-1725

Catherine I, 1725-1727

Peter II, 1727-1730

Anna I, 1730-1740

Ivan VI, 1740-1741

Elizabeth I, 1741-1762

Peter III, 1762

Catherine II, 1762-1796

Paul I, 1796-1801

Alexander I, 1801-1825

Nicholas I, 1825-1855

Alexander II, 1855-1881

Alexander III, 1881-1894

Nicholas II, 1894-1917

1   *Alef, Gustave. "The Adoption of the Muscovite Two-Headed Eagle:
    A Discordant View." Speculum, 41, no. 1 (1966): 1-21.
    The stated purpose of this article is "to suggest that the two-
    headed eagle as a device on the Muscovite coat-of-arms came
    into being as a reaction to some of the diplomatic maneuver-
    ings of the Habsburg rulers and their emissaries," and not
    as part of an attempt by Ivan III to symbolize the transfer
    of the Byzantine religio-political heritage to Muscovy.

2   *_____. "Aristocratic Politics and Royal Policy in the Late
    Fifteenth and Early Sixteenth Centuries." Forsch Ost Ges,
    27 (1980): 77-109.
    An analysis of the "corrective actions taken between 1499 and
    1505" by Ivan III and Vasily III as they attempted to deal with
    the discontent of those middle-rank aristocratic servitors who
    felt that their opportunities for advancement within the Musco-
    vite political system were being circumscribed. Alef states that
    the appointments and demotions made during the years under
    study suggest that they were not a consequence of problems as-
    sociated with dynastic succession or differences over ecclesiasti-
    cal and foreign policy but rather were an attempt by the grand
    princes to redress legitimate grievances held by middle-rank
    servitors and princely newcomers without wholly alienating the
    aristocratic elite. However, dissatisfaction continued and the
    jockeying for position actually accelerated during Vasily III's
    reign, particularly when the crown was hard pressed by a cri-
    sis of any sort. Alef concludes with a brief discussion of Ivan
    IV's attempt, in the late 1540s and early 1550s, "to defuse the
    selfish conflicts that had caused so much grief in the past" by
    making a flood of appointments from outside the ranks of the
    competing groups.

3   *_____. "Muscovite Military Reform in the Second Half of the
    Fifteenth Century." Forsch Ost Ges, 18 (1973): 73-108.
    A discussion of Ivan III's creation of a large and effective
    army through increased pressure on landholders to give mili-
    tary service, absorption into the military of impoverished
    members of the gentry, coercion of contingents from weaker
    independent neighbors, and the use of dependent Mongols.
    Alef concludes that in addition to its obvious internal military
    value, the greatly expanded Muscovite army "enhanced the

figure of the monarch" and "provided some of the means by which the monarch could exert his will at home."

4 *_____. "The Origin and Development of the Muscovite Postal Service." Jahr Ges Ost, 15 (1967): 1-15.
An account of the growth of the Muscovite postal service in the fifteenth century with considerable reference to the support given by Ivan III to this enterprise. Alef discusses the construction of postal stations along the principal routes of travel in newly won territories and the methods used to enhance the efficiency and security of the mail system. By the end of Ivan III's reign, "the Muscovite government had established one of the best systems of internal communications to be found upon the European scene."

5 *_____. "Reflections on the Boyar Duma in the Reign of Ivan III." Slavonic E Eur R, 45 (Jan. 1967): 76-123.
An examination of the "duma membership of Ivan's reign and its changing character and functions." Alef contends that while there was a "severe reduction in the duma's membership during Ivan III's reign, ... there is no substantiation for the view that the duma was invaded by new princely immigrants." Alef appends a genealogical list of some 90 individuals who were members of the duma during Ivan's rule.

6 Andreyev, N. "Filofey and His Epistle to Ivan Vasil'yevich." Slavonic E Eur R, 38, no. 90 (Dec. 1959): 1-31.

A study of the life and historical times of the Elder Filofey, a monk of the Eleazarov monastery in Pskov, in order to determine why he wrote his epistle and to whom it was addressed. Andreyev concludes that the epistle was designed to reinforce Muscovy's claim to the existing Russian lands and was addressed to Ivan III, not Ivan IV as some historians have claimed.

7 *Arans, David. "A Note on the Lost Library of the Moscow Tsars." J Lib Hist, 18 (Summer 1983): 304-16.
A review of nearly a century of Russian language writings on the possible existence of a large collection of ancient Greek manuscripts acquired by Ivan III from his wife, Princess Sophia Paleologue, who allegedly brought them to Moscow as part of her dowry as the niece of the last Byzantine emperor.

8 *Bakhrushin, S. V. "The Emergence of Muscovy: Consolidation." RRPDH (anthology), 6-8. Excerpt from Nauchnye trudy, Vol. II. Moscow, 1954, 258-61.
A brief survey of the steps taken by Ivan III to tighten "the thread of administration of the united Russian lands around himself in Moscow." Bakhrushin maintains that despite Ivan's shrewdness and adaptation of a number of important administrative measures, the Muscovite state at the turn of the century was far from being a centralized one.

9 Barbaro, Josafa and Ambrogio Contarini. "Contarini's Impression

of Muscovy in 1476." MRSB (anthology), 152-58.
A 1476 description of Muscovy, Ivan III's physical appearance, and his favorable treatment of the author (Venetian
ambassador Ambrosio Contarini) at a court dinner held in
his honor.

10 *Bazilevich, K. B. "The Emergence of Muscovy: Political Unification." RRPDH (anthology), 1-6. Trans. from Vneshnaia
politika russogo tsentralizovannogo gosudarstva: vtoraia
polovina XV veka. Moscow, 1952, 15-21.
A Soviet discussion of Ivan III's contribution to "the liquida-
tion of feudal disintegration and the final destruction of the
rule of the Golden Horde" and his efforts to counter Swedish,
Polish and Lithuanian attempts to perpetuate political dis-
unity within Russia. Bazilevich maintains that the foreign
policy pursued by Ivan is best viewed as an integral part of
"the general process of the formation of the Russian centralized state."

11 *Croskey, Robert M. "The Diplomatic Forms of Ivan III's Relationship with the Crimean Khan." Slav R, 42, no. 2
(1984): 257-69.
A discussion of diplomatic practice between Ivan III and the
Crimean Khan during the latter part of the fifteenth century
as an indication that the forms of diplomacy between Muscovy
and the Crimean Khanate did not, as of that time, reflect the
independent status that Muscovite Russia had come to enjoy
following its 1480 victory over the Great Horde at the Ugra
River. Croskey establishes that the forms used in ceremonies
and documents "indicate that the subordination which Russia
experienced during the rule of the Golden Horde was retained,
at least formally, in the relationship to the Crimea" even
though Ivan, in reality, was the dominant partner in this
relationship. Croskey speculates that the "disparity between
the political reality of the relationship with the Crimea and
the forms in which it was conducted" was most likely due to
"calculated flattery on Ivan's part" and to the persistence of
traditional forms in a static society such as Muscovy.

12 _____. "Muscovite Diplomatic Practice in the Reign of Ivan
III." University of Washington, 1980 (dissertation)

13 *Dewey, Horace W. "The 1497 Sudebnik: Muscovite Russia's
First National Law Code." ASEER, 15, no. 3 (Oct. 1956):
325-38.
An examination of the 1497 legal code's historical background,
principal sections, and significance for Muscovite legal history. Dewey states that the code was incomplete and often
neglected but was important "as a first step in the direction
of all-Russian legislation" and because it provided a foundation for the 1550 Sudebnik of Ivan IV.

14 *"The Economic Policy of Ivan III." HRET (anthology), 91-103.
     A Soviet discussion of Ivan III's economic policy as one
     geared toward the consolidation of feudal production rela-
     tionships within the political superstructure of the emerging
     Russian centralized state. The author gives most attention
     to Ivan's establishment of the pomestie system of land tenure
     as an inextricable link in the formation of a centralized state
     at the expense of Russia's feudal lords. Ivan's financial
     and commercial policies also receive favorable review.

15 "Ending the Mongol Yoke in 1480." MRSB (anthology), 159-61.
     Excerpt from Polnoe Sobranie Russikh Letoposei, Vol. 8.
     Basil Dymytryshyn, trans. St. Petersburg, 1885, 205-07.
     A selection from a Muscovite chronicle which describes Ivan
     III's 1480 victory over Khan Akhmad of the Golden Horde as
     a product of the latter's unwillingness to cross the Ugra
     River and confront the Muscovite forces without the Lithu-
     anian aid he had expected to receive.

16 *Esper, Thomas. "Russia and the Baltic, 1494-1558." Slav R,
     25, no. 3 (Sept. 1966): 458-74.
     A reassessment of the periodization of Russian commercial
     relations with Western Europe with considerable reference to
     the Baltic policies of Ivan III and Ivan IV. Esper discusses
     the continuity in Russian commercial policy from Ivan III's
     1494 dissolution of the Hanseatic establishment in Novgorod
     to the 1558 conquest of the Baltic port of Narva by Ivan IV.
     Esper sees both of these events as steps toward establishing
     free and direct trade between Russian and Western merchants.

17 *Fennell, J. L. I. "The Dynastic Crisis 1497-1502." Slavonic
     E Eur R, 39 (1960-61): 1-23.
     An investigation of the evidence on and conflicting interpre-
     tations of the dynastic crisis faced by Ivan III as a conse-
     quence of his selection as his successor Dimitry, the son of
     the deceased heir to the throne, rather than Vasily, Ivan's
     eldest surviving son.

18 *_____. Ivan the Great of Moscow. London: Macmillan and
     Company, 1961, 386pp., bib. 367-71.
     The purpose of this study is to present, for the first time
     in English, an account of the foreign policy and diplomatic
     methods followed by Ivan III as he expanded the principality
     of Moscow. To this end, Fennell examines the negotiations,
     wars, annexations, and treaties associated with Ivan's deal-
     ings with the Khanate of Kazan, the Tartars to the south of
     Muscovy, Lithuania, Moldavia, Novgorod, and Tver. Ivan
     emerges from this study as a farsighted, shrewd, and force-
     ful leader who relentlessly pursued his goal of gathering
     together into a centralized state the various principalities of
     Russia. Although domestic policy is beyond the stated

purpose of this study, Fennell includes a one chapter survey
of internal developments during Ivan's reign and appends a
selection of Soviet interpretations of the dynastic crisis
which occurred at the close of the fifteenth century.
DK101.F4
Reviewed in:
Am Hist R, 68 (1962):   448
Can Hist R, 44 (1963):   72
Eng Hist R, 79 (1964):   164
History, 48 (1963):   72
Hist Today, 12 (1962):   142
Slav R, 22, no. 1 (1963):   139

19   *Fine, John V. A.   "The Muscovite Dynastic Crisis of 1497-
1502."   Can Slav P, 8 (1966):   198-215.
An examination of the role played by Lithuania in both Ivan
III's selection of his grandson, Dimitry, rather than his son,
Vasily, as heir to the throne and the subsequent deposition
of Dimitry through Vasily's efforts.

20   Grey, Ian.   Ivan III and the Unification of Russia.   New York:
Collier Books, 1967, 181pp., bib. 175-76.
A semi-popular study which aims "to recount briefly the main
events in Ivan III's reign, leading up to the unification of
Great Russia under Moscow's rule."   Within this context,
Grey discusses Ivan's annexation of Novgorod, Pskov, and
Vyatka, his struggle against powerful neighbors, efforts to
create a unified administration, and his attempt to deal with
the dynastic crisis which developed towards the end of his
reign.   Grey concludes that, among the early rulers of
Muscovy, Ivan III was "the chief architect of Russian unity."
DK100.G73

21   *Herberstein, Sigismund von.   Description of Moscow and Muscovy.   Bertold Picard, ed.   J. B. Grundy, trans.   New
York: Barnes and Noble, 1969, 105pp.
The earliest relatively accurate Western account of Muscovy,
its court life, and internal politics.   Herberstein, who
traveled to Muscovy in 1517 and 1526 as a special envoy of
Holy Roman Emperor Maximilian commissioned to resolve the
military conflict between Muscovy and Lithuania, describes
his reception at the court of Vasily III, the relationship between Vasily and leading boyars, the customs and habits
of the Muscovites, the practices of the Orthodox Church,
and a host of court affairs and festivities.   Of particular
interest is his account of Vasily's opposition to any accord
with Lithuania without the sovereign of that state first ex-
pressing directly his own desire for peace.   DK21.H5313
For a discussion of the influence of Herberstein's book
upon sixteenth- and seventeenth-century Western writings
about Muscovy, see Walter Leitsch's "Herberstein's Impact

on the Reports about Muscovy in the 16th and 17th Centuries: Some Observations on the Technique of Borrowing."
Forsch Ost Ges, 24 (1978): 163-77.

22 *Howes, Robert Craig, ed./trans. The Testaments of the Grand
    Princes of Moscow. Ithaca: Cornell University Press, 1967,
    445pp., bib. 391-95.
    A commentary on the testaments left by Muscovite rulers to
    their heirs. Howes presents thirteen such documents, written by rulers from Ivan Kalita through Ivan the Terrible,
    which collectively represent a valuable source of primary
    information on Muscovy of the fourteenth to sixteenth centuries. Most notable among the testaments' contents are
    records of territorial acquisitions, information on the changing nature of princely power and administration, and insights into the rulers' personalities and family affairs.
    DK70.A2H6

23 "Ivan III's Conquest of Novgorod in 1471." MRSB (anthology),
    138-52 from The Chronicle of Novgorod, 1016-1471. C. R.
    Beazley, intro. Robert Mitchell and Nevill Forbes, trans.
    London: Royal Historical Society, 205-20.
    A dramatic Muscovite version of Ivan III's conquest of
    Novgorod as a consequence of its "wrong doings" (defiance
    of Ivan's authority) and its "lapsing into Latinism (seeking
    aid from a Catholic Lithuanian prince).

24 *Keenan, Edward L. "The Jarlyk of Axmed-Xan to Ivan III:
    A New Reading." Int J Slav Ling Poetics, 12 (1969): 33-
    47.
    An argument that the jarlyk allegedly sent by Akhmad Khan
    of the Great Horde to Ivan III is not an acceptable source
    of information on the events which transpired between the
    Mongolian and Muscovite forces which faced each other at
    the Ugra River in October of 1480. Keenan maintains that
    the form, grammar, and vocabulary of the jarlyk prove that
    it is not an authentic diplomatic document but rather "a
    poetical pamphlet, the purpose of which was to point out,
    in entertaining form, the importance of Muscovy's triumph
    over the other Golden Horde successor states, by exaggerating her erstwhile subservience and the hauteur of the Tartar Khans."

25 _____. "Muscovy and Kazan: Some Introductory Remarks on
    the Patterns of Steppe Diplomacy." Slav R, 26, no. 4
    (1967): 548-76.
    In part, a discussion of the diplomacy pursued by Ivan III
    and Vasily III in regard to the stabilization of Muscovy's
    eastern and southern borders and the promotion of trade
    in these regions.

26 *Kleimola, A. M. The Duty to Denounce in Muscovite Russia."
    Slav R, 31, no. 4 (1972): 759-79.
    A discussion of the origin and evolution of the duty of Mus-
    covites to inform the sovereign about any matter involving
    the security of his realm. Kleimola establishes that this
    practice began "in agreements or contracts concluded by the
    princes among themselves" as early as the mid-fourteenth
    century. By the end of the fifteenth century, such contracts
    had been converted into a more general obligation and ex-
    tended to the lesser Russian princes. In succeeding decades,
    oaths of allegiance became even more common and specific,
    and by the seventeenth century "all subjects of the tsar
    were bound by their oath of allegiance to report anyone
    plotting against the sovereign." Through denunciations,
    rulers were able to gain valuable information about political
    intrigue, and they held the duty to denounce in sufficiently
    high regard to punish severely those who failed to report
    whatever they knew about disloyal deeds and thoughts.

27 Lamb, Harold. "The Dominion." The March of Muscovy. Ivan
    the Terrible and the Growth of the Russian Empire, 1400-
    1648. Garden City: Doubleday Press, 1948, 75-90.
    Ivan III is not the sole focus of this chapter, but it contains
    a discussion of his annexation of surrounding territories,
    marriage to Sophia Paleologue, and struggle against the
    Mongols to the east of Muscovy. DK71.L3

28 *Majeska, George P. "The Moscow Coronation of 1498 Recon-
    sidered." Jahr Ges Ost, 26, no. 2 (1978): 353-62.
    An argument that the similarities between the 1498 corona-
    tion of Dimitry and Byzantine coronation ritual should not
    be linked to any attempt by Ivan III to demonstrate Muscovy's
    claim to leadership in the Orthodox world but rather is best
    viewed as an effort to establish a Byzantine justification for
    naming his grandson, not his son, as his successor. Majeska
    claims that the misrepresentation of the parallels between Mus-
    covite and Byzantine coronation ceremonies was a deliberate
    one on the part of sixteenth century chroniclers who, under
    the leadership of Metropolitan Macarius, sought to construct
    an ideological justification for Ivan IV's centralized, absolute
    rule.

29 *Martin, Janet. "Muscovite Relations with the Khanates of Kazan
    and the Crimea (1460s to 1521)." Can Am Slav S, 17, no. 4
    (1983): 435-53.
    An argument that Muscovy's relations with the Khanate of
    Kazan during the reigns of Ivan III and Vasily III are best
    understood when placed within the confines of Muscovite
    policy toward the Crimean Khanate rather than viewed as a
    consequence of the goals pursued by Muscovy in the West,

particularly with respect to Lithuania. Martin states that
the Khanate of Kazan and Muscovy "were not fundamentally
and consistently hostile to one another" and, in fact, engaged in a profitable commerce. However, their positive
relations deteriorated as a consequence of the collapse of
the Muscovite-Crimean Tartar alliance which prompted each
of the former allies to attempt to bind the Kazan Khanate
to an alliance against the other. Martin concludes that
"the rivalry engendered by the collapse of their alliance ...
remained a critical factor influencing Muscovy's policies
toward Kazan, including, ultimately, its decision to annex
that khanate."

30 Melencamp, Noble Merrill. "Foreign and Domestic Policies of
    Ivan III, 1462-1505." University of California, Berkeley,
    1956. (dissertation)

31 "Milanese Architect Who Worked for Ivan III." Architect
    (19 Nov. 1915): 398-401.
    Unavailable for annotation.

32 Orchard, George Edward. "Economic and Social Conditions in
    Muscovy during the Reign of Ivan III." McGill University,
    1967. (dissertation)

33 _____. "The Stand on the Ugra." New R E Eur Hist, 5, no.
    1 (1965): 34-41.
    A discussion of the nature and significance of the 1480 Ugra
    River confrontation between Ivan III and Akhmad Khan of the
    Golden Horde. Orchard maintains that Ivan's behavior and
    strategy are best understood as a response to a complex
    political and military situation which dictated caution on
    Muscovy's part. Ivan was threatened simultaneously by
    Livonian, Polish-Lithuanian, and Tartar military forces, and
    he feared the consequences of the disaffection of his two
    brothers, Boris and Andrei. The threat posed by these
    rivals and the tactical disadvantages associated with a frontal
    assault on the Tartar forces across the Ugra led Ivan to
    withdraw his troops and consolidate his position to the west
    of the river. When the Tartars failed to pursue the Mus-
    covites, Ivan was able to claim victory. Orchard concludes
    that the true significance of the Ugra episode is that Ivan
    emerged unscathed from a situation which could have resulted
    in a catastrophe for him and Muscovy.

34 *Presniakov, Alexander E. "The Gathering of Power." The
    Formation of the Great Russian State. A Study of Russian
    History in the Thirteenth to Fifteenth Centuries. A. E.
    Moorehouse, ed./trans. Alfred J. Rieber, intro. Chicago:
    Quadrangle Books, 1970, 340-91.
    A scholarly assessment of Ivan III's reign forms the concluding

chapter to a study of the evolution of princely power as a response to the increasingly complex problems which confronted Muscovite leaders. Presniakov, an eminent Russian historian (1870-1929), discusses Ivan's treatment of Novgorod, Pskov, Tver, and Riazan within the confines of a policy which predates Ivan's reign and which aimed at destroying the foundations of the votchina system and replacing them with the principle of hereditary autocracy. DK90.P713

35 * _____ . The Tsardom of Muscovy. Robert F. Price, ed./ trans. Charles Halperin, intro. Gulf Breeze, Fla.: Academic International Press, 1978 (translation of 1918 edition), 157pp.
This scholarly study of "the development of Muscovite autocracy in its relationship to Muscovite society and institutions" does not include a separate chapter on any one ruler but contains an analysis of the forces which influenced the grand princes along the path of autocracy. Presniakov maintains that such factors as northeast Russia's sparse population, backward economy, and hostile bordering states provided a powerful and pressing impetus for the emergence of a centralized and autocratic political apparatus during the reigns of Ivan III, Vasily III, and Ivan IV. DK100.P7413

36 *Raba, Joel. The Authority of the Muscovite Ruler at the Dawn of the Modern Era." Jahr Ges Ost, 24, no. 3 (1976): 321-44.
An examination of the scope and nature of the powers held by Muscovite rulers in the half century that preceded the reign of Ivan IV. Devoting most attention to the reign of Vasily III, Raba demonstrates that, in addition to Byzantine influences, there were significant trends toward the creation of a legal and ideological foundation for the grand princes' claim to the title 'autocrat.' At the same time, the absence within society of a structure which would have allowed the development of an "independent political initiative" encouraged Muscovite rulers to envision and move towards a political absolutism of a more extensive and modern kind. Raba concludes that by the end of Vasily III's reign "a specifically Russian form of government was evolved. Autocratic absolutism was born."

37 * _____ . "The Fate of the Novgorodian Republic." Slavonic E Eur R, 45, no. 105 (1967): 307-23.
An evaluation of the political and military dissimilarities between Muscovy and Novgorod, and an account of the spasmodic nature of Ivan III's efforts to incorporate the Novgorodian republic into the growing Muscovite state.

38 * _____ . "Novgorod in the Fifteenth Century: A Re-examination." Can Slav S, 1, no. 3 (1967): 348-64.

An argument against the existence of the "political passivity, economic dependence, military weakness, and widespread lack of support" in fifteenth century Novgorod to which Muscovite rulers pointed in justifying the republic's absorption into the Muscovite state. Raba contends that since Novgorod was a vital and stable state, its absorption "can only be explained by the collision of and ensuing struggle between two fundamentally opposed political systems: the autocracy of Muscovy and the democratic oligarchy of Novgorod."

39 Rywkin, Michael. "Russian Colonial Expansion Before Ivan the Dread: A Survey of Basic Trends." Rus R, 32, no. 2 (1973): 286-93.
A discussion of three centuries of Muscovite attempts to expand to the east with most attention given to the efforts of Ivan III and Vasily III. Rywkin states that by the time Ivan IV became tsar, Russia had "arrived at the very verge of a genuine colonial expansion," a development upon which Ivan IV capitalized in the form of his Kazan campaign.

40 *Soloviev, Sergei M. History of Russia. Vol. VII. The Reign of Ivan III the Great. John D. Windham, ed./trans. Gulf Breeze, Fla.: Academic International Press, 1978, 164pp.
A classic study of the expansion of Muscovy and the emergence, under Ivan III, of a state more centralized and autocratic than that which existed under the rule of Ivan's predecessors. Drawing upon an impressive array of primary sources, Soloviev examines in detail Ivan's diplomatic relations with and military campaigns against rival principalities, the Mongols to the south and east of Muscovy, and the powerful Lithuanian state to the west. He portrays Ivan as a farsighted ruler who showed remarkable flexibility in the methods employed to further the size and security of his state. He also discusses Ivan's 1472 marriage to Sophia Paleologue (niece of the last Byzantine Emperor, Constantine XI) as a shrewd political move which enhanced Muscovy's status by establishing imperial lineage for Ivan's successors thereby encouraging them to look southward for future expansion. DK40.S6213

41 *_____. History of Russia. Vol. VIII. Russian Society in the Age of Ivan III. John D. Windham, ed./trans. Gulf Breeze, Fla.: Academic International Press, 1979, 183pp.
A scholarly examination of court, urban, and rural life, religion and culture, and the financial, legal, and administrative characteristics of Muscovy under Ivan III. DK40.S6213

42 *_____. History of Russia. Vol. IX. The Age of Vasily III. Hugh F. Graham, ed./trans. Gulf Breeze, Fla.: Academic International Press, 1976, 273pp.
A detailed discussion of the reign of Vasily III within the

confines of the view that "the course of Russian history constituted a slow and inexorable forward movement that tri-
umphed over every obstacle." Soloviev synthesizes a large
body of primary source material as he examines court life,
Vasily's personal qualities and relationships, domestic policy,
and, especially, foreign and military affairs. Vasily emerges
from this study as a dynamic and intelligent ruler who continued successfully Ivan III's policy of annexing rival principalities and centralizing control over his domain at the expense of feudal lords. Soloviev concludes this volume with
an examination of Ivan IV's early years during which political
intrigue was rampant. He asserts that the early death of
Ivan's parents, the disrespect and disloyalty shown toward
him by leading boyars, and the generally insecure nature of
his environment were of paramount importance in Ivan's
development of an unstable personality and an overly suspi-
cious nature. DK40.S6213

43 *Szeftel, Marc. "The Title of the Muscovite Monarch up to the
End of the Seventeenth Century." Can Am Slav S, 13,
nos. 1-2 (1979): 59-81.
An examination of the evolution of the royal title employed
by Muscovy's rulers for insight into the growth of the rulers'
authority, the "place claimed by the Muscovite monarch for
himself in the community of nations," and the influence exerted by outside forces in shaping Muscovite political thought.

44 Toumanoff, Cyril. "Moscow the Third Rome: Genesis and Significance of a Politico-Religious Idea." Cath Hist R, 40,
no. 4 (1955): 411-17.
A scholarly study of the genealogy of the Third Rome theory
with some reference to Ivan III's reaction to the theory's
formulation by the Pskovian monk Philotheus.

45 *Treadgold, Donald W. "The Meeting of Moscow and Rome in
the Reign of Vasilij III." The Religious World of Russian
Culture. Russian Orthodoxy. Vol. II. Essays in Honor of
Georges Florovsky. Andrew Blane, ed. The Hague: Mouton, 1975, 55-74.
A discussion of the conflict, during the reign of Vasily III,
between two religious movements, the trans-Volga elders and
the Josephites, as a "cultural encounter between Moscow and
Rome" which both "inaugurated the modern period in which
Russia has experienced successive waves of West European
influence" and foreshadowed the weakening of ecclesiastical
autonomy and princely resistance to the progress of Muscovite centralization. Treadgold states that Western influence
on the Josephites was neither organized nor intentional. The
Josephites, like Ivan III and Vasily III, selected from Western thought and practices that which might best serve their
interests. The Josephites' development of the idea of

"Moscow, the Third Rome" had as its aim the glorification
of the rapidly centralizing Muscovite state in return for the
grand prince's support and protection of their landholdings
and his recognition of their privileged position with regard
to the state. However, Treadgold concludes, the ultimate
victor in the Josephite/trans-Volga elders contest was Muscovite autocracy. BX250.R87

46 *Vernadsky, George. "The Heresy of the Judaizers and Ivan
III." Speculum, 8 (1933): 436-54.
A study of the beliefs of the Judaizers, the extent of their
numbers and influence, and the source of Ivan III's favorable
attitude toward this heretical group. Vernadsky maintains
that Ivan's support was not due to any religious sympathy
with the Judaizers but rather to "political motives in regard
to both domestic and foreign policy," most notably concerning the secularization of church land (which the Judaizers
favored), and Ivan's desire to impress favorably the large
Jewish population of Lithuania, Muscovy's rival to the west.

47 Volgin, A. "In Commemoration of the 500th Anniversary of the
Liberation of Russ from the Mongol-Tartar Yoke." J Moscow
Patr, no. 2 (1981): 69-75.
Unavailable for annotation.

48 Wolff, Robert L. "The Three Romes: The Migration of an
Ideology and the Making of an Autocrat." Daedalus, 88
(Spring 1959): 291-311.
An examination of the roots of the third Rome theory and the
theory's connection to Russian political behavior. Wolff sees
the doctrine as being of paramount importance in providing
Muscovite rulers, especially Ivan III and Ivan IV, with "the
ideological assistance needed in transforming themselves into
autocrats."

GENERAL STUDIES AND ASSESSMENTS/
PERSONAL AFFAIRS AND CHARACTER

49 *Alexandrova, Vera. "New Concepts of Ivan the Terrible."
    Bks Abroad, 17 (1943): 318-24.
    A review of the favorable revaluation of Ivan IV by Soviet
    writers during World War II. Alexandrova places the Soviet
    transformation of Ivan's image as an oppressive tyrant to a
    progressive and patriotic ruler within the broad context of
    the regime's turn to totalitarianism under Stalin's leadership:
    "What profound doubts must have arisen in the justification
    of the dictatorship of the Communist Party, how shaken must
    be faith in the liberating idea of the great Revolution, if in
    the ideological domain a retreat has been undertaken all the
    way to the foot of the ancient image of the Leviathan State."

50 Apsler, Alfred. Ivan the Terrible. Folkstone: Bailey Brothers
    and Swinen, 1971, 191pp., bib. 186.
    A colorful narrative geared toward the non-specialist. Apsler
    presents a balance of information on Ivan and his domestic,
    foreign, and military policies, and, while noting Ivan's
    cruelties, contends that he "was no worse than many other
    high-born contemporaries in a most violent period of man's
    history." DK106.A65 1971b

51 Backer, George. The Deadly Parallel. Stalin and Ivan the
    Terrible. New York: Random House, 1950, 250pp.
    The general premise behind this work is that "history is only
    the recreation of the past in the image of the present.
    Therefore, the interpretation of its past which a nation ac-
    cepts is the authentic presentation of its concept of national
    destiny and the goals to which its strength is directed."
    Backer thus argues that the attempt by Soviet historians to
    rehabilitate the reputation of Ivan the Terrible indicates a
    similarity between Ivan's goals, values, and methods and
    those of the Stalin regime, particularly in regard to their
    respective concepts of the state, treatment of dissent, and
    efforts to expand Russia's borders. DK268.S8B15

52 Barry, Philip B. "Ivan 'the Terrible' of Russia." Twenty Human
     Monsters in Purple and in Rags from Caligula to Landau.
     London: Jarrolds, 1929, 64-80.
     An account of Ivan IV's "monstrous crimes and devilries" as
     by-products of his genuine "love of suffering" rather than
     political need. There follows a lurid account of the tortures
     Ivan gleefully inflicted upon thousands of his subjects.
     HV6245.B3

53 *Berry, Lloyd E., and Robert O. Crummey, eds. Rude and
     Barbarous Kingdom. Russia in the Accounts of Sixteenth
     Century English Voyagers. Madison: University of Wiscon-
     sin Press, 1968, 391pp.
     Excerpts from the sixteenth-century writings of Chancellor,
     Jenkinson, Randolph, Tuberville, Fletcher, and Horsey
     which collectively provide considerable insight into the char-
     acter and policies of Ivan the Terrible, Feodor, and Boris
     Godunov as well as into the nature of the Russia over which
     they ruled. The editors provide a series of excellent intro-
     ductions in which they comment on the travelers' experiences
     in Russia as well as on the veracity and historical merits of
     their respective writings, particularly those of Fletcher and
     Horsey. A detailed subject index makes for easy access to
     information pertinent to the study of the monarchs of this
     time period. DK19.B4

54 *Bolsover, G. H. "Ivan the Terrible in Russian Historiography."
     Trans Roy Hist S, series 5, 7 (1957): 71-89.
     A survey of the evolution of Russian historical judgments on
     Ivan IV and his reign including the early negative assess-
     ment advanced by Karamzin, the reassessments of Soloviev
     and Kliuchevsky, and the favorable interpretations of Plato-
     nov and Wipper. Bolsover describes the general trend as
     one characterized by a shift away from an image of Ivan as
     a deranged sadist pursuing pointless policies and toward a
     portrayal of him as a farsighted and systematic state builder.

55 Brodsky, P. P. "The Russian Source of Rilke's Wie der Verrat
     nach Russland kam." Germanic R, 54 Spring (1979): 72-77.
     A discussion of a historical song about Ivan IV, "How
     Treachery Was Brought to Russia," as the source for Rainer
     Maria Rilke's story Wie der Verrat nach Russland kam.

56 Carr, Francis. Ivan the Terrible. Totowa, N.J.: Barnes and
     Noble, 1981, 220pp., bib. 215.
     A popular biography of Ivan IV which stresses the negative
     and grotesque features of his reign. Carr maintains that
     Ivan's reign was "undoubtedly a success in terms of immedi-
     ate territorial aggrandizement ... but it was also a disaster
     culturally, socially and spiritually" and was by far the most
     oppressive and brutal era in Russia's history. DK106.C37

57 *"The Debate on Ivan the Terrible in 1956." RRC, Vol. I
    (anthology), 110–17. Originally in Voprosy Istorii, (1956):
    195–203.
    A summary of the views presented at a 14–15 May 1956
    meeting of Soviet historians in regard to the erroneous Soviet
    interpretations of Ivan IV and his policies advanced during
    the era of Stalin. The article consists of the reactions of
    five historians to S. M. Dubrovsky's argument that Ivan was
    not a "tsar of the people" whose policies were progressive
    and aimed primarily at the centralization of the state but
    rather was a landowners' tsar who advanced serfdom and
    practiced "predatory expansionist policies." Dubrovsky also
    maintains that since feudal fragmentation was already a
    phenomenon of the past, Ivan should not be credited with
    the establishment of a centralized state but instead with
    giving the state an autocratic form it need not have assumed.
    While Dubrovsky's colleagues agreed with his assertion that
    the idealized image of Ivan IV established by Wipper, Bakh-
    rushin, and other historians is in need of serious revision
    they took issue with his interpretation of the oprichnina
    terror, the state of Russia's political development in the
    mid-sixteenth century, and the leading role played by Ivan
    in determining the direction taken by Russia during his
    reign.

58 Dumas, Alexandre. "Ivan, 'the Terrible'." CCRC (gen. study),
    1–13.
    A presentation of Ivan IV's upbringing and experiences as
    a youth as the keys to understanding his bizarre behavior
    and cruel policies. Dumas provides colorful examples of
    Ivan's misdeeds but also notes that his reign was character-
    ized by several progressive features, particularly in regard
    to foreign policy.

59 Eckardt, Hans von. Ivan the Terrible. Catherine A. Phillips,
    trans. New York: Alfred Knopf, 1949, 421pp., bib. 411–
    14.
    A general, somewhat impressionistic biography of Ivan IV
    which concentrates on his youth, character, and the motiva-
    tion behind his main policies. Eckardt maintains that Ivan's
    reign "marks the end of the age of disintegration," hence-
    forth, the Russian people "possessed a center, a sense of
    solidarity, they were no longer a confused medley of stars."
    DK106.E313

60 *Eisenstein, Sergei M. Ivan the Terrible: A Film. A. E.
    Ellis, trans. London: Lorrimer, 1970, 264pp.
    The script of Eisenstein's monumental film portrayal of Ivan
    IV. Useful as an example of the positive Soviet reassess-
    ment of Ivan and his rule that characterized the 1940s.
    PN1997.E3713

61 Errol, Joseph. "Ivan the IV." <u>Belgravia</u>, 88 (Nov. 1895):
        262-76.
        A sketch of Ivan IV's character and life with emphasis placed
        upon the atrocities he committed and the influences which
        made him such a brutal individual.

62 Ewart, Andres. "Ivan the Terrible." <u>The World's Wickedest</u>
        <u>Men</u>. New York: Taplinger Publishing Company, 1965, 115-
        29.
        A gory account of Ivan IV's cruelties and misdeeds, and a
        brief description of his death. CT9980.E9

63 *Farrer, J. A. "A Russian Bear." <u>Gent M</u>, 265 (Aug. 1888):
        168-78.
        A critical review of the image of Ivan IV's character, be-
        havior, and policies propagated by his contemporaries.
        Farrer states that the accounts written by Horsey, Fletcher,
        Kurbsky, Oderborn, and others contain so many errors,
        contradictions, and exaggerations that they cannot possibly
        be accepted as viable sources of information on Ivan or his
        reign. Farrer contrasts these accounts with the positive
        portrayals of Jenkinson, Cobenzel, and others, and con-
        cludes that the latter are far more accurate than the former.
        He sees Russian aristocrats, whose power was circumscribed
        by Ivan's policies, and Polish nobles, who feared that Ivan
        might be elected king of Poland after the 1576 death of
        Sigismund, as being the prime sources of "the wildest exag-
        gerations and calumny which appeared to have gathered
        round his (Ivan's) name."

64 *Fennell, J. L. I., ed./trans. <u>Prince A. M. Kurbsky's History</u>
        <u>of Ivan IV</u>. Cambridge: Cambridge University Press, 1965,
        314pp., bib. 302-04.
        A classic, contemporaneous assault on Ivan IV's methods and
        policies during the first 40 years of his reign. Kurbsky
        provides a dramatic characterization of Ivan and an assess-
        ment of his policies as being at odds with Russia's best in-
        terests and traditions. Although clearly a biased source,
        Kurbsky's account is valuable for its contemporary quality
        and, more importantly, for providing the reader a glimpse at
        Ivan from the perspective of his victims. To quote the edi-
        tor: "Even when distorting the facts, Kurbsky sheds light
        on his viewpoint and on the viewpoint of that sector of the
        community he professed to represent--the conservative op-
        position to the tsar." DK107.K8A3
        Reviewed in:
        <u>Am Hist R</u>, 71 (Jan. 1966): 625-26
        <u>Eng Hist R</u>, 81 (Oct. 1966): 827-28
        <u>History</u>, 52 (1967): 200
        <u>Slav R</u> , 25 (1966): 691-92

65   *Gerasimov, M. M. "Ivan the Terrible, Tsar Ivan IV (1530-1584),
       Son of Basil III." The Face Finder. Alan H. Brodrick,
       trans. New York: J. B. Lippincott Company, 1971, 184-89.
       A description of Ivan IV's physical appearance and medical
       condition, based upon the findings of Soviet forensic experts
       who, in 1963, opened his tomb and examined its contents.
       Gerasimov, who was commissioned to reconstruct Ivan's facial
       features, states that Ivan was about six feet in height,
       weighed about 200 pounds, and suffered great pain from poly-
       arthritis. GN64.G413 1971

66   *Graham, Hugh F., ed./trans. "A Brief Account of the Char-
       acter and Brutal Rule of Ivan Vasil'evich, Tyrant of Muscovy
       (Albert Schlichting on Ivan Grozny)." Can Am Slav S, 9,
       no. 2 (1975): 204-72.
       A critical portrayal of Ivan IV, written by a German resident
       of Muscovy in the 1560s. Schlichting's negative image of
       Ivan was used by the papacy's envoy in Poland (Vincenzo
       dal Portico) to convince the pope to abandon a plan to seek
       assistance from Ivan in countering the Turks and in reunit-
       ing the Eastern and Western churches. As stated in an
       introduction by Hugh Graham, although Schlichting "is prej-
       udiced, clumsy, disorganized, cavalier in matters of chronol-
       ogy and careless of detail," his information provides some
       useful and interesting insights into Ivan's reign, particularly
       in regard to the oprichnina episode.

67   Graham, Stephen. Ivan the Terrible. Life of Ivan IV of Russia.
       Hamden, Conn.: Archon Books, 1968 (reprint of 1933 edi-
       tion), 335pp., bib. 322-23.
       The stated purpose of this popular study of Ivan IV is "to
       reveal his personality and character (rather) than to give
       a history of his reign." To this end, Graham provides de-
       tails on Ivan's behavior, personal relationships, and psycho-
       logical makeup. He portrays Ivan as a cruel ruler whose
       brutal policies were carefully calculated measures against
       perceived rivals to his authority and obstacles to the expan-
       sion of the Russian state. Graham concludes that Ivan's
       policies, methods, and goals bear comparison to those of
       Peter the Great. DK106.G7 1968

68   Grey, Ian. "Ivan the Terrible." Hist Today, 14, no. 5 (1964):
       326-33.
       A sympathetic portrayal of Ivan IV which clearly delineates
       his accomplishments in unifying and expanding the size of
       his realm. Grey criticizes Ivan's biographers for exaggerat-
       ing his negative qualities and disregarding his progressive
       policies and the tragic nature of his personal life.

69   _____. Ivan the Terrible. London: Hodder and Stoughton,
       1964, 256pp., bib. 247-49.

A general study of the life and policies of Ivan IV. Grey
presents a balance of information on Ivan's personality,
character, domestic policies, foreign and military affairs, and
impact on Russia's development as a nation. He portrays
Ivan as a leader who "laid the foundations of the Russian
empire by opening the way for the colonizing drive eastward," created the machinery necessary for a centralized
government, and "struggled to secure access to the Baltic
so that Russia would share in trade and free intercourse
with the rest of Europe." Grey concludes that although
cruel in method, Ivan was "far less terrible than the tsar
of legend," especially when his policies and behavior are
judged by the standards of their time. DK106.G72

70   *Hellie, Richard. "In Search of Ivan the Terrible." S. F.
     Platonov. Ivan the Terrible. Joseph L. Wieczynski, ed./
     trans. Gulf Breeze, Fla.: Academic International Press,
     1974, ix–xxxviii.
     An interesting historiographical essay on the changing nature
     of the image of Ivan IV. Hellie traces the evolution of Ivan's
     image through the writings of such historians as Tatishchev,
     Pokrovsky, Platonov, Kliuchevsky, and Skrynnikov, and then
     turns to a discussion of the oprichnina and the matter of the
     tsar's sanity. He maintains that "it is reasonable to conclude
     that Ivan was a classic paranoid" and that the many bizarre
     happenings during his reign are best considered in light of
     his less than stable mental condition. DK106.P5513

71   Hook, Donald D. "Ivan IV." Madmen of History. Middle Vil-
     lage, N.Y.: Jonathan David Publishers, 1976, 1–18.
     A discussion of Ivan IV as an individual possessed by "a
     persecution complex which had begun in his childhood as a
     result of the machinations of power-hungry boyars" and
     which deepened in response to the disloyalty shown by rep-
     resentatives of this class during his near fatal illness in
     March of 1553. Hook contends that this paranoia took a fatal
     turn with the 1560 death of Ivan's beloved wife, Anastasia,
     and that thereafter Ivan's behavior and policies "were to
     bring a new meaning to the word 'terrible.'" D110.H66

72   Inge, William R. "Three Human Monsters. Part Three. Ivan
     the Terrible." A Pacifist in Trouble. London: Putnam
     Press, 1939, 210–15.
     A brief portrayal of Ivan IV as an individual who became a
     homicidal maniac following the tragic death of his first wife.
     With an eye on Nazi aggression, Inge questions how people
     can be so morally bankrupt to follow obediently deranged
     rulers such as Ivan IV and Adolf Hitler. AC8.I525

73   Ireland, W. W. "Ivan the Terrible." The Blot upon the Brain.
     Studies in History and Psychology. Freeport, N.Y.:

Books for Libraries Press, 1972, 125-40.
An argument that Ivan IV's experiences as a youth led to his
development of sociopathic tendencies which remained latent
under the benevolent influence of his wife, Anastasia, and
advisers Sylvester and Adashev but surfaced after Anatasia's
death to result in unbounded cruelties. RC458.I73 1972

74 "Ivan the Corpse, Tomb Opened." Newsweek, 62 (23 Aug. 1963):
     38.
     A review of the findings of Soviet specialists who disinterred
     Ivan IV in 1963. The report maintains that the remains
     "bore traces of a lewd and stormy life."

75 "Ivan the Terrible." St. James M, 22 (July 1868): 449-57.
     An account of the tyrannical features of Ivan IV's reign with
     much reference to the Kurbsky-Ivan IV correspondence.
     The author also reviews Ivan's efforts to marry into the Eng-
     lish royal family.

76 Johler, Phyllis Penn, ed./trans. "The Soul of the Kremlin."
     Journey for Our Time. The Journals of the Marquis de
     Custine. Walter B. Smith, intro. New York: Peleguini
     and Cudahy, 1951, 257-84.
     A discussion of the rule of Ivan IV as an "assemblage of
     abominations," a charge supported by numerous graphic de-
     scriptions of cruelties and tortures inflicted by Ivan and
     his oprichniki on innocent victims. Custine, whose critical
     account of Russian society and institutions was widely read
     during the reign of Nicholas I, asserts that the root of
     Ivan's brutal behavior was not so much his personal defects
     as it was a by-product of the Russian autocratic system:
     "Absolute power ... would, in the long run, derange the
     soundest mind; despotism blinds men; people and ruler all
     become drunk on the cup of tyranny." DK25.C98

77 *Keenan, Edward. "Vita: Ivan Vasil'evich." Harv M, 80
     (Jan./Feb. 1980): 49.
     A brief argument that the results of a 1963 study of the re-
     mains of Ivan IV by Soviet specialists indicate that Ivan "was
     chronically ill as an adult with a most painful form of arthro-
     sis" which, coupled with the harmful side effects of the large
     doses of alcohol and various mercurials that he took to alle-
     viate pain, makes it unlikely that he had the will or ability
     to function as the forceful and omnipotent autocrat that
     many believe him to have been.

78 Klonsky, Milton, ed. "Ivan the Terrible." The Fabulous Ego.
     Absolute Power in History. New York: Quadrangle Books,
     1974, 204-29.
     A brief discussion of the Soviet rehabilitation of Ivan IV's
     historical reputation, and a series of excerpts from Jerome

Horsey's Travels which describe Ivan's military exploits, abdication in favor of Simeon Bekbulatovich, talent for creative cruelty, and, especially, his attempt to forge a military alliance with England. DK105.K55

79 Koslow, Jules. Ivan the Terrible. New York: Hill and Wang, 1961, 271pp., bib. 261–62.
    A general, undocumented account of Ivan IV's life and reign with most attention given to the brutalities associated with the oprichnina. Koslow does not see madness in Ivan's political actions but rather views them as a logical result of Ivan's conclusion that "conditions in Russia had reached such a critical point that he ... had to take extreme measures to save the throne and the country." Adding impetus to the oprichnina was Ivan's "personal ambition for unlimited power." Koslow concludes that "Ivan's vision of the greatness and power of Russia, and the political and military means to be used to realize this vision, were matched only by those of Peter the Great." DK106.K58 1961a

80 *Likhachev, Dmitri S. "The Histrionics of Ivan the Terrible: To the Question of the Farcical Style of His Works." A Lit ASH, 18, nos. 1–2 (1976): 1–10.
    An argument that the style of writing which characterizes Ivan IV's literary works provides considerable insight into the nature of his behavior as tsar. Likhachev contends that Ivan's principal stylistic traits, his "emotionalism and excitability, drastic alterations of lofty Church Slavonic language and brusque popular speech are derived not so much from an adopted literary school or literary tradition as from his nature and are part of his behavior. They are pregnant with the traditions of buffoonery rather than elements of literary tradition."

81 MacLaurin, C. "Ivan the Terrible." Mere Mortals. Medico-Historical Essays. New York: George H. Doran Company, 1926, 103–16.
    An assertion that Ivan IV suffered from "diffuse cerebral syphilis of the aortic valve," and that this affliction, which produces violent mental irritation, largely accounts for his "murderous political activity" and, ultimately, his death.

82 *McNally, Raymond T. "The Image of Ivan IV 'The Terrible' in the Works of Peter Chaadaev, Ivan Kireevskii and Aleksei Khomiakov." RSH (anthology), 91–104.
    The threefold purpose of this article is to demonstrate similarities in the images of Ivan IV put forth by Chaadaev, Kireevsky, and Khomiakov; to "trace the reasons behind this common negative image, given the differing ideological positions of these three writers; and to analyze the meaning of their final evaluations of Ivan IV for Russian intellectual

history during the 1840s." McNally maintains that although
all three writers portrayed Ivan negatively, Chaadaev believed "Ivan had unfortunately grown organically out of historical conditions in Russia whereas to Kireevsky and Khomiakov, Ivan had been an essential aberration." The assessments of all three, however, besides being historically inaccurate show a concern for the general pattern of historical
development rather than for research into the factual data of
history, and, as such, pre-shadow developments in Russian
intellectual history of the 1840s.

83 *Manning, C. A. "The Songs of Ivan the Terrible and His
    Sons." Todd Memorial Volumes. Philological Studies, Vol.
    II. John D. Fitzgerald and Pauline Taylor, eds. Freeport,
    N.Y.: Books for Libraries Press, 1968 (reprint of 1930
    edition), 17-24.
    A discussion of regional variations of the historical song
    which tells of Ivan IV ordering the execution of one of his
    sons because Ivan suspected, wrongly, that he was guilty
    of conspiring against him. The son's life was saved by the
    daring intervention of Nikita Romanovich, an act that went
    unpunished as the grieving Ivan reacted with jubilation upon
    learning that his son was still alive. Manning groups by
    region the 43 examples of this song, notes their peculiarities
    and historical inaccuracies, and links these variations to
    both the time during which they were composed and the
    culture of the region in which they were sung. He con-
    cludes that "whether or not the theme be an allusion to the
    tsar's murderous attack on (his son) Ivan, the songs give
    us a powerful portraiture of the impulsive ruler with his
    fits of anger and his spells of mercy and hence are important
    in picturing to us the impression which Ivan the Terrible
    made upon his court, his subjects, and his victims."
    PC14.T74 1968

84 Menken, Jules. "Ivan the Terrible." Hist Today, 43, no. 3
    (1953): 167-73.
    A sketch of Ivan IV's personal life and reign with most at-
    tention given to him as the "founder of modern Russia and
    the originator of the disciplining system by means of which
    many Russian rulers since have held their power."

85 *Miller, David B. "The Coronation of Ivan IV of Moscow."
    Jahr Ges Ost, 15 (1967): 559-74.
    An analysis of the coronation rite of 1547, and a comparison
    of it to the 1498 coronation of Dimitry, grandson of Ivan III.
    Miller maintains that the 1547 coronation had far more Byzan-
    tine imperial overtones than that of 1498.

86 "New Soviet Supermovie Makes a Hero out of Czar." Life, 18
    (12 Mar. 1945): 90-95.

A review of the favorable portrayal of Ivan IV in Sergei
Eisenstein's film Ivan the Terrible.

87 Payne, Robert, and Nikita Romanoff. Ivan the Terrible. New
    York: Thomas Y. Crowell, 1975, 502pp., bib. 451-63.
    A detailed semi-popular biography of Ivan IV. The authors
    discuss the standard highlights of Ivan's life and reign while
    painting a picture of him as a remarkably vicious and de-
    structive ruler whose cruelties are best viewed as a conse-
    quence of his precarious and fear-ridden childhood. Payne
    and Romanoff are especially critical of Ivan's oprichniki who
    are described as a "vast swarm of maggots eating away at
    his throne" and of Ivan's involvement in the oprichnina as
    he became "almost an abstraction of pure evil." They con-
    clude that Ivan "left his country in disarray, exhausted
    by his savagery," and they add that "his greatest gift to
    the Russian people was his own death." Included are a
    number of interesting illustrations depicting events and in-
    dividuals associated with Ivan's reign. DK106.P39

88 Peatman, Mary N. "Sergei Eisenstein's Ivan the Terrible as a
    Cinematic Realization of the Concept of the Gesamtkunstwerk."
    Indiana University, 1975. (dissertation)

89 Pember, Austen. Ivan the Terrible, His Life and Times. Lon-
    don: A. P. Marsden, 1895, 262pp.
    Unavailable for annotation.

90 *Perrie, Maureen. "The Popular Image of Ivan the Terrible."
    Slavonic E Eur R, 56, no. 2 (1978): 275-86.
    The stated purpose of this article is "to explore the origins
    of the popular image of the tsar, and to put forward an
    explanation for its emergence." Perrie establishes that
    Ivan IV's popular image as a "just tsar" came about not only
    because of the people's support of Ivan in his struggles with
    the boyars but also because Ivan himself "sought to create
    such an image by populist devices and appeals to the people
    for support."

91 *Platonov, S. F. Ivan the Terrible. Joseph L. Wieczynski,
    ed./trans. Gulf Breeze, Fla.: Academic International Press,
    1974, 166pp.
    A scholarly examination of "the motivation of Ivan the Ter-
    rible in his political work ... and the influences that caused
    his reign to assume its peculiar behavior." Platonov, an
    eminent Russian historian, contends that the drastic and
    seemingly bizarre nature of Ivan's policies, especially the
    oprichnina, were carefully calculated steps in the systematic
    obliteration of the power of those groups opposed to the
    establishment of absolute and centralized control over Mus-
    covy by the tsar. Ivan thus emerges from this study as an

astute politician and a statesman of considerable stature whose
positive qualities and accomplishments have been obscured by
critics blind to his true goals and the historical circumstances
which confronted him. DK106.P5513
Reviewed in:
Can Am Slav S, 9, no. 1 (1975): 113-14.
Slav R, 34, no. 2 (1975): 383-84

92 *_____. "Ivan the Terrible in Russian Historiography."
Sidney Harcave, trans. RRH, Vol. I, 188-94. Originally in
Russkoe Proshloe, no. 1 (1923): 3-12.
An examination of the evolution of Russian historical judgments on Ivan the Terrible and the significance of his reign.
Platonov states that the study of Ivan IV has been complicated by the paucity of material available on sixteenth century Muscovy and by the extremely subjective and often
tendentious character of the writings of Ivan's contemporaries. In reviewing the principal works and major schools
of thought concerning Ivan, Platonov identifies as the basic
trend the growth of Ivan's "stature as a statesman and administrator" and "the minimization of the significance of his
personal qualities and shortcomings." Platonov concludes
that the principal features of Ivan's policies remained consistent throughout his reign and that these policies were
"at all times marked by powerful initiative, broad conceptions, and ... energetic execution...."

93 Potter, George W. "Ivan the Terrible." Royal Blood. Garden
City, N.Y.: Doubleday Press, 1964, 135-72.
A description of various cruelties perpetrated by Ivan IV,
and an account of his accidental murder of his son, written
to entertain the general public by presenting Ivan as a
prime example of "the various murderers, maniacs, perverts
and monsters who pursued the bloody route to royalty."
HV6278.P66

94 Rappoport, Angelo A. "Madman of the Kremlin." Mad Majesties
or Raving Rulers and Their Submissive Subjects. London:
Greening and Company, 1910, 273-92.
A portrayal of Ivan IV as "the degenerate offspring of an
already degenerate, neuropathic family." Rappoport contends
that Ivan's deranged mental condition shaped his perception
of the world around him and determined the grotesque nature of the policies he adopted in dealing with that world.

95 *Sakharov, A. M., and D. H. Kaiser, eds. "Historical Knowledge in the Sixteenth Century." Sov St Hist, 18, no. 3
(1979-80): 86-110.
In part, a discussion of the exploits of Ivan IV and the expansion and strengthening of the Russian state under his
rule as expressed first in folktales and later in sixteenth-
century official histories.

96   *Skrynnikov, Ruslan G. <u>Ivan the Terrible</u>. Hugh F. Graham,
     ed./trans. Gulf Breeze, Fla.: Academic International Press,
     1981, 219pp.
     A scholarly study of Ivan IV's reign with most attention
     given to his internal policies. Skrynnikov, a Soviet special-
     ist on sixteenth century Russia, presents a detailed analysis
     of the complex historical, economic, political, and personal
     factors which shaped Ivan's thought and actions. Although
     he does not directly attack the view that Ivan's reign
     marked the emergence of an autocratic state in Russia, he
     offers a new interpretation of the <u>oprichnina</u> as a move back-
     wards towards appanage Russia and a perversion of the
     course of political development being followed in the sixteenth
     century. Skrynnikov concludes that the rulers who succeeded
     Ivan were even more dependent upon the very nobles who
     were the targets of the <u>oprichniki</u>. In an interesting intro-
     duction, Hugh Graham reviews critically the principal his-
     torical writings on Ivan IV. DK106.S4513

97   *_____. "An Overview of the Reign of Ivan IV: What Was
     the <u>Oprichnina</u>?" <u>Sov St Hist</u>, 24, nos. 1-2 (1985): 62-82.

98   *Staden, Heinrich von. <u>The Land and Government of Muscovy.
     A Sixteenth Century Account</u>. Thomas Esper, ed./trans.
     Stanford: Stanford University Press, 1967, 142pp.
     Although Ivan IV is not the sole focus of any one chapter
     in this work, it contains a number of firsthand observations
     on his policies of the 1560s and 1570s. The book is divided
     into three sections: the land and government of Muscovy,
     a "plan for the conquest of Russia," and Staden's autobiog-
     raphy. Of particular interest is Staden's description of the
     <u>oprichnina</u> (the only account in existence written by an
     <u>oprichnik</u>) which de-emphasizes the cruel and terroristic
     features of the <u>oprichnina</u> and stresses Ivan's use of terror
     as a political and psychological weapon against the opponents
     of autocracy. In an introductory essay, Thomas Esper dis-
     cusses the career of Staden and the nature of the <u>oprichnina</u>.
     DK106.S7513

99   "Subway Workers Dig up Ivan the Terrible's Terrors." <u>News-
     week</u>, 6 (20 July 1935): 15.
     A brief review of "the horrors of Ivan IV's reign," prompted
     by the unearthing of a sixteenth-century "torture chamber"
     by workers laboring on the construction of the Moscow metro
     system.

100 *Szeftel, Marc. "The Epithet <u>Groznyj</u> in Historical Perspective."
     <u>The Religious World of Russian Culture. Russia and Ortho-
     doxy: Essays in Honor of Georges Florovsky</u>, Vol. II.
     Andrew Bond, ed. The Hague: Mouton, 1975, 101-15.

The purpose of this essay is to illustrate that a close examination of the historical background of Ivan IV's epithet
"Grozny" shows a much more complicated origin of this term,
and its much richer significance" than is indicated by those
interpretations which connect the term to Ivan's harsh
policies and cruel behavior. Szeftel maintains that the
epithet "was used in different forms even before it was applied to Ivan IV, and that in no instance did it pertain to
the sternness or cruelty of the times. The epithet was not
given to Ivan for the brutalities which he introduced in the
latter part of his reign, but for the shining glory which he
brought to its beginning." Only well after Ivan's era did
the negative connotations associated with the epithet replace,
and eventually obscure from historical memory, the original
meaning of the term. BX250.R87

101 Thomas, Lowell. "Ivan the Terrible." The Vital Spark. Garden City, N.Y.: Doubleday Press, 1959, 262-65.
A brief portrayal of Ivan IV as an intelligent but coarse and
brutal ruler whose foreign policy foreshadowed that of Peter
the Great. CT104.T537

102 *Thompson, K. "Ivan the Terrible and Stalinist Russia: A
Re-examination." Cinema J, 17, no. 1 (1977): 30-43.
An evaluation of Dwight MacDonald's assessment of Eisen-
stein's film Ivan the Terrible as a subtle anti-Stalinist al-
legory. In the process of challenging the validity of
MacDonald's interpretation, Thompson reviews the evolution
of historical scholarship on Ivan IV, the favorable image of
Ivan propagated by Soviet historians in the 1940s, and
Stalin's personal interest in Eisenstein's direction of the
film version of the tsar's life. While Thompson notes the
existence of similarities between the policies and actions of
Ivan and Stalin, he fails to find sufficient grounds to support an anti-Stalinist reading of the film.

103 Troyat, Henri. Ivan the Terrible. Joan Pinkham, trans.
New York: E. P. Dutton, 1984, 283pp., bib. 267-69.
A stylish, popular account of Ivan's life and reign. Troyat,
who has authored similar biographies of Catherine II and
Alexander I, discusses Ivan's reforms, domestic policies,
and military ventures, but he is at his best when describing
Ivan's character, behavior, and personal life. Concentrating
on Ivan's deeds and actions rather than the motivation behind them, Troyat portrays Ivan as a paranoic wielding a
heavy fist in cruel and sadistic ways against real and, more
often than not, imaginary enemies. He suggests that Ivan
was driven to madness, toward the end of his life, by guilt
over the pain and death he had inflicted upon a suffering
Russian people: "Ivan discovered that there were instruments

real authors of the letter. Auerbach also contends that
Kurbsky's writings best fit within a mid-sixteenth- rather
than mid-seventeenth-century historical context.

110 *Backus, Oswald P. "A. M. Kurbsky in the Polish-Lithuanian
State (1564-83)." Acta Balt-Slav, 6 (1969): 29-50.
The Lithuanian career of Kurbsky is the focus of this article, but it includes an interesting discussion of the nobility's
inability to counter the growth of Muscovite absolutism and
of Kurbsky's motives for opposing Ivan IV.

111 *_____. "Treason as a Concept and Defections from Moscow
to Lithuania in the Sixteenth Century." Forsch Ost Ges,
15 (1970): 119-44.
An argument that, during the mid-sixteenth century, the
existence of an "appanage psychology and the slowness of
the development of a legal concept of treason not only call
into question the extent to which the powers of the Muscovite ruler had grown but also suggest that the idea of a
state developed less quickly in Muscovy than some would
have us believe." Backus points to the treatment of two
instances of flight from Muscovy to Lithuania (by Princes
Belsky and Kurbsky) to show that "the concept of the
right of departure was not truly dead" and that the concept
of treason lacked any clear definition.

112 *Bakhrushin, S. V. "The Emergence of Muscovy: The Tsar's
Authority." RRPDH, Vol. I (anthology), 8-10. Translation
from Nauchnye trudy, Vol. II, Moscow, 1954, 267-69, 274-75.
A brief Soviet discussion of the influence exerted upon Ivan
IV by representatives of the service nobility (especially
Ivan Peresvetov) who attempted to advance their class in-
terests by encouraging him to strengthen the monarchy at
the expense of the boyars.

113 *Baron, Samuel H. "Ivan the Terrible, Giles Fletcher and the
Muscovite Merchantry: A Reconsideration." Slavonic E Eur
R, 56 (Oct. 1978): 563-85.
An argument that the prevalent view of the nature of the
Muscovite trading class "underestimates the status, influence,
and role of the merchantry, at least its upper strata." Baron
asserts that the merchants "were listened to, and sometimes
they were heeded" by Ivan IV, although "their influence was
distinctly limited by considerations of state interest as defined by the ruler."

114 *Blum, Jerome. "Absolutism and Aristocracy." Lord and
Peasant in Russia from the Ninth to the Nineteenth Century.
New York: Atheneum, 1964, 135-51.
In part, a discussion of the circumstances and motives which
led Ivan IV to attempt to unify his realm by breaking the
power of the aristocracy through the creation of the

oprichnina. Blum sees this policy as an insane one which
not only failed to achieve its objective but ultimately led
the nation into the Time of Troubles.   D210.G6

115 *Cherniavsky, Michael. "Ivan the Terrible and the Iconography
of the Cathedral of Archangel Michael." Rus Hist, 2, no. 1
(1975): 3-28.
An interpretation of the iconography of the Cathedral of
Archangel Michael as an attempt by Ivan IV to add another
dimension to the official rationale for Muscovite absolutism by
presenting the royal family as "a biological entity" and
thereby creating a type of self-justification for its claim to
power.

116 *_____. "Ivan the Terrible as Renaissance Prince." Slav R,
27, no. 2 (1968): 195-211.
An analysis of Ivan's epithet "the Terrible" with much reference to the image of the ruler in Western renaissance writings (most notably the works of Petrarch and Machiavelli),
Ivan's own political thought, and the writings of Ivan Peresvetov, a member of the service gentry. Cherniavsky sees
similarities between Ivan's views and those prominent in
renaissance political thought, although Ivan believed evilness
moved men more than greed and ambition.

117 *Crummey, Robert O. "The Kurbskii Controversy." Can Slav
P, 14, no. 4 (1972): 684-89.
A review article on Keenan's The Kurbskii-Groznyi Apocrypha.
Crummey commends Keenan for his imaginative and insightful argument and for stimulating further inquiry into the
Kurbsky-Ivan IV correspondence, but he believes that Keenan
may have created a methodological straightjacket as counter-
productive to fruitful inquiry as the conventional compla-
cency of the historians who Keenan criticizes. Crummey also
questions Keenan's contention that "the future discussion of
the literary heritage of both Ivan and Kurbskii is to be
carried on entirely within the context of the rich literature
of the seventeenth century" rather than in the context of
both the sixteenth and seventeenth centuries.

118 *Culpepper, Jack M. "The Kremlin Executions of 1575 and the
Enthronement of Simeon Bekbulatovich." Slav R, 24, no.
3 (1965): 503-06.
An argument that Ivan IV's 1575 abdication and enthronement
of Simeon Bekbulatovich was a direct response to the un-
covering of a boyar conspiracy against Ivan. Culpepper does
not speculate on how Bekbulatovich's accession to the throne
would have protected Ivan from the conspirators.

119 Deriabin, Peter. "Ivan the Terrible." WT (gen. study), 34-37.
A brief account of the circumstances which led Ivan IV to
create the oprichnina, and a few graphic details on his use

of the oprichniki as a police force to eliminate enemies,
real or imaginary.

120 _____. "Streltsy and Oprichniki." Ibid., 104-14.
A discussion of the Muscovite security forces as the brain
children of a tsar gone mad. Deriabin concentrates on the
cruelties, death, and destruction meted out by the oprichniki under the maniacal leadership of the "chief criminal,"
Ivan IV.

121 *Dewey, Horace W. "Charters of Local Government Under
Tsar Ivan IV." Jahr Ges Ost, 14 (1966): 10-20.
An analysis of the origins, purpose, and results of Ivan IV's
1556 reform of local government. Dewey argues that "the
tsar and his immediate advisers were the primary benefici-
aries of the reform" not the bourgeoisie, gentry, or general
populace as asserted by some historians. In fact, the reform was less a response to popular request than it was the
product of Ivan's need for increased state revenues to fund
his military ventures.

122 * _____. "The 1550 Sudebnik as an Instrument of Reform."
Jahr Ges Ost, 10, no. 2 (1962): 161-80.
An argument that "no one can deny the reforming purpose
of the Sudebnik's articles on judicial administration, maintenance of public safety, and its general attempt to put
Russian society on a more carefully regulated basis," but "as
Ivan became more and more a true autocrat" his personal
attitude toward law and administration became increasingly
arbitrary and was directly contrary to the spirit of the
Sudebnik. Dewey concludes that within a decade after its
promulgation, the Sudebnik lost its meaning as an instrument of reform, although it "lived on in the minds of some
Russians as a model legal document."

123 Ezergailis, Andrew. "U.S.S.R. Totalitarian State or Oprichnina?" Il Pol, 35, no. 2 (1971): 329-48.
A portrayal of the Soviet Union as a "failed and burned out
utopia" bearing more resemblance to Ivan IV's oprichnina
than to a modern totalitarian state.

124 *Fedotov, George P. St. Filipp. Metropolitan of Moscow--
Encounter with Ivan the Terrible. Richard Haugh and
Nikolaus Lupinin, trans. Belmont, Mass.: Nordland, 1978,
207pp.
The purpose of this scholarly study of Metropolitan Filipp's
opposition to the brutal policies of Ivan IV is to counter the
interpretation that the Orthodox Church was an obedient
servant of autocracy. Fedotov traces carefully the events
and developments which led Filipp to oppose Ivan and the
latter to stage the trial which resulted in Filipp's incarceration and execution. Fedotov maintains that "from St. Filipp's

feat we understand the Russian saints did not serve the
almighty Muscovite secular power but rather they served
the light of Christ which shone in the Tsardom and only
while this light shone." Appended is a series of historical
revaluations of the oprichnina. BX597.F5F413

125 *Fennell, J. L. I., ed./trans. The Correspondence Between
Prince A. M. Kurbsky and Tsar Ivan IV of Russia. Cambridge: Cambridge University Press, 1955, 275pp., bib.
266-67.
This series of letters between Ivan IV and Prince Kurbsky,
who was a trusted and valuable servitor in Muscovy prior to
his defection to Lithuania, is considered by many historians
to be one of the most important and revealing documents of
the sixteenth century. In them, Kurbsky assails Ivan, his
policies, and his political philosophy, while Ivan responds
with an impressive defense of divine right monarchy. Recently, the authenticity of this correspondence has been
questioned by Edward Keenan (see entry 137). DK106.A25
    Reviewed in:
    Eng Hist R, 71 (1956): 485
    Slav R, 16 (1957): 415
    Slavonic E Eur R, 35 (1956-57): 304

126 *Graham, Hugh F., ed./trans. "The Missio Muscovita." Can
Am Slav S, 6, no. 3 (1972): 437-77.
An account of conditions in Muscovy, written by the Italian
priest and diplomat Antonio Possevino who was sent to Moscow by Pope Gregory XIII upon Ivan IV's request for papal
mediation in the Livonian War. Of particular interest is
Possevino's account of the occupations of Ivan's former
oprichniki. In a preface, Hugh Graham provides historical
background for Possevino's mission and experiences.

127 *Grobovsky, Antony N. The 'Chosen Council' of Ivan IV: A
Reinterpretation. Brooklyn: Theodore Gaus and Sons, 1969,
171pp., bib. 159-64.
A scholarly examination of the historical context, membership,
and significance of the Izbrannaia rada, Ivan IV's "chosen
council." Grobovsky reviews the various historical interpretations of the rada's structure, composition, and leadership
and its relationship with and influence on Ivan IV. He
concludes that the existence of a powerful "party" of individuals who limited Ivan's authority and greatly influenced
his decisions is a historiographic construct without foundation in reality. DK106.5.G7
    Reviewed in:
    Am Hist R, 76 (Feb. 1971): 166
    Slav R, 30, no. 1 (1971): 136-37

128 _____. "The 'Chosen Council' of Ivan IV: A Reinterpretation." Yale University, 1969-70. (dissertation)

129 *Gudzy, N. K. "Publistic Literature in the Sixteenth Century:
     Works of Ivan Peresvetov, A. Kurbsky, Ivan the Terrible."
     History of Early Russian Literature. Susan W. Jones, trans.
     New York: Octagon Books, 1970 (reprint of 1949 edition),
     333-40.
     An analysis of Peresvetov's Legend of Sultan Mahomet and
     Tale of a Man Who Loved God, both of which support Ivan
     IV's political policies and foreshadow the creation of the
     oprichnina. Gudzy also presents a brief, stylistic assess-
     ment of the Kurbsky-Ivan IV correspondence. PG3001.G762

130 *Halperin, Charles J. "Keenan's Heresy Revisited." Jahr Ges
     Ost, 28, no. 4 (1980): 481-99.
     A review article on a decade of reactions to Edward Keenan's
     The Kurbsky-Groznyi Apocrypha.

131 *Hellie, Richard. Enserfment and Military Change in Muscovy.
     Chicago: University of Chicago Press, 1971, 432pp.
     This scholarly examination of the evolution of serfdom and
     military service in Muscovy does not contain a chapter which
     focuses solely upon the role played by any one monarch in
     these twin developments, but it includes numerous references
     to policies pursued by Tsars Ivan IV, Boris Godunov, and
     Alexis pertinent to the subjects under study. HT807.H44

132 _____. "The 'Forbidden Years.'" Readings for Introduction
     to Russian Civilization: Muscovite Society. Chicago:
     University of Chicago Press, 1967, 110-22.
     A study of the circumstances surrounding the initial (1581)
     suspension of the Russian peasants' freedom of movement
     from estate to estate. Hellie sees this decision as being
     prompted, in part, by Ivan IV's desire to address the in-
     creasing need of landowners to protect their labor supply
     in light of the disastrous consequences of the oprichnina
     and Livonian War and by his eagerness to provide additional
     favors to the service gentry upon whom he relied so heavily
     for support. There follows a series of documents which
     illustrate the use of "forbidden years" in the 1581-1649
     period. KR280.H3

133 *Hulbert, Ellerd. "The Zemskii Sobor of 1575: A Mistake in
     Translation." Slav R, 25, no. 2 (1966): 320-22.
     An argument that Ivan IV did not convene a zemsky sobor
     in 1575, as claimed by V. I. Koretsky in a 1959 Istoricheskii
     arkhiv article (no. 2, 148-56), but rather only a council of
     military advisers.

134 Huttenbach, Henry R. "The Zemsky Sobor in Ivan IV's Reign."
     University of Washington, 1961. (dissertation)

135 *"Ivan the Terrible's Principles of Economic Policy." HRET

(anthology), 145-75.
A favorable, Soviet discussion of the economic policy of Ivan IV as one which "was subordinated to two basic aims: consolidation of the Russian state and strengthening of the autocratic power of the tsar." Within this context, the authors discuss the economic content of the Sudebnik of 1550, the 'tsarist inquiries' of the Stoglav Council of 1551, Ivan's "various decrees which determined the reforms of the 1550s and thereafter," his correspondences with Prince Kurbsky and Queen Elizabeth, his judicial, financial, and administrative reforms, and, especially, his creation of the oprichnina.

136 "Ivan the Terrible's Punishment of Novgorod in 1570." MRSB (anthology), 203-07. Excerpt from Polnoe Sobranie Russikh Letopisei (Complete Collection of Russian Chronicles), Vol. III. St. Petersburg, 1885, 254-62.
An account of Ivan IV's brutal destruction of Novgorod in 1570 because he suspected that the city was about to seek Polish-Lithuanian protection against Muscovy. The Chronicle speaks of Ivan conducting ingenious tortures "in various spiteful, horrible, and inhuman ways" including death by roasting, mass drownings in the Volkhov River, and mutilation by ravenous animals.

137 *Keenan, Edward. The Kurbskii-Groznyi Apocrypha. The Seventeenth Century Genesis of the "Correspondence" Attributed to Prince A. M. Kurbskii and Tsar Ivan IV. Cambridge: Harvard University Press, 1971, 241pp., bib. 231-37.
A reassessment of the content, context, language, and structure of the correspondence between Ivan IV and Prince A. Kurbsky. Keenan maintains that the letters, long prized by historians as a unique and valuable source of information on Ivan IV and sixteenth century Muscovy, were written "neither by Ivan nor by Kurbsky, nor indeed in their time." He asserts that the initial letters were most likely the work of Semen Shakhovskoi, and the remainder, and Kurbsky's History of Ivan IV, were written during the last quarter of the seventeenth century by persons in the upper level of state service. DK106.5K4
Reviewed in:
Can Am Slav S, 6 (1972): 490-93
Can J Hist, 7 (1972): 188-89
Can Slav P, 14 (1972): 684-89
J Mod Hist, 45 (1973): 489-90
Rus R, 32 (1973): 299-311
Slav R, 31 (1972): 882-83
Slavonic E Eur R, 16 (1972): 223-36

138 _____. "Paper for the Tsar: A Letter of Ivan IV of 1570." Ox Slavonic P, 4 (1971): 21-29.

An examination of the watermark on the paper on which a
26 September 1570 letter was written by Ivan IV to King
Frederik II of Denmark for insight into determining the date
of the first Russian paper mill. Keenan states that the
watermark (which usually indicates the origin of the paper)
suggests that there was a short-lived mill on the Ucha River
in the 1560s under the control of Merten Saver.

139 *_____. "Putting Kurbskii in His Place, or: Observations
and Suggestions Concerning the Place of the History of the
Grand Prince of Moscow in the History of Muscovite Literary
Culture." Forsch Ost Ges, 24 (1978): 131-61.
An argument that an "examination of the manuscript tradition, the language and style of the text, its genre and literary sources" leads to the hypothesis that Kurbsky's
History was "composed in several stages in Moscow around
1675, and its author or authors were persons whose literary
culture was very much like that of the individuals whom one
usually associates with the Chudov circles ... and 'grecophile'
literary activities of that time."

140 *_____. "R. G. Skrynnikov, Perepiska Groznogo i Kurbsko-
go. Paradoksy Edvarda Kinana." Kritika, 10, no. 1 (Fall
1973): 1-36.
A detailed review of Skrynnikov's critical analysis of the
author's controversial work on the inauthenticity of the Kurbsky-Ivan IV correspondence. Keenan asserts that "Skrynnikov concentrates on the lesser probabilities as clearly defined
in the book, on matters perhaps insufficiently treated and
on the weaving of new possible explanations of the 'para-
doxes' that surround the whole matter" and appears to be
"content with the old answers and with contriving new variations of explanation within the traditional conceptual bounds."
While Skrynnikov's book does raise some new and interesting questions, Keenan concludes, the question of the authorship of the correspondence cannot be determined conclusively unless the Soviet Academy of Sciences publishes all rele-
vant manuscripts.

141 *_____. "Reply." Jahr Ges Ost, 22, no. 4 (1974): 593-
617.
A questioning of C. Halperin's assertion (Jahr Ges Ost, 22,
1974:161-213) that the best evidence in support of the hypothesis that the Kurbsky-Ivan IV correspondence is a forgery
rests on the pattern of the letters' preservation rather than
on textual issues.

142 *_____. "Some Observations on R. G. Skrynnikov's Views
Concerning the Kurbskii-Groznyi Apocrypha." Slav R, 38,
no. 1 (1979): 89-91.
A response to Skrynnikov's claim (Slav R, 37, no. 1, 1978:

107-15)   of the first letter
in the   ias been resolved.
Keenan   g "definite proof
of auth(he several versions
of Ivan'   is still in doubt,"
and tha   isitively dated within a dec   ely that Kurbsky
had no j   er to Ivan.

143 *Kleimola, A   e Muscovite Autocracy; the .... ᴜᴇɴtury: Sources of Weakness."
Jahr Ges Ost, 25, no. 4 (1977): 481-93.
An argument that although the actions of the oprichniki
certainly played a significant role in restricting and eliminating "would-be aristocratic challengers" to Ivan IV's power
and authority, his reign's "most important contribution to
weakening the aristocracy lay in its fostering increased
factionalism and atomization within the elite."

144 *_____. The Muscovite Autocracy at Work: The Use of
Disgrace as an Instrument of Control." Russian Law:
Historical and Political Perspectives. William E. Butler, ed.
Leyden: A. W. Sitjhoff, 1977, 29-50.
An account of the Muscovite grand princes' use of opala (the
sovereign's "disgrace" or "disfavor" which led to loss of
rank, position, wealth, and/or property) as an instrument
of political control. Kleimola states that opala was used
selectively, but effectively, by Ivan's predecessors, but in
his reign, particularly during the oprichnina period, political
denunciations occurred on a massive scale and the punishments meted out to the disgraced became more severe and
were extended to entire families. Ivan's gross abuse of
opala "severely shook the social foundations of the state"
and precipitated such a crisis that he relented in his use of
this device, in the early 1580s, and granted "posthumous
amnesty to a group of several thousand persons who had
perished in the oprichnina terror." After Ivan's death, a
reaction set in against the use of opala, and, as a result,
"in practice, disgrace as a political weapon nearly disappeared
in the seventeenth century" though it continued through the
reign of Peter I.

145 *"The Kurbskii Controversy." RSH (anthology), 212-59.
Opening remarks by Edward Keenan (pp. 212-17) on the
current status of the study of the authorship of the Kurbsky-
Ivan IV correspondence precede papers by D. Waugh and I.
Auerbach (see entries 109 and 164) presented at the First
International Slavic Conference (Banf, 1974). Also included
(pp. 251-59) are the reactions of Keenan and other historians
in attendance to these two papers.

146   *McCormick, Donald. "Ivan the Terrible and His Oprichniki."
        HRSS (gen. study), 11-23.
        A portrayal of Ivan IV's oprichniki as the forerunners of
        the Okhrana and Cheka. McCormick examines the circum-
        stances which prompted Ivan to form the oprichniki, and
        then he discusses this agency as "a nation-wide organization
        of spies, informers, torturers, and executioners to smell out
        and put down enemies wherever they were to be found."
        The excesses of the oprichniki and the opposition which they
        aroused eventually led Ivan to realize "what a monstrous
        force he had created." McCormick discounts the theory that,
        in forming the oprichniki, Ivan was following a carefully
        conceived plan to advance the centralization of the Russian
        state.

147   Magnus, L. A. "Ivan the Terrible." The Heroic Ballads of
        Russia. New York: E. P. Dutton, 1921, 125-28.
        A brief, critical review of Ivan IV's reign with most atten-
        tion devoted to the activities of the oprichniki: "The un-
        concealed lawlessness and savagery of these devastating vis-
        itations have made Ivan IV's name a deathless byword."
        PG3104.M33 1967

148   Marcu, V. "Ivan the Terrible and Stalin." Cur Hist, 48 (May
        1938): 50-52.
        A brief comparison of the political methodology and goals of
        Ivan IV and Joseph Stalin.

149   Miller, David B. "The Literary Activities of Metropolitan
        Macarius: A Study of Muscovite Political Ideology in the
        Time of Ivan IV." Columbia University, 1970. (disserta-
        tion)

150   *_____. "The Viskovatyi Affair of 1553-54: Official Art,
        the Emergence of Autocracy, and the Disintegration of
        Medieval Russian Culture." Rus Hist, 8 (1981): 292-332.
        An examination of Ivan Viskovaty's 1553-54 trial on the
        charge that he publicly criticized the new icons and frescoes
        that decorated the Church of the Annunciation and the royal
        palace following the fire of 1547. Miller discusses the trial,
        which was presided over by Ivan IV and Metropolitan Macari-
        us, as an example of "incipient paranoia" which developed
        in Ivan IV after the dynastic crisis associated with Ivan's
        near death in 1553.

151   *Nørretranders, Bjarne. "Ivan Groznyj's Conception of Tsarist
        Authority." Scando-Slav, 9 (1963): 238-48.
        An investigation of the complex roots of Ivan IV's political
        ideology. Nørretranders discusses the influence of Byzantine
        tradition and the thought of Joseph of Volokolamsk while
        noting the independent and original elements in Ivan's own
        thinking on the secularization of autocratic power.

152 *_____. The Shaping of Czardom Under Ivan Groznyj.
London: Variorum Reprints, 1971 (reprint of 1964 edition),
188pp.
The stated purpose of this scholarly study is to analyze
"the formation of Muscovite Czarism under Ivan Groznyj by
considering the fundamental decisions and actions of the
period in relation to ideological and practical motives."
Nørretranders maintains that th---   -ical behavior of the
crown. churc'   nobility was determined
far   y any cohesive set of
prin   d a distinct ideology
(one   ential means of support
for l   willingly sanctioned
autoc   ogical integrity and
sovei   privileges and political in   implicated set of practical l   d the absence of any
"canal   could take the form
of an   ---- policy," Ivan reacted
pragma   _ _y attempting to deal with Russia's domestic
problems and foreign challengers by concentrating power in
his own hands and ruling without compromise. Nørretranders
concludes that Ivan's "upbringing, conditions, and situations
compelled him to rule on the basis of a religious axiom, and
his concrete tasks urged him to liberate himself from that
religious axiom. In his statements of principle, he clearly
showed how far he had moved towards a secularized way of
thinking." JN6541.N63 1971
    Reviewed in:
    Slav R, 33, no. 4 (1974): 711.

153 *Ostrowski, Donald. "Review of Perepiska Ivana Groznogo s
Andreem Kurbskim by Iakov Solomonovich Lur'e and Iurii
Dmitrievich Rykov." Kritika, 17, no. 1 (Winter 1981): 1-
17.
A review of a new Soviet edition of the Prince Kurbsky-Ivan
IV correspondence and the interpretive essays appended to
this work. Ostrowski comments on the merits of Soviet research on the thorny question of the authorship of the correspondence and provides support for Keenan's hypothesis
as being the most acceptable in light of the available evidence.

154 *Owen, Thomas C. "A Lexical Approach to the Kurbskii-Groznyi
Problem." Slav R, 41, no. 4 (1982): 686-91.
An argument for the study of the vocabulary of the Kurbsky-
Ivan IV correspondence as a means of dating the letters and
resolving the question of the authenticity of these much
studied letters. Owen adds that while a purely lexical approach could advance the likelihood of resolving the historical
debate over the letters' authorship, such an inquiry could
not be conducted successfully without extensive cooperation
from Soviet historians and archivists.

155 *Pokrovsky, M. N. "Oprichnina: A Marxist Interpretation."
     RIRH (anthology), 67-75.
     An interpretation of Ivan IV's creation of the oprichnina
     as a premature attempt "to found a personal autocracy like
     the Petrine monarchy." Pokrovsky, a noted Soviet historian,
     criticizes those historians who have presented the oprichnina
     as a bizarre product of a demented tyrant. He argues in-
     stead that the oprichnina was a carefully designed innovation
     in response to pressing economic and political concerns. Of
     particular interest is Pokrovsky's description of the domain
     of the oprichnina and the composition of its army.

156 *Rossing, Niels, and Birgit Rønne. Apocryphal--Not Apocry-
     phal? A Critical Analysis of the Discussion Concerning the
     Correspondence Between Tsar Ivan Groznyj and Prince Andrej
     Kurbskij. Copenhagen: Rosenkilde and Bagger, 1980,
     189pp., bib. 174-78.
     An analysis of Edward Keenan's The Kurbskii-Groznyi
     Apocrypha and the academic debate spawned by this work
     among specialists in Russian history, literature, and lan-
     guage who have criticized, supplemented, and/or supported
     Keenan's argument. Upon careful analysis of the textologi-
     cal issues associated with the manuscript tradition of the
     correspondence, the authors conclude that while Keenan's
     writings have advanced scholarly understanding of the cor-
     respondence, his fundamental thesis is incorrect; the corres-
     pondence is a genuine one. DK106.5.R6713
          Reviewed in:
          Can Slav P, 32 (Dec. 1981): 469
          Rus R, 40, no. 4 (1981): 444-45

157 *Ševčenko, Ihor. "A Neglected Source of Muscovite Political
     Ideology." SRH (anthology), 80-107.
     A scholarly study of the influence of the Byzantine theorist
     Agapetus on Muscovite political ideology with considerable
     reference to the thought of Ivan IV, Joseph of Volokolamsk,
     and Metropolitan Filipp. Following an intricate comparative
     examination of the political writings of the individuals under
     study, Ševčenko concludes that Agapetus affected political
     thought in Muscovy to such an extent that his views "proved
     almost a substitute for such thinking," particularly in re-
     gard to the most often quoted passages from the works of
     Muscovite political theorists.

158 *Skrynnikov, Ruslan G. "Edward Keenan's Textological Experi-
     ment." St Sov Hist, 24, nos. 1-2 (1985): 83-112.

159 *_____. "On the Authenticity of the Kurbskii-Groznyi Cor-
     respondence: A Summary of the Discussion." Slav R, 37,
     no. 1 (1978): 107-15.
     A review of the negative reaction of historians to Edward

Keenan's The Kurbskii-Groznyi Apocrypha, and a defense
of the reviewer's own work on this subject against criticisms
raised by John Fennell in regard to the grouping of the letters and the relationship between Kurbsky's first letter and
the works of the monk Isaiah.

160 *_____. "The Synodicon of Those Who Fell into Disgrace
Under Tsar Ivan the Terrible: An Attempt at a Textological
Reconstruction of the Lost Oprichnina Archive." Sov St
Hist, 24, nos. 1-2 (1985): 45-61.

161 Tschebotarioff-Bill, Valentine. "National Feudalism in Muscovy."
Rus R, 9, no. 3 (1950): 209-18.
A discussion of the emergence of "medieval practices, ways
and features" in Muscovite Russia with considerable reference
to Ivan IV's oprichnina as an impetus to Russian serfdom.

162 *Tumins, Valerie A., ed. "Introduction." Tsar Ivan IV's Reply
to Jan Rokyta. The Hague: Mouton, 1971, 11-46.
An analysis of the origin, style, and substance of the 1570
manuscript in which Ivan IV stated his position in regard
to the religious dissent and dissenters championed by Jan
Rokyta, a minister of the Czech Brethren. According to
Tumins, careful study of the manuscript reveals that Ivan
was not merely curious in regard to other creeds but rather
investigated them systematically and was stating here his
final (and negative) pronouncement on the issue of freedom
of worship. Tumins analyzes the form of the manuscript and
the language, type of argument, and style employed by Ivan
in writing it. BX324.5.I9 1971
Reviewed in:
Slavonic E Eur R, 51, no. 123 (1973): 3066-67
Renais Q, 25, no. 4 (1972): 481

163 _____. "The Polemics of Tsar Ivan IV Against the Czech
Brother Jan Rokyta." Radcliffe, 1959. (dissertation)

164 *Waugh, Daniel Clark. "The Lessons of the Kurbsky Controversy Regarding the Study and Dating of Old Russian Manuscripts." RSH (anthology), 218-37.
An argument that without more careful study of the manuscripts of the Kurbsky-Ivan IV correspondence and related
works the 'Kurbsky controversy' cannot be resolved. In
assessing the genuineness of the letters, Waugh supports
Crummey's assertion that "the careful study of the manuscripts has not ... provided conclusive grounds for a
precise redating...," but adds that "neither has it provided
any grounds whatsoever for a convincing confirmation of
the traditional attribution."

165 *Yaresh, Leo. "Ivan the Terrible and the Oprichnina."

Rewriting Russian History. Soviet Interpretations of Russia's
Past. Cyril E. Black, ed. New York: Random House, 1962,
216-32.
A scholarly assessment of the significance of Ivan IV's reign
with most attention devoted to a review of Soviet interpretations of the oprichnina. Yaresh states that Ivan's reign is
generally regarded by Soviet historians as being a crucial
one because they credit Ivan with "the overcoming of feudal
fragmentation within the unified Russian state" through farsighted reforms and the concerted use of force against the
opponents of modernization. They also maintain that Ivan's
reign "marked the start of an offensive by the Great Russian
state against its neighbors," thus making Ivan "a true fore-
runner of the long line of rulers of the new multinational
'Russia.'" Yaresh believes that Soviet historians have added
little to the study of Ivan IV because of their "adherence to
certain fixed assumptions," most notably that Ivan's oprichnina
was a practical, necessary, and desirable policy in dealing
with feudal opposition to the creation of a centralized state.
DK 38.B5

166 *Yarmolinsky, Avrahm. "Ivan the Terrible contra Martin
     Luther: A Sixteenth Century Russian Manuscript." NY
     Pub Lib B, 44, no. 6 (June 1940): 455-60.
     An account of Ivan IV's 1570 debate with Jan Rokyta over
     the Lutheran faith, and a summary of a pamphlet written by
     Ivan in which he "attacked Luther and condemned his fol-
     lowers as enemies of Christianity." Yarmolinsky also traces
     the publication history of the pamphlet, a photostat facsimile
     of which is in the collection of the New York Public Library.

167 *Zenkovsky, Serge A. "Prince Kurbsky-Tsar Ivan IV Corres-
     pondence: Reflections on Edward Keenan's The Kurbskii-
     Groznyi Apocrypha." Rus R, 32 (1973): 299-311.
     A discussion of Keenan's The Kurbskii-Groznyi Apocrypha
     as a confused and contradictory work which draws very
     questionable conclusions from flimsy and unacceptable evi-
     dence.

FOREIGN POLICY AND MILITARY AFFAIRS

168 Bennigsen, George. "Queen Elizabeth and Ivan the Terrible."
     Nineteenth C, 99 (Mar. 1926): 432-41.
     An account of Ivan IV's attempt to marry the niece of Queen
     Elizabeth, the Lady Mary of Hastings.

169 *Billington, James H. "The Germans." IA (gen. study), 97-
     102.
     A discussion of the increase of political and economic inter-
     course between the north European Protestant states and

and Russia as a consequence of Ivan IV's aggressive foreign
policy. Of particular interest are Billington's connection of
the Livonian War to the formation of the oprichnina and
zemsky sobor and his analysis of Ivan's reign as the product
of a type of schizophrenia: "Ivan was, in effect, two
people: a true believer in an exclusivist, traditional ideology and a successful practitioner of experimental, modern
statecraft."

170 *Bogoushevsky, Nicholas C. "The English in Muscovy During
the Sixteenth Century." Trans Roy Hist S, 7 (1878): 58-
129.
An account of Richard Chancellor's voyage to Russia, the
establishment of commercial relations between Russian and
England, and Ivan IV's subsequent efforts to form a military
alliance with England. Bogoushevsky includes a copy of
the 1568 secret treaty proposed by Ivan as well as copies
of the letters which ensued as Ivan sought to pressure
Elizabeth into a military accord with Russia.

171 Casmir, Nicholas (Bogoushevsky). "Historical Notes Relating
to Czar John 'the Terrible' of Russia and to Queen Elizabeth
of England." Reliquary, 16 (July 1875): 1-18.
An examination of Ivan IV's attempt to marry Queen Elizabeth and, later, her niece, Mary Hastings. Bogoushevsky
questions Elizabeth's near sacrifice of her niece to appease
"the cruel sovereign of a semi-savage, scantily-clad people."

172 *Croskey, Robert M. "Hakluyt's Accounts of Sir Jerome
Bowes' Embassy to Ivan IV." Slavonic E Eur R, 61 (Oct.
1983): 546-64.
An investigation into the reasons for the withdrawal of the
original account of Bowes' 1583-84 embassy to Muscovy which
had appeared in the 1589 edition of Hakluyt's Principall
Navigations, Voyages and Discoveries of the English Nation.
Croskey examines the contents of the original account written
by Bowes, the official Russian version, and the anonymous
account included in later editions of Principall Navigations.
He concludes that Hakluyt produced a second, inaccurate
version of the embassy which intentionally failed to mention
Bowes' unsuccessful attempt to negotiate an Anglo-Russian
alliance. This was done to advance the chances of such an
accord being negotiated anew by Jerome Horsey and to present to prospective investors in the Muscovy Company a
more favorable image of Anglo-Russian relations.

173 *Eaves, Richard G., and Robert E. Simmons. "Anglo-Russian
Relations in the European Diplomatic Setting: 1572-1584."
New R E Eur Hist, 13, no. 3 (1973): 40-51.
An argument that Anglo-Russian relations during Ivan IV's
reign were not linked to any desire on Ivan's part to

Westernize his realm but rather reflected his concern for
both improving the technical quality of Russia's military
forces by drawing upon English technology and for advancing the likelihood of Russia's military success against northern
neighbors by securing English assistance.

174   Grey, Ian. "Ivan the Terrible and Elizabeth of England."
       Hist Today, 12 (Sept. 1962): 648-55.
       An account of Ivan IV's attempts to develop economic, mili-
       tary, and matrimonial relations with England as revealed in
       the letters he exchanged with Queen Elizabeth.

175   *Hakluyt, Richard. The Principall Navigations, Voyages,
       Traffiques and Discoveries of the English Nation, Vols. I-II.
       New York: Macmillan, 1903.
       A collection of reports, letters, and other primary materials
       related to the travel, experiences, and endeavors of English
       voyagers to Muscovy. Of special interest is Richard Chan-
       cellor's often cited account of his 1553 reception by Ivan IV
       in which he describes the tsar's bearing, wealth, and power.
       More significantly, Chancellor's unintentional stop in Mus-
       covy (he was part of a three ship expedition seeking a north-
       ern route to China) resulted in the establishment of commer-
       cial and diplomatic ties between Muscovy and England. Many
       of the documents contained in this work shed light on the
       origin and evolution of the Anglo-Russian commercial relations
       which began with Ivan's 1555 granting of privileges to Eng-
       lish merchants trading in northern Russia. G240.H144

176   *Hamel, J. (Joseph K. Gamel). England and Russia. John
       Leigh, trans. London: Frank Cass and Company, 1968
       (reprint of 1854 edition), 422pp.
       An account of the travels and experiences of a number of
       English visitors to old Russia, including the voyages of
       Chancellor, Jenkinson, Willoughby, and Tradescant. Gamel
       provides most detail on the four diplomatic missions of
       Anthony Jenkinson which dealt with the status of the Mus-
       covy Company, Anglo-Russian commercial relations in gen-
       eral, Ivan IV's attempt to establish a military alliance with
       England, and Ivan's proposal of marriage to Queen Elizabeth.
       DK21.G313 1968

177   *Horsey, Jerome. "The Travels of Sir Jerome Horsey." Russia
       at the Close of the Sixteenth Century. Edward A. Bond, ed.
       New York: Burt Franklin, 1967, 156-266.
       Observations on the character and policies of Ivan IV, Feo-
       dor, and Boris Godunov and on a number of historical in-
       cidents of interest, written by an agent of the Muscovy
       Company and an envoy of Queen Elizabeth who was in Russia
       during the 1575-1591 period. Horsey writes of Ivan's "cruel,
       bloody, and merciless" deeds, his superstitious nature,

desire to secure possible political asylum in England, attempt
to wed Lady Mary Hastings, and last few days of life.
Horsey also comments on Anglo-Russian commerical and diplomatic relations during the latter part of Ivan's reign. In
an interesting and lengthy introduction, Edward Bond discusses Horsey's experiences and observations, Ivan IV's
correspondence with Queen Elizabeth, and the diplomatic
missions of Anthony Jenkinson. G161.H22

178 *Huttenbach, Henry R., ed./trans. "Anthony Jenkinson's 1566
and 1567 Mission to Muscovy Reconstructed from Published
Sources." Can Am Slav S, 9, no. 2 (1975): 179-203.
A discussion of two missions to Muscovy made by the English
merchant-diplomatic envoy Anthony Jenkinson. Huttenbach
devotes most of his attention to proving that Jenkinson did,
in fact, undertake an "off the record" mission in 1567 when
Ivan IV was pressing for a military alliance with England
and threatening to sever Anglo-Russian trade relations unless such an accord were established soon. The author
maintains that the sensitivity of these negotiations accounts
for Jenkinson's failure to mention them in his autobiographical
writings.

179 *_____. "The Correspondence Between Queen Elizabeth I
and Tsar Ivan IV: An Examination of Its Role in the Documentation of Anglo-Muscovite History." Forsch Ost Ges,
24 (1978): 101-30.
A discussion of the slow emergence into print of the 43 letters exchanged between Elizabeth I and Ivan IV, and an
examination of the inner unity of the correspondence. In
spite of long lapses in the correspondence and the absence
of at least eight letters, Huttenbach states, there is still
a discernible flow of reply, counter-reply, and acknowledg-
ment concerning: "1) the activities of the Muscovy Company;
2) which deals with disputes over the so-called 'rebel merchants' and the issue of the port of Narva; 3) which involves
the controversy surrounding the drafting of an Anglo-Muscovite treaty and the question of political asylum; 4) which has
to do with the supply of military shipments to Muscovy."

180 *_____. "New Archival Material on the Anglo-Russian Treaty
of Queen Elizabeth and Tsar Ivan IV." Slavonic E Eur R,
49 (1971): 535-49.
An examination of six documents (housed in the Public
Records Office in London) which deal with the timing and
substance of Ivan IV's proposal of an alliance with England.

181 *_____, ed./trans. "The Search for and Discovery of New
Archival Materials for Ambassador Jenkinson's Mission to
Muscovy in 1571-72: Four Letters of Queen Elizabeth to
Tsar Ivan IV." Can Am Slav S, 6, no. 3 (1972): 416-36.

A discussion of the 1571-72 mission of Anthony Jenkinson to
the court of Ivan IV for the purpose of restoring trade
relations between England and Muscovy. Huttenbach examines
four letters of Elizabeth to Ivan for insights into the exact
nature of Jenkinson's mission. He concludes that, in essence, "Jenkinson was to win back the coveted trade privileges but without committing her (Elizabeth) to the political
alliance which Ivan had made the sine qua non of future
Anglo-Muscovite relations."

182 *Kirchner, Walther. "Ivan Grozny's Livonian Policy: Some
      Addenda to Norbert Angermann's Studien zur Livland-
      Politik Ivan Groznys." J Baltic S, 4, no. 2 (1973): 143-47.
      A review article which questions Angermann's interpretation
      of Ivan IV's motives for launching the Livonian War.

183 *_____. "A Milestone in European History: The Danish-
      Russian Treaty of 1562." Commercial Relations Between
      Russia and Europe, 1400-1800. Bloomington: Indiana Uni-
      versity Press, 1966, 78-89. Originally in Slavonic E Eur R,
      22, 1944.
      An examination of Ivan IV's motives for securing the Danish-
      Russian Treaty of 1562, and a discussion of this accord as
      "the first ever to be peacefully negotiated by Russia with
      one of the great powers of western Europe which was based
      on complete equality." Kirchner contends that although the
      treaty turned out to be of little practical value, it was none-
      theless significant as a step toward bringing Russia into the
      European family of nations, a step which might have led to
      normal relations with other Baltic states were it not for "the
      military disasters during the later years of Ivan's reign."
      HF3628.E9K5

184 *_____. "The Russians." The Rise of the Baltic Question.
      Westport, Conn." Greenwood Press, 1970 (reprint of 1954
      edition), 86-122.
      A scholarly discussion of the origin, development, and sig-
      nificance of Ivan IV's efforts to incorporate Livonia into the
      growing Muscovite state. In analyzing the specific motives
      which moved Ivan to commence hostilities against Livonia,
      Kirchner maintains that the economic factors traditionally
      considered to have been of paramount importance cannot
      alone account for the Russian invasion. He asserts that
      one must also take into account "the personality of the tsar,
      his lust for power, his political expansionist drive, his op-
      position to the boyar class, his ambition to continue his
      grandfather's policy, and his vanity." In light of these
      factors and the sources of Polish and Swedish intervention
      on Livonia's behalf, Kirchner examines the ebb and flow of
      the military campaigns and diplomatic initiatives launched by
      Ivan IV during his protracted yet unsuccessful war to gain

for Muscovy an outlet to the Baltic Sea. Kirchner concludes
that despite Ivan's failure to secure such an outlet, he exercised "the decisive influence on the rise of the Baltic
Question" and set the stage for its eventual decision in Russia's favor. DL59.K5

185 Lamb, Harold. "Ivan the Terrible, 1533-84." The March of
Muscovy. Ivan the Terrible and the Growth of the Russian
Empire 1400-1648. Garden City, N.Y.: Doubleday Press,
1948, 119-98.
A general review of Ivan IV's youth, character, military affairs, and international policies. Lamb provides most detail
on Ivan's policy toward England, destruction of Novgorod,
and motives for launching the Kazan campaign and Livonian
War. He portrays Ivan as a farsighted, dynamic ruler responsible for impressive gains in the territory and power of
the Russian state. DK171.L3

186 *Lantzeff, George A., and Richard A. Pierce. "Liberation and
Advance." Eastward to Expansion. Exploration and Conquest on the Russian Open Frontier, to 1750. Montreal:
McGill-Queens University Press, 1973, 51-73.
A discussion of the leading role played by Ivan IV in the
1552 decision to launch a military expedition to seize Kazan
and in the strategy pursued during the campaign itself.
In assessing the importance of Ivan's conquest of Kazan,
the authors state that the victory opened for Muscovy "vast
possibilities for colonization, exploration of natural wealth,
commercial relations with the Caucasus region, Persia, and
central Asia, and new expansion.... The expansionist tendencies of Russia restrained by alien rule and hostile neighbors for almost three centuries, were now released as of
yore." DK43.L33

187 *Lubimenko, Inna. "The Correspondence of Queen Elizabeth
with the Russian Czars." Am Hist R, 19, no. 3 (1914):
525-42.
A review of the correspondence of Elizabeth and Ivan IV
concentrating on his desire to draw England into a political
alliance and Elizabeth's efforts to avoid such an accord while
still maintaining England's newly established commercial ties
with Russia. Lubimenko also discusses Ivan's attempt to wed
Lady Mary Hastings and his consideration of a journey to
England, perhaps to seek asylum from internal enemies.

188 Meyendorf, A. F. "Anglo-Russian Trade in the 16th Century."
Slavonic E Eur R, 25, no. 4 (Nov. 1946): 109-21.
In part, a discussion of Ivan's desire for a political alliance
with England to accompany Anglo-Russian commercial relations
and of Queen Elizabeth's reluctance to forge such an agreement.

189 *Pelenski, Jaroslaw. "Muscovite Imperial Claims to the Kazan
      Khanate." Slav R, 26, no. 4 (1967): 559-67.
      An investigation of Muscovite legal, religious, historical, and
      dynastic claims to the Kazan Khanate as they evolved, in
      part, under Ivan III and Ivan IV. Pelenski maintains that
      while "Muscovite imperial claims to Kazan were not of a very
      sophisticated sort," Ivan IV's annexation of this territory
      nonetheless served to enhance Muscovy's image as a "power-
      ful and influential empire in international affairs" and helped
      to make territorial expansion "a national virtue and political
      goal, an aim common to most centralized national states."

190 *_____. Russia and Kazan. Conquest and Imperial Ideology
      (1438-1560s). The Hague: Mouton, 1974, 368pp., bib.
      335-48.
      This scholarly study of "Russia's first major expansion beyond
      the ethnic frontiers of the Great Russian nationality" does not
      contain a separate chapter on the role played by any one
      Muscovite ruler in this development, but it is nonetheless a
      valuable source of information on the contributions made by
      Ivan III, Vasily III, and, especially, Ivan IV in the trans-
      formation of Muscovite Russia into a multinational empire.
      DK100.P44

191 Pritsak, Omeljan. "Moscow, the Golden Horde, and the Kazan
      Khanate from a Polycultural Point of View." Slav R, 26,
      no. 4 (1967): 577-83.
      Contains some discussion of Ivan IV's claims on the Kazan
      Khanate and his enthronement of Simeon Bekbulatovich.

192 Rowse, A. L. "Europe's First Glimpse of the Russians, Eliza-
      beth I and Ivan the Terrible." Slav R, 41 (7 June 1958):
      9-11+.
      A survey of early Anglo-Russian relations with emphasis on
      the discordant aims of Ivan IV and Elizabeth and the lack of
      understanding each had in regard to the other's conventions
      and customs.

193 Ševčenko, Ihor. "Muscovy's Conquest of Kazan: Two Views
      Reconciled." Slav R, 26, no. 4 (1967): 541-77.
      An analysis of Muscovy's conquest of Kazan and the justi-
      fication employed to explain the absorption of the first major
      non-Slavic region into its domain with some reference to
      Ivan IV's motivation in launching the Kazan campaign.

194 *Steveni, W. Barnes. "Queen Elizabeth and Ivan the Terrible."
      Nineteenth C, 34 (Dec. 1893): 944-54.
      A review of a French translation of a series of documents
      issued by the Russian Ministry of Foreign Affairs in regard
      to Anglo-Russian relations prior to the reign of Alexander I.
      Steveni devotes most of his attention to discussing the conflict

that developed between Ivan IV and Elizabeth over the latter's
refusal to form a military alliance with Russia against Poland
and Sweden, the difficulties encountered by English merchants
in Russia as a consequence of this conflict, and Ivan's attempt to arrange a marriage between himself and Mary Hastings, Elizabeth's niece.

195 *Tolstoy, George, ed. The First Forty Years of Intercourse
     Between England and Russia, 1553-1593. New York: Burt
     Franklin, 1963 (reprint of 1875 edition), 441pp.
     A collection of Russian and English language primary source
     material on Anglo-Russian contacts and relations during the
     reigns of Ivan IV and Feodor. Tolstoy includes letters, of-
     ficial papers, and observations made by English voyagers to
     Muscovy gathered from the holdings of the British Museum
     and the London State Papers Office and from the writings of
     Chancellor, Hakluyt, Horsey, and Fletcher. The 82 docu-
     ments which he includes represent a useful source of infor-
     mation on the diplomatic and commercial relations between
     England and Muscovy established by Ivan IV. DK106.F64
     1963

196 Urban, William. "The Origin of the Livonian War." Lituanus,
     29, no. 3 (1983): 11-25.
     Unavailable for annotation.

197 *Wilson, Francesca. "1553-1600. Tudor Discoveries of Mus-
     covy." RTFE (anthology), 19-64.
     A discussion of the observations and experiences of five
     English travelers in the Russia of Ivan IV. Included are
     the writings of Chancellor, Jenkinson, Burrough, Horsey,
     and Fletcher.

198 *Yakobson, S. "Early Anglo-Russian Relations (1553-1613)."
     Slavonic E Eur R, 13, no. 39 (1934-35): 597-610.
     A review of the origins and development of Anglo-Russian
     relations with most attention devoted to the commercial ties
     established by Ivan IV and used by him as a means of
     coaxing England into a formal alliance with Muscovy. Yakob-
     son stresses the role played by Anglo-Polish commercial re-
     lations in Queen Elizabeth's rejection of Ivan's political ad-
     vances and in her support of the status quo in the Baltic
     region.

FEODOR I (1584-1598), BORIS GODUNOV (1598-1605), AND
THE TIME OF TROUBLES: 1605-1613
(Feodor II, False Dimitry, Vasily Shuisky)

199 Afanasyev, George. "Boris Godunov and the First Pretender."
     Rus R (Liverpool), 2, no. 4 (1913): 31-53.
     Unavailable for annotation.

200 *Allen, E. D. "The Georgian Marriage Projects of Boris Godu-
     nov." Ox Slavonic P, 12 (1965): 69-79.
     An account of Boris Godunov's 1603 turn to the Georgian
     Bagratid dynasty as a source for a husband for his twenty-
     one-year-old daughter, Kseniya. Allen states that Boris
     did not want Kseniya to marry a powerful Russian aristocrat
     for fear that such a person might try to rule as a regent
     for the youthful son of Boris in the event of Boris' prema-
     ture death. The project came to naught because Boris died
     before his ambassador could return to Moscow with the po-
     tential husband, Prince Khozdrov.

201 *_____. "The Embassy of Tatishchev and Ivanov (1604-5)."
     Russian Embassies to the Georgian Kings (1589-1605). Vol.
     II. Cambridge: Cambridge University Press, 1970, 379-516.
     A documentary record of Russian-Georgian relations during
     the reign of Boris Godunov. Of particular interest are the
     documents pertaining to Godunov's efforts to find spouses
     for his son and daughter among Georgian royalty. G161.H2

202 Appleby, Jon H. "Doctor Christopher Reitinger and a Seal of
     Tsar Boris Godunov." Ox Slavonic P, n.s. 12 (1979): 32-
     39.
     An account of the medical services rendered to Boris Godu-
     nov by the English physician Christopher Reitinger, and a
     description and history of the bronze medallion given to
     Reitinger by the tsar.

203 *Barbour, Philip L. Dimitry. Called the Pretender. Tsar and
     Prince of All Russia, 1605-06. Boston: Houghton-Mifflin,
     1966, 387pp., bib. 361-76.

A lively history of the career and brief reign of Dimitry,
the pretender to the throne of Russia. Barbour presents
Dimitry in a sympathetic light and asserts that the pretender's many fine qualities and popularity outside of court
circles have been obscured by the slander of the conspirators who deposed him. Although Barbour states that the
real Tsarevich Dimitry most likely died accidentally in 1591,
he suggests, in an appendix on the identity of the Dimitry
crowned tsar in 1605, that the tsarevich and the pretender,
Grishka Otrepiev, may well have been one and the same
person. Barbour's work is also useful as a source of information on the circumstances which led to Boris Godunov's
unpopularity and inability to counter Dimitry's rise to power.
DK112.B3813
  Reviewed in:
  Rus R, 26, no. 3 (1967):   303-05
  Slav R, 27, no. 1 (1968):   135

204 Baumann, Hans. Dimitri and the False Tsars. Anthea Bell,
     trans. New York: Henry Walck, 1970, 188pp.
     A colorful account of the life and death of Tsarevich Dimitry.
     Baumann devotes most of his attention to the imposters who
     surfaced in the early sixteenth century claiming to be the
     tsarevich. Intended for youthful readers. DK112.B3813

205 *A Bloudie Tragedie-The Reporte of a Bloudie and Terrible
     Massacre in the City of Mosco." FDRRT (anthology), 27-62.
     An eyewitness, graphic description of the overthrow and
     execution of Dimitry and his Polish supporters. The author
     also discusses the circumstances which prompted the bloody
     uprising, the most noteworthy being Dimitry's lack of re-
     spect for the Orthodox faith, reliance on foreigners for
     counsel, disregard for Russia's traditions and customs, and
     neglect of Russia's best interests as a nation.

206 *Blustain, Jonah. "'Boris Godunov': For the Descendents of
     the Orthodox." Rus R, 27, no. 2 (April 1968): 177-94.
     A discussion of Mussorgsky's Boris Godunov as the national
     opera of Russia because of its masterful illumination of "a
     tragic period and a tragic tsar" in the nation's history.
     Blustain identifies three themes in the opera which, during
     the Time of Troubles and afterward, came to have great
     meaning for the Russian people: "the misfortunes which
     must follow when a disorganized Russian states falls prey
     to foreigners; the struggle between Russian Orthodoxy and
     Polish Roman Catholicism" and the "slippery, selfish, and
     boastful" nature of the nobility of both Russia and Poland.

207 Boutwell, Jane. "The Highest Power." Opera N, 40 (24 Jan.
     1976): 11-13.
     An overview of the circumstances associated with Boris

Godunov's accession to and fall from power. Designed to
make more intelligible Mussorgsky's opera, Boris Godunov.

208   "Brereton's Account of the Wars in Russia--Newest of the
      Present Miseries of Rushia." FDRRT (anthology), 69-150.
      A detailed, first-hand account of the military struggle be-
      tween Vasily Shuisky and the Polish forces of the second
      false Dimitry.

209   *Brody, Ervin C. "The Demetrius Legend in History." The
      Demetrius Legend and Its Literary Treatment in the Age of
      the Baroque. Rutherford, N.J.: Fairleigh-Dickinson Uni-
      versity Press, 1972, 19-51.
      A discussion of the unstable social, economic, and political
      condition of late sixteenth century Russia, and an account
      of the death of Tsarevich Dimitry and the emergence of the
      legend of his survival. Brody also reviews the various
      historical interpretations of this episode which he divides into
      contemporary, romantic, scientific, and Soviet schools of
      thought. He concludes that, although there is a great deal
      of contradictory evidence in regard to Dimitry's death and
      the identity of the pretender, Dimitry most likely died in 1591.
      PN1821.B7
          Reviewed in:
          Can Am Slav S, 8 (1974): 587
          Rus R, 32, no. 3 (1973): 329-30
          Slav R, 32 (1973): 656-57

210   *Bussow, Konrad. "Bussow's Account of the Russian Famine,
      1601-1604." MRSB (anthology), 224-26. Excerpt from
      Moskovskaia Khronika, 1584-1613, B. Dmytryshyn, trans.
      Moscow-Leningrad: Akademia Nauk, 1961, 97-98.
      An eyewitness account of the horrible famine which swept
      Russia in the early 1600s, written by a German merchant who
      resided in Moscow from 1584 to 1613. Bussow also describes
      Boris Godunov's futile attempt to cope with the famine by
      requisitioning grain supplies and establishing a system for
      distributing food to urban areas.

211   DeJonge, Alex. "Around 'Boris Godunov.'" Boris Godunov.
      Modest Mussorgsky. John Nicholas, ed. New York:
      Riverrun Press, 1982, 29-34.
      A brief overview of the themes "the death of the tsarevich"
      and "the pretender-tsar" in Pushkin's drama and Mussorg-
      sky's opera Boris Godunov. DeJonge also discusses the his-
      torical value of Boris Godunov, particularly as a source of
      insight into pre-Petrine Russian society and culture.

212   *Evans, Norman E. "The Anglo-Russian Royal Marriage Nego-
      tiations of 1600-1603." Slavonic E Eur R, 61, no. 3 (July
      1983): 363-87.

An examination of the complex negotiations between Boris
Godunov and Queen Elizabeth in regard to both the marriage
of Tsarevich Feodor and a member of the English royal family and English concern over the possible harmful effects of
the proposed marriage of Archduke Maximilian of Austria
and Boris' daughter Kseniya. Evans states that since Elizabeth's offer came at a time when the Austrian marrige project was already collapsing, Boris eagerly pressed her to
identify the person being proposed as a wife for Feodor.
Elizabeth's inability to find readily such a person placed her
in a difficult diplomatic position which threatened Anglo-
Russian trade. The Queen's death on 24 March 1603 saw the
marriage project come to an end without a specific candidate
ever having been named.

213 *Emerson, Caryl. "Pretenders to History: Four Plays for
     Undoing Pushkin's Boris Gudunov." Slav R, 44, no. 2
     (1985): 257-79.

214 *_____. "Queen Elizabeth I and Tsar Boris: Five Letters,
     1597-1603." Ox Slavonic P, 12 (1965): 29-68.
     A discussion of five letters exchanged between Queen Eliza-
     beth and Boris Godunov which collectively deal with the
     status of English merchants in Russia, the death of Tsar
     Feodor, the election of Boris to the throne, alleged English
     assistance to the Turks, and the possible marriage of Boris'
     son Feodor to an English young lady of high birth.

215 *Fletcher, Giles. Of the Russe Commonwealth. R. Pipes, intro.
     Cambridge: Harvard University Press, 1966 (reprint of
     1591 edition), 214pp., bib. 65-68.
     A firsthand account of the political system, institutions,
     religion, customs, and manners of Russia of the late 1580s.
     Fletcher, who was sent to Russia in 1588 as a special am-
     bassador of Queen Elizabeth to confirm the trade concessions
     negotiated by Jerome Horsey, is at his best when describing
     the extent of the tsar's powers and the manner in which he
     exercised them. He does, however, present some informa-
     tion on Feodor's character, piety, and daily routine, the
     character and power of Boris Godunov, and the 1591 death
     of Tsarevich Dimitry. In an introduction, Richard Pipes
     discusses Fletcher's diplomatic mission and experiences in
     Russia and the historical value of Fletcher's book. DK21.F57

216 Gerasimov, M. M. "Tsar Feodor Ivanovich (1557-1598), Son
     of Ivan the Terrible." The Face Finder. Alan H. Brodrick,
     trans. New York: J. B. Lippincott, 1971, 189-91.
     A brief description of Tsar Feodor's physical appearance,
     based upon the findings of a Soviet team of specialists who
     opened his sarcophagus in 1963 for the purposes of scientific
     and historical investigation. Feodor apparently was five feet,

three inches in height, plump, and frail. GN64.G413

217 Graham, Stephen. Boris Godunof. New Haven: Yale Univer-
     sity Press, 1933, 290pp., bib. 283-84.
     A general study of the life and brief reign of Boris Godunov.
     Graham devotes most of his attention to Boris' years in power
     as tsar and the sources of the revolt which deposed him. In
     regard to the Uglich affair, Graham suggests that Boris had
     a hand in a conspiracy to kill Tsarevich Dimitry and does
     not reject the interpretation that the tsarevich survived the
     attempt on his life and resurfaced as the "pretender" to
     claim the throne which was rightfully his. DK109.G7

218 Grey, Ian. "Boris Godunov." Hist Today, 22 (Jan. 1972):
     44-53.
     A sympathetic overview of Boris Godunov's reign. Grey
     presents Boris as a honest, humane, hard working sovereign
     genuinely concerned with the welfare of his subjects. Grey
     believes that the difficult period during which Boris ruled
     made effective government and substantial reforms virtually
     impossible, a fact ignored by critics such as N. Karamzin.

219 _____. Boris Godunov. The Tragic Tsar. Joan Pinkham,
     trans. New York: Charles Scribner's Sons, 1973, 188pp.,
     bib. 180-82.
     Aimed at the nonspecialist and based upon secondary sources,
     this study presents a favorable account of Boris Godunov's
     character and reign. Grey maintains that "Boris has been
     misrepresented and treated by most historians with extra-
     ordinary prejudice and even malice," a trend promoted by
     the writings of Karamzin and Pushkin. Far from being a
     conniving boyar responsible for the death of Tsarevich
     Dimitry, Grey sees Boris as a man of unusually high prin-
     ciples and intelligence who was committed to advancing the
     welfare of the Russian people and pursued sound policies in
     their interest. Boris emerges from this study as a far-
     sighted, progressive, and humane ruler whose demise came
     about not because of his own policies and behavior but
     rather as a result of "the turbulence of a period when Russia
     was struggling to survive as a nation." DK109.G73

220 *Horsey, Jerome. "The Travels of Sir Jerome Horsey." Russia
     at the Close of the Sixteenth Century. Edward A. Bond,
     ed. New York: Burt Franklin, 1967, 156-266.
     A commentary on various incidents in late sixteenth-century
     Russia and on the character and policies of Tsars Feodor and
     Boris. Horsey, who was in Russia at various times between
     1575 and 1591 as an agent of the Muscovy Company and a
     representative of Queen Elizabeth, describes his reception at
     the Russian court, the ornate coronation ceremony for Feodor,
     domestic and foreign responses to Feodor's granting amnesty

to a number of individuals imprisoned by Ivan IV for political offenses, and the mysterious death of Tsarevich Dimitry. Of special interest is Horsey's account of his negotiations with Boris Godunov in regard to the privileges enjoyed by English merchants in Russia. For additional information on these privileges, see Appendix V, pp. 356-81, "Papers Relating to Horsey's Mission to Russia in 1590-1591." G161.H22

221 *Kleimola, A. M. "Boris Godunov and the Politics of Mest-
nichestvo." Slavonic E Eur R, 53 (July 1975): 355-69.
A study of Boris Godunov's victory over Prince Ivan Sitsky in a 1578 legal case dealing with their respective places in Ivan IV's service hierarchy. On the basis of an examination of the service registers, Kleimola concludes that Godunov did in fact have seniority over Sitsky, and, therefore Ivan IV's decision in Godunov's favor was based upon legal evidence not favoritism.

222 Klyuchevsky, Vasili. "Chapters I-IV." The Rise of the
Romanovs. Liliana Archibald, ed./trans. London and New York: Macmillan/St. Martin's Press, 1970, 371pp.
A scholarly examination of the origin, development, and historical significance of the Time of Troubles. Kliuchevsky, a prominent Russian historian at the turn of the nineteenth century, states that neither the 1598 extinction of the Kalita dynasty, the slanderous rumors which circulated about Boris Godunov, nor the appearance of the false Dimitry were suf-ficient causes for the outbreak of the Time of Troubles. Both the advent and prolongation of the Time of Troubles were the product of a complex series of long-standing griev-ances harbored by each of the major social classes in Russia. Boris Gudonov's election as tsar in 1598 merely provided an opportunity for these grievances to take concrete form and, therein, to convert a dynastic crisis into a broad political, economic, and, eventually, an international crisis. Kliu-chevsky sees the effects of the Time of Troubles as being both numerous and far-reaching. A new dynasty was created, the powers of the sovereign and the authority of the zemsky sobor were revised, the standing of the service ranks under-went complete change, the nation's relations with neighboring states had been poisoned, and the government's domestic problems reached new heights. In essence, Kliuchevsky concludes, the institutional developments, national uprisings, and protracted foreign struggles which marked the seven-teenth century were spawned amidst the turbulence of the Time of Troubles.   DK114.K573
Reviewed in:
Hist Today, 20 (1979): 437-48
Lib J, 95 (1970): 2472
Slav R, 32, no. 2 (1973): 374-75
Ukr Q, 26 (1970): 320-22

223 *Konovalov, S. "Thomas Chamberlayne's Description of Russia,
     1631." Ox Slavonic P, 5 (1954): 107-16.
     An argument in favor of the genuineness of Russian interest
     in offering the crown to James I of England as a means of
     terminating the Time of Troubles. The possibility of such an
     offer was made known to James I by way of a 1612 proposal
     submitted by Thomas Chamberlayne which called for the
     restoration of order in Russia through English military as-
     sistance and "the establishment of a kind of English pro-
     tectorate over the whole or parts of the country." As evi-
     dence, Konovalov appends a copy of a 1631 petition submitted
     by Chamberlayne to Charles I which made reference to the
     1612 proposal and suggested that it might be rekindled in
     view of the likelihood of Russia's defeat in the impending war
     with Poland.

224 *Lantzeff, George A., and Richard A. Pierce. "The Frontier
     Policies of Boris Godunov." Eastward to Empire. Explora-
     tion and Conquest on the Russian Open Frontier, to 1750.
     Montreal: McGill-Queens University Press, 1973, 109-26.
     An argument that "a study of Russian frontier policies dur-
     ing the two decades while Boris Godunov was at the helm
     of the State would seem to reveal new aspects of his gener-
     ally recognized statecraft." In support of this statement,
     the authors discuss Godunov's efforts to promote commerce
     and communication by establishing terminals along trade
     routes, protect the Russian frontier, and provide staging
     points for further Eastward expansion through the construc-
     tion of a series of forts. They conclude that "if the one
     man most responsible for the early establishment of the Rus-
     sian Asiatic Empire were to be chosen, he should be Boris
     Godunov." DK43.L33

225 *Loewenson, Leo. "Sir Roger Manley's History of Muscovy
     The Russian Imposter." Slavonic E Eur R, 31, no. 76
     (1951-52): 232-40.
     A detailed review of Manley's The Russian Imposter. Loewen-
     son discusses Manley's background and the book's contents
     and influence, and, in the process, comments on the events
     associated with Tsarevich Dimitry's death, the emergence of
     the false Dimitry, and the demise of Boris Gudunov.

226 Lyubavsky, M., ed./trans. "Leo Sapieha, Chancellor of
     Lithuania, On the Events of the Time of Troubles." Rus R
     (Liverpool), 3, no. 2 (1914): 47-59.
     Unavailable for annotation.

227 Manley, Sir Roger. The Russian Imposter; or, The History of
     Muskovie Under the Usurpation of Boris and the Imposture
     of Demetrius, Late Emperors of Muskovy. London: Thomas
     Basset, 1674, 250pp.

228 *Margeret, Jacques. The Russian Empire and the Grand Duchy
     of Moscow. A 17th Century French Account. Chester S. L.
     Dunning ed./trans. Pittsburgh: University of Pittsburgh
     Press, 1983, 216pp.
     A 1607 account of the political and military circumstance which
     attended the collapse of the Godunov regime and the short-
     lived reign of Dimitry. Margeret was a multitalented pro-
     fessional soldier who attained high rank in the military forces
     of Boris, Dimitry, and Vasily Shuisky, and who had ample
     opportunity to observe court politics and the public mood in
     Muscovy. His account is therefore a particularly insightful
     one which has been acknowledged by historians as an ac-
     curate and valuable source of information on Muscovy of the
     early seventeenth century and the roots of the Time of
     Troubles. Of special interest is Margeret's intricate argu-
     ment that the Dimitry who became tsar in 1606 was, in fact,
     the real Dimitry, son of Ivan IV. Adding further value to
     this source are Chester Dunning's introduction and notes on
     Margeret's career and the historical setting within which he
     wrote his book. DK111.M313 1983

229 *Massa, Isaac. A Short History of the Beginnings and Origins
     of These Present Wars in Moscow Under the Reign of Various
     Sovereigns Down to the Year 1610. G. Edward Orchard, in-
     tro./trans. Toronto: University of Toronto Press, 1982,
     235pp.
     A detailed account of the complex origins and development of
     the Time of Troubles, written by a Dutch resident of Moscow
     during the first decade of the seventeenth century. Massa
     discusses the banishment of Dimitry to Uglich, the tsarevich's
     death, and the legend of his survival, but he is at his best
     when describing the events he witnessed or about which he
     was able to acquire firsthand information. This work is a
     much cited one by historians because of its depth and the ac-
     curacy of its information on the reigns of Boris Godunov and
     Vasily Shuisky and Muscovite reaction to the confusing and
     trying events of this era. D111.M37

230 Mérimée, P. "Boris Godunov." RIRH (anthology), 85-87.
     Excerpt from Episode de l'Histoire de Russe-Les Faux Deme-
     trius. Paris, 1854.
     A brief account of Boris Godunov's accession to the throne
     of Russia in 1598. Mérimée portrays Boris as an ambitious
     yet patient regent who cleverly orchestrated his "election"
     so that it appeared to be the result of the people's will
     rather than his own machinations.

231 "Narrative of an Englishman Who Was with the Poles When
     Besieged in Moscow." FDRRT (anthology), 184-200.
     An eyewitness English account of the deterioration of the
     Polish army as a consequence of a two-year siege of the

Kremlin by Russian patriotic forces under the leadership
of Prince Dimitry Pozharsky.

232 Nicholas, John, ed. Boris Godunov. Modest Mussorgsky.
     New York: Riverrun Press, 1982, 112pp.
     As part of the English National Opera Guide series, this
     volume consists of the text of Mussorgsky's opera Boris
     Godunov and a series of short essays by various authors
     on the opera's plot, characters, themes, and historical
     setting. ML50.M993.B62

233 *Nikolaieff, A. M. "Boris Godunov and the Ouglich Tragedy."
     Rus R, 9, no. 4 (Oct. 1950): 275-85.
     An investigation of the question "was Boris Godunov ...
     really responsible for the tragic death of the nine year old
     son of Ivan IV at the city of Ouglich on 15 May 1591?"
     Nikolaieff reviews the conflicting interpretations on this
     question and the evidence on which they are based. He
     concludes that the case against Boris is purely circumstantial
     and not very believable in light of his character and integ-
     rity.

234 Orchard, G. E. "The Frontier Policy of Boris Godunov."
     New R E Eur Hist, 9 (1969): 113-23.
     Unavailable for annotation.

235 *Perrie, Maureen. "Jerome Horsey's Account of the Events of
     May 1591." Ox Slavonic P, n.s. 13 (1980): 28-49.
     An examination of the evidence presented by Jerome Horsey, a
     sixteenth-century intermediary between the English and Rus-
     sian governments, in regard to the alleged murder of Tsare-
     vich Dimitry. Perrie compares Horsey's findings to those of
     the official investigation committee, the interpretation advanced
     by seventeenth-century chroniclers, and the views of sev-
     eral modern historians. He concludes that although Horsey's
     account has some inaccuracies, omissions, and unconfirmed
     references, none of the sources disprove Horsey's evidence
     that Boris Godunov was responsible for Dimitry's death.

236 _____. "Russian Pretenders of the Early 17th Century."
     Hist Today, 31 (Feb. 1981): 11-16.
     A popular review of the claims and careers of the various
     pretenders to the throne during the Time of Troubles.
     Perrie devotes most of her attention to the two false Dimitrys
     but also chronicles the fate of a dozen less known pretenders.
     In all, a useful overview of a complex political phenomenon.

237 *Platonov, Sergei F. Boris Godunov. John Alexander, intro.
     L. Rex Pyles, trans. Gulf Breeze, Fla.: Academic Inter-
     national Press, 1973 (reprint of 1921 edition), 230pp., bib.
     222-23.

A scholarly and positive portrayal of the life and career of
Boris Godunov within the broader context of the turmoil
which plagued Russian society in the late sixteenth century.
Platonov presents Boris as a caring and talented leader confronted with insurmountable obstacles as a consequence of the
disintegration of old Muscovite society which occurred following Ivan IV's reign: "Boris was placed at the head of
the Russian government during a period of complex crises.
He was forced to attempt to reconcile the irreconcilable and
to bring together that which could not be joined." Platonov
commends Boris for his brilliance, devotion to duty, and for
his many fine personal qualities, and defends him against
the charge that he was responsible for the death of Tsarevich
Dimitry, an allegation made by Boris' personal and political
enemies who were jealous of his powerful position at the
court of Tsar Feodor. Platonov concludes that the "blighted
image" of Boris developed by his contemporaries and perpetuated by the Russian state and Orthodox Church must be
rejected in favor of one more in tune with his high character
and progressive qualities as a ruler. DK109.P513
Reviewed in:
Slav R, 34, no. 2 (1975): 383-84

238   *_____. The Time of Troubles. A Historical Study of the
Internal Crisis and Social Struggle in Sixteenth and Seventeenth Century Muscovy. John T. Alexander, intro./trans.
Lawrence: University of Kansas Press, 1970, 197pp., bib.
183-91.
Although written 60 years ago, this examination of the Time
of Troubles is still considered to be among the most authori-
tative studies available on this complex period in Russia's
history. Platonov presents here a summation of his previous
scholarly publications made palatable for the general public
by the exclusion of documentation as well as intricate detail.
He traces the origins of the Time of Troubles to the social
and economic dislocation caused by Ivan IV's oprichnina
and the Livonian War and then divides the era under study
into three stages: dynastic confusion, the social struggle,
and the struggle for nationhood. Platonov sees the Time of
Troubles as having been responsible for significantly altering
Muscovy in four basic ways: the center of gravity of the
Muscovite social structure shifted from the boyars to the
service gentry; the personal authority of the monarch was
complemented by the collective authority of a council of "all
the land" (zemsky sobor); Muscovites experienced an "intellectual ferment" spawned by a dramatic increase in contact
with foreigners; and Muscovy's loss of territory to Sweden
and Poland gave birth to the idea of retribution which fueled
Russian foreign policy for the next century. DK111.P5813
Reviewed in:
Can Slavonic P, 14, no. 4 (1972): 578-89

Eng Hist R 82 (1972):   863
Slav R, 32, no. 1 (1973):   160
Slavonic E Eur R, 49 (1971):   619

239   Poole, Stanley B.   "The False Dimitrys."   Royal Mysteries and
        Pretenders.   London: Blanford Press, 1969, 45-53.
        A brief discussion of the circumstances which led to the
        regency of Boris Godunov and his election as tsar, and a
        standard account of the activities of the successive pre-
        tenders to the throne who claimed to be Dimitry, Ivan IV's
        youngest son.   D107.P58

240   *Pushkin, Alexander.   Boris Godunov.   New York: Viking
        Press, 111pp.
        Although works of fiction are not the subject of this bibli-
        ography, Pushkin's Boris Godunov is listed here as an ex-
        ception because his dramatization of Boris' rise to and fall
        from power was influential in shaping nineteenth century
        opinion on this subject.   The theme of misguided personal
        ambition leading to tragic consequences is central to Pushkin's
        drama as he attributes to Boris the 1591 murder of Tsarevich
        Dimitry, an act which allegedly haunted Boris and led to his
        demise.   PG3347.B6

241   Pushkin, N.   "Story of the False Dimitri."   Tablet, 215 (23
        Dec. 1961):   1227-28.
        An argument, by the grandson of Alexander Pushkin, that
        Gregory Otrepiev was the real Dimitry, son of Ivan IV,
        and rightful heir to the throne, a fact supposedly acknowl-
        edged by Boris Godunov.

242   "Report of Captain Gilbert, of Dmitri's Bodyguard."   FDRRT
        (anthology), 63-68.
        A defense of the reputation of Dimitry the pretender, and
        a critical account of the character and motives of Vasily
        Shuisky, Dimitry's successor.   Gilbert also describes how a
        Polish general summoned him to meet and support as a re-
        placement for the recently deceased Dimitry a man who "dif-
        fered from this ... person, as night from day."   Gilbert
        goes on to discuss the calamities that befell "miserable Rus-
        sia ground betwixt these two mill-stones, the pretending
        Demetrius and the super-intending Pole."

243   Salgaller, Emanuel.   "The Demetrius-Godunof Theme in the
        German and Russian Drama of the Twentieth Century."
        New York University, 1956.   (dissertation)

244   Sandler, Stephanie.   "The Problem of History in Pushkin:
        Poet, Pretender, Tsar."   Yale University, 1982.   (disserta-
        tion)

245 *Skrynnikov, Ruslan G. Boris Godunov. Hugh F. Graham,
      ed./trans. Gulf Breeze, Fla.: Academic International Press,
      1982, 175pp.
      A scholarly and well-balanced analysis of the rise and fall of
      Boris Godunov. Skrynnikov, a Soviet specialist on sixteenth-
      century Russian history, connects Godunov's political diffi-
      culties and demise as Muscovy's ruler to the intensely nega-
      tive popular reaction to his restrictive policies toward the
      peasantry and his ineffective assistance to those suffering
      due to protracted crop failures. Besides alienating the com-
      moners and gentry alike, Boris failed to win the favor of
      the boyars to whom his policies catered. In spite of these
      difficulties and the consequent brevity of Boris' reign, the
      author maintains that Boris deserves praise for his concern
      for education, interest in Western technology and culture, and
      for at least attempting to point Russia in the direction which
      it later was to take under Peter the Great. DK109.S4413
      Reviewed in:
      History, 68 (Feb. 1983): 158

246 *_____. "Boris Godunov's Struggle for the Throne." Can
      Am Slav S, 11, no. 3 (1977): 325-53.
      The stated purpose of this article is to answer two questions:
      "How was the first elected Russian tsar chosen and how valid
      are the documents pertaining to his election?" Drawing upon
      a series of primary materials, Skrynnikov concludes that the
      existence of two significant forgeries in Boris Godunov's
      electoral documents warrants a reassessment of the circum-
      stances surrounding his accession. The author maintains
      that the first assembly (1598) which elected Boris was neither
      representative nor duly convened, whereas the second as-
      sembly (1599) was "the most representative assembly convoked
      in the sixteenth century" but cannot be considered as an
      electoral body since it merely confirmed a political reality.

247 *_____. "The Rebellion in Moscow and the Fall of the God-
      unov Dynasty." Sov St Hist, 24, no. 1-2 (1985): 137-52.

248 Soloviev, S. M. "A Letter from the False Dmitri to Boris
      Godunov, 1604." MRSB (anthology), 226-28. Excerpt from
      Istoriia Rossii s drevneishikh vremen (History of Russia
      since Ancient Times), Vol. 8. B. Dmytryshyn, trans.
      Moscow: Izdatelstvo sotsialnoekonomicheskoi literatury,
      1960, 413-14.
      A reproduction of a letter by the false Dimitry to Boris
      Godunov in which the former explains how he escaped murder
      at the hands of assassins instructed by Boris to kill him.
      Dimitry concludes with a plea for Boris to abdicate in favor
      of the rightful heir to the throne.

248a *Thompson, A. H. "The Legend of Tsarevich Dimitriy: Some

Evidence of an Oral Tradition." Slavonic E Eur R, 46 (Jan. 1968): 48-59.
A review of the circumstances surroudning the 1591 death of Tsarevich Dimitry, and an examination of folksongs and bliny devoted to Dimitry, Boris Godunov, and the False Dimitry.

249 Treue, Wilhelm. "Russia: Boris Godunov." DAC (gen. study), 45-49.
The recollections of Daniel Collins, an English physician, who attended to Boris Godunov's health, serve as the basis for a brief discussion of Boris' intense religious convictions and his predilection for excessive fasting during the observance of holy days.

250 *Vernadsky, George V. "The Death of the Tsarevich Dimitry: A Reconsideration of the Case." Ox Slavonic P, 5 (1954): 1-19.
A scholarly review of the various interpretations of the 1591 death of Tsarevich Dimitry. Vernadsky divides the sources reviewed into two categories, those which precede the 1819 publication of the proceedings and findings of the official investigation of the affair, and those which came afterwards. He concludes that neither the sources contemporary with the event nor those published since (including the seventeenth-century chronicles) offer acceptable evidence that the official report is not an accurate and trustworthy one.

MICHAEL ROMANOV (1613-1645), ALEXIS I (1645-1676), AND FEODOR III (1676-1682)

251 Alexeyev, Basil. "The Restoration of Order and the First
  Romanovs." Rus R (Liverpool), 2, no. 2 (1913): 14-50.
  Unavailable for annotation.

252 *Billington, James A. "The Split Within." IA (gen. study),
  121-62.
  In part, a discussion of the 1666-67 subordination of the
  church to the state as a symbol of the secularization process
  at work during the latter part of Alexis' reign. Billington
  states that the "Westernizing changes of Alexis' late years
  were profoundly revolutionary" and prompted traditionalists
  in Russian society to believe that "the reign of the Anti-
  christ had begun." On a broader level, Alexis' reign
  "meant the end of any serious efforts to maintain a civilization completely distinct from that of the West."

253 Buxhoeveden, Baroness Sophie. A Cavalier in Muscovy. London: Macmillan, 1932, 325pp., bib. 324-25.
  The focus of this study is the Russian life of General Patrick
  Gordon, an English observer/military adviser who had numerous contacts with Tsars Alexis and Peter I (to 1699),
  but it contains considerable discussion of Muscovite policy
  of the second half of the seventeenth century. Of particular
  interest are Buxhoeveden's sections on Alexis' personal life,
  clash with Patriarch Nikon, and relations with England.
  DK115.5.G6B8

254 Collins, Samuel. The Present State of Russia, in a Letter to
  a Friend at London; Written by an Eminent Person Residing
  at the Great Tsar's Court at Mosco for the Space of Nine
  Years. London: Printed by J. Winter for D. Newman,
  1671, 141pp. Excerpt in RTFE (anthology), 77-84.
  Unavailable for annotation. Collins served as Tsar Alexis'
  personal physician, 1660-69. For a discussion of Collins'
  work see Leo Loewenson, "The Works of Robert Boyle and
  The Present State of Russia by Samuel Collins (1671)."
  Slavonic E Eur R, 33 (1954-55): 470-85.

255   *Crummey, Robert O. "Court Groupings and Politics in
         Russia, 1645-1649." Forsch Ost Ges, 24 (1978): 203-22.
         An examination of court alignments of the late 1640s for in-
         sight into the source of Tsar Alexis' "fateful decisions to
         complete the enserfment of the peasantry, tie down the urban
         taxpayers and limit the legal autonomy of the church."
         Crummey establishes that from 1645 to 1648 the court group
         led by B. I. Morozov dominated the Muscovite government
         because of the favor which Morozov enjoyed with Alexis
         since serving as the tsar's tutor. However, the inequities
         of Morozov's rule and the unpopularity of the policies as-
         sociated with his name (particularly the salt tax) spawned
         such powerful opposition to him that a rebellion broke out in
         June of 1648 and Alexis was forced to exile Morozov to a
         distant monastery. In the chaotic months which followed the
         revolt, the court group associated with Prince Cherkassky
         became dominant, and Alexis' "fateful decisions" were reached
         as Cherkassky "looked desperately for support wherever he
         could find it. One after another, the most powerful interest
         groups in society ... extracted concessions they had long
         sought."

256   *_____. "Crown and Boiars Under Feodor Ivanovich and
         Michael Romanov." Can Am Slav S, 6, no. 4 (1972): 549-71.
         An analysis of the relationship between the crown and the
         members of the Boyar Duma during the reigns of Feodor I
         and Michael. On the basis of a statistical account of the
         tsar's appointments to top military and civil positions, Crum-
         mey concludes the "despite Michael's use of almost identical
         criteria in making appointments and setting conditions of
         service," a small group of royal favorites was able to rise
         far above the other members of the Boyar Duma in power
         and wealth.

257   Dukes, Paul. "Russia and the 'General Crisis' of the Seven-
         teenth Century." New Zealand Slavonic J, 2 (1974): 1-17.
         An examination of the roots of the 1648 revolt in Muscovy,
         Alexis' reaction to the disturbance, and the connection be-
         tween this event and contemporaneous revolts in Europe.

258   Ellersieck, Heinz E. "Russia Under Aleksei Mikhailovich and
         Feodor Alekseevich, 1645-1682, the Scandinavian Sources."
         University of California, Los Angeles, 1955. (dissertation)

259   *Evans, Norman. "A Russian Royal Letter of 1682." Prisca
         Monumenta. Studies on Archival and Administrative History.
         Presented to Dr. A. E. J. Hollander. Felicity Ranger, ed.
         London: University of London Press, 1973, 108-15.
         An analysis of a June 1682 royal letter, sent to Charles II
         of England, for insights into the nature of the "administra-
         tive machinery" which produced the document. Evans states
         that the letter, which announced the death of Alexis and

the accession of the joint sovereignty of Peter I and
Ivan V, reveals through its paper, ink, calligraphy, style,
and design that the Russian administrative system of 1682
was an anachronistic one. In comparing this letter to an
October 1709 letter sent by Peter I to Queen Anne, Evans
demonstrates that the anachronistic features of Russian diplomatic correspondence had all but disappeared, a development
which he discusses as a symbolization of Peter's Westernization of Russia's administrative system. CD1041.P74

260 Field, Cecil. The Great Cossack. The Rebellion of Sten'ka
     Razin Against Alexis Michaelovitch, Tsar of All the Russias.
     London: Herbert Jenkins Limited, 1947, 126pp., bib. 126.
     This account of the Razin Rebellion does not include a
     separate chapter on Alexis but contains a number of ref-
     erences to both the policies pursued by Alexis which prompted
     the revolt and his efforts to suppress the disturbance.
     DK118.5.F5

261 *Fuhrmann, Joseph T. Tsar Alexis. His Reign and His Russia.
     Gulf Breeze, Fla.: Academic International Press, 1981,
     250pp., bib. 232-39.
     The stated goals of this semi-popular biography are "to
     present Alexis' life in a readable way, to capture the passion,
     drama—even the coarseness—which so often escape scholarly
     studies of seventeenth century Russia" and to clarify the
     role played by Alexis in the important developments of this
     period. Fuhrmann is relatively successful on both counts
     as he presents a colorful, informative, and fairly detailed
     account of the highlights of Alexis' life and reign. Alexis
     emerges as a dynamic, Western-oriented leader whose reign
     marks the eclipse of Poland as the dominant power in eastern
     Europe and the emergence in Russia of a centralized, auto-
     cratic state. Fuhrmann praises Alexis for the depth of his
     piety and devotion to duty but sees flaws in his character,
     particularly in regard to his excessive vanity and conse-
     quent susceptibility to manipulation by friends and advisers.
     Fuhrmann also discusses the stark contrast between Alexis'
     personal Christian life and the coarse policies he often fol-
     lowed in dealing with the nation's peasant class. DK118.F83
     Reviewed in:
     Am Hist R, 87 (Apr. 1982): 500
     History, 67 (June 1983): 334
     Slav R, 41, no. 2 (1982): 324-25

262 Grey, I. "Tsar Alexei, 1645-1676." Hist Today, 18, no. 9
     (Sept. 1968): 606-13.
     A favorable overview of the life, character, and accomplish-
     ments of Tsar Alexis. Grey portrays Alexis as a "humble
     man and a humane ruler in a barbaric age" whose acquisition
     of Kiev and the eastern Ukraine, subjugation of the church,

and pro-Western policies laid the foundation for the advancements later made by Peter the Great.

263 Joliffe, John. "Lord Carlisle's Embassy to Moscow." Cornhill,
     176 (Autumn 1967): 217-22.
     In part, an account of a rift which occurred in Anglo-Russian
     commercial relations during the middle part of Alexis' reign.
     Joliffe also comments on Alexis' concept of diplomatic proto-
     col.

264 *Keep, J. L. H. "The Regime of Filaret (1619-1633)."
     Slavonic E Eur R, 38, no. 91 (1960): 334-60.
     A critical assessment of the policies pursued by Filaret
     Romanov during the fourteen years when he ruled Russia
     in the name of his son, Michael. Keep states that Filaret
     was "a 'reactionary,' who sought to solve present problems
     by applying the formulas of a bygone age." Autocratic in
     temperament, Filaret pursued as his basic goal the consolida-
     tion of "the new dynasty's position by winning for it the
     support of the most powerful social elements." He viewed
     this consolidation as an essential prerequisite to the establish-
     ment of autocratic power in its pre-Time of Troubles form.
     While his policies heavily favored the boyars and service
     gentry at the expense of the townsmen and peasants, Filaret
     promoted an image of "the autocratic power as an impartial
     arbitrator concerned only with the general welfare." Keep
     concludes that when all things are considered, Filaret's suc-
     cess in consolidating the monarchy's authority was primarily
     due to the general desire of Muscovites for a return to nor-
     mality after the chaos of the Time of Troubles and to the
     consequent absence of any organized or institutionalized op-
     position to absolutism.

265 *Kliuchevsky, Vasili. The Rise of the Romanovs. Liliana
     Archibald, ed./trans. London/New York: Macmillan/St.
     Martin's Press, 1970, 371pp.
     This classic study of pre-Petrine seventeenth century Russia
     does not contain a chapter devoted to any one of the Romanov
     tsars who ruled the nation during this period but nonetheless
     is regarded as an essential source for the study of early
     Romanov history. Kliuchevsky, a renowned turn of the
     century historian, artfully recreates the historical conditions,
     forces, and personalities responsible for the birth of the
     Romanov dynasty and a new era in the nation's history.
     While he devotes most of his attention to the nature and
     evolution of administrative and social institutions, the condi-
     tion of the various estates (especially the serfs), and the na-
     tion's involvement in exhausting civil and international strug-
     gles, he also discusses the personality, character, principal
     policies, and historical significance of each of the first three
     Romanov sovereigns. Of special interest are his sections
     dealing with the election of Michael as tsar, the Ulozhenie

of 1649, the zemsky sobor, the church schism, and the be-
ginnings of the modernization process which took concrete
form during the reign of Peter the Great.   DK114.K573
Reviewed in:
Hist Today, 20 (1970):   437-38
Lib J, 95 (1970):   2472
Slav R, 32, no. 2 (1973):   374-75
Ukr Q, 26 (1970):   320-22

266   Konovalov, Sergey.   "Seven Letters of Tsar Mikhail to King
       Charles I, 1634-1638."   Ox Slavonic P, 9 (1960):   32-63.
       An introduction to Tsar Michael's 1634-1638 letters to King
       Charles I of England, and a brief commentary on the histori-
       cal value of the Russian royal letters of 1613-1645 contained
       in British archives.

267   Krupnytsky, Borys.   "Treaty of Pereyaslav and the Political
       Orientation of Bohdan Khmelnytsky."   Ukr Q, 10 (1954):
       32-40.
       Unavailable for annotation.

268   Lamb, Harold.   "The Two Gates of Muscovy."   The City of the
       Tsar.   Peter the Great and the Move to the West 1648-1762.
       Garden City, N.Y.:   Doubleday Press, 1948, 1-49.
       A popular study which presents Alexis as the tsar who set in
       motion the policies which, under Peter the Great, led to the
       modernization and expansion of the Muscovite state.   DK113.L3

269   Lapman, Mark C.   "Political Denunciations in Muscovy, 1600 to
       1649.   The Sovereign's Word and Deed."   Harvard University,
       1982.   (dissertation)

270   Lewitter, L. R.   "Poland and the Ukraine, and Russia in the
       Seventeenth Century."   Slavonic E Eur R, 27, no. 68 (1948):
       151-71.
       Includes some information on the Westernizing policies adopted
       by Tsar Alexis as part of his attempt to place Russia on a
       par with the leading powers in Europe.   Lewitter also devotes
       considerable attention to the reaction of the Orthodox Church,
       especially through Patriarch Nikon, to the "Russian Renais-
       sance" of the mid-seventeenth century.

271   Lodge, Henry Calvin.   "The Urban Crowd During the Reign of
       Alexis Mikhailovich."   Rutgers University, 1970.   (disserta-
       tion)

272   Loewenson, Leo.   "The Moscow Rising of 1648."   Slavonic E Eur
       R, 27, no. 68 (1948):   145-56.
       A survey of the causes of the 1648 revolution and Alexis'
       reaction to it, and a reproduction of a document, from the
       Oxford University archives, which contains an eyewitness
       account of the uprising.

273 *Longworth, Philip. Alexis. Tsar of All the Russias. New
     York: Franklin Watts, 1984, 305pp., bib. 280-85.
     A favorable reassessment of Tsar Alexis and his accomplish-
     ments. Longworth presents Alexis as a forceful and progres-
     sive ruler whose reign witnessed the development of a central
     bureaucracy, the repatriation of Slavic peoples to Muscovy's
     south and west, the creation of a modern army, and the ad-
     vancement of political centralization despite challenges from
     the aristocracy, church, and peasantry. Given these de-
     velopments, which bear comparison to the policies pursued by
     Peter the Great, Longworth questions the neglect of Alexis'
     rule shown by Soviet historians and the portrayal of him
     by various Western historians as a pious weakling.
     DK118.L66 1984
          Reviewed in:
          History, 70 (June 1985): 303
          TLS, (7 Dec. 1984): 1421

274 _____. "Tsar Alexis Goes to War." Hist Today, 31 (Jan.
     1981): 14-18.
     A brief discussion of Alexis as a tsar whose domestic, foreign,
     and military policies mark the beginning of Russian moderniza-
     tion and expansion and foreshadow those pursued by his
     celebrated son, Peter the Great.

275 *Lubimenko, Inna. "The Correspondence of the First Stuarts
     with the First Romanovs." Trans Roy Hist S, 1, 4th series
     (1918): 77-91.
     A description of the form and substances of the 128 letters
     exchanged between the first two Stuart kings and Michael
     Romanov and his father, Filaret. Commercial concerns are
     at the forefront of most of the letters, though the corres-
     pondence in 1623 nearly brought a political alliance between
     England and Russia (James I died before the details could be
     settled). The letters also refer to the affairs of Russian
     students in England and to the military assistance rendered
     by England in the reorganization of the Russian army.

276 Lupinin, Nikolas. "The State of Religion in a Religious State:
     The Russian Church in the Reign of Tsar Aleksei, 1645-76,"
     New York University, 1973. (dissertation)

277 Lyubavsky, M. "The Accession of the Romanovs: March 3,
     1613 in the History of Russia." Rus R (Liverpool), 2, no. 1
     (1913): 11-31.
     Unavailable for annotation.

278 O'Brien, C. Bickford. Muscovy and the Ukraine; from the
     Periaslav Agreement to the Truce of Andrusovo, 1654-1667.
     Berkeley: University of California Press, 1963, 138pp., bib.
     134-38.

This scholarly study of Muscovite-Ukrainian relations in the thirteen years between the Treaties of Periaslav and Andrusovo does not contain a titled section on Alexis' role in promoting the union of Russia and the Ukraine but still merits consultation for its scattered references to his part in this momentous event in Russia's history.   DK508.2.02

279 *_____. "Russia and Turkey, 1677-1681: The Treaty of Bakhchisarai." Rus R, 12, no. 4 (Oct. 1953): 259-68.
A discussion of the Treaty of Bakhchisarai as a document which "established important precedents which Russia was to expand in subsequent agreements with the Turks." O'Brien thus sees Feodor's reign as one which marks a crucial turning point in Russo-Turkish relations.

280 *Olearius, Adam. The Travels of Olearius in Seventeenth Century Russia. Samuel H. Baron, ed./trans. Stanford: Stanford University Press, 1967, 347pp.
A translation of the 1656 German edition of Olearius' A New Enlarged Description of Travels to Muscovy and Persia, a work hailed for its accurate and perceptive commentary and one which was widely read in seventeenth-century Europe. Olearius, a member of several embassies sent by the Duke of Holstein to Muscovy between 1634 and 1643, is at his best when describing Muscovite religion, social life, manners, and customs, but he also presents a series of observations on the coronation of Alexis, his wealth, daily habits, and servitors, and, particularly, the 1648 revolt in Moscow. In discussing the rebellion (an event which he did not witness), Olearius does not comment on the underlying causes of the opposition to Alexis but rather focuses on its external features and Alexis' efforts to quell the disturbance. DK22.06133

281 *Palmer, William. The Patriarch and the Tsar, 6 Vols. London: Trubner and Company, 1871-1876.
This six-volume, 3,400-page work presents an impressive collection of primary source material dealing with the 1666-1667 trial of Patriarch Nikon and an interpretation of this affair as a disaster for both Russia and the Romanov dynasty. Volumes one and two contain the court testimonies of Alexis, boyar leaders, and ecclesiastic authorities as well as Nikon's statement of defense. Volume three presents an account of the pre-trial relationship between Alexis and Nikon and an interpretation of the rift which developed between them as being caused by Alexis' interference in church affairs, in part because of his egomania and jealousy of Nikon, but mostly because he was encouraged to do so by scheming boyars and clerics who convinced him that Nikon was attempting to usurp his authority as tsar. Following a defense of Nikon's thought, policies, and behavior, and a discussion of the broader issue of the limits of spiritual and civilian authority in mid-

seventeenth-century Russia, Palmer, in volumes four through six, turns to an account of the punishments meted out by God to all the individuals responsible for the degradation of Nikon and the Russian Orthodox Church. For Alexis' leading role in "the creation in Russia of a merely national Church under the supremacy of the state," he suffered divine retribution (foretold by Nikon) in the form of "dynastic suicide" at the hands of his son, Peter the Great. BX597.N5P3

282 Schakovsky, Zinaida. "Tsar Alexis (1657-1676)." The Fall of Eagles. Precursors of Peter the Great. J. M. Brownjohn, trans. New York: Harcourt, Brace and World, 1964, 15-134. A favorable, popular account of the reign of Alexis from the time of the birth of the tsar's daughter Sophia until his death in 1676. Schakovsky discusses in dramatic style the growth of the Russian economy, the acquisition of the Ukraine, and the removal of Patriarch Nikon within the confines of her belief that the reigns of Alexis and Feodor and the regency of Sophia heralded the modernization of Russia which later occurred under Peter the Great, a modernization which Peter's predecessors carried out in a more humane fashion than did he. DK114.S3213

283 _____. "Tsar Theodore Alexeyevitch (1678-1682)." Ibid., 135-90.
A favorable review of the reign of Feodor as one which helped pave the way for the modernization of Russia wrought by Peter the Great. Schakovsky states that although Feodor's frail nature and lack of concern for the mechanics of political power led him to delegate much of his authority to advisers, his reign nonetheless witnessed steady progress and a humane treatment of Russia's populace. Receiving particular praise are Feodor's abolition of the right of precedence, his successful conclusion of a protracted war with the Turks, and his modernization of the Russian army. DK114.S3213

284 *Soloviev, Sergei M. History of Russia, Vol. 24. The Character of Old Russia. Alexander V. Muller, ed./trans. Gulf Breeze, Fla.: Academic International Press, 1980, 301pp. This volume does not contain any one chapter which focuses on the rule of Alexis, but it places his reign squarely at the crossroads between old and new Russia. Drawing upon an impressive amount of primary source material, Soloviev presents an analysis of Russia's development from Kievan times, when popular urban assemblies in Russia's oldest cities dominated the political scene, to the end of Alexis' reign by which time Muscovy had not only consolidated its position as the successor to the Kievan state but showed distinct signs of "the type of secularization and modernization inspired by the West that would become prevalent under Peter the Great."

Within this context, Soloviev discusses Alexis' struggle with
and triumph over Patriarch Nikon, use of foreigners as state
servitors, and his generally favorable attitude toward Westernization. DK40.S6213

285   *Spinka, Matthew. "Patriarch Nikon and the Subjugation of the
      Russian Church to the State." Church Hist, 10 (1941): 347-
      66.
      An examination of the roots of Patriarch Nikon's conflict with
      Tsar Alexis, the patriarch's trial, and the overall significance
      of this episode. Spinka states although Nikon misinterpreted
      the Epanagoge (a Byzantine law code dealing with Church-
      State relations) so did those who judged and condemned him,
      a condemnation which symbolized the establishment of complete
      supremacy of the Russian state over the Orthodox Church.

286   Uroff, Benjamin Philip. "Grigorii Karpovich Kotoshikhin on
      Russia in the Reign of Alexis Mikhailovich. An Annotated
      Translation." Columbia University, 1970. (dissertation)

287   *Vernadsky, George V. "The Hetman and the Tsar." Bohdan,
      Hetman of Ukraine. New Haven: Yale University Press, 1941,
      99-109.
      A description of the resistance encountered by the envoy
      sent by Alexis to B. Khmelnitsky to secure Ukrainian alle-
      giance to Muscovy by way of an oath to be taken by the
      Zaporozhian Cossacks. Khmelnitsky insisted, before taking
      the oath, that the envoy "swear first in the name of the tsar
      that the privileges of the Kozak Host would be kept intact."
      Reluctantly the Cossack elders agreed to swear allegiance to
      the tsar with only a vague guarantee that their autonomy
      would be preserved. In the second half of this chapter,
      and in various other sections, Vernadsky discusses carefully
      the complex relations that existed between Khmelnitsky and
      Alexis' government. DK508.V44

288   Wren, M. "The Early Romanovs." WITR (gen. study), 12-20.
      In part, a discussion of the popularization of Western customs
      by Alexis, his reliance on advisers sympathetic with Westerni-
      zation, and his implementation of various Western-oriented
      policies, most notably in regard to the subjugation of the
      Orthodox Church to secular authority. Wren also describes
      the negative popular reaction to the growth of Western influ-
      ence during Alexis' reign.

289   Yakovliv, Andriy. "Bohdan Khmelnytsky's Treaty with the
      Tsar of Muscovy in 1654." Ann Ukr Soc Arts Sci, 4, no.
      3 (1955): 904-16.
      Unavailable for annotation.

290   *Zenkovsky, Serge A. "The Russian Church Schism: Its

Background and Repercussions." Rus R, 16, no. 4 (1957): 37-58.

An argument that the church reform of 1666-1667 was primarily a consequence of the conviction shared by Patriarch Nikon and Tsar Alexis that "the time had come for Russia to play a decisive role in the Orthodox world" and, in order to do so, Russian church life and practices had to be made consistent with those of the more Western-oriented Orthodox population to Russia's south and west. Zenkovsky maintains that this conviction, itself a consequence of Alexis' annexation of the Ukraine and subsequent interest in adding to Russia the Orthodox population which bordered on that region, led to the sacrifice of Muscovy's cultural harmony and ideological integrity to the new imperial ideal. Zenkovsky concludes with an account of the plight of the Old Believers who "lived in a state of internal emigration as a result of their refusal to cooperate with the Empire and its reformed church."

REGENCY OF SOPHIA (1682-1689)

291 *Coxe, William. "Of the Princess Sophia Alexiefna. Sister of Peter the Great." TPRSD (gen. study), 353-75.
An argument that Sophia's positive qualities have been obscured and her accomplishments grossly misrepresented simply because she headed a party in opposition to Peter. Singling out the works of Gordon, Neuville, and Voltaire as the principal sources of Sophia's dismal historical image, Coxe maintains that these authors wrongly linked Sophia to the revolt of the streltsy which preceded the establishment of joint rule by Peter and Ivan V. Sophia was merely selected by the party representing Ivan V's interests to rule in his minority (and Peter's) because of her "imperial lineage, popular manners, respectable character, and great abilities." Coxe admits that as a regent Sophia probably became ambitious and may have been unwilling to relinquish "a power which she had long enjoyed, and which she exercised with great ability," but he asserts that there is "no positive evidence which should induce us to believe that she conspired against her brother's life." Coxe concludes by citing Peter I's own tribute to Sophia's competence as a ruler: "What a pity that she persecuted me in my minority, and that I cannot repose any confidence in her; otherwise, when I am employed abroad she might govern at home."

292 *De la Neuville, Foy. An Account of Muscovy, As It Was in the Year 1689. London: Edward Castle, 1699, 119pp.
An account, by a diplomatic envoy representing the King of Poland, of the political intrigue at the Russian court of the 1680s which attended the joint rule of the youthful Peter I and his half-brother, Ivan V, and which culminated in the 1689 abortive coup d'etat of the Regent Sophia. In relating the events which took place, Neuville provides a number of interesting anecdotal comments on the conspiracy of Sophia and Peter's violent reaction to it. PG3447.Z2I82 v.2

293 Hayes, Alice M. "The Regent Sophia and the Tzarina Eudoxia."
     Ang-Rus Lit Soc Proc, 27 (Feb.-Apr. 1900): 41-55.
     Unavailable for annotation.

294 Hughes, Lindsey. "Sofiya Alekseyevna and the Moscow Rebel-
     lion of 1682." Slavonic E Eur R, 63, no. 4 (1985): 518-39.

295 _____. "Sophia, Regent of Russia." Hist Today, 32 (July
     1982): 10-15.
     A description of Sophia's rise to power in the male-dominated
     society of late seventeenth-century Russia, and a discussion
     of her regency as a productive one, particularly in regard
     to cultural advancements. Hughes also relates the bloody
     events surrounding Sophia's overthrow.

296 *Keep, John. "Mutiny in Moscow, 1682: A Contemporary
     Account." Can Slavonic P, 23, no. 4 (1981): 410-42.
     A translation of Heinrich Butenant's eyewitness account of
     the bloody mutiny of the streltsy in Moscow on 15-17 May
     1682. Butenant, a German merchant involved in various bus-
     iness activities in Muscovy during the decade which preceded
     the revolt, provides a particularly graphic description of the
     streltsy's brutality and the terror which swept the city amidst
     their rampage. More importantly, Butenant does not make any
     reference to the Miloslavskys' complicity in the outbreak of the
     mutiny but rather links the revolt to long standing grievances
     which the streltsy held. In an introduction, Keep maintains
     that Peter the Great was primarily responsible for the vitality
     of the theory that partisans of the Miloslavsky clan engineered
     the mutiny so as to advance the regency of Sophia over
     Peter's half-brother Ivan V, a fiction which rendered sup-
     port for Peter's claim that Sophia tried to usurp autocratic
     power.

297 O'Brien, Carl B. "Russia Prior to Peter the Great: The
     Regency of Tsarevna Sophia." University of California,
     Berkeley, 1943. (dissertation)

298 *_____. Russia Under Two Tsars, 1682-1689. The Regency
     of Sophia Alekseevna. Berkeley: University of California
     Press, 1952, 178pp., bib. 159-71.
     An argument that the regency of Sophia deserves far more
     attention from historians as a period of significant advances
     in many spheres and as a precursor of the reign of Peter
     the Great. In summarizing Sophia's accomplishments, O'Brien
     states that "new trade and diplomatic relations were estab-
     lished with the nations of the East and West. Internally, a
     number of reforms were effected. A strong impulse was
     given to education. The national propensity toward cultural
     isolation was attacked. Efforts were made to bring better
     order into international trade and to landed property, and to

Peter I and Ivan V   73

free the state from an excessive dependence on foreign
industry. Not only the events themselves but their relation
to the reforms of Peter's epoch gave extraordinary signifi-
cance to the regency of Sophia." DK125.037
Reviewed in:
Am Hist R, 59, no. 1 (1953): 116
Ann Am Acad, 285 (1953): 221
Slav R, 12, no. 2 (1953): 263

299 *Palmer, William. "The Ambitious and Unnatural Daughter."
PAT, (gen. study), 923-54.
A discussion of the political intrigue of Sophia as one example
of the type of punishments, "which came chiefly from without,
by the will of God, upon the person and family and dynasty
of the Tsar Alexis" as both "chastisement" and "penal retribution" for his role in the degradation of Patriarch Nikon and
the Russian church.

300 *Schakovsky, Zinaida. "Regent Sophia (1682-1689)." The Fall
of Eagles. Precursors of Peter the Great. J. M. Brownjohn,
trans. New York: Harcourt, Brace and World, 1964, 191-
302.
An examination of the political maneuverings which led to
the regency of Sophia, and an account of her reign as an
enlightened one. Schakovsky praises Sophia for "the spirit
of logic that guided her reforms and the methodical manner
in which she straightened out the country's tangled affairs,"
particularly in regard to her economic policies, forging of
closer links with European powers, and stabilization of Russia's southern border at the expense of the Crimean Tartars.
The author commends Sophia for her humane and progressive
policies and presents a sympathetic recreation of her struggle
with Peter I. In all, Schakovsky sees Sophia's reign as an
enlightened one consistent with the very best characteristics
of Peter the Great's more celebrated rule. DK114.S3213

GENERAL STUDIES AND ASSESSMENTS

301 Abbott, Jacob. Peter the Great. New York: Harper and
Brothers, 1901, 368pp.
A popular biography with most attention devoted to Peter's
personality, family relationships, and Westernization of court
life, dress, and customs. Abbott highlights Peter's volatile
nature and vigorous pursuit of foreign and domestic policies
designed to make Russia a great European nation. DK132.A32

302 *Aksakov, Konstantin Sergeevich. "On the Internal State of
Russia." RIH (anthology), 230-51. Excerpt in PG (anthol-
ogy), 148-52.
A classic Slavophile statement on the perversion of Russia's

culture, values, and institutions at the hands of Peter the
Great. Aksakov, who submitted his essay to Alexander II
in hope of persuading him to erase the harm done by Peter I
and perpetuated by his successors, presents an idealized
version of life in old Muscovy and attacks Peter for tearing
asunder Muscovy's civic harmony and cultural integrity by
Westernizing the upper class and therein separating it from
the Russian people. Aksakov warns that "the longer Peter's
system of government continues ... the more will foreign ideas
infiltrate Russia, the greater will be the number of people
who lose touch with their native Russian soil, ... and the
more terrible will be the revolutionary attempts which in the
end will destroy Russia."

303   *Anderson, M. S. "The Age of Peter the Great." Britain's
Discovery of Russia 1553-1815. New York: St. Martin's
Press, 1958, 49-79.
An examination of the changing image of Russia and Peter
the Great reflected in British writings of the first quarter
of the eighteenth century. Anderson states that despite
Peter's 1698 visit to England little was written to dispell the
image of Russia as a primitive Asiatic kingdom until Peter's
victory over Charles XII at Poltava. Thereafter, fear of the
harmful effects of Russian expansion into Northern Europe
prompted a number of works, especially The Northern Crisis,
which exaggerated the danger posed to British interests by
Peter's diplomatic and military policies. However, when
"Sweden's defeat and loss of her Baltic empire were found to
involve no immediately disastrous results either for Great
Britain or for Protestantism," the majority of British publications concerning Peter swung to the opposite extreme and
generally presented him in an exceptionally favorable light
not only since he seemed less threatening but also because
"exaggerated ideas of the scope and novelty of Peter's reforms could take root in Britain" due to "the ignorance of
many aspects of Russian life which still prevailed there."
DA47.65.A77

304   *_____. English Views of Russia in the Age of Peter the
Great." ASEER, 13 (April 1954): 200-14.
An account of the growth of English interest in Russia as a
consequence of the Northern War. Anderson states that English views of Peter, his policies, and the Russia he ruled were
simplistic and contributed much to the establishment of the
myth of Peter the Great as a wonder-working, enlightened
despot.

305   _____. Peter the Great. London: The Historical Association, 1969, 32pp., bib. 31-32.
A brief review of the highlights of Peter's reign and its
place in the evolution of Russia as a nation. Useful as an

introduction to the issues most central to the study of Peter
and his accomplishments. DK131.A49

306 *_____. Peter the Great. London: Thames and Hudson,
1978, 207pp., bib. 189–193.
A scholarly overview of the character of Peter the Great,
the policies he implemented, and the historical context within
which he functioned. Synthesizing much of the modern scholarship on Peter, Anderson discusses the seventeenth-century
roots of the Petrine program, the pressures (material and
personal) which influenced the shape and pace of Peter's
reforms, the principal reforms themselves, and the personality
and character traits of Peter which so colored (often negatively) his reign. In assessing Peter's place in history,
Anderson maintains that the tsar's failures, the incomplete-
ness of much of his work, and the existence of predecessors
for his more successful policies seriously limit his claim to
greatness, though he must be admired for the energetic and
tenacious manner in which he pursued his goal of creating a
more powerful and enlightened Russia. DK131.A492

307 Bailey, H. "From Peter the Great to Lenin." Fortn R, 114
(Oct. 1920): 564–72.
An examination on the parallel efforts of Peter the Great and
Lenin in their respective attempts to "graft a Western civiliza-
tion on an Eastern people."

308 Baker, Nina Brown. Peter the Great. New York: Vanguard
Press, 1943, 310pp., bib. 305–06.
A general, favorable, and colorful account of Peter and his
accomplishments. Nondocumented, somewhat fanciful, this
work is designed for the young reader. DK131.B17

309 Banks, John. A New History of the Life and Reign of the Czar
Peter the Great. Montpelier, Vt.: Wright and Sibley, for
P. Merrifield and Company, 1811 (reprint of 1740 edition),
316pp.
An early English language account of the backward condition
of late seventeenth-century Russia and Peter's attempt to
improve Russia through the modernization of its institutions,
culture, economy, and military forces. Banks draws heavily
from the works of Fontenelle and Voltaire as he presents a
detailed sketch of Peter's personality, character, and behavior,
and chronicles the principal events in Peter's life and reign.
Long on anecdotes, short on analysis. DK131.B121

310 Barrow, John. The Life of Peter the Great. New York: A.
L. Burt and Company, 1903, 405pp.
The stated purpose of this work is to "bring together and
arrange the scattered fragments of histories, lives, anecdotes,
and notices, ... in manuscript or in print of one of the most

extraordinary characters that ever appeared on the great
theater of the world." Principal among the sources utilized,
in quiltwork fashion, by Barrow in his favorable account of
Peter and his reign are those by Gordon, Bell, Bruce, Mottley, Staehlin, and Voltaire. DK131.B27

311 _____. A Memoir of the Life of Peter the Great. New York:
A. L. Fowle, 1900 (reprint of 1832 edition), 320pp.
A favorable account of Peter's character, leading policies,
and accomplishments. The author states, quite correctly,
that he has done "little more than bring together and arrange the scattered fragments of histories, lives, anecdotes,
and notices" concerning Peter in an attempt to review and
provide insight into Peter's extraordinary accomplishments.
Based primarily on the writings of Mottley, Staehlin, Voltaire,
Bruce, Bell, and Gordon, and on the journals of Peter the
Great. The lack of a subject index and an adequate table of
contents makes this work a somewhat difficult one to use.
DK131.B27 1900

312 *Belinsky, Vissarion. "The Miracle of Peter the Great." MMR
(anthology), 126-28.
A portrayal of Peter the Great as a miracle worker who effectively redressed the political, economic, military, and cultural shortcomings under which Russia suffered as a consequence of 250 years of Tartar domination. Belinsky, a noted
Russian radical, journalist, and literary critic of the mid-
nineteenth century, adds that Peter "opened his nation's door
to the light of the world," but since his death Russians have
become a people with a character of their own--Russians in
the European spirit not Europeanized Russians.

313 *_____. "Russia and the West." MMR (anthology), 119-26.
An argument that Peter the Great's reforms did not pervert
native Russian culture but rather cleansed form it the harmful effects of the Tartar yoke and pointed the way for Russia
to proceed if she were to achieve the progress denied the nation by centuries of misfounded traditionalism. Belinsky paints
a dismal portrait of Muscovite culture and portrays Peter as a
colossus among the giants of history not only for his accomplishments but also for his paving the way for Russia to become a contributing member of the European community of
nations.

314 Birkhead, Alice. Peter the Great. London, 1913, 188pp.
Unavailable for annotation, but an excerpt, titled "Peter the
Great" appears on pages 137-44 in the author's Heroes of
Modern Europe (Freeport: Books for Libraries Press, 1916.
D106.B55) in which she portrays Peter as a revolutionary
tsar who transformed Russia from a primitive nation to one
modern and European.

315   *Black, C. E. "The Reforms of Peter the Great. <u>Rewriting</u>
      <u>Russian History</u>. Cyril E. Black, ed. New York: Random
      House, 1962, 233-59.
      A scholarly review of the interpretations of Peter's reforms
      advanced by Soviet historians. Black states that the central
      task confronting Marxist historians who study Peter's reign
      has been to identify his role "in a period of declining 'feudal-
      ism' and incipient 'capitalism' and to place Peter's reforms in
      their proper relationship to the 'class struggle.' " Within
      this context, Black discusses the writings of Pokrovsky
      (who sees Peter's reforms in light of the needs of the mer-
      chant class), Roshkov (who argues that the Petrine era was
      the final phase of the revolution of the court nobility),
      Syromyatnikov (who contends that Peter's reforms, in the
      mold of enlightened despotism favored the bourgeoisie at the
      expense of feudal landowners), Voskresensky, Andreev, and
      others. Throughout, the author stresses that Soviet histori-
      ans have had to adapt their interpretations to the changing
      needs of the Communist Party's leaders, particularly in re-
      gard to the role played by the individual in history, and to
      the need to present favorably those tsarist rulers whose ad-
      vancement of state interests (even through brutal policies)
      might serve as "a justification of the strains and stresses of
      Soviet policies." DK38.B5

316   Black, J. L. "N. M. Karamzin's Views on Peter the Great."
      <u>New R E Eur Hist</u>, (6 Dec. 1966): 20-37.
      Unavailable for annotation.

317   Blamberg, Margaret O. "The Publicists of Peter the Great,"
      Indiana University, 1974. (dissertation)

318   Bouvet, J. <u>The Present Condition of the Muscovite Empire,</u>
      <u>till the Year 1699....</u> Jococus Crull, ed./trans. London:
      Printed for F. Coggan, 1699, 109pp.
      Unavailable for annotation.

319   Bradford, Sarah H. <u>The History of Peter the Great, Czar of</u>
      <u>Russia</u>. New York: D. Appleton and Company, 1858, 233pp.
      A general and somewhat fanciful biography of Peter I, written
      for youthful readers.

320   Browning, Oscar. <u>Peter the Great</u>. London: Hutchinson and
      Company, 1898, 347pp.
      Synthesizing the works of Ustrialov, Soloviev, and Waliszew-
      ski, Browning chronicles Peter's reforms, policies, and ac-
      complishments, and presents a reasonably sympathetic review
      of Peter's personal qualities and impact on Russia's develop-
      ment.

321   Bruce, Peter H. <u>Memoirs of Peter Henry Bruce, Esquire. A</u>

Military Officer in the Services of Prussia, Russia, and Great
Britain.... London: Frank Cass and Company, 1970 (reprint
of 1782 edition), 527pp.
More of an account of the author's travels and adventures
than a commentary on Peter I and his reign, this work is of
value primarily for its insights into the Russian military, in
which the author served for a number of years, and for its
anecdotes and observations on Peter's travels, military exploits, personal behavior, and relationship with Tsarevich
Alexis. D285.8.B7A3

322 Buzzi, Giancarlo. The Life and Times of Peter the Great.
Philadelphia: Curtiss Publishing Company, 1967, 75pp.
As part of the Portraits of Greatness series, this work presents a beautifully illustrated outline of Peter's life and accomplishments. Buzzi's text to this pictorial work is succinct
and quite readable and therefore provides an overview of
Peter's reign useful for the general public. DK131.B813

323 Chaadaev, Peter. The Major Works of Peter Chaadaev. Richard
Pipes, intro. Raymond T. McNally, trans./commentary.
Notre Dame: University of Notre Dame Press, 1969, 216pp.
Excerpts in IEH, 237-40; PG, 139-44; RIH, 159-73; RICA,
303-14; MMR, 50-57 (anthologies).
In a number of the writings contained in this volume, Peter
Chaadaev, a noted Russian philosopher/essayist during the
reign of Nicholas I, discusses the place of the Petrine reforms in Russia's historical evolution as he develops his views
in regard to the nature of and proper relationship between
the civilizations of Russia and Western Europe. Chaadaev's
essay, "A Philosophical Letter" (1836) spawned an immense
furor among Russian intellectuals because of its assertion
that Russia was a stagnant, cultural wasteland prior to its
Westernization at the hands of Peter the Great. For his criticism of native Russian culture and lack of respect for Russia's pre-Petrine past, Chaadaev was declared insane by order
of Nicholas I and was placed under house arrest. During this
time, he wrote "Apology of a Madman" which contains further
favorable discussion of Peter the Great as the civilizer of
Russia. Chaadaev argues in the "Apology" that Peter was
able to impose Western civilization upon Russia because he
"found only a blank page when he came to power"; Peter,
therefore, could not have robbed the nation of its past because it had no viable traditions: "We were so obedient to
the voice of a prince who led us to a new life because our
previous existence apparently did not give us any legitimate
grounds for resistance." B4238.C52F5

324 Cobb, James F. The Story of the Great Czar. A Sketch of
the Life of Peter the Great. London, 1875, 127pp.
Unavailable for annotation.

325 Cowie, Leonard W. "Russia Under Peter the Great." Seven-
     teenth Century Europe. London: G. Bell and Sons, 1960,
     342-64.
     A favorable portrayal of Peter as a ruler whose devotion to
     work and country and pursuit of bold and progressive poli-
     cies brought Russia into the modern era. Cowie notes that
     Peter was cruel, obstinate, and sometimes showed poor judg-
     ment and that his policies in no way altered the historical
     direction in which Russia was heading but nonetheless con-
     cludes that Peter was a great leader because he so success-
     fully shaped and accelerated existing trends and aspirations.
     DK246.C6

326 *Cracraft, James. "More 'Peter the Great.'" Can Am Slav S,
     14, no. 4 (1980): 535-44.
     A review article on recent works on Peter the Great by Troyat,
     Bagger, Pavlenko, DeJonge, Anderson, Peterson, and Gasio-
     rowska. With the exception of Peterson's book, Cracraft be-
     lieves these publications do little to advance understanding of
     Peter's reign and, especially in the case of Troyat and De
     Jonge, serve to perpetuate the Petrine legend.

327 Cross, Anthony G., ed. "The Reign of Peter the Great."
     RUWE (anthology), 125-74.
     Excerpts from the writings of Western travelers to Petrine
     Russia which deal, in part, with Peter's character, suppres-
     sion of the streltsy revolt, entry into Moscow after his vic-
     tory at Noteborg, and his social reforms. The excerpts are
     from the works of Y. Ides, J. Korb, C. LeBrun, J. Perry,
     F. Weber, and J. Bell.

328 *Cuppy, William J. "Peter the Great." The Decline and Fall
     of Practically Everybody. New York: H. Holt and Company,
     1950, 132-40.
     A humorous portrayal of Peter's character, personal relation-
     ships, and customs. As a sample of Cuppy's wit and style,
     consider the following: "Peter's son, the Tsarevich Alexis,
     was no good. Everything bored him and he had a funny
     feeling on the top of his head. He wore an old dressing gown
     with missing buttons and he would sit on the stove all day
     eating pickled mushrooms and salted cucumbers. Peter often
     beat Alexis. This hurt Alexis more than it did him. Some
     people say that he beat Alexis to death. Well, he only did
     it once. And besides, he was drunk at the time."
     PN6161.C787

329 *Daniels, R. L. "Peter the Great and the Westernization of
     Russia." Harold T. Parker, ed. Problems in European His-
     tory. Durham: Moore Publishing Company, 1979, 36-44.
     An interpretive overview of the origin, extent, and signifi-
     cance of the Petrine policy of Westernization. Daniels discusses

80   Russian Autocrats

Peter's youthful fascination with the West and consequent
travels to various parts of Europe as the beginnings of the
tsar's lifelong interest in the West and desire to modernize
his realm along European lines. Daniels does not believe that
Peter followed "a 'time table' or systematic program" in
Westernizing Russia and agrees that "the exigencies of war
may have modified the reform effort to some extent," but
nonetheless maintains that Peter certainly "set out to remake
Russia into a Western European state" and devoted the vast
majority of his time and energy to the accomplishment of this
enormous task." Despite Peter's herculean efforts, Daniels
concludes, "Russia did not lose or reject its original Muscovite essence" since "the vast majority of Russians retained
Muscovite values and identity." D6.P738

330 Day, Helene R. "Voltaire's Portrayal of Peter the Great."
     Boston University, 1971. (dissertation)

331 DeFoe, Daniel. Impartial History of the Life and Actions of
     Peter Alexowitz, the Present Czar of Muscovy ... Written
     by a British Officer in the Service of the Czar.... London:
     W. Chetwood, J. Stagg, J. Botherton, and T. Eldin, 1723,
     420pp. Also published under the title A True, Authentick,
     and Impartial History of the Life and Glorious Actions of the
     Czar of Muscovy: From His Birth to His Death. London:
     A. Bettesworth, 1725, 429pp.
     A highly flattering account of Peter I's life and reign. DeFoe
     blends with his narrative a large number of lengthy citations
     from the writings of foreign diplomats and observers as well
     as from letters written to and by Peter. The tsar's extensive
     foreign travels, diplomacy, and military affairs receive more
     attention than do his domestic policies and personal life. Al-
     though DeFoe notes that Russia's rulers prior to Peter had
     begun Westernizing the nation, he nonetheless portrays Peter
     as the source of all that is good in Russia.

332 DeJonge, Alex. Fire and Water. A Life of Peter the Great.
     New York: Coward, McCann, and Geoghegan, 1980, 279pp.,
     bib. 267-70.
     A sympathetic, popular biography which provides most detail
     on Peter's personal life and foreign and military policies. In
     a free-flowing fashion, DeJonge delves into Peter's character
     and personality. He notes the tsar's ruthlessness when pur-
     suing desired ends but sees a "joyful side" to Peter who
     loved life and lived it to its fullest in an unpretentious and
     exuberant manner. In assessing Peter's reforms, DeJonge
     states that Peter did not follow any conscious program of
     change but rather devised and implemented reforms as he
     identified obstacles that stood in the way of Russia becoming
     a great power. His reforms, nonetheless, had a revolutionary
     effect on Russia's development: "it is thanks to the actions

and attitude of this one man that Medieval Muscovy became
Imperial Russia within the span of some twenty-five years."
D132.D42

333 Dilworth, W. H. The Father of His Country: Or the History
of the Life and Glorious Exploits of Peter the Great, Czar of
Muscovy. London: H. Woodgate and S. Brooks, 1760, 135pp.
A fanciful and favorable description of the travels, exploits,
and accomplishments of Peter I published for "the improvement
and entertainment of the British youth of both sexes."
DK131.D58

334 *Dmytryshyn, Basil, ed. "Modernization of Russia Under Peter
I." Modernization of Russia Under Peter I and Catherine II.
New York: John Wiley and Sons, 1974, 9-84.
As part of the Major Issues in History series, this volume aims
to expose students "to both the finest historical thinking" on
Peter's modernization of Russia and "some evidence on which
this thinking is based." Following a general introduction to
the problem of interpreting the modernizing efforts and accomplishments of Peter I and Catherine II, the editor presents
selections from Peter's decrees and orders and excerpts from
three contemporary foreign assessments of Peter's modernization (J. Perry, F. C. Weber, and J. G. Vockerodt), V. O.
Kliuchevsky's Peter the Great, and a textbook prepared for
Soviet university students. DK133.D58

335 Dumas, Alexandre. "The Romance of Peter the Great (1689-
1725)." CCRC (gen. study), 31-66.
An anecdotal survey of the highlights of Peter's personal life
and accomplishments. Dumas, inspired by an 1863 visit to
St. Petersburg where he saw "Peter's spirit hovering over
all," devotes most of his attention to Peter's establishment of
St. Petersburg and victory over Charles XII.

336 _____. "The Romance of the Strelitz Guard." Ibid., 67-83.
A colorful account of the intrigues and foul deeds of the
streltsy during the regency of Sophia and the first few years
of Peter's reign as tsar. Dumas also describes vividly the
harsh punishments the rebellious streltsy suffered at the
hands of Peter upon his return from Europe in 1698.

337 Fitzmaurice-Kelly, James. "Peter the Great." New R, 17
(Aug. 1897): 163-74.
A favorable review of Waliszewski's Peter the Great, and a
discussion of Peter's character and accomplishments. The
author emphasizes that although Peter's dedication to coarse
debauchery and his ruthless and often cruel behavior cannot
be denied, he unquestionably was personally responsible for
"placing his country on a level with the proudest kingdoms
of the Continent." Fitzmaurice-Kelly concludes that within the

context of early eighteenth-century Russia Peter's behavior
is acceptable and his progressive policies deserve praise in
any context.

338   Gibson, Michael. Peter the Great. London: Wayland Publishers, 1975, 96pp., bib. 95.
As part of the Wayland Kings and Queens series, this book
consists of a generously illustrated and well-balanced introduction to the highlights of Peter I's life and reign. A useful survey for the non-specialist. DK131.G5

339   Gooch, G. P. "Voltaire as Historian" and "Charles XII and
Peter the Great." Catherine the Great and Other Studies.
London: Longmans, Green and Company, 1954, 199-274.
A generally favorable review of Voltaire's writings on Charles
XII and Peter the Great. Gooch notes that while Voltaire
tended to be uncritical in his treatment of Peter's reforms
and accomplishments and chose to overlook the questionable
features of Peter's behavior, the depth of his research and
the fluidity of his style make his work an admirable one.
DK170.G65

340   *Gordon, Alexander. History of Peter the Great, 2 Vols.
Aberdeen: F. Douglasss and W. Murray, 1755.
A praiseful biography of Peter the Great, written by a Scottish officer who served (1696-1711) as a major-general in
Peter's army. Gordon's account is most detailed on Peter's
military affairs and campaigns (particularly those in which he
served Peter) but also includes information on diplomatic relations with bordering nations. In general, Gordon describes
Peter as an energetic, dramatic, and highly effective sovereign who "almost instantaneously" revolutionized the condition
of "a barbarous and uncivilized people" by pursuing policies
designed to eliminate superstition, improve Russia's institutions, and develop its economy and military forces. In support
of this image of Peter, Gordon discusses, often in anecdotal
form, Peter's Western travels, recruitment of foreigners for
service in Russia, personal command of the army, construction
of St. Petersburg, victory over Sweden, promotion of education, concern for efficient administration of his realm, and
generosity toward all who served Russia well. Gordon describes Peter as being practical, determined, inspirational,
accomplished in many fields, generous to the deserving and
harsh toward his enemies, unpretentious, impetuous, and
fun-loving.

341   Gordon, Patrick. Passages from the Diary of General Patrick
Gordon in the Years 1635-1699. New York: DeCapo Press,
1968 (reprint of 1859 edition, originally published in 1724),
244pp.
Observations on Peter by an English soldier of fortune who

through years of service in Russia won for himself a high
place at the Russian court. Gordon recollects numerous pre-
1700 incidents involving Peter which collectively shed light
on the young tsar's activity, character, and behavior. A
detailed table of contents and subject index makes this source
a convenient one to consult for anecdotal information on
Peter's early years as tsar of Russia. DK114.5.G6A33

342   Graham, Stephen. Peter the Great. A Life of Peter I of
      Russia. London: Ernest Benn Limited, 1950, 376pp.
      A popular biography of Peter I which is at its best when
      describing his war with Charles XII, foreign travel, and
      personal relationships, especially with Alexis. Peter emerges
      from this discussion as a man of extremes so taken with his
      absolute power as to be guilty of megalomania. DK114.5.G6A33

343   *Grey, Ian. Peter the Great. Emperor of All Russia. Phila-
      delphia: J. B. Lippincott, 1960, 505pp., bib. 445-48.
      A comprehensive, semi-popular account of Peter I's life, in-
      ternal policies, and foreign and military affairs. Grey draws
      upon a variety of Russian and English language primary
      sources as he discusses the highlights of Peter's reign.
      While giving most attention to Peter's improvement of his
      nation's position in respect to the European powers, Grey
      states that Russia's rulers in the decades prior to the eight-
      eenth century had outlined the policies followed and reforms
      adopted by Peter but that it took a man with the energy,
      dedication, and force of personality of Peter to impose changes
      of such magnitude in so short a span of time. Peter thus
      accelerated the pace of change, rather than determined its
      path, yet in the process transformed Muscovy into the Rus-
      sian Empire. DK131.G75
         Reviewed in:
         Am Hist R, 66 (Jan. 1961): 527-28
         Ann Am Acad, 334 (Mar. 1961): 162-63
         Hist, 48 (1963): 223
         Rus R, 20, no. 2 (1961): 157
         Sat R, 42 (20 Aug. 1960): 18

344   *Grunwald, Constantin de. Peter the Great. Viola Garvin,
      trans. London: Douglas Saunders, 1956, 224pp.
      A vivid, popular study of Peter the Great and his accomplish-
      ments. Grunwald paints a negative picture of the conditions
      in pre-Petrine Russia and then proceeds to portray Peter as
      a revolutionary figure who brought a primitive nation into the
      mainstream of European development. He denies that Peter's
      various internal reforms were part of any preconceived plan
      but rather sees them as necessary by-products of Peter's
      drive to convert Russia into a modern European power.
      Peter's tireless labor in this direction Grunwald commends
      heartily in a lengthy section on Peter's character, personality,

and habits. However, Peter's political, educational, religious,
and economic reforms do not receive a great deal of attention,
as Grunwald concentrates instead on the tsar's creation of an
effective military machine and a Western oriented political
capital to symbolize the modernization process to which he was
dedicated. DK142.G72
   Reviewed in:
   Am Hist R, 62 (Oct. 1956): 221
   Commonweal, 64 (4 May 1956): 130
   Hist Today, 6 (1956): 359
   Newsweek, 47 (16 Apr. 1956): 120
   Rus R, 16, no. 2 (1957): 75
   Sat R, 39 (7 July 1956): 12
   Slav R, 16, no. 1 (1957): 91
   TLS, (17 Feb. 1956): 104

345 Hamlyn, Paul. The Life and Times of Peter the Great. Felt-
     ham, Middlesex (U.K.): Hamlyn Publishing Group Limited,
     1968, 75pp.
     A short outline of the reign of Peter the Great accompanies
     an interesting series of 130 paintings, drawings, photographs,
     and engravings depicting Peter and his contemporaries as well
     as events and locales of significance in his life. Part of the
     Portraits of Greatness series under the general editorship of
     Enzo Orlandi.

346 Institute of History of the Academy of Sciences. "Peter the
     Great: Views of Soviet Historians." IEH, Vol. I (anthology),
     253-58.
     An excerpt from the conclusion of the 1954 official Soviet
     history of early eighteenth-century Russia. The achievements
     of Peter's reign are portrayed as anonymous victories gained
     in the struggle "waged against the economic as well as mili-
     tary, administrative, and cultural backwardness of Russia"
     which, through promoting "the political and economic independ-
     ence" of Russia, "increased the domination of the landed
     gentry and the oppression of the serfs."

347 Johnston, John T. M. "Peter the Great--Russia's Masterful
     Man." World Patriots. New York: World Patriots Company,
     1917, 95-108.
     A portrayal of Peter I as "the embodiment of the Russian
     characteristics of his age," and a brief, favorable account of
     his reforms as the foundation for modern Russian technology
     and culture. D106.J57 1924

348 Joseph, Joan. Peter the Great. New York: Julian Messner,
     1968, 190pp., bib. 185.
     A fanciful, undocumented account of Peter the Great's life
     with emphasis on his personal relationships, travels, and mili-
     tary exploits. Juvenile literature. DK131.J66

349 *Karamzin, N. M. "Peter I." Karamzin's Memoir on Ancient
     and Modern Russia. R. Pipes, ed./trans. Cambridge:
     Harvard University Press, 1959, 120-27. Excerpts in IEH,
     232-37 and PG, 133-38 (anthologies).
     A critical portrayal of Peter I as a leader who subverted
     Russia's cultural heritage in order to create a Western oriented,
     powerful state. Karamzin, a noted historian and writer in
     early nineteenth-century Russia, criticizes Peter for failing to
     see that "the national spirit constitutes the moral strength of
     states, which is as indispensible to their stability as is their
     physical might." Karamzin also questions Peter's methods,
     policy toward the Russian church, and relocation of the cap-
     ital to St. Petersburg. DK71.K343

350 *Klyuchevsky, Vasili. Peter the Great. Liliana Archibald,
     trans. New York: Random House, 1958, 282pp. Excerpts
     in IEH, 240-45; PG, 153-60, and PGCR, 21-39 (anthologies).
     A translation of the 1937 edition of volume four of Kliuchev-
     sky's classic five-volume History of Russia, which focuses
     more on the history of the nation during the first quarter of
     the eighteenth century than it does on Peter I as an individ-
     ual. Kliuchevsky develops the thesis that Peter's reforms
     were a continuation of policies outlined by his predecessors
     and were in no way part of any pre-conceived program of
     change. What separated Peter from his forerunners was his
     immense energy and remarkably practical nature, character-
     istics which colored his responses to contemporary conditions
     and circumstances unlike those that existed in the previous
     century. Of these circumstances, Kliuchevsky identifies the
     war with Sweden as being of paramount importance: the war
     not only determined the sequence and tempo of Peter's pro-
     gram, but "the difficulties and demands of war forced Peter
     to do everything hastily." Also having a negative impact
     on the reforms were the several internal struggles and con-
     spiracies in part caused by strains associated with the re-
     forms: "Peter went against the wind, and his rapid motion
     increased the resistance he encountered." Kliuchevsky con-
     cludes with a critical account of Peter's methods, lack of
     judgment, and consistency, but counter balances these re-
     proaches with praise for Peter's devotion, energy, sacrifices,
     and love for his country. In all, a comprehensive and bal-
     anced work highly regarded by specialist on Petrine Russia.
     DK131.K553
         Reviewed in:
         Can F, 39 (1959): 191
         Can Hist R, 40 (1959): 250
         Cath Hist R, 45 (1960): 515
         Eng Hist R, 75 (1960): 166
         Historian, 22 (1959): 95
         History, 44 (1959): 164
         Hist Today, 9 (1959): 288

J Cent Eur Aff, 15 (1955–56):   79
Pol Sci Q, 75 (1960):   479
Rus R, 19, no. 1 (1960):   91
Slav R, 22, no. 3 (1963):   140

351   Kochan, Miriam, and Lionel Kochan.   "From Peter the Great to
      Bolshevism."   Russian Themes.   A Selection of Articles from
      History Today with an Original Introductory Essay by Miriam
      and Lionel Kochan.   London: Oliver and Boyd, 1967, 1–26.
      A general survey of Romanov policy beginning with a dis-
      cussion of Peter the Great in terms of "the forces he set in
      motion from which his successors would benefit," most notably
      "a proven army and navy, the rudiments of an industrial and
      mining structure, and an improved administration and, ... a
      new capital—St. Petersburg."   DK42.R8

352   Korb, Johann-Georg.   Diary of an Austrian Secretary of Lega-
      tion at the Court of Czar Peter the Great.   London: Brad-
      bury and Evans, 1863, 340pp.   Also published under the
      title Scenes from the Court of Peter the Great.   New York:
      N. L. Brown, 1921.
      This diary is of value primarily for its observations on Peter
      I's return from his European travels, crushing of the streltsy
      rebellion, and his initial policies as tsar of Russia.   Korb,
      who was in Moscow in 1698–99 as secretary to the Austrian
      embassy sent by Emperor Leopold I to bolster the Austro-
      Russian alliance against the Ottoman Turks, additionally pro-
      vides an incident-oriented account of Peter's behavior and
      personal relationships.   DK130.K83

353   Lamb, Harold.   The City and the Tsar.   Peter the Great and
      the Move to the West, 1648–1762.   Garden City, N.Y.:
      Doubleday and Company, 1948, 368pp.
      A popular study of Peter the Great's reign as one representa-
      tive of a struggle between urban, centralized Russia and its
      vast, Eurasian hinterland.   Drawing upon various Western
      language works, Lamb relates the standard episodes in Peter's
      life and presents an anecdotal account of the tsar's personal-
      ity and character, but it is the author's discussion of the
      impact of and popular reaction to Peter's reforms that separ-
      ates this study from others of its genre.   Lamb states that
      Peter's prime goal was the creation of a modern military force
      as means of transforming Russia into a formidable European
      power.   The reforms devised by Peter in pursuit of this
      goal were ruthlessly implemented at the expense of the people,
      resources, and traditions of Russia's hinterland, and conse-
      quently were resented by "the forces of the land."   The op-
      ponents to these reforms rebelled in various ways during and
      after Peter's reign, and eventually Petrine Russia was "changed
      inexorably into something adapted to the land itself."
      DK113.L3

354   LeBovier de Fontenelle, Bernard. "Memoirs of Peter I, Emperor
      of Russia." The Northern Worthies: Or, the Lives of Peter
      the Great and of His Illustrious Consort Catherine the Late
      Czarina. London: E. Mory, 1728, 76pp.
      A eulogy of Peter the Great, written for the French Academy
      of Sciences of which Peter was a member. Fontenelle reviews
      in a general fashion Peter's principal accomplishments, par-
      ticularly in foreign and military affairs, and then describes in
      glowing detail the emperor's active promotion of science, medi-
      cine, and education. Peter emerges from this work as a
      gifted, forceful, and successful sovereign who single-handedly
      forged Russia into a powerful and reasonably modern state.

355   Lentin, A. "The Age of Peter the Great." Russia in the
      Eighteenth Century. London: Heinemann Educational Books,
      1973, 3-43.
      A general study of the reign of Peter I as part of a synopsis
      of the significant features of eighteenth-century Russia.
      Written for the nonspecialist. DK127.L46

356   *_____. "Voltaire and Peter the Great." Hist Today, 18
      (Oct. 1968): 683-89.
      A favorable review of Voltaire's History of the Russian Em-
      pire Under Peter the Great, and a discussion of his contem-
      poraries' reaction to this work. Drawing upon "decrees,
      confidential reports, Peter's letters and journals, and other
      documents ... hitherto entirely untapped by scholars," Len-
      tin states, Voltaire constructed a masterful interpretation
      of Peter as a creator of the first rank responsible for re-
      markable and progressive institutional, economic, social, and
      cultural changes. The general public and European royalty,
      with the exception of Frederick II of Prussia, reacted enthusi-
      astically to the book, but Voltaire came under fire from critics
      and scholars who questioned the reliability of his sources,
      his lack of understanding of Russian history, and his failure
      to deal with Peter's personal shortcomings and some of the
      less attractive features of the tsar's reign. While Lentin
      admits that the limitations and biases of the book are quite
      real, he nonetheless believes that Voltaire deserves credit
      for "the sweeping fluency of his narrative, his clear and
      vivid descriptions and the depth and cogency of his inter-
      pretive insight."

357   Lewitter, L. R. "Monarch into Myth." Listener, 71 (5 Mar.
      1964): 390-92.
      A brief account of the sources of the myth that has come to
      surround Peter the Great as both an individual and a re-
      former.

358   Liversidge, Douglas. Peter the Great. The Reformer-Tsar.
      New York: Franklin Watts, 1968, 152pp.

A popular introduction to Peter's principal accomplishments
with most attention given to his domestic reforms, especially
in regard to education and culture. The author consistently
notes Peter's coarse and brutal methods and disregard for
the welfare of Russia's peasants but nonetheless credits him
with setting Russia on the path of modernization. Written
for youthful readers. DK131.L5

359   *Lomonosov, Mikhail, V. "Panegyric to the Sovereign Emperor
      Peter the Great." RIH (anthology), 32-48. Ronald Hingley,
      trans. from Sochineniia, Vol. IV, St. Petersburg, 1898, 361-
      91. Excerpt in Makers of the Western Tradition. J. Kelley
      Sowards, ed. New York: St. Martin's Press, 1975, 326-32.
      A 26 April 1775 speech, delivered in commemoration of the
      coronation of Empress Elizabeth, which portrays Peter as the
      creator of modern Russia. Lomonosov, a multitalented Russian
      scholar and enthusiastic admirer of Peter the Great, reviews
      Peter's fundamental accomplishments and attributes them di-
      rectly to the tsar's genius and personal leadership. As M.
      Raeff aptly states in his brief introduction to this oration,
      Lomonosov, by asserting that "only the personal qualities
      of the Emperor made the country's transformation possible,"
      did much to advance "the process of mythologizing Peter's
      reign" and thereby "contributed to the formation of a political
      tradition that assigned absolute value to voluntaristic and
      rational leadership in social and cultural change."

360   McCullagh, Francis. "Peter the Great and Lenin." Studies,
      19 (Dec. 1930): 564-76.
      A portrayal of Peter I as a tyrant who, like Lenin, "forced
      on Russia a system which ninety per cent of the Russian
      people did not want," but unlike Lenin was miserably educated,
      disgustingly coarse in manner, and pursued a predatory
      foreign policy.

361   *McNally, Raymond T. "Chaadaev's Evaluation of Peter the
      Great." Slav R, 23, no. 1 (Mar. 1964): 31-44.
      An examination of the historical development of P. I. Chaad-
      aev's evaluation of Peter the Great for insight into Chaadaev's
      intellectual evolution. McNally identifies two stages in Chaad-
      aev's estimation of Peter's place in Russia's history. Initially,
      as expressed in his "First Philosophical Letter," Chaadaev
      argued "that although Peter the Great had tried to civilize
      Russia he had basically failed to do so." A year later, in
      "Apology of a Madman," he "emphasized the positive aspects
      of Peter the Great's program" and presented a more favorable
      estimate of the progress made by Russia since Peter's death.
      Drawing upon a hitherto unpublished letter written by Chaad-
      aev, McNally identifies a third stage in Chaadaev's thought
      on this subject marked by an admission of error in his initial
      negative appraisal of Peter's reforms and an argument in sup-
      port of not only Peter's goals and accomplishments but

also his methodology. McNally sees the "change of
heart" to be a reflection of Chaadaev's "increasing disen-
chantment with contemporary West European society" and the
stark contrast between the policies of Nicholas I and the
Petrine spirit.

362 *Massie, Robert. Peter the Great. His Life and World. New
     York: Knopf, 1981, 909pp., bib. 861-67.
     A comprehensive and highly readable popular account of
     Peter's life, policies, and accomplishments with considerable
     attention given to the historical setting within which Peter
     functioned. As a narrative, Massie's is a classic one as it
     contains a dramatic and colorful rendering of nearly all the
     standard highlights of Peter's personal life and reign, though
     military and foreign affairs receive most attention. Massie
     presents both the negative and positive features of Peter and
     his policies, and refrains from drawing any pointed conclu-
     sions on Peter's legacy: "Peter has been idealized, condemned,
     analyzed again and again, and still ... remains essentially
     mysterious.... He was a force of nature, and perhaps for
     this reason no final judgement will ever be delivered."
     DK131.M28
        Reviewed in:
        Mod Age, 26 (1982):   434-36

363 *Miliukov, Paul. "In Advance of His Century." PG (anthology),
     161-67. Excerpt from A History of Russia, Vol. I. Charles
     L. Markmann, trans. New York: Funk and Wagnalls, 1968,
     212-13, 232-33, 238, 305-06, 309-10, 330-31.
     An argument that although the Petrine reforms were not incon-
     sistent with the general direction in which Russia was head-
     ing, their scope and rapid implementation served to render
     them "premature and beyond the capacities of a country as
     poor and as backward as Russia." Miliukov, a prominent
     liberal and historian in turn of the century Russia, states
     that Peter's reign marked Russia's transition from a spon-
     taneous to a conscious evolution toward a more European char-
     acter, and that even though his reform could not be under-
     stood by his Russian contemporaries and was in advance of
     its time, "nevertheless, over the next two centuries, events
     justified what was essential in it. Peter had foreseen the
     road that Russia was destined to follow."

364 *_____. "Social and Political Reforms." PGCR, (anthology),
     63-67. From Gosudarstvennoe Khoziaistvo Rossii v Pervoi
     Chetverti XVIII Stoletiia i Reforma Petra Velikogo (The Na-
     tional Economy of Russia in the First Quarter of the Eight-
     eenth Century and the Reform of Peter the Great). Mirra
     Ginsburg, trans. Second Edition: St. Petersburg, 1905,
     542-43, 545-46; First Edition: St. Petersburg, 1896, 730-32
     734-36.

A discussion of Peter's social, economic, and political reforms as fitful responses to needs created by his diplomatic and military policies. Miliukov not only asserts that Peter's reforms were unplanned, disjointed, and sometimes contradictory, but that they were inconsistent with Russia's basic domestic needs at that time, though militarily expedient. He concludes that "Russia had been raised to the rank of a European power at the cost of the country's ruin."

365   *Morley, Charles. "Peter the Great." IEH, Vol. I (anthology), 227-58.

A brief assessment of Peter the Great's accomplishments and place in Russia's history precedes excerpted assessments from the writings of N. Karamzin, P. Chaadaev, V. Kliuchevsky, P. Miliukov, B. Sumner, M. Pokrovsky, and the Institute of History of the Soviet Academy of Sciences. Morley's overview is a useful one for students unfamiliar with the principal questions asked by historians in regard to Peter's reign. Although none of the excerpts is from writings contemporary with Peter's era, they provide a decent representation of the views of nineteenth-century Russian historians and contemporary Soviet analysts.

366   *Motley, John L. "Peter the Great." No Amer R, 129 (Oct. 1845): 269-319. Reprinted as Peter the Great. New York: Maynard, Merrie and Company, 1893, 70pp., and as "Peter the Great" in Great Short Biographies of the World. Barrett H. Clark, ed. New York: McBride, 1928, 846-85.

A review article on M. de Custine's Russia in 1839 and J. Barrow's A Memoir of the Life of Peter the Great in which the author develops at length his own views on Petrine Russia, the motivation for Peter's reforms, and the significance of his reign. Motley, who was Secretary of the American Legation in St. Petersburg in 1841, takes issue with Custine's "sweeping condemnation of Peter's policy in building St. Petersburg and establishing a Navy," and asserts instead that both of these accomplishments only served to advance the import of the Western civilization Russia so badly needed. Following a generally favorable assessment of Peter's program of Westernization, Motley criticizes Peter for weakening the Russian aristocracy to a point where there was "nobody left to civilize," and suggests that behind Peter's reforms "the activating motive was his own fame rather than the good of the country."

367   *Mottley, John. History of the Life of Peter I Emperor of Russia, 3 Vols. London, 1739.

As the most comprehensive and detailed biography of Peter I of its time, this three volume work is a rich source of information on the tsar's character, behavior, personal life, and principal policies and accomplishments. Mottley neither

introduces any point of view nor provides any final judgments
but rather presents a chronologically arranged, sympathetic
narrative based upon contemporary opinion of Peter as well
as upon various official papers and documents. Each of the
three volumes contains a detailed subject index thus information on specific events, reforms, personages, etc. can be
readily located, but the archaic nature of the print and language used in this work make it somewhat difficult to read.
DK131.M92

368 Muller, Edwin. "Peter the Great." Read Dig, 54 (Apr. 1949):
     103-08.
     A brief review of Peter I's principal accomplishments, and a
     critique of the overly flattering Soviet writings of the 1940s
     on Peter's reign.

369 Myers, Frederic. "Peter of Russia." Lectures on Great Men.
     London: J. Nisbet and Company, 1861, 114-42.
     A lecture presenting Peter I as a 'great man' because of the
     courage and self-sacrifice he exhibited in attempting to im-
     prove the internal condition and international status of Rus-
     sia. Myers states that Peter inherited "a barbarian province,
     without any one element of civilization," yet bequeathed to
     his successors "the consolidated empire" of a territory the
     largest ever known in the world." Though crude, of a prac-
     tical mind, and violent temper, Meyer conclues, Peter's self-
     less and energetic pursuit of noble goals make him one of the
     greatest monarchs in the world's history.

370 Nechkina, M. V., et al. "An Assessment of Peter I's Moderni-
     zation in Soviet Historiography." MRPC (anthology), 71-84.
     Excerpt and translation from Istoriia SSSR s drevneishikh
     vremen do 1861g (History of USSR from Ancient Times to
     1861). Moscow, 1956.
     This Soviet overview of Peter's reform program emphasizes its
     progressive features and significance for Russia's emergence
     as a modern power of the first rank. The authors devote
     most attention to Peter's efforts to improve education, expand
     industry, and create a formidable military force. Designed
     for Soviet university students.

371 Nicolson, Harold. "The Emergence of Muscovy. Peter the
     Great, 1672-1725." The Age of Reason. The Eighteenth
     Century. Garden City, N.Y.: Doubleday Press, 1961, 70-88.
     An overview of Peter's personal life and principal reforms
     and accomplishments precedes a negative assessment of his
     personality and behavior. Nicolson maintains that Peter,
     through "the superhuman force of will ... rendered his coun-
     try a great power," but his ruthlessness and personal coarse-
     ness must forever qualify any positive assessment of his place
     among the great men of history.

372 Nowak, Frank. "Peter the Great" and "Reforms of Peter the
     Great." Mediaeval Slavdom and the Rise of Russia. New York:
     Cooper Square Publishers, 1970, 65-77.
     A discussion of Peter's accomplishments within the context of a
     larger chapter on the foundation of the Russian Empire. No-
     wak maintains that "while his predecessors played with Western
     culture and suggested many changes that might have influ-
     enced Peter, his reforms were scarcely less than revolutionary.
     He hastened the process of modernization by a century or
     more." DK147.N67

373 *Oliva, L. Jay, ed. "Peter the Great: 1682-1725." RW,
     (anthology), 1-25.
     A series of excerpts from primary and secondary sources
     dealing with Peter's Westernization of Russia. Included are
     Peter's decrees on the employment of foreigners, the founding
     of the Academy of Sciences, and the creation of the Holy
     Synod; contemporary observations by diplomats Korf and LaVie
     on Peter's attempt to advance Western customs and manners;
     and historical assessments of Peter by Sumner, Chaadaev,
     Karamzin, and Kliuchevsky.

374 *_____. Russia in the Era of Peter the Great. Englewood
     Cliffs, N.J.: Prentice-Hall, 1969, 184pp., bib. 177-80.
     An examination of Petrine Russia in terms of both its Muscovite
     legacy and interaction with the forces and trends prevalent
     in early eighteenth-century Europe. Oliva states that "the
     whole drift of internal and external policy" in Muscovy pro-
     moted the nation's membership in the European community of
     nations of the early modern age. He identifies as the char-
     acteristics of this era "the emergence of the nation-state, the
     centralization of the monarchy, the creation of the bureau-
     cracy, the all-European quality of warfare, the triumph of
     state over dynastic foreign policy, the carving out of empires,
     and the flourishing of a secularized learning." He then
     discusses within this context the Northern War and Peter's
     principal domestic policies. Oliva concludes that although
     the general direction of Peter's rule was not inconsistent with
     that of his Muscovite predecessors and typified that of his
     European contemporaries, "Peter can lay claim to substantial
     leadership" because of his grasp of his heritage and the
     forces at work within his environment and his ability to re-
     shape in their light the absolute state as an instrument to
     advance and secure Russia's borders and to promote the in-
     ternal development and stability of his realm. DK131.O4
          Reviewed in:
          Can Slav S, 4 (1970): 351
          Slav R, 29 (1970): 505
          Slavonic E Eur R, 14 (1970): 503-07

375 Oudard, Georges. Peter the Great. F. M. Atkinson, trans.

New York: Payson and Clarke, 1929, 386pp., bib. 375-86.
A critical examination of Peter the Great and his accomplishments. Oudard portrays Peter as a brutal autocrat who ruthlessly forced his will on a nation neither ready nor willing to
accept reform. For this reason Peter's reforms never took
root, and Russia remained a crude, non-European society.
Oudard thus believes that the historical argument between
Peter's supporters and those who contend Peter's Westernization subverted Russia's native culture is based on a false
premise--that Peter in fact did Westernize Russia. Oudard
concludes that Peter, through his military successes, simply
annexed part of Europe to old Muscovy. DK131.083

376 Pashkov, A. I. "Absolutism and the Police-Bureaucratic State."
PG (anthology), 173-77. Excerpt from HRET (anthology),
245-49.
A Soviet interpretation of Peter the Great's reign as one
marked by the strengthening of political absolutism and a
consequent expansion of the economic functions of the Russian
feudal state. Pashkov sees Peter's reforms as being progressive in the sense that they addressed effectively the twin
questions of how to eliminate Russia's backwardness and secure an outlet to the sea, but he maintains that despite
Peter's attempt "to present the principle of 'general welfare'
as a supra-class principle, and the state ... as an extra-
class force," the Petrine reforms benefitted only the nobility
and the rising merchant class.

377 *Perry, John. The State of Russia. New York: DaCapo
Press, 1968 (reprint of 1716 edition), 280pp. Excerpts in
RTFE, 100-14; MRPC, 17-26; RIRC, Vol. II, 233-37 (anthologies).
An early and influential English language account of conditions in Russia and the efforts of Peter I to better them.
Perry, an English engineer who was recruited in 1698 by
Peter to provide assistance in establishing a Russian fleet
and developing a navigable system of internal waterways,
chronicles his travels and labors in Russia during his fourteen years of service, and in the process presents an ex-
ceedingly flattering estimate of Peter's character, activities,
and policies. Heartily supporting Peter's various efforts to
Westernize Russia, Perry is at his best when describing
Peter's military reforms and creation of a modern navy.
Perry's book was widely read in Western Europe and contributed significantly to the image of Peter as a reformer of titanic
proportions. DK131.P35
    Reviewed in:
    MRTFE (anthology), 101-13
    SBIR (anthology), 3-20
    Slavonic E Eur R, 46 (1968): 253

378   Perry, Powell. The Story of Peter the Great. Harcourt M.
      Doyle, Illust. London: Perry Colourprinted Limited, 1944,
      46pp.
      A heavily illustrated, colorful biography of Peter I, written
      for pre-teenage readers.

379   "Peter the Great." Liv Age, 162 (1884): 12-48.
      A detailed and favorable review of Schuyler's Peter the
      Great, Emperor of Russia.

380   "Peter the Great." So Q, 28 (July 1855): 123-48.
      A positive overview of Peter's reign as that of a classic en-
      lightened despot.

381   *"Peter the Great in History." PG (anthology), 122-77.
      A selection of eleven excerpts, spanning two centuries, from
      writings which collectively represent well the evolution of
      Peter's image within his own country. Those excerpts trans-
      lated expressly for this volume have been annotated and listed
      separately by author.

382   *"Peter the Great Viewed by His Contemporaries: The View
      from Europe." PG (anthology), 104-21.
      A series of titled excerpts from the writings of Burnet, Sophia
      Charlotte of Brandenburg, and Saint-Simon which collective-
      ly illustrate the diverse judgments of Peter by his European
      contemporaries. Highlighted are Peter's aggressive foreign
      policy and coarse personal habits. Of particular interest are
      Saint-Simon's observations, drawn during Peter's 1717 visit to
      France, in regard to Peter's intense curiosity, dynamism, and
      unaffected manner.

383   *"Peter the Great Viewed by His Contemporaries: The View
      from Inside the Empire." PG (anthology), 90-104.
      A series of excerpts from the writings of Korb, Kampfer,
      Weber, Bergholz, Munnich, and Manstein which, respectively,
      deal with Peter's brutal suppression of the streltsy rebellion,
      his appearance and impetuousness as a youth, his penchant
      for overindulgence in food and drink and for surrounding him-
      self with men of low birth, his multifaceted genius, and his
      use of foreigners to improve Russia's military forces. Also
      included is an apocalyptic tract found in the Solovievtsky
      Monastery which portrays Peter as the Anti-christ.

384   *Platonov, Sergei F. "The Heritage of Muscovy." Mirra Gins-
      burg, trans. PGCR (anthology), 3-15. From Lektsii po
      Russkoi Istorii (Lectures on Russian History. I. Blinov, ed.
      St. Petersburg, 1904, 367-78.
      A discussion of the foreign policy, central and local adminis-
      tration, and social order of the Russian state inherited by
      Peter the Great. Platonov states that Peter the Great did not

embark on a new course in foreign policy but merely was
more successful than his predecessors in striving towards
long established goals. Similarly, Peter's administrative
policies reflected the long standing desire by Muscovy's leaders for a more ordered, simplified, and efficient central
government.

385 *_____. "Peter the Great, Not a Revolutionary Innovator."
Mirra Ginsburg, trans. PGCR (anthology), 179-82. Ibib.,
457-60.
An argument that "Peter's reforms were not a revolution either
in their substance of their results." Platonov examines Peter's
foreign, political, social, economic, and cultural policies, and
in each sees him following essentially the pattern established
by his Muscovite predecessors. Platonov concludes that the
root of the myth that Peter's reign was a revolutionary one
rests in the nearsighted reaction of Peter's contemporaries
and in the very militant character of his own activities, especially "the needless cruelties, the coercion and the severity
of his measures."

386 Pokrovsky, M. N. "The Bankruptcy of Peter's System."
PG (anthology), 168-72. Excerpt from History of Russia from
the Earliest Times to the Rise of Commercial Capitalism. Jesse
D. Clarkson, ed. Bloomington: Indiana University Press,
1966, 289-90, 326-27.
An argument that Peter's attempt to raise Russia to the rank
of a European power not only led to the ruination of the
nation's peasant class but also resulted in no appreciable
elevation of Russia's military forces. Pokrovsky, one of the
first prominent Marxist historians, also identifies as "bank-
rupt" Peter's attempt to transfer power from the aristocracy
to the new merchant class.

387 *Prokopovich, Feofan. "The Heroic Tsar." PGCR (anthology),
39-43. From "Slovo na pogrebenie vspresvetleishago Petra
Velikogo..." ("Oration at the Funeral of the Most Illustrious
Peter the Great...") in Sochineniia (Works). I. P. Eremin,
ed. M. Raeff, trans. Moscow-Leningrad, 1961, 126-29. Also
in Literature of Eighteenth Century Russia, Vol. I. H. B.
Segal, ed. New York: E. P. Dutton, 1967, 141-48.
A funeral oration which, as editor M. Raeff aptly states,
illustrates "the uncritical admiration and sense of awe which
the collaborators and disciples of Peter displayed towards
their great and beloved 'Tsar Reformer.'" Prokopovich, a
Ukrainian clergyman who was Peter's most loyal and trusted
advisor on matters concerning church affairs and the theoretical aspects of statecraft," eulogizes Peter as a highly progressive, audacious, and successful ruler whose policies
brought a revolutionary advance in Russia's domestic condition and military power.

388   *Putnam, Peter. "John Perry: Engineer to the Great Tsar."
      SBIR (anthology), 3-20.
      An introduction to an extract from Perry's The State of
      Russia Under Peter the Great in which Putnam comments on
      Perry's experiences in Russia as well as on the value of
      Perry's observations. The author states that "to Perry,
      Peter, endowed with a European education, hereditary genius,
      and a despotic political power, represented an irresistable
      force, but in the great Muscovite community he strove to re-
      form he encountered a nearly immovable object."

389   _____. Peter, the Revolutionary Tsar. New York: Harper
      and Row, 1973, 269pp., bib. 255-59.
      A popular account of Peter I's life and accomplishments.
      Putnam presents, in dramatic fashion, an image of Peter as
      a dynamic autocrat so driven by the desire to shape Russia
      into a modern state that he felt compelled to implement rapidly
      and ruthlessly a far-reaching reform program. The author
      concludes that although Peter's accomplishments are impressive,
      the methods which he employed and the suffering which his
      policies caused must limit any positive assessment of his reign.
      Designed for secondary school readers. DK131.P88

390   *Raeff, Marc. "Peter the Great's Revolution." UIR (gen.
      study), 35-55.
      An argument that while Peter the Great is to be commended
      for the goals that he set for Russia and for his energetic
      efforts to achieve them, the ultimate effect of his reign was
      more a destabilizing than a constructive one. Raeff main-
      tains that Peter's attempt to transform Russia into a modern
      society was successful only in regard to the service nobility
      and the intellectual elite; the common people remained Mus-
      covite in their beliefs and habits. The absence of a broad
      social basis for his program of reform resulted in the reforms
      being "suspended in midair" and heavily dependent on the
      personal authority of the sovereign. Therefore, since Peter
      failed to institutionalize the personal authority of the "trans-
      forming tsar" and provide a social foundation for the new
      Russia beyond the service elite upon which he had relied so
      heavily, Raeff concludes that the effect of Peter's reign was
      "to tear Russian society apart, leaving behind a legacy of un-
      certainty and insecurity...."

391   *_____. "Peter's System in Difficulty." Ibid., 57-87.
      An examination of the political, social, and cultural problems
      that Peter the Great bequeathed to his successors. Raeff
      establishes that the rapid growth in the number and scope
      of administrative activities during Peter's reign rendered the
      process of governing Russia far too complex to be controlled
      and directed by one man, yet Peter, though recognizing this
      fact, failed to create the planning and coordinating agencies

necessary for the government to run smoothly. The need to
rationalize government by establishing a centralized super-
visory body became even more pronounced with Peter's death,
but royal favorites, fearful of loss of political influence,
"found it advantageous to encourage the preservation of personal authority and to hamper the development of any regular
institution with enough power to bring order to ... the administration of the empire." Raeff concludes that the absence
of rational government and the rule of law, particularly at
the local level, combined with the social and cultural dislocation generated by the Petrine reforms to produce political instability and pronounced feelings of insecurity within various
segments of the Russian population. Collectively these shortcomings comprised a problem of staggering proportions to be
confronted by Russia's monarchs of the next century.

392   *Riasanovsky, Nicholas V. The Image of Peter the Great in
      Russian History and Thought. New York: Oxford Univer-
      sity Press, 1985, 331pp., bib. 307-26.
      An examination of the image of Peter the Great as projected
      by Russian historians and political theorists during four
      periods in the nation's history: "the Russian Enlightenment"
      of 1700-1826, "the age of idealistic philosophy and romanticism"
      of 1826-1860, "the age of realism and scholarship" of 1860-
      1917, and the Soviet period of 1917-1984. Riasanovsky dis-
      cusses the image of Peter as a wonder-working, progressive
      autocrat, propagated by Peter and his entourage and accepted
      by educated Russians, which prevailed until the 1830s; the
      furthering of this image by the Westernizers of the mid-
      nineteenth century amid the assault on the Petrine legacy
      launched by the Slavophiles; the fragmentation of Peter's
      image as Russian society and historical scholarship became
      more sophisticated during the decades which preceded the
      1917 revolutions; and the evolution of Soviet views on Peter
      and his reign from the hostile position established by Pokrov-
      sky to "a more complex bipolar Petrine image" which "empha-
      sizes both the positive and negative in the reformer and the
      reform in an extreme and contradictory manner...."
      DK132.R53

393   Roetter, J. H. "Russian Attitudes Toward Peter the Great and
      His Reform Between 1725 and 1910." University of Wisconsin,
      1951. (dissertation)

394   *Rogger, Hans. National Consciousness in Eighteenth Century
      Russia. Cambridge: Harvard University Press, 1960, 319pp.,
      bib. 285-95.
      This scholarly study of the problem of national identity and
      culture, as it appeared in Russian life and letters of the
      eighteenth century, does not contain a separate chapter on
      Peter the Great but does make frequent references to the

ways in which he and his accomplishments affected national
consciousness through the works of various Russian writers
of the eighteenth century. DK127.R6

395 Rosenbush, Michael. "The Personality of Peter the Great in
Nineteenth Century Russian Literature." University of Montreal, 1970. (dissertation)

396 Russell, Phillips. "Russian Axman." The Glittering Century.
New York: Charles Scribner's Sons, 1936, 65-81.
A colorful overview of Peter's life and reign with most detail
on his foreign travels, military affairs, and Westernization of
culture. Russell is quite critical of Peter's personal manner
and method of rule, and sees the Petrine reform program as
"mere plaster applied to a huge, resisting body" and ultimately as a failure since after Peter's death "Russia sank back
into its medieval inertia." DK286.R98

397 *Schuyler, Eugene. Peter the Great, Emperor of Russia. A
Study in Historical Biography, 2 Vols. New York: Charles
Scribner's Sons, 1884. Also published in condensed form as
Passages from the Life of Peter the Great. London, 1881.
Serialized in Scrib M, Vols. 19-22 (1880-81).
A detailed study of Peter's life and reign with most concern
shown for his foreign policy and military successes. Schuyler
presents a powerful portrait of Peter as a dynamic autocrat
whose radical policies, ruthlessly implemented, diverted the
nation from its natural course of development and "brought
Russia prematurely into the circle of European politics."
Although Schuyler commends Peter for his dedication and far-
sightedness, he stresses the point that by sacrificing all to
the creation of a modern military machine and the procure-
ment of a prominent position among the great powers in
eighteenth-century Europe, Peter, in effect, diverted the
attention of his successors "away from home affairs and the
regular development of internal institutions to foreign politics
and the creation of a great military power." DK131.S39
Reviewed in:
Athen, (16 Feb. 1884): 209-211
Dial, 5 (May 1884): 4-8
Liv Age, 162 (1884): 579-95
Nation, 38 (1884): 389, 411
Sat R, 57 (1884): 552
Quar R, 158 (1884): 105

398 Segur, General Count Philip de. History of Russia and of
Peter the Great. London: Treuttel and Wurtz, 1829, 447pp.
The first half of this work consists of a history of Russia
up to the end of the seventeenth century; the second half
contains a sympathetic account of Peter the Great's life,
character, policies, and accomplishments. Segur maintains

that historians of the nineteenth century who criticized Peter
did not place him within the context of his age and culture,
and thus failed to realize that the only means Peter could
employ to improve Russia were despotic ones. To Peter's
credit, he used despotism for progressive purposes, and so
improved the condition of Russia that he paved the way for
the emergence of a system far more modern and humane than
the one he inherited: "Peter the Great did more for liberty
than all the dreamers of liberalism have since fancied that he
ought to have done! His people are indebted to him for
their first and most difficult step towards their future emancipation." DK41.S45

399   *Shcherbatov, Mikhail M. "(The Pace of Russia's Modernization)." Valentine Snow, trans. RIH (anthology), 56-60.
From Sochineniia (Works), Vol. II. St. Petersburg, 1898,
13-22.
A survey of the military, economic, and cultural backwardness
of Russia before Peter the Great's reign, and an argument
that without his rapid acceleration of the pace of progress
in Russia the nation would not have reached for two centuries
a comparable level of advancement. Shcherbatov, a noted
conservative writer and public figure during the reign of
Catherine II, expresses here a view of Peter's reign quite
different from that which characterizes his other writings on
this subject.

400   Shirley, Ralph. "Peter the Great." Contemp R, 161 (Apr.
1942): 229-34.
A discussion of how Peter's youthful impetuousness, crudeness,
and fascination with the West combined to determine the pace
and direction of his policies as tsar. After presenting a number of examples of Peter's abrupt and sometimes uncontroll-
able behavior, Shirley concludes that Peter was nonetheless
responsible for drastic improvements in the condition of Russia and for bringing his realm into the comity of European
nations.

401   *Smith, Irving H. "An English View of Russia in the Early
Eighteenth Century." Can Slav S, 1, no. 2 (Summer 1967):
267-83.
A favorable review of Daniel DeFoe's An Impartial History
of the Life and Actions of Peter Alexowitz, the Present Czar
of Muscovy (1723).
Smith states that although DeFoe's vision was somewhat clouded
by his contempt for Muscovite customs and for Peter's despotic
rule he prophetically saw Petrine Russia as a nation with vast
potential which might soon threaten Europe's security.

402   *Soloviev, Sergei M. History of Russia. Vol. XXIX. Peter
The Great. The Great Reform Begins. K. A. Papmehl, ed. /

trans. Gulf Breeze, Fla.: Academic International Press, 1981, 212pp.
As chapter three of volume sixteen of Soloviev's classic Istoriia Rossii s drevneishikh vremen (History of Russia from Earliest Times), this work deals with the major reforms launched by Peter I between 1711-1721. Blending a wealth of primary sources into a readable narrative, Soloviev presents a forceful case for Peter I as a dynamic ruler pursuing progressive policies in Russia's best interests. As noted by Papmehl in a short introduction to this volume, the History was written at a time when the Petrine legacy was "under attack by the proponents of the Slavophile ideologies and Soloviev clearly set himself the task of rebutting their charges and restoring Peter's traditional image as a wise and farseeing, if single-minded and uncompromising reformer." To this end, Soloviev presents positively Peter's administrative, social, economic, cultural, and church reforms and policies while rationalizing the tsar's harsh methods by reference to the necessity for sternness in the face of opposition, mostly passive, from those steeped in the ways of old Muscovy. DK40.S6213

403 *_____. "Peter's Reforms." MMR (anthology), 225-31.
A discussion of Peter the Great's reforms in terms of their Christian elements. Soloviev commends Peter for effectively countering the stultifying provincialism and narrowminded Muscovite piety responsible for Russia's abandonment of Christian universalism and separation from the rest of the world. He concedes that Peter himself was far from being a paragon of Christian virtues and did not willfully seek to give his realm a more Christian orientation, but by countering Muscovite religious chauvinism, expanding greatly contacts with the West, and encouraging the development of "an ever vigilant critical attitude toward her social realities," he was responsible for rekindling the true spirit of Christianity which Russians possessed in Kievan times but had lost sight of as a consequence of centuries of isolation under the Mongol yoke.

404 *Sowards, J. Kelley, ed. "Peter the Great and the Westernization of Russia." Makers of the Western Tradition. Portraits from History. New York: St. Martin's Press, 1975, 322-43.
A brief introduction to the historical controversy surrounding Peter the Great's Westernization of Russia precedes excerpts from three sources which illustrate the range of the interpretations on this subject: M. Lomonosov's "Panegyric to the Sovereign Emperor Peter the Great," M. Shcherbatov's On the Corruption of Morals in Russia, and N. Riasanovsky's A History of Russia. CT104.M29

405 Steinberg, Jonathan. "You, Me and Peter the Great." New Soc, (16 Dec. 1982): 472-73.
Unavailable for annotation.

406 *Sumner, B. H. "Peter the Great." History, 32 (Mar. 1947):
     39-50. Also in PGCR, 188-94 and RRH, 246-55 (anthologies).
     An argument that Peter's actions were revolutionary in form
     but not in substance. Sumner states that Peter's methods
     were "extreme and violent and shocking to many, perhaps
     most, of his subjects ... and in that sense he may be called
     revolutionary ... but he did not seek either to build upon
     entirely new foundations or to sweep away the essentials of
     the Muscovite social structure." Sumner sees seventeenth-
     century precedents for Peter's basic reforms with the excep-
     tion of the founding of the navy, education of Russians
     abroad, construction of St. Petersburg, and the abolition of
     the Patriarchate. Peter's reign constituted a revolution only
     in the respect that it created an ideological schism "between
     the conception of Russia as part of Europe and of Muscovy
     as a world of her own, neither Europe or Asia."

407 *_____. Peter the Great and the Emergence of Russia. New
     York: Collier Press, 1962, 190pp., bib. 183-84. Excerpt in
     IEH (anthology), 247-49.
     A concise and well-regarded introduction to the policies and
     accomplishments of Peter the Great. The first half of the
     book is devoted to a survey of Peter's background and a dis-
     cussion of his foreign policy, while the second half deals with
     his principal reforms and the problem of political succession.
     In assessing the origin of Peter's reforms and their signifi-
     cance, Sumner asserts that Peter began his reforms without
     any clear plan to Westernize Muscovy, but that "in the end
     he grew to entertain broad views that amounted to an all-
     around rennovation of Muscovy." While some of Peter's re-
     forms did not long survive his reign, there can be no doubt
     that he succeeded in revolutionizing Russia's international
     position: "henceforth Russia played her part as one of the
     main participants in European history." DK131.S88
          Reviewed in:
          Ann Am Acad, 278 (1951): 235
          Eng Hist R, 67 (1952): 301
          History, 37 (1952): 245
          Slav R, 12, no. 1 (1953): 144
          Slavonic E Eur R, 29/30 (1950-52): 270

408 Veastnaya, Nais. Peter the Czar-Reformer. Hollywood:
     David Graham Fischer, 1929, 384pp.
     A popular and sympathetic biography of Peter I with a bal-
     ance of information on his personal life, domestic affairs,
     foreign relations, and military exploits. Included are scores
     of interesting portraits and illustrations. DK131.V4

409 *Vockerodt, Johann G. "Contemporary Foreign Assessments of
     Peter I's Modernization: An Assessment by a Prussian Diplo-
     mat." MRPC (anthology), 36-43. From "Rossiia pri Petre

Velikom" in <u>Chteniia v Imperatorskom obshchestve Istorii</u>,
<u>Vol. II</u>, 1874.
An account of Peter's church, administrative, educational,
and military reforms, and an assessment of their impact on
the Russia of his era. Vockerodt, who was Secretary of the
Prussian embassy in St. Petersburg, presents most detail on
the inadequacies of Peter's administrative and educational reforms, the failure of his Westernization of manners to take
root within the middle and upper classes, and the private
criticism of his reform program by the aristocracy.

410   *Voltaire, François M. A. de. <u>Russia Under Peter the Great</u>.
      M. F. O. Jenkins, intro./trans. Rutherford, N.J.: Fair-
      leigh Dickinson University Press, 1983, 281pp. Excerpt in
      <u>PG</u> (anthology), 123-32.
      A new translation of Voltaire's classic two volume work,
      <u>History of the Russian Empire Under Peter the Great</u> (London,
      1759, 1763); also published as pages 261-600 of <u>The History
      of Charles XII King of Sweden, to Which Is Added, the Life
      of Peter the Great</u> (London, 1780). Voltaire presents a flat-
      tering account of Peter's personality and leadership and
      rationalizes Peter's shortcomings by references to his poor
      upbringing and the generally backward nature of turn of the
      century Russia, the only exception being the arrest, torture,
      and execution of Tsarevich Alexis. In an excellent introduc-
      tion, M. Jenkins reviews Voltaire's <u>Russia</u>, the predominant
      theme of which he identifies aptly as being "Peter's astonish-
      ing twofold achievement, first, in overcoming every obstacle
      to educate himself in the broadest sense of the term, and,
      second, in fulfilling his ambition to transform his immense,
      ramshackle, feudal empire into a modern nation-state on the
      West European model." Voltaire's work, which was widely
      read throughout Europe, was an influential one in establishing
      and sustaining an image of Peter as a revolutionary tsar.
      DK131.V913

411   *Waliszewski, K. <u>Peter the Great</u>. Mary Loyd, trans. New
      York: D. Appleton and Company, 1897, 562pp.
      A detailed assessment of Peter and his domestic and foreign
      policies. Waliszewski states that although Peter accomplished
      a great deal in modernizing Russia and improving its inter-
      national standing, his policies represent no break with Rus-
      sia's past nor genius on Peter's account but rather were "the
      inevitable outcome of the historical conditions of the country."
      The hastiness of Peter's major reforms and his harshness in
      implementing them largely account for the impression that they
      did indeed constitute a revolution. Waliszewski admits that
      critics of Peter's methods and policies are on firm ground
      when citing his disregard for human rights and dignity, dis-
      dain for native Russian culture, intensification of serfdom, and
      his overly utilitarian approach to all reform, but he asserts

that a reign such as Peter's was necessary to bring Russia
back into the mainstream of European civilization from which
she had been sidetracked by two centuries of Mongolian domi-
nation. DK131.W17
Reviewed in:
Athen, 2 (Feb. 1897): 58
Citizen, 3 (Jan. 1898): 255-57
Edinb R, 187 (Apr. 1898): 460-84
Lond Q, 89 (Oct. 1897): 26-37
Nation, 65 (Sept. 1897): 296-97, 316-17
New R, 17 (Aug. 1897): 163-74

412 *Weber, Friedrich Christian. The Present State of Russia.
2 Vols. London: Frank Cass, 1968 (reprint of 1723 edition).
Excerpt in MRPC (anthology), 26-35.
A contemporaneous description of social, economic, and cultural conditions in Russia, and a highly positive account of the
character, reforms, and policies of Peter the Great. Weber,
a Dutch diplomat who resided in St. Petersburg from 1714 to
1719, describes Peter's character, habits, speeches, and
family relations, particularly the events which led to the trial
and execution of Tsarevich Alexis. In discussing Peter's reforms, Weber concentrates on the Westernization of court culture, the abolition of the Patriarchate, and those measures
designed to improve and expand Russia's military forces.
Weber notes the shortcomings of some of Peter's policies and
the continued existence of abuses and corruption in Petrine
society, but, collectively, Weber's various anecdotes, descrip-
tions, and observations yield an image of Peter as a revolutionary leader who energetically and personally shaped a
primitive, Asiatic society into a powerful European nation.
DK133.W6

413 Whitworth, Charles. An Account of Russia As It Was in the
Year 1710. Strawberry Hill, England, 1765, 158pp.
Unavailable for annotation. DK133.W6

414 Wight, Orlando W. The Life of Peter the Great. Compiled
from the Most Authentic Sources, 2 Vols. New York: Delis-
ser and Proctor, 1859.
The purpose of this two volume work is to provide "a reliable
and readable life of Peter the Great" for the general public.
To this end, Wight restates, in simplified language, the findings and observations of Tooke, Segur, Staehlin, Voltaire,
Villebois, Bruce, and others as he presents both favorable
and critical judgments on Peter and his accomplishments.
DK131.W7

415 Wren, M. "The Petrine Revolution." WITR (anthology), 21-67.
An examination of the Western roots of Peter's reforms and
Russian society's reaction to his modernization program.

Wren discusses the impact of Swedish, Dutch, and English
examples on Peter's social, economic, administrative, military,
church, and educational reforms. He identifies as Peter's
most spectacular achievement the transformation of Russia into
not just a Baltic power but "a European power of tremendous
force." Wren states that the most apparent Westernization of
Russia was in the realm of government: "Before Peter's accession the central administration would have been unrecogni-
zable and even unintelligible to a Westerner" but by 1725 any
knowledgeable European "would have understood the administrative pattern of Russia because it would have seemed so similar
to that of his own country." The veneer of Western civilization, however, "affected the governing classes profoundly and
the urban and rural masses hardly at all," and consequently
Peter's reign marks the advent of a culturally divided Russia,
"half-Western and half Byzantine-Oriental, half enlightened
and half benighted...."

416 Yakobson, Sergius. "Peter the Great: A Russian Hero."
     Hist Today, 22 (July 1972): 461-69.
     A favorable commentary on Peter the Great's personality, ac-
     complishments, and place in Russian history. Following a
     review of Peter's travels, reforms, and exploits, Yakobson
     concludes that despite Peter's personal coarseness, brutal
     methods, and various failures, the magnitude of the efforts
     which he made to improve his realm and the general success
     that he had in this endeavor make him worthy of consideration
     as a truly heroic figure in Russia's history.

       PERSONALITY/CHARACTER, FAMILY/PERSONAL RELATIONS,/
                          AND COURT LIFE

417 *Anderson, M. S. "Peter the Great: Imperial Revolutionary."
     A. G. Dickens, ed. The Courts of Europe: Politics, Patron-
     age and Royalty 1400-1800. New York: McGraw Hill, 1977,
     267-81.
     A discussion of court life during Peter the Great's reign as
     being atypical of that of contemporary European monarchs.
     Anderson states that Peter's indifference to custom and tradi-
     tion, impatience, often crude behavior, and violent outbursts
     made him a unique figure among European royalty. Similarly,
     his royal court stood out starkly from the other courts of
     Europe, largely because of his disdain for finery, preference
     for things practical, and unwillingness to live the type of
     sedate and immobile existence necessary for the maintenance
     of a formal court of the European style. Anderson concludes
     that although Peter "did not build a great palace he associated
     his name, as no ruler since Alexander the Great had done,
     with a new city," St. Petersburg, and managed to transfer
     to the Russian aristocracy and court a veneer of European

culture. Included are a score of impressive illustrations of
Peter the Great, his family, and royal court.   GT3510.C68
   Reviewed in:
   Can Am Slav S, 14 (Winter 1980): 535-44
   Christ Cent, 96 (21 Feb, 1979): 195
   Lib J, 103 (Aug. 1978): 1500
   TLS, (6 Oct. 1978): 1112

418 *Bain, R. Nisbet. "Catherine Aleksyeevna and Peter." PPG
     (anthology), 36-70.
     A discussion of the character of and support given to Peter
     I by his principal advisers and his consort Catherine Aleks-
     yeevna (formerly Martha Skovronskaya and later Catherine I).
     Referring to this group as "Peter's pupils," Bain states that
     they represented a carefully chosen band of fellow-workers
     who were both "able and willing to build upon the foundations"
     laid by Peter. The group consisted of the "rapacious five":
     P. Tolstoy, F. Apraksin, G. Golovkin, P. Yaguzhinsky and
     A. Menshikov; A. Ostermann, the most able of Peter's fledg-
     lings; and Catherine, Peter's "inseparable companion" and
     most trusted pupil. Although Bain stresses the closeness of
     Catherine and Peter's relationship and the beneficial influence
     exerted by Catherine on Peter's behavior, he devotes consid-
     erable attention to their respective infidelities.

419 *Besancon, Alain. "Emperor and Heir--Father and Son." M.
     Raeff, trans. PGCR (anthology), 160-70. From Le Tsaré-
     vitch immolé--La Symbolique de la loi dans la Culture Russe.
     Paris: Libraire Plon, 1967, 111-22.
     An examination of the conflict between Peter the Great and
     his son Alexis within the confines of Peter's broader struggle
     to modernize Russia. Besancon states that Alexis' opposition
     to Peter "is the sign of the schism that the Petrine reforms
     introduced into Russian socity and the watershed in Russia's
     history between 'a before' and 'an after.' Alexis was as much
     the gangrened member that is cut away as he was the expia-
     tory victim." In discussing the trial of Alexis, Besancon as-
     serts that ironically "Peter wanted an impersonal sentence
     rendered in the name of the state" so that his soul would not
     be burdened with guilt over the execution of his own flesh
     and blood.

420 Bryant, John E. "Peter I (Called Peter the Great) 1672-1725."
     Genius and Epilepsy. Brief Sketches of Great Men Who Had
     Both. Concord: Ye Old Depot Press, 1953, 75-77.
     A brief and favorable review of Peter I's impetuousness,
     diverse tastes, and accomplishments with some mention of the
     seizures from which he suffered throughout life.
     BF416.A87

421 Bunbury, Selina. Anecdotes of Peter the Great.... London,

1843, 187pp.
Unavailable for annotation.

422 Cobb, Irvin A. "Behind the Scenes with Peter the Great."
     Incredible Truth. New York: Cosmopolitan Book Corporation,
     1931, 312-20.
     A journalistic rendering of various anecdotes which illustrate
     the cruel side of Peter I's nature. D24.C6

423 Coxe, William. "Alexey Petrovitch." TPRSD (gen. study),
     513-30.
     A discussion of Alexis' poor upbringing and miserable relations
     with his father, Peter I, as the source of the tsarevich's
     treasonous behavior. Coxe states that "Peter had conceived
     a very early prejudice against his son" and inspired in Alexis
     such terror that his judgment became warped and his mind
     periodically unhinged. His weakness of character and inces-
     sant drunkenness made him easy prey for those opposed to
     Peter's policies." In discussing Alexis' torture and death,
     Coxe states that Alexis was beheaded by direct order of
     Peter, a fact Peter attempted to conceal by having Alexis'
     head "sewn to his body previous to its lying in state."

424 Cracraft, James. "Some Dreams of Peter the Great: A Bio-
     graphical Note." Can Am Slav S, 8, no. 2 (Summer 1974):
     173-97.
     A psychoanalytical assessment of twelve dreams recorded by
     Peter the Great from 1714 to 1716. Cracraft contends that
     Peter's symbolic dreams and Turkish dreams indicate a strong-
     ly compulsive personality fueled by a powerful desire to be
     successful on a grand scale. Peter's dreams of Turkish con-
     quests may perhaps be linked to "a secret ambition to reverse
     the humiliating denouement of the Pruth campaign" as part of
     a "deeply felt need for revenge." Cracraft also evaluates two
     dreams recorded by Peter's wife Catherine in 1719 which re-
     veal fear of and resentment towards Peter and guilt over her
     love affair with William Mons.

425 Dale, Philip M. "Peter the Great." Medical Biographies. Nor-
     man: University of Oklahoma Press, 1952, 58-71.
     A discussion of the medical roots of Peter I's sometimes bi-
     zarre behavior and strange mannerisms. Dale contends that
     habitual alcoholism aggravated an epileptic condition to the
     point where Peter was incapacitated by seizures and psycho-
     motor tics and developed a hysteria induced fear complex.
     Dale also states that Peter was most likely afflicted with
     syphilis. In spite of these various ailments, the author con-
     cludes that Peter died from a simple urinary obstruction as a
     consequence of bladder and kidney infections. R703.D3

426 Dumas, Alexandre. "The Romance of Cinderella the Czarina

Catherine I, 1702-1727." CCRC (gen. study), 84-101.
A fanciful account of Catherine's relationship with Peter
the Great with emphasis placed upon her betrayal of his trust
through her affair with William Mons.

427 Escherny, Francois L. Anecdotes Hitherto Unpublished of the
     Private Life of Peter the Great. London, 1813, 170pp.
     Unavailable for annotation.

428 *Eustaphieve, Alexis. Reflections, Notes, and Original Anec-
     dotes, Illustrating the Character of Peter the Great....
     Boston: Munroe and Francis, 1812, 215pp.
     A hagiographic account of Peter and his accomplishments pre-
     cedes a list (pp. 45-118) of seventy notes/anecdotes illustrat-
     ing Peter's character and a five-act drama (pp. 119-215) on
     his conflict with his son Alexis. Eustaphieve's account and
     his five part drama are arranged in such a way that they
     follow the sequence of the anecdotal observations. The anec-
     dotes, which are taken from Voltaire's History of Peter the
     Great and Staelin's Anecdotes of Peter the Great, are both
     amusing and interesting, and place in a sympathetic light
     Peter's personal relations, tastes, habits, and behavior.
     DK132.E9

429 *Golovin, Ivan, ed. Kamenski's Age of Peter the Great. Lon-
     don: T. C. Newby, 1851, 272pp.
     A series of twenty-two essays on the principal advisors to
     Peter the Great, which collectively provides considerable in-
     sight into the type of individual with whom he surrounded
     himself. DK130.A1B2

430 "The Grand Tour." Dublin U M, 66 (Sept. 1865): 336-49 and
     68 (Sept. 1866): 308-21.
     A pseudo-firsthand presentation of a series of anecdotes
     pertaining to Peter's mannerisms, life style, character, per-
     sonal relationships, and basic policies.

431 Grey, Ian. "Peter the Great and Tsarevich Alexei." Hist
     Today, 24 (Nov. 1974): 754-64.
     A straightforward account of the circumstances which led to
     the disaffection of Tsarevich Alexis for his father and, even-
     tually, to the actions which prompted Peter the Great to order
     Alexis' trial for high treason. Grey discusses as the sources
     of Alexis' behavior an unsupervised childhood, the criticism
     of Peter voiced by those who surrounded Alexis in his youth,
     and the tsarevich's personal shortcomings which were aggra-
     vated by acute alcoholism. Particularly detrimental to his
     fortunes was his mistress, Efrosinia, who testified before Peter
     that he had conspired to stir up a rebellion against his father
     and intended, upon ascending to the throne, to reverse the
     Petrine reforms and policies.

432   Grove, G. L. "Peter the Great as Peter the Little." RR, 5
      (Mar. 1892): 207.
      A series of brief anecdotes on Peter the Great's personality
      and lifestyle.

433   Holland, Rupert Sargent. "Historic Boyhoods: Peter the Great,
      the Boy of the Kremlin." St Nich, 35 (Oct. 1908): 1064-66.
      A dramatic reconstruction of Peter I's narrow escape of death,
      as an eleven-year-old boy, at the hands of enraged members
      of the streltsy guard who the author defines as "savage-
      faced pets of the half-civilized Russian rulers." Holland also
      describes sympathetically Peter's development of a practical,
      inquisitive, and self-confident manner in the years prior to
      assuming personal rule over Russia.

434   Hramov, Konstantin D. "Verb Forms in The Letters and Papers
      of Emperor Peter the Great, 1688-1703." New York Univer-
      sity, 1970. (dissertation)

435   *Kliuchevsky, V. O. "The Artisan Tsar." PGCR (anthology),
      21-39. Excerpt from Peter the Great. New York: St. Mar-
      tin's Press, 1958, 35-56.
      An insightful character sketch which highlights Peter the
      Great's likes and tastes, relationship with various people,
      sense of humor, attitude toward religion, and, especially,
      his practical skills and technical abilities. Kliuchevsky con-
      cludes that where Peter's predecessors "were sedentary men
      who preferred to benefit from the work of others, ... Peter
      was an active, self-taught master craftsman, an artisan-Tsar."

436   *Lewitter, L. R. "Peter the Great and the Modern World."
      Hist Today, 35 (Feb. 1985): 16-23.
      A discussion of Peter the Great's intense intellectual curiosity,
      desire for improvement, and predilection for novelty as out-
      standing qualities of his mental makeup. Lewitter provides
      from Peter's life a number of interesting illustrations of these
      characteristics.

437   *Palmer, William. "Suicidal Extinction of the Dynasty." PAT,
      Vol. VI (gen. study), 1029-1498.
      A discussion of the treason and execution of Tsarevich Alexis
      within the confines of a broader interpretation of the excesses
      and cruelties of Peter's reign as a type of punishment inflicted
      by God upon the Romanov successors of Tsar Alexis for the
      latter's assault upon Patriarch Nikon and the Russian church.
      Palmer examines in detail the upbringing of Tsarevich Alexis,
      his relationship with his father, his torture and execution for
      state treason, and the disinheritance of Alexis' son Peter.

438   *_____. "The Uneducated Materialistic Son." Ibid., 955-1028.
      A discussion of the neglect of Peter the Great's education as

the source of his crudeness and brutality and as a further
example of the punishment inflicted upon the family of Tsar
Alexis for his blasphemous church policy. Following a detailed
account of Peter's childhood upbringing and reign up to 1703,
Palmer asserts "that for Tsar Alexis... to have a son and
successor, born with the greatest natural gifts and with the
brightest promise, develop into a savage, doing acts of monstrous cruelty, lawlessness, and impiety, was certainly a
punishment," and for the boyars and streltsy "who had been
accomplices of servants of iniquity, it was a punishment to
have such a hero-savage set over them as a legislator and a
destroyer." Palmer concludes by citing Peter's own words
on his fits of rage: "I can govern others, but I cannot
govern myself."

439 "Peter the Great." Eclectic M, 49 (Mar. 1980): 412-13.
     A short description of a scene in the Monastery of the Trinity
     depicted by a print in which the youthful Peter and his
     mother were nearly put to death by two members of the
     streltsy who had been incited by a rumor (started by Peter's
     step-sister Sophia) that Tsar Feodor's death was the result
     of poison administered to him by plotters who hoped to have
     Peter placed on the throne.

440 Pilkington, Mary. Parental Care Producing Practical Virtue ...
     with a Description of the Inhabitants of Russia and a Variety
     of Interesting Anecdotes of Peter the Great. London, 1810.
     Unavailable for annotation.

441 Poole, Stanley B-R. "The Tsarevitch Alexis." Royal Mysteries
     and Pretenders. London: Blandford Press, 1969, 54-66.
     A discussion of Peter's neglect of his son Alexis and the lat-
     ter's consequent upbringing by his mother Eudoxia and her
     relatives who were "bitter opponents of Peter's Westernizing
     reforms" as the source of Alexis' becoming "the focal point of
     all the opposition to Peter's policy of reform at home." Poole
     gives a standard account of Alexis' flight to Naples to escape
     the wrath of Peter and the latter's success in securing Alexis'
     return to St. Petersburg where the tsarevich was interrogated,
     tortured, and, eventually, executed. D107.P58

442 Porter, Jane. "Peter I and the Shipwreck." Mus For Lit, 13
     (Aug. 1828): 329-33.
     An account of some of Peter the Great's humanitarian deeds
     with most attention given to his rescue of several drowning
     sailors during a fierce storm, an endeavor which led to his
     illness and death. The tale was introduced by Catherine II's
     unveiling of the famous statue of Peter in St. Petersburg at
     which time one of the sailors saved by Peter fell in veneration
     of the statue.

443 Saint-Simon, Duke of. "His Personality and Habits." PGCR
     (anthology), 19-21. From Memoirs of Louis XIV and the
     Regency, Vol. III. Bayle St. John, trans. Washington and
     London: M. Walter Dunne, 1901, 101-04.
     A French noble, Louis de Rouvroy, Duc de Saint-Simon, de-
     scribes Peter's personality and habits on the basis of a 1717
     visit to the Russian court. Saint-Simon characterizes Peter
     as a robust, forthright, intelligent individual.

444 Spence, Lewis. "The Scot Who Saved the Tsar." Scots M,
     (Sept. 1941): 429-36.
     Unavailable for annotation.

445 *Staehlin, Jakob. Original Anecdotes of Peter the Great.
     New York: Arno Press, 1970, 448pp.
     A collection of anecdotes about Peter the Great from people
     who were acquainted with him in various capacities. Staeh-
     lin's desire to compile the anecdotes was based on his wish
     to "give to the world a picture of the admiration and sublime
     virtues of the creator of Russia." Many of the anecdotes are
     from court members, ambassadors, servitors, and others who
     were in a position to see Peter under positive circumstances.
     Useful as a source of insight into Peter's personality, charac-
     ter, and policies, though undocumented. DK132.S813

446 Traquain, E. M. "The Mother of a Remarkable Man." Cosmo-
     pol, 1 (May 1886): 158-59.
     A brief, fanciful account of how Peter the Great's mother
     came to her exalted position as wife of Tsar Alexis.

447 Treue, Wilhelm. "Peter the Great and His Doctors." DAC
     (gen. study), 50-55.
     A brief account of Peter the Great's interest in promoting
     and advancing medical assistance in Russia and of the many
     physicians who attended him personally. The exact source
     of Peter's death is also a point of discussion with the possi-
     ble causes identified as syphilis, poison, and bladder disease.

448 The Tryal of the Czarewitz Alexis Petrowitz, Who Was Condemned
     at Petersbourg on the 25th of June, 1718, for Treason Against
     the Life of the Czar His Father. London: James Crokatt,
     1725, 110pp.
     A series of documents pertaining to the charges levied against
     Tsarevich Alexis. Officially sanctioned by Peter I, the docu-
     ments were to serve as a justification for Alexis' execution
     and the disinheritance of the tsarevich's son, Peter.

449 Ulanski, Baron Carl Theodor von. The Woeful History of the
     Unfortunate Eudoxia, First Consort of the Czar, Peter the
     Great, Emperor of Russia. John Kortz, trans. Hudson:
     W. E. Norma, 1816, 135pp. Appendix: "The Destruction of

the Strelitzes," 123-35.
A favorable biography of Eudoxia, Peter the Great's first
wife, and a sharp attack on Peter for his abuse of her.
Ulanski discusses the initial "falling out" between Eudoxia
and Peter and the influence exercised by LeFort, Menshikov,
and Catherine (Peter's second wife) in hardening the tsar's
feelings toward Eudoxia and Tsarevich Alexis, their son.
He then presents a lurid account of the execution of Alexis,
the torture and exile of Eudoxia's brother, Abraham Lapus-
chin, and internment of Eudoxia. Ulanski concludes that
Peter's inhuman treatment of Eudoxia must forever qualify
any consideration of his rule as an enlightened one.

450 Vŏgué, Viscount E. M. de. A Czarevitch of the Eighteenth
     Century and Other Studies in Russian History. C. N. Ander-
     son, trans. London: A. L. Humphreys, 1913, 306pp.
     Unavailable for annotation.

                    DOMESTIC POLICY AND AFFAIRS

Politics

451 *Baron, Samuel H. "The Fate of the Gosti in the Reign of
     Peter the Great." Cahiers du monde, 14, no. 4 (1973):   488-
     512.
     An examination of the decline in the number and importance
     of foreigners in the service of Peter's government. Baron
     states that although the gosti was a flourishing privileged
     group in the early years of Peter's reign, between 1710 and
     1720 it all but disappeared from the scene, largely because
     Peter chose not to replenish its ranks with new appointments
     as a result of his belief that, once entrenched, the foreigners
     ceased to be dynamic contributors to the Russian state and
     economy. The gosti was thus cast aside as an instrument
     that had outlived its purpose.

452 *Bennett, Helju Aulik. "Evolution of the Meaning of Chin:
     An Introduction to the Russian Institution of Rank Ordering
     and Niche Assignment from the Time of Peter the Great's
     Table of Ranks to the Bolshevik Revolution." Calif Slav S,
     10 (1977): 1-44.
     The first half of this article deals with Peter the Great's 1722
     creation of the Table of Ranks within "the context of an
     evolving, complex and peculiarly Russian institution, the
     chin system." Although Bennett's focus is the 1722 law's
     impact on the social rank of the nobility, he traces the forma-
     tion of the Table of Ranks to Peter's growing need for a
     way to secure loyal servitors without using threats and force
     or paying substantial salaries.

453 *Benson, Sumner. "The Role of Western Political Thought in
     Petrine Russia." Can Am Slav S, 8 (Summer 1974): 254-73.
     An examination of the use of various Western political theories
     by both the Petrine state and its opponents. Benson discusses
     the employment of medieval Catholic theory by Stefan Yavorsky
     and Patriarch Adrian to counter the state's encroachment upon
     the sovereignty of the church, and then turns to an account
     of the utilization, by both Peter I and Feofan Prokopovich, of
     Protestant theorists who supported the supremacy of the state
     over the church and of secular theorists who argued for ab-
     solutism from the rational perspective of the political contract.
     Benson concludes that the most important consequence of the
     state's use of Western political thought was its success in
     stigmatizing as reactionary and self-serving any attempt to
     place limits on the tsar's absolute authority.

454 *Blackstock, Paul W. "The Testament of Peter the Great:
     From Legend to Forgery." Agents of Deceit. Frauds, For-
     geries and Political Intrigue Among Nations. Chicago: Quad-
     rangle Books, 1966, 25-37.
     A discussion of the complex origins of the forged testament
     of Peter the Great and the employment of this "document" as
     a propaganda weapon by various Western governments to as-
     sail the motives behind Russian foreign policy, tsarist and
     communist, during time of war or heightened political tension.
     DK61.B55

455 *Bogoslovskii, Mikhail M. "Peter's Program of Political Reform."
     Mirra Ginsburg, trans. PGCR (anthology), 47-62. From
     Oblastnaia Reforma Petra Velikogo-Provintsiia, 1719-1727
     (Peter the Great's Reform of Regional Administration-the
     Pronvince in 1719-1727). Moscow, 1902, 1-13, 19-23.
     A discussion of Peter the Great's reforms as a practical mani-
     festation of his basic concept of government. Bogoslovsky, a
     Russian specialist on the Petrine era, states that Peter's be-
     lief that the monarchy was obligated to serve as the driving
     force behind the progressive refashioning of the nation and
     its people led to a state-initiated, implacable struggle against
     backwardness in each of its various forms. Such a philosophy
     of government prompted not only diverse and far-reaching re-
     forms but also led Peter to justify his reforms by references
     to the general good of the nation.

456 *Cherniavsky, Michael. "The Sovereign Emperor." Tsar and
     People. Studies in Russian Myths. New York: Random
     House, 1961, 72-100. Excerpt in PGCR (anthology), 141-59.
     A discussion of Peter's assumption of the title "emperor" as
     symbolic of the secularization of political power which occurred
     during his reign. Cherniavsky states that "the denial of the
     theocratic foundation of the ruler-myth under Peter ... could
     have two alternative consequences within the old Russian

tradition of the saint-prince: the rejection of a tsar who no
longer corresponded ... to the ideal image, or a new and possibly greater exaltation of the tsar on a different ideological
foundation." While popular opposition to Peter in his lifetime
reflected the vitality of the first alternative, the efforts of
court circles, writers, iconographers, and official ideologues
marked the emergence of the latter. Cherniavsky concludes
that the ultimate rationale established for the new monarchy
was the monarchy itself. Peter thus emerged as an autocrat
"truly secular and truly absolute in the sense of owing nothing to anything outside of himself and limited by nothing
outside of himself." DK32.C523

457 *Crummey, Robert O. "Peter and the Boiar Aristocracy, 1689-
     1700." Can Am Slav S, 8 (Summer 1974), 274-87.
     An examination of the effect of Peter's early reign on the
     political and administrative fortunes of the boyars. Crummey
     maintains that Peter made far more use of the traditional
     aristocracy as a source of leadership and advice than is often
     realized by historians: "When Peter needed generals or ad-
     ministrators, he turned, more often than not, to families whose
     members had for generations supplied the state's leading ser-
     vitors.... In short, from one generation to the next the
     Golitsyns stood around the throne; the Gordons and Leforts
     of this world did not."

458 *Daniels, Rudolph L. V. N. Tatishchev: Guardian of the
     Petrine Revolution. Philadelphia: Franklin Publishing Com-
     pany, 1973, 125pp., bib. 117-25.
     Although this work does not contain a separate chapter on
     Peter the Great, it does discuss the service rendered by
     Tatishchev to Peter during the latter's lifetime and, more
     importantly, Tatishchev's efforts to preserve the Petrine re-
     forms and continue enlightened absolutism as the foundation
     of the Russian government. Of special interest is Daniels'
     account of Tatishchev's efforts to win aristocratic support
     for the Table of Ranks by arguing that aristocrats could re-
     gain their social status by acquiring the education and culture
     which their service demanded of them. DK127.5.T3D3

459 Deriabin, P. "Peter the Great." WT (gen. study), 48-56.
     A brief discussion of Peter the Great's 1698 crushing of the
     streltsy mutiny as the greatest purge Russia was to experi-
     ence until the Stalin purges of the 1930s. Deriabin also de-
     scribes other instances of cruelty in Peter's political behavior.

460 Ginsburg, Saul M. "Peter Shafiroff; Jewish Adviser to Peter
     the Great." Judaism, 22 (Fall 1973): 409-17.
     A review of the career of Peter Shafiroff, a converted Jew
     who served Peter the Great in a number of capacities. Shafi-
     roff, who was fluent in several languages, traveled to the

West with Peter, played a major role in securing Polish, Prussian, and Danish assistance in Russia's war with Sweden,
initiated the negotiations with the Turkish sultan which led to
the rescue of Peter and the Russian army encircled by the
sultan's forces, and concluded trade agreements with France
and Prussia. Despite his accomplishments, Peter the Great,
under the influence of Menshikov who hated Shafiroff, con-
firmed a judgment by the Senate that Shafiroff was to be
stripped of his titles and fortune and executed by ax on 15
February 1723 because of his misappropriation of government
funds. At the last moment, the tsar commuted Shafiroff's
sentence to lifelong exile in Siberia, a judgment reversed
after Peter I's death when Shafiroff returned to government
service under Empresses Catherine I and Anna.

461   Hassell, James. "Implementation of the Table of Ranks During
       the Eighteenth Century." Slav R, 29, no. 2 (June 1970):
       283-95.
       Peter is not the focus of this article, but it includes some
       discussion of his motives for establishing the Table of Ranks
       and the fate which befell this reform following Peter's 1725
       death. Hassell concludes that "fundamentally the Table of
       Ranks was an attempt to establish merit instead of birth as
       the basis of awarding government positions. Since eighteenth-
       century Russia was a class society with the nobility in a
       strongly dominating position, this attempt failed. Only those
       provisions of the Table of Ranks that reinforced prevailing
       attitudes met with general acceptance."

462   *Meehan-Waters, Brenda. Autocracy and Aristocracy. The
       Russian Service Elite of 1730. New Brunswick, N.J.: Rut-
       gers University Press, 1982, 274pp., bib. 245-59.
       A scholarly study of the composition of the 1730 generalitet
       for insight into "the impact of Petrine reform on the social
       composition of the service elite" and the social, economic, and
       political attributes which this group possessed. Meehan-Waters
       establishes that contrary to the view that foreigners and Rus-
       sians of non-noble birth dominated the top positions in the
       Petrine bureaucracy, it was the old Muscovite elite which still
       held these positions in the Russian government and society.
       The persistence rather than the replacement of the aristocracy's
       hold on high positions was a reflection of Peter's interest in
       revitalizing rather than removing them as the nation's service
       elite. This revitalization was achieved by Peter through his
       establishment of advancement by merit as a fundamental prin-
       ciple of the Russian bureaucracy and by his provision for
       substantial material benefits for those who served him best.
       Meehan-Waters adds that the powerful advantages gained by
       the aristocratic service elite did not result in any advancement

of the aristocracy's political position with respect to the tsar
since he was still "the source of all power and the distributor
of all rewards." This work may also be consulted with profit
for information on the generalitet's unsuccessful attempt to
use to its own advantage the succession crisis of 1730.
DK150.M43

463 * _____. "The Muscovite Noble Origins of the Russians in the
Generalitet of 1730." Cahiers du monde, 12, no. 1-2 (1971):
28-75.
An analysis of the social origins of the Russians in the generalitet of 1730 for insight into "the working relationship between
Peter and the Muscovite nobility, the effect of the Table of
Ranks on that nobility, and the question of social mobility
in general under Peter." Meehan-Waters concludes that Peter
was not so much interested in social mobility as he was "with
transforming the existing nobility and demanding that they
operate within his structure." Included in an appendix is a
detailed record of the service backgrounds of the families
represented in the 1730 generalitet.

464 * _____. "The Russian Aristocracy and the Reforms of Peter
the Great." Can Am Slav S, 8, no. 2 (1974): 288-302.
An argument that Peter the Great's reforms, particularly his
creation of the Table of Ranks, were without "profound effect
upon the nature and composition of the Russian nobility."
Drawing upon a considerable body of statistical evidence,
Meehan-Waters reasons that "Peter was not concerned with
social mobility or opening opportunities for all, but rather
with transforming the existing nobility. He seems to have
guaranteed first preference for the old service nobility,
provided they operate within his new structure."

465 Merguerian, Barbara J. "Political Ideas in Russia During the
Period of Peter the Great (1680-1730)." Harvard University,
1971. (dissertation)

466 *Peterson, Claes. Peter the Great's Administrative and Judicial
Reforms. Stockholm: A. B. Nordisha Bohhandeln, 1979,
448pp., bib. 418-37.
The stated aim of this study is to "investigate the preconditions for the administrative and judicial reforms carried out in
Russia between 1715 and 1722 with special regard for the influence of Swedish administrative institutions and Swedish law
upon them." Peterson demonstrates that Peter I was both
the initiator and driving force behind these reforms but adds
that Heinrich Fick, who was commissioned in 1716 by Peter to
study Swedish administrative practices at first hand, deserves
credit for substantial influence on the reforms' shape. The

reforms launched demonstrated more dependence "upon Swedish prototypes than has hitherto been assumed," particularly in regard to fiscal administration. Peterson sees scant sign of any of the "creative reworking" of the Swedish administrative model by Peter and his advisers noted by several Soviet historians. Rather, Peter believed, quite simplistically, that the Swedish administration, which presented a unitary pattern and a strictly hierarchical organization with clearly defined areas of responsibility and jurisdiction, was readily adaptable to Russian circumstances and state needs. JN6524.P47
Reviewed in:
Can Am Slav S, 14, no. 4 (1980): 535-44
J Mod Hist, 53, no. 4 (1981): 760-61

467 *Petschauer, Peter. "In Search of Competent Aides: Heinrich Van Huyssen and Peter the Great." Jahr Ges Ost, 26, no. 4 (1978): 481-502.
A discussion of the career of Heinrich Van Huyssen, a foreign servitor in the employment of the Russian state, and an examination of Peter I's difficulty in finding suitable aides and advisers. Petschauer demonstrates that Van Huyssen had the education and emotional make-up needed to be a successful courtier in Western Europe but lacked the qualities necessary to serve Peter as a capable politician, administrator, or statesman.

468 *_____. "The Philosopher and the Reformer: Tsar Peter I, G. W. Leibniz and the College System." Can Am Slav S, 13, no. 4 (1970): 473-87.
A discussion of the influence had by Gottfried Liebniz on the conceptualization and establishment of Peter's collegial system. Petschauer examines the various memoranda and recommendations that shaped Peter's thought on the college system and concludes that the suggestions made by Liebniz had a major impact on Peter, both in regard to the very need for a college system and on the nature of the individual colleges to be established, particularly in the fields of science, technology, and education.

469 *Plekhanov, G. V. History of Russian Social Thought. Boris M. Bekkar et al., trans. New York: Howard Fertig, 1967, 224pp.
A discussion of the nature of Peter the Great's reforms and their influence on the development of Russian social and political thought. Plekhanov, who was a force in Russian Marxism in the decades before the October Revolution, states that the Petrine reforms did not change the foundation of the sociopolitical order of old Russia but nonetheless Peter's contemporaries (both opponents and advocates) believed that such change had occurred, largely because they failed to distin-

guish the fundamental from the subordinate features of social life. The legend of Peter as an omnipotent reformer was disseminated particularly by the "Learned Guard" (F. Prokopovich, V. Tatishchev, and A. Kantemir) whose efforts to promote Peter's reforms, exalt his personality, and defend royal absolutism Plekhanov examines at length. Of particular interest is Plekhanov's discussion of the impact had upon subsequent political thought by the development during Peter's reign of the precept that "great reorganization in Russia could be promoted best from the top." DK32.7.P515

470 _____. "Peter the Great--An Oriental Despot." M. Raeff, trans. PGCR (anthology), 183-87. From Istoriia Obshchest-vennoi Mysli, Vol. II. Moscow, 1918, 91-92.
An argument that the extent of Russia's backwardness and the pressing nature of the need to Westernize left Peter with no options but to use the unlimited power of the monarchy to create the conditions necessary for Russia's modernization.

471 The Prerogative of Primogeniture, Shewing That the Right of Succession to an Hereditary Empire Depends Not upon Grace ... but ... upon Birth-right. (Written on the Occasion of the Czar of Muscovy's Reasons, in His Late Manifesto, for the Disherison of His Eldest Son). London: Printed for W. Boreham, 1718, 44pp.
Unavailable for annotation.

472 *Prokopovich, Feofan. "Sermon on Royal Authority and Honour." Horace G. Lunt, trans. PGCR (anthology), 14-30. From "Slovo o vlasti i chesti tsarskoi..." in Sochineniia Feofana Prokopovicha. I. P. Fremin, ed. Moscow, 1906, 76-93.
An April 1718 sermon which provides a theoretical justification for autocratic power. Drawing upon scriptural writings for support, Prokopovich argues for obedience to a legitimate monarch and against those who dared challenge or subvert the sovereign's will. As M. Raeff points out in a brief introduction, the sermon "was meant to justify the Tsar's disinheritance of his first-born and to warn of the dire consequences--a new Time of Troubles--that would inevitably follow if the Tsar's will were opposed."

473 Rasmussen, Karen M. "Catherine II and Peter I: The Idea of a Just Monarch," University of California, Berkeley, 1973. (dissertation)

474 *Wortman, Richard. "Peter the Great and Court Procedure." Can Am Slav S, 8 (Summer 1974): 303-10.
An argument that those historians who measure Peter's reform of legal procedure in light of modern concepts involving inquisitorial and adversarial justice misconstrue the thrust of

this legislation. Wortman maintains that Peter was far more
concerned with improving the efficiency of the court system
than he was with implementing any one specific concept of
legal procedure. Peter believed that, given Russia's social
fabric, inquisitorial procedure offered the best hope of a
swift and honest dispensation of justice.

Economics

475   *Blanc, Simone. "The Economic Policy of Peter the Great."
       Russian Economic Development from Peter the Great to Stalin.
       W. L. Blackwell, ed. New York: New Viewpoints, 1974,
       21-49. Reprint from Cahiers du monde, 3 (1962): 122-39.
       An investigation into the origin and nature of Peter the
       Great's economic policies. Blanc places the Petrine economic
       reforms within a broad Russian historical context as she dem-
       onstrates that they did not represent any rupture with the
       general trend of Russia's economic development and were not
       a mere copy of Western mercantilist policies of the early
       eighteenth century. She concludes that Peter's mercantilism
       was nothing but a logical response to a Russian economic
       situation. Peter sought only to provide for the economic
       needs of the state as a customer while instilling in his sub-
       jects patriotic pride and faith in "potentials until then unknown
       or neglected," a feat which he accomplished admirably.

476   Drew, Ronald F. "Siberia: An Experiment in Colonialism. A
       Study of Economic Growth Under Peter I." Stanford Uni-
       versity, 1957. (dissertation)

477   *"The Economic Views and Principles of Peter I." HRET
       (anthology), 245-94.
       A Soviet discussion of Peter I's economic thought and policies
       as a manifestation of his desire to eliminate the backwardness
       of Russia within the confines of the traditional feudal-
       absolutist system. The authors first discount the "supra-
       class principles" behind Peter's economic and political pro-
       gram and then examine in detail his efforts to use the state
       as an agent to transform Russia's industry, agriculture,
       finances, transportation, and trade. While the authors note
       the similarities between Peter's practical economic policies
       and those of West European mercantilists, they maintain that
       his economic principles "were significantly broader than the
       theoretical views formulated by the spokesmen of West Euro-
       pean mercantilism in respect to the nature of wealth and the
       basic method of its increase.... For their time, Peter's
       economic views were advanced and progressive. They helped
       the development of the productive forces of Russia."

478   *Gerschenkron, Alexander. "Lecture Number Three." Europe

in the Russian Mirror--Four Lectures in Economic History.
Cambridge: Cambridge University Press, 1970, 62-96. Also
in PGCR (anthology), 82-102.
An examination of Peter I's mercantilist policies, their place
in Russia's economic development, and relation to European
mercantilism. In isolating the unique aspects of Petrine mercantilism, Gerschenkron states that "nowhere else in the mercantilist world do we encounter a comparable case of a great
spurt, compressed within such a short period" where "the
starting point was so low" and "the obstacles that stood in
the path of development so formidable.... Nowhere else was
it so strongly dominated by the interests of the state." Also
unique to Russian mercantilism was its lack of preoccupation
with foreign trade and precious metals, and "the almost complete absence in it of general theorizing." The most distinc-
tive feature of Petrine economics, however, was the state's
attempt to counter backwardness through the use of severe
and compulsory measures and at the cost of a further intensification of serfdom. In the sense that Petrine mercantilism
created obstacles to the very economic development which it
sought to perpetuate, it was similar to its West European
counterpart, but the magnitude of these obstacles was far
greater due to the relative backwardness of the Russian
economy. HC334.G45

479 *Kahan, Arcadius. "Continuity in Economic Activity and Policy
During the Post-Petrine Period in Russia." SRH (anthology),
191-211. Reprint from J Eco Hist, 25 (Mar. 1965): 61-85.
An argument that "the economic process set in motion during
the Petrine period continued during the post-Petrine period
and that the policies that supported the early industrialization
drive were not abandoned by Peter's successors." Kahan
establishes the fundamental character of Peter's economic
policies and concedes that since Peter was the driving force
behind them, his death in 1725, "could not but leave a mark
upon the economic life of the country." However, he rejects
the thesis (advanced by Miliukov and Kliuchevsky) that
Peter's economic policies were not sustained by his successors
on the grounds that statistical evidence shows further development, after 1725, of private-sector manufactures as a response
to a government policy which favored the interests of the
entrepreneurial groups.

480 *_____. "Observations on Petrine Foreign Trade." Can Am
Slav S, 8, no. 2 (Summer 1974): 222-36.
The author's stated goal is "to demonstrate that regardless
of what happened in other areas of economic activity, ... the
foreign trade of Russia certainly expanded" during Peter's
reign. Kahan discusses the impetus behind the expansion of
foreign trade, problems which confronted Russian merchants,
the composition and extent of the trade itself, and Peter's

general approach to international commerce. Kahan questions
those who claim that Peter's policy was mercantilistic since the
pre-conditions for mercantilism were lacking in Russia. He
stresses the point that Peter's expansion of trade is best seen
as a consequence of his political objective of transforming Russia into a powerful Western nation rather than as an end in
itself.

481   Kelpsh, A. E.   "Rubles of Peter the Great." Numismatist, 62
      (Mar. 1949):   161-74.
      An account of Peter the Great's interest in minting, and a de-
      scription of the type of coins minted during his reign.

482   *Lyashchenko, Peter I.   "The National Economy." PGCR
      (anthology) 67-82. From History of National Economy of Rus-
      sia to the Revolution of 1917. L. M. Herman, trans.   New
      York, 1949, 267-70, 283-88, 291-97.
      A Marxist interpretation of Russia's economic development of
      the eighteenth century and the influence exerted on it by
      Peter's reform program. Lyashchenko, a noted Soviet econom-
      ic historian, describes the Petrine era as the formative period
      of Russia's capitalist development, the period "that brought
      into view the trend and organizational forms of later industrial
      development in all its characteristics and peculiarities." With-
      in this context, Lyashchenko discusses Peter's industrial,
      fiscal, and commercial reforms while emphasizing the hard-
      ships which Peter's program brought to the broad mass of the
      Russian people.

483   *Mavor, James.   "The Military, Fiscal, and Commercial Policy
      of Peter the Great" and "The Industrial Policy of Peter the
      Great and His Reforms." An Economic History of Russia,
      Vol. I. New York: E. P. Dutton, 1925, 100-63.
      A detailed examination of the steps taken by Peter to improve
      the quality of Russia's military forces and to increase the pro-
      ductive powers of its people. Mavor discusses Peter's reor-
      ganization of the army, use of the military as a "police, tax-
      gathering, and centralizing force," imposition of the poll tax,
      fusing of the peasantry into one social class, and, especially,
      his efforts to create industrial enterprises where few of the
      preconditions for such were in existence. Mavor commends
      Peter for his tireless energy, broadness of vision, and mani-
      fest economic ability, but does not see him as being either a
      revolutionary or the source of Russia's Westernization: "Peter
      took from the West technical, educational, administrative and
      financial methods; he took nothing of the spirit of the West,
      and for this reason he is entitled neither to the credit nor
      the blame of having Westernized his country." The author
      concludes that Peter succeeded admirably in increasing the
      state's material resources and military power, but his use of
      excessive force in implementing reforms and failure to elevate

the general standard of life in Russia make impossible the
labeling of his reign as an economically progressive one.
HC333.M3

Education, Science, and Culture

484 Alexander, John T. "Medical Developments in Petrine Russia."
     Can Am Slav S, 8, no. 2 (1974): 198-221.
     A favorable account of Peter the Great's involvement in medical
     affairs. Alexander discusses Peter's fascination with the field
     of medicine and efforts to develop medical science in Russia
     both through importing foreign specialists and promoting medi-
     cal education. The author also discusses the treatment of epi-
     demics in Petrine Russia and the causes of Peter's death.

485 *Billington, James A. "The Westward Turn." IA (gen. study),
     163-205.
     An insightful examination of Westernization during Peter the
     Great's reign and the nature of the negative response which it
     prompted among Russian traditionalists. Billington demon-
     strates that although the substance of Petrine modernization
     was consistent with seventeenth century proposals for West-
     ernization, Peter's reform program was so broad and ruthless-
     ly enforced that it generated a passionate reaction, most
     notably on the part of "merchant Old Believers, peasant in-
     surrectionaries, and monastic ascetics." Of particular inter-
     est is Billington's discussion of St. Petersburg as the symbol
     of the secularized society and monarchy which Peter sought to
     create.

486 *Black, Joseph. "Peter I: Ideas and Their First Practitioners."
     Citizens for the Fatherland. Education, Educators and Peda-
     gogical Ideals in Eighteenth Century Russia. New York:
     Columbia University Press, 1979, 23-43.
     A discussion of Peter's educational reforms as an expression
     of his belief that "education was the panacea for Russia's
     weakness." In addition to presenting within this context
     Peter's creation of the school of artillery, promotion of sec-
     ondary education, and promulgation of the Spiritual Regulation
     of 1721, Black chronciles the efforts of Prokopovich, Tatish-
     chev, and Kantemir to promote education along the lines sug-
     gested by Peter. Black also notes that while Peter's educa-
     tional reforms yielded few favorable, practical results, they
     were at least a beginning and influenced substantially the
     educational thought and policies of his successors.
     LA831.5.B44

487 *Brechka, Frank T. "Peter the Great: The Books He Owned."
     J Lib Hist, 17, no. 1 (1982): 1-15.
     An interesting account of the nature of the 1,663 books and

manuscripts known to have been in Peter I's personal library.
Brechka states that although the library contained a number
of religious and historical works that Peter either inherited or
received as gifts, the vast majority of its contents consisted
of scientific and technical books. Nearly half of the books
were in Western European languages (296 were in German,
only twelve in English), and most of these were purchased
abroad in one year (1722) by Peter's librarian, Daniel Schu-
macher, in anticipation of the establishment of the St. Petersburg Academy of Sciences. Brechka concludes that Peter's
library reflects well the tsar's secular tastes and "impatient
and impetuous life style."

488   *Brown, William Edward. "Literature in the Age of Peter the
      Great." HECRL (gen. study), 9-30.
      A portrayal of Peter I's reign as "the most unliterary period
      in Russian history." Brown states that "Peter neither knew
      nor cared anything about such a civilized refinement as liter-
      ature.... If there was a vast increase during his reign of
      the amount of printed material available in the empire, this
      was largely made up of hurried translations from West Euro-
      pean languages of works on mathematics, navigation, fortifi-
      cation, medicine and the like. And in so far as there was
      literary composition during his reign, it was backward-looking
      and old-fashioned, and in no way in keeping with the 'Westerniz-
      ing' character of other aspects of Peter's reign." In support of
      this statement, Brown discusses the primitive qualities of
      Petrine poetry and drama (including Peter's attempt to create
      a theater that did not dwell on love and intrigue) and the
      overly utilitarian character of the prose of the era, especially
      that of Feofan Prokopovich and Ivan Pososhkov.

489   *Cracraft, James. "The Tercentenary of Peter the Great in
      Russia." Can Am Slav S, 8 (Summer 1974): 319-26.
      An account of the Soviet commemoration of the 300th anniver-
      sary of Peter the Great's birth, including a description of
      the exhibitions at the Russian Museum, Hermitage, and State
      Public Library as well as of the displays of Petrine memora-
      bilia at libraries, schools, and commemorative scholarly con-
      ferences.

490   Hans, Nicholas. "Henry Farquarson: Pioneer of Russian
      Education, 1689-1739." Aberdeen Un R, 38 (1959-60): 26-29.
      An account of the influence exerted on Russian education by
      the Scottish mathematician Henry Farquarson who was recruited
      in 1698 by Peter the Great to be the director of the newly
      established School of Navigation in Moscow. Hans maintains
      that Farquarson's "many-sided activities, and especially
      participation in the training of all the Russian teachers of the
      first school system established by Peter, make him an out-
      standing pioneer of Russian education."

491 *_____. "The Moscow School of Mathematics and Navigation."
     Slavonic E Eur R, 29 (June 1951): 532-36.
     The focus of this article is a refutation of Professor Medyn-
     sky's claim that "Russia has the distinction of having opened
     the first non-classical school in the world" (The Moscow School
     of Mathematics and Navigation). Hans maintains that Peter I
     used English and French schools as models for this institution.

492 _____. "Peter the Great." HREP (gen. study), 10-16.
     An overview of Peter's educational reforms and their effective-
     ness. Hans concludes that the reforms are significant in that
     they mark the beginning of organized educational policy in
     Russia but must not be considered as an attempt by Peter to
     establish a true system of education since they were designed
     "solely for the utilitarian purpose of furnishing educated offi-
     cials for various departments."

493 Haskins, John. "Golden Hoard of Peter the Great." Art N,
     57 (Dec. 1958): 63-65.
     An account of Peter's collection of Sarmatian and Scythian
     gold objects with some attention given to his role in their
     preservation.

494 _____. "Sarmatian Gold Collected by Peter the Great: The
     Demidov Gift and Conclusions." Artibus Asiae, 22 (1959):
     64-78.
     A discussion of the origin and contents of the collection of
     Sarmatian gold held by the Hermitage.

495 *Holquist, Michael. "St. Petersburg: From Utopian City to
     Gnostic Universe." Virg Q R, 48 (1972): 537-57.
     A discussion of St. Petersburg as the symbol of the Petrine
     spirit and as a theme in Russian literature. Holquist contrasts
     the features of Moscow, as the spiritual capital and very
     symbol of old Russia, with those of St. Petersburg as "the
     expression of a total--and totalitarian--vision, social, reli-
     gious, esthetic." He notes that while Peter's reforms were
     generally based on European models, "the project for the new
     capital was the product of a unique utopian vision ahead of
     its time by nearly a century particularly in respect to its
     philisophico-urban aspirations." Holquist concludes with an
     analysis of the evolution of the city's image in eighteeenth-
     and nineteenth-century Russian literature and the portrayal
     of the capital, particularly in the works of Gogol and Dostoev-
     sky, as an oppressive and sterile manifestation of a utopian
     plan turned sour.

496 Johnson, William H. E. "The Rise of the State Universities
     (1700-1760)." Russia's Educational Heritage. Pittsburgh:
     Carnegie Press, 1950, 27-42.

A review of Peter I's accomplishments in the field of education, particularly his creation of the School of Mathematical
and Navigational Sciences at Moscow (1701), renovation of
ecclesiastical schools, and promotion of the establishment of
the Academy of Sciences (1725). Johnson commends Peter
for his role in the formation of these institutions and for his
attention to staffing them with qualified teachers. LA831.J6

497 *Kopelevich, Iu. Kh. "The Creation of the Petersburg Academy
of Sciences as a New Type of Scientific and State Institution."
GBR (anthology), 204-11.
A discussion of both Peter the Great's role in the founding of
the St. Petersburg Academy of Sciences and the unique features of this institution in comparison to its European counterparts of the same era. Kopelevich states that although Peter
visited both the Royal Society of London (in 1698) and the
Paris Academy of Sciences (in 1717) and discussed at length
with Liebnitz the creation of a Russian equivalent to these
European institutions, Peter "did not copy the academies
and scientific societies existing in other countries" but
rather carefully devised "a peculiar type of scientific corporation, with clearcut features of a state institution." In
its capacity as a state institution, the academy performed a
number of valuable services, particularly in regard to cartog-
raphy and the exploration of Russia's remote regions, and in
turn enjoyed special support and benefits. However, through
these obligations to the state the academy became limited in
its ability to function as an educational institution and engulfed in mounds of red tape through contact with numerous
state agencies.

498 Leary, D. B. "Peter to Catherine II, 1689-1762." EAR (gen.
study), 30-37.
A general survey of the Petrine educational reforms and the
obstacles which they encountered.

499 *Likhachev, D. S. "The Petrine Reforms and the Development
of Russian Culture." Avril Pymans, trans. Can Am Slav S,
13, no. 1 (1979): 230-34.
An interpretation of Peter the Great's cultural reforms as an
expression of a centuries-long process at work within Russia.
Likhachev maintains that such pre-Petrine developments as
Russia's departure from medieval traditionalism, the growing
demand for scientific and technical knowledge, the emergence
of specialization in all forms of art, and the general spread of
secularized culture combined to make "the appearance of
Western culture possible." Peter, who was himself a product
of this indigenous cultural transformation, accelerated this
process and changed the "sign-system" (trappings) of Russian
culture but can neither be credited nor blamed for diverting
Russia from its natural course of development.

500 Lipski, A. "The Foundation of the Russian Academy of Sci-
     ences." Isis, 44 (Dec. 1953): 349-54.
     A discussion of Peter the Great's effort to establish an aca-
     demy of sciences in St. Petersburg as a manifestation of his
     belief that it was imperative for Russia to assimilate Western
     scientific knowledge.

501 Mantsevich, A. P. "Finds in the Zaporozhe Barrow: New
     Light on the Siberian Collection of Peter the Great." Am J
     Archeol, 86 (Oct. 1982): 469-74.
     An enumeration and description of the items discovered at
     the Zaporozhe barrow and collected by Peter the Great.

502 Marsden, C. Palmyra of the North; The First Days of St.
     Petersburg. London, 1952.
     Unavailable for annotation.

503 *Miliukov, Paul N. "Secular Schools Under Peter the Great."
     PGCR (anthology), 127-37. From Ocherkii po Istorii Russkoi
     Kul'tury (Essays in the History of Russian Culture), Vol. II,
     Part II. Paris, 1931, 732-43.
     An examination of Peter's secular schools and the problems
     which attended their establishment. Miliukov, a renowned
     historian and liberal leader in early twentieth-century Russia,
     states that the secular school "did not aim either at bringing
     up its pupils or at imparting general education to them; it
     aimed mainly at giving technical training for professional
     purposes, ... learning became a form of (state) service."
     The element of compulsion associated with Peter's secular
     schools, Miliukov concludes, along with the fact that they
     were attended by a reluctant and poorly prepared body of
     students, largely accounts for their deterioration in the dec-
     ades following Peter's death.

504 Okenfuss, Max J. "Education in Russia in the First Half of
     the Eighteenth Century," Harvard University, 1971. (dis-
     sertation)

505 *_____ . "The Jesuit Origins of Petrine Education." ECR
     (anthology), 106-30.
     An argument that the nature of the Kiev and Moscow Aca-
     demies and the system of Russian diocesan schools modeled
     in their image "testifies against any characterization of Petrine
     education as narrowly technical or utilitarian." Okenfuss dem-
     onstrates that the Kiev Academy, which Peter the Great se-
     lected as the model for restructuring the Orthodox school in
     Moscow, was founded on the Jesuit notion of education and
     was therefore both a seminary and a school of general edu-
     cation. Far from being mere "church schools," these insti-
     tutions educated many of the figures who shaped Russian
     secular culture in the eighteenth century and must be seen

as a complement to the schools and academies which provided
technical training in Petrine Russia.

506   *_____. "Russian Students in Europe in the Age of Peter
the Great." Ibid., 131-48.
A reassessment of the origins, nature, and significance of
Russian study in Europe during the Petrine period. Following
an interesting examination of whom was sent where and why,
Okenfuss concludes that, contrary to the opinion of many
historians, "the practice of sending students abroad was not
an unfortunate whim of Peter the Great, not a 'stopgap'
measure prior to the creation of schools in Russia, and not
a lightly considered attempt to 'enlighten' Russia," but
rather was the result of a carefully and rationally conceived
plan to educate Russians in all aspects of international sea-
faring."

507   *_____. "Technical Training in Russia Under Peter the
Great." Hist Ed Q, 13 (Winter 1973): 325-45.
A reassessment of the goals and accomplishments of Petrine
technical education. Okenfuss questions the often repeated
assertion that technical schooling was intended to serve as a
replacement for the religious education of Muscovy and "the
old literacy sequence of primer, Breviary and Psalter." Using
as examples the Moscow School of Mathematics and Navigation,
the St. Petersburg Naval Academy, and the network of elementary ciphering schools established by Peter, Okenfuss
demonstrates that the goals of these institutions "were not
educational, that is, not directed to the forming of the individual, but to training him to perform certain desirable
tasks in a nation engaged in European wars."

508   *Papmehl, K. A. "The First Half of the Century." FEER
(gen. study), 1-12.
An account of Peter I's attempt to shape public opinion in
Russia by holding strictly accountable to his authority the
educational institutions and printing presses that came into
existence through his efforts. Papmehl also discusses Peter's
attempt to ban writings not having official authorization and
to encourage patriotic Russians to denounce and inform on
those who spoke out against his policies. The cultural and
educational institutions and printing presses which came into
existence through Peter's efforts were strictly accountable to
"the supreme political authority whose ends it was their purpose to serve."

509   *Rozhdestvenskii, S. V. "Educational Reforms." PGCR (anthology), 122-27. From Ocherki po Istorii Sistem Narodnogo
Prosveshcheniia v Rossii v XVIII-XIX (Essays in the History
of the Systems of National Education in Russia in the Eighteenth and Nineteenth Centuries, Vol. I. M. Raeff, trans.

St. Petersburg, 1912, 1-5, 8-10.
A discussion of Peter the Great's reforms as a profound boundary mark in the history of Russian education. Rozhdestven-
sky, a specialist in Russian education, agrees with the standard interpretation that the Petrine educational reforms originated in response to the state's need for technical specialists
and competent government servitors rather than as an expression of any cohesive reform plan, but adds that the reforms
served, beside practical requirements, "the broader cultural
interests of society" and, more importantly, introduced a
secular purpose for education where previously none had
existed.

510 Salmony, A. "Gold Collected by Peter the Great." Gaz Beaux
     Arts, 631 (Jan. 1947): 5-14.
     This article is centered upon the collection of Sarmatian gold
     as an art form, however it includes some discussion of Peter
     the Great's contribution to the preservation of these pieces
     and his efforts to develop an institution to preserve antiqui-
     ties in Russia.

511 *Segal, Harold B. "The Age of Peter the Great (1689-1725)."
     The Literature of Eighteenth Century Russia, 2 Vols. New
     York: E. P. Dutton, 1967, 117-48.
     A discussion of the paucity of literature during the reign of
     Peter the Great as a reflection of the overly practical nature
     of his interests and policies. Segal highlights the utilitarian
     quality of Petrine literature by enumerating the technical
     manuals which dominated the book publishing trade and by
     reviewing the service oriented writings of Feofan Prokopo-
     vich, "the most powerful and most influential literary figure
     of the times." Appended is a series of excerpts from the
     literature of this era. PG3213.S4

512 *Shcherbatov, Mikhail M. "Petition of the City of Moscow on
     Being Relegated to Oblivion." Valentine Snow, trans. RIH
     (anthology), 50-55. From Sochineniia. Vol. II. St. Peters-
     burg, 1898, 53-64.
     A recollection of the historical tribulations and glory associ-
     ated with the city of Moscow, and a portrayal of Peter's
     transfer of Russia's capital to St. Petersburg as an act dis-
     dainful of the country's most sacred traditions. Shcherba-
     tov, a leading conservative intellectual and author during the
     reign of Catherine II, writes from the perspective of the city
     itself as he describes its role in Russia's history and pleads
     for its restoration on both cultural and economic grounds as
     the nation's capital.

513 *Shmurlo, Eugene F. "The Opposition of the Traditionalists."
     Mirra Ginsburg, trans. PGCR (anthology), 170-76. From
     Petr Velikii v Ostenske Sovremennikov i Potomstva, Vvp I,

XVIII vek (Peter the Great in the Judgement of Contemporaries and Posterity Fascicle I, the Eighteenth Century). St.
Petersburg, 1912, 1-6.
An examination of the roots of the popular opposition to Peter
the Great and his policies. Shmurlo, a specialist on Russian
culture, identifies as the basic foundation of this opposition
"the anti-national, non-Orthodox character" of Peter's reforms,
policies, and style of rule. Peter's seemingly heretical goals
when combined with the harsh and abrupt means he employed
to realize them led traditionalists to conclude that he was "a
super-human creature, possessed by the devil, born of an
impure virgin-the Anti-Christ himself."

514   Slonim, M. L.   "Peter the Great and the Western Influence."
       Outline of Russian Literature. New York: Oxford Univer-
       sity Press, 1958, 235pp.
       In part, a discussion of the impact of Peter the Great's re-
       forms upon Russian culture. Slonim credits Peter with liberat-
       ing science and the arts from church domination and for pav-
       ing the way for the birth of a native Russian literature later
       in the century but criticizes him for Westernizing only the
       nation's elite and thereby separating it culturally from the
       Russian common people. PG2951.S53

515   *Spassky, I., and E. Shchukina, comps. Medals and Coins of
       the Age of Peter the Great. Leningrad: Aurora Art Pub-
       lishers, 1974, 68pp.
       This collection of color photographs of the coins and medals
       minted during Peter I's reign is of value as an illustration of
       the events and developments which Peter saw fit not only to
       commemorate but to publicize in Russia and Western Europe.
       In a preface, Spassky and Shchukina discuss Peter's influ-
       ence on the theme, subject matter, and artistic design of
       specific coins, most notably those issued in commemoration
       of the Poltava victory, the creation of the Russian navy, the
       founding of St. Petersburg, and the signing of the Nystad
       Treaty. Also of interest is the editors' discussion of Peter's
       use of coins as a means of disseminating abroad an image of
       Russia as a modern and powerful state. CJ6245.L46

516   "Statue of Peter I, St. Petersburg." Liv Age, 5 (28 June
       1845): 591-93.
       An account of the construction and erection of a statue to
       honor Peter the Great for founding the city of St. Peters-
       burg.

517   *Tompkins, S. R.   "Education Under Peter and His Successors."
       RM (gen. study), 29-52.
       A discussion of Peter's various educational reforms and a
       critical assessment of their merits and enduring results.
       Tompkins maintains that the "narrowly utilitarian" view which

Peter I had toward education "permeated the schools and prevented them from achieving much that would have been sound
and lasting." While Peter did have some practical successes
in education, they came through and were dependent upon his
personal initiative and compulsion. Thus following Peter's
death, the schools quickly fell into a state of disrepair and
little of value was left to build upon when attention to education was renewed during the reign of Catherine II.

518   *Vucinich, Alexander. "Peter the Great: Science by Decree."
      Science in Russian Culture. A History to 1860. Stanford:
      Stanford University Press, 1963, 38-74.
      An examination of Peter's various efforts to introduce in Rus-
      sia Western culture by promoting education, particularly in
      the area of science and technology. Vucinich states that the
      wide variety of methods used by Peter to open Russia's doors
      to Western learning was less a tribute to his ingenuity than
      it was a reflection of the failure of cultural Westernization to
      take root. In this sense, the 1725 establishment of the St.
      Petersburg Academy of Sciences was "a last drastic measure"
      to achieve this end and "an admission of the hopelessness of
      doing anything at a lower level and in harmony with the grad-
      ual secularization of Russian society." Vucinich concludes
      that although "more than any other person, Peter opened his
      country to the ideas of modern science," his most important
      and lasting contribution "lay in the realm of the control and
      guidance of scientific pursuits: he made science a govern-
      ment science, a body of knowledge guided and guarded by
      the state." Q127.R9V8

Church and Religion

519   *Bissonnette, Reverend Georges. "The Church Reforms of
      Peter the Great As a Problem in Soviet Historiography."
      Etudes Slav, 1, no. 3 (1956-57):   146-57 and 1, no. 4 (1956-
      57):   195-207.
      An argument that the post-1946 Soviet critics of M. N. Pok-
      rovsky failed to put forth any interpretation to rival his nega-
      tive assessment of the significance of Peter the Great's church
      reforms. Bissonnette maintains that the only Soviet historians
      to diverge at all from Pokrovsky's assessment are Pavlov-
      Silvansky and Platonov, who wrote prior to the establishment
      of an official line on the presentation of Peter's ecclesiastical
      reforms.

520   *_____. "Peter the Great and the Church as an Educational
      Institution." Essays in Russian and Soviet History in Honor
      of Geroid Tanquary Robinson, J. S. Curtiss, ed. New York:
      Columbia University Press, 1963, 3-19.
      An examination of the measures taken by Peter the Great to

harness to a secular cause the Russian church as an educational institution. Bissonnette establishes that Peter diluted
the spiritual content of the studies previously undertaken in
church schools and insisted that the schools teach "absolute
subjection to the will of the Tsar." The church was also to
make the non-Orthodox inhabitants of Russia pliable to Peter's
will by converting them to Orthodoxy. These policies, along
with the increase in the number of ecclesiastical schools serving state needs, lead Bissonnette to conclude that the Russian
church under Peter became "the Tsar's 'Ministry of Education.'" DK4.C8

521   *Consett, Thomas. The Present State and Regulations of the
      Church of Russia Established by the Late Tsar's Royal Edict.
      2 Vols. London: S. Holt, 1729.
      The bulk of volume one of this work consists of documents
      pertaining to Peter's church policy, most notably The Regula-
      tion of the Spiritual College. The author does include, how-
      ever, a lengthy preface (i-lxxvi) in which he maintains that
      the creation of the Holy Synod was necessitated by the fail-
      ure of the Patriarchate to provide effective leadership for the
      church. More specifically, Consett, who served during Peter's
      reign as Chaplain to the British Factory in Russia, states
      that the church was plagued by economic mismanagement,
      superstition, and the miserably low level of education of many
      of its spokesmen, and that a radical restructuring of its ad-
      ministration was essential if its spiritual, educational, and
      economic improvement were to be advanced. Volume two con-
      tains documents relating to a number of Peter's accomplish-
      ments and exploits, including his creation of the Russian fleet
      and his expedition to Derbent in 1722. Consett, who comments
      glowingly on the deeds of Peter reflected in these documents,
      also describes the tsar's sickness and death and gives an ac-
      count of the various orations delivered at his funeral. Con-
      sett's work has been reprinted recently under the title For
      God and Peter the Great. The Works of Thomas Consett,
      1723-1729 (New York: Columbia University Press, 1982),
      edited by James Cracraft. In a preface, Cracraft discusses
      Consett's book as "the first scholarly work on Russia ever
      published in English." DK133.C7

522   *Cracraft, James. The Church Reform of Peter the Great.
      Stanford: Stanford University Press, 1971, 336pp., bib.
      308-22.
      A scholarly discussion of the church reforms of Peter the
      Great as "the decisive step in the secularization of Russian
      society" and therein an essential advance in the broad his-
      torical process of modernization. Drawing on a considerable
      body of primary sources (including official acts, writings by
      Peter and other protagonists in the reform process, memoirs
      and reports of foreign observers, and the proceedings of the

Holy Synod), Cracraft analyzes "the sequence of events
which began in 1700 and which led in the course of twenty
years to the definitive reform of the church, as it was embodied in the provisions of the Ecclesiastical Regulation, as
well as the establishing, official opening, original membership,
and initial administrative problems of the Holy Synod." Cracraft stresses that Peter's radical reorganization of church administration stemmed directly from the influence of Feofan
Prokopovich "who gave concrete expression to the impulsive
dictates of the Tsar." Cracraft concludes that "for all the
achievements of Peter's reign his church reform constituted
the most decisive break with the past." BR935.C7 1971
Reviewed in:
Am Hist R, 29 (1974): 197
Eng Hist R, 88 (1973): 190
Historian, 34 (1972): 508-09
J Eur S, 2 (1972): 116
J Mod Hist, 45, no. 1 (1973): 120-21
Rus R, 31 (1972): 77-79
Slav R, 31 (1972): 153-54
*Slavonic E Eur R, 50 (1972): 276-87

523 *_____. "Feofan Prokopovich." ECR (anthology), 75-105.
An account of how Prokopovich came to the attention of Peter
the Great through preaching sermons in support of Peter and
his accomplishments precedes an examination of Prokopovich's
activities and writings as Peter's chief ideologist from 1718
to 1725. Cracraft states that although Prokopovich's writings
and sermons provided a theoretical justification for Petrine
absolutism and against resistance to the sovereign's will, such
works were only for "the few who cared about politics and
could be reached by logic and learning." It is the Ecclesiastical Regulation, written in 1721 upon a direct request from
Peter the Great, which constitutes Prokopovich's most impressive literary work and his greatest service to Peter, the
spirit of which Cracraft captures well in his description of the
Regulation's finer qualities. Prokopovich emerges from this
essay as a dynamic, learned, and gifted theoretician/politician
who was "devoted to Peter and his memory, and until his
death in 1736 remained a champion of what came to be called
enlightened absolutism."

524 Crummey, Robert O. The Old Believers and the World of the
Anti-Christ. Milwaukee: University of Wisconsin Press, 1970,
258pp., bib. 227-47.
This scholarly work does not contain a separate section on
Peter the Great but includes a number of references to his
Westernization of Russia, church reforms, and treatment of
the Old Believers as the sources for the myth that he was
the Antichrist. Of particular interest is Crummey's discussion of the monarchy's policy toward the Old Believers as a

microcosm of the general Petrine program of modernization.
BX601.C78

525 *Duin, Edgar C. "Peter the Great and the Lutheran Church."
     LUTS (gen. study), 132-37.
     A discussion of Lutheran influence on Peter the Great and his
     policies. Duin states that Peter, through his boyhood fre-
     quenting of the German Quarter and his travels throughout
     Northern Europe, had numerous and favorable contacts with
     a number of Lutherans. These contacts were an important
     source of influence on Peter's attitude toward church-state
     relations as he sought to reshape the organization of the
     Russian church in line with that of the Lutheran state churches
     in Prussia and Sweden and to draw from Protestant theory
     support for his belief in divine right monarchy. Peter also
     sought "to vitalize Russian society by adopting those aspects
     of Protestantism responsible for the vigor of Western society."

526 Graham, Hugh F. "Theophan Prokopovich and the Ecclesiasti-
     cal Ordinance." Church Hist, 26 (1956): 127-35.
     A discussion of the Ecclesiastical Ordinance, written by the
     Ukrainian ecclesiastic Feofan Prokopovich, and sanctioned by
     Peter the Great, which created, in place of a single Patri-
     arch, a college to control and regulate the affairs of the
     church. Graham points out that the Ecclesiastical Ordinance
     was designed to improve the church as an institution (partic-
     ularly in regard to the education of its leaders) but ultimately
     served as a source of enfeeblement by making the church
     "practically defenseless against encroachments by the secular
     authority."

527 *Kartashev, A. A. "Church Reform." PGCR (anthology),
     103-10. From Ocherkii po Istorii Russkoi Tserkvi (Essays on
     the History of the Russian Church), Vol. II. Mirra Gins-
     burg, trans. Paris: YMCA Press, 1959, 311-14, 317-20.
     An argument that, contrary to the claims of historians who
     see Peter's abolition of the Patriarchate and establishment of
     the Holy Synod as the decapitation and emasculation of the
     Orthodox Church, the church in fact "raised its cultural
     standards and expanded its missionary activities" as a conse-
     quence of Peter's reform. Kartashev, a Russian emigré and
     dean of the Russian Orthodox Theological Seminary in Paris
     until his death in 1960, states that during the Synodal period
     following Peter's death, the Orthodox Church expanded almost
     tenfold under the influence of "active and systematic domestic
     and foreign missionary work." Even more impressive was
     the "inner growth of its forces and the forms of its existence,"
     a growth characterized by a tremendous "educational and
     theological upsurge in the energies of the Russian Church."

528 *Lewitter, L. R. "The Church Reform of Peter the Great."

Slavonic E Eur R, 50 (Apr. 1972): 276-87.
A lengthy and favorable review of J. Cracraft's book of the
same title.

529   *Muller, Alexander V. "The Inquisitorial Network of Peter
the Great." Robert L. Nichols and Theofanis G. Stavrou.
Russian Orthodoxy Under the Old Regime. Minnesota:
University of Minnesota Press, 1978, 142-53.
A discussion of Peter the Great's selection of certain church
leaders to serve as inquisitors as a means of improving the
quality of ecclesiastical administration. Muller states that
Peter was particularly concerned with expanding, tightening,
and rationalizing the supervision of and control over inter-
mediate and lower levels of the church hierarchy. The network of inquisitors that Peter established, however, was both
a superficial and short-lived approach to dealing with this
concern, but, Muller concludes, "it provides an illuminating
insight into the intentions, methods, and goals of the Petrine
reform movement." BX491.R87

530   *_____, ed/trans. The Spiritual Regulation of Peter the
Great. Seattle: University of Washington Press, 1972, 150pp.,
bib. 123-36.
A discussion of the roots of Peter the Great's church policy
precedes a translation of The Regulation (Statute) of the
Spiritual College and the supplement to the Spiritual Regulation. In examining the historical background and intellectual
sources of the Spiritual Regulation, Muller places Peter's
formation of an established church within the context of a
general movement occurring at about the same time in other
parts of Europe (especially in Sweden and England) although
"the relationship that came into being between church and
state in Russia did not exactly duplicate other attempted
solutions of this problem in other countries." Muller concludes
that Peter's ecclesiastical reforms were not a mere by-product
of the successive stages of the Petrine program, but rather
they were an integral and highly important part of the sizable
body of legislation that initiated and directed the transformation of the Muscovite state in the first quarter of the eighteenth century...." KR110.S8
Reviewed in:
Can Am Slav S, 8 (1974):   327
Can Slavonic P, 5, no. 3 (1973):   390-91
History, 1, no. 4 (1973):   85
J Ch State, 5, no. 3 (1973):   476-78
Rus R, 32 (1973):   451
Slav R, 32, no. 4 (1973):   804-05

531   *Palmer, William. "Of the Public Punishments Which Fell upon
the Clergy as a Class or Order of Society in Russia." PAT,
Vol. VI (gen. study), 1499-1655.

A detailed discussion of Peter's church policy both as the
natural consequence of the ecclesiastical policy pursued by his
father, Tsar Alexis, and as a form of punishment inflicted by
God upon the clergy for its slavish acceptance of the tsarist
state as the final authority in matters of religion.

532 *Serech, Jurij. "Stefan Yavorsky and the Conflict of Ideologies
in the Age of Peter I." Slavonic E Eur R, 30, no. 74 (1952):
40-62.
In part, an account of the conflicting relations between Peter
I and the Ukrainian churchman/ideologue Stefan Yavorsky.
Serech's discussion illuminates the nature and sources of the
conservative opposition, led by Yavorsky and the Ukrainian
party, which sought to counter Peter's emasculation of the
Orthodox Church.

533 *Zernov, Nicholas. "Peter the Great and the Establishment of
the Russian Church." Church Q R, 125 (Jan. 1983): 265-93.
Also in PGCR (anthology), 111-22.
A critical assessment of the origin and impact of Peter the
Great's reform of the Russian Orthodox Church. Zernov, a
specialist in the history of the Russian church, states that
Peter's ecclesiastical policy was inspired by three concerns:
fear of the church as an institutional rival to the Westernized
monarchy; the desire to use the church as an instrument in
the Westernization of Russia's citizenry; and the need to appropriate ecclesiastical revenue as a means of funding his
military ventures. Zernov maintains that Peter's radical
attack on the church came as a shock to a defenseless clergy
and its lay supporters alike since traditionally the tsars had
been the principal protectors of the Orthodox faith. More
importantly, the tsar's reforms, by depriving the church of
the right to judge the actions of the crown, ultimately led to
the popular impression that the church was but a stooge for
the monarchy and to a consequent decline of the church's
authority in all sections of Russian society and an acceleration
of the secularization process which led eventually to the 1917
revolutions.

534 *Zguta, Russell. "Peter I's 'Most Drunken Synod of Fools and
Jesters.'"
A discussion of the activities of Peter's "Most Drunken Synod
of Fools and Jesters," and an analysis of its origins, particularly its relation to the West European Feast of Fools.

FOREIGN TRAVEL, DIPLOMACY, AND
MILITARY AFFAIRS

535 *Altbauer, Don. "The Diplomats of Peter the Great." Jahr
Ges Ost, 28, no. 1 (1980): 1-16.

An examination of the careers and socio-economic backgrounds
of Peter I's diplomats "in order to ascertain to what extent
Peter had professional or 'amateur' diplomats." Altbauer establishes that of the twenty-three individuals who served
Peter as diplomatic representatives, eighteen were members
of the aristocracy, and, with very few exceptions, this
elite group was a well-educated and exceptionally professional
one which served Peter well and was not at all inferior to
foreign services of other countries. Moreover, Peter's diplomats "were praised and respected in many European courts,
not only as representatives of an emerging power, but also
for their own personality."

536 _____. "The Diplomats of Peter the Great, 1689-1725."
Harvard University, 1976. (dissertation)

537 Anderson, M. S. "Great Britain and the Growth of the Russian
Navy in the Eighteenth Century." Mariner's M, 42, no. 2
(1956): 132-46.
An account of the beneficial influence exerted on the growth
and development of the Russian navy by British shipbuilders
and skilled workers who helped construct and maintain Russian
ships, British subjects who served on these ships (especially
as high ranking officers), and British naval instructors who
trained Russian officers and seamen on British men-of-war.
Anderson devotes most of his attention to the reigns of
Peter I and Catherine II.

538 Anderson, R. C. "Chapters VII-X, 1680-1722." Naval Wars
in the Baltic During the Sailing-Ship Epoch, 1522-1850. London: C. Gilbertwood, 1910, 136-226.
A detailed account of the naval engagements between the
Russian and Swedish fleets during the Northern War with
some reference to Peter's role in the emergence of the Russian
fleet as the foremost naval force in the Baltic. V47.A6

539 Andrusiak, Nicholas. "From Muscovy to Russia: The Battle
of Poltava, 1709." Ukr Q, 18, no. 2 (1962): 167-74.
An argument that the Battle of Poltava was more than a contest between Russia and Sweden, "it was a trial of strength
between two civilizations, that of Europe and of Asia, and
because this was so, the Muscovite victory ... was destined
to be one of the most portentous events in the modern history
of the Western world.... In shadowy forms Poltava was
Marathon in reverse."

540 *Bakhrushin, S. V., and S. D. Skazkin. "Diplomatic Institutions Under Peter I." RRPDH (anthology), 54-60. Excerpt
from "Diplomatiia evropeiskikh gosudarstv v XVIII v" in
Istoriia diplomatii, Vol. I, Moscow, 1959, 344-69.
A favorable Soviet discussion of Peter I's reform of Russia's

diplomatic institutions and selection of capable men to staff
them. The authors state that the scope and complexity of
Peter's foreign policy and the relatively low caliber of the
Russian diplomats at the end of the seventeenth century made
major reform necessary. Although Peter based his innova-
tions on Western models and practices, he did not abandon
Russia's old diplomatic system and customs but rather blended
them with those of the West. In the second half of Peter's
reign Russian diplomats, particularly P. Tolstoy and B. Kura-
kin, were among the most able in Western Europe, although
at all times Peter held "the threads of Russian diplomacy
firmly in his own hands." The authors conclude that "the
strength of Peter's foreign policy consisted in the fact that
Peter concentrated on one problem at a time and was remarkably tenacious in pursuit of his immediate goal."

541   *Benningsen, Alexandre. "Peter the Great, the Ottoman Empire,
      and the Caucasus." Can Am Slav S, 8, no. 2 (Summer 1974):
      311-18.
      A highly critical assessment of Peter the Great's military ven-
      tures on Russia's southern border. Citing Peter's various
      miscalculations, misguided efforts, and defeats in his dealings
      with the Ottoman Empire, the Crimean Tartars, and Persia,
      Benningsen contends that not only do they reflect poorly on
      Peter's claim to military greatness, but they had "lasting and
      tragic results for the Russian monarchy" by embroiling the
      nation in affairs which cost the Romanovs dearly in terms of
      prestige, financial expenditures, and human lives.

542   *Bohlen, Avis. "Changes in Russian Diplomacy Under Peter the
      Great." Cahiers du monde, 7, no. 3 (1966): 341-58.
      An argument that among Peter's reforms, "there were few
      where the transformation was as unequivocal, or its progress
      as readily observable as in diplomacy." In support of this
      contention, Bohlen discusses Peter's establishment of diplo-
      matic missions abroad, recruitment and training of professional
      diplomats, restructuring of the diplomatic corps' organization,
      and his sophistication of diplomatic technique. Bohlen con-
      cludes that Peter's reforms "produced an efficient and coor-
      dinated system of diplomacy which bore little resemblence to
      its Muscovite predecessor."

543   Borshak, Elie. "Early Relations Between England and Ukraine."
      Slavonic E Eur R, 10 (1931-32): 138-60.
      In part, a discussion of George I's contact with and sympathy
      towards the Ukrainian separatist leader Philip Orlik, successor
      to Mazepa, as a facet of the conflict between Peter the Great
      and George I over Baltic affairs.

544   *Bridge, Vice-Admiral Cyprian A. G., ed. History of the Rus-
      sian Fleet During the Reign of Peter the Great by a Contem-
      porary Englishman (1724). London: Navy Records Society,

1899, 161pp.
This anonymous history of Peter the Great's navy focuses on
technical matters dealing with the 1710-1724 operations of the
Russian Baltic fleet, however, it includes some discussion of
his leading role in the fleet's creation and of those instances
in which he personally commanded the navy at sea. The
editor includes an interesting introduction in which he speculates on the identity of the author (most probably an English
officer in Peter's service) and places Peter's naval policy
within a broad historical context. DA70.A1

545 *Bruce, Maurice W. "Jacobite Relations with Peter the Great."
     Slavonic R, 14 (Jan. 1936): 343-62.
     An examination of "the efforts made to interest Peter the
     Great in the Jacobite cause, and to involve him in the prob-
     lems of the English succession by playing on the clash of
     interests between him and George I...." Drawing upon the
     Stuart manuscript collection at Windsor Castle, Bruce estab-
     lishes that, despite the Jacobites' belief that Peter had a
     genuine interest in their cause and would some day undertake
     a campaign against Britain for the restoration of James III,
     the negotiations between St. Petersburg and the Stuart court
     in Rome illustrate that Peter made advances toward the Jacob-
     ites only when to do so would somehow serve the needs of
     Russia. More importantly, Peter refused to consider supply-
     ing military aid to the Jacobites without the direct support
     and participation of the French. Thus when, in 1724-25, the
     moment seemed ripe for Russian action on behalf of the Jacob-
     ites, the coolness of the French government's response to
     the proposal put forth by Peter's emissary led to the tabling
     of the plan.

546 Bulgarin, T. "Charles XII and Peter the Great." New Mo M,
     78 (1846): 17-25.
     Unavailable for annotation.

547 Burnett, Gilbert. "Peter's Journey to England in 1698." RFR
     (anthology), 144-46.
     A brief, firsthand account of Peter I's interests and behavior
     while in England, written by an English bishop who was
     assigned to inform the tsar about the nature of the English
     religion and constitution.

548 Buxhoeveden, Baroness Sophie. A Cavalier in Muscovy. Lon-
     don: Macmillan, 1932, 325pp., bib. 324-25.
     This study focuses on the Russian life of General Patrick
     Gordon, but as an account of the activities of an English
     observer/military-adviser who had numerous contacts with
     Tsars Alexis and Peter I (to 1699) it warrants attention.
     Buxhoeveden discusses the assistance Gordon rendered to
     Peter in reforming the Russian army, conducting the Azov

military campaign, and suppressing the <u>streltsy</u> revolution.
DK114.5.G6B8

549 Cahen, Gaston. <u>History of the Relations of Russia and China</u>
     <u>Under Peter the Great</u>. W. Sheldon Ridge, ed./trans.
     Bangor, Me.: University Prints and Reprints, 1967 (reprint
     of 1914 edition), 128pp.
     This study does not focus upon Peter the Great but contains
     an account of the diplomatic and commercial relations carried
     on in his name from the Treaty of Nerchinsk (1689) to the
     Treaty of Kiakhta (1728). DK68.7.C5C32

550 *Chance, J. F. "George I and Peter the Great After the Peace
     of Nystad." <u>Eng Hist R</u>, 26 (1911): 278-309.
     A discussion of the complex diplomatic negotiations and maneu-
     vers that took place between France and Britain in regard to
     a settlement with Russia in the years immediately following the
     1721 conclusion of the Peace of Nystad. Chance demonstrates
     that George I's desire to protect his Hanoverian possessions
     from a perceived Russian threat led him to do his best to de-
     prive Russia from securing the Baltic territories taken from
     Sweden during the Northern War. The enmity which devel-
     oped between George I and Peter the Great, which had been
     building since 1717, over the Baltic prevented France from
     reaching agreement with Peter with respect to the provisions
     of the Treaty of Nystad because George I insisted that "no
     treaty should be made between France and Russia to which
     he were not a party." While the French were able to obtain
     some small concessions on this matter, the depth of the dif-
     ferences between George I and Peter the Great were such
     that upon Peter's death in February of 1725 essentially "the
     situation remained unchanged."

551 *_____. "Northern Affairs in 1724." <u>Eng Hist R</u>, 27 (1912):
     483-511.
     An intricate account of European reaction to a treaty con-
     cluded between Russia and Sweden in February 1724 which
     contained a clause calling for strong efforts to be made "to
     obtain for the duke of Holstein-Gottorp restitution of his share
     of Sleswick," a proposition which directly threatened Denmark
     and Prussia as well as the Hanoverian possessions of George I
     of Britain. Chance establishes that the concern which the
     treaty prompted led to an acceleration of French efforts to
     reconcile Peter the Great and George I as a means of clearing
     the way for an accord on the Baltic situation mutually accept-
     able to Russia, Britain, and France and the Baltic states con-
     cerned. Negotiations to this end were making guarded prog-
     ress until suspended as a result of Peter's death and the suc-
     cession to the Russian throne by Catherine I who "was credited
     with a hatred of Hanover even greater than his and with a
     special affection for the duke of Holstein-Gottorp."

552 _____. George I and the Northern War: A Study of British
Hanoverian Policy in the North of Europe in the Years 1709
to 1721. London: Smith, Elder and Company, 1909, 516pp.
DA499.C4
Unavailable for annotation.

553 Christien, J. H. L. The Will of Peter the Great; and Little by
Little, or How Russia the Little Has Become Russia the Great.
London, 1854.
Unavailable for annotation.

554 *Clifford, J. Garry. "President Truman and Peter the Great's
Will." Diplo Hist, 4, no. 4 (1980): 371-85.
A discussion of President Truman's perception of Soviet
foreign policy in light of his belief that Peter the Great's alleged "will" constituted "a genuine blueprint" for Russian,
worldwide domination.

555 Coblentz, Stanton A. "Sweden, Russia, and Prussia." From
Arrow to Atom Bomb; the Psychological History of War.
New York: Beechhurst Press, 1953, 252-67.
In part, a discussion of Peter the Great's success in modernizing Russia's military forces as being dependent upon his
ruthlessness, personal vitality, and impatience with the grad-
ualist approach to reform as well as upon the unlimited authority which he possessed. U21.C57

556 Collins, Ruth P. "Birth of a Fleet." Am Merc, 86 (May 1958):
92-96.
A popular account of the birth of the Russian navy as a consequence of Peter's mania for things nautical. Collins describes Peter's first encounter with the sea, travel to England,
and education in navigation and shipbuilding.

557 DeBalbain, Verster J. F. L. Peter the Great at Zaandam and
Amsterdam, 1697-1698. Amsterdam, 1924, 14pp.
Unavailable for annotation.

558 DeKorostovetz, A. "An Ambassador in Trouble." Contemp R,
176 (Sept. 1949): 179-81.
An account of Peter the Great's angry letter to Queen Anne
of England demanding immediate and severe punishment of the
culprits responsible for an attack on the Russian ambassador
to England.

559 *Donnelly, Alton S. "Peter the Great and Central Asia."
Can Slavonic P, 17, no. 2/3 (1975): 202-17.
An examination of Peter the Great's goals and accomplishments
in Central Asia and the degree to which his policies departed
from those of his predecessors. Donnelly establishes that
Peter's interest in Central Asia was essentially commercial

meaning that he hoped to make Russia "the major bridge in
the trade between Asia and Europe." Unfortunately for Russia, Peter's efforts to win over or conquer the Central Asian
Khanates and to construct forts in this region were not only
costly but unsuccessful. Donnelly adds that while Peter's
attempt to control the trade routes to India was consistent
with Russia's Central Asian policy of the seventeenth century,
novel was his plan to divert the flow of the Amu-Darya River
so that his Caspian fleet could be used to assist Russia's advance into Khiva and Bukhara.

560   *Duffy, Christopher. "Peter I, 'the Great' 1682-1725." RMWW
       (gen. study), 9-41.
       An examination of Peter I's military reforms and an assess-
       ment of the quality of the military forces which he created
       and the ways in which he used them. Duffy states that
       although Peter clearly based his reforms on foreign models
       and drew heavily on foreigners for assistance, Peter's success
       in warfare was due primarily to his tenacity, quick intelli-
       gence, and ability to learn from "hard-won experience."
       Within this context, Duffy discusses the Battles of Narva and
       Poltava, reviews the contents of Peter's Military Code of the
       Year 1716, and appraises carefully the manpower and material
       foundations of the Petrine army at the close of the Northern
       War. He concludes that given the underdeveloped nature of
       the Russian economy, the relative smallness of the monarchy's
       revenues, and the "paucity of physical and organisational
       means" for tapping needed resources, Peter created a remark-
       ably effective military machine.

561   *Dvoichenko-Markov, Eufrosina. "William Penn and Peter the
       Great." Proc Am Philo Soc, 97, no. 1 (1953): 12-25.
       A discussion of Peter the Great's interest in and contact with
       English Quakers during his 1698 visit to London. Dvoichenko-
       Markov establishes that Peter found the Quakers to be of in-
       terest not only for their religious beliefs but also because of
       their practical-minded and industrious nature. Peter came to
       meet William Penn because the Quakers who met with the tsar
       initially contacted Penn for assistance in conversing with him
       since both men knew the Dutch language. Dvoichenko-Markov
       draws upon a letter written to Penn by Peter and excerpts
       from the writings of Thomas Story and George Whitehead to
       illustrate the nature of the conversations held between Peter
       and the Quakers and the impressions which the Quakers formed
       in regard to his views and intellect. The author also comments
       on the influence that Peter's English experience may have had
       upon his reform of the Russian Orthodox Church.

562   Edwards, H. Sutherland. Russian Projects Against India from
       Czar Peter to General Skobeleff. London, 1885.
       Unavailable for annotation.

563 Ellis, Sir Henry. History of the Boat Which Gave Peter the
     Great the First Thought of Building the Russian Fleet. Lon-
     don, 1856, 7pp.
     Unavailable for annotation.

564 Eplett, R. W. The Will of Peter, the Great, Emperor of All the
     Russias. Showing the Foundation of Russian Politics for the
     Past Two Hundred Years. London: Ratcliff, 1896.
     Unavailable for annotation.

565 Frederiksen, O. J. "Virginia Tobacco in Russia Under Peter
     the Great." Slavonic E Eur R, 21 (March 1943): 40-56.
     An account of the complexities associated with the 1698 open-
     ing of American tobacco trade to Russia. Frederiksen provides
     most information on the technical difficulties encountered by
     the American merchants who initiated the trade but also places
     the tobacco contract negotiations within the context of Anglo-
     Russian relations in general. Of special interest is the account
     of Peter I's attempt to pirate the secret of tobacco manufactur-
     ing.

566 Golding, Claud. "Peter, Greatest of All the Tsars." Great
     Names in History 356 B.C.--A.D. 1910. Philadelphia: J. B.
     Lippincott, 1935, 173-78.
     A colorful, anecdotal account of Peter's travels, actions, and
     behavior during his four month stay in England in 1698.
     CT104.C6

567 Grey, Ian. "Peter the Great and the Creation of the Russian
     Navy." Hist Today, 11 (Sept. 1961): 625-31.
     An overview of Peter the Great's personal role in the creation
     of the Russian navy. Grey supplements his narrative with a
     number of amusing anecdotes in regard to Peter's Western
     European travels and study of English and Dutch shipbuilding
     and naval technology.

568 _____. "Peter the Great in England." Hist Today, 6 (April
     1956): 225-34.
     A colorful account of Peter I's behavior, interests, and travels
     while in England. Grey devotes most of his attention to de-
     scribing Peter's interest in shipbuilding, naval advancements,
     minting, and other Western technology but also comments on
     Peter's study of the church in England and his visits with
     King William II.

569 Gyllenborg, Count C. The Northern Crisis, or Impartial Re-
     flections on the Policies of the Czar. Occasioned by Mynheer
     Von Stocken's Reasons for Delaying the Descent upon Schoen
     (Memorandum Issued on Behalf of the King of Denmark 10
     October 1716. London: J. Morphew, 1716, 28pp.
     Unavailable for annotation.

570 Hayward, J. F. "A Clock-watch Made for Peter the Great."
     Connois, 158 (Feb. 1965): 86-90.
     A general account of Peter's passionate study of Western
     technology, in its many forms, during his 1698 visit to Eng-
     land, and a description of the technical and artistic character-
     istics of a clock-watch which he purchased in London.

571 *Hellie, Richard. "The Petrine Army: Continuity, Change, and
     Impact." Can Am Slav S, 8, no. 2 (Summer 1974): 237-53.
     A discussion of the changes brought by Peter the Great to
     the Russian army within the confines of the argument that
     "there was no decisive step taken by Peter which was not pre-
     pared in some way by his predecessors." Hellie notes that
     collectively Peter's military reforms resulted in the emergence
     of an army superior to that of seventeenth century Muscovy
     but does not believe that this development in any way alters
     the fact that these reforms only continued established Muscovite
     military trends and policies.

572 Latchford, Henry. "William Penn and Peter the Great." Arena,
     11 (Dec. 1894): 80-89.
     A re-creation of the 1698 meeting between Peter the Great and
     William Penn, and an amusing projection of the different direc-
     tion Russia might have taken if Penn had become Peter's main
     adviser.

573 *Lehovich, Dimitry V. "The Testament of Peter the Great."
     ASEER, no. 2 (1948): 111-24.
     A scholarly investigation of the origins of Peter the Great's
     forged testament. Lehovich states that historians generally
     agree that the 'will' was fabricated in France and was first
     mentioned in print in 1812 by Charles Lesur, of the French
     Ministry of Foreign Affairs, in a propaganda book against
     Russia titled Des Progrès de la puissance russe, but the iden-
     tity of the author of the forgery has not met with such agree-
     ment. Following a review of various theories on this matter,
     Lehovich concludes that the full text of the "will" was the
     product of Frederic Gaillardet who, in an 1836 work titled the
     Memoires du Chevalier d'Eon, forged the testament and at-
     tributed the discovery of the "document" to Chevalier d'Eon,
     a French adventurer of the mid-eighteenth century. Gaillardet
     based his forgery on inflammatory, anti-Russian memoranda
     submitted to the government of Louis XV by Gregory Orlik, an
     embittered Ukrainian emigré and son of Ivan Mazepa. Orlik's
     "gloomy forebodings of Russian expansion," Lehovich adds,
     were also the likely basis of Lesur's forged summary of Peter's
     will.

574 Lemercier-Quelquejay, Chantal. "An Unpublished Document on
     the Campaign of Peter the Great in the Caucasus." Roy Cent
     As J, 54 (June 1967): 174-78.

A translation of a 27 February 1723 letter by the Grand Vizier
of the Ottoman Porte to Hajji Davd Khan, Sovereign of Shirvan
and South Daghestan, which proposed joint action against Peter
the Great as a consequence of his Derbent campaign.

575 *Lewitter, L. R. "The Apocryphal Testament of Peter the Great."
Polish R, 6, no. 3 (Summer 1961): 27-44.
A point by point comparison between the so-called will of Peter
the Great and the policies pursued by Peter and his succesors
serves as the basis for an argument that the document is a
forgery.

576 *_____. "Peter the Great and the Polish Dissenters."
Slavonic E Eur R, 33, no. 80 (1954-55): 75-101.
An examination of Peter's lukewarm support of the Orthodox
population of Poland. Lewitter states that Peter did not want
to appear to be "the champion of Polish disserters" for fear
of driving the Polish oligarchs into an anti-Russian alliance.

577 *_____. "Peter the Great and the Polish Election of 1697."
Camb Hist J, 12, no. 2 (1956): 126-43.
An agrument that Peter the Great's interference in the 1697
Polish election was not the decisive factor in Frederick Au-
gustus' victory but rather was only one of a half-dozen factors which determined the election's outcome. Lewitter maintains that Peter intervened only to secure the election of a
sovereign who would support Russia in its war against Turkey
and not to become the arbiter of Poland. Peter's diplomatic
and military interference achieved this goal and paved the
way for Polish participation in the soon to be established
anti-Swedish coalition.

578 *_____. "Peter the Great, Poland and the Westernization of
Russia." J Hist Ideas, 19, no. 4 (Oct. 1958): 493-506.
An examination of the cultural relations that existed between
Russia and Poland during the reign of Peter the Great for
insight into the nature of Peter's Westernization policy. Lewitter concludes that since "none of the processes that were
transforming the West were at work in Poland" that nation
ceased to be a viable source of enlightenment, in Peter's eyes,
for Russia's governing class. Thus the pronounced Polish
cultural influence on Russia that had existed for a century
came to a halt (with the exception of the Russian clergy) as
Peter looked farther to the West for enlightenment of a more
practical kind than that offered by Poland.

579 *_____. "Poland, Russia and the Treaty of Vienna of 5
January 1719." Hist J, 13, no. 1 (1970): 3-30.
A discussion of the 1719 Treaty of Vienna as an instrument
designed to prevent a possible Russo-Swedish-Prussian alliance
that would redistribute the disputed lands of Europe's Baltic

coast. Lewitter states that although the death of Charles XII
just prior to the defensive Treaty of Vienna served to end all
chances of the feared alliance being formed, the diplomatic preliminaries to the treaty had had such a dampening effect on
Russo-Prussian relations that an alliance between the two nations
was quite unlikely. Although the immediate aims of the Treaty
of Vienna were met even before it was concluded, its ultimate
aim, the re-establishment of peace in northern Europe and the
limiting of Peter's territorial ambitions, could not be accomplished without converting the alliance into an offensive coalition which would include Poland and Prussia.

580 *_____. "Russia, Poland and the Baltic, 1697-1721." Hist J,
      11, no. 1 (1968): 3-34.
      A discussion of the circumstances which led Peter I and Augus-
      tus II of Poland to agree on joint military action against Lith-
      uania and Sweden, and an examination of Peter's nullification
      of his agreement with Augustus and unilateral pursuit of a
      legalization of Russia's Baltic acquisitions. Lewitter concludes
      that Augustus was the victim of an over-powerful ally who
      saw fit to draw upon Polish support until Russia gained the
      upper hand over Sweden and then ignore Poland when the
      time arrived to share in the spoils of war at Sweden's expense.

581 *Lockhart, Laurence. "The 'Political Testament' of Peter the
      Great." Slavonic R, 14, no. 41 (1935-36): 438-41.
      A history of the 'will' of Peter the Great precedes an analysis
      of the portion of the testament which relates to Persia. Lock-
      hart questions the authenticity of the will because it advocates
      Russian penetration to the Persian Gulf, a move which con-
      flicts historically with Peter's policies in that region and with
      his known desire for a trade route far to the east of Persia.

582 Loewenson, Leo. "The First Interviews Between Peter I and
      William II in 1697: Some Neglected English Historical Material."
      Slavonic E Eur R, 36, no. 87 (June 1958): 308-16.
      An argument in favor of the veracity of eighteenth-century
      reports that Peter I delivered to William II a praiseful speech
      during a private conference with him in Utrecht in September
      of 1697. Drawing primarily on the diary of Narcissus Luttrell,
      Loewenson not only demosntrates that the speech certainly was
      given by Peter but also that William and Peter met twice at this
      time. While the eighteenth-century accounts of Peter's speech
      take liberties with its wording, Loewenson concludes, the
      essence of the speech "is certainly in keeping with Peter's
      mind and mood at the time."

583 _____. "People Peter the Great Met in England: Moses
      Stringer, Chymist and Physician." Slavonic E Eur R, 37
      (1958-59): 459-68.
      An account of the meeting between M. Stringer and Peter

where the former entertained the tsar with certain scientific
experiments and was impressed by Peter's scientific knowledge.

584 *_____. Some Details of Peter the Great's Stay in England
     in 1698." Slavonic E Eur R, 40 (June 1961-62): 431-43.
     Drawing from a wide range of previously untapped sources,
     this article provides new facts and amusing anecdotes on Pe-
     ter I's arrival in London, the entertainment provided for him,
     the individuals who came to his establishment in Deptford,
     and the places he visited.

585 Magrúder, A. B. "The Will of Peter I, and the Eastern Ques-
     tion." Atlan M, 42 (July 1878): 34-37.
     A warning that Russia is on the verge of solving the Eastern
     Question in a manner consistent with that prescribed in the
     "will" of Peter the Great.

586 Maland, David. "The Great Northern War, 1700-21." Europe
     in the Seventeenth Century. New York: St. Martin's Press,
     1966, 413-36.
     A portrayal of the Northern War as the principal manifestation
     of Peter I's desire "to acquire for Russia not merely a window
     to the West but a place within the European concert of na-
     tions." Maland discusses Peter's Western travels, military re-
     forms, and various efforts to modernize Russia's institutions
     and culture as offshoots of the tsar's more fundamental con-
     cern for establishing Russia as a European power of the first
     rank. The author concludes that while Peter's domestic re-
     forms failed to Europeanize Russia, the victory in the Northern
     War guaranteed the realization of his primary goal.
     DK246.M28

587 Marble, E. "The Will of Peter the Great." New Eng M, n.s.
     32 (July 1905): 579-84.
     A discussion of the Russo-Japanese War as a manifestation of
     the aggressive foreign and military policies outlined in Peter
     I's will.

588 *Marriott, Sir J. A. R. "The Emergence of Russia Under Peter
     the Great." Anglo-Russian Relations. 1689-1943. London:
     Methuen, 1944, 27-37.
     A portrayal of Peter I's reign as one which "not only marked
     the opening of a new phase in the history of Russia, but
     fundamentally upset the political system of Northern Europe,
     the Near East, and indeed the whole of Europe, ... (and)
     opened the way to the prolonged rivalry between Russia and
     England." Within this context, Marriott discusses Russia's
     military and diplomatic relations with Turkey, Sweden, and
     England, including Peter's 1722 involvement in a Jacobite plot
     to depose George I who, as the Elector of Hanover and King
     of England, opposed Peter's Northern policy. DA47.65.M35

589 A Memorial Presented to His Britannik Majesty, by Monsieur
     Wellelowsky, Minister from His Czarish Majesty. London:
     J. Roberts, 1717, 15pp.
     An official Russian denial of the charge that Peter the Great
     was involved in a conspiracy designed to incite rebellion among
     George I's Hanoverian subjects. Wellelowsky, a special envoy
     from St. Petersburg, asserts that anti-Russian elements within
     the British government were the source of the allegations made
     against Peter. As proof of Peter's innocence, Wellelowsky re-
     lates Peter's desire "to give fresh instances" of Russia's
     friendship toward Britain by granting new trade advantages
     and by working in common to promote a lasting peace in the
     Baltic region. DA503.1717.R9

590 *Mitchell, Donald W. "Peter the Great: Father of the Russian
     Navy." A History of Russian and Soviet Sea Power. New
     York: Macmillan, 1974, 16-41.
     In discussing Peter I as the father of the Russian navy, this
     chapter presents a balance of information on Peter as both a
     naval architect and strategist. Mitchell establishes that Peter
     was far more successful in constructing ships than in staffing
     them, and that while shipbuilding during his reign was impres-
     sive quantitatively, the quality of Russian ships left much to
     be desired. As a strategist, however, Peter was quick to
     learn from errors and shortcomings revealed in battle and was
     always prompt to exploit success. DK56.M48

591 *Nikolaieff, Alexander M. "Peter the Great as a Military Lead-
     er." Army Q Def J, 80, no. 1 (April 1980): 76-86.
     A favorable account of Peter the Great's treatment of Russia's
     defeat at Narva at the hands of Charles XII as an experience
     from which to learn how to reshape Russia's army and military
     strategy and tactics. Nikolaeff states that Russia's victory
     over Sweden at Poltava was the direct result of Peter's mili-
     tary reforms, careful preparations for battle, skillful position-
     ing of troops, and construction of redoubts to neutralize
     Charles XII's skill at maneuvering troops on the battlefield.

592 *The Northern Crisis, or Reflections on the Policies of the Tsar.
     London, 1716.
     An anonymous inflammatory publication which aroused anti-
     Russian feeling in England by ascribing to Peter the Great
     vast schemes for territorial conquest. The pamphlet, which
     was widely read, develops an image of Peter as a power-crazed
     tyrant who intended to seize for Russia the entire Baltic
     coastline. It also highlights the danger posed by the Russian
     fleet to British interests and security.

593 The Northern Heroes; or, The Bloody Conflict Between Charles
     the Twelfth, King of Sweden, and Peter the Great, Czar of
     Muscovy.... London: M. Cooper, 1748, 35pp.

The script of a historical drama, staged in 1748 London, on
the circumstances surrounding Charles XII's decision to invade
the Ukraine and his eventual defeat at Poltava by the forces
of Peter the Great.   PR1241.L6V33

594 O., V. "The Abduction of Andriy Voynarovsky by Tsar Peter
     I." Ukr R, 10, no. 4 (1963):   46-59.
     A discussion of the 1716 abduction by Peter the Great of the
     Ukrainian leader Andrei Voynarovsky, nephew of Ivan Mazepa,
     and an examination of the ruthless and inhuman methods em-
     ployed by Russian rulers then and in the twentieth century.
     The author sees a threefold purpose for the abduction: to
     acquire knowledge of Sweden's activities and plans, gain in-
     formation about relations between Ukrainian emigres and their
     native countrymen so as to root out the liberation movement's
     leaders and supporters, and shatter Ukrainian hopes that the
     successor to Mazepa as hetman would be one of his close rela-
     tives.

595 O'Conor, C. P. "Peter I at Deptford." New Mo M, 171 (1883):
     174.
     Unavailable for annotation.

596 "Peter the Great and Syria." Blackw M, 127 (May 1880):   561-
     77.
     An argument that Peter the Great's interest in Russian expan-
     sion into Central Asia infected his successors with the same
     ambition.

597 "Peter the Great in England." House W, 12 (6 Oct. 1855):   223-
     28.
     A general review of Peter I's motives for visiting England in
     1698, his itinerary while in England, the personal contacts
     that he had, and the "barbarous lifestyle" of Peter and his
     entourage.

598 "Peter the Great Would Be Proud." Nat R, 30 (18 Aug. 1878):
     1005-06.
     A discussion of the Soviet military presence in South Yemen
     as yet another sign of the vitality of Peter the Great's "politi-
     cal testament."

599 Peter the Great's Last Will and Testament.   And Russian Versus
     Bulgarian Atrocities.   Southsea: Mills and Sons, 1876, 17pp.
     Unavailable for annotation.

600 Pinci, A. R. "Peter the Great: Stalin's Ghost; Soviet Russia
     Adopts Controversial Will As Its International Blueprint."
     Cath W, 171 (July 1950):   246-52.
     A point by point application of the aggressive military pre-
     scriptions in Peter I's "will" to the post-1945 foreign policy
     followed by Joseph Stalin.

601 Pool, Bernard. "Peter the Great on the Thames." Mariner's
     M, 59, no. 1 (Feb. 1973): 9-12.
     An account of Peter the Great's firsthand study of English
     shipbuilding and navigation and his recruitment of British
     shipwrights and seamen for service in Russia. Pool also
     describes how Peter's mishandling of the Dove, a small yacht,
     twice nearly resulted in collisions with other vessels on the
     Thames River.

602 *Resis, Albert. "Russophobia and the 'Testament' of Peter
     the Great, 1812-1980." Slav R, 44, no. 4 (1985): 681-93.

603 *Roberts, Louise B. "Peter the Great in Poland." Slavonic R,
     5, no. 15 (Mar. 1927): 537-51.
     A review of Peter's "policy of influence" in Poland. Roberts
     argues that "Peter's success in establishing his system in Po-
     land, a system made up of bribery, intimidation, and skillful
     manipulation of the differences between the King (Augustus
     II) and his subjects," set the tone for Russian policy toward
     Poland in the mid-eighteenth century, and thus contributed
     significantly to Poland's eventual loss of sovereignty.

604 *Ross, O. C. Dalhousie. "The Chevalier d'Eon and Peter the
     Great's Will." Gent M, 242 (Feb. 1877): 159-75.
     A discussion of the assertion made by M. Gaillardet, the
     author of a biography of the French diplomat Chevalier d'Eon,
     that d'Eon, on his return from Russia in 1757, had given a
     copy of Peter the Great's "will" to the Minister of Foreign
     Affairs of Louis XV, the Abbé Bernis. If true, this refutes
     the Russian claim that the will was a forgery of Napoleon I,
     who first published the document on the eve of his 1812 in-
     vasion of Russia. Ross maintains that the most interesting
     feature of the will is not its authorship but rather its accuracy
     as a record, if not a blueprint, of Russia's conquests and ter-
     ritorial ambitions. This article was written as a response to
     an 1877 formal protest issued by Alexander II to the British
     government in regard to the credence being given in London
     to the legitimacy of Peter the Great's will.

605 Ryan, W. F. "Peter the Great's English Yacht. Admiral Lord
     Carmarthen and the Russian Tobacco Monopoly." Mariner's
     M, 69 (Feb. 1983): 65-87.
     Unavailable for annotation.

606 Scott, Richenda C. "Peter the Great Has Visitors and Catherine
     the Great an Englishman." Quakers in Russia. London:
     Michael Joseph, 1964.
     An account of Peter the Great's contacts while in England in
     1698 with various Quakers. Scott discusses the substance of
     Peter's conversation with the Quakers, his attendance at
     Quaker meetings in Deptford, and his later contact (during

the Northern War) with a group of Quakers in the town of
Friedrichstadt in Holstein. BX7710.R8S35

607 *Shafirov, P. P. A Discourse Concerning the Just Causes of
the War Between Sweden and Russia: 1700-1721. William E.
Butler, intro. Dobbs Ferry, N.Y.: Oceana Publishers, 1973
(reprint of 1723 edition), 351pp.
The official Petrine version of the legal grounds for Russia's
war with Sweden. The Discourse is not only a valuable source
of information on Peter's views on the Northern War and
Swedish-Russian relations in general, but, as stated in an
introduction by William E. Butler, it "provides one of the
earliest and best indicators of the extent to which Russia
had assimilated, linguistically and conceptually, the principles
and practices of international law generally accepted in Western
Europe of that day." More generally, Butler discusses Shafirov's work as a "landmark in Russian international legal history." DK136.S45

608 *Subtelny, Orest. "Mazepa, Peter I, and the Question of
Treason." Harv Ukr S, 2, no. 2 (June 1978): 158-83.
An examination of the charge of treason associated with
Ukrainian Hetman Ivan Mazepa's abandonment of Peter's cause
for that of Charles XII. Subtelny maintains that "by repeatedly charging Mazepa with treason, Peter was not attempting merely to establish guilt or to make propaganda; he was
imposing on the Ukrainians a new set of values--those of the
state--and judging them by it. The issue of Mazepa's treason
marked the point when the conception of the all-Russia state
as an institution capable of encompassing both societies had
entered the Ukrainian-Russian relationship."

609 *_____. "'Peter I's Testament': A Reassessment." Slav R,
33, no. 4 (Dec. 1974): 663-78.
An examination of the forged "Testament of Peter I" with stress
on misconceptions about the document's title, origins, and
authorship. Subtelny concludes that "the roots of the document reach into the beginning, rather than the end of the
eighteenth century, that it evolved over a period of time
and was not therefore the creation of one person; that it was
used not only to sway public opinion but also court politics;
and that 'Peter's plan' typically resurfaced whenever Eastern
European political emigrés and members of the French Foreign
ministry met."

610 *_____. "Russia and the Ukraine: The Difference That
Peter I Made." Rus R, 39, no. 1 (Jan. 1980): 1-17.
The stated purpose of this study is "to examine more closely
the nature of Peter I's reforms in the Ukraine and to assess
their impact on the ties between Russia and the Ukraine."
Subtelny concludes that Peter transformed the Russian-Ukrainian

relationship from one which "was ambiguous, limited and loose"
to one which enabled Peter "to have direct control, through
the traditional institutions of statehood, over the Ukraine and
thereby exploit the human and material resources of the region."

611 *Sumner, B. H. Peter the Great and the Ottoman Empire.
     Hamden, Conn.: Archon Books, 1965, 80pp.
     A scholarly survey of the diplomatic and military policies fol-
     lowed by Peter I in regard to the Ottoman Empire. Sumner
     establishes the goals of Peter's southern policy and discusses
     the factors which stood in the way of their realization. He
     maintains that although Russia had little military success in
     the south, Peter did establish Russia's claim as protector of
     the Ottoman Empire's Orthodox population, advance the princi-
     ple that freedom of navigation should prevail on the Black
     Sea, and promote more rational communication with Turkish
     leaders through the establishment of permanent diplomatic
     representation in Constantinople. DK135.S8
         Reviewed in:
         Ann Am Acad, 278 (Nov. 1951): 235
         Slav R, 10, no. 1 (1951): 76
         Slavonic E Eur R, 29/30, no. 2 (1950-52): 270
         TLS, (29 June 1951): 407

612 Thoms, William J. "Will of Peter I." Nineteenth C, 4, no. 17
     (July 1878): 88-97.
     An argument that those who contend that the so-called will
     of Peter the Great was forged by Napoleon are in error and
     that even if the will is not genuine it nonetheless is an accu-
     rate portrayal of the course of Russian foreign policy in the
     150 years since Peter's death.

613 Thomson, Gladys Scott. "Peter the Great and the Russian
     Frontier." Geog M, 28 (1955): 201-15.
     A discussion of Peter the Great's efforts to expand Russia's
     borders to the south and north as a means of gaining access
     to sea. Thomson states that early setbacks suffered by Peter
     at the hands of the Turks and his inability to win Western
     support for future campaigns against the Ottoman Empire led
     him to look toward the Baltic coast for an outlet to the sea.
     Thomson reviews the highlights of Peter's Northern War against
     Charles XII of Sweden, and she concludes with a straight-
     forward summary of the significance of the gains made by
     Peter at the expense of Sweden.

614 *Tokarzewski-Karaczewicz, Prince Jan. "The Battle of Poltava."
     Ukr R, 6, nos. 2-3 (1959): 13-20, 49-67.
     A discussion of Peter's victory at Poltava as a disaster both
     for Ukrainian independence and the security of all Europe.
     The author also gives an account of the battle itself and

Hetman Mazepa's participation in it to prevent Peter from
realizing his goal.

615   Van Amstel, Marie.   "Will of Peter the Great."   Am Merc, 77
       (Dec. 1953):   77-79.
       A reproduction of Peter the Great's alleged "will," and a
       discussion of Russian international behavior.

616   Wayne, T. G.   "The Naval Aid to Russia: Those Were the
       Days."   Tablet, 185 (14 April 1945):   173-74.
       A brief account of Peter I's use of foreign technology and
       manpower in the construction, maintenance, and staffing of
       the Russian navy; based primarily on Vice-Admiral Cyprian
       Bridge's History of the Russian Fleet 1724.

617   White, Percy E.   The Will of Peter the Great.   The History of
       the Will and Russian Policy.   London: Colston Press, 1920.
       Unavailable for annotation.

618   Whitton, F. E.   "Peter: A Navy Builder."   Blackwood's M,
       (Oct. 1933):   528-41.
       Unavailable for annotation.

619   "The Will of Peter the Great."   Liv Age, 138 (1878):   320.
       A brief discussion of the authenticity of Peter the Great's
       will.

620   "William Penn and Peter the Great."   Russia, no. 170 (1957):
       9-15.
       Unavailable for annotation.

621   Williams, Basil.   Stanhope.   A Study in Eighteenth Century War
       and Diplomacy.   Westport, Conn.:   Greenwood Press, 1979
       (reprint of 1932 edition), 478pp.
       This study of English diplomacy during the Northern War
       does not include a separate section on Peter I, but it can be
       consulted with profit for insights into England's reaction to the
       startling emergence of the Russian navy as a force to be con-
       tended with in the Baltic region and to the military reverses
       suffered by Charles XII at the hands of Peter's modernized
       army.   DA497.S8W5

622   Woodward, David.   "Into the Baltic (1703-1725)" and "Into the
       Black Sea (1975-1738)."   The Russians at Sea.   London:
       William Kimber, 1965, 20-37.
       An account of the engagements between the Russian fleet
       and the navies of Sweden and the Ottoman Empire with con-
       siderable mention of Peter's qualities as a naval strategist
       and tactician and his efforts to staff the Russian navy with
       competent officers and crew.   DK56.W6

623 Wren, Sir Christopher. "Peter the Great at Sayes Court,
     Deptford." Notes & Q, no. 19 (10 May 1856): 365-67.
     A list of the damages sustained by the house at which Peter
     the Great and his entourage resided while in England in 1698.
     Also included is the owner's petition to the English govern-
     ment for compensation for the cost of repairs.

624 Wykoff, George S. "The History of a Leter." Penn M, 66
     (1942): 94-105.
     The history of a letter written by William Penn to Peter the
     Great in which Penn implores Peter to rule with fairness,
     charity, and Christian morality.

                               FICTION

625 *Gasiorowska, Xenia. The Image of Peter the Great in Russian
     Fiction. Madison: University of Wisconsin Press, 1979,
     199pp., bib. 191-94.
     A presentation of the composite image of Peter the Great
     "established in the popular mind primarily by historical novel-
     ists." Gasiorowska divides her study into three parts. Part
     one deals with "the genre of historical fiction; its interrela-
     tionship with history and the anecdotic and undocumented
     materials known as petite histoire, and the techniques which
     writers use in blending facts with fiction," while parts II
     and III "present the characterization of Peter the Great in
     Russian historical novels achieved, respectively, through his
     appearance and actions, and through human relationships"
     and interaction with his environment. Gasiorowska analyzes
     over sixty fictional works and, in the process, sheds consid-
     erable light on the origin, nature, and dissemination of the
     Petrine legend. She does not address the question of whether
     the image of Peter in Russian fiction "is true to the historical
     original." PG3098.H5G3
         Reviewed in:
         Can Am Slav S, 14, no. 4 (1980): 535-44
         Mod Lang S, 64 (Autumn 1980): 374-75
         TLS, (4 Jan. 1980): 17
         World Lit T, 54 (Spring 1980): 300-01

626 Merezhkovsky, D. S. Peter and Alexis. London: A. Constable,
     1905, 556pp.
     An artistic portrayal of the clash between Peter I, as the
     symbol of the "new Russia," and Alexis, his heir, as the per-
     sonification of the traditions of old Muscovy. Merezhkovsky
     bases his novel on the 1716-1718 period (though flashbacks
     to Alexis' youth do appear) and draws upon a rich store of
     primary source material as he presents a compelling account of
     the opposition to Peter and Petrine Russia. PG3467.M4K512

627   Morton, Peter, and William Peterson. "Peter the Great and Rus-
      sia in Restoration and Eighteenth Century Drama." Notes &
      Q, 199 (Oct. 1954): 427-32.
      A brief survey of English eighteenth-century drama stimulated
      by Peter the Great's trip to England.

628   *Pushkin, Aleksander. The Bronze Horseman. T. E. Little,
      ed./intro. Hertfordshire, England: Bradda Books, 1974,
      84pp.
      As the product of Russia's greatest poet, The Bronze Horse-
      man is at once an artistic masterpiece and an intriguing por-
      trayal of not only Peter the Great but also the city of St.
      Petersburg as the symbol of the Petrine spirit and reforms.
      Pushkin's motivation for writing The Bronze Horseman, the
      symbolism which he employs in it, and the poem's overall
      meaning have been the focus of a considerable body of scholar-
      ship, a small sample of which is listed in the following seven
      entries (628a-628g).

628a Banerjee, Maria. "Pushkin's The Bronze Horseman: An
      Agnostic Vision." Mod Lang S, 8, (Spring 1978): 47-64.
      An argument that the dramatic contest in The Bronze Horse-
      man between Peter the Great and the poor clerk Evgeny is
      not best interpreted as a victory or defeat for one or the
      other of the characters but rather as a somewhat open-ended
      statement made by Pushkin in regard to Russia's historical
      destiny: "Pushkin's apostrophe of the Horseman ... is not an
      epigrammatic summary of things as they stood, but an open
      question thrown at the future of Russia."

628b Burton, Dora. "The Theme of Peter as Verbal Echo in Mednyj
      Vsadnik." Slav E Eur J, 26 (Spring 1982): 12-26.
      An argument that, contrary to what many analysts claim, there
      is consistency in Pushkin's conception of Peter the Great as
      presented in The Bronze Horseman.

628c Call, Paul. "Pushkin's 'Bronze Horseman': A Poem of Motion."
      Slav E Eur J, 11 (Summer 1967): 137-44.
      A study of the dynamism ("the sensation of motion") created
      by Pushkin in The Bronze Horseman, with some discussion of
      the contrasts in the poem between Peter and Evgeny.

628d Gregg, Richard. "The Nature of Nature and the Nature of
      Eugene in The Bronze Horseman." Slav E Eur J, 21 (1977):
      167-79.
      Within the broader context of the polarity in The Bronze Horse-
      man between the forces of chaos and order, Gregg advances
      the interpretation that Evgeny's rebellion against the image of
      Peter is psychologically rooted in Evgeny's character and his
      tragic life.

628e *Lednicki, Waclaw. Pushkin's Bronze Horseman. The Story
      of a Masterpiece. Westport, Conn.: Greenwood, Press, 1978
      (reprint of 1955 edition), 163pp.
      A scholarly analysis of the genesis and fundamental themes
      of Pushkin's The Bronze Horseman. Lednicki focuses on the
      influence exerted on Pushkin by the monument to Peter the
      Great sculpted by Falconet and Mickiewicz's poem Monument
      of Peter the Great, and then traces through The Bronze
      Horseman the themes of Petersburg, Peter the Great, and
      the Emperor. He maintains that the poem is characterized by
      a tragic, irreconcilable dualism between the omnipotent state,
      symbolized by Peter, and individual freedom, symbolized by
      Evgeny, a dualism Pushkin sorely felt in his own conflict with
      tsarist authority. PG3343.M43L4
         Reviewed in:
         J Cent Eur Aff, 16 (1956–57): 430
         Rus R, 16, no. 2 (1957): 79
         Slavonic E Eur R, 35 (1956–57): 319

628f Newman, John K. "Pushkin's 'Bronze Horseman' and Epic
      Tradition." Comp Lit S, 9 (June 1972): 173–95.
      A discussion of The Bronze Horseman for consistencies with
      the European epic tradition. Newman states that Pushkin's
      "emphasis on the unexpected, introduction of the anti-hero,
      purification of language, combined with colloquialisms, learn-
      ing and musicality, were all employed to revivify the decaying
      Homeric manner," and, therefore, the poem should not be
      viewed as simple social satire nor as an example of contem-
      porary European poetry. Although Pushkin failed to recon-
      cile the public and private domains in The Bronze Horseman,
      Newman maintains, he suggests that without such an accommo-
      dation Russia's future would be a bleak one.

628g Trensky, Paul. "Peter the Great in Pushkin." Zapiski Russ
      Akad Gr, 7 (1973): 239–50.
      Unavailable for annotation.

629   *Tolstoi, Alexis. Peter the Great. Edith Bone and Emile
      Burns, trans. London: Victor Gollancz Limited, 1936, 463pp.
      A thoroughly researched historical novel which presents an
      intriguing and insightful portrait of the early life and reign
      of Peter the Great. Tolstoi, a noted Soviet writer, intended
      to conclude his novel with Peter's 1709 victory over Sweden
      at the Battle of Poltava but died before completing his work.
      DK131.T6
         Reviewed in:
         Nation, 142 (22 Apr. 1936): 522
         New Rep, 88 (19 Aug. 1936): 53
         Sat R, 13 (28 Mar. 1936): 5
         Spectator, 155 (8 Nov. 1935): 790
         TLS, (16 Nov. 1935): 748

630 "After Peter the Great." Nation, 71 (July 1900): 48-49.
As part of a review of K. Waliszewski's L'Hérédité de Pierre
le Grand, this article surveys the political instability which
attended the reigns of Catherine I and Peter II.

631 Bain, R. Nisbet. "Catherine Aleksyeevna on the Throne."
PPG (gen. study), 71-113.   NA
This positive survey of Catherine I's brief tenure as empress
focuses primarily on foreign policy and the court influence of
A. Yaguzhinsky, P. Tolstoy, and A. Menshikov. Bain states
despite Catherine's generally intelligent rule and pursuit of
a policy of conciliation toward those aristocrats who resented
her because of her low birth, court intrigue was rampant
during her reign. Given the powerful nature of this opposition and Catherine's political inexperience, Bain maintains, the
empress deserves considerable credit for being able to maintain Russia on the course set by Peter I.

632 _____. "Reign of Peter II." Ibid., 114-57.
A discussion of the influence exerted during Peter II's brief
reign by two of Peter the Great's 'pupils', A. Menshikov
and A. Ostermann. Bain presents Menshikov as a vigorous,
capable, and economical regent who was nonetheless despised
because he had usurped the position of regent and exercised
his authority in a tyrannical fashion. The consequent overthrow of Menshikov by "a junta of narrow-minded, self-seeking
Patricians" might have led to the ruination of Russia had it
not been for the counter-acting influence of Ostermann who
had the favor of his pupil, the youthful Peter II. The attempt by members of the Dolgoruky family to shape to their
advantage governmental policy as well as the personal predilections of Peter occupies the last section of this chapter.
Bain concludes that although Peter lacked the qualities necessary to be a great ruler, he most likely could have been a
capable one had he relied more upon the counsel of Ostermann.

633 Coxe, William. "Of Catherine I." TRPSD (gen. study), 493-512.

947.01
C83

An account of Catherine I's "early adventures" precedes a
discussion of her relationship with Peter the Great and her
brief reign as empress. Coxe devotes most attention to Catherine's initial relationship with Peter, the question of succession to the throne upon Peter's death, and the rule of Russia
by Menshikov, in Catherine's name, a political eventuality she
accepted willingly since she had "neither the inclination nor
abilities to direct the helm of government." Primarily based
on the writings of Weber, Bruce, and Voltaire.

634 *Kirchner, Walther. "The Death of Catherine I." Am Hist R,
     5, no. 2 (1946): 254-61.
     A discussion of a previously unpublished report, written
     sometime between 1730 and 1733 by the Danish Ambassador
     Hans Georg von Westphalen, which describes the intrigues
     which characterized the court of Catherine I in regard to the
     identity of her successor. Westphalen records his efforts to
     oppose the candidacy of the Duke of Holstein, the husband
     of Catherine's eldest daughter, with that of Grand Duke
     Peter, the grandson of Peter the Great. Westphalen's efforts
     were successful because he was able to enlist the support of
     Alexander Menshikov by proposing that Menshikov's daughter
     marry Grand Duke Peter. Menshikov in turn secured the
     approval of the seriously ill Catherine, but she died before
     actually signing the will which would have legitimized Peter's
     claim to the throne. Menshikov therefore arranged for Cath-
     erine's daughter Elizabeth to sign the will in the name of her
     mother thus making the testament "the greatest forgery on
     earth."

635 LeBovier de Fontonelle, Bernard. "Memoirs of Catherine, Em-
     press and Sovereign of All Russia." Northern Worthies; or,
     The Lives of Peter the Great and of His Illustrious Consort,
     Catherine the Late Czarina. London: E. Mory, 1728, 92pp.
     An account of Catherine's relationship with and influence on
     Peter the Great, and a favorable review of her 1725-1727
     reign. The author provides a number of examples to illustrate
     his claim that Peter valued Catherine's opinion and sought her
     advice on all important affairs of state. In examining Cath-
     erine's rule as empress, Fontonelle commends her for follow-
     ing the same general policies as Peter the Great. He con-
     cludes that "if the Empress Catherine had not succeeded to
     the Crown fully instructed in all the views of Peter the
     Great" the deceased emperor's policies most certainly would
     not have been followed: "she took up the thread, and fol-
     lowed him."

636 Longworth, Philip. "Catherine I." The Three Empresses.
     Catherine I, Anne and Elizabeth of Russia. New York:
     Holt, Rinehart and Winston, 1973, 1-76.
     An unflattering portrait of Catherine I as "a simple, meek and

undemanding woman who yearned only for security and love."
Longworth devotes most attention to describing Catherine's
relationship with Peter the Great and dismisses her brief
reign as one in which she played no positive role: "she
allowed herself to be put on public display, she enjoyed being
surrounded with all the pomp and panoply of power, but she
left more and more decisions to her Ministers, above all to
Alexander Menshikov." By the end of her reign, Longworth
asserts, Catherine was a pathetic creature wholly absorbed
with excessive drinking and pleasure seeking as a means of
soothing her feelings of inadequacy. DK151.L65

637 Mottley, John. The History of the Life and Reign of the Empress Catharine, 2 Vols. London: William Meadows and M.
Read, 1744.
Volume I of this narrative contains a history of Russia through
the early eighteenth century, while volume II contains a detailed account of Catherine's relationship with Peter I, accession to the throne, and principal policies. In describing
Catherine I's reign, Mottley concentrates on the empress'
dealings with Turkey, Persia, Denmark, and Sweden, while
merely reviewing her domestic concerns and personal life.
Although Mottley offers no overall judgment of Catherine's
effectiveness as a ruler, he presents her in a generally favorable light and attributes to her prudence, dignity, and
magnanimity.

638 The Northern Heroine. Being Authentik Memoirs of the Late
Czarina, Empress of Russia. London: H. Curll, 1727, 28pp.
Unavailable for annotation.

639 Scott, George R. "Catherine I." Ten Ladies of Joy. London:
Torchstream Books, 1950, 91-104.
Unavailable for annotation.

640 Shipman, Henry Robinson. "Russian Foreign Policy Under
Catherine I." Harvard University, 1904. (dissertation)

641 Stong, Philip. Marta of Muscovy. The Fabulous Life of Russia's First Empress. Garden City, N.Y.: Doubleday Press,
1945, 274pp., bib. 263-65.
A positive and amusing account of the life and brief reign of
Catherine I. Drawing upon a wide variety of anecdotes,
Stong presents Catherine as a caring, sagacious, and sincere,
if not faithful, wife and companion to Peter I. He also commends Catherine for ruling with humanity while preserving
the Petrine legacy from dismantlement at the hands of traditionalists. DK151.S8

642 "After Peter the Great." Nation, 71 (26 July 1900): 68-69.
As part of a review of K. Waliszewski's L'Héredite de Pierre
le Grand, this article describes the 1730 succession crisis
and the general tone of Anna's reign.

643 *Bain, R. Nisbet. "Chapters V-VIII." PPG (gen. study),
153-318.
A discussion of Anna's reign as a generally positive one in
Russia's history. Bain states that because Anna had the
wisdom to heed the advice of those more experienced in affairs
of state than herself, impressive improvements were made in
Russia's military forces, and victories, if not territorial gains,
were achieved in conflicts with Poland and Turkey. He portrays Anna as neither disinterested in political affairs nor the
object of manipulation of her ambitious advisers but rather as
a sagacious monarch who invited open discussion and took wise
counsel so as to rule more effectively. Despite her successes,
however, Anna was hated by many of her subjects because of
the severity of her rule, the extravagance of her court, and,
most importantly, the predominance of foreigners in high positions in her government. Bain concludes with an account of
the intrigues which developed within the royal court as Anna's
death neared and the regency question remained unanswered.

644 *Cassels, Lavender. "The Czarina and Her Advisers." The
Struggle for the Ottoman Empire 1717-1740. London: John
Murray, 1966, 29-43.
An account of the pomp and pageantry associated with the
Russian court precedes a discussion of the diverse ways in
which Ostermann, Munnich, and Biron were able to maintain
their influence with Anna. In succeeding chapters, Cassels
discusses Russia's Turkish policy of the 1730s as the product
of Anna's three principal advisers who, for different reasons,
favored aggression against the Ottoman Empire. Biron sought
"to flatter his mistress by holding before her the vision of
herself as the ruler of a great and expanding empire"; Munnich
wanted to satisfy his ambition "to lead the Russian army to

victory on the battlefield"; and Ostermann hoped to reverse "the defeat of the Pruth ... in order to give Russia access to the Black Sea." DR542.C3

645 *Cracraft, James. "The Succession Crisis of 1730: A View from the Inside." Can Am Slav S, 12, no. 1 (1978): 60-85. An examination of the insights provided into the 1730 succession crisis by the writings of Feofan Prokopovich. Cracraft states that the writings reveal that Prokopovich was far more involved in the crisis than previously thought and was not merely a supporter of Anna's position but rather favored a relatively radical solution to the crisis through the convocation of a national assembly. Prokopovich's writings reinforce the interpretation that the Supreme Privy Council lacked well-conceived constitutional goals and was moved primarily by the selfish desire to establish an unrestrained oligarchy for itself. Cracraft concludes that during the crisis no one, except Prokopovich, showed "any notion of basic legal procedure in government or even of the need for some. Rather, the operation of familial and personal patronage, improvisation ... and outright physical coercion remained the rule."

646 *Curtiss, Mina. "The Empress Anna's Ice Palace." Hist Today, 23, no. 2 (1973): 122-27. A description of the ice palace, constructed on the Neva River in St. Petersburg during the winter of 1739-1740 upon order from Anna, which served as the intensely frigid scene for the wedding of Prince Golitsyn and his bride. Curtiss points out that the inspiration for the strange pageant came from Peter the Great who was fond of combining elaborate amusements with some concern of state. In the case of Golitsyn's wedding extravaganza, Anna arranged for participants and observers from each of nationalities living within her realm so as "to impress allies, rivals and enemies with the size and power of the Russian empire."

647 * _____. A Forgotten Empress. Anna Ivanovna and Her Reign 1730-1740. New York: Frederick Ungar Publishing Company, 1974, 355pp., bib. 309-20. A favorable reassessment of Anna and her accomplishments. Curtiss maintains that Anna's faults and extravagances were "typical of a Russian autocrat" of the eighteenth century and therefore are undeserving of the critical attention they have received from historians. These same critics have failed to realize that Anna played a positive role in Russia's development of a seminal culture, a phenomenon usually credited to her more "seductive and dynamic" successors, Elizabeth and Catherine the Great. Similarly, her astuteness, attention to detail, and pursuit of sound internal and foreign policies has been obscured by those who mistakenly portray her reign as one in which Russia's best interests were cast aside

by the "German Party" which governed the nation in Anna's
name. In fact, both Ostermann and Munnich were a credit
to Russia and to Anna's talent for delegating authority to
capable advisers. While Curtiss focuses primarily on court
culture, she draws the broad conclusion that Anna's reign
was a continuation of the Westernizing policies of Peter the
Great. DK146.C87 $\mathcal{B}A\mathcal{R}\mathcal{U}A\mathcal{R}\mathcal{D}$
   Reviewed in:
   Nation, 222 (4 Oct. 1975): 312-14
   Slav R, 34 (1975): 588
   Slavonic E Eur R, 53 (1975): 439-40

648   *Daniels, Rudolph L. "V. N. Tatishchev and the Succession
      Crisis of 1730." Slavonic E Eur R, 49 (1971): 550-59.
      A reassessment of Tatishchev's role in the events associated
      with the 1730 attempt of the Supreme Privy Council to limit
      the autocratic prerogatives of Anna. Daniels examines the
      project authored by Tatishchev ("Unrestrained and Concerted
      Discourse and Opinion of the Assembled Russian Gentry on
      State Government") and compares it to similar documents writ-
      ten during the succession crisis. He concludes that "the
      whole tone of Tatishchev's project differs from that of the
      others" in that Tatishchev sought to rationalize and further
      strengthen the centralized state whereas the other plans had
      as their aim the advancement of the interests of a particular
      social group at the expense of the monarch's absolute power;
      "in a word, the nobles as a whole wanted to return to their
      pre-Petrine privileges; Tatishchev and his group wanted to
      continue the 'enlightenment' and reforms introduced by Peter
      the Great."

649   Dawson, P. M. S. "Cowper and the Russian Ice Palace."
      Rev Eng S, 31 (Nov. 1980): 440-43.
      A physical description of the Neva ice palace, built at the
      command of Anna, and a critique of the several sources which
      inaccurately describe the palace's features and use.

650   *Duffy, Christopher. "The Age of Marshal Munnich 1725-41."
      RMWW (gen. study), 41-54.
      A portrait of Field-Marshal Burchard Christopher von Mun-
      nich as "the eighteenth century military adventurer par
      excellence" and "the dominating personality in Russian mili-
      tary affairs" during the reign of Anna. Duffy states that,
      in general, the reign of Anna was "one of good management
      and positive achievement" as exemplified by Munnich's activi-
      ties as head of Anna's Military Commission established in June
      of 1730 to improve the military forces of Russia which had
      fallen into decay since Peter the Great's death. Specifically,
      Munnich founded an academy to provide systematic military
      education for native Russian officers, raised the wages of re-
      cruits, improved living conditions within the military, increased

the size of the army, and established a separate corps of
military engineers. Duffy also discusses Munnich's leading
role in the origin and direction of Russia's war with Turkey
(1735-39) from which Russia gained little territory but lost
great numbers of troops to disease and fatigue.

651 *Dukes, Paul, and Brenda Meehan-Waters. "A Neglected Account
of the Succession Crisis of 1730: James Keith's Memoir."
Can Am Slav S, 12, no. 1 (1978): 170-82.
An examination of A Fragment of a Memoir of Field Marshal
James Keith, 1714-1734 for insights into the 1730 succession
crisis. Keith, a general in the Russian army and a member
of the generalitet at the time of the crisis, states in his
memoir that V. Dolgoruky, not D. Golitsyn, was "the chief
projector" of the plan to limit Anna's powers, and that the
Supreme Privy Council was divided internally on the proper
course of action that it should follow. In an introduction,
Paul Dukes and Brenda Meehan-Waters suggest that Keith's
penning of his memoir some five years after the events being
described may have colored his account.

652 *Lipski, Alexander. "A Re-examination of the 'Dark Era' of
Anna Ioannovna." ASEER, 15 (1956): 477-88. Also in
RRH, Vol. I (anthology), 256-64.
An argument that Russian resentment against the Germans
who ruled the nation under Empress Anna has led to an unwarranted condemnation of Anna's entire reign. Lipski contends that Anna's German dominated government continued
the internal policies of Peter the Great and effectively pursued
Russia's traditional goals in foreign policy.

653 *_____. "Some Aspects of Russia's Westernization During the
Reign of Anna Ioannovna, 1730-1740." ASEER, 18 (Feb. 1959):
1-11.
An argument that historians, in concentrating on the negative
aspects of German rule during Anna's reign, have neglected
the fact that during the 1730s "the Westernization of Russian
culture not only continued but in some areas assumed new
forms and new directions" through the efforts of such well-
educated men as Ostermann, Munnich, Korf, Kantemir, and
Prokopovich. Lipski maintains that Westernization at the
hands of these gifted men was less utilitarian than that which
occurred through the efforts of Peter the Great and was established on a more firm foundation since it no longer was
dependent on "one over-powering personality."

654 _____. "Russia Under Anna Ivanovna: A Study of Internal
Government Policies During Her Reign." University of California, Berkeley, 1954. (dissertation)

655 Longworth, Philip. "Anne." The Three Empresses, Catherine,

Anne, and Elizabeth. New York: Holt, Rinehart and Winston, 1973, 77-152.
A critical account of the character, personality and policies of Anna. Longworth describes Anna as a cruel and vindictive individual who "used terror to keep down opposition to policies which had no great moral, visionary purpose, and sometimes just to vent her private spleen." Longworth suggests that Anna's shortcomings were due "to the unhappiness and disappointments she suffered in her youth" but asserts that such misfortunes scarcely warrant so sadistic a response. In spite of military successes and cultural advancements within the Russian court, Longworth concludes, few Russians mourned Anna's death and her reign must be seen as a negative decade in Russia's history. DK151.L65

656 Maristen, General Christopher H. Contemporary Memoris of Russia from the Year 1727 to 1744. London: Frank Cars and Company, 1968 (reprint of 1856 edition, originally published in 1770), 416pp. Excerpt in RRPDH, Vol. I, 65-76; RFR, 147-49 (anthologies).
The memoirs of a Prussian general who served in the Russian army from 1727-1744. Maristen most often describes military affairs during Anna's reign, but he also comments on various domestic matters and court politics. DK156.M283

657 *Raeff, M. "The Succession Crisis of 1730." PPR (anthology), 41-52.
Following a broad overview of the events and circumstances surrounding the 1730 attempt of the Supreme Privy Council to impose "conditions" on Anna upon her accession to the throne, Raeff presents various documents which respectively illustrate the aims of the Supreme Privy Council, the "ideas of the group of general officers," and the views of the "rank-and-file noblemen." Raeff maintains that "the majority of the nobility preferred the re-establishment of full autocratic rule to any kind of 'constitutional' or limiting settlement.... The noblemen's political horizon did not extend beyond an expression of hope that the worst abuses and hardships would be alleviated in time."

658 Ransel, David L. "The Political Perceptions of the Russian Nobility: the Constitutional Crisis of 1730." Laurentian Univ R, 3 (1972): 20-38.
Unavailable for annotation.

659 *Rondeau, Lady Jane (Mrs. Jane Vigor). Letters from a Lady Who Resided Some Years in Russia, to Her Friend in England. With Historical Notes. London, 1777, 207pp.
A series of letters, written between 1728 and 1739, which contain a number of illuminating references to court life and politics during the reign of Anna. Lady Rondeau, through

her successive marriages to two ranking members of the
British mission in St. Petersburg, was able to attend a number of royal functions and gain access to the gossip which
flowed freely within the Russian court. She describes at
length official court ceremonies of various types, the behavior
and influence of Anna's German advisers, and the personal
qualities of the empress. While Mrs. Rondeau's flattering
portrayal of Anna is of interest, the letters more often describe the haughty and contemptuous manner of the empress'
German favorites and their unpopularity with those Russians
affiliated with the court. For a discussion of the historical
value of Lady Rondeau's letters see Leo Loewenson, Slavonic
E Eur R, 35 (1956-57): 399-408.

660   *Soloviev, Sergei M. History of Russia. Volume XXXIV.
Empress Anna. Favorites, Policies, Campaigns. Walter J.
Gleason, Jr., ed./trans. Gulf Breeze, Fla.: Academic International Press, 1984, 218pp.
Comprised of sections from volumes nineteen and twenty of
Soloviev's classic twenty-nine volume Istoriia Rossii s drevneishikh vremen (History of Russia from Earliest Times), this
work focuses on the constitutional crisis of 1730 and its
aftermath, and the international policy followed by Anna
during the first half of the 1730s. Soloviev, a leading historian in nineteenth century Russia, synthesizes a rich store
of primary source materials as he presents Anna's reign as a
negative one in Russia's history due largely to the rift that
developed between the government and the nobility and, more
importantly, to the harmful influence exercised by foreigners
in high position in the royal court. Soloviev asserts that
the 1730 succession crisis was settled at the expense of the
monarchy through concessions made to the nobility in the form
of the 1731 repeal of the law of inheritance and the establishment of the Cadet Corps. Anna's compromises with the forces
of political reaction, Soloviev maintains, were less harmful to
Russia's best interests than were her depletion of state resources, through extravagant court expenditures and ruinous
military campaigns, under the pernicious influence of the
"German clique" which advised and controlled her. More
importantly, as a result of Anna's ten-year reign, Russia
strayed from the course on which it had been placed by the
farsighted rule of Peter the Great. In an interesting introduction to this volume (pp. x-xxi), W. J. Gleason, Jr. questions the validity of Soloviev's interpretation, particularly
in respect to the political antagonisms which Soloviev alleges
characterized the relations between Anna and the nobility.
DK40.S6213

661   *_____. History of Russia. Volume XXXV. The Rule of
Empress Anna. Richard Hantula, ed./trans. Gulf Breeze,
Fla.: Academic International Press, 1982, 217pp.

As chapters two and three of volume twenty of Istoriia Rossii
s drevneishikh vremen, this study deals with the 1735-39
war with Turkey and with domestic affairs during Anna's
reign. Again drawing on a mass of documentary and memoir
literature, Soloviev continues the line of thought established
in his previous analysis of Anna's rule (see entry 660) as he
portrays her reign as a generally wasteful, misdirected one
often at odds with Russia's capacities, needs, and interests.
Highly critical of Anna's German favorites, especially E.
Biron, Soloviev sees few bright spots during her reign with
the exception of the contributions made to Russian historiography and literature by Tatishchev and Kantemir, "fledglings"
of Peter the Great. DK40.S6213

662   *Tambs, Lewis A. "Anglo-Russian Enterprises Against Hispanic
      South America, 1723-1737." Slavonic E Eur R, 48 (1970): 357-
      72.
      An account of the efforts of Anna and Ostermann to expand
      both Russia's navy and extend the objectives of Russian
      foreign policy to the south Atlantic so as "to place Russia
      in the mainstream of eighteenth century European mercantil-
      ism."

663   Wren, M. "The German Period." WITR (gen. study), 69-73.
      A brief discussion of the 1730 attempt of the Supreme Privy
      Council to limit the power of Empress Anna, and an account
      of the hostile reaction of Russian aristocrats who were ap-
      palled by her preference for Germans over Russians as imperi-
      al appointees.

664   *Yanov, Alexander. "The Drama of the Time of Troubles."
      Can Am Slav S, 12, no. 1 (1978): 1-59.
      An argument that the 1730 failure of the nobility to secure
      for itself an institutional basis for its opposition to the
      autocratic monarchy condemned Russia to follow a non-European
      political, social, and economic course of development. Yanov
      stresses the point that the enslavement of Russia's peasants
      and the stifling of the third estate (and therein economic
      progress) were disastrous by-products of the aristocracy's
      failure to limit Anna's royal prerogatives.

ᗡK 161 . B18
1969

665 *Bain, Robert N. The Daughter of Peter the Great. Westminster: Archibald Constable and Company, 1899, 328pp.,
bib. xv-xviii.
An examination of Russian diplomacy under Elizabeth I with
some attention given to court affairs. Bain contends that
"there are few epochs of modern history at once so momentous and so obscure as the period of Empress Elizabeth"
which "marked a turning point in the political history, not
merely of Muscovy, but of Europe." Bain sees the difficulty in studying Elizabeth's reign as being due to the mass
of ambiguous and contradictory documents associated with the
intrigue which was rampant within her court. In addition to
commending Elizabeth for her impressive gains in foreign
policy, Bain gives a favorable account of her character and
personality. DK161.B18
Reviewed in:
Eng Hist R, 12 (1900): 370
Nation, 71 (11 Oct. 1900): 292-93

666 _____. "History of Russian Diplomacy Under Elizabeth."
Athen (Lon.), 1 (10 Feb. 1900): 170.
Unavailable for annotation.

667 *Butterfield, Herbert. "The Reconstruction of an Historical
Episode: The History of the Enquiry into the Origins of the
Seven Years' War." Man on His Past. Boston: Beacon
Press, 1960, 142-70.
As part of an inquiry into the composition of historical nar-
ratives, Butterfield discusses historical writings on the
origins of the Seven Years' War and, in the process, discounts traditional interpretations of this event. In particular, he asserts that Elizabeth and Chancellor Bestuzhev-
Ryumin played a far more decisive role in the diplomacy associated with the war and its outbreak than historians of this
event have recorded.

668 Coughlan, Robert. Elizabeth and Catherine. New York: G.

P. Putnam's Sons, 1974, 55-174.
A popular and sympathetic account of Elizabeth's personal life
and principal accomplishments. Coughlan portrays Elizabeth
as an effervescent individual and an astute monarch whose
promotion of Western culture and Russia's international position and prestige warrants her being placed beside Catherine
II in "the pantheon of Russian and world history." He concludes that without Elizabeth's successes, Catherine II would
have been unable to achieve the level of greatness that she
realized. DK161.C68

669   *Coxe, William. "History of Prince Ivan." TPRSD, Vol. I (gen.
      study), 29-56.
      An account of the circumstances surrounding the deposition
      of Ivan VI by Elizabeth, his imprisonment, and death in July
      of 1764. Coxe describes the miserable conditions under
      which Ivan suffered while imprisoned in the fortress of
      Schlusselburg, the consequent deterioration of his mind and
      body, the visits to him by Elizabeth and Peter III, and the
      1764 murder of Ivan by his guards in reaction to an attempt,
      led by V. Mirovich, to free him from captivity. Of particular
      interest is Coxe's discussion of the roots of the conspiracy
      to free Ivan and the trial of Mirovich and his co-conspirators.

670   *Duffy, Christopher. "Elizabeth Petrovna 1741-1761/2."
      RMWW (gen. study), 55-124.
      The leadership, strategy, and tactics of the Russian army
      during the Seven Years' War is the focus of this chapter,
      but it includes some discussion of Elizabeth's support for
      military reform and her role in the decision to go to war with
      the Prussia of Frederick the Great. Duffy states that Eliza-
      beth's political apathy created a void in leadership which was
      filled by a number of highly capable advisers, particularly
      A. Bestuzhev-Ryumin and P. Shuvalov, who pursued such
      effective diplomatic and military policies that Elizabeth's
      reign marked Russia's "supreme military effort in the eight-
      eenth century." Duffy supports this statement with a de-
      tailed account of the rebuilding of the Russian military ma-
      chine and the impressive performance of the Russian army in
      the Seven Years' War. He concludes that "thanks largely to
      the presence which had been established by Elizabeth, her
      successor Catherine was able to advance Russia's borders
      deep into Poland and the Middle East, and become the arbiter
      of the quarrels of Western Europe."

671   Dumas, Alexandre. "The Legend of Lestocq." CCRC (gen.
      study), 102-12.
      A colorful account of the role played by Hermann Lestocq,
      physician to Elizabeth, in the 24 November 1741 coup which
      put an end to the regency of Princess Anne and elevated
      Elizabeth to the throne at the expense of the infant Ivan VI.

672 _____. "The Romance of the Boy Czar." Ibid., 113-27.
An account of the life of Ivan VI with most attention devoted
to the unsuccessful 1764 attempt of V. Mirovich to free him
from imprisonment and elevate him to the Russian throne in
place of Catherine II.

673 *Dyck, Harvey L. "New Serbia and the Origins of the Eastern
Question, 1751-55: A Habsburg Perspective." Rus R, 40
(Jan. 1981): 1-19.
In part, a discussion of how "Elizabeth's pretensions to head-
ship of the larger Orthodox community turned Russia into an
active protagonist of Orthodox interests in the Austrian and
Turkish Balkans." Dyck maintains that this turn of affairs
not only led to the termination of the Austro-Russian alliance
but also to the advent of the 'Eastern Question' which came
to plague Russia, Austria, and all of Europe in the next
century.

674 "Elizabeth and Her Court." Temp Bar, 53 (1877-78): 494.
Unavailable for annotation.

675 *Forfar, James. "The Czarina Elizabeth." Gent M, 250 (May
1881): 598-614.
A discussion of the circumstances and motivations which led
Elizabeth to act upon her dormant royal aspirations." Forfar
states that the indecisiveness shown by Elizabeth in 1730,
when forceful action on her part might have won the throne
for her instead of Anne of Courland, was still evident in 1741,
but the insistence of her advisers, the support of the gren-
adiers, and the weakness shown by the young Ivan VI's
regent (Princess Anne of Mecklenberg) produced in her the
resolve necessary to seize control of the government. Forfar
also discusses the steps taken by Elizabeth to secure her
succession and ensure that of her designated heir. Included
is an account of the inhumane treatment and 1764 murder of
Ivan VI.

676 *Kaplan, Herbert. Russia and the Outbreak of the Seven Years'
War. Berkeley: University of California Press, 1968, 165pp.,
bib. 131-60.
A reassessment of Russia's role in the outbreak of the Seven
Years' War. Kaplan maintains that the actions of Empress
Elizabeth are far more central to an understanding of the
war's outbreak than historians have traditionally thought.
He supports this contention with a detailed examination of
the roots of Elizabeth's eagerness for war with Prussia and
the schemings at the Russian court which shaped the empress'
thought. Kaplan discusses the creation of the Imperial Court
Conference as an administrative reform implemented by Elizabeth as part of her mobilization of Russia for war. Since Russia's military preparations preceded those of Prussia and

Austria, Kaplan concludes, Elizabeth was most responsible for precipitating the Seven Year's War. DD411.5.K3

677 *Keep, John L. H. "The Secret Chancellery, the Guards and the Dynastic Crisis of 1740–1741." Forsch Ost Ges, 26 (1978): 169–93.
An account of the origins and activities of the Secret Chancellery and the guards regiments as rival security agencies, and an analysis of their respective roles in the dynastic crisis of 1740–41. Keep states that Ushakov, head of the Secret Chancellery, followed a policy of "benevolent neutrality" towards Elizabeth Petrovna and her supporters and thereby allowed them to stage the coup which removed from power Ivan VI and his regent. The crisis also served to diminish the guards regiments' involvement in matters of state security, a development which Keep sees as being part of the broad process of specialization in the institutionalization of all functions of government.

678 Longworth, Philip. "Elizabeth." The Three Empresses. Catherine, Anne, and Elizabeth of Russia. New York: Holt, Rinehart and Winston, 1973, 153–229.
A highly critical portrayal of Elizabeth, her policies, and accomplishments. Longworth describes Elizabeth as a passionate, pleasure seeking spendthrift whose prime concern as empress was "improving standards at the court." The author surveys Elizabeth's foreign and domestic policies but focuses primarily on the intrigue, gossip, gambling, and festivities that so characterized her court. DK151.L65

679 McCormick, D. "Comic Opera Espionage." HRSS (gen. study), 24–33.
An interesting discussion of the court of Empress Elizabeth as a prime center of European espionage. McCormick states that "intrigues at the Russian court were numerous. Everyone in the court was playing some game of his or her own with a foreign power gleaning a certain amount of intelligence for his own country no doubt, but also giving away a great deal." McCormick details in particular the activities of Alexander Shuvalov, the head of the Russian Imperial Secret Service, Imperial Chancellor Bestuzhev, the French spy Chevalier Charles de Beaumont (disguised as Mademoiselle Lia de Beaumont), and the English Ambassador Sir Charles Hanbury-Williams.

680 Molloy, Fitzgerald. The Russian Court in the Eighteenth Century, 2 Vols. London: Hutchinson and Company, 1905.
The reigns of Elizabeth, Catherine II, and Paul are the focal points of this anecdotal account of court functions, activities, and intrigues. Besides providing amusing and sometimes insightful observations on a wide range of court incidents,

Molloy describes the personality, tastes, daily routine, and
personal relationships of the three monarchs under study.
The lack of a subject index makes this work a difficult one
to access readily, while the absence of documentation leaves
the reader with no way to measure the veracity of Molloy's
accounts and observations. DK127.M72

681 *Oliva, L. Jay. Misalliance. A Study of French Policy in Russia During the Seven Years' War. New York: New York
University Press, 1964, 218pp., bib. 201-09.
The stated purpose of this scholarly study is to "analyze the
origins, content, character, and results of French policy in
Russia from 1755 to 1762, in order to discover whether there
ever existed in the Franco-Russian relationship any elements
of mutality, desirability, or durability." Oliva states that
France entered into the Russian alliance with the ill-founded
attitude that "Russia could be bought, cajoled, and used for
French interests," meaning that Russia could be utilized as
an ally against Prussia, to hasten the end of the Seven Years'
War, without Russia receiving any territorial compensation for
its efforts. The French leaders, however, failed to realize
that "Russia had specific territorial ends in view, sharpened
by the hatred of Empress Elizabeth for Frederick of Prussia
and directed by the intelligence and determination of Aleksei
Bestuzhev." Ironically, during the course of the alliance,
France "was used effectively by Russia as an instrument to-
ward the fulfillment of Russia's own war aims." DC133.5.04
Reviewed in:
Am Hist R, 70 (1965): 1187
Cath Hist R, 51 (1965-66):   114
Eng Hist R, 81 (1966): 175
Historian, 27 (1964): 109
History, 50 (1965): 232
Rus R, 24 (1965): 206
Slav R, 24 (1965): 127

682 Rice, Tamara Talbot. Elizabeth Empress of Russia. London:
Weidenfeld and Nicolson, 1970, 231pp., bib. 216-18.
A popular and favorable biography of Elizabeth with a balance
of concern for both her domestic and foreign affairs. Rice
maintains that, in spite of Elizabeth's lack of training and her
early difficulties as empress, she "succeeded in greatly developing her country's resources and in providing her people
with new outlets and new areas of habitation. She had done
much to raise living and cultural standards and, by signing
Russia's first treaty of alliance with France, she had opened
the road along which French ideas were to reach Russia.
While she had herself freed the country from a German hold
her armies had set a limit to Prussian expansion." DK161.R5

683 Sergeant, Philip. "Woman Rule in Russia." Dominant Women.

Freeport, N.Y.: Books for Libraries Press, 1969 (reprint of 1929 edition), 208-30.
An overview of the character, accession to power, and main policies of Catherine I, Anna, and Elizabeth. Sergeant provides most detail on the private life and cultural achievements of Elizabeth. D109.S4

684 Treue, Wilhelm. "Count Lestocq and M. A. Weikard in Russia." DAC (gen. study), 56-59.
A brief account of the court activities of Hermann Lestocq, personal physician of Empress Elizabeth, who lost favor for too often combining "medicine with politics." Treue also describes the relationship between Catherine II and her physician, M. A. Weikard.

685 *Wren, M. "The Daughter of Peter the Great." WITR (gen. study), 73-82.
A brief review of the spread of Western culture at the court of Elizabeth precedes an examination of the diplomatic and military policies pursued during her reign. Wren states that although Count A. Bestuzhev-Ryumin was the driving force behind Russia's foreign policy, Elizabeth's deep hatred for Frederick II of Prussia made her an enthusiastic supporter of Bestuzhev-Ryumin's pro-Austrian diplomacy. Elizabeth's "stubborn insistence upon destroying Prussian military strength and political influence in the affairs of Europe" may well have led to the annihilation of Prussia had she not died in January of 1762.

GENERAL STUDIES AND ASSESSMENTS

686 Almedingen, E. M. Catherine. Empress of Russia. New York:
Dodd, Mead, and Company, 1961, 312pp., bib. 304. Also
published as Catherine the Great: A Portrait. London:
Hutchinson, 1963.
A popular, undocumented, and sympathetic biography of
Catherine II which concentrates on her personal life and
treats only generally her internal and foreign policies. Almedingen portrays Catherine as an intelligent, astute, and
ambitious ruler who, though very much a social being, never
allowed her personal life to interfere in any way with her
duties as Russia's sovereign. A realist in politics, Catherine
accomplished as much as any monarch in Russia's history and
"certainly compares favorably with Peter the Great." Almedingen sees Catherine as "possibly the greatest woman
sovereign of all ages," not due to her military triumphs, reforms, and similar achievements but because "she created the
perfect fusion between her personality and her work."
DK170.A59

687 *Anderson, M. S. "Russia: Catherine the Great." Historians
and Eighteenth Century Europe, 1715-1789. Oxford: Clarendon Press, 1979, 157-76.
A critical review of the evolution of Western and Russian historical assessments of Catherine II and her accomplishments.
Anderson states that eighteenth-century commentators generally presented a "flattering view of Catherine as both progressive in her politics and glorious in their execution."
Those who criticized her concentrated on specific personal
issues, such as her role in the 1762 overthrow and murder of
Peter III, her questionable personal morals, and the corruption
of her favorites, but overlooked "the intensification and geographical extension of serfdom" which occurred during her
reign. Even among Russian historians, it was not until the
last quarter of the nineteenth century that critical attention
was given to Catherine's serf policy. Criticism of this policy

has increased, particularly at the hands of Soviet historians
who have labeled Catherine as a hypocrite because of the
stark contrast between her liberal ideals and despotic policies.
Modern Western historians, on the other hand, while agree-
ing that Catherine failed to reduce the burdens which serfdom imposed on the peasantry and contributed much to widen
its geographical scope, have pointed to various circumstances
which mitigate her responsibility for the plight of Russia's
serfs. Catherine's peasant policy, however, has not been as
central a concern of contemporary Western scholarship as has
her administrative reforms. Anderson concludes that while a
biography of Catherine has yet to be written which truly does
her justice, "the good press abroad which Catherine so much
desired she has now very largely attained. It is based,
moreover, on a knowledge of her achievements and understanding of her problems far more detailed and complete than
was ever possible in her own lifetime." D284.5.A52

688   Anthony, Katherine. <u>Catherine the Great</u>. Garden City,
      N.Y.: Garden City Publishing Company, 1925, 331pp.
      Excerpt in <u>Century</u>, 110, no. 5 (512-25); 110, no. 6 (Oct.
      1925): 731-44; 111, no. 1 (Nov. 1925): 59-72.
      A popular and favorable account of the life of Catherine the
      Great. Anthony very generally surveys Catherine's principal
      domestic, foreign, and military affairs, and then turns to a
      folksy review of the empress' personal and family life, es-
      pecially her relationships with Poniatowski, Orlov, Potemkin,
      Empress Elizabeth, Peter III, her son Paul, and her grand-
      son Alexander.

689   Aretz, Gertrude. <u>The Empress Catherine</u>. London: Godfrey
      and Stephens Limited, 1947, 244pp.
      A popular and sympathetic narrative on the highlights of
      Catherine II's personal and public life with most concern for
      her relationship with her various favorites.

690   Baily, F. E. "Catherine of Russia (1729-1796)." <u>Film Stars of
      History</u>. London: Macdonald and Company, 1945, 63-88.
      The purpose of this essay is to provide an accurate and
      readable overview of Catherine II's private life and reign as
      empress for "the great inarticulate mass of cinema-goers who
      ... see historic characters butchered to make a Hollywood
      holiday, and believe what they see to be true." The film
      <u>Catherine the Great</u>, starring Elisabeth Bergner as Catherine,
      is the cinema for which this biographical sketch is to provide
      background.

691   Bruun, Geoffrey. "Catherine the Great of Russia." <u>The En-
      lightened Despots</u>. Gloucester: P. Smith, 1963 (reprint of
      1929 edition), 48-51.
      An argument that Catherine II's "enlightenment was largely

Bain : PII 92 P444
B

a pose." While noting Catherine's admiration for the philosophes and concern for improving the over-all condition of
Russia, Bruun stresses that there was "a vast discrepancy
between Catherine's theories and her practices," and that in
the face of "the resistance of the privileged orders" she
was unwilling to pursue any programs that would change the
traditional order of things in Russia.   D286.B71967

692 *Bushkoff, Leonard.   "State, Society and the Eighteenth Cen-
tury Russian Nobility."   Can Slav S, 3 (Spring 1969):   121-
27.
A review article on P. Dukes' Catherine the Great and the
Russian Nobility and M. Raeff's The Origins of the Russian
Intelligentsia.

693 *Castera, Jean Henri.   The Life of Catherine II.   Empress of
Russia, 3 Vols.   William Tooke, trans.   London: T. N.
Longman and O. Rees, 1799.   Excerpt in RFR (anthology),
157-58.
An early, detailed account of Catherine II's life and rule and
the condition of Russia during her reign.   Drawing upon official documents and records and the memoirs and opinions of
individuals who knew Catherine, Castera presents a chronologically arranged, somewhat gossipy review of court, domestic,
and foreign affairs and Catherine's personal relationship with
successive favorites and prominent European intellectual and
political figures of her era.   He portrays Catherine as an
ambitious, calculating, and prideful individual whose remarkable composure rendered impossible the fathoming of her
thoughts and emotions by any study of her exterior.   He
commends her for promoting art, literature, and science but
at the same time labels as 'scandalous' her private life and
bestowal of wildly extravagant gifts on her favorites.   Included in appendices are hundreds of pages of documents,
ukazes, treaties, and other state papers pertinent to Catherine's major policies and accomplishments.   A significant por-
tion of this work consists of additions to the French language
original made by the translator, William Tooke.   Unfortunately,
Tooke failed to indicate which parts of this work are his own
and which are Castera's.   DK170.T6

694 "Catherine the Great of Russia."   New Mo M, 120 (1860):   431-
41.
A translated excerpt from the two volume French language
work Catherine II et son Regne, by E. Jauffret, which presents Catherine and her accomplishments in a sympathetic light.

695 "Catherine II, Empress of Russia."   Eclectic M, 64 (May 1865):
641-48.
A standard overview of Catherine II's life and accomplishments.

696   Coughlan, Robert. Elizabeth and Catherine. New York: G.
      P. Putnam's Sons, 1974, 198-323.
      A discussion of Catherine II's relationship with and debt to
      Empress Elizabeth, and a review of the standard highlights
      of Catherine's reign. Coughlan presents most detail on the
      coup which deposed Peter III, Catherine's affairs with various
      favorites, and the Pugachev Revolt. He does not provide
      much information on her major victories in foreign policy or
      her domestic reforms. Designed for the nonspecialist.
      DK161.C68

697   Cronin, Vincent. Catherine. Empress of All the Russians.
      New York: William Morrow and Company, 1978, 359pp.
      A popular, sympathetic survey of the highlights of Catherine
      II's personal life and her policies as empress. Cronin portrays
      Catherine's reign as a positive one in Russia's history since
      under her leadership impressive advancements were made in
      education, science, and literature and the nation's borders
      were extended significantly. Although many of Catherine's
      ideas for reform were not implemented, she at least "narrowed
      the gap between Russia and Europe" and pointed the way for
      her successors to proceed. Cronin characterizes Catherine
      as an exceptionally dedicated monarch possessed of an indomit-
      able will, and he sees her many love affairs as being a conse-
      quence of her unwillingness to form a permanent relationship
      with any one man for fear that by so doing she would be di-
      verted from her state duties and thus become less effective as
      a ruler. DK170.C76

698   Cross, Anthony G. "An Oxford Don in Catherine the Great's
      Russia." J Eur S, 1 (1971): 166-74.
      A discussion of the 1971 publication of the travel diaries of
      John Parkinson (A Tour of Russia, Siberia and the Crimea,
      1792-94) as a "notable addition to English eighteenth century
      travel literature and a new and important source for the stu-
      dent of Russia and the reign of Catherine the Great."

699   * _____, ed. "The Reign of Catherine the Great." RUWE
      (anthology), 196-253.
      A series of selections from the writings of Western travelers
      to Catherine II's Russia which deal with serfdom, the nobility,
      religion, popular culture, and court life as well as with
      Catherine's triumphant tour of the Crimea and her rule in
      the closing years of her reign. The excerpts are from the
      works of J. Chappe D'Auteroche, W. Richardson, G. Macart-
      ney, W. Coxe, E. Dimsdale, E. Craven, C. DeLigne, J.
      DeLesseps, A. Swinton, C. Masson, and E. Clarke.

700   Dark, Sidney. "Catherine the Great." Twelve Royal Ladies.
      New York: Thomas Y. Crowell, 1929, 253-72.
      A critical account of Catherine II's character, rise to power,

and personal life as empress. Dark describes Catherine as
a woman wiht the morals of an alley-cat who came to the
throne of Russia as the result of sheer luck and maintained
herself in that exalted position for thirty-nine years through
the same good fortune. He asserts that Catherine is undeserving of the title 'the great' since "she did nothing to add
to the happiness of the Russian people and little to add to
the prestige of the Russian crown." D107.3.D3

701 *DeMadariaga, Isabel. Russia in the Age of Catherine the Great.
New Haven: Yale University Press, 1981, 698pp., bib. 653-
75.
A detailed, scholarly, and favorable study of the reign of
Catherine II. DeMadariaga states that "if one is to analyze
the significant aspects of Catherine's reign, three areas of
her activity spring to mind: Her relationship with the
philosophes and the Enlightenment in general; her social
policies; and her foreign policy." As an avid reader, correspondent, and conversationalist, Catherine quite naturally was
subjected to the main intellectual currents of the Enlightenment, many of which she attempted to adapt to Russian circumstances. Most importantly here, Catherine blended the
political thought of Montesquieu and Blackstone, with German
cameralist writings, and worked diligently to devise a system
of government in Russia which rested on a combination of
the best elements of this thought. In social policy, Catherine
sought to create a society based upon estates to enable her
to communicate more effectively with organized social groups
and to provide administrative assistance for the government
in the absence of a well trained and substantial bureaucracy.
Similarly, Catherine's extension of the rights and privileges
of the nobility vis-à-vis the serfs is best understood as a
"delegation by the Crown to the nobility of certain functions
it could not hope to fulfill by means of a non-existent bureaucracy it could not afford to pay." Moreover, the entire administrative and political apparatus of Russia was demilitarized
under Catherine's rule, and consequently government became
far more concerned with civilian interests. In the area of
foreign policy, however, Catherine demonstrated brash and
brutal behavior and, for the sake of territorial aggrandize-
ment, engulfed Russia in costly wars. The author concludes
that in spite of Catherine's weaknesses and failings she
"rendered signal service to Russia. Her greatness lies not
so much in her territorial acquisitions but in the new relationship between rulers and ruled which she fostered."
DK171.D45
Reviewed in:
Economist, 279 (25 Apr. 1981): 115
History Today, 31 (Feb. 1981): 50
Lib J, 106 (15 Feb. 1981): 448
NY R Bks, 28 (28 May 1981): 38

176   Russian Autocrats

Spectator, 246 (4 Apr. 1981): 23
TLS, (17 July 1981): 807
Virg Q R, 57 (Summer 1981): 86

702 *Dmytryshyn, Basil. "Modernization of Russia Under Catherine
II." Modernization of Russia Under Peter I and Catherine II.
New York: John Wiley and Sons, 1974, 85-157.
As part of the Major Issues in History series this volume
presents a sampling of primary materials and secondary historical assessments suitable for classroom use. Dmytryshyn
provides a general introduction to the problem of interpreting
the modernizing efforts and accomplishments of Peter I and
Catherine II, and then presents excerpts from Catherine's
Instruction to the Legislative Commission of 1767-68, two
critical contemporary assessments of Catherine's reign (Shcherbatov and Masson), a pre-revolutionary Russian study by
V. S. Ikonnikov (The Significance of Catherine II's Reign),
and a text prepared for Soviet university students.

703 *Forfar, James. "The Light of the North." Gent M, 251 (Nov.
1881): 609-24.
An interesting discussion of Catherine's personal life and domestic and foreign policies within the context of the assertion
that "an insatiable appetite for 'glory,' and an unregulated
animal desire were the two mainsprings of notice to which all
her actions can be traced." Forfar concludes that while
Catherine's private life was wholly scandalous and immoral
and she wasted much energy in attempts to "impress other
nations with a sense of the prosperity and greatness of her
reign, and of the striking stides of her empire towards the
van of civilization," her rule led to an impressive development
of Russia's natural resources and to highly effective legal and
administrative reforms.

704 *Gooch, G. P. "Catherine the Great." Catherine the Great
and Other Studies. London: Longmans, Green and Company,
1954, 1-108.
An essay on Catherine's personal life with a brief account of
her principal reforms and reaction to the French Revolution.
Gooch examines Catherine's "years of apprenticeship," relationship with her son Paul, her court favoritism, and contacts
with Voltaire and Friedrich Melchior von Grimm. He concludes
that Catherine was truly an enlightened autocrat but that
her "vision was too circumscribed" to see that absolutism of
the type she practiced could not survive long as a political
system since it required "a never-failing supply of such
gifted persons" as herself, Frederick the Great, and the
other enlightened despots of the eighteenth century. The essay is based upon a series of articles which Gooch wrote for
the Contemporary Review, Volumes 181-183, April, 1952-Feb.
1953. DK170.G65

705 Grey, Ian. Catherine the Great. Autocrat and Empress of All
     Russia. New York: J. B. Lippincott, 1962, 254pp., bib.
     246-47.
     A popular, balanced study of Catherine the Great and her
     principal policies and accomplishments. Grey, who has written
     a number of works of this type on other Russian monarchs,
     portrays Catherine as a wholly unoriginal ruler with a pro-
     nounced talent for seizing "on the ideas of others and on the
     advantage of the moment" and exploiting them effectively. He
     grants that her foreign policy was relatively successful but
     maintains that her domestic policies were not only unimpres-
     sive but reactionary. He concludes that "as a story of per-
     sonal ambition and achievement her career inspires admira-
     tion," but in "dedication, selflessness, and creativeness" her
     reign is sorely lacking and certainly not comparable to that
     of Peter the Great. DK170.G68

706 *Griffiths, David M. "Catherine II: The Republican Empress."
     Jahr Ges Ost, 21, no. 3 (1973): 323-44.
     An analysis of Catherine's republicanism from the perspective
     of her perception of the concept's meaning. Griffiths con-
     cludes that Catherine's policies "were very much in harmony
     with the ideas of the age," and that "within the context of
     pre-revolutionary European political thought her professions
     and practices earned for her the right to bestow upon her-
     self a 'republican soul.'" He notes that as the meaning of
     the term 'republican' changed with the French Revolution,
     Catherine ceased to refer to herself as a republican but con
     tinued to pursue the principles associated with her lifelong
     concept of republicanism.

707 Haslip, Joan. Catherine the Great. A Biography. New York:
     G. P. Putnam's Sons, 1977, 383pp., bib. 368-72.
     A biography of Catherine the Great aimed at the nonspecialist.
     The author states that her book "makes no pretensions to
     original scholarship or to the discovery of any startling new
     material" but rather is "merely an attempt to depict the char-
     acter and justify the actions of one of the most extraordinary
     women of her age." To this end, Haslip relies heavily on
     Catherine's autobiographical writings, the memoirs and letters
     of the empress' contemporaries, and dispatches of foreign am-
     bassadors to the St. Petersburg court. Although Haslip re-
     views favorably Catherine's main policies, it is the empress'
     relationship with court favorites and family members (Eliza-
     beth, Peter III, Paul, and Alexander) that receives most at-
     tention. DK170.H37 1976

708 Heilprin, N. "Catherine II." Nation, 38 (1884): 320-21.
     A review of a German language biography of Catherine II
     written by Alexander Bruckner.

709 Hodgetts, E. A. Brayley. The Life of Catherine the Great of
     Russia. New York: Brentano's Publishing Company, 1914,
     335pp.
     A general and sympathetic account of Catherine's life and
     reign. Hodgetts presents Catherine as the tragic victim of
     an arranged marriage to Tsar Peter III, who, extricating her-
     self from a hopeless marital situation, served Russia with a
     devotion, energy, and wisdom that is admirable. He states
     that the scandalous side of Catherine's love life has been sen-
     sationalized and sees most of her poor behavior as being a
     consequence of the decadent and corrupt influence of Potem-
     kin. He also questions those who charge Catherine with in-
     sincerity because of the disparity between her lofty sentiments
     and practical accomplishments, claiming that the backward
     condition of Russia and "the ignorant and unenlightened na-
     ture of her administrators" largely account for her failure to
     achieve desired goals. DK170.H6

710 Holland, Cecelia. "Catherine the Great." Cosmopol, 178 (Jan.
     1975): 148-51.
     A popular account of Catherine II as a remarkable woman rul-
     ing in a man's world.

711 Holliday, Kate. "How Great Was Catherine the Great?" Man-
     kind, 1, no. 1 (1968): 10-15. Also in Women in History.
     Don Sheperd, ed. Los Angeles: Mankind Publishing Com-
     pany, 1973, 107-31. CT3202.S5
     A balanced overview of Catherine the Great's life and accom-
     plishments. While noting Catherine's efforts to modernize
     Russia and her successes in foreign and military affairs, Hol-
     liday sees as the empress' most outstanding achievement her
     successful promotion of intellectual pursuits by Russia's no-
     bility. Holliday tempers her praise by noting Catherine's
     callousness in dealing with "the sufferings and privations of
     the serfs" but nonetheless concludes that Catherine so "solid-
     ified into adulthood the adolescent nation nurtured by Peter
     the Great" that the title "the Great" is one well-bestowed
     upon her.

712 *"Inedited Memoirs of a Russian Minister of State." Am Eclectic,
     2 (July 1841): 70-86.
     A recreation of Admiral Chichigov's assessment of Catherine
     II's rule. Chichigov maintains that although Catherine could
     not erase the evils that had for centuries reigned in Russia,
     she did the best that she could to advance Russia socially,
     economically, politically, and culturally. He defends Catherine
     against her critics, and asserts, in particular, that she was
     not responsible for the partition of Poland, was not among
     the conspirators who dethroned and murdered Peter II, and
     did not neglect the education and general upbringing of her
     son Paul.

713 Johnson, W. Knox. "The Empress Catherine II." Fortn R,
     66 (Nov. 1896): 664-79. Also in Liv Age, 211 (19 Dec. 1896):
     796-806.
     The centennial of Catherine II's death prompted this broad
     review of the empress' accomplishments and a portrait of her
     as an ambitious, practical, and affable monarch though fickle
     as a reformer and lover.

714 Jones, Arthur E. "Catherine the Great." Cent Lit M, (Jan.
     1938): 192-97.
     Unavailable for annotation.

715 *Karamzin, Nicholas M. "Catherine II." Memoir on Ancient and
     Modern Russia. R. Pipes, ed./trans. Cambridge: Harvard
     University Press, 1959, 130-35. Also in CG (anthology),
     122-25.
     A much discussed 1811 memoir, sent to Alexander I, in which
     Catherine's policies, though not her personal behavior, are
     presented as a model for Alexander to emulate. Karamzin,
     a noted Russian historian and novelist, commends Catherine
     for humanizing autocracy without emasculating it, for improv-
     ing the efficiency of the crown's government, and for her
     success in advancing the security and international standing
     of Russia. DK71.K343

716 Kaus, Gina. Catherine. The Portrait of an Empress. June
     Head, trans. New York: Literary Guild, 1935, 384pp.
     A popular and well balanced biography of Catherine II with
     most attention given to her personal relationships. Kaus
     portrays Catherine as a truly remarkable personality--dy-
     namic, intelligent, humorous, and giving, but capable of
     ruthless behavior when circumstances so dictated. The
     author sees little in Catherine's accomplishments that warrants
     her title "the Great," but notes that Catherine could not pos-
     sibly have overcome the conditions and circumstances in Rus-
     sia which blocked reform: "the people themselves benefitted
     by neither her kindness nor her victories. She was not to
     blame. She had aspired to the best, and achieved the pos-
     sible ... she had recognized the force of circumstance and
     bowed to it, therein lay her greatness." DK170.K35

717 *Kizevetter, Aleksandr A. "Portrait of an Enlightened Auto-
     Crat." CG (anthology), 3-20. Mary Mackler, trans. from
     "Ekatrina II." Istoricheskie Siluety-Liudi i sobytiia. Ber-
     lin: Parabola, 1931, 7-28.
     A critical examination of Catherine II's personality and char-
     acter for insights into the successes she had as ruler of
     Russia. Kizevetter, a representative of the liberal tradition
     in Russian historiography, contends that the source of Cath-
     erine's success was her "extraordinary personality, with its
     rare combination of two ordinarily mutually exclusive traits--

impassioned desires and calculating self-control in the selection of ways and means to gain those desires." Most significant was Catherine's habit of advancing towards her goals
"along the path of least resistance, not overthrowing one's
enemies but taming them, not outstripping the surroundings,
but keeping in step with them.... She was incapable of challenging destiny in order to satisfy her ambitions." Kizevetter
also notes Catherine's skill at propagating, through her own
words as well as those of others, an exceptionally favorable
image of herself and her policies.

718 *Kliuchevsky, V. O. "Catherine's Man of Letters." CG
(anthology), 133-38. From A History of Russia. London:
J. M. Dent and Sons, 1931, 110, 112-13, 115-19.
Excerpts from Kliuchevsky's monumental history of Russia in
which the distinguished Russian historian argues that Catherine's policies were both contradictory and inequitable. Kliuchevsky criticizes Catherine for liberating the nobles from
bonded service to the state without doing the same for the
peasantry, freeing from a foreign yoke millions of Slavs only
to subject them to internal servitude, and for entrusting "the
future guidance of the Russian community along the road of
development to the very class which stood least willing for,
and least capable of, the task ... the cultured dvorianstvo."

719 Kochan, Miriam. Catherine the Great. London: Wayland Publishers Limited, 1976, 96pp., bib. 93.
A heavily illustrated, popular introduction to the principal
highlights of Catherine's personal life and, to a lesser extent,
her reign. DK170.K54

720 _____. Life in Russia Under Catherine the Great. New York:
G. P. Putnam's Sons, 1969, 182pp., bib. 175.
A well illustrated survey of the fundamental features of the
Russia which Catherine II ruled. For a basic and very read-
able introduction to the economic, social, and cultural char-
acteristics of Catherine's Russia, this work is a useful one.
DK171.K6

721 Krieger, Leonard. Kings and Philosophers 1680-1789. New
York: W. W. Norton and Company, 1970, 369pp., bib. 344-
53.
This work does not contain a titled section on Catherine the
Great but includes a significant number of references to her
method of rule, policies, and accomplishments within the context of a discussion of enlightened despotism. D288.K7

722 Lawrence, E. "Catherine II." Harper's M, 38 (April 1869):
624-35.
A popular recreation of the standard highlights in Catherine's
personal life with the exception of the assertion that she and

her husband Peter were lovers until he was disfigured by
smallpox and consequently became mean and cranky.

723 Lentin, A. "The Age of Catherine the Great." Russia in the
     Eighteenth Century. London: Heinemann Educational Books,
     1973, 79-123.
     A general introduction to the highlights of Catherine II's
     reign as part of a synopsis of the significant features of
     eighteenth-century Russia. Designed for the nonspecialist.
     DK127.L46 1973

724 * _____. "Catherine the Great and Enlightened Despotism."
     Hist Today, 21, no. 3 (Mar. 1971): 170-77.
     A defense of Catherine II's claim to enlightened rule. Lentin
     maintains that Catherine's failure to implement a broad pro-
     gram of reform consistent with her liberal sentiments was not
     due to any fickleness or insincerity on her part but rather
     to the opposition posed by conservative nobles. Catherine
     nonetheless followed a progressive course in her educational
     and religious policies and maintained a positive relationship
     with the most prominent philosophers of the Enlightenment
     as an integral part of her statecraft.

725 *Meehan-Waters, Brenda. "Catherine the Great and the Problem
     of Female Rule." Rus R, 34 (July 1975): 293-307.
     An examination of the reaction to Catherine II's rule by her
     Western and Russian contemporaries whose observations and
     judgments were influenced by the fact that Catherine was a
     woman. Meehan-Waters sees Western commentators reacting
     in a sexist fashion far more frequently and pointedly than
     their Russian counterparts.

726 Morris, W. O. "The Empress Catherine II." Edinb R, 178
     (July 1893): 168-98.
     A lengthy review article on the French language edition of
     K. Waliszewski's Empress Catherine II of Russia. The
     reviewer summarizes the book's contents and presents it as
     a comprehensive assessment of Catherine II's striking character
     and powerful influence on Russia and the Europe of her era.

727 Mowat, R. B. "Enlightened Monarchs: Catherine II." The
     Age of Reason. New York: Russell and Russell, 1971, 121-
     35.
     A general sketch of Catherine's career with much reference to
     the concept of enlightened despotism. Mowat maintains that
     Catherine was well-schooled in the principles of the Enlighten-
     ment, but the reform plans which she devised in their light
     came to little because of her preoccupation with foreign af-
     fairs and the dampening of her liberalism as a consequence of
     the Pugachev and French Revolutions. D286.M58

728 Nicolson, Harold. "Semiramis. Catherine the Great, 1729-1796."
     The Age of Reason. The Eighteenth Century. Garden City,
     N.Y.: Doubleday Press, 1961, 128-48.
     A general review of the highlights of Catherine II's personal
     and public life. Nicolson portrays Catherine as an ambitious
     yet cautious monarch "subtly aware that politics is the art
     of the possible" and wholly convinced that "it is better to
     inspire a reform than to enforce it." He concludes that her
     mastery of "thrust and parry" politics made her both an ef-
     fective diplomat and reformer and a sovereign deserving of
     the epithet "the Great." CB411.N5

729 Noble, Iris. Empress of All Russia. Catherine the Great.
     New York: Julian Messner, 1966, 191pp., bib. 183-84.
     A general biography designed for young readers. DK170.N6

730 *Nowak, Frank. "Catherine the Great (1762-1796)." Mediaeval
     Slavdom and the Rise of Russia. New York: Cooper Square
     Publishers, 1970, 78-113.
     A discussion of Catherine the Great's reign as the end of
     Russia's formative period. Nowak states that by the end of
     the eighteenth century Russia had completed its basic terri-
     torial expansion and had emerged as a modern nation no longer
     in need of "the prodding of despotic sovereigns like Peter the
     Great and Catherine" since the Russian people "had developed
     an initiative of their own in bringing about the social, intel-
     lectual, and economic transformation of the nation." He notes
     the important role played by Catherine in this process and
     identifies as the foundation of her success a situation in
     Europe favorable for territorial aggrandizement, the support
     of the gentry (purchased at the expense of the peasantry),
     and her "great willpower and cleverness in managing men and
     inspiring them with her own unbounded optimism and courage."
     D147.N67

731 *Oliva, L. Jay, ed. "The Eighteenth Century: 1725-1801."
     RW (anthology), 27-54.
     A series of brief excerpts from primary and secondary
     sources dealing with Catherine the Great and her foreign
     and domestic policies. Included are selections from Catherine's
     Nakaz and correspondence with Voltaire as well as from the
     works of historians R. H. Lord, R. R. Palmer, G. P. Gooch,
     and D. M. Lang.

732 O'Sullivan, J. M. "Catherine the Great and Russian Policy."
     Studies, (Sept. 1915): 397-410.
     Unavailable for annotation.

733 Powys, Lewelyn. "The Great Catherine." Mentor, 16 (Oct.
     1928): 3-10.

A popular, somewhat sensationalized account of Catherine's life and accomplishments.

734 *Raeff, M. "Postscript." CGP (anthology), 301-21.
A survey of the various schools of thought on Catherine's reign and a review of contemporary scholarship on her polices and accomplishments. Raeff identifies certain "problem areas" in the study of Catherine's reign and suggests as a fruitful line of inquiry that historians turn to "a thorough examination and dynamic interpretation of the social, economic, and administrative institutions in Catherine's Russia and attempt to discover and define the purposes and methods of her legislation." Such a line of investigation should enable analysts "to see more clearly the factors that fostered innovation and creativity (as well as those which hampered them) and implanted conceptions of rationality and modernity, traits which Catherine II herself exemplified by her political genius and intellectual energy."

735 *_____. "Random Notes on the Reign of Catherine II in Light of Recent Literature." Jahr Ges Ost, 19 (1971): 541-56.
A review of various articles written for the fall 1970 issue of Canadian Slavic Studies which was devoted to the reign of Catherine II. Raeff generally commends the authors of these highly specialized articles for the insights they have provided into the nature of Catherine's Russia and for illuminating areas in need of further investigation. He suggests a systematic follow up to the lines of inquiry identified.

736 Russell, Phillips. "Dark Sea." The Glittering Century. New York: Charles Scribner's Sons, 1936, 167-76.
A brief overview of Catherine the Great's life and accomplishments. Russell maintains that Catherine's Western ideas were imposed on Russia from above and were so at odds with the backwardness of the nation that they influenced only a tiny educated elite. D286.R98

737 Scherman, Katharine. Catherine the Great. New York: Random House, 1957, 184pp.
A popular, undocumented biography which portrays Empress Catherine and her policies in a most favorable fashion. Scherman states that Catherine was "a perfect expression of her age: the age of reason, of philosophy, of courtly elegance, of polished wit--and of uncompromising autocracy," who brought to Russia "its first breath of equality and justice" and therein "helped to shape the democracy which was to destroy all of her kind." DK171.6.S30

738 Schmucker, Samuel M. Memoirs of the Court and Reign of Catherine the Second. Empress of Russia. Philadelphia:

Porter and Coates, 1855, 338pp.
A balanced description of Catherine and her reign drawing
heavily upon the reminiscences of those who knew or simply
observed the empress. Schmucker presents Catherine as a
woman of extraordinary genius with remarkable accomplishments in domestic and foreign policy, but whose sordid personal life must qualify any final assessment of her reign:
"the empress was, beyond question, one of the most corrupt,
sensual, and licentious of women. There was no depth or
excess of impurity which she had not fathomed and exhausted."
Appended is a catalog of Catherine's presents to her favorites.
DK170.S35

739 Self, Gloria. "The Joy of Russia and the Hope of Europe."
San Diego M, 27 (Aug. 1975): 94-97, 108-14.
A review of Catherine II's various efforts to promote Western
education and culture in Russia and to expand the nation's
borders at the expense of Poland and the Ottoman Empire.

740 *Shcherbatov, Mikhail N. On the Corruption of Morals in Russia.
A Lentin, ed./trans. London: Cambridge University Press,
1969, 338pp. Excerpts in CG, 101-10, MRPC, 109-22 (anthologies).
A highly critical assessment of Catherine and her policies.
Shcherbatov, a publicist and historian who held a variety of
posts in the government of Catherine II, states that the empress, though clever and enterprising, "is licentious, and
trusts herself entirely to favourites, ... is full of ostentation
in all things, infinitely selfish, and incapable of forcing herself to attend to any matters which may bore her." Shcherbatov devotes considerable attention to describing Catherine's
favorites (especially Orlov and Betskoy) and her immoral and
decadent lifestyle. He concludes that Catherine's disreputable
behavior and policies have led to a general decline in the
moral fiber of the nobility and the general wellbeing of the
Russian nation.

741 *Smirnov, A. "The Soviet View: New Capitalist Relations."
CG (anthology), 143-58. From A Short History of the U.S.S.R.
Moscow, 1965, 172-87.
A Soviet presentation of Catherine's reign as one in which
feudalism was being replaced by capitalism and the class
struggle was intensified in the form of the Pugachev Revolt.
Within this context, Smirnov discusses the challenges which
faced Catherine as she sought to bolster serfdom and the
interests of the gentry while at the same time cope with the
problems and needs which attended the growing commercial
and industrial sectors of the Russian economy.

742 Thomson, Gladys Scott. Catherine the Great and the Expansion
of Russia. London: Hodder and Stoughton, 1947, 294pp.,
bib. 284-86.

As part of the Teach Yourself History series, this work seeks
to provide a general and popular account of the life and reign of
Catherine the Great. Thomson devotes most of her attention to
Catherine's promotion of Western science and culture and extension of Russia's borders at the expense of Poland and Turkey.

743 *Tooke, William. View of the Russian Empire During the Reign
of Catherine the Second, 3 Vols. London: T. N. Longman
and O. Rees, 1800.
More of a compilation of information on the nature and condition of the Russian Empire in the second half of the eighteenth
century than a study of Catherine the Great's reign, this detailed and widely read work presents a mass of information
on Russia's people, culture, geography, economy, administrative system, and military forces. Tooke, who spent much of
his life in Russia and was dedicated to promoting West European understanding of the Russian nation and people, bases
his account on the best scholarship of his era and on the
findings of Russian scientists commissioned in 1767 by Catherine II to travel into and study the nation's interior. In addition to his "view of the Russian Empire," Tooke discusses
Catherine's basic policies and in the process generally presents
her as a most capable successor to Peter the Great and the
chief source of all that was positive in the Russia of her era.
Catherine receives most praise, however, for opening Russia
to the West by publicizing abroad Russia's basic features and
promoting amicable relations with the major Western powers.
For a discussion of Tooke's writings on Russia and Catherine
II and his translation of the works of Castera, Georgi, and
Storch, see A. Cross' "The Reverend William Tooke's Contribution to English Knowledge of Russia at the End of the 18th
Century." Can Slav S, 3 (Spring 1969): 106-15. DK23.T66

744 *Troyat, Henri. Catherine the Great. Joan Pinkham, trans.
New York: E. P. Dutton, 1980, 377pp., bib. 358-61.
A popular and highly readable biography of Catherine II.
Troyat, who has written several works of this type on other
Russian monarchs, presents, with considerable dramatic flair,
a sympathetic narrative on Catherine, her rise to power, and
her principal policies and accomplishments. Drawing upon a
wide range of eighteenth-century French and English language
sources, especially Catherine's autobiographical writings,
Troyat projects the reader into the empress' environment and
innermost thoughts and feelings. Although Troyat presents
a balance of information on Catherine's foreign and domestic
affairs, it is very much the personal side of her life with
which he is most concerned. No new interpretation or scholarly judgment emerges from this biography, but it is among the
best of the popular accounts of Catherine and her reign.
DK170.T613
Reviewed in:
Hist Today, 30 (Sept. 1980): 57
Nat R, 32 (11 July 1980): 850

New Rep, 183 (27 Dec. 1980):   77
TLS, (25 Apr. 1980):   476
Virg Q R, 57 (Spring 1981):   47

745 Wenzlaff, Theodore C. "The Great Catherine the Great."
     Heritage R, 16 (Dec. 1976): 16-21.
     A generally favorable review of Catherine II's life and reign
     with special attention given to her encouragement of foreign
     settlements of the Russian interior. Written for the North
     Dakota Society of Germans.

746 Wren, M. "The Empress Catherine II." WITR (gen. study), 82-110.
     A survey of Catherine II's policies and accomplishments within
     the context of her concern for continuing the Westernization
     of Russia began by Peter I. Wren presents a balance of infor-
     mation on Catherine's political philosophy, administrative and
     cultural reforms, and foreign affairs. He concludes that Cath-
     erine deserves as much credit for the intellectual and cultural
     Westernization of aristocratic Russia as does Peter I for admin-
     istrative and technological Westernization, and he notes that
     Catherine, like Peter, did not aim at converting Russia into a
     Western nation but rather "to appropriate and adapt the best
     of what the West had to offer."

747 *Yaresh, Leo. "The Age of Catherine II." Two Essays in
     Soviet Historiography. New York: Research Program on the
     U.S.S.R., 1955, 30-42, 57-59.
     A review of Soviet writings of the 1930s and 1940s on Cath-
     erine II and her reign. Yaresh states that none of these
     writings can be considered to be substantial or comprehensive
     since they neglect her significant accomplishments. Those
     Soviet writers who identified important developments and
     achievements during her reign failed to credit her with being
     responsible for any of them. DK1.E35 no. 76

PERSONALITY/CHARACTER, FAMILY/PERSONAL RELATIONS,
                   AND COURT LIFE

748 Aldanov, M. A. "How a German Princess Became Empress of
     Russia." Liv Age, 315 (7 Oct. 1922): 33-36.
     A sketch from the author's historical novel dealing with how
     Frederick the Great conceived the idea of making the fifteen-year-
     old Princess Ficke of Zerbst the bride of the Grand Duke Peter.

749 Almedingen, E. M. The Young Catherine the Great. New York:
     Roy Publishers, 1965, 141pp.
     A somewhat fanciful account of Catherine II's youth up to the
     time of her departure for Russia. Almedingen draws heavily
     from Catherine's memoirs as she projects herself into the
     future empress of Russia's mind in order to reconstruct the
     family setting, personal relationships, and principal experi-
     ences in the life of the youthful Catherine. The author

depicts Catherine as an intelligent, pensive, romantic, and
ambitious young woman. DK170.A598

750 Altenhoff, Herbert T. Catherine the Great. Art. Sex. Politics. New York: Vantage Press, 1975, 114pp.
An account of Catherine II's love life with some attention
given to its relationship to her political behavior and successes.
Altenhoff, an officer in the German army during World War II
who served on the Russian front, supplements his discussion
of Catherine's relationship with Peter III and her various lovers
with a series of photographs which he took of the bedchambers
of Catherine's summer palace where furnishings and art work
abounded depicting phalli, genitalia, and sexual acts. In
regard to the political significance of Catherine's amorous affairs, Altenhoff poses, but does not answer fully, the question: "did she only fulfill her need for satisfaction in love
or were her affairs the vehicle for gaining power?" DK170.A6

751 Anthony, K. "Catherine Herself." New Rep, 7 (3 June 1916):
113-15.
A favorable review of Catherine II's life and accomplishments
serves as the basis for an attack on George B. Shaw's portrayal of the empress in his play "Great Catherine."

752 "Au Revoir, Potemkin?" Time, 105 (19 May 1975): 53-54.
Following an account of Catherine II's refusal of Great Britain's request for a force of 20,000 Russian mercenaries to
help suppress the American insurrection, the author describes
Catherine's political and romantic relationship with Potemkin
and speculates that the latter may not have become the empress' favorite by his own choosing.

753 Authentic Memoirs of the Life and Reign of Catherine II Empress
of All the Russias. Collected from Authentic Manuscripts,
Translations of the King of Sweden, Right Honorable Lord
Malmesbury, M. De Volney, and Other Indisputable Author-
ities. London: B. Crosby, 1797, 291pp.
Unavailable for annotation.

754 *"The Autobiography of Catherine II." Nat R, 8 (Jan. 1859):
32-64.
The 1859 publication of Catherine II's memoirs serves as the
basis for this discussion of Catherine's unhappy life as grand
duchess and her involvement in those political intrigues of the
Russian court which resulted in the assassination of Peter III
and her enthronement as empress of Russia.

755 *Bil'bassov, Vasilii A. "The Intellectual Formation of Catherine
II." CB (anthology), Robert Drumm, trans. 21-40. From
Istoricheskie Monografii, Vol. IV, St. Petersburg, 1901, 241-
72.

An analysis of the forces which helped to shape Catherine II's character and thought. Bilbassov, a conservative Russian historian and specialist on the reign of Catherine, discusses as formative influences upon Catherine's character the modest environment within which she was reared, her girlhood dreams about the luxury and glory of the Russian court, and the challenging circumstances which she encountered during her years as grand duchess. He states that Catherine was by nature of a philosophical mind and her years of solitude as a youth gave her ample time to read at length, especially the works of Diderot, Montesquieu, and Voltaire. However, while Catherine was heavily in debt to the French philosophers for her intellect, she was never in their tutelage but rather used their ideas selectively and practically to advance her public image and policies.

756   Bischoff, Ilse. "Madame Vigee Le Brun at the Court of Catherine the Great." Rus R, 24, no. 1 (1965): 30-45.
An account of the relationship between Catherine II and Madame Le Brun, a renowned French portrait painter living in exile as a result of the French Revolution. Bischoff discusses Le Brun's opinion of Catherine and the Russian court and the artist's painting of the empress' granddaughter.

757   Bradford, Gamaliel. "Eve Enthroned: Catherine the Great." Daughters of Eve. Port Washington: Kennikat Press, 1969 (reprint of 1939 edition), 156-97. Also in Yale R, 19 (Sept. 1929): 95-113.
A stylish portrayal of Catherine II as a loving and compassionate woman who enjoyed life immensely. Bradford discusses Catherine's love life and mental and spiritual constitution and comments incidentally on her domestic policies, particularly her active promotion of West European culture among the Russian nobility. CT3202.B68

758   *Buckinghamshire, John Hobart, Second Earl. The Despatches and Correspondence of John, Second Earl of Buckinghamshire, Ambassador to the Court of Catherine II of Russia, 1762-1765, 2 Vols. Adelaide D'Arcy Collyer, ed. London: Longmans, Green and Company, 1900-1901. Excerpts in CG, 95-100, RIRH, 181-84, 191-95 (anthologies).
A valuable and primary source of information on Catherine II's character, accession to power, and first few years of rule as empress. Buckinghamshire identifies as Catherine's assets her courage, resolution, industriousness, enlightened views, and laudable ambition to distinguish herself, while he sees as her shortcomings her amoral love life, preoccupation with trifling amusements, susceptibility to manipulation at the hands of unscrupulous favorites, lack of affection for her son Paul, and her tendency to be more concerned with grand and general plans than the details of their implementation.

In regard to the 1762 coup, Buckinghamshire states that
Peter III's ill-considered policies and miserable treatment of
Catherine apologize for her support of his removal from the
throne but not for her failure to punish those responsible for
his unnecessary murder. Buckinghamshire also comments on a
wide range of other incidents and developments within the
Russian court and in the process presents an interesting,
insider's view of Catherine's initial political position.
DA20.R91

759 *Catherine II, Empress of Russia. The Memoirs of Catherine
the Great. Lowell Blair, trans. A. Herzen, pref. New
York: Bantam Books, 1957, 305pp. Excerpts in CG (an-
thology), 126-32, Royal Memoirs. New York: Cooperative
Publication Society, 1901, 79-109, Milton Klonsky, ed.
The Fabulous Ego. Absolute Power in History. New York:
Quadrangle Books, 1974, 350-95.
In a preface to Catherine's memoirs of the years 1729-59,
Herzen, who smuggled a manuscript copy of the memoirs out
of Russia in 1858 and published them in their original French
language form, discusses the history of this valuable primary
source and the image of Catherine and Russia which they project. He also notes that the Memoirs' publication has "serious
consequences for the imperial family of Russia: they show
that not only does this family not belong to the Romanovs,
but that it does not even belong to the Holstein-Gottorps..."
since "the father of Tsar Paul I was Sergei Saltikov." In a
lengthy and perceptive epilogue (pp. 251-305), Lowell Blair
examines Catherine's relationship with Peter III, the coup
d'etat of 1762, the empress' various amorous affairs, and the
legacy of her reign.
For another translation, see The Memoirs of Catherine the
Great. Dominique Maroger, ed. Moura Budberg, trans.
G. P. Gooch, intro. New York: Macmillan, 1955, 400pp.
This publication includes a discussion, by G. P. Gooch, of
the historical setting of the Memoirs and their value as a
source of information on Catherine, and a series of letters,
documents, and autobiographical fragments beyond those con-
tained in the Herzen edition. DK172.A262
Herzen edition reviewed in:
Colburn's, 115 (1859): 218-26
Nat R, 8 (Jan. 1859): 32-64

Maroger edition reviewed in:
Hist Today, 5 (1955): 347
Rus R, 15, no. 2 (1956): 138
Sat R, 38 (30 Apr. 1955): 128-30
Spectator, (4 Mar. 1955): 261
TLS, (29 Apr. 1955): 194

760 "Catherine of Russia at Home." Chambers' Edinb J, 31 (Mar.
1859): 166-69.

A brief, sympathetic portrayal of Catherine's early life in
Russia; based upon Catherine's Memoirs.

761   Cérenville, Jeanne Elénore de. Memoirs of the Life of Prince
      Potemkin; Comprehending Original Anecdotes of Catharine
      II and of the Russian Court. London: Printed for Henry
      Colburn, 1812, 256pp.
      Although the career of Prince Gregory Potemkin is the focus
      of these memoirs, they shed considerable light on Catherine
      II's relationship with and delegation of power to this influ-
      ential court favorite. Cérenville discusses the origins of
      Potemkin's favor with Catherine, his military exploits in the
      Crimea, and subsequent administration of that region.
      Cérenville concludes that Potemkin's obvious vices obscured
      the great service he rendered to Catherine II: "for the
      space of 16 years, Catharine had no designs but what were
      his, and did nothing but through him. It was in this power
      that he found means to perform great things." DK169.P8M3

762   Chula, Prince of Siam. "Catherine II." The Education of the
      Enlightened Despots. London: Eyre and Spottiswoode, 1948,
      120-44.
      An examination of Catherine II's formal education at the hands
      of various nurses, tutors, and governors/governesses as
      well as that which she received from her unofficial teachers,
      most notably the English Ambassador Sir Charles Hanbury-
      Williams and the French philosopher Voltaire. In the process,
      Chula discusses Catherine's education in the humanities,
      religion, kingship and statecraft, military service, manners,
      love and marriage, and health and sports. LC4945.A1C47

763   Coolidge, Susan. "Girlhood of an Autocrat." Atlan M, 74
      (Aug. 1894): 166-80.
      An account of Catherine's arrival in Russia and early years
      of marriage to Grand Duke Peter. Using lengthy quotations
      from Catherine's Memoirs, Coolidge discusses the influence
      that this difficult time in Catherine's life had upon her char-
      acter, particularly in regard to her willpower and resource-
      fulness.

764   Crocker, L. G. "A Philosopher Queen." The Embattled Phi-
      losopher: A Life of Denis Diderot. London: Neville Spear-
      man, 1955, 373-400.
      A discussion of Diderot's conversations with Catherine II and
      the difficulties which he encountered at the imperial court as
      a consequence of aristocratic suspicion of his "radical ideas"
      and jealousy over the favor he enjoyed with Catherine.
      Crocker also reviews Diderot's correspondence with and serv-
      ice to Catherine after the former's March 1774 departure from
      St. Petersburg. Although Catherine rejected Diderot's politi-
      cal prescriptions because of their impracticality, and, therefore,

his attempt to influence her thought was fruitless, Crocker
concludes that "the Russian episode was the great adventure
of Diderot's life.... He returned richer in experience and
broader in horizons. At the same time, association with
royalty imparted to him an aura of respectability which he
had never before enjoyed." B2016.C68

765 *Cross, A. G. "John Rogerson: Physician to Catherine the
     Great." Can Slav S, 4 (1970): 594-601.
     A discussion of John Rogerson's activities at the Russian
     court as both a confidant of Catherine II and "a pillar of the
     English community." Although Rogerson treated the ailments
     of a number of members of the royal court, Catherine's affec-
     tion for him was not due to his medical skills (which she in
     fact questioned) but rather to her "recognition of his un-
     doubted loyalty and devotion to her ... as well as his extreme
     usefulness as a storehouse of information about court affairs."

766 Cuppy, William. "Catherine the Great." The Decline and Fall
     of Practically Everybody. New York: H. Holt and Company,
     1950, 141-48.
     A witty sketch of Catherine II's private life as both grand
     duchess and empress. Particularly amusing is Cuppy's de-
     scription of Potemkin as "the only one of Catherine's men who
     was not strikingly handsome. He was one-eyed, hook-nosed,
     bow-legged, and mostly drunk. He would live for days on
     kvass and raw onions, mooching around the palace barefoot
     in a dirty old dressing gown, biting his nails. Nobody could
     understand what Catherine saw in him. Well, when you got
     him alone, he could imitate the voice of a dog, a cat, and a
     rooster to perfection, the only form of art Catherine honestly
     loved. She could imitate a cat herself, but nothing to brag
     of." PN6161.C787

767 Dale, Philip M. "Catherine the Great." Medical Biographies.
     Norman: University of Oklahoma Press, 1952, 91-101.
     A description of Catherine II's medical condition from her
     youth up to and including her 1796 death. Dale notes Cath-
     erine's bouts with pleurisy and pneumonia while a child and
     again during her early years in Russia, including on the eve
     of her marriage, and speculates on the possibility that the
     unstable mentality of her son Paul may have been due to her
     contraction of syphilis from one of her lovers. Catherine's
     death, he concludes, was most likely the result of a cerebral
     hemorrhage due to arteriosclerosis and prolonged high blood
     pressure. R703.D3

768 *Dashkov, Princess. The Memoirs of Princess Dashkov. Kyril
     Fitzlyon, ed./trans./intro. London: John Calser, 1958,
     322pp. Excerpt in The Fabulos Ego. Absolute Power in
     History. Milton Klonsky, ed. New York: Quadrangle Books,

1974, 350-95.

Recollections, by a confidante of Catherine II, of various
court affairs, the behavior and character of the empress,
and, most importantly, the 1762 coup d'etat which removed
Peter III from the throne. The Memoirs, written when the
princess was 60 years old and initially translated into English from the original French in 1840, is one of the most
valuable sources of information on the conspiracy behind the
1762 coup since Dashkov was among the conspirators and thus
was able to provide an inside view of the foundation and implementation of the plot. In an interesting and insightful
introduction, K. Fitzlyon discusses the relationship between
the princess and the empress and the historical merits of the
Memoirs. He portrays Dashkov as "the guiding spirit of the
conspiracy" which brought Catherine to the throne of Russia.
DK 169. D2A 42

769 *DeLigne, Prince Charles Joseph. The Prince DeLigne. His
Memoirs, Letters, and Miscellaneous Papers. Katharine
Prescott Wormeley, ed./trans. Boston: Hardy, Pratt and
Company, 1899.
Included in this work are the 1780-96 letters exchanged between Catherine II and Prince DeLigne and a wide range of
observations and commentaries by the latter in regard to the
empress and a number of her policies. DeLigne, a confidant
and emissary of Joseph II of Austria, had considerable contact with Catherine and her favorites, and accompanied Potemkin and Catherine on their "triumphal tour" of the Crimea in
1787. While the author's insights into court affairs and politics are of value, it is his description of the splendor and
frivolity of the Crimean entourage that is most noteworthy.
Of additional interest is the prince's commentary on Catherine's
non-involvement in the 1762 murder of Peter III. For a discussion of the Memoirs, see G. Norton. "Crimean Journey of
Catherine II." Nation, 44 (1887): 60-61.

770 DeSégur, Count Louis Philippe. Memoirs and Recollections of
Count Louis Phillipe DeSégur. New York: Arno Press, 1973.
This work, written by the French ambassador to Russia
(1784-89), sheds considerable light on the character, intellect,
and tastes of Catherine II and various individuals prominent
in her court. DeSégur, who enjoyed the favor of the empress
because of his quick wit and well-developed social skills, also
recollects his efforts to promote Franco-Russian commercial
and political relations, largely at the expense of England's
long-standing favor with Russian rulers. Of special interest
is his eyewitness account of the pomp and majesty which
characterized the tour of the Crimea orchestrated for Catherine by Prince Potemkin. DC146. S37A 42
For a discussion of the historical setting of DeSégur's embassy to Russia and the reasons for his successfulness while

in St. Petersburg, see Alelaide D'Arcy Collyer's "A French
Ambassador at the Court of Catherine II." Liv Age, 202
(July 1984): 131-44. Also in Temp Bar, 102 (1894): 169+.

771 Diderot, Denis. "Portrait of the Empress." CG (anthology),
     117-20. From "Diderot to Catherine II, October 17, 1774,"
     and "Propos de Diderot sur l'imperatrice de Russie," in
     Maurice Tourneaux's Diderot et Catherine II. L. J. Oliva,
     trans. Paris: Calmann Lévy, 1899, 495-98, 579-82.
     A letter of Diderot to Catherine II and a series of brief,
     favorable observations by Diderot on the empress' intelli-
     gence and character.

772 Dreifuss, Jerome. Catherine and Potemkin. An Imperial Ro-
     mance. New York: Covici Friede Publishers, 1937, 343pp.,
     bib. 339-43.
     Although this work reads more like a romantic novel than a
     historical monograph, it is based upon Catherine II's various
     correspondences, especially her letters to Potemkin, and on
     a good number of Russian, German, and English language
     secondary sources on Catherine and her most important lover,
     Prince Gregory Potemkin. Projecting himself into the inner-
     most thoughts of Catherine and Potemkin, Dreifuss presents
     a colorful and graphic account of the origin, development,
     and termination of Catherine's relationship with Potemkin.
     DK170.D77

773 Durant, Mary. "Catherine's Boat Ride." Horizon, 8, no. 4
     (1966): 98-104.
     An account of Catherine II's Crimean tour with special atten-
     tion given to the "window-dressing" of the region by Potemkin
     to impress the empress and the foreign dignitaries who ac-
     companied her. Durant maintains that Potemkin's "special
     effects" were far less extensive than portrayed by many
     critics and were "in keeping with Catherine's and Potemkin's
     inordinate love of ostentation."

774 Feltman, Jeffrey. "Catherine the Great's Correspondence with
     Voltaire." Indiana Soc St Q, 31 (Autumn 1978): 40-46.
     Unavailable for annotation.

775 *"The French Embassy: Paternity of Grand Duke Paul." CG
     (anthology), 111-12. From "Notes from Saint Petersburg,
     September 8, 1758," in Archives of Foreign Affairs of France,
     Russian Correspondence, Vol. 57. L. J. Oliva, trans.
     A 1758 French document which asserts that Sergei Saltykov
     fathered Catherine's son Paul, but, "frightened by his pre-
     dicament," took measures to remedy the cause of Grand Duke
     Peter's impotency so that Peter could consummate his marriage
     and therein appear to be the source of Catherine's pregnancy.

776 George, Walter L. "Catherine the Great." Historic Lovers.
     London: Hutchinson and Company Limited, 1926, 161-82.
     A popular account of Catherine II's personal life. George
     sees Catherine's claim to greatness as resting on the intelli-
     gence and nerve which she displayed in rising to power and
     using her lovers to advance her political interests rather
     than on any improvements which she made in Russia's politi-
     cal, economic, or cultural condition.

777 "Giddy Empress' Golden Rules." Lit D, 88 (30 Jan. 1926):
     42-48.
     A glimpse of the social mores personified by Catherine at
     royal functions.

778 Gip, Bernard. Passions and Lechery of Catherine the Great.
     London: Skilton, 1971, 74pp.   DK171.5.G56313
     Unavailable for annotation.

779 Golder, Frank. John Paul Jones in Russia. Garden City, N.Y.:
     Doubleday and Page Company, 1927, 230pp.   DR555.7.J6
     Unavailable for annotation.

780 *Golovina, Countess C. N. "The Last Years of the Reign of
     Catherine II." Memoirs of Countess Golovine. A Lady at
     the Court of Catherine II. G. M. Fox-Davies, trans. K.
     Waliszewski, pref. London: David Nutt, 1910, 121pp.
     An illuminating series of observations and commentaries on
     Catherine II and court life during the last two decades of her
     reign. Golovine, who was a favorite of Catherine and an
     intimate of Grand Duchess Elizabeth (the wife of the future
     Alexander I), focuses on those who surrounded the empress
     but also comments upon Catherine's personality, character,
     and private life as well as on court reaction to her death.
     In a lengthy preface, K. Waliszewski discusses Golovine's
     life and the historical importance of her memoirs.
     DK188.6.G6A3

781 *Gooch, G. P. "Mother and Son." Catherine the Great and
     Other Studies. London: Longmans, Green and Company,
     1954, 20-36.
     A discussion of Catherine's estrangement from and rivalry
     with her son Paul as "the most embarrassing problem of her
     reign." DK170.G65

782 Gribble, Francis. The Comedy of Catherine the Great. Lon-
     don: Grayson and Grayson, n.d., 368pp.
     A vivid, popular recreation of Catherine II's personal life.
     Drawing heavily upon the writings of Waliszewski and the
     empress herself, Gribble describes Catherine as a marvelous
     social creature, thoroughly charming, and a master conver-
     sationalist. The author criticizes those who portray her as

a licentious, amoral hedonist and presents instead an image
of her as a vivacious, overly sentimental woman and an able,
if not great, ruler. DK170.G7

783 *Griffin, Frederick C. "Catherine the Great and Voltaire."
St Hist Soc, 4, no. 1 (1972): 12-18.
A discussion of the mutually beneficial nature of the relationship between Catherine the Great and Voltaire. Griffin asserts that Catherine effectively used Voltaire as a propa-
gandist for her image as an enlightened ruler. Voltaire was
aware of the role he was playing and realized that Catherine's
enlightenment was only a facade but believed that he could
win support for his progressive views by describing them in
the form of the empress' deeds, policies, and principles.

784 *Hadley, Michael. "The Sublime Housewife: An 18th Century
German View of Catherine the Great." Germano-Slavica, 2
(Spring 1977): 181-88.
An analysis of A. F. Geisler's Katharine die Zweite, Kaiserin
von Rusland und Selbstherrscherin aller Reussen. Ein bio-
graphisch-karakterisches [sic] Germälde (1797) as a typifica-
tion of the eighteenth-century German portrayal of Catherine
as "a model of both political and domestic virtue." Hadley
also speculates on why German writers, unlike their British
and French counterparts, did not write of Catherine's scandalous personal life or role in the overthrow of her husband
Peter III.

785 Hanemann, H. W. "The Facts of Life. A Series of Parody
Biographies. Catherine the Great. A Loose Lady Friend of
Vina Delmar's." Bookman, 70 (Oct. 1929): 157-63.
A witty and spicy re-creation of the highlights of Catherine
II's personal life.

786 *Harris, James, Earl of Malmesbury. Diaries and Correspond-
dence of James Harris, First Earl of Malmesbury. 4 Vols.
London: Richard Bentley, 1844.
Observations and comments on Catherine II, her advisers,
and her court by the British ambassador to St. Petersburg,
1777-82. Harris' many references to Catherine and court
politics are scattered throughout the letters and memoirs of
this four-volume set but nonetheless constitute a valuable
source of firsthand information on a wide range of subjects
and incidents. Of special interest are his comments on Potemkin, with whom Harris formed a close relationship, and on
Catherine's character, personal relationships, political conduct,
attitude toward England and the American Revolution, and
policy toward Poland and Turkey. In general, Harris portrays Catherine as an able and astute ruler, though an ex-
cessively vain one, committed to an ambitious and aggressive
foreign policy. D364.M2

For a discussion of Harris' use of bribery as a diplomatic
tool, see Isabel DeMadariaga's "The Use of British Secret
Funds in St. Petersburg, 1777-1782." Slavonic E Eur R,
32 (1954): 464-74.

787 Hill, Georgiana. "Catherine II and the Comte de Ségur."
Gent M, 291 (July 1901): 62-65.
A brief description of "the foremost place in the circle of
Catherine II's admirers and flatterers" occupied by the French
courtier, the Comte de Ségur, because of his quick wit, well-
developed social graces, and ability to excel at the court
games which the empress loved to play.

788 *Hyde, H. Montgomery. The Empress Catherine and Princess
Dashkov. London: Chapman and Hall, 1935, 282pp.
A study of the life of Princess Dashkov and her relationship
with and influence on Catherine II. Drawing primarily on
Dashkov's Memoirs and correspondence with Catherine and
various prominent Russians, Hyde asserts that "in spite of
repeated quarrels and reconciliations, the facts remain that
Dashkova helped to put Catherine on the Russian throne,
and between them they advanced immeasurably the cause of
letters and science in the country...." He defends Dashkov
against the charge, advanced by her contemporaries, that
she was "an unscrupulous intriguer" and maintains that the
actual source of her disfavor was her lack of tact and consequent "fatal facility for making enemies." The princess was
not in any way deceitful or manipulative in her dealings with
Catherine but rather was "the willing tool of a dominant personality." DK169.D3H9

789 *Ilchester, Earl of, and Mrs. Langford-Brooke, eds./trans.
Correspondence of Catherine the Great when Grand Duchess
with Sir Charles Hanbury-Williams and Letters from Count
Poniatowski. M. Sergei Gorianov, intro. London: T.
Butterworth, 1928, 288pp.
The letters contained within this volume constitute a valuable
source of primary information in regard to Catherine II's
relationship with Elizabeth and Grand Duke Peter, love affair
with K. Poniatowski, and status within the Russian court in
the years prior to her assumption of the throne. Hanbury-
Williams, British ambassador to Russia in the mid-1750s, was
a formative influence in the shaping of young Catherine's
political ambitions and was responsible for the advent of her
affair with Poniatowski. The letters indicate the nature and
extent of this influence and the favor Hanbury-Williams enjoyed with the grand duchess and shed light on the attempt
of Count Bestuzhev to undermine the position of both Poniatowski and Hanbury-Williams.

790 _____. The Life of Sir Charles Hanbury-Williams, Poet, Wit,

Diplomatist. London: Thornton Butterworth, 1929.
The last six chapters of this study deal with Sir Charles
Hanbury-Williams' two years in St. Petersburg as British
ambassador to Russia during which time he formed a close
relationship with Grand Duchess Catherine. Drawing primarily from Hanbury-Williams' correspondence with Catherine and
various members of the British Foreign Office, the authors
discuss his role in establishing and maintaining Poniatowski
as Catherine's lover and his provision of financial aid, to
enable her to counter French influence within the Russian
court, as well as political counsel. DA501.W615

791 Johnson, C. A. "Wedgwood and Bentley's 'Frog' Service for
Catherine the Great." GRB (anthology), 123-33.
An account of Joseph Wedgwood's manufacture and decoration
of "the most famous dinner service in Europe," the 952-piece
"frog" service purchased by Catherine the Great in 1774.
Johnson also discusses Catherine's use of the service for dinner parties in honor of distinguished English visitors and
ambassadors. DK67.5.G7G73

792 Kelly, Alison. "Wedgwood's Catharine Service." Burlington M,
122 (Aug. 1980): 554-61.
An account of the commissioning and production of the famous
952-piece Wedgwood dinner service with most attention given
to the cost and difficulties encountered in manufacturing the
enormous set.

793 Kemble, James. "Catherine the Great of Russia." Idols and
Invalids. Garden City: Doubleday, Doran and Company,
1936, 221-43.
A somewhat disjointed review of Catherine II's personal life,
and a sympathetic assessment of her character. CT105.K38

794 Klonsky, Milton, ed. "Catherine the Great." The Fabulous
Ego. Absolute Power in History. New York: Quadrangle
Books, 1974, 350-95.
A brief commentary on the zestful personal life of Catherine
II precedes a series of excerpts from Castera, Dashkov, and
Catherine's memoirs which deal with her life as grand duchess,
role in the overthrow and assassination of Peter III, romantic
relationships with various favorites, and her claim to historical
greatness. The section concludes with the statement "Catherine had two passions which never left her but with her last
breath: the love of man, which degenerated into licentious-
ness, and the love of glory, which sank into vanity."
D107.K55

795 Kotzebue, August Friedrich Ferdinand von. The Most Remarkable Year in the Life of August von Kotzebue, 3 Vols. London:
R. Phillips, 1802. The appendix of this work is listed as containing an examination of Masson's Secret Memoirs of the

Court of Russia.
Unavailable for annotation.

796 Krasinski, Count Henry. The Cossacks of the Ukraine: Com-
     prising Biographical Notes of the Most Celebrated Cossack
     Chiefs or Attamans, and a Description of the Ukraine with a
     Memoir of Princess Tarakanof, and some Particulars Respect-
     ing Catherine II of Russia and Her Favourites. London:
     Partridge and Oakey, Paternoster Row, 1848, 312.
     This work contains a section which sharply attacks Catherine
     II's Polish policy and scandalous personal life. Krasinski
     criticizes Catherine's wasteful spending on gifts which she
     lavished upon her favorites, and he portrays her as a dia-
     bolical and vindictive tyrant. DK35.K89

797 Le Corbeiller, C. "Grace and Favor: Catherine the Great's
     Orloff Service." Met Mus, 27 (Feb. 1969): 289-98.
     Unavailable for annotation.

798 *Lentin, A. "Catherine the Great and Denis Diderot." Hist
     Today, 22, no. 5 (1972): 313-20.
     An account of the 1773 visit of French philosopher Denis
     Diderot to the court of St. Petersburg. Lentin states that
     Catherine II invited Diderot to visit her because of the
     favorable publicity that she believed could be gained from
     such an act, while Diderot responded favorably to the em-
     press' request not out of any desire to thank Catherine for
     support of his writings or to gain additional financial aid
     but rather to try to persuade her to act upon her enlightened
     views and thereby set an example of reform for Europe's
     monarchs to emulate. However, in his conversations with
     Catherine, Diderot gradually came to realize that she regarded
     his political philosophy as a utopian one particularly inappli-
     cable to Russia given her political position and the nation's
     economic backwardness. On the other hand, Catherine
     found Diderot's familiar manner irksome and her conversations
     with him futile.

799 Lewis, Dominic B. W. "Potemkin." Four Favourites. New
     York: Longmans, Green and Company, 1949, 172-232.
     An examination of the origin and nature of Potemkin's relation-
     ship with Catherine II. Lewis portrays Catherine as a virile
     and amoral woman with an aversion to marriage after her
     disastrous experience with Peter III. Her relationship with
     Potemkin was a physically and emotionally satisfying one even
     though Potemkin attempted to make her "totally dependent on
     him" and to establish himself as tsar, a capacity in which he
     was well on the way toward functioning despite his avarice
     and the opposition it inspired within the Russian court.
     Lewis concludes that Potemkin's death "robbed Catherine the
     Great of an irreplaceable servant, ally, friend, and counsellor;

(and) Russia of an unrivalled and very expensive publicity
agent." D107.7.L48

800 Lorenz, Lincoln. The Admiral and the Empress. John Paul
Jones and Catherine the Great. New York: Bookman Associates, 1954, 194pp., bib. 185-86.
A sympathetic account of John Paul Jones' ventures and misfortunes in Russia. Lorenz portrays Catherine as an unscrupulous, vain, and ambitious tyrant who lured the naive
and idealistic Jones into service in the Russian navy in hope
of securing victory in her war with the Ottoman Turks and
then, under the influence of the jealous Potemkin, allowed
Jones' reputation to be ruined by the malicious charge that
he molested a ten-year-old girl. E207.J7L77

801 *Luppol, Ivan K. "The Empress and the Philosophe." CGP
(anthology), 41-63. From his "Didro i Ekaterina II" in
Deni Didro-Ocherki zhizni i mirovozreniia. Mary Mackler,
trans. Moscow: 1960, 91-115.
A scholarly assessment of the intellectual and personal relationship between French philosopher Denis Diderot and
Catherine II. Luppol, a Russian specialist on eighteenth-
century intellectual history, states that Diderot, in his
conversations with Catherine, presented ideas wholly unacceptable to her as the monarch of a semi-feudal society, but
in her response she did not overtly reject them largely because "she valued him as a means of gaining publicity in
Europe." Luppol notes that Diderot apparently did not
expect Catherine, as a sovereign, to take his proposals
seriously but did assume that the empress, as a philosopher
in her own right, would find his ideas meritorious.

802 Masson, Charles. Secret Memoirs of the Court of St. Petersburg Particularly Towards the End of the Reign of Catherine
II and the Commencement of That of Paul I. London: Wilson
and Company, 1802, 423pp. Excerpt in MRPC (anthology),
123-36.
A series of observations and commentaries on Catherine II's
reaction to the French Revolution, the financial condition of
the Russian Empire at the close of her reign, and the relations between Catherine, her son Paul, and her grandson
Alexander. Masson, who was an officer in Catherine's Imperial Guards and served as tutor to Grand Duke Alexander,
is critical of Catherine's extravagant life style, burdensome
financial policy, and reactionary attempt to crush the liberalism epitomized by the French Republic. Masson reserves the
majority of his criticisms, however, for Emperor Paul who had
expelled him from Russia upon assuming the throne. The
scandalous nature of some of the incidents and behavior described by Masson (particularly in the section titled "Historical Anecdotes") led to the Memoirs creation of a public

sensation in Western Europe when first published in 1800.
DK171.M43

803   Murat, Princess Lucien. The Private Life of Catherine the
      Great. Garnett Saffery, trans. New York: Louis Carrier
      and Company, 1928, 212pp.
      A fanciful, anecdotal account of Catherine's love of life.
      DK171.5.C515

804   Nikolaev, Vsevolod A., and Albert Parry. The Loves of Cath-
      erine the Great. New York: Coward, McCann and Geoghe-
      gan, 1982, 287pp., bib. 264-77.
      An account of Catherine's relationship with her first three
      lovers, Sergei Saltykov, Stanislas Poniatowski, and Gregory
      Orlov. The authors assert that each man "was responsible
      for awakening passions lying dormant in Catherine. And
      these passions, the source of her indomitable will, combined
      with her innate gift for intrigue to propel Catherine along
      the road to despotism and empire." Saltykov, who was
      selected by Empress Elizabeth to provide Catherine with the
      child that Peter III was apparently incapable of producing,
      certainly aroused Catherine's passions but most likely was
      not the father of her son Paul. Peter III, after "corrective
      surgery," was probably Paul's father, a fact intentionally
      concealed by Catherine in her Memoirs so that Paul's claim
      to the throne would be seen as less deserving than her own.
      Poniatowski, a dashing Polish aristocrat, was Catherine's
      second lover and father of her second child, Anna. In this
      affair, the authors concentrate on the romance and intrigue
      which attended the relationship Catherine and Poniatowski
      conducted behind the backs of Peter III and Empress Eliza-
      beth. In discussing Orlov's relationship with Catherine, the
      authors devote most attention to his crucial part in the con-
      spiracy which led to Peter III's overthrow and Catherine's
      accession to the throne of Russia. DK171.5.N54

805   O'Hare, John. "Catherine." Uneasy Lies the Head. London:
      Alvin Redman Limited, 1955, 87-109.
      A sympathetic popularization of Catherine's youth, life as
      grand duchess, and seizure of power at the expense of Peter
      III. CT105.045

806   Oldenbourg, Zoe. Catherine the Great. Anne Carter, trans.
      New York: Random House, 1965, 387pp., bib. 377-78.
      A popular account of "the slow shaping and maturing of the
      future empress" during her years as grand duchess. Olden-
      bourg discusses the influence of Empress Elizabeth, Peter III,
      and Russian court conditions of the 1750s and 1760s in deter-
      mining Catherine's character, methods, and successes, and in
      the process portrays Catherine as an astute, energetic, and
      vivacious individual, but calculating, vain, and prideful.
      DK170.0373

807   Orr, Lyndon.   "The Empress Catharine and Prince Potemkin."
      Famous Affinities of History.   Vol. II.   New York: Harper
      and Brothers, 1909, 3-22.
      A short description of the life of Catherine II with emphasis
      on her relationships with her husband and lovers, particular-
      ly Count Potemkin.   Orr devotes most of his attention to Po-
      temkin's satisfaction of Catherine's needs and desires as a
      woman.   CT3203.07

808   Permenter, Hannelore R.   "The Personality and Cultural Inter-
      ests of the Empress Catherine II as Revealed in Her Corres-
      pondence with Friedrich Melchior Grimm."   University of
      Texas, 1970.   (dissertation)

809   Pitcher, Harvey.   "A Scottish View of Catherine's Russia:
      William Richardson's Anecdotes of the Russian Empire, 1784."
      Forum Mod Lang St, 3, no. 3 (1967):   236-51.
      A discussion of William Richardson's Anecdotes as "the best
      work by a British writer on Russia during the eighteenth
      century."   Pitcher describes Richardson (secretary to Lord
      Cathcart, British ambassador to Russia) as an exceptionally
      astute observer, particularly in regard to the nature of the
      Russian political system and national character and the short-
      comings of the nobility and clergy.

810   Polovtsoff, Alexander.   The Favourites of Catherine the Great.
      London: Herbert Jenkins Limited, 1940, 288pp.
      A study of Catherine's relationship with twelve of her fav-
      orites: S. Saltykov, S. Poniatowski, G. Orlov, A. Vassil-
      chikov, G. Potemkin, P. Zavadovsky, S. Korich, I. Rimsky-
      Korsakov, A. Lanskoy, A. Yermolov, A. Deimitriev-Mamonov,
      and P. Zubov.   Polovtsoff discusses the lives of each of
      these men, the origin and nature of their relationships with
      Catherine, and the reasons which prompted the empress to
      part from their company.   He criticizes those biographers who
      have depicted Catherine as a sensation-seeking nymphomaniac
      and maintains instead that she was far more of a sentimental-
      ist than a sensualist and was, in fact, faithful to her lovers
      throughout the duration of her relationship with each of them.
      Polovtsoff concludes that it is unfortunate that most commenta-
      tors on Catherine and her reign have dwelled upon the em-
      press' love affairs at the expense of her many accomplishments
      as an exceptional and noble monarch.

811   Polter, George W.   "Catherine the Great of Russia."   Royal
      Blood.   Garden City, N.Y.:   Doubleday, 1961, 35-58.
      A popularization of Catherine II's relationship with Peter III,
      accession to power, and love affairs with various court
      favorites.

812   *Putnam, Peter.   "Sir James Harris: Lion in the Vixen's Den
      (1777-1783)."   SBIR (anthology), 179-95.

A perceptive commentary on the experiences and writings of
the British diplomat, Sir James Harris. Of particular interest
is Putnam's discussion of Harris' involvement in court politics
and his inability to utilize the information which he garnered
from his intrigues in any way that would enable him to predict
or shape Russian foreign policy.

813   *_____. "William Richardson: Humanist Scholar of Slavery
(1768-1772)." Ibid., 125-40.
A discussion of Richardson's travels in and writings on the
Russia of Catherine the Great. Putnam commends Richardson
for his vivid and amusing anecdotes and perceptive analysis
of the Russian political system and national character but
sees him as a shortsighted commentator on the empress' diplomacy.

814   *Rasmussen, Karen. "Catherine II and the Image of Peter I."
Slav R, 37, no. 1 (1978): 51-69.
The stated purpose of this article is to answer two questions:
"What was Catherine's opinion of Peter the Great" and "How
closely did she feel her reign and reputation measured up to
his." Rasmussen concludes that Catherine "was not an uncritical admirer of Peter the Great" ... but rather, "found
the image of Peter as a farsighted and triumphant ruler per-
suasive or helpful in some contexts, inadequate or uncomfort-
able in others." The author draws upon Catherine's legislation and less public remarks and correspondence to support
her argument.

815   *Reddaway, W. F., ed. Documents of Catherine the Great.
The Correspondence with Voltaire and the Instruction of 1767
in the English Text of 1768. Cambridge: University of Cambridge Press, 1931, 349pp.
In a perceptive introduction, Reddaway provides background
to and commentary on Catherine's 1763-77 correspondence with
Voltaire (the letters are collected here in their original French
language form) and on the 1768 English language translation
of the text of Catherine's 1767 Instruction or Nakaz to the
Legislative Commission. Reddaway discusses the opinion that
Catherine and Voltaire had toward each other, the question
of the authorship of Catherine's letters, and the benefits
gained by Catherine and Voltaire from their correspondence.
He also examines the sources of the ideas expressed by Cath-
erine in her Nakaz, the basic content of the document, and
the impact that it had on contemporary European opinion of
her. DK168.C4
Reviewed in:
Am Hist R, 37 (1932): 794
Eng Hist R, 47 (1932): 710
History, 17 (1932): 268

816   *Richardson, William. Anecdotes of the Russian Empire. Lon-
      don: W. Strahan and T. Cadell, 1784, 478pp. Excerpts in
      CG, 113-16 and SBIR, 141-78, (anthologies).
      A series of 1768-72 letters, written by a Scottish observer
      who served as secretary to British ambassador to St. Peters-
      burg Lord Cathcart, which provides a vivid portrayal of Rus-
      sian society and court life, and includes comments on Cather-
      ine's behavior, personality, character, and daily habits as
      well as on her convocation of the Legislative Commission.
      Richardson states that the distinguishing feature of Cather-
      ine's character, and one that motivated a great many of her
      actions, was her "desire of doing good" as a means of ac-
      quiring public acclaim. DK1717.R52
      For a discussion of the merits of Richardson's ancedotes
      see SBIR (anthology), 141-78, and S. Pitcher, "A Scottish
      View of Catherine's Russia." Forum Mod Lang St, 3, no. 3
      (1967): 236-51.

817   Savill, Rosalind. "'Cameo Fever': Six Pieces from the Serves
      Porcelain Dinner Service Made for Catherine II of Russia."
      Apollo, 116 (Nov. 1982): 304-11.
      A description of six pieces of the Serves dinner service,
      and a discussion of Catherine's passion for collecting stone-
      ware carved in relief.

818   Self, Gloria. "Catherine and Potemkin." San Diego M, 27
      (Sept. 1975): 106-24.
      A discussion of Potemkin's role in shaping various policies
      pursued by Catherine the Great, most notably her attempts
      to solve by force the Eastern Question and to Russify newly
      acquired territories. Self also discusses Catherine's turn
      toward conservatism in the last years of her reign and her
      reaction to Potemkin's death.

819   Sergeant, Philip W. The Courtship of Catherine the Great.
      New York: Brentano's Publishers, n.d., 337pp. For a con-
      densed version of this work, see the author's Dominant Women.
      New York: Books for Libraries Press, 1969, 203-30.
      An account of Catherine's rise to power and her personal life
      as empress of Russia. Sergeant devotes nearly half of his
      book to Catherine's amorous relationships, especially with
      Orlov and Potemkin, and, in the process, describes Cather-
      ine's attitude toward and practice of the favoritism which was
      so prevalent at the court of many of Russia's rulers. Ser-
      geant concludes with a rather lengthy assessment of Cather-
      ine's character and claim to greatness in which he presents
      her as a charming, amiable, and intelligent woman who well
      deserves the title "the Great" primarily because of her re-
      markable successes in foreign policy. DK170.S5

820   Shaw, Bernard. "Great Catherine: A Thumbnail Sketch of

Court Life in the 18th Century." Everybody's M, 32 (1915): 193-212.
Unavailable for annotation.

821 Soloveytchik, George. Potemkin. A Picture of Catherine's Russia. London: Thornton Butterworth Limited, 1938, 349pp. Also published as Potemkin. Soldier, Statesman, Lover and Consort of Catherine of Russia. New York: W. W. Norton, 1947.
Although Potemkin, not Catherine, is the focus of this study, it presents a significant amount of information and detail on Catherine and her internal and foreign policies. Most notably, Soloveytchik provides a very readable and comprehensive account of the empress' relationship with Potemkin and the power which the later wielded in her name. The author asserts that Potemkin has been erroneously portrayed as just another of Catherine's favorites, and a scurrilous one at that, when, in fact, he was an astute and energetic individual with many positive achievements to his credit.
DK169.P8S65

822 Stander, Edith A. "The Mistress and the Widow." Met Mus, 25 (Jan. 1967); 185-96.
The portraits of Catherine the Great and Peter III's mistress, which are part of the collection of the New York Metropolitan Museum of Art, prompt the author to discuss Peter III's relationship with both women and to present a favorable image of Catherine as a patron of the arts.

823 Steel, Mortimer. "John Paul Jones and Catherine the Great." Mentor, 14 (July 1926): 33-34.
A brief account of Jones' departure from Russia because of fear that Catherine II was about to take hostile action against him.

824 Trease, Geoffrey. "Catherine the Great." Seven Sovereign Queens. New York: Vanguard Press, 1968, 149-78.
A popular, favorable review of Catherine's life as grand duchess and reign as empress. Trease commends Catherine for coping courageously with a difficult situation during her years of marriage to Peter III and for her "continuation of the policies of Peter the Great to magnify Russia and make her a world power." D107.3.T7

825 Treue, Wilhelm. "The Empress Catherine and Doctor Zimmerman." DAC (gen. study), 60-64.
A brief account of the relationship between Catherine II and Dr. Zimmerman, a Swiss physician with whom the empress came to carry on a long-lived and lively correspondence following her reading of Zimmerman's book On Solitude. Treue describes the general tone and substance of the correspondence and, in particular, the moral support and ego strength

gained by Catherine from Zimmerman's letters.

826   . "A Famous Vaccinator and an Influential Scottish
Doctor." Ibid., 65-68.
A brief account of the vaccination of Catherine II and Grand
Duke Paul by Dr. Thomas Dimsdale. Treue also discusses the
fame and financial rewards which Dimsdale gained from his
service to Catherine.

827 Tuttle, Herbert. "Bridal Journey of Catherine the Great."
Cosmopol, 3 (May 1887): 147-50.
An account of the politics involved in Catherine being selected
as the wife of Grand Duke Peter, and a description of Catherine's journey to St. Petersburg and initial meeting with
Peter and Empress Elizabeth. Tuttle also notes that while
Frederick of Prussia was instrumental in arranging Catherine's
marriage to Peter, she refrained from favoring Frederick with
a political alliance once she assumed the throne of Russia.

828 *Voltaire, François Marie Arouet de. Voltaire and Catherine
the Great. Selected Correspondence. A. Lentin, trans./
intro. Cambridge, England: Oriental Research Partners,
1974, 191pp.
The correspondence between Catherine the Great and the
French philosopher Voltaire are of value not only as a source
of information on the empress' intellect and political thought
but also for the light which they shed upon her place within
the Enlightenment personified by Voltaire. As A. Lentin aptly
points out in his introduction to this work, Catherine admired
Voltaire for his wit and talent as a writer but it was not for
his views but his vogue that she cultivated their relationship.
Lentin adds that Catherine's rule "might or might not be
enlightened, but it was essential to her public image that it
should seem to be." PQ1084.C313

829 *Waliszewski, K. The Romance of an Empress. Catherine II
of Russia. New York: D. Appleton and Company, 1900,
458pp. Excerpt in William Trowbridge, ed. These Splendid
Women. New York: J. H. Sears, 1926, 264-89.
A general biography of Catherine with special attention given
to her personal life. Waliszewski has short sections on home
and foreign policy but devotes most of his time to an account
of Catherine's rise to power, her personality, character and
ideals, family and romantic relationships, and, to a lesser extent, her cultural policy. While Waliszewski commends Catherine for her dedication, will power, and pursuit of policies
progressive for her era, he questions her intellect and creativity and criticizes her for allowing "shameless sensuality"
to dominate her private affairs. DK170.W27
Reviewed in:
Edinb R, 178 (July 1893): 168-98
Naton, 58 (28 June 1894): 481-83

Sat R, (22 June 1895): 811-12
Spectator, 72 (24 Feb. 1894): 269

830 *_____. The Story of a Throne. Catherine II of Russia.
London: William Heinemann, n.d., 435pp.
A study of Catherine II's personal relationships. Waliszewski
discusses, in a dramatic fashion, Catherine's relationships
with three groups of individuals: statesmen and soldiers,
prominent men of the Enlightenment, and members of her
inner court, and in the process covers her dealings with
Panin, Viazemsky, Poniatowski, Potemkin, the Orlovs, the
Zubovs, Voltaire, von Grimm, Diderot, and Dashkov. For information on Catherine's private life and for insight into the
nature of her personality, character, tastes, habits, and intellect, this often cited work is a useful one. DK170.W23
Reviewed in:
Nation, 56 (16 Feb. 1893): 120-21

831 Wallace, Irving, et al., eds. "Mother of the Country. Catherine II of Russia." The Intimate Sex Lives of Famous People.
New York: Delacorte Press, 1981, 304-06.
A brief review of Catherine II's personal life with emphasis
placed upon her relationships with various lovers and her
zestful lifestyle. Wallace concludes by citing Catherine's
favorite toast "God, grant us our desires, and grant them
quickly." CT105.155

832 Williams, Sir John H. "Catherine the Great and Some of Her
Portraits." Connois, 109-10 (Mar. 1942): 3-13.
An interesting collection of pictures and prints of Catherine
II obtained form the author's ancestor Sir Charles Hanbury
Williams, British ambassador to Russia and a confidant of
Catherine during the 1750s. The author also provides a
flattering portrayal of Catherine's appearance and manner as
described by several of her contemporaries.

833 Williamson, George Charles. The Imperial Russian Dinner
Service; A Story of a Famous Work by Josiah Wedgwood.
London: G. Bell and Sons, 1909, 114pp. NK4335.W6
Unavailable for annotation.

834 *Wilson, Arthur. "Diderot in Russia, 1773-1774." ECR (anthology), 166-99.
Although Diderot is the focus of this essay, it includes considerable discussion of his relationship with Catherine the
Great during his year long stay in St. Petersburg at Catherine's request. Diderot's memoranda show that his discussions
with the empress were most typically on "political, economic,
social and legal matters," rather than cultural or intellectual
ones, and were "reformist in tone." Wilson states that Diderot's ambition was to convert Catherine II to the philosophy
of the Enlightenment, or at least to reinforce what there were

of her liberal convictions," but he notes that Catherine
viewed her conversations with Diderot "with more curiosity
than profit." Wilson concludes that while Diderot's image and
financial status were both advanced by his sojourn to the
Russian court, the empress "profited greatly, both intellect-
ually and in public esteem."

DOMESTIC POLICY AND AFFAIRS

Politics

835   *Alexander, John T. Autocratic Politics in a National Crisis:
The Imperial Russian Government and Pugachev's Revolt,
1773-1775. Bloomington: Indiana University Press, 1969,
346pp., bib. 315-34.
A scholarly investigation of the imperial government's response
to the Pugachev Revolt for insight into the operation of Catherine II's regime, the conclusions she drew from the rebellion,
and the influence the revolt had upon subsequent government
policies. Alexander establishes that news of the uprising
was slow to reach St. Petersburg and the government initially
misinterpreted the disturbance as "a typical small-scale,
localized mutiny" requiring only a minor military force for its
suppression. Once Catherine realized the actual extent of
the revolt, she began to consider ways to terminate the war
with the Ottoman Turks and improve her support within the
Russian court to facilitate quelling the rebellion as quickly as possible. Alexander sees Catherine's 1775 provincial
reform as an attempt to reduce the "enormous gap between
the government in St. Petersburg and its subordinates in the
provinces," revealed by the Pugachev Revolt, by giving the
nobility a greater role in local government and affairs. The
over-centralization of the imperial government persisted, however, at the very top of the political edifice due to "Catherine's own determination to personally govern so much of her
Empire" with the assistance of assorted favorites and occasion-
al special commissions. Alexander concludes that while the
government attempted "to repair institutional faults and
ameliorate obvious abuses" suffered by the serfs so as to
reduce the likelihood of future peasant disturbances, it "refused to concede that serfdom had conceived and nurtured"
the Pugachev Revolt. DK183.A44 1969
Reviewed in:
Am Hist R, 76 (1971): 169
Can Slav S, 4 (1970): 618
History, 56 (1970): 106
Rocky Mt Soc Sci J, 7, no. 2 (1970): 177
Rus R, 29 (1970): 337
Slav R, 29 (1970): 507
Slavonic E Eur R, 49 (1971): 619

836 _____. "Western Views of the Pugachev Rebellion." Slavonic
        E Eur R, 48 (Oct. 1970): 520-36.
        A discussion of contemporaneous Western reaction to the Puga-
        chev Revolt with some reference to Catherine the Great's re-
        sponse to the rebellion.

837 Allen, Robert V. "The Great Legislative Commission of Cath-
        erine II of 1767." Yale University, 1950. (dissertation)

838 Andre, P. F. "Catherine II as a Politician." Victoria M, 5
        (1865): 213.
        Unavailable for annotation.

839 *"Apology for Serfdom in the Nakaz of Catherine II." HRET
        (anthology), 421-23.
        A Soviet argument that Catherine II's Nakaz and the economic
        policies which she pursued as empress demonstrate that the
        foundation of her domestic policy was the maintenance of
        autocratic rule at the expense of Russia's peasant class. The
        author maintains that Catherine cloaked behind the concept of
        "enlightened absolutism" the exploitive features of her rule:
        "she adorned even her cruelest laws against the peasants with
        fancy phrases about being filled with 'motherly concern' for
        the 'welfare of her subjects.'" The author also contends that
        Catherine's views on the development of agriculture, industry,
        and commerce do not bear comparison to those of the French
        Physiocrats, despite arguments to the contrary. In short
        sections scattered throughout part five of this work, other
        facets of Catherine the Great's economic thought and policies
        receive critical attention. HB11.A2A43

840 *Bain, R. Nisbet. Peter III, Emperor of Russia. Westminster:
        Archibald Constable and Company, 1902, 208pp., bib. ix-xvi.
        A favorable reassessment of the life and brief reign of Peter
        III. Bain contends that Peter III possessed a number of
        positive qualities and pursued well-considered domestic and
        foreign policies but these facts have been obscured by the
        brilliant reign of Caterine II and the slander of those who
        suffered at his hands and/or were involved in the conspiracy
        which led to his overthrow. Bain notes that Catherine was
        anxious for Peter's removal from power (and her life) and
        had been involved in several plots against the emperor but
        does not link her directly to the coup which deposed him.
        DK166.B2
            Reviewed in:
            Athen, 1 (15 Mar. 1902): 330
            Nation, 74 (24 Apr. 1902): 328

841 *Bartlett, Roger P. "J. J. Sievers and the Russian Peasantry
        Under Catherine II." Jahr Ges Ost, 32 (1984): 16-33.
        A discussion of Jacob Sievers' views on the peasant question

and attempts at agricultural reorganization on the court
estate of Korostina over which he presided as Governor-
General of Novgorod Province. Drawing upon various reports which Sievers sent to Catherine II, Bartlett establishes
that Sievers understood well the peasantry's ills and was
sincere in his efforts to ameliorate them, however, his approach to the peasant question, like Catherine's, was a conservative, paternalistic one counter-productive to fundamental,
effective reform. Thus while Sievers' proposals to improve
the condition of the peasantry went beyond what Catherine
was prepared to approve, he shared with her both the desire
to rationalize rather than abolish serfdom and a view of the
peasants as "dependents under tutelage to be directed, dis-
ciplined and used, incapable of controlling their own lives."

842   *Billington, James. "The Dilemma of a Reforming Despot."
IA (gen. study), 217-26. Also in CG (anthology, 167-76.
An examination of Catherine's attempt to cope with the trouble-
some question of "how can one retain absolute power and a
hierarchical social system while at the same time introducing
reforms and encouraging education?" Billington states that
Catherine, under the influence of the utilitarianism of Bent-
ham and the political thought of Montesquieu, sought to
serve the common good through a fully rationalized autocratic
government. However, a combination of internal obstacles to
enlightened reform, the lure of territorial expansion, and the
dampening effect exerted on European liberalism by the French
Revolution, led Catherine to turn away from her early ideas
and retreat to a more traditional conception of autocratic rule.
Billington concludes that Catherine's philosophical writings
and her encouragement of education within the ranks of an
aristocracy "burdened" with idle time as a consequence of
being freed from obligatory state service contributed greatly
to the emergence of an intelligentsia hostile to the very
monarchy she sought to preserve.

843   Butler, W. E. "The Nakaz of Catherine the Great." Am Book
Coll, 16, no. 5 (1966): 19-21.
A brief review of the contents, purpose, and publication his-
tory of Catherine II's Nakaz submitted to the 1767 Legislative
Commission. Butler also discusses the favorable reaction to
the Nakaz by Catherine's European contemporaries.

844   *Cizova, Tatiana. "Beccaria in Russia." Slavonic E Eur R,
40, no. 96 (1962): 384-408.
A discussion of the impact of Beccaria's On Crimes and Punishments on the section of Catherine's Nakaz dealing with criminal law. Cizova notes that while the Nakaz is laden with
"direct borrowings from and paraphrases of Beccaria," Catherine used Beccaria's ideas more as an "apology for Russian
absolutism" than as a real guide for legislative reform.

845 *Clardy, Jesse. "Alexander Radishchev-A Revolutionist?"
     John C. White, ed. The Consortium on Revolutionary Europe.
     1750-1850. Athens, Ga.: Consortium on Revolutionary
     Europe, 1978, 127-34.
     An argument that although Radishchev's political views cer-
     tainly "ran counter to the existing philosophy and policies
     of Catherine II," he should not be considered a revolutionist
     since he "did not advocate propagandizing and mobilizing the
     strength of the masses to secure the violent overthrow of
     the government." Clardy asserts that Radishchev was a
     liberal who "never propounded any views that Catherine
     herself had not espoused during her early years in Russia."
     However, Catherine, under the influence of the Pugachev Re-
     volt, the conservative Russian gentry, and the French Revo-
     lution, turned so far away from her initial progressive views
     that the ideas expressed by Radishchev in A Journey from
     St. Petersburg to Moscow and Ode to Liberty, particularly in
     regard to natural law, appeared to her as truly revolutionary
     ones, a misconception perpetuated by such individuals as
     Herzen and Lenin who idealized Radishchev as the father of
     the radical intelligentsia. D299.C625

846 *DeMadariaga, Isabel. "Catherine II and the Serfs: A Re-
     consideration of Some Problems." Slavonic E Eur R, 52,
     no. 126 (1974): 34-62.
     An argument that Catherine II's serf policy was neither
     radically different than that of her predecessors nor a con-
     sequence of her political dependence on the nobility but
     rather is best understood within "the wider context of the
     problems facing the crown, notably public order, finance,
     economic development, public administration, and war."

847 Deriabin, P. "Catherine the Great." WT (gen. study), 63-68.
     A brief account of Catherine's involvement in the conspiracy
     which led to the overthrow of Peter III, and a discussion
     of her reaction to the threat posed by pretenders and re-
     bellion during her reign.

848 *Dukes, Paul. Catherine the Great and the Russian Nobility.
     A Study Based on the Materials of the Legislative Commission
     of 1767. Cambridge: Cambridge University Press, 1967,
     269pp., bib. 253-60.
     An examination of the role played by the attitudes and in-
     terests of the Russian nobility in shaping Catherine's domestic
     policies. Drawing upon documents concerning the Legislative
     Commission of 1767 published by the Imperial Historical So-
     ciety, Dukes asserts that "Catherine's failures, as well as
     her successes, must be seen in the context of the necessity
     of appeasing the desires of the dvorianstvo" (the Russian
     nobility). More specifically, Catherine's two principal legis-
     lative acts, the provincial reform of 1775 and Charter of the

Nobility of 1785, were motivated by the need to maintain the
support of the social class upon which her autocratic power
rested while at the same time improve the administration of
her realm by this same social class. Similarly, Catherine's
failure to deal with serfdom and its related evils was due to
her recognition of the nobility's firm opposition to any radical
alteration of this institution. Dukes concludes with a favorable assessment of Catherine's domestic accomplishments within
the context of the circumstances associated with her accession
to power and the limits placed upon her by the interests of
the dominant class in Russian society and the general conditions existent in eighteenth-century Russia. DK172.D84
Reviewed in:
Am Hist R, 74 (1969): 669
Can Slav S, 3, no. 1 (1969): 121-27
Historian, 30 (1968): 658-59
History, 55 (1970): 469
Irish Hist S, 16 (1968-69): 523
Rus R, 26 (1969): 97
Slav R, 27 (1968): 645-46
Slavonic E Eur R, 47 (1969): 270

849 * _____. "Catherine II's Enlightened Absolutism and the
Problem of Serfdom." William E. Butler, ed. Russian Law:
Historical and Political Perspectives. Leyden: A. W. Sijthoff,
1977, 93-115.
An argument that if Catherine II's "own peculiar brand of
enlightened absolutism," and her policies toward serfdom in
particular, are placed "in a broad spatial and chronological
setting, in both a comparative and stadial manner," the traditional negative appraisal of her serf policies "appears less
than balanced." Dukes maintains that the unbalanced nature
of the writings which vigorously condemn Catherine's peasant
policy can be seen if one considers serfdom as a variant of
slavery and then contrasts the condemnation of Catherine
with the leniency shown by historians in judging Thomas
Jefferson's record on slavery. Similarly, the negative effect
on Catherine's serf policy exerted by the Pugachev Revolt is
not unlike the effect had on governmental policy by slave
rebellions in America and other slave societies. DK43.R8

850 * _____, ed./trans. Russia Under Catherine the Great, 2
Vols. Newtonville, Mass.: Oriental Research Partners,
1978.
A valuable collection of documents pertaining to the political
thought of Catherine II and the general character of the
government and society over which she ruled. In volume
one, Dukes includes documents pertaining to the condition of
the serfs, Pugachev's Revolt, the 1775 administrative reform,
and 1785 Charter of the Nobility. Volume two contains Catherine's Instruction (Nakaz) to the Legislative Commission of

1767 which Dukes prefaces with an insightful introductory
essay on the document's source, content, and significance.
DK168.C3

851 Dumas, Alexandre. "The Romance of Catherine the Great."
     CCRC (gen. study), 128-64.
     A dramatic account of the overthrow of Peter III and the
     acceptance of Catherine as his successor. Dumas presents
     Catherine's official version of the coup and Peter's death
     in the form of a lengthy letter written by her to K. Ponia-
     towski, and then contrasts it with an account far less flatter-
     ing with respect to Catherine's poise, courage, and political
     morality.

852 _____. "A Romance of the Russian Bastille." CCRC (gen.
     study), 165-75.
     An undocumented account of Catherine II's orchestration of
     the 1764 abduction from Italy of Princess Elena Tarakanov
     who, as the daughter of Empress Elizabeth, had a claim to
     the Russian throne. Dumas asserts that Catherine was fear-
     ful that the princess was about to become the political pawn
     of Prince Charles Radziwill who intended to marry her as
     part of a scheme to unite the crowns of Poland and Russia.
     The empress thus commissioned Prince G. Orlov to seduce and
     abduct Elena and incarcerate her in the "darksome dungeon
     of the St. Andrew Ravelin" where she remained for twelve
     years until she drowned when the Neva River flooded her
     cell.

853 *Gershoy, Leo. "Absolutist to the Core." CG (anthology),
     159-66. From From Despotism to Revolution, 1763-1789.
     New York: Harper and Row, 1944, 109-117.
     A presentation of Catherine as "a farsighted and capitalist-
     minded absolutist who worked for the greater glory of the
     Russian crown." Gershoy states that Catherine well under-
     stood that Russia's best interests would be served by encour-
     aging the growth of commerce and industry but hoped to
     promote such growth without jeopardizing, in any way, the
     traditional order of things in Russia. To this end she en-
     couraged the landowning aristocracy, by way of privileges
     granted in the Charter of the Nobility, to join with merchant
     capitalists in developing Russia's economic potential.

854 Givens, Robert D. "Supplication and Reform in the Instruction
     of the Nobility." Can Am Slav S, 11, no. 4 (1977): 483-502.
     A discussion of the nobility's recommendations to Catherine
     II through the Legislative Commission as an extension of the
     petitionary tradition in Russia's political history. Givens
     states that the nobles regarded their role in drafting the in-
     structions as a passive one and retained the servile mentality
     of petitioners more concerned with specific local affairs than
     with altering the sway of autocracy.

855 *Gleason, Walter J. Moral Idealists, Bureaucracy, and Cather-
     ine the Great. New Brunswick, N.J.: Rutgers University
     Press, 1981, 252pp., bib. 233-44.
     Catherine II is not the focus of this scholarly work, but it
     nonetheless provides considerable insight into the critical
     reaction to her political philosophy and policies by Nikolai
     Novikov, Ippolit Bogdanovitch, and Denis Fonvizin.
     DK171.5.G58

856 Griffiths, David M. "Eighteenth Century Perceptions of Back-
     wardness: Projects for the Creation of a Third Estate in
     Catherinean Russia." Can Am Slav S, 13, no. 4 (1979):
     452-72.
     An examination of eighteenth-century commentaries on urban
     development and of the proposals submitted to Catherine II
     to deal with conditions in and the population of the empire's
     towns. Griffiths maintains that the proposals and projects
     were characterized by a belief, shared by Catherine, that a
     third estate could be created in Russia "without impinging
     upon already existing estates" or the authority of the mon-
     archy.

857 Hans, Nicholas. "Francois Pierre Pictet: Secretary to Cath-
     erine II." Slavonic E Eur R, 36 (1957-58): 481-91.
     A brief account of the services rendered by F. P. Pictet who,
     as secretary to Catherine II from 1762 to 1764, drafted letters
     in French for the empress. Hans establishes that Pictet was
     also "instrumental in bringing together Catherine and Voltaire
     who through him began their famous correspondence." There
     follows the original French language text of an August 1762
     letter by Pictet to Voltaire in regard to the coup d'état which
     removed Peter III from the throne in favor of Catherine.
     Subsequently Pictet came to serve as a recruiting agent for
     the settlement of the foreign colonies established by Catherine
     in her first few years as empress.

858 Hartley, Janet M. "The Implementation of the Laws Relating to
     Local Administration, 1775-1796, with Special Reference to
     the Guberniya of St. Petersburg." University of London,
     1980. (dissertation)

859 *_____. Town Government in Saint Petersburg Guberniya
     After the Charter to the Towns of 1785." Slavonic E Eur R,
     62, no. 1 (1984): 61-84.
     A study of town government in St. Petersburg Guberniya
     for insight into the effectiveness of Catherine II's reform of
     municipal administration by way of her 1785 Charter of the
     Towns. Hartley demonstrates that the charter was deficient
     in several respects. Its division of the town population into
     six groups "did not correspond to the actual social composi-
     tion of most Russian towns." It failed "to define clearly the
     responsibilities of the new town institutions which it created,"

and it left unclear the new institutions' relationship with
existing local governmental agencies. However, Hartley
adds, through local adaptations of the charter, the new town
dumas generally were representative of the population which
they served, met regularly, and often dealt with matters of
substantial importance. Moreover, the problems associated
with the new town government, particularly in regard to dup-
lication of functions and protection against institutional
rivals, were characteristic of every branch of local administration, therefore the charter should not be singled out as
a reform uniquely deficient.

860 *Hassell, James A. "Catherine II and Procurator-General
      Vjazemsky." Jahr Ges Ost, 24, no. 1 (1976): 23-30.
      A discussion of Alexander Viazemsky's career as procurator-
      general as an illustration of how the Russian machinery of
      government was transformed during Catherine II's reign from
      "an essentially passive instrument to one capable of initiating
      change." Hassell states that the growth of the Russian state
      and its activities made it impossible for Catherine to rule Rus-
      sia personally. Consequently there emerged a large state
      bureaucracy which gradually came to operate "according to
      its own inner logic." Because Viazemsky "alone had a grasp
      of the entire administrative apparatus," he developed exten-
      sive authority and power during his years of service as
      procurator-general.

861 *Jones, Robert E. "Catherine II and the Provincial Reform of
      1775: A Question of Motivation." Can Slav S, 4, no. 3
      (1970): 497-512.
      An analysis of the question "was the reform of 1775 the final
      culmination of long-standing efforts to improve provincial ad-
      ministration..., or was it simply a direct and desperate re-
      action" to the Pugachev Revolt? Jones concludes that prior
      to the rebellion, "Catherine regarded provincial reform as
      desirable but not at all urgent or vital," while afterwards
      such reform "was treated as a matter of the very highest
      priority." Thus the Pugachev Revolt "provided the crucial
      difference between her earlier interest in provincial reform
      and her subsequent determination to make provincial reform
      a fact."

862 *_____. The Emancipation of the Russian Nobility. Prince-
      ton, N.J.: Princeton University Press, 1972, 326pp., bib.
      300-12.
      This scholarly study of the "redefinition and reorganization
      of the Russian nobility carried out between 1762 and 1785"
      does not focus on Catherine per se but contains an analysis
      of her general role in this process and her legislative acts
      which sought to resolve the problems associated with the
      1762 emancipation of the nobility by Peter III. Jones

discounts the interpretation that "the fate of the nobility
was ultimately decided as part of a political accommodation
or compromise between a usurping empress and the dominant
social and economic class." He maintains instead that Catherine's position as empress was sufficiently secure for her to
approach the question of the nobility's legal status from a
supra class perspective. Thus her treatment of the nobility
is best understood "in terms of the problems she encountered
in trying to provide Russia, especially the vast and under-
developed provinces, with a government capable of defending
and promoting national interest." HT647.J65

863 *_____. "Jacob Sievers, Enlightened Reform, and the Development of a 'Third Estate' in Russia." Rus R, 36, no. 4
(1977): 424-37.
This examination of the efforts of Jacob Sievers, Governor
General of the Novgorod viceregency, to promote the development of a third estate in Russia provides considerable insight
into "the context of Catherine's urban reforms and the process through which they were introduced." Jones states that
"although Catherine personally favored the development of an
urban middle class in Russia, she was careful not to impose
her views by fiat. Instead, she allowed Sievers to take the
initiative in proposing measures ... and then gave his opponents ample time to air their contrary opinions." The result
was a policy which "emulated both tutelage and liberty" as
the monarchy worked to create the conditions necessary for a
third estate to evolve.

864 _____. Provincial Development in Russia: Catherine II and
Jakob Sievers. New Brunswick, N.J.: Rutgers University
Press, 1984, 255pp., bib. 227-47.
An examination of the attempt by the government of Catherine
II to apply, largely through the efforts of Jacob Sievers,
eighteenth century ideas of development in the guberniya
of Novgorod. Jones defines "development" as "an increase in
prosperity, productivity, and happiness," and sees Catherine
II as generally successful in its promotion given "the administrative capabilities of the Russian state and the current condition of the provinces." JN6511.J66

865 *_____. "Urban Planning and the Development of Provincial
Towns in Russia During the Reign of Catherine II." ECR
(anthology), 321-44.
A discussion of the urban planning of Catherine the Great as
"one of the important legacies of the 18th century in Russia"
because "it established the appearance and character of the
modern Russian city." Jones examines Catherine's efforts to
rebuild Russian towns "so as to give them a more European
appearance," particularly by way of her 1763 decree which
called for the creation of a general urban plan applicable to

all of Russia's towns and cities. In appraising the effectiveness of this decree as well as Catherine's attempt to create
hundreds of new, "modern" towns, Jones states that although
"Catherine and her contemporaries took exaggerated pride in
her programme, later historians more than compensated for it
by treating the programme with exaggerated scorn." Jones
defends Catherine's urban policy against critics who emphasize
only "its most ridiculous failures," such as Potemkin's project
for Ekaterinoslav, and maintains that while her plans far out-
distanced the government's ability to implement them and did
not produce ideal results they nonetheless led to significant
improvements in nearly all of Russia's provincial capitals.

866   *Kizevetter, Aleksandr A. "The Legislator in Her Debut."
      CGP (anthology), 247-66. From "Pervoe Piatiletie pravleniia
      Ekateriny II." Istoricheskie silutey-Liudi i sobjtiia. Mary
      Mackler, trans. Berlin: Parabola, 1931, 29-54.
      An analysis of the policies pursued by Catherine in her first
      five years of power for insight into the character and direction
      of her entire reign. Kizevetter, a noted liberal Russian his-
      torian, maintains that contrary to the traditional interpreta-
      tion of Catherine's reign as a steady retreat (in the face of
      aristocratic opposition) from early liberal and idealistic re-
      form hopes, the empress' "very first program never went
      beyond the aspirations of the representatives of public opinion
      of the time." She was from the very beginning of her reign
      a proponent of the rights and privileges of the nobility and
      an opponent of serf emancipation, though she did wish to
      regulate lord-serf relations.

867   *Lang, David Marshall. The First Russian Radical: Alexander
      Radishchev, 1749-1802. London: George Allen and Unwin,
      1959, 298pp., bib. 280-88.
      This scholarly study does not contain a separate section on
      Catherine II but includes numerous references to the intel-
      lectual climate which characterized her reign, her role in
      promoting Radishchev's education, and, most importantly, her
      furious reaction to the criticism of her rule and the condition
      of Russia expressed by Radishchev in his A Journey from St.
      Petersburg to Moscow. DK169.R3L3

868   *_____. "Radishchev and Catherine II: New Gleanings from
      Old Archives." J. S. Curtiss, ed. Essays in Russian and
      Soviet History in Honor of Geroid Tanquary Robinson. New
      York: Columbia University Press, 1963, 20-33.
      An examination of "the manuscript despatches of western en-
      voys reporting to their courts from St. Petersburg in 1790"
      for insight into the circumstances which surrounded Radish-
      chev's publication of A Journey from St. Petersburg to Moscow
      and the effect the book had on the thinking of contemporary
      Western diplomats. Lang focuses on the dispatches of Charles

Whitworth (British minister to St. Petersburg) and Edmond
Genêt (French chargé d'affaires), who sympathized with
Radishchev's exposé and viewed Catherine's reaction to it as
a hysterical one. DK4.C8

869 *Lappo-Danilevskii, Aleksandr S. "The Serf Question in an
     Age of Enlightenment." CGP (anthology), 267-90. From
     "Ekaterina II, krest'ianskii vopros." A. K. Dzhivelegov
     et al., eds. Velikaia Reforma-Russkoe obshchestvo i
     krest'ianskii vopros v proshloni i nastoiashchem. Mary
     Mackler, trans. Moscow, 1911, 163-90.
     A critical review of the evolution of Catherine's policy
     toward Russia's serfs. Lappo-Danilevsky, a noted Russian
     social historian, states that Catherine, upon assuming the
     throne, quickly abandoned her youthful liberal views on
     the matter of serf emancipation and instead turned her at-
     tention to the consideration of measures to mitigate the
     serfs' hard life not because of any humanitarian concern
     for the serfs but out of fear of a peasant revolt due to
     the intolerable conditions under which they lived. However,
     Catherine's proposals to restrict serfdom were so negatively
     received by the 1767 Legislative Commission that she aban-
     doned them in favor of a policy geared toward "ensuring
     the peasants' unquestionable obedience to their landlords"
     and increasing the latter's power over the serfs. Lappo-
     Danilevsky concludes that the final result of Catherine's
     peasant policy was a massive extension and intensification
     of serfdom.

870 Le Donne, John P. "Appointments to the Russian Senate,
     1762-1796." Cahiers du monde, 16, no. 1 (1975): 27-65.
     Although containing scant mention of Catherine the Great,
     this study of the professional and family background of her
     appointees to the Senate demonstrates the dominant influence
     of the circles centered about the offices of the procurator
     general and the chancellor.

871 _____. "Catherine's Governors and Governors-General."
     Cahiers du monde, 20, no. 1 (1970): 15-42.
     An examination of Catherine II's appointments to the top
     positions in the provincial administration reformed by the
     empress' Organic Law of 7 November 1775. Le Donne argues
     that "the governor-general, not the post-reform governor,
     was the successor of the pre-reform governor and that the
     provincial voevoda survived in the post-reform governor."
     Le Donne also establishes that Catherine's appointees gener-
     ally had military backgrounds and came from a small number
     of prominent families.

872 _____. "The Judicial Reform of 1775 in Central Russia."
     Jahr Ges Ost, 21, no. 1 (1973): 29-45.

A discussion of the creation of local courts as part of the
decentralization process associated with Catherine's provincial
government reform of 1775. Le Donne analyzes the need for
and shape of the new courts as well as the reform's deficiencies.

873 _____. "The Provincial and Local Police Under Catherine the
Great, 1775-96." Can Slav S, 4, no. 3 (1970): 513-28.
An examination of the restructuring of the provincial and local
police that occurred as part of Catherine II's local government
reforms of 1775-1785. Le Donne states that although the
governors-general retained considerable power, Catherine's
reforms served to make the provincial and local police, along
with the gentry, petty autocrats in rural Russia: "Servility
toward the great, unrestrained despotism toward the power-
less, such were the characteristic features not only of the
behavior of those whose duty it was to maintain peace and
order, but also of those who constituted the privileged group
of Russian local society toward the end of the eighteenth
century."

874 *_____. "The Territorial Reform of the Russian Empire
1775-1796. Part I: Central Russia, 1775-1784." Cahiers
du monde, 23 (1982): 147-85.
Catherine the Great's role in the administrative-territorial
reform of the Russian Empire which occurred under her rule
is not central to the theme of this article, but Le Donne's
study should nonetheless be consulted by researchers who
seek to understand the roots of the reform and the geographic
and demographic complexities associated with its scope and implementation. Drawing upon a substantial body of statistics,
Le Donne demonstrates the pressing nature of the need for
the reform as well as the long-term considerations which
argued in its favor. He concedes that the Pugachev Rebellion acted as a catalyst to the reform but believes that "the
considerable work done in the 1760s to prepare a systematic
reform applicable to the whole of Great Russia militates against
accepting a theory that overemphasizes the importance of a
regional revolt." In part II of this study, Le Donne intends
to discuss the territorial reform in the borderlands which
surrounded Great Russia.

875 Leonard, Carol S. "A Study of the Reign of Peter III of
Russia," Indiana University, 1976. (dissertation)

876 *Lincoln, W. Bruce. "The Russian State and Its Cities:
A Search for Effective Municipal Government, 1786-1842."
Jahr Ges Ost, 17, no. 4 (1969): 531-41.
An analysis of the failure of Catherine II's 1785 reform
which attempted to create an all-class municipal governing
body with some limited rights of self-government. Lincoln

sees Catherine's failure as being rooted in an idealized view
of Russian urban society which, in fact, "bore little resemblance to reality."

877 *McConnell, Allen. "Arrest and Trial." A Russian Philosophe:
     Alexander Radishchev. Westport, Conn.: Hyperion Press,
     1981 (reprint of 1964 edition), 106–22.
     An account of the arrest and trial of Alexander Radishchev
     following Catherine II's reading of his book A Journey from
     St. Petersburg to Moscow. In discussing Catherine's critical
     reaction to the Journey, McConnell states that the empress
     misinterpreted Radishchev's intent in writing the book as
     well as its overall message. She saw in it a radicalism akin
     to that which had provoked revolution in France rather than
     the humanitarianism of a Russian patriot who yearned for the
     betterment of his country through enlightened reform, espe-
     cially in regard to Russia's enserfed peasantry. More impor-
     tantly, her overly negative reaction to the Journey and her
     consequent Siberian exile of Radishchev "symbolized a fatal
     split between the government and the country's best minds..."
     as Catherine "tried to turn time back to unfettered, irre-
     sponsible autocracy." This scholarly study also contains
     many references to and short sections on Catherine's encour-
     agement of the intellectual development of Russia's nobility
     prior to the 1789 outbreak of the French Revolution.
     PG3317.R3Z735

878 *   . "The Empress and Her Protégé: Catherine II
     and Radishchev." J Mod Hist, 36, no. 1 (1964): 14–27.
     Also in CGP (anthology), 156–78.
     A discussion of Catherine's trial of Radishchev, for the radi-
     cal views which he expressed in his book A Journey from St.
     Petersburg to Moscow, as "one of the darkest spots in her
     reign" and an illustration of "how far she had lapsed from
     her early published liberal aims." McConnell contends that
     Catherine wholly misunderstood Radishchev's intent in writing
     the Journey since she condemned him for conspiracy and in-
     citement to rebellion when in fact he wrote the book to pre-
     vent the rebellion which he believed would come unless the
     crown addressed the terrible conditions which plagued Russia's
     enserfed peasantry. McConnell also discusses similarities in
     the thought and intellectual tastes of Catherine and Radish-
     chev and concludes with an account of the alterations which
     Radishchev made, in later life, in his general view of the
     Russian monarchy.

879 McCormick, D. "Catherine's 'Secret Expedition' and the 'Yellow
     Box.'" HRSS (gen. study), 34–37.
     A brief account of Catherine's role in the overthrow of Peter
     III, the abolition of his spy service, and her creation of a
     new security agency titled the "Secret Expedition."

880 *Miliukov, Pavel N. "Voices of the Land and the Autocrat."
     CG (anthology), 113-55. Norman K. Sloan, trans. From
     Ocherki po istorii russkoi Kul'tury. Paris, 1930, 293-328.
     An analysis of the origin and evolution of Catherine II's
     political philosophy. Miliukov contends that during her
     years as grand duchess Catherine developed a concept of
     statecraft based upon the premise that effective rule must be
     founded upon lofty principles openly expressed. Her faith
     in the applicability of general principles to life was rooted
     in her belief that "principled rule" was advantageous rather
     than philosophically necessary. Consequently, she believed
     that if her principles were to diverge from her best interests
     as sovereign they would have to be compromised. With the
     1767 convening of the Legislative Commission, Catherine's
     idealism cooled in the face of the provincialism and selfish
     class interests which she encountered. Later, as she came
     to realize that through her encouragement of learning among
     the Russian nobility there had emerged a small, critically
     thinking, independent body of public opinion, she rejected
     completely the liberal/critical thought to which she had once
     subscribed. Miliukov concludes that the close of Catherine's
     reign marks the advent of the fatal rift between the monarchy
     and the intelligentsia which became so dominant in nineteenth-
     century Russia.

881 Morazé, Charles. "The Domestic Policies of Frederick the
     Great, Maria Theresa, and Joseph II." Shephard C. Clough,
     ed. The European Past, Vol. I. Reappraisals in History
     from the Renaissance to Waterloo. New York: Macmillan,
     1966, 375-94. Reprint of "Finance et despotisme: essai sur
     les despotes éclairés." James Friguglietti, trans. Annales:
     Economies-Sociétes-Civilisations, 3 (1948): 279-96.
     An argument that the domestic policies of Catherine II, like
     those of the other enlightened despots of her era, were
     founded more on political and economic practices current in
     England and France than on the philosophy of the Enlighten-
     ment. Morazé cites several examples in support of this con-
     tention, the most noteworthy being Catherine's utilization of
     "an English invention" to create a national bank and bank
     notes as a means of securing a monetary instrument to pro-
     mote the modernization process in Russia. He suggests that
     Catherine's favorable relations with various philosophes and
     her verbalization of progressive philosophic views and prin-
     ciples largely account for the birth of the myth that her
     domestic policies were based on contemporary French political
     thought. CB358.C55

882 *Morrison, Kerry R. "Catherine II's Legislative Commission:
     An Administrative Interpretation." Can Slav S, 4, no. 3
     (1970): 464-84.
     An appraisal of "the role played by Catherine II's Legislative

Commission of 1767 within the continuing dynamics of 18th
century Russian institutional development." Morrison rejects
the argument that Catherine dissolved the Legislative Commission because she doubted its ability "to respond construc-
tively to her enlightened program" and contends instead that
the Commission was a successful administrative device designed to test "the temper of public reaction and solicit the
stamp of public approval with regard to reform projects
which ... were not of its own making." The themes of
several of the drafts completed by Commission members
"reaffirm the generic relationship" between the work of the
Legislative Commission and Catherine's major reforms of
1775-1785. Morrison concludes that the Legislative Commissions of both Elizabeth and Catherine were merely an "administrative method of preparing for reform, a part of the
process rather than its cause," ... and therefore "were no
more derived form the Enlightenment than were the needs
which brought them into being."

883   *Papmehl, K. A.   Freedom of Expression in Eighteenth Century
      Russia.   The Hague: M. Nijhoff, 1971, 166pp., bib. 152-61.
      This scholarly study of the origin and evolution of the con-
      cept of freedom of expression as a basic civil liberty is
      centered upon the reign of Catherine II.   Papmehl states that
      Catherine was responsible for "a considerable extension of
      freedom in the realm of thought, speech, and the press,"
      and therefore inadvertently set the stage for a confrontation
      between autocracy and political liberty as rival principles.
      Once she realized the impossibility of maintaining a clear
      dividing line between civil and political liberty, she resorted
      to restrictive measures, particularly in response to the chal-
      lenge posed by Radishchev's A Journey from St. Petersburg
      to Moscow.   Papmehl concludes that, while Catherine's reign
      clearly ended on a negative note, her pre-1790 policies
      "towards freedom of expression were more liberal, and her
      contribution to its growth more positive and significant than
      is generally believed."   JC599.R9P36 1971

884   *_____.   "The Problem of Civil Liberties in the Records of
      the 'Great Commission.'"   Slavonic E Eur R, 42 (1962-63):
      274-91.
      A discussion of Catherine II's "attitude toward civil liberties,
      as expressed in her 'Instruction'," and an investigation into
      the matter of "whether or not any demand for them was
      raised by the representatives of Russian society." Papmehl
      regards Catherine's views on civil liberties as being quite
      enlightened but does not see a similar level of thought by
      representatives to the Legislative Commission whose attention
      was absorbed by the pressing problems of the day and who
      lacked sufficient time to take advantage of the open forum
      given to them by the empress.

885 Petschauer, Peter. "The Education and Development of an En-
     lightened Absolutist: The Youth of Catherine the Great,
     1729-1762." New York University, 1969. (dissertation)

886 _____. "Enlightened Mentors of Catherine the Great." Enl
     E, 2 (1971): 167-75.
     Unavailable for annotation.

887 *Pokrovsky, M. N. "The Serfowners' State." CG (anthology),
     139-42. From A Brief History of Russia. New York: Inter-
     national Publishers, 1933, 12-24.
     A Marxist portrayal of Catherine II as "a dissolute and
     criminal woman" who acquired historical fame solely because
     her policies were "necessary and useful to the social forces
     that built up the capitalists' and serfowners' empire." In
     light of this contention, Pokrovsky, a noted Soviet historian,
     discusses Catherine II's territorial acquisitions and her ex-
     tension and intensification of serfdom.

888 Poole, Stanley B. R. "Peter III and Pugachev." Royal Myster-
     ies and Pretenders. London: Blanford Press, 1969, 67-80.
     A popular portrayal of the miserable relationship between Peter
     III and Catherine and the ill-advised policies pursued by him
     as the twin sources of the 1762 conspiracy that led to his re-
     moval from power and this world. Poole also discusses the
     "constant stream of pretenders who claimed to be Peter III,"
     most notably the Cossack rebel E. Pugachev. D107.P58

889 *Radishchev, Aleksandr Nikolaevich. A Journey from St.
     Petersburg to Moscow. Leo Wiener, trans. Roderick Page
     Thaler, ed./intro. Cambridge: Harvard University Press,
     1958, 286pp. Excerpt in RIRC (anthology), 261-79.
     A sharp and influential critique of the government and insti-
     tutions of Catherinean Russia. Radishchev, a formative in-
     fluence in the emergence of the Russian liberal intelligentsia,
     criticizes Catherine's domestic policies (especially in regard
     to the peasants, law, and censorship) and the officials who
     implemented them. Although Radishchev did not call for a
     revolution but rather for major reforms to prevent one, the
     sharpness of his criticism, particularly in reference to serf-
     dom and its related evils, and the fact that the Journey was
     published simultaneous with the French Revolution, led Cath-
     erine to interpret this work as a revolutionary one whose
     author was "full of the French madness." Catherine ordered
     the imprisonment and execution of Radishchev but later re-
     duced his sentence to ten years of exile in Siberia. The criti-
     cal notes made by Catherine as she read the Journey are in-
     cluded in an appendix. HN525.R313
         Reviewed in:
         J Cent Eur Aff, 19 (1959-60): 84
         New W R, 27 (1959): 45

Rus R, 18, no. 1 (1959): 77
Slav R, 19 (1960): 108
Slavonic E Eur R, 37 (1958-59): 516
World Aff Q, 30 (1959): 373

890 *Raeff, Marc. "Domestic Policies of Peter III and His Overthrow." Am Hist R, 75 (June 1970): 1289-1310.
A reassessment of the domestic policies pursued by Peter III
and their relationship to his overthrow. Raeff asserts that,
contrary to the traditional interpretation, Peter III's reign
represents a logical continuation of the social and economic
policies pursued by Russia's leaders in the first half of the
eighteenth century. However, Peter's legislation was devised
by a new group of advisers whose existence was a threat to
the Senate's authority and position. Raeff maintains that
Peter III's demotion of the Senate and creation of a new group
of "in" servitors were more responsible for the 1762 coup than
the specific content of the policies which he implemented.

891 *_____. "The Empress and the Vinerian Professor. Catherine
II's Projects of Government Reforms and Blackstone's Commentaries." Ox Slavonic P, 7 (1974): 19-41.
An examination of the 1776 notes made by Catherine II when
reading William Blackstone's Commentaries on the Laws of England for insight into her views on judicial and administrative
reform. Raeff states that the notes reveal, among other
things, that Catherine intended to create a Chief Executive
Chamber (the members of which were to be, in part, elected)
to serve as a legislative consultant to the monarchy and to
supervise the administration of justice. Unfortunately, Raeff
concludes, Catherine did not create such an institution, perhaps because she believed it to be premature given the backwardness of Russian society.

892 *_____, ed. "The Memorandum of Nikita Panin, 28 December
1762." PPR (anthology), 53-68.
A brief introduction to the genesis and ultimate fate of N.
Panin's proposal to establish an imperial council, and a series
of excerpts from the proposal and the manifesto drafted to
announce the council's formation. Panin hoped that the council would provide an orderly procedure for formulating basic
policy and thereby make the monarch less susceptible to the
harmful influence of selfish favorites and courtiers. Catherine initially supported Panin's proposal out of concern for
making government more rational but reversed her position
after several advisers convinced her that the council posed a
threat to her royal prerogatives.

893 _____. "Pugachev's Rebellion." R. Forster and J. P.
Greene, eds. Preconditions of Revolution in Early Modern
Europe. Baltimore: Johns Hopkins Press, 1970, 161-202.

Catherine II is not central to the focus of this essay, but it
contains a discussion of the policies of Peter III and Catherine which, in part, prompted the Pugachev Revolt. Of particular interest is Raeff's discussion of the popular reaction
to the crown's taking the "seemingly paradoxical step of eliminating direct communication with the people by allowing the
serf-owning nobles to become a barrier between peasantry and
ruler." D231.P7

894   *_____. "The System of Peter the Great: To Reform or Not
to Reform." UIR (gen. study), 89-111.
An examination of the nature and effectivenss of Catherine II's
attempt to advance the modernization process began by Peter
I and to address the shortcomings of the Petrine administrative system. Raeff demonstrates that Catherine's efforts to
improve her realm were hampered by the absence of a governmental structure, particularly at the local level, sufficiently
rational or well-ordered to mobilize Russian society in support
of the desired improvements. Catherine's reform of provincial
government and establishment of charters for the nobility
and the cities were designed to provide an administrative
foundation that would "shape the development of a dynamic
and productive, yet peaceful and harmonious society, which
would proceed to acquire power, prosperity, and happiness
under the guidance of the autocratic sovereign." Raeff concludes that, despite considerable success in reshaping Russian
society and advancing the nation's cultural life, Catherine's
stern paternalistic outlook and distrust of local initiative combined with the absence of a "coherent system of law enforced
by an independent judiciary" to render impossible the establishment of a Rechtsstaat in Russia. Moreover, the arbitrary
features of the autocratic state served to alienate the nation's
cultural elite and therein sow unwittingly the seeds for the
revolutionary discontent that emerged in the next century.

895*   _____. "Uniformity, Diversity, and the Imperial Administration in the Reign of Catherine II." Hans Lemberg, Peter
Nitsche and Erwin Oberlander, eds. Osteuropa in Geschichte
und Gegenwart. Köln: Böhlav, 1977, 97-113.
An examination of how "the cultural-human diversity and the
physical size" of Russia were dealt with administratively by
the imperial government during the reign of Catherine II.
Raeff states that Catherine and her advisers, under the influence of cameralist and mercantilist thought, treated the empire's economic, ethnic, and cultural diversity as an obstacle
which had to be removed if a smoothly functioning, well-
ordered and progressive autocratic state were to be established.
In accord with Catherine II's directives, the Russian government gave "temporary recognition of local and cultural differences but only as a step in the process of integration;
integration was to lead to uniformity, first administrative and

economic, then institutional and social, and finally cultural.
In fact, the goal may be termed institutional russification."
Raeff notes that in pursuing this goal the administrators of
Catherine's era moved more gradually and demonstrated more
flexibility than Russia's administrators of the next century,
but nonetheless they set the foundations for a policy which
was to have disastrous consequences for the monarchy.
DJK.9.087

896   Ransel, David L. "Bureaucracy and Patronage: The View
from an Eighteenth Century Russian Letter Writer." Frederick C. Jaher, ed. The Rich and Wellborn and the Powerful:
Elites and Upper Classes in History. Urbana: University
of Illinois Press, 1973, 154-78.
An examination of an anonymous 1788 letter-writer, or style
manual, for insight into the survival of the patronage system
as the foundation of relations among noble servitors. Ransel
maintains that the failure of Catherine II's administrative,
social, and legal reforms to "produce more than the pretense
of legality to protect values of property, status, and personal
security" largely accounts for the undiminished vigor of the
patronage system after the close of her reign. HM141.J25

897 *_____. "Catherine II's Instruction to the Commission on
Laws: An Attack on Gentry Liberals?" Slavonic E Eur R,
50 (Jan. 1972): 10-28.
A refutation of the argument that Catherine II's 1767 Instruction to the Legislative Commission represents an attempt by
the empress to assert herself against a liberal faction of the
gentry which, under the leadership of N. Panin, was anxious
to place limits on royal absolutism. Ransel maintains that the
Panin group did not pose such a challenge to Catherine's
autocratic prerogatives but rather was simply trying to out-
maneuver rival factions within the Russian court. As a further indication of the absence of such a challenge, and the
consequent unlikelihood that the Instruction was intended as
a rebuke of the liberal circle headed by Panin, Ransel points
to the excellent working relationship which Panin maintained
with Catherine.

898 *_____. "The 'Memoirs' of Count Munnich." Slav R, 30,
no. 4 (1971): 843-52.
An examination of the role played by the elderly Count
Burchard Christoph von Munnich in a mid-1763 struggle between the Panin party and a group led by A. P. Bestuzhev-
Ryumin to win Catherine II's support for their respective and
divergent policies. Ransel demonstrates that Munnich, who
enjoyed considerable prestige in court circles and with the
empress herself, submitted a proposal for reform (since
referred to as his "memoirs") similar to that of Panin, and
consequently, when his proposal won the approval of the

empress the balance in the court struggle shifted to the
favor of the Panin party.

899 *_____. The Politics of Catherinean Russia. The Panin
Party. New Haven: Yale University Press, 1975, 327pp.,
bib. 291-314.
Nikita Panin and his supporters are the central figures in
this scholarly study, but it includes a great deal of information on Catherine's political and administrative activities and
her relationship with the Panin party. Ransel rejects the
traditional interpretation that Panin led a "full fledged
'gentry opposition' movement" against the absolute monarch
and asserts instead that Panin's thought and actions are best
understood if seen as part of a struggle with a "competing
patronage hierarchy vying for position and influence in the
central administration." Ransel does not deny that Panin,
his rivals, and Catherine herself, had a sincere concern for
rationalizing Russian politics, but they nonetheless repeatedly
resorted to and relied on traditional patronage politics when
trying to maintain or advance their respective positions and,
eventually, carry out their policies. For a condensed version
of this thesis, see the author's "Nikita Panin's Imperial
Council Project and the Struggle of Hierarchy Groups at the
Court of Catherine II." Can Slav S, 4, no. 3 (1970): 443-
63.

900 Rasmussen, Karen M. "Catherine II and Peter I: The Idea of
a Just Monarch." University of California, Berkeley, 1973.
(dissertation)

901 *Rulhiere, M. A History, or Anecdotes of the Revolution in
Russia in the Year 1762. New York: Arno Press, 1970
(reprint of 1797 edition), 200pp.
A controversial, firsthand account of the gossip, views and
opinions expressed within Russian court circles in regard to
Peter III's dethronement and assassination. Rulhiere discusses anecdotally the character of Catherine II and Peter III,
their miserable relationship, the inflammatory policies followed
by Peter which spawned the plot to depose him, the leading
role played in the conspiracy by Count Panin, Princess
Dashkov, and Catherine herself, and the course of events on
the evening of Peter's murder. Rulhiere refused a bribe of
30,000 francs offered to block the publication of his Anecdotes,
but, under threat of imprisonment by the French government,
agreed not to publish his work until after Catherine's death.
DK166.R913

902 Self, Gloria. "Catherine and Frederick and Sergi and Orlov.
Love and War for Europe." San Diego M, 27 (July 1975):
96-99, 114-18.
A general review of the personalities, events, and circumstances

associated with Catherine II's accession to power and efforts to expand Russia's borders to the south and west.

903 *Shmurlo, E. "Catherine II and Radishchev." Slavonic R, 17, no. 51 (1939): 618-22.
A reassessment of Catherine II's response to Radishchev's A Journey from St. Petersburg to Moscow. Shmurlo maintains that the zealous nature of Radishchev's attack on autocracy and, implicitly, the empress and her policies, understandably prompted a show of force by Catherine, particularly in light of the outbreak of revolution in France.

904 Soloviev, Sergei. "The Legislative Commission of 1767." RIRC, Vol. II (anthology), 256-60. Excerpt from Istoriia Rossii s Drevneishikh Vremen, Vol. XIV. Moscow, 1965, 75, 77-80, 83, 87-89, 92-95, 104-06, 119.
An account of the thought and views presented by various deputies to the Legislative Commission with some attention to Catherine's motives for convening the Commission and her reaction to its deliberations. Soloviev, a leading Russian historian in the latter part of the nineteneth century, states that while Catherine was upset by a number of the arguments presented in the Commission, she certainly became familiar with the mood of the individuals to whom her policies would be addressed and therein achieved the goal for which she had created the Commission.

905 *Sumner, B. H. "New Material on the Revolt of Pugachev." Slavonic R, 7, no. 19 (1928): 113-27 and 7, no. 20 (1928): 338-48.
A discussion of the dispatches of the French minister at St. Petersburg, Durand, which contain a highly negative description of Catherine II and her internal policies (especially in regard to the Pugachev Revolt), and some speculation on the likelihood of a coup d'etat to remove Catherine in favor of her son Paul.

906 Thaler, Roderick P. "Catherine II's Reaction to Radishchev." Etudes Slav, 2, no. 3 (1957): 154-60.
Unavailable for annotation.

Economics

907 *Alexander, John T. "Petersburg and Moscow in Early Urban Policy." J Urb Hist, 8 (Feb. 1982): 145-70.
An examination of Catherine II's "urban policy to the early 1770's as it evolved through the interaction of her own aspirations ... with her reactions to specific experiences, problems, and proposals." Alexander emphasizes that Catherine's urban policy drew heavily upon German cameralist theory particularly

in regard to measures to ameliorate overpopulation and its
attendant problems such as urban sprawl, unemployment,
crime, and beggary.

908 *Bartlett, Roger P. "Catherine II and the Manifestos of 1762
and 1763." Human Capital. The Settlement of Foreigners in
Russia, 1762-1804. Cambridge: Cambridge University Press,
1980, 31-56.
An examination of Catherine II's populationist views and
measures with special reference to her manifestos of 1762 and
1763 and her general support for foreign settlement of the
Russian hinterland. Bartlett establishes that although Catherine "regarded population increase essentially as a means to
increase the wealth and power of the state," she also believed
by the settlement of frontier regions control over outlying
parts of the Russian Empire could be improved, fugitive
serfs could be more easily reclaimed, and foreigners interested
in migrating to Russia could be accommodated. The plan approved by Catherine to create "an administrative system at a
national level which could organize both the recruitment and
settlement of immigrants from all sources, and supervise their
use in whatever fields the government might find advantageous" was certainly a constructive one, but once the empress' energy waned and she ceased to supervise personally
the settlement project, the plan fell victim to the defects of
the Russian bureaucracy, inadequate funding, and especially
to the lack of attention given to the concrete means of its
implementation. JV8182.B37

909 _____. "Diderot and the Foreign Colonies of Catherine II."
Cahiers du monde, 23, no. 2 (1982): 221-28.
A discussion of an anonymous French language memorandum
acquired by Denis Diderot during his 1773-74 visit to St.
Petersburg in regard to the foreign colonies established along
the Volga River by immigrants who came to Russia in response
to Catherine's edicts of 1762 and 1763 which provided a
variety of incentives for such settlements. The document
contains an analysis of the problems which the colonists confronted and a series of proposals for dealing with these problems and maximizing the economic potential of the Volga region.
Bartlett suggests that François Pictet was the memorandum's
author and that the latter chose to submit his project anonymously because he was at that time in public disgrace due to
the discovery by Russian authorities of his involvement in a
smuggling operation.

910 _____. "Foreign Settlement in Russia Under Catherine II."
N Z Slavonic J, n.s. 1 (1974): 1-22.
Unavailable for annotation.

911 Brown, A. H. "Adam Smith's First Russian Followers." A. S.

Skinner and Thomas Wilson, eds. Essays on Adam Smith.
Oxford: Clarendon Press, 1975, 202-73.
A discussion of Adam Smith's indirect influence on Catherine
the Great by way of his disciple, S. E. Desnitsky, whose
"Proposal Concerning the Establishment of Legislative, Judicial
and Executive Authorities in the Russian Empire" served as
the foundation for parts of the empress' celebrated Nakaz.
HE108.S6E78

912 _____. "S. E. Desnitsky, Adam Smith and the Nakaz of
Catherine II." Oxford Slav P, n.s. 7 (1974): 42-59.
An examination of the influence exerted on Catherine II by
Adam Smith through the writings of S. E. Desnitsky. Brown
demonstrates that Catherine in the Second Supplement (1768)
to her Nakaz, borrowed heavily from Desnitsky's fourth appendix to his Predstavlenie (unpublished until 1905): "no
fewer than 26 articles of the Nakaz (articles 575-600) bear a
definite (and in many cases, verbatim) relationship to Desnitsky's formulations."

913 Clendenning, P. H. "The Background and Negotiations for
the Anglo-Russian Commercial Treaty of 1766." GBR (anthology), 145-63.
An argument that the 1766 Anglo-Russian Commercial Treaty
"quickly became the foundation for almost thirty years of
mutual economic growth," a fact since "ignored by Russians
and the West alike." As part of his examination of the complex negotiations which shaped the substance of the treaty,
Clendenning discusses the influence of Catherine's views,
as expressed in her Nakaz, on Russia's economic needs and
the effect upon her had by the optimism of her economic
advisers in regard to the future of Russian commerce.

914 Cross, Anthony G. "The Sutherland Affair and Its Aftermath." Slavonic E Eur R, 50, no. 119 (1972): 257-75.
In part, a discussion of Catherine II's angry reaction to the
revelation that Baron Richard Sutherland (court banker responsible for Russian financial transactions abroad) misap-
propriated nearly two million rubles and that both Prince
Potemkin and Grand Duke Paul were involved in the "Sutherland Affair."

915 Daniel, Wallace. "The Merchantry and the Problem of Social
Order in the Russian State: Catherine II's Commission on
Commerce." Slavonic E Eur R, 55, no. 2 (1977): 185-203.
Catherine II is not the focus of this article, but as a study
of the deliberations and proposals of her Commission on
Commerce it warrants the attention of those researching the
problems which confronted the empress as she sought to
modernize and develop Russian trade.

916 _____. "The Merchants' View of the Social Order in Russia

as Revealed in the Town Nakazy from Moskovskaia Guberniia
to Catherine's Legislative Commission." Can Am Slav S, 11,
no. 4 (2977): 503-22.
As an examination of the merchants' "conceptions of themselves
as presented in the Nakazy they helped to prepare," this
article provides some useful insights into the problems which
confronted Catherine II as she sought to create a viable third
estate. Daniel states that "if there is one central theme in
all the urban Nakazy, it is the reliance on the laws to overcome weaknesses in commerce," a reliance contrary to the
very spirit of the European bourgeoisie.

917   *Dmytryshyn, Basil. "The Economic Content of the 1767 Nakaz
      of Catherine II." ASEER, 19, no. 1 (1960): 1-9.
      A presentation of Catherine's ideas on economics as expressed
      in her Instruction to the Legislative Commission of 1767-68.
      Dmytryshyn discusses Catherine's enlightened views on science,
      agriculture, individual ownership of property, industriousness,
      self-sufficiency, desirability of a population increase, freedom
      of trade, and the government's role in promoting a healthy
      economy.

918   *Duin, Egar C. "The Decrees of Catherine the Great and the
      Early Colonists." LUTS (gen. study), 179-96.
      An examination of the immigration of German Lutherans to
      Catherine II's Russia as a consequence of the empress' policy
      of encouraging foreigners to settle in the nation's newly ac-
      quired lands. Duin discusses the actions of Catherine's re-
      cruiters in Western Europe, the motives which led German
      Lutherans to respond favorably to the recruiters' effforts,
      the warm reception received by the Lutherans upon arrival
      in St. Petersburg, and especially, the life of the immigrants
      who settled along the lower Volga River. In regard to the
      latter, Duin reviews the implementation of Catherine's April
      1769 "Instructions for the Colonists on the Volga" which
      dealt with various economic, administrative, and religious
      matters associated with the settlements. Duin goes on to dis-
      cuss Alexander I's active interest in the Volga German com-
      munity and support for continued immigration to this region.

919   *Duran, James A., Jr. "Catherine II, Potemkin and Coloniza-
      tion Policy in Southern Russia." Rus R, 28, no. 1 (1969):
      23-36.
      A discussion of the colonization policy pursued by Catherine
      II as she sought to develop as quickly as possible newly
      acquired territories in southern Russia. Duran states that
      Catherine entrusted to Potemkin the development of this cru-
      cial region not as a political gift to a court favorite but be-
      cause she had an intense personal interest in the success of
      southern colonization. The author favorably reviews the
      specific policies followed to encourage colonization and economic

expansion and concludes that "the greatest permanent monu-
ment to the relationship of Prince Potemkin and Catherine the
Great was the assimilation of these territories into the Russian
Empire."

920 *_____. "The Reform of Financial Administration in Russia
During the Reign of Catherine II." Can Slav S, 4, no. 3
(1970): 485-96.
A favorable examination of Catherine II's reform of Russia's
financial administrative system. Duran establishes that
Catherine saw as a high priority the reordering of the cha-
otic and mismanaged financial system which she had inherited.
Through her own efforts and those of her chief financial adviser, Prince A. A. Viazemsky, a centralized system of ad-
ministering the nation's finances, under the control of a
single responsible state official, replaced the ineffective and
disorganized collegial institutions of the first half of the
century. While the new system had its shortcomings, Duran
concludes, "it is from Catherine's reign not from that of
Peter, Paul, or Alexander I that the beginnings of an effective state financial administration must be dated."

921 "The First Statistical Report on the Volga Colonies Dated
February 14, 1769. Presented to Empress Catherine II by
Count Orlov." Adam Gresinges, trans. AHSGR, 25 (Winter
1977): 4-9.
A statistical report presented to Catherine II on the more
than 5,000 families recruited in Germany to settle in the Volga
region. Among the statistics are the size of each family, the
agricultural skills possessed by adult males, the livestock
owned by the settlers, and the amount and type of foods which
the Volga Germans produced.

922 *Foust, Clifford M. "Catherine and the China Trade." Muscovite and Mandarin: Russia's Trade with China and Its Setting,
1727-1805. Chapel Hill: University of North Carolina Press,
1969, 280-329.
An account of the rapid growth of Russian trade with China
during Catherine II's reign as a consequence of the empress'
successful adaptation of Russia's eastern commercial policy to
the circumstances and forms of the region and the times.
Foust states that although Catherine was sincerely interested
in easing the restrictions on private trade and her enactments
and policies with regard to the China trade reflected this
concern, it would be a mistake to seek as the source of her
actions the free trade philosophy which she expressed in her
Nakaz. In fact, her policy toward trade with China was
based far less on any theoretical predilections on her part
than it was on "the experiences accumulated in the decades
before Catherine came to the throne." HF 3628.C45F66

923 Hittle, J. Michael. "Catherinean Reforms, Social Change, and
    the Decline of the Posad Commune." RSH (anthology), 274-
    300.
    An account of the nature and functions of the posadsky mir
    (a communal organization of tax-paying townsmen), and a dis-
    cussion of its decline as a consequence of reforms in urban
    administration, tax policies, the growth of the state bureau-
    cracy, and socio-economic changes that occurred during
    Catherine II's reign.

924 *Hudson, Hugh D., Jr. "Urban Estate Engineering in Eight-
    eenth Century Russia: Catherine the Great and the Elusive
    Meshchanstvo." Can Am Slav S, 18, no. 4 (1984): 393-410.
    An argument that careful study of Catherine II's concept of
    the meshchanstvo as a social class and efforts to improve her
    realm by reshaping the nature of Russian towns and the
    meshchanstvo reveals lack of support for "the image of the
    Catherinean state as an organized, rational entity consciously
    attempting to modernize society according to a well-formulated
    plan." Hudson contends that Catherine's policy in regard to
    the meshchanstvo was a confused and contradictory one. On
    the one hand she sought to maintain a rigid estate system
    while on the other she wanted to promote a more prosperous
    and dynamic urban economy: "She sought in a revolutionary
    manner to transform her urban subjects' values while pre-
    serving the rigid estate society that had thwarted those
    very values of entrepreneurship and self-reliance."

925 *Kamendrowsky, Victor. "Catherine II's Nakaz, State Finances
    and the Encyclopédie." Can Am Slav S, 13, no. 4 (1979):
    545-54.
    A refutation of the thesis that the chapter on state finances
    in Catherine II's Nakaz was essentially based upon the writings
    of Adam Smith, Quesnay, Justi, Bielfeld, and the Encyclopédie
    of Diderot and D'Alembert. Kamendrowsky maintains that the
    chapter consists for the most part of borrowings from Pes-
    selier's Encyclopédie article and an essay written for Catherine
    by S. E. Desnitsky.

926 *Kamendrowsky, Victor, and David Griffiths. "The Fate of the
    Trading Nobility Controversy in Russia: A Chapter in the
    Relationship Between Catherine II and the Russian Nobility."
    Jahr Ges Ost, 26, no. 2 (1978): 198-221.
    A review of the eighteenth-century, European-wide debate in
    regard to whether or not the nobility should be allowed to
    engage in commerce, and an analysis of Catherine II's position
    on this issue. Kamendrowsky states that Catherine was firmly
    opposed to the prospect of nobles engaging in commerce be-
    cause she believed that such activity would lead the nobility
    to place personal interest above corporate duty, "thereby
    weakening its sense of obligation to the state, and in this

way undermining the very foundations of monarchy."

927 Le Donne, John P. "Indirect Taxes in Catherine II's Russia:
     The Salt Code of 1781" and "The Liquor Monopoly." Jahr
     Ges Ost, 23, no. 2 (1975): 161-90, 24, no. 2 (1976): 173-
     207.
     Catherine II is not the focus of either of these articles, but
     they are of considerable value for the insights which they
     provide into how such necessities as salt and liquor served
     as prime sources of revenue for the aristocracy and the state
     and indirectly as a means of expanding the Russian economy.
     In regard to the state's attitude toward the welfare of its
     subjects, Le Donne notes that while the government was
     "fulfilling a moral purpose" in securing a constant supply of
     salt, by encouraging the production and consumption of liquor,
     the government "contributed to the spread of drunkenness
     and moral turpitude."

928 MacMillan, David S. "The Scottish-Russian Trade: Its
     Development, Fluctuations and Difficulties." Can Slav S,
     4, no. 3 (1970): 426-42.
     In part, a discussion of the negative effect exerted upon
     Scottish-Russian trade by Catherine II's restrictive tariffs of
     1793. The tariffs, which marked the ascendancy of protec-
     tionists within the Russian court, led to a shift in Scottish
     commercial interest from the Baltic region to North America.

929 Morrison, Daniel. "'Trading Peasants' and Urbanization in
     Eighteenth Century Russia: The Central Industrial Region."
     Columbia University, 1981. (dissertation)

930 *Munro, George E. "The Empress and the Merchants: Response
     in St. Petersburg to the Regulation of Commerce Under Cath-
     erine II." Soc Sci J, 13, no. 2 (1976): 39-50.
     An examination of the response of the St. Petersburg mer-
     chantry to the elaborate controls and regulations legislated by
     Catherine II in regard to the rights, duties, and activities
     of the nation's merchant class. Munro contends that the prime
     goal of this mass of commercial legislation was to enhance the
     growth of trade, but Catherine's policies often "thwarted
     genuine merchant efforts to develop entrepreneurial possi-
     bilities" and ultimately served to stifle rather than encourage
     economic expansion and modernization by conditioning mer-
     chants "to expect the state to take the first step in develop-
     ing the economy."

931 Schmidt, K. Rahbek. "The Treaty of Commerce Between Great
     Britain and Russia, 1766: A Study in the Development of
     Count Panin's Northern System." Scando-Slav, 1 (1954):
     115-34.
     In part, a discussion of Catherine II's opposition to the

maintenance of British trading privileges in Russia since
they conflicted with her plans to improve Russia's industry,
commerce, and navigation.

Education, Science, and Culture

932   *Alexander, John T.   "Catherine the Great and Public Health."
      J Hist Med Pub H, 36, no. 2 (1981):   185-204.
      An argument that Catherine II played a far more significant
      role in improving the administration of public health than she
      is traditionally credited with.   Alexander establishes that
      Catherine developed from cameralist and physiocrat literature
      a broad conception of the domain of public health and an
      appreciation for its importance.   In the process, she con-
      ceived "a more active notion of medical assistance, preventive
      and curative alike," which led her to promote the collection
      of vital statistics on health, the construction of medical fa-
      cilities, and an extensive smallpox vaccination campaign.

933   *_____.   "Catherine II, Bubonic Plague, and Industry in
      Moscow."   Am Hist R, 79, no. 3 (1974):   637-71.
      An investigation into the origins and meaning of an unpub-
      lished 1771 note by Catherine II which called for the removal
      of all large factories from the city of Moscow.   Alexander
      places Catherine's proposal within the framework of her gen-
      eral concern for improving conditions in Moscow, a city
      burdened with disease, fires, crime, and poverty.   The pro-
      posal's exact timing was determined by a devastating outbreak
      of bubonic plague in Moscow, the origins of which were traced
      to the squalid conditions of bondaged labor in the city's large
      textile factories.   Alexander concludes that since the plague
      killed such a high percentage of the bondaged labor force,
      the relocation of the factories in which they worked became
      unnecessary, thus Catherine's note was never acted upon.

934   _____.   "Ivan Vien and the First Comprehensive Plague
      Tractae in Russia."   Med Hist, 24, no. 4 (1980):   419-31.
      In part, a discussion of Catherine II's contacts with Ivan Vien,
      a German-Russian medical practitioner, and her promotion of
      him to the position of Secretary of the Medical Collegium as
      means of fostering Russian medical research and publication.

935   Bischoff, Ilse.   "Etienne Maurice Falconet-Sculptor of the Statue
      of Peter the Great."   Rus R, 24 (1965):   369-86.
      An account of Catherine II's commissioning of the French
      sculptor E. M. Falconet to produce a statue of Peter the
      Great and of the difficulties which he encountered in creat-
      ing a work unique and worthy of the trust which the empress
      placed in his talent.   Bischoff also describes the positive
      relationship which developed between Catherine and Falconet
      and the enthusiastic response of the empress and official

Russia in general to his artistic creation which was unveiled
on 18 August 1782.

936   *Bishop, W. J. "Thomas Dimsdale, M.D., F.R.S., and the
       Inoculation of Catherine the Great of Russia." Ann Med Hist,
       n.s. 4 (July 1932): 321-38.
       An account of the smallpox vaccination of Catherine II, her
       son, and grandchildren by British physician Thomas Dimsdale.
       Bishop relates various anecdotes dealing with Catherine's
       recruitment, treatment, and reward of Dimsdale, and her ef-
       forts to introduce smallpox inoculation throughout the Russian
       empire.

937   *Black, J. L. "Catherine II's Imperial Society for the Educa-
       tion of Noble Girls as Russia's Saint-Cyr." Slav E Eur Ed R,
       2 (1980): 1-11.
       An argument that Catherine II's Imperial Society for the Educa-
       tion of Noble Girls, founded in 1764 and better known as
       Smolny, was not modeled upon the famous French school at
       Saint-Cyr. Black maintains that Catherine, in founding
       Smolny, drew upon the expertise of Betskoy and current
       education theory and practice rather than simply copying the
       program at Saint-Cyr. Although the two schools did have a
       number of similarities, there were several, more fundamental
       differences between them, particularly in regard to "the type
       of graduate they were expected to produce." At Saint-Cyr
       the goal was to produce young women with "strong moral
       character and completely devoted to domestic life," while
       Smolny girls were to have character and domestic skills but
       also were to serve as potential foils to the vulgarity which
       Catherine believed was prevalent among Russia's gentry.
       A second basic difference between the two schools was that
       Saint-Cyr was a religious institution whereas Smolny was
       completely secular. Moreover, Smolny came into existence as
       "an integral part of a far-reaching program designed to bring
       education to all of Russia's youth except those of the serf
       caste," Saint-Cyr's origins were less premeditated and the
       school was not part of any grand design to promote education
       in France.

938   *_____. "Chapters 4-7." Citizens of the Fatherland: Edu-
       cation, Educators and Pedagogical Ideas in 18th Century
       Russia. New York: Columbia University Press, 1979, 70-
       171.
       A critical review of Catherine II's practical accomplishments
       in the field of education. Black states that although Cather-
       ine genuinely respected education and believed that it had to
       be improved if Russia were to become a modern nation, her
       various educational plans, though important, failed to result
       in the creation of an effective public school system. Her
       initial efforts to develop educational facilities in which moral

training was emphasized as a means of creating "the new
Russian man" failed due to public apathy and the lack of
good teachers and proper funding. Her attempt, in the
1780s, to invest public education with less idealistic goals
by patterning Russia's schools on those of Austria faltered
because she "ignored those operating principles" which made
the Austrian schools work. More generally, Black criticizes
Catherine because she compromised her pedagogical principles
by placing the maintenance of the political and social status
quo in Russia ahead of the advancement of the nation's
system of education: "Thus schooling tended to remain a
preserve for nobility and bureaucrats, and the masses remained illiterate, kept in place by their own ignorance and
superstition." LA831.5.B44

939 *_____. "Educating Women in Eighteenth Century Russia:
Myths and Realities." Can Slav P, 20, no. 1 (1978): 23-43.
An examination of Catherine II's schools for girls serves as
the basis for an argument that the empress' endeavors in the
area of education have been at best ignored and often misrepresented. Black states that the creation of the Imperial
Educational Society for Noble Girls (Smolny School), a comple-
mentary school for girls from bourgeois families, and other
agencies for the education of young females provided an institutional basis for bringing Russia's middle and upper-class
women out of the terem and for instilling in them the skills,
values, attitudes, and knowledge which they needed to function well within the confines of their station in life. While
the schools did not wholly realize the initial hopes of Catherine and her prime educational adviser Ivan Betskoy, their
graduates, especially those from Smolny, were far from the
naive and penniless creatures described by Catherine's
critics and a number of her "objective" biographers.

940 Brown, William Edward. "Catherine II as a Dramatist."
HECRL (gen. study), 215-18.
A brief critical review of Catherine's efforts as a dramatist,
most notably her attempt to write light-hearted comedies with
a slight social sting to them. Brown maintains that although
Catherine's good-humored comedies are "light and witty,"
her dramas are generally more noteworthy as a barometer
for the changing genre of the times than they are meritorious
in plot, characterization, and style.

941 *_____. "Journalism: Catherine II, Nikolai Novikov et al."
HECRL (gen. study), 162-82.
A critical review of Catherine II's attempt to use satire as a
means to "combat some of the evils of ignorance and bad man-
ners which she observed in Russian Society around her."
To this end, Catherine founded, in 1769, the satirical journal
Vsiakaia vsiachina (All Sorts of Things) and, "with surprising

unawareness of possible consequences," invited "other journalists to follow her lead." Much to Catherine's dismay, some
of the journals which came into existence as a response to
her invitation contained satire far more pointed than that
which she envisioned. This was particularly true of N. Novikov's The Drone, the tone and influence of which she at first
sought to counter with her own pen and later through censorship. Brown concludes that the journalistic clash between
Caherine and Novikov affords a perfect example of the contra-
dictions which attended her cultural policy as a consequence
of her desire to bring enlightenment to Russia while preserving all of her autocratic prerogatives.

942   "Catherine's Campaign for Culture." Life, 58 (2 Apr. 1965):
      82-83.
      A brief discussion of Catherine's purchase and patronage of
      art as an expression of her interest in gaining European
      recognition of Russia as a cultured nation.

943   Cross, Anthony G. "British Freemasons in Russia During the
      Reign of Catherine the Great." Oxford Slav P, 4 (1971):
      43-72.
      Catherine II is not the focal point of this article, but as an
      examination of Freemasonry in Russia in the 1780s and 1790s
      it contains some discussion of her disapproval of masonic
      activity in St. Petersburg and Moscow.

944   * _____ . "A Royal Blue-Stocking: Catherine the Great's
      Early Reputation in England as an Authoress." R. Auty,
      L. R. Lewitter, and A. P. Vlasto, eds. Gorski Vijenats.
      A Garland of Essays Offered to Professor Elizabeth Mary
      Hill. Cambridge: Modern Humanities Research Association,
      1970, 85-99.
      A survey of the generally favorable English reaction to
      Catherine II's writings with most attention devoted to her
      dramatic works of the 1780s. Cross establishes that whereas
      Catherine's Nakaz and The Antidote: Or an Enquiry into the
      Merits of a Book Entitled a Journey into Siberia (by Abbé
      Chappe d'Auteroche) were her only early writings to receive
      foreign attention, by the 1780s "the general interest which
      her reign and personality had generated in Europe" served
      to focus attention on her literary works of that decade,
      especially on her comic operas. While the operas' texts were
      at best mediocre, the high quality of the actors, dancers,
      and composers employed by Catherine and her use of "ela-
      borate scenery and stage machinery, rich costumes and ...
      veritable multitudes in ... crowd scenes" made the operas
      popular with foreigners residing in or visiting St. Petersburg
      and therein contributed to her reputation as an author of
      some talent. DK4.G67

945 *_____. "Russian Literature in the Age of Catherine:
     Synchronic Tables." Russian Literature in the Age of Cath-
     erine the Great. Oxford: Meeuws, 1976, 185-93.
     A year by year listing of the output of Russian literature in
     the fields of poetry, drama, prose, and journalism during
     Catherine II's reign. Cross also lists some 50 foreign works
     translated into Russian and records the main public and lit-
     erary events of the era. PG3007.R87

946 *DeMadariaga, Isabel. "The Foundation of the Russian Educa-
     tional System by Catherine II." Slavonic E Eur R, 37, no.
     3 (1979): 369-95.
     A sympathetic reassessment of Catherine II's educational
     principles and reforms. DeMadariaga contends that critics
     have given insufficient attention to the chaos and disrepair
     which characterized Russia's schools at the time of Catherine's
     accession to the throne and consequently have failed to realize
     that the empress' use of her authority to dictate and impose
     educational policy was necessary if backwardness and illiter-
     acy were to be countered effectively.

947 "An Empress Editress." RR, 1 (Feb. 1890): 141.
     A brief review of a Russian Archives article written by E.
     S. Shumigorsky in regard to Catherine II's purpose in found-
     ing the satirical journal All Sorts of Things.

948 Epp, George. "The Educational Policies of Catherine II of
     Russia, 1762-96." University of Manitoba, 1976. (dissertation)

949 Felbrigg, Henry. "Collector and Patron of the Arts. The
     Empress Catherine II." Antiq Coll, 50 (May 1979): 86-89.
     Unavailable for annotation.

950 *Gukovskii, Grigorii A. "The Empress as Writer." CGP
     (anthology), 64-89. From "Ekaterina II" in Grigorii A.
     Gukovskii and V. A. Desnitskii, eds. Literatura XVIII veka.
     Istoriia russkoi literatury. Vol. IV, Part II. Mary Mackler,
     trans. Moscow-Leningrad, 1947, 364-80.
     An evaluation of the style, form, and substance of Catherine's
     many and varied literary works. Gukovsky states that Cath-
     erine was without talent as a writer and that even after years
     of effort was unable to produce any single work that came
     close in quality to the literary standards of her time. Her
     writings are of interest primarily because "they express the
     real and official literary policy of the government ..." while
     at the same time reflect well the changing artistic styles of
     the period. Gukovsky also notes that with the coming of
     the French Revolution Catherine "gave up her writing, in
     which she was always more of a monarch lecturing her sub-
     jects than a genuinely creative artist."

951   Hans, Nicholas. "Catherine II." <u>HREP</u> (gen. study), 17-32.
      A favorable review of Catherine II's efforts to construct a
      nationwide system of schools. Hans devotes most of his at-
      tention to a discussion of the 5 December 1786 Statute of
      Schools as the most important legislation in the field of educa-
      tion during the entire eighteenth century. He adds that the
      act was deficient because it pertained only to the town popula-
      tion and did not make school attendance compulsory but none-
      theless represented a significant advancement toward the
      creation of a free, secular, and relatively democratic school
      system.

952   _____. "Dumaresq, Brown, and Some Early Educational
      Projects of Catherine II." <u>Slavonic E Eur R</u>, 41 (1961-62):
      229-35.
      A brief account of the advice and assistance provided to
      Catherine II by British educators Daniel Dumaresq and
      John Brown in regard to the improvement of education in
      Russia. Dumaresq served on a 1764 commission on Russian
      school reform and influenced its recommendations as did Brown
      who corresponded with Dumaresq while the former was in the
      service of the empress.

953   Hilles, Frederick W. "Sir Joshua and the Empress Catherine."
      <u>Eighteenth Century Studies in Honor of Donald F. Hyde.</u>
      New York: n.p., 1970, 267-77.
      An account of the circumstances surrounding Sir Joshua
      Reynolds' production of and reward for painting "the Infant
      Hercules" for Catherine II. Hilles establishes that the impetus
      for the painting came from Lord Carysfort who pointed out to
      Catherine that the English school was not represented at all
      in her collection of paintings. Hilles also discusses Reynolds'
      choice of theme for the painting, the mixed reaction to the
      work by English art critics, and Catherine's generous reward
      of Reynolds in the form of a jeweled snuff-box, a most flat-
      tering handwritten note, and the payment of 1,500 guineas to
      Sir Joshua's estate the year after his death. PR442.E4

954   Home, R. W. "The Scientific Education of Catherine the
      Great." <u>Melbourne Slav S</u>, 11 (1976): 18-22.
      A short account of Grand Duchess Catherine's study of the
      natural sciences under the guidance of tutor Franz Aepenēes.
      Home notes that while Catherine had a genuine desire to
      extend her knowledge in this field, the immediate impetus for
      her studies came when she turned toward a more contempla-
      tive lifestyle as a consequence of Empress Elizabeth's dis-
      covery of her involvement in political intrigue within the
      Russian court.

955   *Ikonnikov, V. S. "An Assessment of Catherine II's Reign by
      a Pre-Revolutionary Russian Historian." <u>MRPC</u> (anthology),

137-48. Excerpt from <u>Znachenie tsarstovovaniia Ekateriny II</u>.
Kiev, 1897.
A positive account of Catherine II's promotion of education,
science, medicine, literature, and art. Ikonnikov enumerates
the contributions made by various Russians in each of these
fields during Catherine's reign and relates the overall development of culture during this age to the empress' intense personal interest in the advancement of learning and knowledge
within Russia.

956 Johnson, William H. E. "The Creation of State Schools (1760-
1800)." <u>Russia's Educational Heritage</u>. Pittsburgh: Carne-
gie Press, 1950, 43-62.
A favorable review of Catherine II's efforts to extend the
scope and improve the quality of education in Russia. Johnson notes that while Catherine generally sought to advance
the reforms initiated by Peter the Great, her pedagogical
views were far less utilitarian than those of her illustrious
predecessor in that she saw education as "a social force
which could mold the future, produce cultured citizens, form
character, and control behavior." Johnson sees the 1786
Statute for Public Schools in the Russian Empire, drawn up
by the Commission for the Establishment of Schools which was
chaired by Jankovich de Mirievo, as a noble attempt to advance the nation's educational program, which, after initial
rapid progress, fell victim to lack of funds, students, and
local support. LA831.J6

957 Jones, G. Gareth. "Novikov's Naturalized 'Spectator.'" <u>ECR</u>
(anthology), 149-65.
As part of an examination of Nikolay Novikov's 1769 creation
and editorship of the satirical journal <u>The Drone</u> (modeled
after Addison and Steele's <u>The Spectator</u>), this essay includes
a discussion of Catherine II's role in the emergence of a
distinct literary coterie in Russia.

958 *Key, Mary Ritchie. <u>Catherine the Great's Linguistic Contribu-
tion</u>. Carbondale, Ill.: Linguistic Research, Inc., 1980,
200pp., bib. 157-80.
A discussion of Catherine II as a pioneer in the comparative
study and classification of languages on a worldwide basis.
Key states that Catherine gathered systematically through a
wide-ranging correspondence samples of vocabulary from
various languages, and then constructed a series of lists to
facilitate the comparative analysis of the words collected for
insight into the origin, nature, and interrelationship of the
languages under study. Key commends Catherine not only
for the diligence which she displayed in this endeavor but also
for making available the results of her findings in the form of
her <u>Linguarum Totius Orbis Vocabularia Comparativa</u> (edited by
P. Pallas and published in St. Petersburg, 1786-89) and for

her role in the publication of the first Russian dictionary.
P85.C37K4

959 Leary, D. B. "Catherine II to Alexander I. 1762-1801." EAR
(gen. study), 38-44.
A brief discussion of Catherine's intellectual qualities and educational reforms.

960 Leonard, Gerald Irwin. "Novikov, Shcherbatov, Radishchev:
The Intellectual in the Age of Catherine the Great." State
University of New York at Binghamton, 1980. (dissertation)

961 Lukomski, George K. "Charles Cameron, Architect. Bronze
Work at Tsarskoje-Sélo." Connois, 97 (Mar. 1936): 152-56.
This article, as well as the next two entries written by the
same author, deals more with the work performed by architect Charles Cameron while under commission to Catherine II
than with the empress herself but is a useful source of information on the artistic and architectural styles of her era.

962 _____. "Charles Cameron, Architect to Catherine the Great."
Connois, 95 (Apr. 1935): 190-96.

963 _____. "Charles Cameron, Architect to Catherine the Great
of Russia." Roy Inst Br Arch J, 43, no. 18 (1936): 961-73.

964 *McArthur, Gilbert. "Catherine II and the Masonic Circle of
N. I. Novikov." Can Slav S, 4, no. 3 (1970): 529-46.
An examination of Catherine's view of the Society of Freemasons and the reasons for her harassment and persecution
of N. Novikov. McArthur maintains that although Catherine
and Novikov shared a concern for advancing the enlightenment
of Russia's citizenry, the empress came to resent and fear
Novikov because of his leading role in Russian Freemasonry,
her suspicion that he was attempting to win Grand Duke Paul
over to Freemasonry, and most importantly, her belief that
private initiative for reform posed a threat to her royal
prerogatives.

965 McKenna, Kevin J. "Catherine the Great's Vsiakaia Vsiachina
and The Spectator Tradition of the Satirical Journal of Morals
and Manners." University of Colorado, 1970. (dissertation)

966 Massie, Stephanie. "Crowning Achievement of the Jewelers'
Art." Antiq W, 3 (Apr. 1981): 68-70.
A description and history of the crown created by Posier for
Catherine II's coronation with some reference to Catherine's
accession to the throne and delight over the magnificence of
Posier's creation.

967 *Miliukov, Pavel N. "Educational Reforms." Norman K. Sloan,

trans. CG (anthology), 93-112. From Ocherki po istorii
russkoi Kul'tury. Vol. II, Part 2. Paris, 1931, 750-65.
A critical review of the educational program of Catherine II.
Miliukov, a noted Russian liberal and historian, divides
Catherine's educational reforms into two phases. During
the first phase, prior to 1780, Catherine assigned to the
schools the task of nurturing children, a job previously
performed by the family. The schools were thus to create
"a new race of men" through humane and enlightened child
rearing. This attempt to reshape Russia's educational institutions as a means of implementing her goals failed miserably,
and consequently the empress "cooled to the idea of rearing
a new race" and turned instead to the establishment of a
general program of education with the assistance of Jankovich
de Mirievo, a Serbian disciple of the Prussian educator Fell-
bieger. However, because of the entrenched nature of "the
old habits of family and school" and the "grievous material
and moral condition of the teacher in the Russian school,"
Catherine's reforms resulted in but a partial improvement of
secondary education only.

968   "The Mystery of the Tsaritsyno Ruins." Sov Life, 279 (Dec.
      1979):   45-58.
      A discussion of Catherine II's decision to demolish the royal
      estate at Tsaritsyno just prior to the completion of its con-
      struction. The empress' action was prompted by the concern
      that Vasily Bazhenov, the architect and an alleged Freemason,
      had mocked Russian Orthodoxy by cleverly incorporating into
      the estate's design Masonic symbols.

969   Nechkina, M. V., et al., eds. "An Assessment of Catherine
      II's Reign in Soviet Historiography." MRPC (anthology),
      148-57. Excerpt from Istoriia SSSR s drevneishikh vremen
      do 1861 g. Moscow, 1956.
      A Soviet characterization of Catherine II's reign as one
      marked by creativity and noteworthy successes in the fields
      of science, literature, and the arts despite the reactionary
      policies of a corrupt and morally bankrupt monarchy.

970   *Okenfuss, Max J. "Education and Empire: School Reform
      in Enlightened Russia." Jahr Ges Ost, 27, no. 1 (1979):
      41-68.
      An analysis of the 1786 Statute of Schools for insight into
      the reform's origin and consistency with Catherine II's repu-
      tation as an enlightened ruler. Okenfuss contends that the
      reform is best understood when placed within a Central
      European context and viewed as an attempt to maintain the
      political-social status quo rather than as an expression of
      sympathy with the ideals of the Western Enlightenment.

971   Rice, Tamara Talbot. "Charles Cameron: Catherine the

Great's British Architect." Connois, 165 (Aug. 1967): 240-
45.
The focus of this article is the architectural skill of Charles
Cameron, but it includes some discussion of Catherine's
approval of his work in the construction of Tsarskoe Selo.

972 Rosenfeld, Albert. "Biggest Medical Fee in History." Coronet,
     47 (Nov. 1959): 101-03.
     An account of the smallpox inoculation of Catherine II and
     Grand Duke Paul by Dr. Thomas Dimsdale, who received royal
     treatment and the equivalent of 130,000 dollars for his serv-
     ices.

973 Ryu, In-Ho Lee. "Freemasonry Under Catherine the Great:
     A Reinterpretation." Harvard University, 1967. (disserta-
     tion)

974 Scott, Richenda C. "Peter the Great Has Visitors and Catherine
     the Great an English Physician." Quakers in Russia. Lon-
     don: Michael Joseph, 1964, 40-43.
     A brief account of Catherine II's recruitment of Dr. Thomas
     Dimsdale for the introduction of inoculation as a method of
     preventing smallpox in Russia. BX7710.R8S35

975 *Segal, Harold B. "The Reign of Catherine II (1762-1796) and
     Paul I (1796-1801)." Literature of 18th Century Russia, Vol.
     I. New York: E. P. Dutton, 1967, 69-116.
     A survey of the literary explosion which occurred during
     Catherine the Great's reign. Segal devotes most of his at-
     tention to a discussion of journals published between 1769
     and 1774, the literature based on foreign travel, Radishchev's
     Journey, and Karamzin's Letters of a Russian Traveler. Of
     particular interest is Segal's account of the literary dispute
     between Catherine and N. Novikov in regard to the tasks
     and goals of satire. PG3213.S4

976 Selden, Margery S. "An Operatic Success of Catherine the
     Great." J Am Mus S, 10 (Fall 1957): 212-13.
     An abstract of a paper, read at a 1957 meeting of the Ameri-
     can Musicological Society, in which the author discusses the
     plot, themes, and music of Catherine II's opera Nachal'noye
     Upravleniye Olega (The Early Reign of Oleg).

977 *Simmons, E. J. "Catherine the Great and Shakespeare."
     PMLA, 47 (Sept. 1932): 790-806.
     A discussion of Catherine II's four "Shakespearian" plays.
     Simmons establishes that Catherine in her "free rendering"
     of Shakespeare's The Merry Wives of Windsor transformed
     the play into a vehicle for satire. In reworking Timons of
     Athens, Catherine diverged radically from the Shakespearian
     original to enable her to play the role of a moralist and

provide an ending to the play acceptable to her Russian audience. Catherine's attempts at historical drama, The Life
of Rurik and The Early Reign of Oleg, were referred to by
her as "imitations of Shakespeare" but, beyond the initial
inspiration provided by Shakespeare for the broad, historical
sweep of the play, Catherine's dramas "have little of the manner and none of the poetry of the master.... Of Shakespeare's genius for portraying a huge canvas containing a
variety of characters that breathe with genuine pathos, tragedy, and comedy of life, she has none." Separate from the
quality of Catherine's plays, Simmons concludes, the empress'
work is significant because it stimulated "an interest in
Shakespeare by introducing him in a new light to the Russian
public."

978   *Simmons, Robert W., Jr. "Catherine II: The Stimulation of
      Literature by Royal Decree." Kent For Lang Q, 9, no. 1
      (1962): 52-57.
      A discussion of the flowering of satirical journals in Russia in
      response to Catherine II's founding of her own journal
      All Sorts of Things. Of particular interest is Simmons' ac-
      count of the literary debate which ensued between Catherine
      and N. Novikov in regard to the purpose of such satirical
      publications. Simmons concludes that the 1769-1774 period
      was the only time in the history of Russian literature that
      "relative freedom of expression was encouraged."

979   Slonim, Marc. "Poets, Playwrights, and Satirists of the Eight-
      eenth Century." The Epic of Russian Literature. New York:
      Oxford University Press, 1964, 29-48.
      An overview of the growth of secular Russian literature as
      the most important expression of the "blossoming of national
      consciousness" that occurred during Catherine II's reign.
      Although Slonim notes that Catherine became more practical
      and conservative as her reign progressed, he nonetheless
      commends her for the support which she gave to education,
      publishing, and literature of various types. PG2951.S5

980   Taylor, Francis Henry. "The Great Catherine." The Taste of
      Angels. Boston: Little, Brown and Company, 1948, 526-31.
      A brief discussion of Catherine II as a voracious collector of
      art works. Taylor enumerates Catherine's principal purchases
      and maintains that the haste and lack of discrimination shown
      by Catherine in buying objects of art show that "her connois-
      seurship was as superficial as her philosophy." N380.T3

981   *Tompkins, S. R. "Education Under Catherine and Her Suc-
      cessors." RM (gen. study), 76-97.
      A favorable review of Catherine II's educational philosophy
      and reforms. Tompkins establishes that Catherine's convic-
      tion, as expressed in her 1767 Nakaz, that "true education

should be moral as well as intellectual" contrasted sharply
with Peter the Great's view that the nation's schools should
serve as a training ground for state servitors. Tompkins
notes that while Catherine's attempt to give concrete shape
to her pedagogical views in the form of a nationwide school
system was fitful and deficient in a number of respects, she
nonetheless was responsible for the creation, by 1800, of
over 300 public schools with a total enrollment of nearly
20,000 students.

982 *_____. "Freemasonry." Ibid., 53–75.
A discussion of the origins and development of Russian Freemasonry during the reign of Catherine II. Tompkins states
that the impressive growth and early accomplishments of
Freemasonry in Moscow were effectively countered by Catherine who, out of distrust of "spontaneous movements of any
kind among the people" and resentment over Masonic activity
in education ("a field which the government had taken for its
own"), harassed and eventually imprisoned the driving force
in the Masonic movement, N. N. Novikov.

983 *_____. "The Press." Ibid., 98–119.
In part, a discussion of Catherine II's patronage of Russian
literature and journalism, and her later turn to repressive
policies, particularly in regard to Novikov and Radishchev,
as she came to fear that she had unleashed a force she could
no longer control.

984 *Von Herzen, Michael. "Catherine II: Editor of Vsiakaia
Vsiachina? A Reappraisal." Rus R, 38, no. 3 (1979): 283–
97.
The stated goals of this article are to establish the sources
for the conclusion that Catherine II was the editor of the
satirical journal Vsiakaia vsiachina (All Sorts of Things); to
demonstrate that there never has been any direct evidence
that Catherine was the editor of this publication; and to speculate as to reasons for the perpetration of the myth that she
was the journal's editor. Von Herzen states that scholars
have used an 1863 essay by P. Perkavsky, which contains
portions of articles in Catherine's handwriting addressed to
Vsiakaia vsiachina, to demonstrate that she was in fact the
editor of the journal. Perkavsky's discovery however reveals
that Catherine was only a contributor to Vsiakaia vsiachina,
but scholars anxious to determine which articles could be
attributed to the empress conveniently jumped to the conclusion that the entire journal was hers, and "in a flash all problems of attribution vanished." Von Herzen concludes that the
ready acceptance and longevity of the myth of Catherine's
editorship can be traced to the desire of populist, liberal,
and Soviet historians to present Catherine in a negative light
and "to make a place for Novikov in the Pantheon of Russian

heroes ..." by connecting her with the "conservative"
Vsiakaia vsiachina and explaining her later persecution of
Novikov as an expression of her desire to avenge the drub-
bing she took at his hands during the literary debates between Vsiakaia vsiachina's anonymous editor and Novikov
over the proper form of satire.

985 *Vucinich, Alexander. "Science, Enlightenment and Absolutism."
Science in Russian Culture. A History to 1860. Stanford:
Stanford University Press, 1963, 125-83.
Includes a discussion of Catherine II's efforts to develop a
public school system in Russia, her support of the Academy
of Sciences, role in the founding of the Free Economic Society,
and the growth of the scientific spirit in Russia during her
reign. Q127.R9V8

986 Waliszewski, K. "The Bondage of the West-Catherine II."
A History of Russian Literature. Port Washington, N.Y.:
Kennikat Press, 1969 (reprint of 1927 edition), 88-127.
A sharp attack on Catherine II for stifling the creativity
of Russia's writers through censorship and excessive imitation
of Western artistic styles and practices. Waliszewski maintains that in addition to stunting the development of an indigenous body of literature through her "excessive Occidental-
ism," Catherine so overreacted to any sign of outside, independent, or creative thought that "by the end of her reign
scarcely anyone wrote." Within this context, Waliszewski discusses the sterility of Catherine's various literary works and
the harshness of her reaction to the writings of N. Novikov
and A. Radishchev. PG2951.W3

987 Watts, G. B. "Catherine II, Charles Joseph Panckovcke, and
the Kehl Edition of Voltaire's Works." Mod Lang Q, 18 (Mar.
1957): 59-62.
A brief account of Catherine II's decision to provide financial
support for Charles Joseph Panckovcke's project for editing
and publishing Voltaire's complete works. Watts also describes
the circumstances which prompted Panckovcke to sell the
product of his labors to Beaumarchais before learning of the
empress' generous offer.

Church and Religion

988 *Ammann, A. M. "Church Affairs." CGP (anthology), 290-300.
From Abrisse der ostslawischen Kirchengeschichte. Brigitte
McConnell, trans. Wein: Thomas Morus Presse in Verlag
Herder, 1950, 403-13.
An examination of Catherine's church policy in terms of its
unique qualities as well as the features which it shared with her
predecessors' policies. Ammann, professor of Western church

history at the Pontifical Oriental Institute in Rome, states
that the problem of the administration of church property
and the question of how best to reintegrate the Old Believers
into the Russian national community were concerns which
Catherine inherited, however in the area of clerical education
and in the general spiritual development of educated Russians
Catherine's reign is a unique one because of the intensity and
scope of the empress' efforts to promote secularization.

989 Baron, Salo W. "Under Catherine II and Alexander I." RJTS
     (gen. study), 15-30.
     A survey of Catherine II's initial progressive policy towards
     Russia's Jewish population and the circumstances which led
     her to replace this policy with one more restrictive. Baron
     contends that at the root of Catherine's decision to restrict
     Jewish settlement to Russia's newly acquired territories was
     her desire to limit geographically the toleration of the existence
     of the Jewish kahal as "a state within a state" and to avoid
     further complicating internal conditions in old Russia where
     Jews faced "the perennial hostility of the population" and
     where their presence was seen as an economic threat by Rus-
     sian merchants.

990 *Dubnow, S. "The Jewish Policy of Catherine II." HRJP,
     Vol. I (gen. study), 306-20.
     A discussion of the evolution of Catherine II's Jewish policy
     from an initial quasi-liberal one to a conservative one which
     foreshadowed the anti-Semitic policies to be pursued by sub-
     sequent Romanov rulers. Dubnow states that the first par-
     tition of Poland, in 1772, so swelled the Jewish population of
     Russia that Catherine was perplexed as to the best policy to
     adopt. She wavered between placing Russia's Jews under
     the general laws of the empire and allowing them to retain
     their own laws and institutions. Under pressure from Russian
     merchants who resented business competition from the Jews,
     Catherine began to restrict Jewish rights. With the second
     partition of Poland and a new influx of Jews, Catherine re-
     sorted to the Law of the Pale Settlement and other measures
     which limited Jewish rights and established the first Jewish
     territorial ghetto. Thus Catherine the Great set in motion
     the trend which led to the compression of the Jewish popula-
     tion into certain areas and the institution of restrictive meas-
     ures on Jewish freedom.

991 *Fisher, A. W. "Enlightened Despotism and Islam Under
     Catherine II." Slav R, 27 (Dec. 1968): 542-53.
     A favorable assessment of Catherine II's policy toward Russia's
     Muslim subjects. Fisher states that when Catherine came to
     power, she inherited a militant Orthodox program of religious
     conversion that was the target of a bitter protest by Russian
     Muslims. She eliminated this program in favor of a new

conversion policy based upon economic incentives. However,
in reaction to the critical reports of the 1767-68 Legislative
Commission, Catherine abandoned this policy in favor of a
more progressive one which tolerated the Islamic religion but
still aimed to assimilate Muslims into the mainstream of Russian
society through bureaucratic methods. Under the expert
guidance of Baron Igelstrom, the Russian state, in the last
decade of Catherine's reign, made substantial gains in this
direction.

992   *Klier, John D. "The Ambiguous Legal Status of Russian
      Jewry in the Reign of Catherine II." Slav R, 35 (Sept. 1976):
      504-17.
      A discussion of the disjointed and contradictory policies pur-
      sued by Catherine II in regard to Russian Jews. Klier main-
      tains that "the formulation of a distinct legal status for the
      Jews ... was not influenced solely by anti-Semitic calculations,
      but also by a pervasive ignorance about, and apathy toward,
      the Jews." Klier traces the evolution of Catherine's policy
      from one based on maintaining the autonomy of the Jews with-
      in Russia to one geared toward their segregation.

993   *Petschauer, Peter. "Catherine the Great's Conversion of
      1744." Jahr Ges Ost, 20, no. 2 (1972): 179-93.
      An analysis of Catherine's conversion from Lutheranism to
      Russian Orthodoxy for insights into her views on religion
      and their effect on her politics. Petschauer maintains that
      Catherine's "conversion to Orthodoxy instilled in her the
      idea about the superficiality of the outside framework of re-
      ligion, but it did not erase her basic trust in the power of
      God as inculcated by her father." While retaining her faith
      in God, Catherine also realized that "religious establishments
      should not stand in the way of her drive ... to get ahead in
      the world."

994   *Pipes, Richard. "Catherine II and the Jews: The Origins
      of the Pale Settlement." Sov Jew Aff, 5, no. 2 (1975): 3-
      20.
      A reassessment of the Jewish policies of Catherine II. Pipes
      criticizes Jewish historians for the narrow-mindedness of their
      approach to the history of Russia's Jews. He asserts that
      Catherine's policies were not anti-Semitic but rather were in-
      tended to benefit the Jews and certainly were more enlightened
      than those pursued by her European counterparts. Her at-
      tempt to give Jews status met with failure because of the op-
      position of Poles living in Russia's western provinces and the
      resistance of Russia's merchant class. Pipes concludes that
      Catherine's limitation of the area open to Jewish settlement
      was not intended to be a repressive measure but became so
      under the reactionary policies of her successors.

995 Shahan, Thomas J. "Catharine II and the Holy See (1772-
     1769)." Am Cath Q, 30, no. 117 (1905): 1-27.
     An argument that Catherine II's dealings with Poland, the
     Holy See, and the Roman Catholic population of the terri-
     tories she annexed during her reign were more damaging to
     the interests of Catholicism than "even the hydraheaded
     revolution of the doctrinaires and Jacobins of France."
     Shahan maintains that Catherine "robbed the Roman Catholic
     Church of more millions of souls than ever were in Ireland
     in the days of its greatest population, and she built up be-
     tween them and Rome a Chinese Wall of exclusion that
     stands today...."

996 *Smal-Stocki, Roman. "Catherine II of Russia and the Jesuits."
     Ukr Q, 26, no. 1 (1970): 73-78.
     An examination of Catherine's motivation for allowing the
     Jesuits to continue to function in Russia following the 21
     July 1773 suppression of the Order by the Pope. Smal-
     Stocki argues that Catherine did not preserve the Jesuit
     Order out of any admiration for the Jesuits as teachers but
     rather hoped that "in gratitude for permitting them to con-
     tinue their existence" they would persuade Polish Jesuits to
     help lessen opposition in Poland to the 1772 partition by
     Russia.

997 Springer, Arnold. "Enlightened Absolutism and Jewish Re-
     form: Prussia, Austria, and Russia." Calif Slav S, 11
     (1980): 237-67.
     In part, a discussion of the question of Jewish emancipation-
     integration in Russia under Catherine II and Alexander I.
     Springer maintains that the enlightened absolutist regimes
     of Russia and east central Europe failed to make substantial
     progress in their treatment of the "Jewish question" due to
     "lack of sufficient financial resources and an underdeveloped
     and unsympathetic bureaucracy" and because their inclination
     toward "sweeping reform of the Jewish community in theory"
     was not matched by a commitment to a systematic and rigor-
     ous follow-through on actual reform legislation.

                  FOREIGN POLICY AND MILITARY AFFAIRS

998 Anderson, M. S. "Great Britain and the Russo-Turkish War
     of 1768-74." Eng Hist R, 69 (1954): 39-58.
     In part, a discussion of Catherine II's efforts to conclude a
     formal military alliance with Britain during the first decade
     of her rule. Despite Britain's diplomatic isolation at this
     time and Catherine's willingness to come to Britain's aid in
     the event of war in North America, the empress' various
     proposals in regard to an alliance were rejected, a decision
     which Anderson labels "a disastrous mistake" on the part of
     Great Britain.

999   *_____. "The Great Powers and the Russian Annexation
        of the Crimea, 1783-84." Slavonic E Eur R, 37 (Dec. 1958):
        17-41.
        An investigation of why the great powers--France, Britain,
        and Prussia--proved so impotent and/or indifferent in the
        face of Catherine II's annexation of the Crimean state
        whose independence Russia and the Ottoman Empire had
        agreed to recognize in 1774 by way of Article III of the
        Treaty of Kuchuk-Kainardji. Anderson maintains that the
        antagonisms which separated the great powers served to
        prevent them from intervening in this affair while the mili-
        tary weakness of the Turks made for the bloodlessness of
        Russia's victory. He also links Catherine's success in this
        endeavor to "the tenacity and cool-headedness with which
        she had faced the representations and protests of France
        and the obstinacy of the Turks. Her determination and self-
        reliance contrasted forcibly with the confusion and weakness
        of her opponents."

1000 _____. "The Ottoman Empire and the Great Powers, 1774-
        98." The Eastern Question, 1774-1923. A Study in Inter-
        national Relations. New York: St. Martin's Press, 1966,
        1-27.
        In part, an account of Catherine II's attempt to consolidate
        the gains made by Russia in its war with Turkey by way of
        the Treaties of Kuchuk-Kainardji (1774) and Jassy (1792).
        Anderson devotes most of his attention to a discussion of
        why France and Britain were unable to prevent Catherine's
        restructuring of Russo-Ottoman affairs to her advantage.
        D371.A43

1001 *Bakhrushin, Sergei V. and Sergei D. Skazkin. "Diplomacy."
        CGP (anthology), 181-96. From their "Diplomatiia evrope-
        iskikh gosudarstv v XVIII veke" in Istoriia Diplomatii.
        V. P. Potemkin, ed. Mary Mackler, trans. Moscow, 1941,
        283-95. Excerpt in RRPDH (anthology), 63-95.
        A review of Catherine's foreign policy goals, methods, and
        accomplishments. The authors state that "Russian diplomacy
        between 1726 and 1762 prepared the ground for the solution
        of the basic foreign policy problems that confronted Russia
        from the end of the 17th century," but it was left to Cath-
        erine to accomplish in the main the tasks inherited from that
        century. More specifically, Catherine consolidated Peter
        the Great's achievements in the Baltic region, repatriated
        the Ukrainians and Byelorussians who inhabited the territory
        to the south and west of Russia, gained a firm foothold on
        the Black Sea, and won a decisive voice for Russia in the
        affairs of Europe as a whole. The authors also credit Cath-
        erine with the introduction of several new diplomatic tech-
        niques, including the dissemination of propaganda in foreign
        countries, and with the establishment of personal contact
        with foreign monarchs.

1002 Batalden, Stephen K. Catherine II's Greek Prelate: Eugene
      Voulgaris in Russia, 1771-1806. New York: Columbia Uni-
      versity Press, 1982, 197pp., bib. 145-89.
      This work does not contain a separate section on Catherine
      II, but as a scholarly discussion of E. Voulgaris' motivation
      for encouraging Catherine to pursue an expansionist southern
      policy it is a useful source of information on the formative
      stages of the Eastern Question which came to dominate Rus-
      sian foreign policy in the next century.

1003 *Baylen, Joseph O., and Dorothy Woodward. "Francisco de
      Miranda in Russia." Americâs, 6 (Apr. 1950): 431-49.
      A discussion of Miranda's attempt to enlist the aid of Cath-
      erine II in liberating Spanish America. Baylen and Wood-
      ward establish that Catherine treated Miranda well and was
      intrigued by the possibility of securing political allegiance
      and trade privileges from those American colonies that
      could be separated from Spain, but she refrained from active
      involvement for fear that Spain might close Mediterranean
      ports important to Russia. Catherine, however, continued
      her favoritism toward Miranda most likely so that she might
      use him as a pawn in Russo-Spanish diplomacy.

1004 *Bolkhovitinov, Nikolai N. Russia and the American Revolu-
      tion. C. J. Smith, trans. Tallahassee: Diplomatic Press,
      1976, 277pp., bib. 250-72.
      This study, by a Soviet specialist on American diplomatic
      history, includes an analysis of the policies pursued by
      Catherine II in regard to America and Britain during the
      American Revolution. Drawing on unpublished Russian
      archival material, Bolkhovitinov examines Catherine's rejec-
      tion of an alliance with England, formulation of a position of
      "armed neutrality," efforts to serve as mediator in the dispute
      between the American colonies and Britain, and treatment
      of the American envoy F. Dana. The author asserts that
      Catherine's actions, notably her Proclamation of Armed
      Neutrality, improved the international position of America
      and were vital, in the final analysis, to the colonial victory.
      He notes that it was not sympathy with America's cause that
      inspired Catherine but rather "considerations of real politik--
      the ever growing discontent with the policy of the British
      cabinet" and her desire "to play the role of arbitrator of
      European affairs." B249.B6413

1005 *Carter, Harold Burnell. "Sir Joseph Banks and the Plant
      Collection from Kew Sent to the Empress Catherine II of
      Russia, 1795." Bull Br Mus, 4, no. 5 (1974): 283-385.
      A series of records kept by Sir Joseph Banks serve as the
      basis for an investigation into the motivation behind George
      III's plant gift to Catherine II. Carter maintains that the
      gift, which consisted of an extensive collection of plants from
      the Royal Gardens at Kew, was prompted by Sir Charles

Whitworth who was laboring to secure Russian support for
a coalition against the French Republic. Of particular interest is Carter's account of the difficulties which attended
the delivery of the collection.

1006 *"Catherine of Russia." Quar R, 146 (July 1878): 203-32.
      Also in Liv Age, 138 (1878): 707-15.
      Drawing upon a number of German language works of the
      1860s and 1870s and Catherine II's correspondence with
      Emperor Joseph of Austria, the author discusses Catherine's
      "Eastern policy" and "the wars and transactions in which her
      ambition involved herself, her rivals, and her allies." He
      concludes that "Catherine was the first of her time to con-
      ceive, and to install as a national object, that system of
      unremitting Russian crusade against Turkey, which has
      proved so permanent and so dangerous a disturber of
      Europe's diplomatic repose. Her towering ambition trans-
      formed the latent aims of the houses of Rurik and Romanov
      into a conscious and systematic resolve for the destruction
      of a neighboring Empire."

1007 "Catherine II and Frederick the Great." Bentley's M, 64
      (1868): 307.
      Unavailable for annotation.

1008 Cresson, W. P. Francis Dana: A Puritan Diplomat at the
      Court of Catherine the Great. New York: L. MacVeagh,
      Dial Press, 1930, 397pp.
      This study of the diplomatic mission of American envoy
      Francis Dana does not contain a separate section on Cath-
      erine II but is of value for its illumination of court politics
      and the American perspective on the empress' neutrality in
      the struggle between the colonies and Great Britain. Dana
      was appalled by the cynicism of the courtiers and favorites
      who surrounded Catherine and shielded her from his entreat-
      ies. He also harbored a low opinion of Catherine's political
      behavior, particularly in regard to her motives in offering
      to mediate the British-American conflict. E302.6.D16C92

1009 *Cross, Anthony G. "The British in Catherine's Russia:
      A Preliminary Survey." ECR (anthology), 233-67.
      Catherine II is not the focus of this essay, but it includes
      an interesting examination of her reign as "the halcyon days"
      of British influence in Russia. In support of this statement,
      Cross presents an account of Catherine's commissioning of
      various British subjects, including sculptors, painters, en-
      gravers, gardeners, physicians, naval officers, and techni-
      cal advisers.

1010 *Davison, Roderic H. "'Russian Skill and Turkish Imbecility':
      The Treaty of Kuchuk-Kainardji Reconsidered." Slav R,

35 (Sept. 1976): 463-83.
A refutation of the interpretation of the Treaty of Kuchuk-
Kainardji as a document which, through the cleverness of
Catherine II and the skill of her diplomats, accorded Russia
the right to act as the protector of all Ottoman Christians.
Davison contends that Catherine was far more interested in
the political, territorial, and commercial terms of the treaty
than she was in the rights of the Christians living under
Turkish control. Consequently she was content with the provisions of articles VII and XIV of the treaty which limited
Russia's protectorship to the Christians of Moldavia and
Wallachia. Davison also maintains that during the negotiation of the treaty's various provisions, the Russian statesmen displayed less skill, and the Turkish more, than historians have credited them with.

1011 *DeMadariaga, Isabel. Britain, Russia, and the Armed Neu-
      trality of 1780. New Haven: Yale University Press, 1962,
      496pp., bib. 464-82.
      A scholarly analysis of the origins and development of the
      League of Armed Neutrality within the broader context of
      Anglo-Russian relations of the previous two decades.
      DeMadariaga develops carefully the thesis that launching of
      the league was not "a policy suddenly embarked on by the
      empress in a fit of vanity or pique," as some historians have
      asserted, but rather stemmed from "a slowly maturing inter-
      est in the problems of neutral trade, in the relations of both
      belligerent sides with the neutrals, and above all in the
      vexed question of British relations with the United Provinces,
      the biggest carriers of Russian exports after Britain." More
      generally, Catherine was striving to put an end to Russia's
      subservience to Great Britain, and to establish relations "on
      the basis of a real reciprocity of interests." DeMadariaga
      also asserts that "the idea of forming a league of neutral
      powers ... stemmed from Catherine herself" who also imple-
      mented and understood well its political and economic signifi-
      cance. D295.M23
          Reviewed in:
          Am Hist R, 68 (1962): 414
          Can Hist R, 43 (1962): 359
          Eng Hist R, 79 (1964): 864
          Slav R, 22 (1963): 142

1012 _____. "The Use of British Secret Funds at St. Petersburg,
      1777-82." Slavonic E Eur R, 32 (June 1954): 464-74.
      An account of the efforts of James Harris, the British envoy
      to St. Petersburg during the American Revolution, to gain
      information on the motivation behind Catherine II's American
      policy and to promote the cause of an Anglo-Russian alliance
      through the use of bribery. Drawing upon British diplomatic
      records, DeMadariaga establishes that Harris did not spend

nearly as much money on bribes as contemporary rumor pro-
jected nor was Potemkin the recipient of any such funds.
With few exceptions, Harris confined himself to bribing lower
level court officials and apparently gained very little in return for his expenditures.

1013 *Duffy, Christopher. "Catherine II, 'the Great' 1762-96."
      RMWW, (gen. study), 165-99.
      This account of the emergence of Russia as a major military
      power in the last quarter of the eighteenth century focuses
      on the improvement, growth in size, and deployment of the
      Russian army rather than on Catherine II's role in military
      developments and events, but it is a useful source of infor-
      mation on the place of the military in securing territorial
      gains nominally credited to the empress. Duffy establishes
      that through the efforts of G. Orlov, Z. Chernyshev, P.
      Rumiantsev, G. Potemkin, and A. Suvorov, the Russian army
      was able to win an impressive series of victories and, in
      the process, advance the nation's self-esteem and internation-
      al status to such a degree that Catherine's reign must be
      considered to be the golden age of the Romanov dynasty.

1014 Ehrman, John. "The Younger Pitt and the Oczakov Affair."
      Hist Today, 9 (July 1959): 462-72.
      An examination of the struggle which ensued between William
      Pitt and opposition leader Charles Fox as a consequence of
      the former's 27 October 1791 ultimatum to Catherine II de-
      manding peace between Russia and Turkey and a restoration
      of conquered land. Ehrman's discussion provides consider-
      able insight into the mounting British fear of Russian expan-
      sion under Catherine II.

1015 Fisher, Alan W. The Russian Annexation of the Crimea, 1772-
      1783. Cambridge: Cambridge University Press, 1970, 180pp.,
      bib. 163-76.
      This study does not contain a separate chapter on Catherine
      II but nonetheless warrants consultation for insight into her
      motives, methods, and success in the expansion of Russia's
      borders southward and integration of the Crimea into the
      Russian Empire. D511.C7F5

1016 Goetz, Vera. "Catherine II on the Dnieper." Cath W, 18
      (1874): 420.
      Unavailable for annotation.

1017 Golder, Frank A. "Catherine II and the American Revolution."
      Am Hist R, 21 (Oct. 1915): 92-96.
      A brief discussion of both England's attempt to gain Russian
      aid in crushing the American Revolution and Catherine II's
      offer to act as a mediator in the resolution of the conflict.

1018 *Goldsmith, Margaret Leland. "Catherine the Great (1792-
      1796)." Studies in Aggression. London: Evans Brothers,
      1948, 105-54.
      A critical review of Catherine II's foreign policy. Goldsmith
      asserts that the slick diplomacy pursued by Catherine in the
      three partitions of Poland and the aggressive military policy
      which she followed in regard to the Ottoman Empire demon-
      strate that she was one of the boldest adventuresses in his-
      tory. Although the empress' territorial gains certainly were
      impressive and did much to advance Russia's reputation as
      a European power of the first rank, her policy of expansion,
      along with those of Frederick the Great of Prussia and Maria
      Theresa of Austria, upset the entire European balance of
      power and bequeathed to her successors burdensome nation-
      alistic and political problems. D285.7.G66

1019 *Griffiths, David M. "Catherine II, George III, and the
      British Opposition." GRB (anthology), 306-15.
      A discussion of Catherine II's spring 1971 attempt, amidst
      the Russo-Turkish War, "to conspire with the British opposi-
      tion in a joint effort to frustrate Prime Minister William Pitt's
      project to arm the Royal Navy and wield it to thwart Russia's
      war aims." Griffiths maintains that in addition to "concrete
      political exigencies of the moment" ... Catherine's actions
      were motivated "by almost three decades of unremitting,
      accumulated scorn for King Goerge III and the politicians
      he had hand-picked to govern Great Britain."
      DK67.5.G7G73

1020 *_____. "Nikita Panin, Russian Diplomacy, and the Ameri-
      can Revolution." Slav R, 28 (Mar. 1969): 1-24.
      An examination of Russian policy towards the American Rev-
      olution as one which was marked by two distinct phases, the
      first associated with Nikita Panin, and the second with Panin's
      successors, Grigory Potemkin and A. A. Bezborodko. Grif-
      fiths maintains that from 1776 to 1780, Catherine supported
      Panin's policy of trying to find a peaceful settlement of the
      war and secure independence for the colonies, but by mid-
      1781 she removed Panin from office and altered her policy
      to one which favored a prolongation of the fighting in Ameri-
      ca as means of diverting European attention from her newly
      formed policy of expansionism.

1021 *_____. "The Rise and Fall of the Northern System: Court
      Politics and Foreign Policy in the First Half of Catherine
      II's Reign." Can Slav S, 4, no. 3 (1970): 543-69.
      A discussion of the rise and fall of the set of alliances
      termed the Northern System for insight into the sources of
      Russian foreign policy and the workings of court politics
      during Catherine II's reign. Griffiths establishes that
      Catherine selected Nikita Panin to serve as director of the

College of Foreign Affairs largely because his views on the
merits of the Northern System paralleled her own at that time.
However, with the improvement of Austro-Russian relations
that came with Joseph II's accession to the throne and with
Catherine's return to a policy of territorial expansion, the
Northern System and the men who supported it no longer had
the empress' favor. The efforts of Panin and his political
clique, which included Grand Duke Paul, to save the Northern
System only served to provoke Catherine's wrath and hasten
her replacement of the Paninites in the foreign office with
individuals supportive of her new policy. Griffiths concludes
that this episode reveals the tenuous status of "proto-political
parties in an autocratic state" and the absolute nature of the
monopoly had by the autocrat in the determination of foreign
policy.

1022 _____. "Russian Court Politics and the Questions of an Ex-
      panionist Foreign Policy Under Catherine II, 1762-83."
      Cornell University, 1968. (dissertation)

1023 *Kaplan, Herbert. The First Partition of Poland. New York:
      Columbia University Press, 1962, 215pp., bib. 197-209.
      A comprehensive, scholarly examination of the historical
      circumstances and political maneuvers which surrounded the
      1772 partition of Poland by Austria, Prussia, and Russia.
      In assessing Catherine II's responsibility for the partition,
      Kaplan states that she was content with her pre-partition
      exclusive domination of Commonwealth Poland but in response
      to Austria's unilateral occupation of part of Poland and the
      urgings of Orlov and Chernyshev (who hoped to undermine
      Panin's influence over Catherine's foreign policy) allowed
      herself to be manipulated into the tripartite partition of 1772.
      Kaplan concludes that Catherine's "lack of diplomatic shrewd-
      ness ... allowed Austria and Prussia to share in an influ-
      ence in Poland which had never been accorded to them."
      DK434.K33

1024 Keep, John L. H. "Catherine's Veterans." Slavonic E Eur R,
      59 (July 1981): 385-96.
      A study of the social composition and educational level of the
      non-commisioned officers and privates in the Yaroslavl'
      Regiment of 1795 with some mention of Catherine II's policies
      toward military servitors without rank.

1025 Kramer, Gerhard F. and Roderick E. McGrew. "Potemkin, the
      Porte, and the Road to Tsargrad: The Shumla Negotiations,
      1781-90." Can Am Slav S, 8 (Winter 1974): 467-87.
      A study of the unpublished journal kept by Major Ivan Baroz-
      zi, Potemkin's special envoy to the Turks, which contains an
      account of the talks with Selim III's grand vizir at Shumla
      from November 1789 to December 1790. Barozzi's journal

shows that "the diplomacy of European states was less significant in conditioning Russo-Turkish relations in this
period than has generally been assumed to be the case."
Catherine II emerges from this journal as a ruler more concerned with establishing a secure boundary in southernmost
Russia than in gaining the Turkish straits and Constantinople. The authors conclude that Russian southward expansion threatened the Ottoman Empire's control of the Balkan
Peninsula thus the Turks had legitimate cause for worry.

1026 Laserson, Max. The American Impact on Russian Diplomacy
      and Ideology--1784-1917. New York: Macmillan, 1950,
      441pp.
      This study includes a brief discussion of Catherine II's
      policy toward the American Revolution and the difficulties
      had by Francis Dana who, as an unrecognized envoy of the
      colonies, attempted to gain Russian recognition of America
      and secure a treaty for the protection of commerce. Laser-
      son concludes that Catherine's generally favorable policy
      toward the colonies was motivated not by any concern for
      America but by her dislike of Britain for reasons of her
      own. DK183.3.R9L35

1027 Le Donne, John P. "Outlines of Russian Military Administra-
      tion 1762-1796. Part I: Troop Strength and Deployment."
      Jahr Ges Ost, 31 (1983): 319-47.
      This survey of the composition and deployment of the Russian
      army in the 1762-96 period establishes that the strength of
      the regular army trebled during Catherine II's reign while
      the concept of a strategically mobile fighting force gave way
      to that of territorial defense by way of static frontier posi-
      tions as a consequence of the changing nature of Russia's
      military-political position with respect to Poland and the
      Ottoman Empire.

1028 *Leitsch, Walter. "Russo-Polish Confrontation: The Partition
      of Poland." Taras Hunczak, ed. Russian Imperialism; From
      Ivan the Great to the Revolution. New Brunswick, N.J.:
      Rutgers University Press, 1974, 156-63.
      An analysis of the motives and circumstances associated with
      Catherine II's decision to partition, rather than maintain the
      Russian protectorate over Poland. Leitsch states that from
      the very beginning of Catherine's reign the annexation of
      Poland was under consideration. With the 1768 outbreak of
      Russian hostilities with Poland and Turkey, and with the
      deterioration of Austro-Russian relations, Catherine saw the
      partition plan as a way to settle the Polish question, appease
      Austria, and free Russian troops for the war on the Turkish
      front. The second and third partitions were inevitable since
      Poland was bound to attempt to reverse the initial partition
      and therein prompt a hostile response from Russia.
      DK43.H86

1029   *Lentin, A. "Prince M. M. Shcherbatov as Critic of Catherine
        II's Foreign Policy." Slavonic E Eur R, 49 (1971): 365-81.
        A discussion of the critical opinions recorded by the con-
        servative spokesman M. M. Shcherbatov in regard to Cath-
        erine II's policy of expansion at the expense of Poland and
        the Ottoman Empire. Lentin establishes that Shcherbatov's
        various criticisms of Catherine's policy as a morally inde-
        fensible one which needlessly drained Russia's resources
        "were among the most comprehensive and incisive of their
        time."

1030   *Lobanov-Rostovsky, Andrei A. "Catherine II and Paul I."
        Russia and Europe 1789-1825. Durham: Duke University
        Press, 1947, 3-30.
        A discussion of Catherine II's passivity in the struggle
        against the revolutionary French republic and in the
        second and third partitions of Poland. In regard to the
        latter event, Lobanov-Rostovsky defends Catherine's actions
        on the grounds that the initiative for the policy did not
        come from her, she took only territory previously held by
        Russia, and such partitions were "the stock in trade of the
        diplomacy of the century." DK197.L6

1031   *Lojek, Jerzy. "Catherine II's Armed Intervention in Poland:
        Origins of the Political Decisions at the Russian Court in
        1791 and 1792." Can Slav S, 4 (Fall 1970): 570-93.
        An argument that the matter of Russia's 1792 intervention
        in Poland was far from being decided upon readily, as many
        historians contend, but rather was debated at length by
        Catherine's advisors and favorites as part of the struggle
        for influence within the imperial court. Lojek maintains that
        Catherine's failure to respond quickly and decisively to the
        provocative actions of the Polish patriot party was due to
        the argument advanced by Potemkin against a military inter-
        vention.

1032   *Lord, Robert H. The Second Partition of Poland. A Study in
        Diplomatic History. Cambridge: Harvard University Press,
        1915, 586pp., bib. 557-72.
        A detailed and scholarly analysis of the Austro-Prussian-
        Russian diplomatic maneuverings that led to the second par-
        tition of Poland. In assessing Catherine II's responsibility
        for this event, Lord questions those historians who contend
        that she "disliked partitions (and) ... would have preferred
        to rule over the whole of Poland by influence rather than
        make territorial acquistions at its expense" and argues in-
        stead that she saw the partition as a desirable, permanent
        solution to the Polish problem. She merely gave the impres-
        sion that Prussia was the instigator as a bit of stage-play
        for the sake of her image as an enlightened monarch. Lord
        concludes that Catherine "more than any other, stands

responsible for the violent and ... unfortunate solution
which the Polish Question" received.   DK434.L7

1033   *_____. "The Third Partition of Poland." Slavonic R, 3
(Mar. 1925): 481-98.
A reconstruction of the complexities associated with the
third and final partition of Poland in 1795. Lord asserts
that the final shape of the partition settlement was a reflection of the strengths and weaknesses of the three Eastern
powers. Russia received the lion's share of Polish territory
because of the power of its military forces and the skillful-
ness with which Catherine II conducted diplomacy. More
specifically, when General Suvorov was able to crush the
Polish uprising virtually unaided by Prussia or Austria,
Catherine became determined to capitalize on Russia's favorable military position and the rivalry between Austria and
Prussia to force through a partition exactly in accord with
her own desires. The decline in Prussia's military strength
caused by the war with revolutionary France led the two
German powers to accept reluctantly and with some small
modifications the partition terms literally dictated by Catherine.

1034   *Marcum, James W. "Catherine II and the French Revolution:
A Reappraisal." Can Slav P, 16 (Summer 1974): 187-201.
An attack on those historians who contend that "Catherine
never intended to assist in the counter-revolutionary effort
and that her florid appeals for a restoration of order in
France were merely a smokescreen to hide her true and dark
design to destory the Polish state." Marcum maintains that
Catherine failed to intervene in the French Revolution not
because of any preconceived policy but rather because she
was unable to gain international support for the restoration
of the Bourbon dynasty in France. Her motives in parti-
tioning Poland, far from being a product of the events in
France, were a result of "a battery of events and circumstances involving Prussian and Austrian policy and a French-
inspired nationalist uprising in Poland."

1035   *Mitchell, Donald W. "Catherine the Great: The Turkish Wars
and the War with Sweden." HRSSP (gen. study), 54-102.
A favorable assessment of Catherine II's role in the growth
of the Russian navy and use of it as both a military force
and an effective tool of diplomacy. Mitchell commends Catherine for the support which she gave for the expansion of
the navy's size, the construction of fortifications to protect
naval bases, the establishment of a new outlet to the nation's
south, and the exploration of Russia's northern coastline
and extensive system of Siberian waterways. He also credits
Catherine with the possession of "an almost infallible sense
of timing" in her "use of seapower both in peacetime

diplomacy and in war." The increase in the size and effectiveness of the Russian navy and the consequent impressive
performance of the fleet in its various engagements with its
Turkish and Swedish counterparts lead Mitchell to the conclusion that "the reign of Catherine II was a Golden Age of
Russian seapower."

1036 *Persen, William. "The Russian Occupation of Beirut, 1772-
      1774." Roy Cent As J, 43 (1955): 275-86.
      A discussion of Catherine II's 1768-75 Mediterranean policy
      as a short-sighted one and a foreshadowing of the line pur-
      sued by her successors in regard to the Eastern Question
      which dominated tsarist diplomacy in the next century. Per-
      sen contends that Catherine II erred in overlooking the
      possibility of gaining control of the Straits by eroding Turk-
      ish power through encouraging revolt in the Arab regions
      of the Ottoman Empire rather than by way of a costly
      frontal assault.

1037 Petrovich, Michael B. "Catherine II and a False Peter III in
      Montenegro." ASEER, 14 (April 1955): 169-94.
      A colorful account of the activities of one of the lesser known
      false Peter IIIs. Petrovich discusses how Stephen the Small
      of Montenegro came to be accepted by the Montenegrins as
      Peter III of Russia and how Catherine II was able to unmask
      the pretender before the Montenegrin people through the
      efforts of Prince Yuri Dolgoruky.

1038 *Raeff, Marc. "The Style of Russia's Imperial Policy and
      Prince G. A. Potemkin." G. N. Grob, ed. Statesmen and
      Statecraft of the Modern West: Essays in Honor of Dwight
      E. Lee and H. Donald Jordan. Barre: Barre Publishing
      Company, 1967, 1-51. Also in CGP (anthology), 197-246.
      An analysis of Prince Potemkin's diplomatic, military, and
      economic activities in the south of Russia for insights into
      the character of Catherine's imperial policy. Raeff states
      that in expanding southward, Catherine combined with the
      long standing goal of securing the steppelands the rational
      goal of modernizing the empire by exploiting its resources
      to the fullest and by assimilating border areas into the
      social, economic, and political fabric of the growing auto-
      cratic state. However, in pursuit of this goal, Catherine
      (through Potemkin) followed a Russification policy counter-
      productive to the very entrepreneurial energies the regime
      needed to cultivate if the economy of the newly acquired
      territory were to be modernized effectively. Raeff concludes
      that unlike most societies where the conflict between the old
      and new is resolved, the Russian state "pursued ambivalent
      goals with ambivalent methods and did not evolve a synthe-
      sis which would overcome the ambivalence."

1039 "Russia and George Washington." Sov Life, 4 (April 1982):
      53-55.
      A brief review of early Russian-American relations with most
      attention devoted to Catherine II's refusal to render aid to
      Britain in countering the American Revolution and to her
      efforts to gain through the assistance of George Washington
      a list of words spoken by American Indian tribes to facili-
      tate her compilation of a comparative dictionary of languages.

1040 *Schweizer, Karl W. and Carl S. Leonard. "Britain, Prussia,
      Russia and the Galitzin Letter. A Reassessment." Hist J,
      26 (1983): 531-56.
      An argument that careful study of the Galitzin dispatch of
      26 January 1762 reveals that Peter III pursued consistent
      and sustained objectives in his effforts to bring the Seven
      Years' War to a conclusion and to open the way to new and
      favorable alliances for Russia. Galitzin, who was the Russian
      ambassador to England, reported to Chancellor Vorontsov
      that Britain was anxious to force its ally Frederick the Great
      to conclude peace with Austria and to have Russia assist in
      this endeavor. Schweizer and Leonard contend that Peter
      III demonstrated considerable statesmanship as he exploited
      the dispatch and his peace-maker's role "to gain advantage
      with Frederick ..." and "to gain peace and alliance in
      Europe.... Calculation, not 'flights of imagination,' under-
      lined his foreign policy moves.... By defining a new posture
      for Russia in Europe, creating the peace and furthering a
      northern alliance, Peter III left a legacy that Catherine II
      would preserve and extend."

1041 Sorel, Albert. The Eastern Question in the Eighteenth Cen-
      tury. The Partition of Poland and the Treaty of Kuchuk-
      Kainardji. New York: Howard Fertig, 1969 (reprint of 1898
      edition), 270pp.
      An analysis of the events and maneuverings associated with
      the partial dismemberment of Poland and the Ottoman Empire
      in the 1770s. Sorel stresses that the ambition of Catherine
      II, rather that Frederick II of Prussia or Maria Theresa of
      Austria, was the driving force behind this sordid episode in
      Europe's diplomatic history.

1042 Struve, Gleb. "A Chapter in Russo-Polish Relations." Rus R,
      (Autumn 1946): 56-68.
      A favorable review of the diplomatic career of Count S.
      Vorontsov with some reference to his opposition to the two
      partitions of Poland supported by Catherine II in 1792 and
      1795.

1043 Tarsaidzé, Alexandre. "Empress' Doorstep." CP (gen. study),
      3-22.
      A discussion of Francis Dana's fruitless efforts to gain

Russian diplomatic recognition of America during the latter's
revolt against England. Tarsaidzé states that Catherine's
rejection of Dana's overtures was due to her realization that
as long as "England was the lifeline of Russian commerce"
it would be a mistake to recognize American independence
before it had been permanently established. Tarsaidzé concludes that "only when Russia and the United States were
both friendly or both hostile toward England could their own
friendship thrive." Also included in this chapter is a brief
but interesting account of John Paul Jones' misfortunes in
the empress' naval service.

1044 Almedingen, E. M. So Dark a Stream. A Study of the Emperor Paul I of Russia, 1754-1801. London: Hutchinson,
1959, 249pp.
A negative popular portrayal of Paul I and his reign. Almedingen presents Paul as an unbalanced and cruel tyrant
possessed by a "monstrous disregard for individual value
and privilege, and a blind resolve to turn his own Empire
into an 18th century equivalent of a concentration camp."
She asserts that he pursued ineffective, unsound, and often
irrational domestic and foreign policies, and she sees the
only positive feature associated with his reign as being its
brevity. DK189.A57

1045 Anthony, Evelyn. Royal Intrigue. New York: Thomas Y.
Crowell, 1954, 279pp.
A sympathetic and somewhat fanciful account of the tragic
life of Paul I as both grand duke and emperor. PZ4.S832

1046 *Atkin, Muriel. "The Pragmatic Diplomacy of Paul I: Russia's
Relations with Asia, 1796-1801." Slav R, 38, no. 1 (1979):
60-74.
An argument that Paul I's Asiatic policy, particularly in regard to Iran, India, and the Caucasus region, was "generally
level-headed and pragmatic, much more so than the policies
of his mother, Catherine, or his son, Alexander."

1047 Brockman, Eric. "Background to Betrayal (June, 1798)."
Ann Ord Souv Mil M, 8, no. 3 (1960): 9-24.
Unavailable for annotation.

1048 Bryant, John E. "Paul I of Russia, 1754-1801." Genius and
Epilepsy. Brief Sketches of Men Who Had Both. Concord:
Ye Old Depot Press, 1953, 87-89.
A brief review of the atmosphere of "intrigue, corruption,
and moral degradation" within which Paul I was raised, and
an argument that his epilepsy was precipitated by environ-
mental factors. BF416.A87

1049 Carr, Sir John. "A Gloomy Catastrophe." A Northern Summer:
      Travels Round the Baltic, Through Denmark, Sweden, Russia,
      and Part of Germany in the Year 1804. London: Richard
      Phillips, 1805, 302-20.
      An account of the circumstances and actions which led to the
      overthrow and assassination of Paul I. Carr states that
      while Catherine II's mistreatment of Paul must be seen as
      the ultimate source of his erratic behavior and policies which
      prompted the 1801 coup against him, the immediate source of
      his demise was the scheming of Talleyrand and Sieyes who
      were able to estrange Paul from his family by ensnaring him
      in the clutches of the beautiful French actress M. Chevalier.
      D965.C31

1050 Cross, Anthony. "The Russian Literary Scene in the Reign
      of Paul I." Can Am Slav S, 7, no. 1 (1973): 39-51.
      A discussion of the decline of the quantity and quality of
      Russian literature during Paul I's reign as a consequence
      of the censorship policy which he pursued. Cross does note
      a few exceptions to the generally dismal literary works of
      the era, namely the early writings of N. Karamzin and I.
      Krylov and the publications carried by several short-lived
      but impressive literary journals.

1051 *Czartoryski, Adam. Memoirs of Prince Adam Czartoryski,
      2 Vols. Adam Gielgud, ed. New York: Arno Press, 1971
      (reprint of 1888 edition).
      Recollections of Paul I's behavior and policies, written by a
      Polish aristocrat who served as an aide-de-camp to Grand
      Duke Alexander while Paul was emperor. Czartoryski pre-
      sents a number of anecdotes which illustrate the vagaries
      and eccentricities of Paul's character and actions, and he
      comments on the origin and execution of the coup which
      deposed Paul as well as on Alexander's reaction to this
      event. DK435.5.C83A313 1971

1052 *Day, Edward. "When Russia 'Almost' Became Catholic."
      Liguorian, 49 (Apr. 1961): 45-49.
      An examination of Paul I's efforts to reunite the Russian
      Orthodox and Catholic Churches. Day commends Paul for
      recognizing the significance of such a reunion and for the
      sincerity of his convictions on the reunification question but
      maintains that Paul grossly underestimated the importance
      of the doctrinal differences which separated the two churches,
      a miscalculation that limited his ability to promote a reconcil-
      iation.

1053 Deriabin, P. "The Last Palace Revolution." WT (gen. study),
      68-70.
      A brief account of the policies and actions of Paul I as the
      source of the coup d'etat which terminated his reign. Deria-
      bin sees Paul's overthrow as a watershed in Russian history:

"It was the last time a Russian monarch fell in a palace revolution; from then on all serious threats to the tsar came
from the people who wanted not the throne but an end of
autocracy."

1054 *Duffy, Christopher. "Paul I, 1796-1801." RMWW (gen. study),
      200-32.
      An examination of Paul I's military reforms, and an account
      of the military operations conducted by General Suvorov
      during Paul's reign. Duffy discusses Paul's restructuring
      of military organization and administration as well as his
      penchant for military parades and spot inspections as a re-
      flection of his desire to manage personally Russia's fighting
      forces. The drastic nature of his reforms and his disre-
      gard for the military traditions of Russia led him to be "at
      war with elements in his own army." Nonetheless, Duffy
      credits Paul with showing good judgment in borrowing from
      Prussian military examples to address the principal deficiencies
      in the quality and management of the Russian army.

1055 Dumas, Alexandre. "The Romance of a Czaricide." CCRC
      (gen. study), 197-217.
      A dramatic account of the assassination of Paul I at the
      hands of a band of aristocratic conspirators outraged over
      his despotic and irrational behavior and policies. Dumas
      states that through the schemings of Count Pahlen, Paul
      was convinced that Grand Dukes Alexander and Constantine
      and Empress Marie were part of a plot to depose him. Upon
      securing from Paul orders to arrest the three "royal con-
      spirators," Pahlen was able to convince Alexander that since
      Paul was on the verge of insane actions against the royal
      family an immediate coup was necessary. Dumas goes on to
      describe how the conspirators, under the leadership of
      Counts Bennigsen and Zubov, gained entry to Paul's bed-
      chambers, strangled him to death, and proclaimed Alexander
      the new sovereign of Russia.

1056 _____. "A Romance of the Frigid Neva." Ibid., 176-96.
      A reconstruction of the 1798 secret execution of an aged,
      anonymous prisoner by order of Paul I. Dumas states that
      an acquaintance related to him a meeting with an eccentric
      recluse who told of his being commissioned by Paul to super-
      vise the midnight drowning of an emaciated prisoner whose
      last words were, "so the Empress has remembered me. I
      thought I had escaped her mind."

1057 *Eidel'man, N. "The Flip-side of Providence (A Historical
      Essay)." Sov St Hist, 21, no. 1 (1982): 47-82.
      An investigation of the foundation for an 1861 anonymous
      article which asserted that the real Grand Duke Paul was
      stillborn and another infant was substituted for him because
      Grand Duchess Catherine was so hardpressed by Empress

Elizabeth to produce an heir to the throne. Allegedly, the
changeling Paul had a brother, Afanasy, who so resembled
him that years after Paul's death Alexander I was informed
of the existence of a 'possible uncle' residing in Krasnoiarsk,
Siberia and ordered an inquiry into this rumor. Eidelman's
investigation of this affair reveals that not only did Afanasy
actually exist, but his identity was carefully investigated
in 1822-23 by several representatives of the imperial government. No evidence of any royal lineage was discovered, but
the attention Afanasy received served to sustain the rumor
of his being the brother of the deceased Paul I.

1058   *Feldbaek, Ole. "The Foreign Policy of Tsar Paul I, 1800-
       1801: An Interpretation." Jahr Ges Ost, 30, no. 1 (1982):
       16-36.
       A review of the conflicting interpretations of Paul I's foreign
       policy, and a favorable revaluation of its foundations and
       execution. Feldbaek identifies as Paul's prime goal the
       rational and conservative one of safeguarding Russia's bor-
       ders. The inconsistencies in Paul's diplomacy, Feldbaek as-
       serts, were not due to any lack of conviction or reason on
       the tsar's part but rather to his need to adjust constantly
       his short-term goals and strategies in the face of the insta-
       bility which so characterized the international scene during
       his reign.

1059   *Golovina, Varvara N. "The Reign of Paul I." Memoirs of
       Countess Golovine A Lady in Waiting at the Court of Cath-
       erine II. London: David Nutt, 1910, 122-238.
       An illuminating series of observations and commentaries on
       Paul I, his court, and the intrigue which abounded there
       during his five-year reign. Golovine, who was a confidante
       of Grand Duchess Elizabeth (the wife of Grand Duke Alex-
       ander), comments mostly upon Paul's personality and be-
       havior and, particularly, court reaction to his general re-
       versal of Catherine II's policies. Golovine also discusses
       the genesis of the coup which removed Paul from power and
       the reaction of Elizabeth and Alexander to Paul's death.
       DK188.6.G6A3

1060   *Gooch, G. P. "Mother and Son." Catherine the Great and
       Other Studies. London: Longmans, Green and Company,
       1954, 20-36.
       A discussion of the strained nature of the relationship that
       existed between Catherine II and Grand Duke Paul. Gooch
       states that Catherine's uncertainty about the exact identity
       of Paul's father and her infrequent contact with Paul during
       his years as an infant and child (due to Empress Elizabeth's
       removal of him from Catherine's care) were the initial sources
       of her estrangement from her son. After Catherine seized
       the throne from Peter III, she came to view Paul as a rival

rather than a son and treated him accordingly. The mistreatment Paul received at the hands of Catherine, along with his resentment of her for usurping the throne he believed to be rightfully his, led him to harbor a deep-seated hatred of his mother which, eventually, served to destabilize his personality. Addressing Catherine in regard to Paul's mental condition, Gooch concludes: "You, more than anyone, made him what he was. You bruised his soul beyond the power of the healer's art." DK170.G65

1061 Grant, Mrs. Colquhoun. The Mother of Czars. A Sketch of the Life of Marie Feodorowna, Wife of Paul I and Mother of Alexander I and Nicholas I. New York: E. P. Dutton, 1905, 292pp.
Drawing primarily on the works of Castera, Masson, and Segur, this popular study presents, in part, an account of Paul's relationship with his wife and children and the reaction of his family to the 1801 coup d'etat. DK186.3.G76

1062 Heier, Edmund. "William Robertson and Ludwig Heinrich von Nicolay, His German Translator at the Court of Catherine II." Scot Hist R, 41, no. 132 (Oct. 1962): 135-40.
In part, a discussion of von Nicolay's service as a tutor for Paul I. Heier asserts that von Nicolay, a prominent figure at the court of Catherine the Great, had little positive influence upon Paul's education and character.

1063 Jones, William A. "Paul I and the Jesuits of Russia." University of Washington, Seattle, 1977. (dissertation)

1064 *Keep, John L. H. "Paul I and the Militarizaton of Government." PIAR (anthology), 91-103. Originally in Can Am Slav S, 7, no. 1 (1973): 1-14.
An argument that Paul I's reign must not be viewed as an aberrant one in the history of Romanov rule but rather as a formative period heralding the bureaucratization of the monarchy which occurred in the nineteenth century. In support of this contention, Keep discusses three interrelated processes which were at work during Paul's reign: "the allocation to the military establishment of definite responsibilities in civil administration; a shift in the locus of executive power from the aristocratic elite to professional administrators; ... and a change in the ethos of the public service best expressed by the term 'militarization.'" Keep identifies as Paul's model for rationalizing the operation of the Russian administrative machine the Polizeistaat of Frederick the Great of Prussia.

1065 *Kenny, James J., Jr. "Lord Whitworth and the Conspiracy Against Tsar Paul I: The New Evidence of the Kent Archive." Slav R, 36, no. 2 (1977): 205-19.

A study of the recently discovered papers of Lord Charles
Whitworth, British minister to St. Petersburg under Paul I,
for insight into British complicity in the plot which led to
Paul's overthrow. Kenny maintains that while the papers fail
to show conclusively any British involvement in the plot,
they do reveal that Whitworth had contact with Count Pahlen,
a principal conspirator, and that he disbursed 28,000 rubles
to "secret service" upon his departure from Russia in May
of 1800, money which Kenny speculates may have been used
to fund the conspiracy against Paul.

1066 *_____. "The Politics of Assassination." PIAR (anthology),
       125-46.
       An argument that since recent writings generally tend to
       view Paul I's reign as a foreshadow of nineteenth-century
       tsarist policies, the traditional interpretation of his assassina-
       tion as an action needed to set right a reign that had gone
       awry must be altered. Investigating Paul's murder from the
       perspective of the individuals who were involved in the con-
       spiracy, Kenny concludes that the plot "was essentially an
       aristocratic revolt against the policy of centralization by an
       'enlightened despot.' The issue was not really whether or
       not the tsar was mad; the fact is that Paul's domestic and
       foreign policies were interpreted by the aristocrats as being
       hostile to their interests...."

1067 Lobanov-Rostovsky, Andrei A. "Catherine II and Paul I."
       Russia and Europe, 1789-1825. Durham: Duke University
       Press, 1947, 3-30.
       A scholarly account of Paul I's reversal of Catherine II's
       foreign policy. Lobanov-Rostovsky devotes most of his at-
       tention to Paul's irrate reaction to the French occupation
       of Malta and to the consequent Russian campaign in the
       Ionian Islands. DK197.L6

1068 *Loewenson, Leo. "The Death of Paul I and the Memoris of
       Count Bennigsen." Slavonic E Eur R, 29 (1950): 212-32.
       An examination of the publication history of the memoirs
       of Count Bennigsen, a principal conspirator in the plot
       which led to the overthrow and death of Paul I. Loewenson
       establishes that despite the Russian government's success in
       securing Bennigsen's memoirs soon after his death in 1826,
       his account of Paul's murder was not erased from history
       since several people had either read, knew about, or copied
       parts of the memoirs before they fell into the government's
       hands. More importantly, a fragment of the memoirs was
       actually published in a Swiss periodical in 1819, the year
       after Bennigsen's departure from Russia, and re-issued in
       other languages and in various countries over the next few
       decades, but since the article was anonymous the source of
       the document remained unknown until the twentieth century.

1069 *McGrew, Roderick E. "Paul I and the Knights of Malta."
       PIAR (anthology), 44-75.
       A discussion of Paul I's relationship with the Knights of
       Malta for insight into his "political style and ideological
       commitments." McGrew sees a logical purpose behind Paul's
       seemingly bizarre attachment to the Order of Malta. Paul
       believed that the Order stood for the type of ethics which
       he felt were sorely lacking in the Russian nobility. However,
       McGrew notes, Paul's enthusiastic support for the Order
       "generated no discernible response among the nobility, and
       Paul himself showed no indication that he could use the Order
       effectively."

1070 *_____. "A Political Portrait of Paul I from the Austrian
       and English Diplomatic Archives." Jahr Ges Ost, 18 (1970):
       503-29.
       A critical review of the recent attempt by a number of his-
       torians to place Paul I and his accomplishments in a more
       favorable light. Drawing upon Austrian and English diplo-
       matic correspondence of the 1790s, McGrew argues that while
       some of Paul's ideas on government may have been well-
       conceived and even progressive their effective implementation
       was rendered impossible by Paul's creation of "antagonisms,
       opposition, and contempt" through his personal style of rule.
       In view of the harmful influence exerted upon Russia's do-
       mestic and diplomatic policies by Paul's unbalanced personality,
       McGrew questions the wisdom of any positive reassessment
       of his reign.

1071 *_____. "The Politics of Absolutism: Paul I and the Bank
       of Assistance for the Nobility." PIAR (anthology), 104-24.
       Originally in Can Am Slav S, 7, no. 1 (1973): 15-38.
       An examination of the organization and operation of the Bank
       of Assistance for the Nobility for insight into "the values
       and political attitudes that characterized Russian absolutism
       under Emperor Paul I." McGrew states that the reform was
       not a progressive one intended to accelerate Russia's econom-
       ic development but rather "reflected Paul's determination to
       stabilize and strengthen the foundations of Russian society
       while intensifying and consolidating the power of the tsar."
       Such a policy "marked a significant reorientation of the
       autocracy toward preserving the existing social order in
       place of forcing the pace and direction of social develop-
       ment" and thus foreshadowed Romanov policies of the nine-
       teenth century.

1072 *Macmillan, David S. "Paul's 'Retributive Measures' of 1800
       Against Britain: The Final Turning Point in British Com-
       mercial Attitudes Towards Russia." Can Am Slav S, 7, no.
       1 (1973): 68-77.
       An analysis of the 1800 collapse of the favored and privileged

status enjoyed by British merchants in Russia. Macmillan
places Paul's embargo on British goods and order to confis-
cate British ships in Russian ports within the broad frame-
work of the decline of Anglo-Russian commercial relations in
the 1770-1812 period. Macmillan concedes that Paul's measures were harsh but maintains that they were consistent
with the general growth of economic nationalism in eighteenth-
century Russia and, more particularly, with the widespread
belief that Russia had been exploited by Britain for too long
as a cheap source of raw materials.

1073   Masson, C. Secret Memoirs of the Court of St. Petersburg.
       Particularly Towards the End of the Reign of Catherine II
       and the Commencement of That of Paul I. London: H. S.
       Nichols, 1895 (reprint of 1802 edition), 390pp. Excerpt in
       RUWE (anthology), 254-74.
       A series of observations on the manners, customs, person-
       alities, and intrigues which marked the courts of Catherine
       II and Paul I. Masson, who was commissioned by Catherine
       II to serve as a tutor for Grand Duke Alexander, was dis-
       missed from service by Paul I and thus repeats fondly many
       of the criticisms voiced against the tsar by those injured or
       offended by his actions and policies. Masson is at his best
       when relating the resentment which developed toward Paul
       within the court, but he also presents some interesting
       observations on Paul's upbringing and relationship with
       Catherine II. DK171.M412

1074   Michelsen, Edward H. "The Death of the Emperor Paul."
       The Life of Nicholas I, Emperor of All the Russias. Lon-
       don: William Spooner, 1854, 91-107.
       A discussion of the despotic policies of Paul I as the source
       of the conspiracy which led to his dethronement and assas-
       sination. Michelsen also describes the reactions of Alexander
       I and Marie Feodorovna to Paul's death, and he comments
       upon the ultimate fate of the conspirators. DK210.M6

1075   Mitchell, Donald W. "Naval Policy of Paul I." HRSSP (gen.
       study), 105-13.
       A review of the Mediterranean operations of the Russian fleet
       under Paul I, and an argument that, despite the Malta epi-
       sode, Paul's naval policy "was in no sense unbalanced."
       Mitchell supports this contention by citing Paul's encourage-
       ment of improvements in Russian shipbuilding and the train-
       ing of naval technicians as well as his efforts to advance
       the size and quality of the Black Sea fleet.

1076   *Papmehl, K. A. "Freedom of Expression Under Paul I."
       FEER (gen. study), 135-46.
       A discussion of the intensification of censorship during the
       reign of Paul I. Papmehl maintains that the main goal of

Paul's censorship policy was "to stop the influx of undesir-
able ideologies from abroad" by increasing the number of
censors and the severity of punishments and by personally
supervising the entire censorship operation, including reading the censors' reports." Papmehl notes that while Paul's
censorship policy is often portrayed as being at odds with
that of Catherine II, in fact he merely intensified the restrictions established by her after the outbreak of the French
Revolution.

1077 _____, ed. "Letters by L. K. Pitt, British Chaplain in St.
Petersburg, on the Person and Policies of the Emperor
Paul." Can Am Slav S, 7, no. 1 (1973): 85–105.
A brief introduction to four letters which describe the char-
acter, personality, policies, and dethronement of Paul I.
The letters were sent by L. K. Pitt to William Coxe to assist
the latter in his study of Russian affairs of the late eighteenth
century.

1078 Parkinson, Roger. "'Mad' Paul." The Fox of the North. The
Life of Kutuzov, General of War and Peace. New York:
David McKay, 1976, 32–43.
An account of the growth of opposition to the rule of Paul I
as a consequence of his irrational and cruel behavior. Parkinson portrays Paul as a "haughty, delusioned megalomaniac"
whose disdain for Russia's military traditions and war heroes
(particularly Suvorov) and whose rapprochement with Napoleon "seemed a slur on Russian honour" and therefore prompted
a number of senior officers to conspire to rid the nation of
the "tsar-traitor." Parkinson notes that General Kutuzov
sympathized with the sentiments of those officers critical of
Paul but refrained from supporting any of the plots to depose
the emperor and remained, as Governor-General of St. Petersburg, a trusted servitor up to the very day of the fatal
coup d'etat. DK169.K8P34 1976

1079 Piechowiak, A. B. "The Anglo-Russian Expedition to Holland
in 1799." Slavonic E Eur R, 41 (1962–63): 182–95.
In part, a discussion of Paul I's commitment of 17,000 Russian
troops to support Britain in its struggle against France in
Holland. Of particular interest is Piechowiak's examination
of Paul's decision to withdraw from the anti-French coalition
because of the Anglo-Russian discord which developed over
the campaign's disastrous outcome.

1080 *Ragsdale, Hugh A. "A Continental System in 1801: Paul I
and Bonaparte." J Mod Hist, 42, no. 1 (1970): 70–89.
An analysis of the circumstances which led Paul I to a reconciliation with Napoleon and the establishment of an economic
blockade against Britain similar in size and substance to that
established by France in 1806. Ragsdale contends that when

England sided with Austria in the latter's dispute with
Russia, Paul became obsessed with "a vindictiveness sustained
by self-righteousness" to the extent that an incident as petty
as the Maltese affair became sufficient reason to open hostilities against Britain. Although the consequent Russian commercial blockade of British goods was short-lived because of
Paul's death, Ragsdale asserts that it nonetheless served to
advance Napoleon's bargaining position at the Amiens peace
conference.

1081 * _____. Detente in the Napoleonic Era. Bonaparte and the
Russians. Lawrence: Regents Press of Kansas, 1980, 183pp.,
bib. 161-76.
A detailed account of the policies pursued by Britain, France,
and Austria toward Russia for the 1799-1801 period, and an
argument that these policies were based upon a misunderstanding of the foreign policy aims and interests of Paul I.
Ragsdale maintains that Napoleon's rapprochement with Paul
was founded upon the false assumption that Russia's international goals were those specified in the forged testament
of Peter the Great. While the existence of this document
was unknown in Britain and Austria, the statesmen of these
nations tended to interpret Paul's actions "in terms of well-
developed eighteenth century cliches about Russian foreign
policy," thus they too failed to realize that Paul did not
subscribe to the policy of aggression and conquest developed
by Catherine II and linked by Napoleon to Peter the Great's
will. Ragsdale adds that the widespread misunderstanding of
Paul's foreign policy has been perpetuated to a significant
degree because of the refusal of Soviet authorities to make
available the primary sources needed to conduct a thorough
historical study of eighteenth-century tsarist foreign policy.
DC59.8.R8R34

1082 * _____. "Documents on the Foreign Policy of Paul I from
the Former Prussian Archives." Can Am Slav S, 7, no. 1
(1973): 106-11.
A brief introduction to a series of French language documents
from the correspondence of the Prussian ambassador to St.
Petersburg (Count von Lusi) and the Prussian chancellor
(Count von Haugwitz). The documents illustrate Paul's dis-
illusionment with Napoleon and growing belief that "a Russo-
Prussian alliance was the best guarantee against excessive
French pretensions."

1083 * _____. "The Origins of Bonaparte's Russian Policy."
Slav R, 27, no. 1 (1968): 85-90.
An investigation of the means employed by Napoleon in se-
curing Russian support for his foreign policy goals. Rags-
dale establishes that the unsolicited concessions made by
Napoleon to Paul in regard to the status of Malta and the

return of nearly 6,000 Russian prisoners of war softened
Paul's enmity toward France. The rapprochement itself,
however, was spurred by Paul's receptiveness to a plan to
partition the Ottoman Empire, to the mutual advantage of
France and Russia, suggested by Count Rostopchin who had
come under the influence of French agents within the Russian
court.

1084 *_____. "The Mental Condition of Paul I." PIAR (anthology),
      17-30.
      An assessment of Paul's mental condition, based upon his writ-
      ings during the 1772-1788 period as well as upon modern
      scholarship on personality disorders. Ragsdale maintains that
      Paul had an "obsessive-compulsive personality" which ac-
      counts for his "quest for order and perfection" in his own
      life and the world around him and for his well known pen-
      chant for moral absolutes.

1085 *_____. "Russia, Prussia, and Europe in the Policy of Paul
      I." Jahr Ges Ost, 31 (1983): 81-118.
      A chronological review of the twists and turns in Paul's
      foreign policy, and an argument that his diplomacy was
      founded upon a unity of purpose neglected by most his-
      torians who study his reign. Ragsdale contends that Paul
      consistently sought a means of restoring and preserving the
      political order of Europe. When he was unable to gain
      Prussian support for this goal and found Austria and Eng-
      land to be unworthy allies in his quest to promote stability
      in Europe, Paul logically turned to Napoleonic France.
      Ragsdale adds that although such a turn led Paul to abandon
      his goal of restoring the Bourbons as the legitimate rulers
      of France, the shift was fully consistent with his desire to
      bring peace and security to Europe.

1086 _____. "Russian Diplomacy in the Age of Napoleon. The
      Franco-Russian Rapprochement of 1800-01." University of
      Virginia, 1965. (dissertation)

1087 *_____. "Russian Influence at Luneville." Fr Hist S, 5,
      no. 3 (1968): 274-84.
      An argument that, separate from the question of whether or
      not Paul I was "a mere cat's paw of Bonaparte," Napoleon
      took his 1800-1801 rapprochement with Russia seriously and
      "derived real advantages from it," particularly during the
      negotiations associated with the Treaty of Luneville during
      which he increased his demands in proportion to the cred-
      ibility of the threat of Russian intervention. Ragsdale points
      out that during the negotiations Paul, at last, was able to
      play the role of the "arbiter of Europe," a role which Austria
      and Prussia had to take seriously given Paul's positioning
      of Russian troops near the Austrian border.

1088 *_____. "Was Paul Bonaparte's Fool? The Evidence of
       Neglected Archives." PIAR (anthology), 76-90. Originally
       in Can Am Slav S, 7, no. 1 (1973): 52-67.
       An examination of Swedish, Prussian, and Danish diplomatic
       records for fresh insights into Paul's relationship with Na-
       poleon. Ragsdale concludes that, contrary to the opinion of
       many Western analysts and observers contemporary with Paul,
       the emperor was not duped by Napoleon into pursuing a
       policy beneficial to France but rather simply followed sound,
       balance of power diplomacy in his relations with France,
       Britain, and Austria.

1089 *Ransel, David. "An Ambivalent Legacy: The Education of
       Grand Duke Paul." PIAR (anthology), 1-16.
       A review of the contradictory sets of ideals and models to
       which Paul was exposed during his years as grand duke.
       Ransel establishes that Paul, through his mentors, came under
       the influence of the principles associated with enlightened
       constitutional monarchy as well as those upon which was
       founded the absolute despotism of Peter the Great. Paul
       took seriously the possibility of ruling as a constitutional
       monarch and "moved very far in that direction, even com-
       mitting to paper a plan for representative government and
       checks on autocratic authority," but once in power moved
       wholly in the direction of Petrine despotism.

1090 Rappoport, Angelo S. "Paul." The Curse of the Romanovs.
       A Study of the Lives and Reigns of Two Tsars: Paul I and
       Alexander I of Russia, 1754-1825. London: Chatto and
       Windus, 1907, 1-250.
       A discussion of the reigns of Paul I and Alexander I as
       representations of "the curse of the Romanovs," the curse
       being that Romanov rulers "either remain faithful to the
       spirit of autocracy, and assassination stares them in the
       face, as in the case of Paul, or they inaugurate an era of
       liberalism, but finding that they thus undermine their own
       existence, they turn reactionaries and lose their mental
       balance, as in the case of Alexander." Within the confines
       of this generalization, Rappoport presents Paul as a tyran-
       nical, mentally unbalanced megalomaniac, and Alexander as a
       weak-willed, well-intentioned ruler whose shallow liberalism
       was destined to end tragically. DK186.R3 1907

1091 *Sablukov, Nikolai A. "Reminiscences of the Court and Times
       of the Emperor Paul I of Russia up to the Period of His
       Death." Fraser's M, 72 (Aug. 1865): 222-41; (Sept. 1865):
       302-27.
       Excerpts from the memoirs of a Russian officer who was well-
       acquainted with Paul I, the royal family, and the leading
       men of government in turn of the century Russia. Among the
       many subjects addressed by General Sablukov are Paul's
       personality and upbringing, predilection for things military,

relationship with Catherine II, and his initial appointments
and actions as tsar. Sablukov also presents a series of
disconnected anecdotes which collectively illuminate the qualities of Paul's rule which spawned staunch opposition within
the Russian aristocracy. Of special interest is his account
of the events which transpired on the eve of Paul's murder,
events which Sablukov witnessed as duty officer in the regiment assigned to protect Paul.

1092 *Saul, Norman E. "The Objectives of Paul's Italian Policy."
PIAR (anthology), 31-43.
The stated purpose of this scholarly essay is "to evaluate
the background of the Russian presence in Italy, the course
of its development, the objectives of Russian policy in the
area, and the results." Saul portrays Paul's concern for
developments in Italy as a logical extension of the growth
of Russian involvement in Italian affairs which followed the
partition of Poland and the consequent increase in Russian
contact with the Catholic Church. More immediately, Paul
hoped to counter French and Austrian incursions in Italy as
a means of maintaining the general balance of power in
Europe. Saul concludes that even though Paul's Italian policy
was unsuccessful, his general objectives "set a precedent
that would be followed by his successors and would influence the leaders of Russia's allies in the coalition wars that
followed."

1093 *_____. Russia and the Mediterranean, 1797-1801. Chicago:
University of Chicago Press, 1970, 23-154, bib. 229-56.
A scholarly examination of Paul I's policies toward the Ottoman Empire, Malta, and the Ionian Republic. Saul addresses
three basic questions: "why did Russia suddenly enter the
Mediterranean in 1798? What were the effects of the Russian
presence there? Why was the Russian withdrawal so complete in 1807?" He sees the initial motive behind Paul's Mediterranean policy as being "the desire to protect the Ottoman
Empire from the direct threat posed by the Eastern ambitions of General Bonaparte." To this motive was added
Paul's desire to protect the Order of Malta to which he felt
a sacred commitment. For a discussion of the reversal of
Paul's policy at the hands of Alexander I, see entry 1262.
DK186.S28

1094 *Schmidt, Christian D. "The Further Study of Paul." PIAR
(anthology), 147-70.
A review of historical scholarship, published documents,
archival materials, and memoir literature dealing with Paul I
and his reign.

1095 Strakhovsky, Leonid I. "The Mad Emperor." Alexander I
of Russia. The Man Who Defeated Napoleon. New York:

W. W. Norton, 1947, 13-24.
A portrayal of Paul I as an unbalanced, paranoid, and ex-
plosive individual who deserved the fate he suffered.
DK191.S75

1096 *Strong, John W. "Russian Plans for an Invasion of India in
1801." Can Slav P, 7 (1965): 114-26.
An argument that Paul I's launching of the Orlov-Denisov
expedition has been wrongly interpreted as being part of a
Franco-Russian campaign against India. Strong maintains
that the campaign was "merely an emotional outlet for Paul's
growing hatred of the English" and was fall too ill-planned
to have been accepted by Napoleon. Strong also asserts
that while the plan was "vaguely prepared and ill-conceived,"
it does not constitute proof of Paul's unbalanced mental condition.

1097 Tucker, Clara J. "The Foreign Policy of Tsar Paul I." Syracuse University, 1966. (dissertation)

1098 *Waliszewski, K. Paul the First of Russia, the Son of Catherine the Great. London: William Heinemann, 1913, 496pp.
A critical evaluation of the character and leadership of Paul
I. Waliszewski maintains that Paul's environment and upbringing severely limited his ability to govern Russia effectively:
"the romantic and humanitarian ideas of the Latin West were
mingled in his mind with Oriental brutalities, the formalism
of Prussia with the fantasy of the East; civilization and bar-
barism jostled in him." Further complicating Paul's reign
was his desire to reverse the policies pursued by Catherine
II, a desire which drove him to rush about recklessly trying
to create a new system of government. Waliszewski concludes
that separate from Paul's reform intentions, his methods and
actual policies certainly do not warrant any favorable reassessment of his reign. DK186.W82

1099 Warner, Richard H. "The Political Opposition to Tsar Paul I."
New York University, 1977. (dissertation)

1100 Whishaw, F. "Paul I." Temp Bar, 106 (1895): 107.
Unavailable for annotation.

GENERAL STUDIES AND ASSESSMENTS/
PERSONAL AFFAIRS AND CHARACTER

1101 "Alexander I." Liv Age, 46 (1855): 546-49.
A translation of an anonymous account of the death of Alexander I apparently written by one of Alexander's attendants and published in Germany for the purpose of quelling the rumor that he had been poisoned.

1102 "Alexander I and His Court." Dial, 28 (1 June 1900): 428-30.
A review of Choiseul-Gouffier's Historical Memoirs of Alexander and the Court of Russia.

1103 Almedingen, E. M. The Emperor Alexander I. New York: Vanguard Press, 1964, 275pp., bib. 238.
A vivid and sympathetic biography of Alexander I written for the general public. Almedingen sees Alexander as a complex personality deeply affected by guilt over the murder of his father, Paul I, and torn between his desire to implement reforms consistent with the liberal political philosophy which he acquired from his tutor, F. La Harpe, and the pressures placed upon him by Russian conservatives and the Napoleonic Wars. Concentrating primarily upon foreign policy and military affairs, Almedingen maintains that, despite Alexander's lackluster domestic program and less than commendable personal conduct, his lofty sentiments and leading role in the liberation of Europe from French domination make him a positive figure in Russia's history. DK191.A65

1104 Bariatinsky, V. "Mysterious Hermit." Fortn R, 99 (May 1913): 988-1001.
A brief argument in favor of the theory that Alexander I staged his own death and lived out the remainder of his life as Feodor Kuzmich, a Siberian hermit.

1105 Choiseul-Gouffier, Madame la Contesse de. Historical Memoirs of the Emperor Alexander I and the Court of Russia. Mary

B. Patterson, trans. Chicago: A. C. McClurg, 1901, 321pp.
An interesting series of remembrances of Alexander I's per-
sonal and public life, written by an intimate of the tsar.
The memoirs shed light upon the coup d'etat against Paul I,
Alexander's character and family life, his early domestic
policies, and, most notably, his struggle against Napoleon.
Throughout, Choiseul-Gouffier portrays Alexander as a kind-
ly, gracious, and dedicated sovereign. DK191.C54

1106   Clapp, Jane. "The Sphinx of the North: Czar Alexander I."
       Vanishing Point. New York: Scarecrow Press, 1961, 43-51.
       A popular review of the theory that Alexander I staged his
       own death so as to escape the burdens imposed upon him by
       his lofty station. G525.C57

1107   *Cross, Anthony G., ed. "The Reign of Alexander I."
       RUWE (anthology), 275-380.
       Excerpts from the writings of Western travelers to Russia
       which provide insight into socio-economic conditions under
       Alexander I as well as into Alexander's character and the
       circumstances surrounding his death. The selections are
       from the works of J. Carr, R. Porter, J. Q. Adams, J.
       Klaproth, G. de Stael-Holstein, P. de Segur, R. Pinkerton,
       J. Johnson, R. Lyall, and R. Lee.

1108   "Czar Who Wouldn't Die." Time, 86 (26 Nov. 1965): 39.
       A general review of the Alexander I/Feodor Kuzmich legend,
       prompted by a report in Izvestia which indicated that Soviet
       authorities intended to open the coffins of both Alexander
       and Kuzmich in an attempt to determine if there is any fac-
       tual basis for the legend.

1109   Deriabin, P. "The Magnificent Myth." WT (gen. study), 70-
       76.
       A brief negative assessment of Alexander I's character and
       accomplishments. Deriabin maintains that "the reign of
       Alexander I has been somewhat overplayed by historians and
       writers" who, under the influence of Alexander's dashing
       image and Russia's victory over France, fail to see that he
       was in no way personally responsible for the defeat of Na-
       poleon but certainly must be held accountable for pursuing
       contradictory, unsuccessful, and often harmful domestic
       policies.

1110   Empaytaz, H. L. A Brief Memoir of Alexander, Emperor of
       Russia. London: 1849.
       Unavailable for annotation.

1111   _____. Sketch of the Religious Character of Alexander,
       Emperor of Russia. New York: American Tract Society,
       1862, 44pp.

An account of the spiritual awakening of Alexander I by way of his conversations with Madame de Krudener in the summer of 1813. Empaytaz, a Swiss clergyman who was present at many of the meetings which took place between Alexander and Krudener, states that the question of personal salvation tormented Alexander, but, through the efforts of Krudener, Alexander was able to find peace of mind as she convinced him that the sins of his life could be expiated through prayer and faith in the word of God. Afterwards, Empaytaz asserts, Alexander became a more compassionate, magnanimous, and Christian ruler, as evidenced by his leading role in the formation of the Holy Alliance.

1112 _____. Some Particulars Relating to the Late Emperor Alexander, Previous to His Arrival, and During His Stay at Paris, in 1815. M. A. Schimmelpennick, trans. London: Bristol, 1830.
Unavailable for annotation.

1113 "Empty Coffin and Runaway Czar." Lit D, 116 (25 Nov. 1933): 35.
A brief note on the veracity of the theory that Alexander I abandoned the throne of Russia in 1825 to assume the identity of Feodor Kuzmich, a hermit-monk residing in Siberia. This article was prompted by the Soviet discovery that Alexander's coffin did not contain his remains.

1114 Gibbon, Edward. Memoirs of the Public Character and Life of Alexander the First, Emperor of All the Russias. Trenton: D. E. Fenton, 1819, 196pp. Appendix by Paul Allen.
Unavailable for annotation.

1115 Golovin, I. History of Alexander the First, Emperor of Russia. London: Guilford, 1858.
Unavailable for annotation.

1116 *Golovina, Varvara N. Countess. "The Reign of Alexander I." Memoirs of Countess Golovine. A Lady in Waiting at the Court of Catherine II. G. M. Fox-Davies, trans. London: David Nutt, 1910, 239-376.
An illuminating and picturesque series of observations and commentaries on Alexander I, his wife, and court life in the years between 1796 and 1817. Golovine, who was a confidante of Alexander's wife Elizabeth during much of the period discussed, provides most detail on Alexander's assumption of the throne, private life, and his character, and court reaction to his domestic and foreign policies.
DK188.6.G6A3

1117 Gribble, Francis. Emperor and Mystic. The Life of Alexander I of Russia. New York: E. P. Dutton, 1931, 291pp.

A popular biography of Alexander I with most attention devoted to his conduct of foreign affairs. In addition to a detailed narrative on Alexander's clash with Napoleon, Gribble
provides considerable information on the tsar's personal relationships (especially with Madame de Krudener) and on the
theory that he did not die in 1825 but rather lived on for
decades as the Siberian hermit Feodor Kuzmich. DK191.G85

1118 Hodgetts, E. A. Brayley. "Alexander I." The Court of
      Russia in the Nineteenth Century, Vol. I. New York:
      Charles Scribner's Sons, 1908, 1-140.
      The stated purpose of this study is to present an unbiased,
      readable account of the character and life of Alexander I.
      To this end, Hodgetts reviews, often anecdotally, the high-
      lights of Alexander's reign, particularly his family life, ro-
      mantic affairs, attraction to political idealism and religious
      mysticism, his latter life depression, and his mysterious
      death. DK189.H75

1119 *Jackman, S. W., ed. Romanov Relations. The Private
      Correspondence of Tsar Alexander I, Nicholas I and the
      Grand Dukes Constantine and Michael with Their Sister
      Queen Anna Pavlovna. London: Macmillan and Company,
      1969, 375pp.
      This volume contains a sizable body of letters exchanged
      among the members of Alexander I's immediate family and
      thus constitutes a valuable source of inside information not
      only on family relations but also on his political behavior
      and the major events which took place during his reign.
      Of particular interest are the various letters of Alexander's
      sister Anna which illustrate the very loving nature of her
      relationship with him and the moral support which she
      rendered at difficult points in his life. DK188.J313
          Reviewed in:
          Can Hist R, 52 (1971): 226.

1120 Jarintzoff, N. "The Legend of Alexander I and the Hermit,
      Theodor Kouzmitch." Contemp R, 101 (June 1912): 856-
      65.
      An account of the motives which allegedly prompted Alex-
      ander I to stage his own death as a means of escape from
      the duties of state in favor of life as a Siberian hermit under
      the name of Feodor Kuzmich. Jarintzoff also describes the
      intricate plot supposedly conceived by Alexander to cloak
      his escape and new identity.

1121 Joyneville, Catherine Johnstone. Life and Times of Alexander
      I. Emperor of All the Russias. 3 Vols. London, Tinsley
      Brothers, 1875.
      A detailed account of Alexander I's life and reign with most
      attention given to his diplomatic and military affairs.

Joneville presents an uncritical, chronologically arranged
narrative on Alexander's upbringing, accession to the throne,
early reforms, and family relations before turning to detailed
accounts of the Russian military campaigns at Austerlitz,
Eylau, and Friedland, the era of Tilsit, the campaigns at
Moscow, Dresden, Leipzig and Paris, and Alexander's leading role at the Congress of Vienna. Joyneville concludes
with a brief survey of Alexander's solitary life as a religious
mystic toward the close of his reign. DK191.J65

1122 *Kulomzin, Anatole. "The Siberian Hermit Theodore Kuzmich."
      Slavonic R, 2, no. 5 (1923): 381-87.
      An interesting and favorable review of the theory that the
      hermit Feodor Kuzmich and Alexander I were the same per-
      son. Kulomzin discusses as evidence Alexander's self-
      expressed desire to retire, irregularities associated with his
      "death" in 1825, similarities between Kuzmich and the tsar,
      and the procession of dignitaries and members of the royal
      family who visited Kuzmich's grave during the course of the
      nineteenth century.

1123 Lee, Robert. "The Last Days of Emperor Alexander." The
      Last Days of Alexander and the First Days of Nicholas.
      London: Richard Bentley, 1854, 1-77.
      A recollection of meetings with Alexander I in the Crimea
      during the autumn of 1825. In addition to recounting con-
      versations with Alexander on matters of no consequence, Lee
      comments on the ailment which led to Alexander's death at
      Taganrog and on the treatment the tsar received from attend-
      ing physicians. Lee concludes with an eyewitness account
      of Alexander's funeral and a critical commentary on his
      passing: "no one regrets the Emperor Alexander as a pub-
      lic loss, and I feel certain that out of Russia few tears will
      be shed on this occasion, except by those wretched despots
      whom he assisted by upholding them in their unlimited and
      unlawful power." DK191.L4

1124 The Life of Alexander I, Emperor of Russia. London: W.
      Mason, 1814, 24pp.
      A short pamphlet which outlines in glowing terms Alexander
      I's reign up to 1814 and relates an incident in which he
      risked his life to rescue a drowning Polish peasant.
      DK191.L5

1125 Lloyd, H. E. Alexander I. Emperor of Russia. A Sketch of
      His Life. London: Treuttel and Wurtz, 1826, 315pp.
      A highly favorable account of the life and reign of Alexander
      I. Lloyd presents a detailed, anecdote-oriented, character
      sketch of Alexander as a most humane, affable, principled,
      and intelligent monarch, and then reviews, in a favorable
      fashion, Alexander's domestic policies and conduct of

international relations, especially his promotion of peace
among the nations of Europe in the years following the
Napoleonic Wars. DK191.L7

1126 "Lloyd's Memoirs of Alexander I." Eclectic R, n.s. 25 (Jan.-
June 1826): 385-92.
A favorable review article on H. E. Lloyd's Alexander I.
Emperor of Russia. A Sketch of His Life (London, 1826).
The reviewer concentrates on Alexander's failure to live up
to the liberal promises made at the start of his reign, and
he does not question Alexander's sincere intentions nor dedication but rather sees the domestic shortcomings of his reign
as being due to the lack of an adequate machinery of government from which to draw support for effecting reforms.

1127 Lockhart, John G. "Alexander I." The Peacemakers 1814-
1815. London: Duckworth, 1932, 130-74.
A general review of the reign of Alexander I and the careers
of the other world leaders present at the Congress of Vienna.
Lockhart states that by studying the beliefs, actions, and
policies of Alexander and his Vienna colleagues, insight can
be gained into the qualities essential to effective statesman-
ship and equitable government. Lockhart maintains that
Alexander possessed few of these qualities hence his dismal
record of domestic reform and negative influence on international diplomacy. He concludes that Alexander's liberalism
in both its domestic and continental forms was largely still-
born as evidenced respectively by his bequeathal of a legacy
of "derelict projects begun with enthusiasm, abandoned at
the first opposition, and soon forgotten," and by his leav-
ing Europe in the grasp of Metternich and the Holy Alliance.
DS249.L6

1128 *McConnell, Allen. Tsar Alexander I. Paternalistic Reformer.
New York: Thomas Crowell, 1970, 232pp., bib. 212-24.
A scholarly study of Alexander I's life and reign with most
attention given to the ideals and motives which fueled his
various policies. McConnell advances the thesis that Alexander was neither a timid and vacillating liberal nor a calculating, power-hungry autocrat but rather was a paternalist
from start to end who, though interested in promoting the
welfare of the Russian people, at no time considered any reform which would diminish his powers as an absolute monarch. The author sees the conspiracy which led to the
assassination of Paul I as being of paramount importance
in influencing Alexander in his decision to guard jealously
his royal prerogatives. DK191.M32
     Reviewed in:
     Slav R, 30 (1971): 392-93

1129 Masters, Peter. "The Tsar Who Crushed Napoleon." Men of

Destiny. London: Evangelical Times, 1968, 9-17.
An account of Alexander I's desertion of his "immoral ways
and vain pursuits" for a Christian based philosophy of life,
and an argument that the defeat of Napoleon at the hands
of Russia's forces was due to Alexander's turn to God for
guidance and support. BV4930.M34

1130 Michelsen, Edward H. "Emperor Alexander's Last Journey to
Taganrog." The Life of Nicholas I. Emperor of All the
Russias. London: William Spooner, 1854, 107-13.
A description of the illness and death of Alexander I, based
on the memoirs of Frederic Fayot, Professor of French at
St. Petersburg University, and the journal of Sir James
Wylie, Alexander's personal physician from 1814 to 1825.
DK210.M6

1131 *Nicholas, Grand Duke of Russia, ed./intro. Scenes of Russian
Court Life. Being the Correspondence of Alexander I and
His Sister Catherine. Henry Havelock, trans. London:
Jarrolds Publishers, n.d., 7-25.
A favorable commentary on the character, policies, and life
of Alexander I, based upon the 1807-18 correspondence between Alexander and his favorite sister, Catherine. According to Grand Duke Nicholas, the letters reveal that Alexander
was neither confused about the direction tsarist policy
should take nor irresolute in his pursuit of policies in which
he had full confidence: "all that was enigmatical to his contemporaries, all that men held to be irresolution of character, vanishes in the new light of today." Nicholas concedes, however, that after the Congress of Vienna, Alexander, exhausted by the demands placed on his time by international affairs, devoted less attention to domestic reform,
and, under the harmful influence of Madame de Krudener,
turned to mysticism. DK191.A3

1132 Paléologue, Maurice. The Enigmatic Czar. The Life of Alexander I of Russia. Edwin and Willa Muir, trans. New York:
Harper and Brothers, 1938, 326pp.
A detailed account of Alexander I's life with most attention
given to foreign policy and personal relationships. Paléologue characterizes Alexander as a man with a great many
positive attributes but whose lack of commitment and con-
sistency prevented him from being a great ruler. According to Paléologue, Alexander's "worst fault, which explains
all his reign, was his mental instability. Imaginative and
neurotic, he acted on nothing but impulse." This resulted
in a host of incongruities which disappointed Russian reform-
ers and confused Alexander's contemporaries who sought a
unified purpose behind his policies and behavior. Paléologue
concludes with an interesting review of the Feodor Kuzmich
controversy. DK191.P32

1133 Palmer, Alan. Alexander I. Tsar of War and Peace. New
      York: Harper and Row, 1974, 487pp., bib. 462-70.
      A broad, popular biography of Alexander I. Palmer devotes
      most of his attention to Alexander's conduct of foreign affairs
      and conflict with Napoleon but also addresses each of the
      principal facets of the tsar's reign. While Palmer does not
      offer any final judgments on Alexander's accomplishments or
      place in Russia's history, Alexander emerges from this study
      as a leader who, despite his questionable personal life and
      pursuit of ambivalent domestic policies, deserves sympathy
      for his attempt to cope with the nation's internal problems
      while advancing the cause of European peace. Of particular
      interest is Palmer's discussion of the confusion of liberal
      and autocratic strands in Alexander's thought and policies
      as a consequence of the contradictory influences exerted by
      his grandmother, Catherine II, and father, Paul I.
      DK191.P348

1134 Parkinson, Roger. "Alexander and Exile (1801-August 1805)."
      Fox of the North. New York: D. McCay Company, 1976,
      44-52.
      A discussion of the August 1802 exile of General Kutuzov as
      a result of Alexander I's distrust of him as a former confi-
      dant of Tsar Paul and a potential source of information on
      Alexander's complicity in Paul's assassination. Parkinson
      also discusses the emperor's August 1805 recall of Kutuzov
      because, "despite his personal feelings toward Kutuzov,
      Alexander realized that no other choice existed for the com-
      mander of the Russian forces." The remainder of this study
      contains a number of references to Alexander's relationship
      with Kutuzov and an argument that Kutuzov has yet to re-
      ceive sufficient credit for his part in bringing about the de-
      feat of Napoleon. DK179.K8P37

1135 Pazos, Don Vincente. The Beauties of Modern History, Com-
      mencing with the Life and Achievements of Alexander the
      First, Emperor of All the Russias; with the Campaigns of
      Bonaparte; Also a Correct History of South America. To
      Which Is Added, the Admirable Works of Nature, and the
      Rights of Women Investigated. Philadelphia: Printed for
      the Publisher, n.d., 206pp.
      Unavailable for annotation.

1136 Phillips, W. A. "Alexander I of Russia." Edinb R, 243
      (Jan. 1926): 50-65.
      A lengthy and favorable review article on K. Waliszewski's
      Le Regne D'Alexandre I.

1137 Poole, Stanley B-R. "Alexander I of Russia and Feodor Kuz-
      mich." Royal Mysteries and Pretenders. London: Blanford
      Press, 1969, 95-108.

An examination of the roots of the rumor that Alexander I
did not die in Taganrog in 1825 but rather fled to Siberia
to live out his life in religious contemplation free from the
demands of his political station. Poole identifies the rumor's
broad basis as being Alexander's despondency over the recent deaths of two close family members, frustration over
his failure to achieve the goals of his domestic and foreign
policies, and his desire to devote more time to religious concerns. More immediately, the lack of witnesses to Alexander's death, the less than credible reputation of Dr. Wylie
who performed the autopsy (Wylie had signed Paul I's death
certificate attributing the death to 'natural causes'), and the
premature sealing of Alexander's coffin led some observers to
question the veracity of the official statement on the tsar's
death. Despite these factors, the similarity between Alexander and the Siberian monk Feodor Kuzmich, and the attention given to Kuzmich by the royal family after Alexander's
death, Poole concludes that there is insufficient evidence to
believe that Alexander did not die at Taganrog.   D107.P58

1138   Royal Humane Society. Resuscitation by His Imperial Majesty
       the Emperor of Russia. London: Royal Humane Society,
       1814, 15pp.
       Unavailable for annotation.

1139   Simpson, J. Y. "Monarch or Monk? A Legend of Tomsk."
       Blackwood's M, 161 (Feb. 1897): 257-68.
       Unavailable for annotation.

1140   *Strakhovsky, Leonid I. Alexander I of Russia. The Man
       Who Defeated Napoleon. New York: W. W. Norton, 1947,
       302pp., 274-92.
       An examination of Alexander I's character, domestic policies,
       and, especially, conduct of foreign and military affairs.
       Strakhovsky concentrates on the decisive effect had upon
       the course of Alexander's reign by the threat posed to Russia
       by Napoleonic France. Specifically, he shows that Alexander's
       attention was diverted from launching major internal reforms
       to countering, diplomatically and militarily, the Napoleonic
       challenge. Following Napoleon's defeat, Alexander became
       consumed by his new role as arbiter of Europe's peace and
       never returned to the great reforms considered during his
       youth. Strakhovsky concludes his study with an argument
       that Alexander, disillusioned by his failure to reform Russia
       and to direct European affairs in line with the ideals of the
       Holy Alliance, staged his death and lived until 1864 under the
       identity of Feodor Kuzmich.   DK191.S75
       For Strakhovsky's account of Alexander's "death," see
       also "Alexander I's Death and Destiny." ASEER, 4 (1945):
       8-9, 33-50.
       Reviewed in:

Cath Hist R, 33 (1947): 317
J Cent Eur Aff, 7 (1947): 91
Pol Sci Q, 62 (1947): 461
R Pol, 10 (1948): 119-20
Rus R, 7, no. 1 (1947): 119-20
Slav R, 6, no. 5 (1947)
J Mod Hist, 19 (1947): 337-39

1141   Strickland, Jane. "The Domestic Life of Alexander Paulowitz,
       Emperor of Russia." Sharpe's Lon M, 12 (1850): 305-309.
       Also in Eclectic M, 22 (1850): 86 and Liv Age, 28 (1850):
       120.
       A general review of Alexander I's personal relationship with
       his grandmother, parents, wife, and mistress; based upon
       the works of Alexandre Dumas.

1142   _____. "The Last Days of the Emperor Alexander."
       Sharpe's Lon M, 14 (1851): 1-5.
       An account of Alexander's despair toward the end of his
       life, his relationship with his wife, and his illness and
       death; based on the writings of Alexandre Dumas.

1143   Tolstoy, Leo. "Alexander I." Independent, 69 (24 Nov. 1910):
       112-27.
       A brief review of the Alexander/Feodor Kuzmich legend.

1144   Troyat, Henri. Alexander of Russia, Napoleon's Conqueror.
       New York: E. P. Dutton, 1982, 335pp., bib. 323-28.
       A balanced and highly readable biography of Alexander I.
       Troyat asserts that the sordid circumstances associated with
       Alexander's accession to power led him to seek atonement
       through total devotion to improving the condition of the realm
       which he inherited. However, because of his "native inde-
       cisiveness," the magnitude of the problems which plagued
       Russia, and the staunch opposition of conservatives who
       opposed radical change, the reforms which he hoped to im-
       plement rarely emerged from the planning stage. Alexander
       thus began to consider making up for his shortcomings
       through "diplomatic successes on the world stage," but even
       his emergence as "the savior of Europe" at Napoleon's ex-
       pense did not bring peace of mind to him. Troyat concludes
       that this fruitless search for personal salvation led Alexander,
       in the latter years of his reign, to turn toward religious
       mysticism and develop a theological/patriarchal concept of
       monarchy, all to no avail as he remained a troubled individual
       until his death in 1825. DK191.T7613

1145   Vinogradoff, I. "The Emperor's Republican Tutor." TLS,
       no. 4042 (19 Sept. 1980): 1017-18.
       A review of a French language work edited by J. Beaudet
       and F. Nicod titled Correspondence Between Alexander and
       His Tutor Frederick La Harpe.

1146 Ward, John L. "Tsar or Hermit? The Mystery of Alexander
I." Chamber's Edinb J, (Dec. 1930): 761-63.
A discussion of the evidence that Alexander I did not die
in 1825 but rather secretly fled to Siberia to live as a hermit,
Feodor Kuzmich; based on the diary of a wealthy landowner
on whose estate Kuzmich lived.

1147 Webster, James. Travel Through the Crimea, Turkey and
Egypt; Performed During the Years 1825-8, Including Particulars of the Last Illness and Death of the Emperor Alexander, and of the Russian Conspiracy in 1825. 2 Vols.
London: Henry Colburn and Richard Bentley, 1830.
The appendix to volume two of this work contains a description of Alexander I's illness, medical care, death, and
autopsy. DR427.W38

1148 Wheeler, Daniel. "Letter to Thomas Shillitoe on the Death of
Alexander I." J Friends Hist S, 26 (1929): 17-19.
A description of the illness and death of Alexander I.
Wheeler bases his account on conversations with several
anonymous individuals who attended to Alexander during
his last few days of life.

1149 Whibley, Charles. "A Famous Tsar." Political Portraits.
Freeport, N.Y.: Books for Libraries Press, 1970 (reprint
of 1917 edition), 150-72.
A short biographical sketch of the life of Alexander I with
emphasis on his sympathy with the liberalism of the Enlightenment and his transformation from a reformer to a warrior/
statesman as a consequence of the Napoleonic Wars. D108.W5

1150 Wilson, Francesca. "1801-1825--The Reign of Alexander I."
RTFE (anthology), 155-212.
A discussion of the observations and experiences of six
Western travelers in the Russia of Alexander I. Included
are the writings of J. Carr, M. and C. Wilmont, R. Porter,
R. Lyall, and D. Wheeler.

1151 *Wren, M. "Alexander I." WITR (gen. study), 113-30.
An examination of Alexander I's domestic and foreign policies
within the context of the process of Europeanization at work
in Russia since the start of the eighteenth century. Wren
states although it is undeniable that after 1815 Alexander
lost his enthusiasm for the reforms planned in the early
part of his reign, it is unfair to assert that he deserted the
liberalism of his youth in favor of reactionary policies. Such
assertions, Wren argues, stem from measuring Alexander's
liberalism by contemporary Western liberal standards rather
than in terms of the eighteenth-century enlightened despotism
to which Alexander subscribed. The administrative reforms
which he launched "brought Russian practice into line with
that of most Western governments," while his reforms in

education "brought Russia abreast of accomplishments in
much of the West." Wren maintains that Alexander's turn
to more conservative policies was not so much a rejection of
the West as it was part of an anti-Enlightenment movement
which itself was Western and within which Alexander was
"somewhwere near the middle of the spectrum." While it is
possible to question the progressiveness of Alexander's
domestic reforms, Wren concludes, it is undeniable that his
foreign policy resulted in Russia being accepted as a Western
power of the first rank.

1152 Young, Ian. "Alexander I: Emperor of Russia." Lionel and
      Miriam Kochan, eds. Russian Themes. London: Oliver and
      Boyd, 1967, 61-75. From Hist Today, 11 (1961): 301-08.
      A two part evaluation of Alexander I's character and accom-
      plishments. The first section consists of an overview of
      political and social developments under Alexander with em-
      phasis on the disparity between his reform plans and actual
      legislation. The second part contains a review of various
      interpretations of why Alexander's reign ended in such an
      anti-climactic fashion. Throughout, Young devotes consider-
      able attention to Alexander's lack of strong convictions and
      a sense of personal commitment as well as to his neglect of
      the mechanical and mundane aspects of government.
      DK42.R8

                    DOMESTIC POLICY AND AFFAIRS/
                    POLITICAL THOUGHT AND PRACTICE

1153 Baron, Salo W. "Under Catherine II and Alexander I."
      RJTS (gen. study), 15-30.
      A brief account of the circumstances surrounding Alexander
      I's 9 December 1804 decree which delineated Jewish rights
      and called for the relocation of Russia's Jews to rural areas
      as a means of converting them into a class of small farmers.
      Baron also discusses Alexander's decision to suspend the re-
      location project due to pressures exerted by war with France.
      He concludes with a review of "the steady retrogression of
      the empire's policies toward Jews" in the last decade of
      Alexander's reign.

1154 *Billington, James. "The Frustration of Political Reform."
      IA (gen. study), 259-68.
      A discussion of the major currents of thought which emerged
      during Alexander I's reign. Billington examines the consti-
      tutional monarchism which arose early in the nineteenth cen-
      tury in response to Alexander's "loosely worded promises of
      reform at his coronation," the autocratic conservatism which
      developed amidst aristocratic fear that Alexander was planning
      to implement reforms overly liberal, and the federal republi-
      canism which took shape after the Napoleonic Wars as a

consequence of Alexander's failure to put into effect progressive political and economic reforms.

1155 Blackwell, William L. "Russian Decembrist Views of Poland."
      Polish R, 3, no. 4 (1958): 30-54.
      In part, a discussion of Alexander I's pro-Polish policy as a
      source of the troubled atmosphere from which emerged the
      Decembrist movement. Blackwell's main focus is the dilemma
      which faced Russian revolutionaries who needed Polish support for the success of the revolution but wished to continue
      traditional tsarist policy toward Poland.

1156 Christian, David. "The Political Ideals of Michael Speransky."
      Slavonic E Eur R, 54 (Apr. 1976): 192-213.
      As a study of the political philosophy of M. Speransky and
      the objectives of his 1809 reform project, this article provides some insight into the 'liberal phase' of Alexander's
      reign and the ultimate fate of Speransky's constitutional
      proposal.

1157 * _____. "The Political Views of the Unofficial Committee in
      1801: Some New Evidence." Can Am Slav S, 12, no. 2
      (1978): 247-65.
      An argument that the political thought of the members of the
      Unofficial Committee was primarily derived from French and
      English liberal sources rather than from the conservative,
      German concept of liberalism as has been recently argued
      by some Soviet and American historians. Christian bases
      his position on a document dealing with the reform of the
      Governing Senate which was prepared by Unofficial Committee
      member N. N. Novosiltsev and submitted to Alexander I on
      5 August 1801.

1158 * _____. "The 'Senatorial Party' and the Theory of Collegial
      Government, 1801-1803." Rus R, 38, no. 3 (1979): 298-
      322.
      As a discussion of the political behavior of the Senatorial
      party, this article contains some interesting insights into
      one of the bodies which attempted to influence the direction
      taken by Alexander I's initial reforms. Christian argues
      that the Senatorial party's efforts should be viewed as an
      attempt to secure access to the monarch rather than as an
      effort to limit his powers in any way.

1159 Cross, Anthony. "Pnin and the Sankt-Petersburgskii zhurnal
      (1798)." Can Am Slav S, 7, no. 1 (1974): 78-84.
      This examination of the place of Ivan Pnin (1773-1805) within the history of the Russian intelligentsia includes some discussion of the financial support which he and the progressive
      Sankt-Petersburgskii zhurnal received from the liberal Grand
      Duke Alexander by way of A. Bestuzhev.

1160 *Czartoryski, Adam. Memoirs of Prince Adam Czartoryski, 2
      Vols. Adam Geilgud, ed. New York: Arno Press, 1971
      (reprint of 1888 edition). Excerpt in RFR (anthology), 158-
      60.
      An illuminating series of observations and recollections on
      the first part of Alexander I's reign, written by a Polish
      aristocrat who was a member of the emperor's Unofficial Com-
      mittee and served as Russian Foreign Minister from 1804 to
      1806. Czartoryski records the alterations which took place
      in Alexander's political philosophy as the broad constitution-
      alism to which he subscribed as grand duke gave way, in
      the face of unsurmountable obstacles, to concern for practi-
      cal improvements in the existing form of government in Rus-
      sia. The memoirs also contain numerous references to Alex-
      ander's conduct of foreign affairs in the years prior to
      Czartoryski's resignation in 1806. Czartoryski's post-1806
      relationship with Alexander I and the latter's Polish policy
      and turn toward conservatism in the aftermath of the Na-
      poleonic invasion of Russia are well illustrated by the diaries,
      letters, and diplomatic papers which editor Adam Geilgud
      has included in this volume. DK435.5.C83A3

1161 *Dubnow. S. "The 'Enlightened Absolutism' of Alexander I"
      and "The Last Years of Alexander I." HJRP (gen. study),
      335-65, 390-413.
      A critical review of Alexander I's policies toward Russia's
      Jewish population. Dubnow sees Alexander I's 9 December
      1804 attempt to deal with the 'Jewish question' by eliminat-
      ing from the economic life of rural Jews all non-farming oc-
      cupations and relocating nearly half a million Jews as an ill-
      conceived scheme so costly and impractical that it had to be
      abandoned by 1810. He portrays Alexander's subsequent
      shift to a policy of "benevolent paternalism" as nothing less
      than an attempt to "rehabilitate" Russia's Jews by Russifying
      Jewish institutions and life. In fact, the author concludes,
      the second half of Emperor Alexander's rule witnessed the
      emergence of each and every one of the oppressive features
      of Nicholas I's Jewish policy.

1162 Edwards, David W. "Count Joseph de Maistre and Russian
      Educational Policy, 1803-28." Slav R, 36, no. 1 (1977):
      54-75.
      A review of Alexander I's early liberal reforms in education,
      and an analysis of de Maistre's influence in their dismantle-
      ment during the latter half of Alexander's reign. In spite
      of the fact that de Maistre left Russia in 1817, Edwards
      states, his philosophy of education, which favored a socially
      restrictive, classical religious education program, fueled
      Russian policy for the next decade.

1163 Egan, David R. "The Origins of the 1810 State Council and

Its Functioning During the Reign of Alexander I." State
University of New York, Binghamton, 1970. (dissertation)

1164 *Flynn, James T. "The Role of the Jesuits in the Politics of
Russian Education, 1801-1820." Cath Hist R, 56, no. 2
(1970): 249-65.
An argument that Alexander I used the Jesuits as pawns in
the debate which developed within official circles over the
reform of higher education. Flynn sees the expulsion of the
Jesuits from Russia in 1820 as being due, in part, to Alexander's deisre to "appease conservative opinion in educational
matters..., while making rather little change in the Russian
educational scene."

1165 *_____. "The Universities, the Gentry, and the Russian
Imperial Services, 1815-1825." Can Slav S, 2, no. 4 (1968):
486-503.
An examination of the relationship between Alexander I's
educational reforms, the needs of the imperial services, and
the demands of the Russian gentry as part of an argument
that "the collision of these interests and needs helps to explain the failure of the educational reform, even before the
period of 'reaction' began."

1166 _____. "The Universities in the Russia of Alexander I:
Patterns of Reform and Reaction." Clark University, 1964.
(dissertation)

1167 Greenberg, L. "The Jewish Policies of Alexander I and
Nicholas I." JR (gen. study), 29-55.
An argument that "while the avowed intention of both Alexander I and Nicholas I was to break down the isolation of
the Jews and to improve their political and economic status,
their legislation served only to perpetuate and even to exag-
gerate those very conditions." Greenberg admits that Alexander's Statute of 1804 was "written in a more liberal spirit
than any Jewish legislation heretofore" but maintains that it
"left the Jews politically rightless and economically in a worse
position than before." Similarly, Alexander's missionary
policies, inducements offered to converts, and use of education to strengthen the appeal of Christianity did nothing to
improve the condition of Russia's Jews.

1168 Griffiths, David and Karen Griffiths, eds./trans. "M. M.
Speranskii as Viewed in L. H. Jacob's Unpublished Autobiography." Can Am Slav S, 9, no. 4 (1975): 481-541.
A translation from the previously unpublished German language memoirs of Ludwig H. von Jacob, who for several
years worked with Speransky on the codification of Russian
law. Jacob provides some insight into Speransky's relationship with Alexander I, the reforms considered by the tsar,
and the circumstances surrounding Alexander's exile of
Speransky.

1169   *Hans, N. "The School System of Alexander I." HREP
       (gen. study), 33-60.
       A favorable discussion of the origins, development, and
       significance of Alexander I's educational policies. Hans
       surveys the influence exerted on Alexander's reforms by
       Polish and French educational thought (especially Czartorski
       and Condorcet), and then analyzes the Educational Statutes
       of 1804. Hans states that while Alexander's reform was
       flawed because it failed to furnish funds for the establish-
       ment of parochial schools, and, more importantly, did not
       contain any provision for the education of the serfs who were
       the majority of Russia's population, it nonetheless expanded
       education to such a degree that "we may rightly regard him
       as the builder of the Russian national school system." The
       author concludes that "if the original principles which animated
       the legislation of Alexander were in a later period entirely
       reversed, the framework of his system survived all the
       fluctuations of Russian educational policy and is recognizable
       even at present after the most radical Revolution in history."

1170   *Herzen, Alexander. "The Emperor Alexander I and V. N.
       Karazin." My Past and Thoughts. The Memoirs of Alexan-
       der Herzen. Constance Garnett, trans., Isaiah Berlin, intro.
       New York: Knopf, 1968, 1515-59.
       A portrayal of Alexander I as a tragic figure in Romanov
       history, and a critical review of his relationship with V. N.
       Karazin, a multitalented, progressive intellectual who served
       him as an adviser during the early years of his reign. Her-
       zen, a leading representative of the Russian intelligentsia of
       the mid-nineteenth century, states that Alexander assumed
       the throne of Russia as a dreamer with an emotional commit-
       ment to humanizing government and improving the general
       condition of his subjects. At this point in his reign, Alex-
       ander received a letter from Karazin laden with optimism
       over the benefits that would come to Russia through pro-
       gressive political, social, and economic reform. The letter
       marked the start of positive relationship between the tsar
       and Karazin during which the latter submitted various re-
       form projects, but this relationship was shortlived as Alex-
       ander dismissed Karazin over a minor incident. As the Na-
       poleonic Wars and military glory 'turned Alexander's head'
       and dreams of reform fell victim to reactionary policies,
       Karazin wrote to the tsar warning him that certain nobles
       were planning revolution. Karazin's refusal to provide "de-
       tails, proofs, and names" led Alexander to imprison and
       later exile him. Herzen concludes that Alexander's reign
       thus ended tragically for the Karazins, Radishchevs, and
       Speranskys, who had placed their trust in the tsar's liberal-
       ism, and for Alexander himself who had a "genuine desire
       to alleviate the lot of his subjects" but proved incapable
       of doing so. DK209.6.H4A33

1171 Hooge, B. and J. B. Toews, eds./trans. "Czar Alexander I
      Visits the Molotschna Colonies." Mennon L, 29, no. 3 (1974):
      57-59.
      A translation of A. Fadeyev's account of Alexander I's visit
      to Mennonite communities in the Ukraine in 1818 and 1825.
      Fadeyev describes Alexander's travels, conversations with
      various Mennonites, and his satisfaction with the accomplish-
      ments of these industrious colonists.

1172 Jenkins, Michael. Arakcheev. Grand Vizier of the Russian
      Empire. New York: Dial Press, 1969, 317pp., bib. 294-95.
      This work does not contain a separate chapter on Alexander
      I, but as a detailed study of the political activities of one
      of his closest advisers it may be consulted for information
      on Alexander's policies and leadership particularly during
      the last decade of his reign. DK190.6.A8J4

1173 *Karamzin, N. M. "The Reign of Alexander I from 1801-1810."
      Karamzin's Memoir on Ancient and Modern Russia. Cambridge:
      Harvard University Press, 1959, 138-89.
      A critical assessment of Alexander I's reforms of the 1801-
      1810 period. Karamzin, a contemporary of Alexander and
      Russia's first modern historian, defends autocracy as Rus-
      sia's traditional form of government and the one best suited
      to the nation's unique needs, and he attacks Alexander's
      excessive involvement in European affairs, institutional re-
      form, consideration of emancipation of the serfs, and fi-
      nancial policies. Throughout, Karamzin maintains that Alex-
      ander and his advisers were pursuing a path contrary to
      Russia's best interests and in conflict with the path followed
      by those who had established the Russian monarchy. In a
      lengthy and interesting introduction, R. Pipes discusses
      Karamzin's political philosophy and the contents and signifi-
      cance of the Memoir. DK71.K343

1174 *Klier, John D. "Alexander I, Soldier's Cloth and the Jews."
      Can Am Slav S, 9, no. 4 (1975): 463-71.
      An analysis of the attempt, under Alexander I, to create "a
      pool of factory workers from the impoverished lower classes
      of Jewish society" in Russia as part of an experiment to
      direct Jews away from middleman activities deemed exploitive
      of Christians. Klier establishes that the Jews trained at the
      Kremenchug factory in Poland, where coarse soldier's cloth
      was produced, were treated so miserably by their employers
      that the factory took on the appearance of a sweatshop and
      therefore ceased to be appealing to Jews seeking gainful
      employment.

1175 *Land, David M. "The Last Months: Radishchev and Alex-
      ander I." The First Russian Radical. Alexander Radish-
      chev, 1749-1802. London: George Allen and Unwin, 1959,

249-70.
A discussion of Radishchev's work on Alexander I's Legislative Commission with some reference to Alexander's reform
plans and the intellectual climate of the first years of his
reign. For a similar study, see Lang's "Radishchev and the
Legislative Commission of Alexander I." ASEER, 6, no. 2
(1947): 11-24.

1176 *Leary, D. B. "Alexander I. 1801-1825." EAR (gen. study),
45-56.
A discussion of Alexander I's attempt, in the first half of
his reign, "to create an adequate and permanent national
system of schools, which should at once avoid the super-
ficialities of Catherine and the too materialistic bias of Peter,
and provide opportunities for all classes of society." Leary
also examines the reasons behind Alexander's turn away from
a progressive educational program to one characterized by
the spirit of reaction.

1177 *McConnell, A. "Alexander I's Hundred Days: The Politics
of a Paternalistic Reformer." Slav R, 28 (Sept. 1969): 373-
92.
An argument that many historians have erred in their assessment of Alexander I's liberalism because they have overlooked
the significance of the very early part of his reign when he
"recovered from his initial demoralization" over the assassination of his father and "formed the paternalistic political conceptions that would guide the next 25 years of his reign."
This paternalistic philosophy, McConnell maintains, fixed the
limits of Alexander's constitutionalism since he could not bring
himself to trust the Russian people enough to grant any significant measure of self-government.

1178 *McCormick, D. "Catherine's 'Secret Expedition' and the
'Yellow Box.'" HRSS (gen. study), 37-50.
A discussion of Alexander I's 1801 abolition of Catherine II's
secret police and his creation of a secret service agency
based on the French police-spy system employed by Napoleon.
McCormick commends Alexander for establishing a secret service which enabled Russia to compete, for the first time, "on
equal terms with the rival espionage operations in Europe."
McCormick goes on to discuss Russian, French, and British
spy operations during Alexander's reign, particularly in regard to the events surrounding the "leaking of details" about
the Tilsit meeting between Alexander and Napoleon.

1179 McMillin, Arnold B. "Quakers in Early Nineteenth Century
Russia." Slavonic E Eur R, 51, no. 125 (1973): 567-79.
A discussion of the Russian experiences of the English Quaker
Daniel Wheeler (commissioned in 1817 by Alexander I to con-
vert into farmland part of the St. Petersburg marshes), with

some reference to Alexander's Quaker contacts in England
and sympathy with Quaker philosophy.

1180 Narkiewicz, Olga A. "Alexander I and the Senate Reform."
      Slavonic E Eur R, 47, no. 108 (1969): 115-36.
      A study of the views of Alexander I, the Senatorial party,
      and, especially, the Unofficial Committee, in regard to wheth-
      er the reformed Senate "should have administrative, judiciary
      or legislative powers, or whether it should combine all three."
      Narkiewicz establishes that whereas the Senatorial party
      thought that the Senate ought to have all these powers, the
      four members of the Unofficial Committee believed that the
      Senate "should not be given too much power, lest it restrict
      the actions of the emperor." Three of the committee's mem-
      bers felt this way because they viewed the Senate as a con-
      servative body that might use its power to thwart the liberal
      reforms that Alexander was then considering. The fourth
      member, N. N. Novosiltsev, shared this view but also believed
      that the Senate's power had to be broken because he hoped
      to become the chief adviser to an all-powerful monarch rather
      than to one whose authority was curtailed in any way. This
      belief prompted Novosiltsev to use his influence with Alex-
      ander and his capacity for intrigue to shape the reform de-
      cree in a restrictive fashion, particularly in regard to the
      Senate's "right to make representations if a new law appeared
      inconvenient." Narkiewicz concludes that while Novosiltsev
      was successful in undermining the Senate's authority, the
      methods that he used angered the other members of the
      Unofficial Committee and contributed substantially to the Com-
      mittee's break-up.

1181 O'Connor, Mark. "Czartoryski and the Goluchowski Affair at
      Vilna University." Jahr Ges Ost, 31 (1983): 229-43.
      Alexander I is not the focus of this article, but as a study
      of the controversy over J. Goluchowski's appointment as pro-
      fessor of philosophy at Vilna University in 1821 it sheds some
      light on the conservative turn taken by Alexander's domestic
      policy during the final decade of his reign.

1182 Raeff, Marc. "Chapter IV-VII." PPR (anthology), 75-120.
      A collection of four prominent proposals submitted to Alex-
      ander I in hope of securing his "formal approval to a docu-
      ment that would set forth the fundamental rights of Russia's
      upper class." The documents are: A Project for a Most
      Graciously Granted Charter to the Russian People (author
      unknown, 1801), Principles of Government Reform (Unofficial
      Committee, 1802), Introduction to the Codification of State
      Laws (M. M. Speransky, 1809), and a Constitutional Charter
      of the Russian Empire (N. N. Novosiltsev, 1818-1820).

1183 *_____. "The Dawn of the Nineteenth Century. UIR (gen.

study), 113-45.

An examination of Alexander I's attempt to rationalize the
structure of the Russian bureaucracy and advance the modernization process, begun by Peter I and continued by Catherine
II, without in any way limiting his autocratic prerogatives.
Raeff establishes that Alexander's reforms greatly enhanced
the efficiency of the central government in many areas of
economic, social, and political life and improved the communication between the capital and the provinces. While conservative critics feared that these reforms would lead to the eclipse
of the Senate by the imperial bureaucracy and, ultimately, to
an unacceptable social transformation, criticism of a more far-
reaching variety came from the ranks of the cultural elite
that had developed rapidly during the first decades of the
nineteenth century. The members of this elite were, particularly after 1815, no longer willing to trust autocratic pater-
nalism to rectify the shortcomings of Russian public life but
wanted civil society to take the lead in developing the country's human and material resources. Raeff concludes that
Alexander's refusal to allow this elite group to "fulfill its
dreams of civic action" removed from the realm of the possible collaboration with the imperial government by society at
large and, in the long run, forced Russian intellectuals to
consider radical means to effect change.

1184   *_____. Michael Speransky. Statesman of Imperial Russia,
1772-1839. The Hague: Martinus Nijhoff, 1969, 394pp.,
bib. 368-75.

A scholarly study of Count Michael Speransky's political
philosophy and administrative activities during his years
of service under Alexander I and Nicholas I. As part of
his study, Raeff examines Alexander I's character and personality, views on governmental reform, and relationship
with Speransky. Raeff rejects the interpretation that Alexander intended to establish constitutional limitations on the
monarchy until, for various reasons, he underwent a conservative change of heart, and argues instead that at no time
did Alexander or the Unofficial Committee construe constitutionalism to mean "representative institutions, checks and
balances, (and) abolition of the autocracy" but rather "defined constitution as the rule of law, and the clear, logical,
hierarchical organization of the administration." Alexander
thus commissioned Speransky to draft administrative reforms
that would advance the cause of rational government in Russia without limiting the authority of the crown, and Speransky's reform projects, Raeff states, certainly were consistent
with the tsar's wishes. However, "confronted with the
legislative act which concretely embodied his dream," Alexander began to fear that Speransky's proposals would some-
how, someday lead to a restriction of his royal prerogatives,
a conclusion primarily responsible for Speransky's dismissal

from service in March of 1812.   DK261.R134

1185   Roach, Elmo E.   "Alexander I and the Unofficial Committee."
       Ohio State University, 1968.   (dissertation)

1186   *_____.   "The Origins of Alexander I's Unofficial Committee."
       Rus R, 28, no. 3 (1969):   315-26.
       A discussion of the roots of the Unofficial Committee as
       resting "in Alexander's youthful thoughts of reform and in
       the close circle of friends with whom he shared his ideas
       and desires."   Roach also reviews Alexander's personal re-
       lationship with each of the Committee's members and com-
       ments favorably on the Committee's reform proposals.

1187   *Schapiro, Leonard.   "The Springtime of Reform."   Rationalism
       and Nationalism in Russian Nineteenth Century Political
       Thought.   New Haven: Yale University Press, 1967, 1-28.
       A discussion of political reform during the reign of Alexander
       I within the context of two rival strands in Russian political
       thought: rationalism (faith in reason as the basis of all
       political decisions and faith in "the uniformity of political
       development") and nationalism (pride in a people's unique
       qualities and belief that "political institutions are not made,
       but evolve as part of the social and historical structure of
       a particular people...").   Schapiro examines the thought,
       proposals, and reforms of M. Speransky as a representative
       of the rationalist mode of thought, the negative nationalist
       reaction of N. Karamzin to the rationalism of Speransky, and
       Alexander I's rejection of Speransky's 1809 constitutional
       project for fear of infringement upon his autocratic preroga-
       tives.   JR84.R9S353

1188   *Schnitzler, J. H.   Secret History of the Court and Govern-
       ment of Russia Under the Emperors Alexander and Nicholas.
       2 Vols.   London: Richard Bentley, 1847.
       The focus of this two volume study is the 1825 Decembrist
       Revolt and its aftermath, but it includes a discussion of the
       policies pursued by Alexander I which prompted the formation
       of the secret societies from which emerged the Decembrist
       conspiracy.   Schnitzler states that Alexander had the intellect,
       desire, and ability to bring needed reforms to Russia but
       "allowed distractions to divide his thoughts, and eventually
       divert them," the most notable distraction being the Napo-
       leonic Wars from which Alexander hoped to win glory and
       world renown for himself in his role as peacemaker.   Schnitz-
       ler provides most information on the decade prior to the
       Decembrist Revolution when Alexander ceased to concern
       himself at all with the regeneration of Russia, became wholly
       disillusioned with his domestic accomplishments, and retreated
       into a semi-mystical existence.   DK189.S36

1189 *Squire, P. S. "The Preliminary Phase: 1801-1825." The
       Third Department. The Establishment and Practices of the
       Political Police in the Russia of Nicholas I. Cambridge: Cam-
       bridge University Press, 1968, 13-47.
       A discussion of the disorganization, inefficiency, and lack of
       professionalism which characterized the political police during
       Alexander I's reign. Squire sees Alexander's unwillingness
       to create a centralized political police organization and "in-
       creasingly apathetic attitude to questions of internal adminis-
       tration" as the twin sources of the miserable condition of the
       security police during the first quarter of the nineteenth
       century. Squire believes that the general inefficiency of the
       political police was, in part, responsible for the growth of
       secret societies during Alexander's reign and the attempt to
       overthrow the monarchy following his death. HV8224.S59

1190 *Strakhovsky, Leonid I. "Pushkin and the Emperors Alexander
       I and Nicholas I." Can Slav P, 1 (1956): 16-30.
       An examination of Pushkins' relationship with Alexander I and
       Nicholas I for insight into the nature of Pushkin's political
       philosophy. Strakhovsky states that Pushkin, a fervent
       Russian nationalist, was appalled by Alexander I's pro-Polish
       policies. Pushkin's disgust turned into hatred following his
       exile for writing poems critical of Alexander. The conserva-
       tive Nicholas I, on the other hand, treated Pushkin far bet-
       ter than had the liberal Alexander. Nicholas allowed Pushkin
       to return from exile, gave him a court position, and thorough-
       ly charmed the poet in a lengthy private meeting with him.
       Pushkin's admiration for Nicholas reached its peak when Rus-
       sia crushed the Polish revolt of 1830, an act which appealed
       to Pushkin's patriotism. Strakhovsky concludes that Push-
       kin's political idealism was that of an enlightened conserva-
       tive.

1191 Vernadsky, George. "Reforms Under Czar Alexander I:
       French and American Influences." R Pol, 9 (Jan. 1947):
       47-64.
       A discussion of French and American influences on Alexander
       I, the Unofficial Committee, M. Speransky, and the Decem-
       brists. Vernadsky establishes that Alexander and the mem-
       bers of the Unofficial Committee were influenced in their
       deliberations on the reform of Russia's central administrative
       institutions by the French Constitution of the Year VIII
       (1799), the national Almanac of France, and a plan submitted
       by Condorcet to the National Assembly in 1792. Speransky,
       who also admired French political thought, drew upon the
       institutions of the French Consulate and Empire in composing
       his reform proposals. Vernadsky sees N. Novosiltsev's 1820
       proposal, a Constitutional Charter of the Russian Empire, as
       being in debt to American constitutional and federative prin-
       ciples. In reviewing the constitutional projects of the

Decembrists, Vernadsky links P. Pestel's plan to French
thought and practices, and N. Muraviev's to American influences.

1192 *Walker, Franklin A. "Popular Response to Public Education
in the Reign of Tsar Alexander I (1801-1825)." Hist Ed Q,
24 (Winter 1984): 527-43.
A discussion of the popular response to Alexander I's reform of elementary and secondary education as a far more
favorable one than traditionally depicted by historians.
Walker contends that there was active and widespread public
participation in the funding of schools and "considerable local
initiative in the opening and maintenance of district and
parish schools." This support and concern was not merely
a dutiful response to programs set by the central government but was an enthusiastic one which involved "assemblies
of the nobles..., individual landlords, merchants, officials
great and petty, clergy and even private and state peasants...." Walker concludes that the very real and significant shortcomings of Alexander's educational reforms should
not detract from the success the government had in making
the school "an important part of town and sometimes village
life."

1193 *Whittaker, Cynthia H. "From Promise to Purge: The First
Years of St. Petersburg University." Paedag Hist, 18,
no. 1 (1978): 148-67.
A discussion of Alexander I's retreat from an enlightened
philosophy of education toward one based upon pietism and
obscurantism as part of his reaction to the revolutions which
took place in Europe in 1820.

1194 *Wieczynski, Joseph L. "The Mutiny of the Semenovsky Regiment in 1820." Rus R, 29, no. 2 (1970): 167-80.
An examination of the causes and significance of the 17
October 1820 mutiny of the Semenovsky Regiment, a favorite
unit of Alexander I under the command of his youngest
brother, Grand Prince Michael. Wieczynski questions those
interpretations which claim that Alexander who was at the
Congress of Troppau when he learned of the mutiny, fell
under the reactionary sway of Prince Metternich as a result
of this event and consequently adopted repressive domestic
policies during the last years of his reign. Wieczynski also
discusses the link between the Decembrist movement and the
members of the Semenovsky Regiment who were exiled when
Alexander disbanded this military unit.

1195 *Wortman, Richard S. "Bureaucratization, Specialization and
Education." DRLC (gen. study), 34-50.
In part, a discussion of the attention given by Alexander I
to the need to bring order to the mass of conflicting and

overlapping laws that existed within his realm and to rationalize the legal procedure followed in Russia's courts. Wortman also discusses Alexander's attempt to introduce "a systematic legal education" so as to train students in "juris-
prudence and a pure writing style appropriate for legal
cases." K91.W6

1196 *Zacek, Judith. "A Case Study in Russian Philanthropy: The
      Prison Reform Movement in the Reign of Alexander I."
      Can Slav S, 1, no. 2 (1967): 196-211.
      An argument that "the reign of Alexander I marks a distinct
      phase in the emergence of Russian philanthropy." In support
      of this contention, Zacek discusses the prison reform move-
      ment, particularly the composition, goals, and activities of
      the Society for the Supervision of Prisons which was created
      by Alexander I on 19 July 1819.

1197 *_____. "The Imperial Philanthropic Society in the Reign of
      Alexander I." Can Am Slav S, 9, no. 4 (1975): 427-36.
      An examination of the activities and significance of the Im-
      perial Philanthropic Society created by Alexander I in 1802.
      Zacek contends that the Society, which was not a govern-
      ment agency but worked closely with various representatives
      of the government, concerned itself only with treating the
      symptoms of poverty rather than with addressing its causes.
      She concludes that the consequent failure of the society to
      make any serious inroads against poverty as a social evil,
      though consistent with the general lack of noteworthy politi-
      cal and social developments during Alexander's reign, was
      primarily due to the failure of the nobility to pursue a po-
      tentially fruitful opportunity provided by Alexander and not
      to any lack of commitment on Alexander's part in regard to
      the reduction of poverty in Russia.

                    FOREIGN POLICY AND MILITARY AFFAIRS

1198 An Account of the Visit of His Royal Highness, the Prince
      Regent with Their Imperial and Royal Majesties the Emperor
      of All the Russias and the King of Prussia to the Corporation
      of London in June 1814. London: Nichols, Son, and Bent-
      ley, 1815, 93pp.
      A description of Alexander I's 1814 visit to London, includ-
      ing a list of those who attended the reception ceremony and
      an account of the royal procession, entertainment, and the
      toasts made at the dinner held in Alexander's honor. An
      appendix contains the address to Alexander I given by the
      Mayor of London who praised the tsar for his part in the
      defeat of Napoleon.

1199 *Adams, Charles Francis, ed. The Russian Memoirs of John

Quincy Adams: His Diary from 1809 to 1814. New York:
Arno Press, 1974 (reprint of Vol. II of the 1874 publication
of The Memoirs of John Quincy Adams).
The first American ambassador to Russia records his observations on diplomatic and domestic affairs in St. Petersburg
during the October 1809 to April 1814 period. Adams describes Alexander I's character and personality, court activities, and domestic and foreign reaction to his policies. The
memoirs are also valuable as a record of the activities of a
man who pioneered the establishment of favorable relations
between America and Romanov Russia. E377.A19

1200 Anderson, M. S. "British Public Opinion and the Russian
Campaign of 1812." Slavonic E Eur R, 34, no. 83 (1956):
408-25.
In part, an account of the growth in England of the stature
and popularity of Alexander I as a model Christian ruler following Napoleon's disastrous 1812 Russian Campaign.

1201 Barnes, G. M. "Alexander I's Visit--June, 1814 as Recorded
in the Journal of Lady Mary Long." Cornhill, (June 1939):
776-93.
Unavailable for annotation.

1202 *Bartley, Russell H. Imperial Russia and the Struggle for
Latin American Independence, 1808-1828. Austin, Tex.:
Institute of Latin American Studies, 1978, 236pp., bib.
203-24.
In part, an examination of Russia's interests in the Western
hemisphere and their relationship to tsarist responses to the
separatist movement in Latin America. Bartley maintains that
Alexander I's doctrine of legitimacy was little more than an
ideological mantle with which to veil the pursuit of Russian
imperial objectives. Russia's various economic concerns,
along with the policy of imperial expansion which Alexander
inherited from his predecessors better explain Russia's actions
than do ideological considerations. Given Alexander's conservative policy of withdrawal and retrenchment in the New
World, Bartley asserts, the Monroe Doctrine should not be
viewed as a response to any Russian threat to America's
interests. F1416.R8B37

1203 Bayard, James A. Papers of James A. Bayard, 1796-1815,
Vol. II. Elizabeth Donnan, ed. Washington, D.C.: Government Printing Office, 1913, 539pp.
Included in these letters are those written by Bayard while
he was in St. Petersburg attempting to secure the assistance
of Alexander I in terminating the War of 1812 between Britain
and America. E172.A60 1913 v.2

1204 Berquist, Harold E., Jr. "Henry Middleton and the Arbitration

of the Anglo-American Slave Trade Controversy by Tsar
Alexander I." So Car Hist M, 82, no. 1 (1981): 20-31.
Alexander I is not the focus of this article, but it includes
an account of his role in the settlement of the Anglo-American
dispute over the return of, or reimbursement for, slaves
seized by the British from American vessels during the War
of 1812.

1205 *_____. "The Russia Ukase of September 16, 1821: The
Noncolonialization Principle, and the Russo-American Con-
vention of 1824." Can J Hist, 10, no. 2 (1975): 165-84.
A discussion of the negotiations which led to the 1824 resolution of the conflict between Russia and the United States
over the northwest coast of America. Berquist stresses that
mutual concern over the power and policies of England was
the determining factor in Russo-American diplomacy of the
time.

1206 Blackwell, William L. "Alexander I and Poland: The Foundations of His Polish Policy and Its Repercussions in Russia,
1801-1825." Princeton University, 1961. (dissertation)

1207 *Bolkhovitinov, Nikolai N. The Beginnings of Russian-American
Relations, 1775-1815. Elena Levin, trans. L. H. Butterfield, intro. Cambridge: Harvard University Press, 1975,
484pp.
A scholarly, Soviet examination of early Russian-American
diplomatic, economic, and cultural relations. Bolkhovitinov
maintains that the expansion of trade, establishment of scientific and cultural contacts, and emergence of generally
amicable relations between America and Russia during Alexander I's reign did not represent any sincere rapprochement
between the two nations but rather "a union of convenience."
He criticizes those twentieth-century studies which dwell
upon the sincere and "forgotten" friendships of the tsars
and presidents as well as those which assert that there has
been an "age-long hostility" between Russia and America.
Bolkhovitinov concludes that the lesson of Russian-American
relationships up to 1815 should not be sought "in the absence of differences and conflicts, but in ... the possibility
of overcoming them--not with weapons, but peacefully, by
means of negotiation." E183.8.R9B613

1208 *Capodistrias, John. Letters to the Tsar Nicholas I. London:
Doric Publications, 1977 (reprint of 1868 edition), 137pp.
A December 1826 autobiographical memorandum to Nicholas I
in which the author outlines his career (1809-1822) in the
diplomatic service of Alexander I and, in the process, sheds
light on Alexander's foreign policy, particularly in regard
to the Congress of Vienna, Holy Alliance, and Mediterranean
affairs. DF815.K3A4

1209   The Christian Conqueror; or Moscow Burnt, and Paris Saved.
       London: Longman and Company, 1814.
       Unavailable for annotation.

1210   Clark, G. J. "Napoleon and Alexander I." Quar R, 177 (Oct.
       1893): 416-42.
       A lengthy review of Albert Vandal's Napoléon et Alexandre,
       Vol. I, Paris, 1891, and Serge Tatischef's Alexandre et
       Napoléon, Paris, 1891.

1211   Clarkson, Thomas. Thomas Clarkson's Interview with Alexan-
       der I at Aix-La-Chapelle. London: Poyser, Printer, Wis-
       bech, n.d., 24pp.
       A reconstruction of an 1818 interview with Alexander I in
       which the author solicited the tsar's assistance in having
       the principal monarchs of Europe abolish the slave trade in
       Africa. Alexander shared Clarkson's feelings in regard to
       the slave trade and went on to talk at some length about the
       duty of every Christian to work for an equitable world in
       which warfare and oppression would have no place.

1212   Clifford, J. "A Glimpse of Three Crowned Heads." Overland
       M, 6 (May 1885): 446-52.
       A firsthand account of the fanfare which attended the 1817
       meeting at Wilhemsbad between Alexander I, Francis II of
       Austria, and Frederick William III of Prussia. The author,
       in describing Alexander's public behavior, notes his charm,
       grace, and, particularly, the attention which he gave to the
       opposite sex.

1213   Cramer, Frederick H. "The Beginning of the End: Five Pro-
       files from the Congress of Vienna." Cur Hist, n.s. 14 (May
       1948): 261-69.
       A general review of Alexander I's personality, character,
       and domestic and foreign policies. Cramer gives special
       attention to Alexander's influence at the Congress of Vienna
       and creation of the Holy Alliance.

1214   *Dorland, Arthur G. "Alexander I and the Origins of the Holy
       Alliance of 1815." Roy S Can, 33, sec. 2 (1940): 59-79.
       An argument that Alexander I's formation of the Holy Alliance
       was far more a response to French, German, and English
       philosophical, humanitarian, and religious trends than it was
       to any influence by Baroness Krudener. Dorland identifies
       the most important personal influences on Alexander's con-
       ceptualization of the Holy Alliance as being F. La Harpe
       (tutor to Alexander when grand duke) and the various
       Quakers with whom Alexander met in 1814, and the prime
       impersonal forces as being the Pietistic and Wesleyan move-
       ments of Germany and England respectively. The author
       finds nothing to mock in the principles of the Alliance but

rather contends that Alexander merely "made articulate the
almost universal longing for peace of that day which has
found expression in somewhat similar forms at other periods
of history."

1215 Dzienwanowski, M. K. Vienna Appeasement. London: The
Library of Fighting Poland, 1945, 15pp. DK435.D9
Unavailable for annotation.

1216 "The Emperor Alexander." Eclectic M, 49 (Mar. 1860): 414-
18.
A review of Alexander I's reign concentrating on his military
exploits and efforts to expand Russian boundaries.

1217 Ferrari, Ellen D. "In the Service of the Tsar: The Autobiography of Count John A. Capodistrias." State University
of New York, Binghamton, 1980. (dissertation)

1218 Fitzgibbon, Edward M. "Alexander I and the Near East: The
Ottoman Empire in Russia's Foreign Relations, 1801-1807."
Ohio State University, 1974. (dissertation)

1219 *Frederiksen, O. J. "Alexander I and His League to End
Wars." Rus R, 3, no. 1 (1943): 10-22.
A sympathetic treatment of Alexander I's attempt to advance
the cause of European peace through the establishment of an
international organization to maintain political stability and
national sovereignty. Frederiksen asserts that although
Alexander's efforts were greeted with suspicion and derision,
they deserve praise as "faltering steps toward a lofty goal;
and it may well be that Alexander I will go down in history
not as the victor over Napoleon but as the far-sighted initiator and champion" of world freedom.

1220 "Friends and the Emperor Alexander." J Friends Hist S, 25
(1928): 56-62.
A series of June 1814 letters, written by Thomas Clarkson
(British journalist, abolitionist, and historian) to his wife,
which contain an account of Alexander I's attendance of a
London Quaker's meeting and his subsequent conversation
with several of the congregation's members. Alexander expressed his admiration for the Quakers and impressed all
with his piety and command of the Bible.

1221 Girnius, Saulius A. "Russia and the Continental Blockade."
University of Chicago, 1981. (dissertation)

1222 *Golder, Frank A. "The Russian Offer of Mediation in the
War of 1812." Pol Sci Q, 31, no. 3 (1916): 380-91.
A defense of the actions of Chancellor Romanzov in his attempt to arrange for Alexander I to serve as a mediator in
the War of 1812 between Britain and America. Drawing

primarily upon Russian diplomatic archives, Golder establishes
that Romanzov's 28 August 1812 restatement of Alexander's
offer to serve as a mediator was made only because Romanzov
was unaware of Alexander's 9 August withdrawal of the mediation offer, by way of a letter submitted to Lord Castlereagh,
because the British government had shown no interest in
employing the tsar's services. Consequently, Romanzov appeared to be an intriguer and came under criticism from both
American and, especially, British statesmen when in fact,
Golder asserts, Alexander's diplomatic duplicity was the prime
source of this unfortunate incident.

1223 *Gooch, George Peabody. "Caulaincourt, Napoleon, and Alexander." Courts and Cabinets. London: Longmans, Green
and Company, 1946, 284-94.
A discussion of the origins and fate of Napoleon's 1812 campaign in Russia. Drawing heavily on the memoirs of Caulaincourt, French ambassador to St. Petersburg, Gooch discusses
favorably the accuracy of Caulaincourt's assessment of Alexander I's intentions toward France and his probable reaction
to a French invasion of Russia. Gooch also gives an account
of Napoleon's miscalculation of Alexander's resolve to continue the war after the French had taken Moscow. Also in
Contemp R, 164 (Nov.-Dec. 1943): 283-91, 342-48.
DK1-7.G6

1224 Grimstead, Patricia K. "Diplomatic Spokesmen and the Tsar-
Diplomat: The Russian Foreign Ministers During the Reign
of Alexander I, 1801-1825." University of California, Berkeley, 1964. (dissertation)

1225 *   . The Foreign Ministers of Alexander I. Political
Attitudes and the Conduct of Russian Diplomacy, 1801-1825.
Berkeley: University of California Press, 1969, 367pp.,
bib. 307-60.
A critical examination of Alexander I's conduct of foreign
affairs and relationship with the individuals whom he selected
to serve Russia as statesmen. Grimstead contends that while
Alexander had considerable success as both a diplomat and
military leader his failure to improve the domestic bases
needed to sustain the exalted international position which
Russia achieved during his reign made it nearly impossible
for his successors to maintain such a position. In fact, the
efforts to this end made by the Russian monarchs of the
nineteenth century who followed Alexander, only "widened
the gap between domestic potential and foreign commitment,"
a development which eventually brought disastrous consequences to the nation. In discussing Alexander's relationship with the eight men who occupied the position of foreign
minister during his reign, Grimstead asserts that Alexander
appointed individuals whom he believed to be personally committed to the policies he was at that moment following, hence

the short-lived nature of the diplomatic careers of most of
these men. DK197.G7 1969
  Reviewed in:
  Am Hist R, 75 (1970): 1493-94
  Rocky Mt Soc Sci J, 8 (1971): 141-42
  Slav R, 29 (1970): 510

1226 Hale, William H. "The Yankee and the Czar." Oliver Jensen,
      ed. American Heritage. America and Russia; a Century and
      a Half of Dramatic Encounters. New York: Simon and Schus-
      ter, 1962, 17-39. Also in Amer Heritage, 9, no. 2 (1958):
      4-9, 82-86.
      An account of J. Q. Adams' four years in Russia as the
      American minister plenipotentiary to the court of Alexander
      I. In addition to describing Adams' conversations with Alex-
      ander I in regard to British violation of freedom of the seas,
      Hale relates Adams' observations on the extravagance of the
      Russian court, Napoleon's 1812 invasion of Russia, and a host
      of lesser subjects. Most obvious is the positive relationship
      that existed between Adams and the emperor. E183.8.R9A73

1227 Hans, N. "Alexander I and Jefferson: Unpublished Corres-
      pondence." Slavonic E Eur R, 32, no. 78 (1954): 215-25.
      A brief introduction to a series of letters exchanged be-
      tween Thomas Jefferson and Alexander I during the years
      1805-08. As Hans states, the letters point out "the great
      interest aroused in Europe and America by the personality
      of young Alexander and by his first reforms."

1228 Herold, J. Christopher. "Great Confrontations. IV: Napoleon
      and Alexander. A Comedy Played on a Raft." Horizon, 5,
      no. 7 (1963): 28-32.
      A portrayal of Alexander I's meeting with Napoleon at Tilsit
      as a comic venture with each sovereign attempting to delude
      the other and gain advantage for himself. Herold also dis-
      cusses the goals of and methods used by both Alexander and
      Napoleon.

1229 *Hildt, John C. Early Diplomatic Relations of the United States
      with Russia. Baltimore: Johns Hopkins Press, 1906, 195pp.
      In part, a discussion of Alexander's American policy as an
      expression of his desire "to cultivate the friendship of America
      in order to secure her as an ally against Great Britain."
      Within this context, Hildt examines such developments as the
      establishment of formal diplomatic relations between Russia and
      America, Russia's offer to mediate the 1812 War between Brit-
      ain and America, and Alexander's position on the independ-
      ence of Spanish-America. H31.J6 Ser. 24

1230 *Hilt, Douglas. "Czar Alexander I." Ten Against Napoleon."
      Chicago: Nelson-Hall, 1975, 177-96.

A discussion of the relations between Alexander I and Napoleon from Tilsit to Waterloo. Hilt maintains that Napoleon
both underestimated Alexander and misjudged his character
most probably because of the latter's superficial passivity
during their Tilsit meetings: "Napoleon's basic assumption
was that he had fully understood every nuance of Alexander's mind.... It was a fatal miscalculation." In the years
immediately following the Tilsit accord, Napoleon became
upset over what he perceived to be a change of mind and
character in Alexander who, beginning with the 1808 Erfurt
talks, presented himself as Napoleon's equal and demonstrated
a reluctance to continue Russia's "undignified position as a
subservient ally" of France. With the renewal of military
hostilities between France and Russia, Napoleon again underestimated Alexander by believing that a single decisive battle
would "knock the bottom out of ... Alexander's fine resolu-
tions." Alexander's resolve only became apparent to Napoleon
when Russia failed to come to terms after the French had
taken Moscow. Hilt concludes that this same resolve led
Alexander to turn the 1812 defeat of Napoleon in Russia
into a tenacious and successful campaign to rid Europe of
Napoleon's control. D309.H54

1231 Hobbs, William H. "Nineteenth Century Visionary." No Amer
     R, 210 (Dec. 1919): 793-99.
     A review of Alexander I's motives for establishing the Holy
     Alliance, and a discussion of its similarity to the League of
     Nations.

1232 Hunt, Leigh. "On the Separation of Russia from the British
     Interests." Leigh Hunt's Political and Occasional Essays.
     New York: Columbia University Press, 1962, 75-79.
     A January 1808 critical review of English reaction to Alex-
     ander I's rapprochement with Napoleon at Tilsit. Hunt
     maintains that those Englishmen who expressed shock and
     bewilderment over Alexander's political fickleness naively
     overlooked the fact that the tsar's diplomacy was, from the
     very beginning of his reign, rooted in crude self-interest.
     Equally naive, Hunt continues, are those who expected the
     weak-willed Alexander to behave in a principled fashion.
     D7.H85

1233 An Impartial and Authentic Life of Alexander, Emperor of
     Russia. London, 1814, 60pp.
     An anonymous, highly favorable account of the foreign pol-
     icy pursued by Alexander I during the Napoleonic Wars up
     to the time of his June, 1814 visit to England. The author
     describes Alexander as a humane, magnanimous, wise, and
     gracious sovereign who delivered Russia and the rest of
     Europe from the hands of a tyrant. He also provides details
     on the wildly enthusiastic response of the English public to

Alexander wherever he appeared. DK191.I3

1234 Jackson, W. G. F. "The French Road." Seven Roads to
      Moscow. New York: Philosophical Library, 1958, 65-186.
      A general review of Alexander I's motives for concluding
      the Treaty of Tilsit, his role in determining the strategy
      to be employed in countering the French invasion of 1812,
      and his relationship with Generals Phull, Barclay de Tolly,
      and Kutuzov. DK51.7.J3

1235 *Jelavich, Barbara. "Alexander I." CRFP (gen. study), 28-
      70.
      A favorable survey of Alexander I's foreign policy. Jelavich
      asserts that, "in contrast to his relative lack of achievement
      at home, Alexander I throughout his career played a brilliant
      role on the international scene. He was able to repel an
      invasion by the foremost military power of the time, to take
      the lead in the organization of peace, and thereafter to
      maintain the position of his country as the strongest single
      power on the continent." She adds that in foreign relations
      Alexander's "propensity to base practical decisions on moral
      principles and general concepts was always apparent, but
      these considerations usually contributed in the end to the
      strengthening of the power of Russia abroad."

1236 Josselson, Michael and Diana Josselson. The Commander. A
      Life of Barclay de Tolly. Oxford: Oxford University
      Press, 275pp., bib. 253-62.
      This work does not include a separate chapter on Alexander
      I, but as a scholarly assessment of the career of General
      Barclay de Tolly, who served Alexander as Minister of War,
      it merits consultation for insight into Alexander's clash with
      Napoleon. DK190.6.B37J6

1237 Kelen, Betty. "The Holy Alliance." The Mistresses. The
      Domestic Scandals of 19th Century Monarchs. London: W.
      H. Allen, 1966, 20-50.
      An account of Alexander I's relationship with Julie de Krud-
      ener and the influence which she exerted upon him. Kelen
      maintains that Krudener was not only the source of Alexan-
      der's new found Christianity but also was responsible for
      instilling in him the principles from which sprang the Holy
      Alliance. Also receiving attention is the theory that Alex-
      ander orchestrated a death scene for himself as a means of
      slipping away to Siberia to live there in isolation absorbed
      in religious contemplation. D352.1.K4

1238 A Key to the Recent Conduct of the Emperor of Russia. Lon-
      don: Jordan and Maxwell, 1807, 68pp.
      Unavailable for annotation.

1239 *Knapton, E. J. "The Origins of the Treaty of Holy Alliance."
      Hist, 26, no. 102 (1941): 132-40.
      An argument that the 16 September 1815 Treaty of Holy Al-
      liance is best understood when placed within the general con-
      text of European religious and humanistic trends current at
      the close of the eighteenth century and viewed as a reflec-
      tion of Alexander I's long standing vision of a new European
      order. Knapton traces the 1804-15 evolution of this vision
      as a means of discrediting the thesis that the Alliance was
      the eccentric product of a tsar turned mystic under the in-
      fluence of Baroness Krudener.

1240 Knollys, W. W. "Memoirs of General Rochechouart." Edinb R,
      178 (Oct. 1893): 375-404.
      A review of the French language publication of the memoirs
      of an officer who served as an aide-de-camp to Alexander I
      during Russia's 1812-14 campaign against Napoleonic France.

1241 Krok, Joseph, E. "Talleyrand and the Foreign Policy of Alex-
      ander I." Pennsylvania State University, 1975. (disserta-
      tion)

1242 *Laserson, Max. The American Impact on Russia--Diplomatic
      and Ideological--1784-1917. New York: Macmillan, 1950,
      441pp.
      Although this study does not contain a titled section on
      Alexander I, it includes, particularly in chapters five and
      six, a discussion of his relationship with T. Jefferson and
      J. Q. Adams, the influence of the American political example
      on the deliberations of the Unofficial Committee, the normali-
      zation of diplomatic and commercial relations between Russia
      and the United States, and the cooling of those relations as
      a consequence of Alexander's conservative policies at home
      and provocative actions in the northwest region of America.
      E183.8.R9L35

1243 Lobanov-Rostovsky, Andrei A. Russia and Europe, 1789-1825.
      Durham, North Carolina: Duke University Press, 1947,
      448pp., bib. 428-33.
      This study does not focus on Alexander I specifically, but as
      a scholarly treatment of Russia's relations with Europe in the
      first quarter of the nineteenth century it is a useful source
      of information for the student of Alexander's foreign affairs.
      The author is particularly attentive to Alexander's relations
      with Napoleon. DK197.L6

1244 *MacMillan, David S. "Russo-British Trade Relations Under
      Alexander I." Can Am Slav S, 9, no. 4 (1975): 437-48.
      An examination of the books and memoranda of the Russia
      Company of London for insight into trade relations between
      England and the Russia of Alexander I. MacMillan devotes

most attention to determining the source of Alexander I's
"new 'hard' attitude" toward trade with the British. He concludes that "the policies adapted by Russia in 1806-10 were
not merely temporary aberrations, the result of rapprochement with Napoleon, but the expression of principles which
the tsar had come to hold firmly," namely that Russia should
no longer serve as a cheap source of raw materials for Britain
and other European powers and Russian industry should be
protected by stiff tariffs.

1245   *Mazour, A.   "The Russian-American, and Anglo-Russian
       Conventions, 1824-1825: An Interpretation." Pacif Hist R,
       14, no. 3 (1945): 303-10.
       An analysis of why Alexander I was so lenient in the 17 April
       1824 and 28 February 1825 conventions delimiting Russian ter-
       ritorial claims in the New World. Mazour maintains that:
       "the main reason for this sacrifice was that the imperial
       government had greater stakes to fight for on the European
       continent than on the American continent and thus for the
       latter it exhibited ony occasional crocodile affection."

1246   Mitchell, Donald W.   "Naval Policy of Alexander I." HRSSP
       (gen. study), 113-34.
       Following an account of naval operations during Russia's
       wars with Napoleonic France, Sweden (1807-09), and Turkey
       (1806-12), this study focuses upon Alexander I's neglect of
       the contributions made by his fleet commanders, and the
       deterioration of the size and quality of the Russian fleet
       during the last decade of his reign as a consequence of his
       lack of appreciation for naval matters.

1247   *Morley, Charles.   "Alexander I and Czartoryski. The Polish
       Question from 1801 to 1813." Slavonic E Eur R, 25, no. 65
       (1947): 405-26.
       An examination of Alexander I's position on the question of
       Polish independence and of the attempt of Foreign Minister
       A. Czartoryski to influence Alexander on this matter. Morley
       concentrates on Czartoryski's efforts to persuade Alexander
       to serve as "the protector of the weak and oppressed" in
       Europe and to restore Poland as a sovereign state. Alexander
       was unwilling to accept the idea of Poland existing as a nation
       apart from Russia but did see merit in improving the political
       status of Poland as a component part of the Russian Empire.
       The resultant liberal constitution which he granted to the
       Kingdom of Poland, Morley states, was welcomed warmly by
       the majority of Poles, but Alexander's soon to follow turn
       toward reactionary policies caused Russo-Polish relations to
       sour abruptly.

1248   _____.   "Czartoryski as a Polish Statesman." Slav R, 30,
       no. 3 (1971): 606-14.

As part of a discussion of the diplomatic career of Prince
Adam Czartoryski this article touches upon Czartoryski's
relationship with and influence on Alexander I, especially
in regard to the tsar's policy toward Poland.

1249 *_____. "Czartoryski's Attempts at a New Foreign Policy
Under Alexander I." ASEER, 12 (Dec. 1953): 475-85.
A discussion of Foreign Minister Adam Czartoryski's efforts
to inaugurate a new era in European international relations
by founding Russia's foreign policy on "the principles of
equity" and "the law of nations." Morely asserts that Alexander I, in his initial years as emperor, appeared to be
sympathetic with the concepts espoused by Czartoryski, but
Alexander's inherent indecisiveness proved to be an insurmountable obstacle to the effective implementation of Czartoryski's ideas.

1250 Nagengast, William E. "Moscow, the Stalingrad of 1812:
American Reaction Toward Napoleon's Retreat from Russia."
Rus R, 8, no. 4 (1949): 302-15.
A review of the mixed American reaction to news of Napoleon's
1812 retreat from Moscow. Nagengast states Russia was both
"hailed as the world's deliverer against an all-powerful militaristic dictatorship" and "damned for its despotism and bar-
barism."

1251 *Nichols, Irby C., Jr. "The Eastern Question and the Vienna
Conference, September 1822." J Cent Eur Aff, 21, no. 1
(1961): 53-66.
An analysis of the sources of Alexander I's neutral stance in
regard to the Greco-Turkish War. Nichols states that both
Britain and Austria, at the Vienna Conference, sought to
prevent Russian intervention by appealing to Alexander's
idealism by reminding him of his solemn commitment to the
peaceful resolution of potential military conflicts. Although
the offensive policies of Turkey and pro-war sentiment in
Russia caused Alexander to waver in his pacifism, the Anglo-
Austrian peace keeping efforts combined with Alexander's
sincere dislike of war and his suspicion that the Greek cause
was "tainted with Jacobinism" led him to refrain from inter-
vening on the Greeks' behalf.

1252 *_____. "The Russian Ukase and the Monroe Doctrine:
A Revaluation." Pacif Hist R, 36, no. 1 (1967): 13-26.
A discussion of Alexander I's motives for issuing and then
later revoking the 1821 ukase which announced restrictions
on foreign travel to Russia's northwestern American territory.
Nichols maintains that Alexander conceived and abrogated the
ukase with purely Russian interests in mind and that neither
American protests nor the recently established Monroe Doctrine
had anything to do with his decision.

1253 *_____. "Tsar Alexander I: Pacifist, Aggressor, or Vacil-
      lator?" E Eur Q, 16, no. 1 (1982): 33-44.
      A review of the conflicting interpretations of Alexander I's
      policy toward Turkey, and a renewed claim that Alexander
      was not plotting a war against the sultan in 1825, as some
      analysts have maintained. Nichols contends that Alexander
      was firmly committed to preserving the peace and security of
      Europe and that the ambivalence and vacillation which char-
      acterized his policies were due to his "suffering-hero person-
      ality" and consequent unstable mental condition rather than
      to any lack of conviction on his part.

1254 Nicolson, Harold. The Congress of Vienna. A Study in Allied
      Unity. New York: Viking Press, 1963 (reprint of 1946 edi-
      tion), 312pp., bib. 297-99.
      This survey of coalition and congress politics in the 1812-22
      period does not contain a separate chapter on Alexander I
      but includes numerous references to his dealings with Rus-
      sia's allies. Receiving most attention are Alexander's Polish
      policy, his negotiation of the Treaty of Fontainebleau, and
      his relationship with various prominent personalities and
      leaders of the age, especially William Pitt, Baroness von
      Krudener, Talleyrand, and Louis XVIII. DC249.N5

1255 Niven, Alexander C. Napoleon and Alexander I: A Study in
      Franco-Russian Relations, 1807-1812. Washington, D.C.:
      University Press of America, 83pp.
      Unavailable for annotation.

1256 *Oliva, L. Jay, ed. "Alexander and Europe: 1801-1825."
      RW (anthology), 60-88.
      A series of brief excerpts from the writings of Alexander I,
      his contemporaries, and various secondary sources illuminat-
      ing his foreign and domestic policies. Included are observa-
      tions by A. Czartoryski, on Alexander's educational back-
      ground and initial foreign policy, and excerpts from E. Tarle
      on Napoleon's retreat from Moscow, A. Lobanov-Rostovsky on
      Alexander's diplomacy, M. Zetlin on the growth of secret
      societies during Alexander's reign, K. Waliszewski on Alex-
      ander's character, and M. Raeff on Alexander's constitution-
      alism.

1257 Penny, Freeland F. Alexander I of Russia. New York:
      Reproduced from typewritten copy, 1942, 22pp.
      A popular account of the "trials and errors" of Alexander I's
      foreign policy. DK195.P4

1258 *Perkins, Dexter. "Russia and the Spanish Colonies, 1817-
      1818." Am Hist R, 28, no. 4 (1923): 656-72.
      A sympathetic examination of Alexander I's attitude toward
      the pacification of the Spanish colonies. Perkins defends

Alexander against those who see ulterior motives behind his 1817 memorandum on the Spanish colonial question and asserts instead that Alexander, in attempting to reconcile the conflicting views of Britain and Spain on this issue, only sought "to practise that concert of action which he preached." If Alexander was guilty of anything in his reconciliation efforts, Perkins concludes, it was excessive idealism.

1259 *Reinerman, Alan J. "Metternich, Alexander I and the Russian Challenge in Italy, 1815-20." J Mod Hist, 46, no. 2 (1974): 262-76.
An argument that Alexander I's policy in Italy during 1815-20 was not an impulsive one motivated by any emotional commitment to liberal principles but rather was "rationally conceived in terms of Russia's interests as a great power." Reinerman notes that Alexander may have cherished "a certain sympathy for the liberal-nationalist cause" but his main goal in Italy (as Metternich correctly perceived) was "the overthrow of Austrian hegemony" as a means of lessening Austria's international reputation and "weakening her ability to resist Russia elsewhere." Similarly, Reinerman asserts, Alexander's decision (1818-19) to reverse this policy was not due to any lack of commitment on his part or to the machinations of Metternich but was simply a consequence of his realization that the revolutionary revival underway in Italy was potentially harmful to Russia's best interests.

1260 Russell, Bertrand, A. W. R., 3rd Earl. "The Holy Alliance." Freedom Versus Organization, 1814-1914. New York: W. W. Norton, 1934, 43-55.
A discussion of Alexander I's conception of the Holy Alliance as "the application to politics of the great religious truths which he had learnt from the Baroness Krudener." Russell also reviews the part played by Alexander in the reactionary application of the principles of the Holy Alliance in the 1815-19 period." D358.R8

1261 _____. "Napoleon's Successors" and "The Congress of Vienna." Ibid., 16-30.
A favorable presentation of the character, intellect, and leadership qualities of Alexander I, and a discussion of his role in the 1814-15 negotiations at the Congress of Vienna. Russell maintains that Alexander was more than a match for Metternich, Castlereagh, and Talleyrand, and that he deserves credit for the positive features of the Vienna peace, namely the lenient treatment of France and "the establishment of an international government as a means of preserving peace." D358.R8

1262 Saul, Norman E. Russia and the Mediterranean 1797-1801. Chicago: University of Chicago Press, 1970, 268pp., bib.

229-256.
Although the vast majority of this work focuses upon the
reign of Paul I, it includes some discussion of Alexander I's
policies in the Mediterranean. Saul traces Alexander's initial
attempt, in 1801, to disentangle Russia from Mediterranean
affairs, the confused and contradictory course of Russian
policy in that area in the 1802-07 period, and the reasons
for Russia's abrupt withdrawal from Mediterranean involvement in 1807. He concludes that "Russia's surprisingly complete withdrawal from the Mediterranean at Tilsit was a logical move" given Alexander's desire to maintain positive relations with the Ottoman Empire as means of keeping the
Straits open for Russian naval traffic. DK186.S28

1263 *Scherer, Stephen P. "Alexander I, the Prussian Royal
      Couple, and European Politics: 1801-1807." Mich Acad,
      13, no. 1 (1980): 37-44.
      An argument that the personal friendship established between
      Alexander I and the Prussian royal couple (King Frederick
      William III and Queen Louise) at their June 1802 meeting at
      Memel exerted a powerful influence on the diplomatic rela-
      tions of these two nations and their dealings with Napoleonic
      France. Scherer examines Russo-Prussian relations in the
      1802-07 period as he argues that the sovereigns' relation-
      ship was instrumental in "preventing Prussia's entry into a
      French-Prussian alliance," solving peacefully "the vexing
      problem of a passage of Russian forces across Prussia,"
      promoting Russo-Prussian cooperation against France, and
      in Alexander's preservation of Prussia from "political anni-
      hilation at the hands of Napoleon."

1264 *Schmitt, Hans A. "1812: Stein, Alexander I and the
      Crusade Against Napoleon." J Mod Hist, 31, no. 4 (1959):
      325-28.
      An investigation of German influence on Alexander I's de-
      cision to carry his war against Napoleonic France beyond
      Russia's borders. Schmitt disagrees with the interpretation
      that the exiled German patriot Baron von Stein was responsi-
      ble for this decision, and argues instead that Alexander
      merely used Stein as a consultant on German affairs and,
      quite naturally, relied upon him for assistance in implement-
      ing, but not designing, the decision to pursue the retreat-
      ing French army.

1265 Scott, Richenda C. Quakers in Russia. London: Michael
      Joseph, 1964, 302pp.
      Chapters three to five in this study contain a discussion of
      Alexander I's relationship with a number of prominent British
      Quakers, most notably William Allen and Daniel Wheeler. Allen
      attended to Alexander's needs while the latter was in London
      in June of 1814; Wheeler was commissioned in 1817 by

Alexander to draw up and implement a plan to reclaim the desolate marshlands which surrounded St. Petersburg. For a discussion of Wheeler's experiences in Russia, see MRTFE (anthology), 197-210. BX7710.R8S35

1266   Shupp, Paul F. The European Powers and the Near Eastern Question 1806-1807. New York: Columbia University Press, 1931, 576pp., bib. 559-66.
This work does not contain a separate chapter on Alexander I, but as a comprehensive and scholarly study of the great powers' Near Eastern policies during the period between the Treaties of Pressburg and Tilsit it warrants consultation. D374.S5

1267   Tarasulo, Yitzhak Y. "The Napoleonic Invasion of 1812 and the Political and Social Crisis in Russia." Yale University, 1983. (dissertation)

1268   Tarsaidzé, Alexandre. "Diplomatic Mélange." CP (gen. study), 45-59.
A general review of the development of friendly relations between Russia and America during the reign of Alexander I.

1269   *Thackeray, Frank W. Antecedents of Revolution: Alexander I and the Polish Kingdom, 1815-1825. New York: Columbia University Press, 1980, 197pp., bib. 182-92.
A scholarly exploration of the evolution, execution, and impact of Alexander I's Polish policy. Thackeray states that although Alexander pursued several different strategies in his dealings with Poland, his goal remained constant--the maintenance of Russian domination over Poland. Thackeray thus views Alexander's initial conciliatory measures toward Poland as merely an attempt to lessen Polish opposition to Russian hegemony, just as his later (post-1820) repressive Polish policy was an attempt to maintain that same hegemony through means more palatable to the Russian gentry and more consistent with his own increasingly conservative views. Thackeray concludes that although Alexander succeeded in maintaining Russian domination over Poland, "this achievement lacked any permanency and, in fact, contained the seeds of its own destruction." DK4351.T48
   Reviewed in:
   Am Hist R, 86, no. 4 (1981): 884-85
   Can Slavonic P, 23, no. 3 (1981): 340-41
   Slav R, 40, no. 4 (1981): 663

1270   _____. "Alexander I and the Polish Congress Kingdom: A Study in Russo-Polish Relations, 1815-1825." Temple University, 1977. (dissertation)

1271   *West, Dalton A.   "The Russian Military Under Alexander I."
       J. G. Purves and D. A. West, eds.   War and Society in the
       Nineteenth Century Russian Empire.   Toronto: New Review
       Books, 1972, 45-58.   Also in New R, 11 (1971):   45-58.
       A discussion of the rapid growth of the Russian armed forces
       and the institutions that supplied and administered them dur-
       ing the reign of Alexander I.   As West chronicles this growth
       in its various forms, he links it not only to the exigencies of
       war but more generally to the extension of governmental ac-
       tivities which accompanied Alexander's program of reform.
       He concludes that by 1825 the military had evolved into "a
       complex and sometimes hydra-headed establishment which
       penetrated into and coloured the entire fabric of Russian
       society" and had become "less the personal instrument of
       the monarch and more the first institution of state."
       DK189.37

1272   *Zawadzki, W.   "The Czartoryski Archive: An Important
       Source for the History of Russia and Poland in the Reign of
       Alexander I."   Can Am Slav S, 9, no. 4 (1975):   472-80.
       The stated purpose of this article is "to offer some guidance
       as to the contents of those of Czartoryski's papers that are
       relevant to the study of Russian international and foreign
       affairs, and of Russo-Polish relations in particular under
       Alexander I."   To this end, Zawadzki presents a list of over
       100 manuscripts in the Czartoryski Archive dealing with
       Alexander and his reign.   The author urges scholars to
       make more extensive use of this archive than they have in
       the past.

GENERAL STUDIES AND ASSESSMENTS/
PERSONAL AFFAIRS AND CHARACTER

1273 Abbott, John S. "Nicholas." Kings and Queens, or Life in
the Palace. New York: Harper and Brothers, 1848, 147-92.
A contemporaneous survey of the domestic policies of Nicholas I precedes an argument that the idea of gaining control
of the straits to the Black Sea became an obsession for
Nicholas who viewed their acquisition as an essential step
towards Russia's "political and commercial ascendency in the
Eastern hemisphere." Abbott warns of the threat posed by
the growth of Russian power and calls for a united front of
European nations to check the tsar's ambitions. D352.1.A3

1274 Adams, Ezra Eastman. The Dead Lion; or, A Discourse on the
Death of Nicholas. Boston: Stove and Halpine, 1855, 20pp.
Unavailable for annotation.

1275 Alexandra Feodorowna, Empress of Russia. A Czarina's Story.
Being an Account of the Early Married Life of the Emperor
Nicholas I of Russia Written by His Wife. Una Pope-Hennessy,
trans./intro. London: Nicholson and Watson, 1948, 61pp.
An anecdotal account of Nicholas I's personality, relations
with family members, and attendance at various court functions while grand duke; based on the 1817-20 memoirs of his
wife, Alexandra. DK210.7.A32

1276 "Anecdotal Memoirs by a Former Page of the Emperor Nicholas."
Cath W, 7 (1868): 683-99.
A series of disconnected observations on court life, the imperial family, the behavior and character of Nicholas I,
and public reaction to his death.

1277 Bourke, Richard S. St. Petersburg to Moscow: A Visit to
the Court of the Czar. New York: Arno Press, 1970 (reprint of 1846 edition). DK25.M43
Unavailable for annotation.

1278 Bremner, Robert. Excursions into the Interior of Russia:
      Including a Sketch of the Character and Policy of the Em-
      peror Nicholas, 2 Vols. London, 1839.
      Unavailable for annotation.

1279 "The Career of Nicholas." Liv Age, 45 (21 Apr. 1855): 171-
      73.
      An obituary stressing Nicholas I's despotic rule and aggres-
      sive Near Eastern policy.

1280 "The Change of Czars." Liv Age, 45 (28 Apr. 1855): 246-47.
      A brief statement on the domestic and military problems be-
      queathed by Nicholas I to Alexander II.

1281 Christmas, Rev. Henry. Lives of the Emperor of Russia,
      Nicholas I and the Sultan of Turkey, Abdul Medjid Khan.
      London: John Farquhar Shaw, 1854, 168pp.
      An examination of the character of Nicholas I, the policies
      which he pursued, and the qualities of Russia as a society.
      Christmas asserts that Western analysts should not attempt
      to evaluate Nicholas' policies from a European perspective
      since Russia as a nation consists of a world unique unto
      itself. Given the generally backward condition of the nation
      and the nobility's opposition to progressive reform, Christ-
      mas contends, the harshness of Nicholas' rule is understand-
      able. However, the author considers Nicholas' foreign policy
      to be completely indefensible since it was founded upon
      crude territorial aggrandizement and neglect for "every law
      of common honour." Writing amidst the Russophobia that
      swept Europe during the early 1850s, Christmas concludes
      that the Crimean War should be viewed as a noble and
      righteous effort to prevent the spread of tsarist absolutism
      to lands where it is wholly unsuited. DK210.C5

1282 Crankshaw, Edward. "Chapters 1-8." The Shadow of the
      Winter Palace. New York: Viking Press, 1976, 13-151.
      A discussion of Nicholas I's failure to deal with Russia's
      internal problems and his errors in leading Russia into the
      disastrous Crimean War. Crankshaw maintains that while
      Nicholas was sincere in his desire to rationalize autocracy,
      "the system he constructed was calculated almost to perfec-
      tion to increase the alienation of men of talent, goodwill and
      critical intelligence, and to deliver the business of justice
      and administration into the suffocating toils of an underpaid
      bureaucracy." DK189.C66

1283 *Custine, Marquis de. The Empire of the Czar, or Observations
      on the Social, Political, and Religious State and Prospects of
      Russia, 3 Vols. London: Longman, Brown, Green and Long-
      mans, 1843. The first English language translation of Russia
      in 1839. For an abridged version see Journey for Our Time.

Phyllis Penn Kohler, ed./trans. London: George Prior,
1980, 240pp.
A classic critical commentary on Russian institutions, society,
and culture under Nicholas I. Custine describes the Nicholas
system as a type of militarized despotism in which brutality,
deceit, censorship, and inhumanity reigned supreme. The
Russian church, nobility, and bureaucracy also receive criticism particularly for their attempt to conceal the true nature
of conditions throughout the country. When referring to
Nicholas by name, rather than the monarchy as an institution, Custine generally refrains from critical comment, but
his grim account of conditions in Russia blackened the emperor's reputation and contributed to the deterioration of
Russia's image in Western Europe and to the growth of Russophobia. DK25.C98
For a cogent assessment of Custine's views and their impact, see George Kennan's The Marquis de Custine and His
Russia in 1839. Princeton, N.J.: Princeton University
Press, 1971, 145pp. (DK25.C986K45).
For a discussion of Custine's criticism as a re-echoing of
"the fears and observations of the age in which he lived,"
see Oscar J. Hammer's "Free Europe versus Russia, 1830-
1854." ASEER, 11, no. 1 (1952): 27-41.

1284 "The Czar Nicholas." Nat R, 6 (Jan. 1858): 147-72. Reprinted in the Eclectic R, 43 (Mar. 1858): 289-304, under
the title "The Character and Times of the Emperor Nicholas."
A synthesis of the views expressed in the works of Korff,
Haxthausen, Golovine, Schnitzler, and Custine in regard to
the character and government of Nicholas I and the Russia
over which he ruled. Although critical of Nicholas' Polish
and Turkish policies and the corrupt and despotic nature of
the bureaucracy which exercised power in his name, the
author concludes that given the scope of the domestic problems which Nicholas faced and the negative qualities inherent
in autocracy as a political system Nicholas was an effective
and basically benevolent ruler.

1285 "Czar Nicholas I and the French Actress." Bentley M, 37
(Mar. 1855): 267-77.
Unavailable for annotation.

1286 Dallas, George M. Diary of George Mifflin Dallas. United
States Minister to Russia 1837-1839. New York: Arno Press,
1970 (reprint of 1892 edition), 214pp.
This work contains a number of references to Nicholas I,
particularly in regard to his fondness for unannounced military and administrative inspections, plan for the emancipation
of the serfs, behavior at military parades and court functions,
and, most notably, his reaction to the accidental burning
of the Winter Palace. However, the lack of an index and

a table of contents makes it difficult to locate specific references to Nicholas.   DK210.D33

1287   Dawson, George. The Death of the Czar. A Discourse:
Delivered at the Church of the Saviour, March 4, 1855.
London: R. Theobald, 1855, 8pp.
Unavailable for annotation.

1288   "Death of Nicholas." Liv Age, 45 (21 Apr.-28 Apr. 1855):
129-30, 170-71, 173-74, 185-87, 248-50; (5 May-19 May):
271-72, 423-31.
A series of articles which appeared in various British newspapers and periodicals upon Nicholas I's death which collectively deal with his policies and accomplishments, the circumstances of his death, and the nature of the Russia which he bequeathed to Alexander II.

1289   Dow, Richard A. and R. L. Wilson. "The Czar's Colts."
Nineteenth C, 6, no. 4 (1980): 34-37.
A description of three Colt revolvers presented to Nicholas I by manufacturer Samuel Colt in 1854.

1290   "The Emperor Nicholas." New Mo M, 52 (Apr. 1855): 489-
500.
An obituary which highlights Nicholas I's support of Russia's laws and cruel punishment of those who violated them to any degree.

1291   "The Emperor Nicholas." Quar R, 96 (Mar. 1855): 493-508.
Also in Liv Age, 45 (26 May 1855): 470-76.
A sketch of the general features of Nicholas I's character and reign, and a detailed account of his illness and death.
Based upon two French language studies of Nicholas and his Russia: Anon., La Vérité sur l'Empereur Nicolas, Histoire intime de sa vie et de son Regne, 1854, and Gallet de Kulture, Le Tzar Nicolas et la Sainte Russie, 1855.

1292   "The Emperor Nicholas, His Nobles, Serfs and Servants."
New Mo M, 70 (1844): 477-93.
A description of the various social strata in Russian society of the mid-nineteenth century, and a critical review of Nicholas' reign and character stressing his harsh and unforgiving nature.

1292   "The Emperor Nicholas and the Present Government of Russia."
Am Eclectic, 1, no. 3 (1841): 411-27; 2, no. 1 (1841):
53-67.
A highly critical assessment of Nicholas I's character and the domestic and foreign policies he pursued in the first fifteen years of his reign. The author maintains that Nicholas, far from being the amiable sovereign described by foreign

observers who focused on his family life and the benevolent
features of his stern rule, was exceptionally cruel by nature,
a character trait which explains the evil and ferocious quality
of the policies which he pursued against his own people and
neighboring states. Cited as examples of such policies are
Nicholas' harsh treatment of Poland, his religious intolerance,
imposition of censorship, and maintenance of a corrupt and
venal administrative and legal system. The author concludes
that of all the rulers in Russia's history "not one has been
so reckless a destroyer of human life by every variety of
means" as Nicholas I.

1294   Gilson, Adrian. "The Czar Nicholas." The Czar and the Sul-
       tan, or Nicholas and Abdul Medjid. New York: Harper and
       Brothers, 1853, 11-61.
       A biographical sketch of Nicholas I, prompted by heightened
       Western interest in Russia and its leader as a consequence
       of the Crimean War. Gilson states that in his work "there
       will be found no trace of political bias" nor any analysis of
       the individuals and events described but rather a straight-
       forward description of the rulers who were locked in combat
       in the East. Though Gilson is reasonably fair in describing
       the conservative domestic policies pursued by Nicholas, he
       sees Russia's Eastern policy as an aggressive one aimed at
       tilting in Russia's favor the entire balance of power in Europe.

1295   *Golovine, Ivan. Russia Under the Autocrat, Nicholas the
       First. Harry Schwartz, intro. New York: Praeger,
       1970 (reprint of 1846 edition), 695pp.
       Described in an introduction by Harry Schwartz as "a gold
       mine of colorful and detailed information about the Russia of
       Nicholas I," this work does indeed warrant consultation for
       critical observations on both Nicholas and his reign. Golo-
       vine (1816-90), a political exile from Nicholas' Russia, at-
       tacks the Russian nobility for having traded freedom for
       privilege and position. He condemns the church for servili-
       ty, the government for being corrupt and rapacious, the
       legal system for being immoral and arbitrary, and Nicholas I
       for using every repressive tool conceivable to maintain a
       despotic state. Golovine describes Nicholas as being poorly
       educated, limited in natural ability, inadequate as a military
       commander, and devoid of courage and compassion.
       DK211.G62

1296   "Grimm, August Theodor Von. Alexandra Feodorowna. Em-
       press of Russia. 2 Vols. Lady Wallace, trans. Edinburgh:
       Edmonston and Douglas, 1870.
       A highly favorable account of the life of Empress Alexandra,
       the devoted wife of Nicholas I. Grimm states that "the chief
       aim of the book is to show that, after the accession of Nicho-
       las I, the womanly charms of the Empress Alexandra Feodorow-
       na cast, for 30 years, over the domestic life at the Winter

Palace, a dignity and a halo such as never previously existed
in the Russian court.... Politics and military affairs are
entirely excluded from this work, or at least only cursorily
alluded to when influencing family life." Drawing heavily
on his personal acquaintance with the empress over a fifteen
year span, Grimm relates anecdotes and incidents concerning
Nicholas' relations with his father, brothers, and children,
his character, personality and constitution, and reaction to
such events as the Decembrist Revolt, Polish uprising, and
the burning of the Winter Palace. DK210.7.G7

1297 *Grunwald, Constantine de. Tsar Nicholas I. Brigit Patmore,
      trans. London: Douglas Saunders with MacGibbon and Kee,
      1954, 294pp.
      A dispassionate discussion of Nicholas I and his reign. Grun-
      wald discusses Nicholas' personality, character, and domestic
      policies but devotes primary attention to his foreign policy,
      all with an eye on presenting Nicholas as a natural product
      of his upbringing and times rather than as an inherently
      cruel autocrat. Grunwald accepts as his own the judgment
      of Nicholas' Polish page who described the tsar as "a bizarre
      mixture of defects and qualities, of meanness and greatness,
      brutal and chivalrous, courageous to foolhardiness and
      faint-hearted as a poltroon, just, yet tyrannical, generous
      and cruel, fond of ostentation and liking simplicity." Grun-
      wald adds that "the personality of Nicholas is of particular
      interest because in him absolutism is shown in its purest
      form." DK210.G72
          Reviewed in:
          Am Hist R, 61 (1956): 1035-36
          Ann Am Acad, 301 (1956): 184
          Jew Soc S, 19 (1957): 151
          J Cent Eur Aff, 16 (1956-57): 289
          Rus R, 15, no. 1 (1956): 70
          Slav R, 15, no. 4 (1956): 553-54

1298 Gurowski, Count A. "The Czar Nicholas." Russia As It Is.
      New York: D. Appleton and Company, 1854, 44-68.
      A grim picture of Nicholas' Russia as a nation burdened by
      administrative inefficiency, economic waste, and cultural back-
      wardness. Gurowski asserts that Nicholas' personal approach
      to ruling Russia, far from ameliorating any of these defi-
      ciencies, only created additional difficulties because he had
      neither the intelligence nor energy to rule Russia alone.
      His "military mania" and costly and shortsighted policies,
      Gurowski concludes, only served to sow the seeds for the
      destruction of absolutism in Russia. DK211.G3

1299 *Hammer, Oscar J. "Free Europe Versus Russia, 1830-1854."
      ASEER, 11, no. 1 (1952): 27-41.
      A discussion of Custine's critical account of conditions in

Russia under Nicholas I as a re-echoing of "the fears and
observations of the age in which he lived." Hammer places
Custine's work within the context of the European Russophobia that developed in response to Nicholas' use of military
force to counter the spread of liberalism and his pursuit of
a domestic policy which "seemed to place Russia in opposition
to European civilization itself."

1300 Harrison, Robert. Notes on a Nine Years' Residence in Russia,
from 1844 to 1853. London: T. C. Newby, 1855, 310pp.
An account of social and economic conditions in Russia during
the reign of Nicholas I, and an assessment of Nicholas'
personal characteristics and leadership. Harrison describes
Nicholas as a man of mediocre intelligence and limited ability
as a statesman and military commander who in an attempt
"to exercise a personal supervision over the whole country
... reduced the entire system of government to one of military uniformity and routine." Harrison concludes that the
fruit of Nicholas' despotic internal rule and aggressive foreign policy represents "a decisive condemnation of the form
of government called 'absolute,' a system in which Nicholas
had placed entire confidence for the regeneration of his
country." DK211.H32

1301 Henningsen, Charles F. Revelations of Russia; or the Emperor
Nicholas and His Empire in 1844, by One Who Has Seen and
Describes. 2 Vols. London: H. Colburn, 1844. DK25.H495
Unavailable for annotation.

1302 Herzen, Alexander. My Past and Thoughts. The Memoirs of
Alexander Herzen. 4 Vols., Constance Garnett, trans.
Isaiah Berlin, intro. New York: Knopf, 1968.
This work does not contain a separate chapter on Nicholas
I, but as the memoirs of a leading representative of the
Russian intelligentsia of the mid-nineteenth century it con-
stitutes a valuable source of information and insight on the
Russia of Nicholas I. To quote Isaiah Berlin's introduction,
"civilized, imaginative, self-critical, Herzen was a marvellous-
ly gifted social observer; the record of what he saw is unique
even in the articulate 19th century." DK209.H4A33

1303 Hodgetts, E. A. Brayley. "Nicholas I." The Court of Russia
in the Nineteenth Century, Vol. I. New York: Charles
Scribner's Sons, 1908, 141-303.
An undocumented review of the life, character, policies, and
accomplishments of Nicholas I; balanced and readable, but
nonanalytical. DK189.H75

1304 *Jackman, S. W., ed. Romanov Relations. The Private Correspondence of Tsar Alexander I, Nicholas I and the Grand
Dukes Constantine and Michael with Their Sister Anna Pavlona.

London: Macmillan and Company, 1969, 375pp.
The royal correspondences included in this volume show
Nicholas I to have been a well-educated, sensitive man who
cared deeply for his family, took his duties seriously, and
had difficulty understanding why he was not more appreciated
by his subjects and the political leaders of Europe.
DK188.J313

1305 Krasinski, Count Henryk. Private Anecdotes of the Late and
      Present Emperors of Russia, the King of Prussia, and the
      Sultan. London: Wells, 1858.
      Unavailable for annotation.

1306 Labenskii, Ksaverii K. A Russian's Reply to the Marquis de
      Custine's "Russia in 1839." London: T. C. Newby, 1844,
      164pp.
      A critical review of Custine's negative assessment of condi-
      tions in the Russia of Nicholas I. DK25.C988

1307 Lagny, Germain de. The Russians or, The Muscovite Empire,
      the Czar, and His People. John Bridgeman, trans. New
      York: Arno Press (reprint of 1854 edition), 266pp.
      A critical account of the nature of Russian society and culture
      during Nicholas' reign, written amidst the Crimean War.
      Lagny describes Russia as a crude, corrupt, and barbarous
      kingdom thoroughly out of tune with the mainstream of Eu-
      ropean culture. Given the primitive conditions which pre-
      vailed in the Russia of this era, Lagny concludes, the harsh-
      ness of Nicholas I's rule is understandable. Nicholas himself
      most likely realized that his subjects were "incapable of liv-
      ing under a regimen more in harmony with the precepts of
      the Gospel." DK189.L3313

1308 *Layton, Susan. "Mind of the Tyrant: Tolstoj's Nicholas and
      Solženicyn's Stalin." Slav E Eur J, 23, no. 4 (1979): 479-
      90.
      A comparison of the highly critical image of Nicholas I pre-
      sented by Tolstoy in Hadji Murat to that of Stalin as presented
      by Solzhenitsyn in The First Circle. Layton also examines
      critically Nicholas' policy toward Russia's minorities, especial-
      ly the Chechens.

1309 Leary, D. B. "Nicholas I. 1825-1855." EAR (gen. study),
      57-66.
      A general review of the repressive qualities of Nicholas I's
      autocratic rule with most attention devoted to his educational
      policies and the reaction of literate Russians to his conserva-
      tism.

1310 *Lincoln, W. B. "God, the Emperor Nicholas I, and the Rev-
      olutions of 1848: A Young Russian's Fantasy Account."
      Slavonic E Eur R, 51 (Jan. 1973): 95-106.

The Russian and French language texts of a contemporaneous
fantasization of the 1848 revolutions, written by A. E. Tsimmerman, which satirizes the reactionary government of Nicholas I.

1311 *_____. Nicholas I. Emperor and Autocrat of All the Rus-
       sias. Bloomington: Indiana University Press, 1978, 424pp.,
       bib. 394-414.
       The stated purpose of this scholarly study is "to present a
       more favorable and balanced historical perspective of Nicho-
       las I" so as to counter the inordinately critical works which
       have most typically been written about the emperor and his
       reign. Lincoln portrays Nicholas as a remarkably dedicated
       and energetic ruler in the mold of Russia's dynamic sover-
       eigns of past centuries who sought to make autocracy as ef-
       ficient and effective a form of government as possible. Well
       aware of the inertia and corruption which characterized the
       Russian bureaucracy, Nicholas believed that to accomplish
       anything noteworthy it would be necessary for him "to take
       power and the resolution of all problems into his hands
       alone." Unfortunately for Russia, Lincoln concludes, Nicho-
       las failed to realize that "devotion to duty and confidence in
       the righteousness of his purpose were not enough, and the
       phenomenon of 18th century absolutism expressed in the per-
       son of the Russian autocrat" was no longer a viable form of
       government in a world as complex and diverse as nineteenth-
       century Europe. DK210.L56
         Reviewed in:
         Economist, 267 (24 July 1978): 130
         Historian, 42 (Feb. 1980): 337
         Slav R, 38 (1979): 109-10
         Spectator, 240 (24 June 1978): 19
         TLS, (6 Oct. 1978): 1112

1312 MacDonald, Dwight. "Bureaucratic Culture: Nicholas I and
       Josef I." Politics, 5 (Spring 1948): 109-13.
       A presentation of a series of parallels between the regimes
       of Nicholas I and Joseph Stalin. MacDonald discusses simi-
       larities between the two leaders' use of the secret police,
       imposition of censorship, and restriction of foreign travel.
       MacDonald concludes that "the similarities are overshadowed
       by the differences in degree. What Czar Nicholas ... was
       able to do only partially, Czar Stalin has done almost com-
       pletely. "

1313 Maxwell, John S. The Czar, His Court and People; Including
       a Tour of Norway and Sweden. New York: Baker and
       Scribner, 1848, 368pp.
       The vast majority of this work is devoted to a description
       of the dismal condition of mid-nineteenth century Russia, but
       it includes some discussion of Nicholas I's domestic and for-
       eign policies. Maxwell admits that the backwardness which

so characterized Russian society quite logically led Nicholas
to the conclusion that autocracy was the only system of
government suitable for Russia but asserts that "the evils
of despotism" only served to worsen the already miserable
state of affairs. DK25.M46

1314   Mayne, F. The Life of Nicholas I, Emperor of Russia. Lon-
       don: Longman Brown, Green and Longmans, 1855, 390pp.
       The stated purpose of this work is to give the general pub-
       lic "a succinct account of the Emperor Nicholas, the vast
       territories under his sway, and the origin and progress of
       the war into which his 'vaulting ambition' has forced the
       Western powers." Mayne devotes most of his attention to
       a discussion of Nicholas I's foreign policy from the perspec-
       tive of Peter the Great's "will," published by the Times on
       13 April 1854, which allegedly contained an outline of Rus-
       sia's plan for European domination. Mayne contends that
       Nicholas was unable to implement successfully the Petrine
       plan because he did not possess "the business habits, the
       power of concentration, or the varied talents of his ancestor."
       The author concludes that it is England's responsibility to
       "clip the talons of the Russian Eagle" and save Europe from
       rule by a barbarous Asiatic power. DK210.M4

1315   *Michelsen, Edward H. The Life of Nicholas I, Emperor of
       All the Russias. London: William Spooner, 1854, 116pp.
       An examination of Nicholas I's upbringing for insight into
       his personality, character, principles, and policies as tsar.
       Drawing primarily on the works of Custine, Golovin, Ustry-
       alov, Grimm, and Haxthausen, Michelsen states that Nicholas,
       upon ascending the throne, lacked mental refinement and
       compassion, was obsessed with the military way of life, and
       had little understanding of the problems which plagued Rus-
       sia: "Nicholas had, as Grand Duke, remained a perfect
       stranger to state affairs, and ascended the throne of the
       Czars, not to rule as a European Emperor of the nineteenth
       century, but to resume again that Asiatic despotism, which,
       in the semi-liberalism of Alexander's reign, had been cast
       aside." Michelsen concludes that Nicholas' lack of experience
       with administrative and foreign affairs coupled with his mili-
       taristic nature and despotic obstinacy account for his blund-
       ering into the Crimean War, a conflict from which he and Rus-
       sia could not profit. DK210.M6

1316   Novikoff, Madame Olga. "The Emperor Nicholas I." Russian
       Memoirs. London: Herbert Jenkins Limited, 1917, 89-98.
       A brief and favorable commentary on the character of Nicho-
       las I and his sincere desire to establish close and cordial
       ties between Russia and England. Novikoff, a turn-of-the-
       century Russian celebrity who worked incessantly to promote
       amicable relations between Russia and England, commends

Nicholas for correctly realizing that the peace of Europe
could best be secured through an accord between Russia and
England. She defends his attempt to promote such an alliance
and bemoans the fact that English leaders misinterpreted his
intentions so badly that war broke out between Britain and
Russia over the fate of the Ottoman Empire. DK189.N6

1317 *Oliva, L. Jay, ed. "Outer Repression and Inner Liberation:
      1825-1855." RW (anthology), 90-116.
      A series of brief excerpts from the writings of several of
      Nicholas I's contemporaries as well as from various secondary
      analysts illuminating his foreign policy and repressive domes-
      tic program. Included are excerpts from the writings of
      contemporary Russian radicals V. Belinsky and A. Herzen
      and from historians S. Monas, N. Riasanovsky, and T.
      Masaryk.

1318 *Presniakov, A. E. Emperor Nicholas I of Russia. The Apogee
      of Absolutism 1825-1855. Judith C. Zacek, ed./trans.,
      Nicholas V. Riasanovsky, intro. Gulf Breeze, Fla.: Aca-
      demic International Press, 1974, 102pp., bib. 98-102.
      A critical reassessment of Nicholas I and his policies. Pres-
      niakov, a noted Russian scholar (1878-1929), contends that
      Nicholas I, far from being a strong ruler leading a powerful
      autocratic state, suffered from a number of personal failures
      which so handicapped him that he was unable to cope system-
      atically and effectively with the problems which so pressed
      the monarchy. Nicholas steadfastly refused to entrust to any
      individual or agency the task of resolving the political,
      social, and economic problems that continued to mount under
      his rule as a consequence of the growing gap between the
      forces of modernization and the old order of state and social
      relations. Instead, he attempted to settle personally all the
      important matters and issues of the day but by so doing only
      further complicated and confused that which he hoped to re-
      solve. Consequently, some of his top administrators re-
      proached him "for the fact that he ruled unsystematically
      destroying through his personal interference any regularity
      in the system of administering, and for the fact that he for-
      got the business of the sovereign is ruling not administering,
      general leadership not current management." Presniakov con-
      cludes that Nicholas and the Russia he ruled may have been
      stable on the surface, but beneath the condition of each was
      far removed from the image which they projected. Nicholas
      was sufficiently disillusioned by 1855 that the claim that he
      took his own life through poisoning can be considered "psy-
      chologically possible and cannot, on the evidence of sources,
      be either proved or disproved." DK210.P713
      Reviewed in:
      Can Am Slav S, 9, no. 3 (1975): 403-04
      Rus R, 33 (1974): 423

1319   *Riasanovsky, Nicholas V. "Nicholas I and the Course of Rus-
       sian History." Emperor Nicholas I of Russia. The Apogee
       of Absolutism 1825-1855, A. E. Presniakov. Judith C.
       Zacek, ed./trans. Gulf Breeze, Fla.: Academic Internation-
       al Press, 1974, ix-xxxvi.
       A comparative analysis of the reigns of Nicholas I and Alex-
       ander I. Riasanovsky sees similarities between the two reigns
       in that "neither sovereign challenged the fundamental Russian
       realities of autocracy and serfdom" but rather contented them-
       selves with the enactment of modest and limited reforms and
       the preservation of the tradition of the emperor as "both the
       all powerful head and the first servant of the state." Nich-
       olas' reign differed, however, in one fundamental way from
       that of his predecessor since in it there was no place for
       the ideals of the Enlightenment to which Alexander sub-
       scribed. Riasanovsky concludes that "Nicholas I transformed
       enlightened despotism into despotism pure and simple. In-
       stead of reason and progress Russians were to rally around
       Orthodoxy, autocracy, and nationality. Instead of winning
       a future, they were to defend the past." DK210.P713

1320   Rodkey, Frederick. "Three American Diplomats on Tsar
       Nicholas I." Slavonic R, 6, no. 17 (1927): 434-47.
       A brief account of the favorable image of Nicholas I con-
       tained in the dispatches of the American diplomats George
       Dallas, Charles Livingston, and James Buchanan.

1321   Russia Under Nicholas the First. Anthony C. Sterling,
       trans. London: John Murray, 1841, 202pp.
       A translation of an anonymous German language study,
       Conversations--Lexicon der Gegenwart, which presents a
       balanced account of the social, economic, political, and
       cultural condition of Russia during Nicholas I's reign. The
       author also discusses Nicholas' attempt "to see everything
       done himself" and to personalize autocratic rule as much as
       possible. For a lengthy, critical review of this work, see
       "Russia under Nicholas I." Eclectic R, 74 (Dec. 1841):
       704-24. DK211.R9

1322   Schmucker, Samuel M. The Life and Reign of Nicholas the
       First, Emperor of Russia, with a Complete History of Russian
       Society and Government. Philadelphia: J. W. Bradley, 1856,
       415pp.
       A critical review of the character, goals, policies, and ac-
       complishments of Nicholas I. Schmucker states that "in
       truth, it may be said that Nicholas was the most destructive
       and cruel despot who disgraced the 19th century." In sup-
       port of this contention, Schmucker points to Nicholas' policies
       towards Poland, political dissenters, Jews, and the general
       Russian population, 250,000 of which Nicholas condemned to
       Siberian exile. Schmucker reserves special criticism for

Nicholas' aggressive Turkish policy which he sees as having
prompted the Crimean War. DK210.S4

1323 Sortain. Joseph. Craft and Ambitition Rebuked: A Sermon
      on the Death of the Emperor of Russia. Brighton, 1855.
      Unavailable for annotation.

1324 Turnerelli, Edward T. What I Know of the Late Emperor
      Nicholas and His Family. London: Edward Churton, 1855,
      164pp.
      A highly favorable commentary on Nicholas I and the mem-
      bers of his family. Turnerelli, an English observer who
      spent sixteen years in Russia, concentrates on Nicholas'
      character, personality, and daily habits as he portrays the
      emperor as an intelligent, good natured, courageous, and
      compassionate individual completely devoted to governing
      Russia in an efficient and equitable manner. Turnerelli con-
      cludes that Nicholas sometimes was stern and even ruthless
      in dealing with those who ran afoul of the monarchy but
      asserts that much of the criticism levied against him by
      various Western authors is unwarranted, particularly during
      the years surrounding the Crimean War. DK210.T9

1325 Ulam, Adam B. "Nicholas Romanov." In The Name of the
      People. New York: Viking Press, 1977, 20–30.
      A brief, interpretive discussion of the reign of Nicholas I.
      Ulam maintains that Nicholas was "very successful in keeping
      Russia in his iron grip, isolated not only from Western ideas
      and progress but seemingly from the forces of history itself."
      By so doing, he "made it almost inevitable that any attempt
      to undo the evil effects of that isolation would be tardy and
      unsatisfactory and that the long-suppressed thirst for free-
      dom would, after a brief interval of relief, turn into lust
      for revolution." DK221.U38

1326 Ustryalov, Nikolai G. An Historical Review of the Reign of
      the Emperor Nikolai I. W. Roberts, trans. London, 1854.
      Unavailable for annotation.

1327 Wortman, Richard. "Power and Responsibility in the Upbring-
      ing of the 19th Century Tsars." Grps Use Psych Hist News,
      4, no. 4 (1976): 18-27.
      Unavailable for annotation.

1328 Wren, C. "Nicholas I." WITR (gen. study), 138-64.
      A discussion of the reign of Nicholas I as one in which there
      continued undiminished "the anti-Enlightenment which had
      emerged as a Russian Francophobia after Tilsit and gathered
      strength during the last decade of Alexander's reign."
      Wren sees the "strong Western flavor of the Decembrist
      movement" and the conservative nature of young Nicholas'

tutors as being the prime source of Nicholas' anti-Western, reactionary policies. As examples of such policies, Wren focuses upon Nicholas' educational reforms and efforts to thwart liberal and revolutionary movements in Europe.

DOMESTIC POLICY AND AFFAIRS/ POLITICAL THOUGHT AND PRACTICE

1329 Allister, Steven H. "The Reform of Higher Education in Russia During the Reign of Nicholas I, 1825-1844." Princeton University, 1974. (dissertation)

1330 *Baker, Jennifer. "Glinka's A Life for the Tsar and 'Official Nationality.'" Renais Mod S, 24 (1980): 92-114.
An argument that the three fundamental principles of the ideology of Official Nationalism "were made manifest even in the opera house" and, in particular, imbued "the most significant Russian operatic achievement of the 1830s, Glinka's ... 'A Life for the Tsar.'" Baker establishes that Glinka's sympathy with the tenets of Official Nationalism, respect for Nicholas I, and desire to create a "national opera" that would be pleasing to the emperor were the sources for the founding of his opera on the story of Ivan Susanin, as presented in the epic ballad of K. F. Rileyev (ironically, a Decembrist). Baker discusses carefully the elements of Orthodoxy, autocracy, and nationality in the libretto as she contends that "the figure of Nicholas I, Glinka's tsar, dominates the opera." She also establishes that Nicholas "took a personal interest in the opera from an early stage, possibly even interfering ... in the choice of a librettist.... Nicholas attended rehearsals, and, to Glinka's delight was present at the first performance, 'thanking' him for his opera and later rewarding him more tangibly with a costly ring."

1331 *Balmuth, Daniel. "The Origins of the Tsarist Epoch of Censorship Terror." ASEER, 19, no. 4 (1960): 497-520.
The stated purpose of this article is to examine the origins of the 'epoch of censorship terror' (1848-1855) and "to explain the reasons for Nicholas' decision, in the spring of 1848, to adopt special emergency measures." To this end, Balmuth discusses the 1848 findings of the Menshikov Committee which investigated the shortcomings of Russian censorship, especially in regard to the journals National Notes and The Contemporary. Nicholas concluded from the committee's report that previous methods of controlling radical journals were wanting, in several respects, and that a new approach, based on complete repression, was needed.

1332 *Baron, Salo W. "Under Nicholas I and Alexander II." RJTS (gen. study), 31-50.

An examination of Nicholas I's Jewish policy as an ill-
conceived one which, though psychologically damaging to
Russian Jews, failed to effect any fundamental change in
Jewish society. Baron asserts that Nicholas' 1827 edict which,
by drafting young Jews for a 25-year term of duty in the
Russian army, sought to use military service as a means of
Christianization won converts only among two percent of the
Jewish population drafted in the 1827-56 period. Similarly,
his punitive and restrictive legislation as well as his attempt
to Russianize the Jewish schools' curriculum did not significantly alter the "Jewish problem" as Nicholas viewed it but
did, unwittingly, steer young Jews toward the revolutionary
movement which eventually toppled the monarchy.

1333 *Blackwell, William L. The Beginnings of Russian Industriali-
      zation, 1800-1860. Princeton, N.J.: Princeton University
      Press, 1968, 484pp., bib. 437-59.
      This scholarly analysis of the msot immediate causes and the
      background of Russian economic growth in the first half of
      the century does not contain a separate chapter devoted to
      the role of Nicholas I in this process but as a standard work
      on the roots of Russian industrialization it can be consulted
      with profit for information on economic conditions in Russia
      during Nicholas' reign and the economic policies and reforms
      implemented in his name. In scattered sections, Blackwell
      discusses Nicholas' economic views, support for the construc-
      tion of railroads and Russia's first telegraph, and concern
      over labor unrest in the nation's factories. HC334.B55

1334 *Blum, Jerome. "The Question of Serfdom Under Nicholas I."
      IEH, Vol. II (anthology), 146-52. Excerpt from Lord and
      Peasant in Russia from the Ninth to the Nineteenth Century.
      New York: Atheneum, 1964.
      An examination of Nicholas I's sincere desire to redress the
      problems engendered by the institution of serfdom. Blum
      establishes that "from the very outset of his reign Nicholas
      made it clear that he believed serfdom had to be reformed"
      or else "another great jacquerie was certainly to sweep across
      the land." However, Nicholas could not bring himself to
      take decisive action for fear of alienating the nobility and
      raising peasant expectations to a level unrealistically high.
      Thus the deliberations of the ad hoc committees created by
      Nicholas to study the peasant question failed to effect any
      fundamental alteration of serfdom. Nonetheless, Blum con-
      cludes, "Nicholas' never-ceasing preoccupation with the
      agrarian question readied the empire for ultimate emancipa-
      tion. By the time he died in 1855 it was clear that reform
      was inevitable."

1335 Crisp, Olga. "The State Peasants Under Nicholas I." Slavonic
      E Eur R, 37 (1959): 387-412. Also in Studies in the Russian
      Economy Before 1914. New York: Barnes and Noble, 1976,

259-68.
An examination of the rights, duties, and condition of the
state peasants during Nicholas I's reign. Crisp establishes
that while in several respects the state peasants were better
off than peasants who belonged to private landlords, the
numerous obligations which they owed to the state and the
severe shortcomings of the administrative system which governed them resulted in conditions sufficiently grim to make
reform imperative. Nicholas I recognized that the peasant
question was an explosive one, thus he commissioned N. D.
Kiselev to effect major changes in the institution of state
serfdom. Crisp commends the tsar and Kiselev for the dy-
namism which lay beneath their reform program and the
enthusiasm they exhibited in implementing specific reforms.
She concludes that despite its flaws, the Kiselev reform substantially improved the administrative organization that super-
vised the state peasants, expanded their landholdings, rationalized the tax system to which they were subject, and improved various other aspects of their lives. Moreover, it
paved the way for public acceptance of the need for serf
emancipation and gave valuable reform experience to a number
of the individuals who played important roles in the commissions which prepared the 1861 Emancipation Act.

1336   *Curtiss, John Shelton. "The Army of Nicholas I: Its Role
       and Character." Am Hist R, 63, no. 4 (1958): 880-89.
       Also in IEH, Vol. II (anthology), 133-40.
       An examination of the quality and domestic role of Nicholas
       I's army. Curtiss states that Nicholas assigned to the army
       a number of duties that were usually performed by local
       governments and the police in other European countries.
       As a result, it became necessary to maintain a huge army,
       the cost of which was a terrible burden on the general pop-
       ulation. In spite of Nicholas' heavy reliance on the army
       there were a number of serious deficiencies in Russia's
       forces, particularly in regard to weaponry, logistics and
       leadership. Curtiss concludes that "it is clear ... that the
       Russian army under Nicholas was less effective than its glit-
       ter and vast numbers would indicate."

1337   *Deriabin, P. "The Corps of Gendarmes and the Third Sec-
       tion." WT (gen. study), 122-32.
       An examination of Nicholas I's modernization of Russia's
       political police by replacing the guards regiments and various
       chancelleries and bureaus with a professional security force.
       Deriabin discusses Nicholas' motives for creating such a force,
       the background of those men who staffed it, and the tsar's
       use of it for a wide range of purposes.

1338   *Dubnow, S. "The Military Despotism of Nicholas I," "Com-
       pulsory Enlightenment and Increased Oppression," and "The

Last Years of Nicholas I." HJRP, (gen. study), II: 13-87,
140-53.
A discussion of Nicholas I's attempt to "correct" Jewish life,
or at least render the Jews innocuous, by "energetic military
methods," most notably by impressing young Jews into military
service. Dubnow states that Nicholas intended the barracks
to serve as schools for "producing a new generation of de-
Judaized Jews, who were completely Russified, and, if possible, Christianized." What followed was a tragic catastrophe
for Russian Jews as tens of thousands of Jewish teenagers
were forced into a 25-year term of military service where
they were beaten and ridiculed into submission to the "Russian way of life." Dubnow also examines Nicholas' role in
the 1835 issuing of the "Charter of Disabilities," which consolidated three decades of restrictive legislation against Russia's Jews, and his attempt to counter Jewish "religious
fanaticism and separatism" by changing the very fabric of
Jewish life once he realized that neither military conscription nor restrictive measures had altered the Jewish community. By the end of his reign, however, Nicholas abandoned
the "mask of enlightenment" and the role of the would-be
reformer and attempted to solve the Jewish problem by police
methods and forced assimilation. Dubnow concludes that the
latter part of Nicholas' reign represents the darkest years
in the history of Russia's Jews.

1339 Dumas, Alexandre. "The Romanticists' Revolution." CCRC
(gen. study), 218-40.
A dramatic recreation of the Decembrist Revolt and Nicholas
I's suppression of it.

1340 *Edwards, David W. "Nicholas I and Jewish Education." Hist
Ed Q, 22 (Spring 1982): 45-53.
An argument that Nicholas I's 1844 decree which was to
establish state controlled Jewish secular education yielded
results far different from those intended. Edwards maintains that the decree led to the creation, at the government's expense, of a Russified Jewish educated elite highly
conscious of its economic, cultural, and political disabilities.
This elite later provided leadership for both the Zionist and
revolutionary movements in Russia.

1341 _____. "Orthodoxy During the Reign of Tsar Nicholas I:
A Study in Church-State Relations." Kansas State University, 1967. (dissertation)

1342 *_____. "Russian Ecclesiastical Censorship During the Reign
of Tsar Nicholas I." J Ch State, 19, no. 1 (1977): 83-93.
An account of how "Nicholas and his favorites worked to
create a system of censorship which could be used both to
explain and to amplify the official ideology." Edwards

establishes that "both secular and ecclesiastical censorship
mirrored the attitudes of Nicholas, becoming bureaucratic
and centralized, negative and punitive.... The changes
made in the character of religious censorship assured Nicholas
of an obedient prop for his regime, but the church suffered
dearly in this relationship, losing the power to publish its
own books and, therefore, to interpret its own faith."

1343   *_____. "The System of Nicholas I in Church-State Rela-
       tions." Russian Orthodoxy Under the Old Regime. Robert
       L. Nichols and Theofanis George Stavrou, eds. Minneapolis:
       University of Minnesota Press, 1978, 154-69.
       A discussion of Nicholas I's efforts "to create a centralized,
       bureaucratic, lay-dominated church administration" as a means
       of enforcing uniformity in matters of belief and transforming
       the administrative structure of the church into an organiza-
       tion "closely paralleling that of the various state ministries."
       Edwards maintains that under Nicholas the state "controlled
       and directed the church more than at any previous period
       in the history of Russian church-state relations."
       BX491.R87

1344   "An Episode in the Reign of the Emperor Nicholas I." Bentley
       Misc, 37 (Apr. 1855): 381-89.
       An account of the Decembrist Revolt and the oppressive
       measures taken by Nicholas I in his attempt to feret out the
       roots of a conspiracy which he mistakenly believed to be a
       widespread one.

1345   Flynn, James T. "Tuition and Social Class in the Russian
       Universities: S. S. Uvarov and 'Reaction' in the Russia of
       Nicholas I." Slav R, 35, no. 2 (1976): 232-48.
       A defense of S. Uvarov against those who claim that his
       introduction of tuition fees for Russian universities was
       designed to keep out students from the lower classes.
       Flynn maintains that "Uvarov carefully drafted the legisla-
       tion so that it was not a barrier to lower class students but
       rather provided funds to support poor students regardless
       of class origins." Flynn compares Uvarov's ideas on tuition
       fees and open education to those of Nicholas I while discuss-
       ing the broader issue of Russia's need to modernize in the
       face of a changing European World.

1346   Galskoy, Constantine. "The Ministry of Education Under
       Nicholas I, 1826-1836." Stanford University, 1977. (disser-
       tation)

1347   Greenberg, L. "The Jewish Policies of Alexander I and
       Nicholas I." JR (gen. study), 29-55.
       A discussion of Nicholas I's ill-conceived efforts to solve
       Russia's "Jewish problem" by secularizing Jewish schools,

relocating Jews in rural areas where they were to become
farmers, and drafting young Jews into the army where coercion was to be used to encourage them to convert to Christianity. In assessing the ineffectiveness of Nicholas' Jewish
policy, Greenberg states that the resettlement program
failed due to the complete lack of means to implement it,
while the military conscription of teenage Jews only served
to terrorize the Jewish community and brutalize thousands
of young men. Greenberg sees the emperor's anti-Jewish
legislation as being an expression of both the post-1815
European-wide swing toward conservatism and Nicholas' own
convictions which "militated against liberal treatment of any
minority."

1348   *Hans N. "The Reaction (1825-1855)." HREP (gen. study),
       61-91.
       An examination of the conservative educational policies imple-
       mented by Nicholas I. Hans states that Nicholas' legislation
       represented a step backwards toward the type of educational
       system established by Peter the Great, meaning one in which
       students studied only to prepare themselves for some specific
       trade or to secure a government post. Hans links Nicholas'
       educational program to his concern for creating a disciplined,
       effective corps of bureaucrats steeped in Russian traditions
       and dedicated to the service of the state.

1349   *Haywood, Richard M. The Beginnings of the Railway Develop-
       ment in Russia in the Reign of Nicholas I, 1835-1842. Dur-
       ham: North Carolina University Press, 1969, 270pp., bib.
       247-58.
       Nicholas I is not central to this scholarly study of railway
       development during his reign, but it contains a number of
       references to his interest in and support for railway con-
       struction in Russia. Haywood asserts that Nicholas' aware-
       ness of the administrative, military, and economic benefits
       of rail transportation led to the establishment of "the princi-
       ple, so necessary for a backward country, that the state
       should take responsibility for the building of railways."
       Thus, Haywood concludes, Nicholas deserves a significant
       share of the credit for the construction of Russia's first
       railroads. HE3138.H38
          Reviewed in:
          Am Hist R, 75 (1970): 1159
          Rus R, 43 (1969): 566
          Slav R, 29 (1970): 310
          Slavonic E Eur R, 49 (1971): 152

1350   *_____. "The 'Ruler Legend': Tsar Nicholas I and the
       Route of the St. Petersburg-Moscow Railway, 1842-43."
       Slav R, 37, no. 4 (1978): 640-50.

A study of the way in which Nicholas I reached his decision
to have the St. Petersburg-Moscow Railway constructed along
a straight line between the two cities, by-passing the town
of Novgorod. Haywood discounts the legend that Nicholas
responded to a request by officials in regard to the railway's
route by "arbitrarily and hastily" drawing a straight line,
with a ruler, between Moscow and St. Petersburg. Haywood
concludes that Nicholas' decision was in fact the product of
"prolonged, rational, and open discussion in government
circles."

1351 *_____. "The Winter Palace in St. Petersburg: Destruction
by Fire and Reconstruction, December 1837-March 1839."
Jahr Ges Ost, 27, no. 2 (1979): 161-80.
A discussion of the burning of the Winter Palace and its
subsequent reconstruction for insights into the "strengths
and weakness of the reign of Nicholas I, his relationship with
his subjects, and his view of his role as tsar." Haywood
states that Nicholas, whose actions during the fire impressed
observers, benefited initially from the catastrophe because it
strengthened the bonds of unity between the crown and its
subjects. Despite this, Haywood contends, Nicholas felt a
deep sense of personal humiliation because the very symbol
of royal authority had been so quickly and utterly destroyed.
However, as an autocratic regime, the government of Nicholas
was more able than a democratic one "to mobilize all available
resources to overcome the effects of the disaster, obliterat-
ing all traces of it and emerging seemingly stronger than
before."

1352 *Korff, Baron M. The Accession of Nicholas I. London:
John Murray, 1857, 304pp.
An officially sanctioned account of Nicholas I's accession
to the throne of Russia and suppression of the Decembrist
Revolt. Korff, who served as Alexander II's secretary of
state and was commissioned by him to produce this work,
draws from the memoirs of Nicholas I, Empress Alexandra
Feodorovna, and Grand Dukes Michael and Constantine, the
recollections of several of the tsar's advisers (including
Michael Speransky), and the findings of the Commission of
Inquiry and Supreme Criminal Tribunal which dealt with the
Decembrist Conspiracy as he presents a detailed justification of Nicholas' claim to the throne and harsh reaction to
the Decembrist Revolt. DK212.K713

1353 *Kucherov, Samuel. "Introduction." Courts, Lawyers and
Trials Under the Last Three Tsars. New York: Fred A.
Praeger, 1953, 3-19.
A short but interesting account of the deplorable state of the
administration of justice during the reign of Nicholas I. In
addition to highlighting "the disorder, the brutality, the

artibrariness and the corruption of justice" under Nicholas
I, Kucherov discusses the interference in the legal system
by the infamous Third Section of His Majesty's Own Chancery and Nicholas' use of this agency to procure information
on various individuals, groups, and government offices.
KR 397. K8

1354   Kutscheroff, Samuel. "Administration of Justice Under Nicholas I of Russia." ASEER, 7 (Apr. 1948): 125-38.
A discussion of the courts, their members, and the dispensation of justice under Nicholas I as being representative of the
reactionary and oppressive characteristics of Nicholas' entire reign. Kucherov contends that "the secret and inquisi-
tional proceedings with their doctrine of formal evidence, the
complexity of the courts and their procedure, the venality
and corruption of judges, the complete dependence of the
judiciary upon the executive--all these factors combined to
reduce the administration of justice to a mere parody of
equity."

1355   *La Croix, Paul. "The Problem of Succession." RIRH (anthology), 256-62. Excerpt from Histoiré de la vie et du regne
de Nicolas Ier Empereur de Russia, Vol. I. Paris, 1864-66,
238-40, 244-47, 326-29, 346, 363, 395-99, 401-02.
A series of royal letters and documents which collectively
illuminate the circumstances surrounding and arrangements
made for the renunciation of the throne by the Grand Duke
Constantine in favor of his younger brother, Nicholas.

1356   La Farge, J. "Pope and the Tsar: Gregory XVI and Nicholas
I, 1845." America, 71 (27 May 1944): 212.
A discussion of Stalin's wartime decision to re-establish the
Orthodox Church in Russia; includes reference to the 1845
meeting between Pope Gregory XVI and Nicholas I during
which the Orthodox Church's function as the monarchy's
political agent was discussed.

1357   *Le Donne, John P. "The Administration of Military Justice
Under Nicholas I." Cahiers du monde, 13, no. 2 (1972):
180-91.
The avowed purpose of this article is "to outline the organization of the military judiciary in peacetime and to illustrate ...
the double standard, based on social criteria, prevailing in
penal law." In the process, Le Donne describes Nicholas'
pedantic exercise of his autocratic prerogatives in military
court cases involving the discipline and punishment of officers and nobles stripped of their status.

1358   *_____. "Civilians Under Military Justice During the Reign
of Nicholas I." Can Am Slav S, 7, no. 2 (1973): 171-87.
An examination of the motivation for the frequent trial of

civilians in military courts under Nicholas I. Le Donne asserts
that Nicholas "personally was responsible for initiating and
gradually extending the practice of military trials of civilians"
largely because of his impatience with the delays of criminal
procedure characteristic of civilian legal channels and his anx-
iousness to inflict punishments (in special cases) more severe
than those typically handed out by nonmilitary courts.

1359   Lee, Robert. "Part II. The First Days of Emperor Nicholas."
       The Last Days of Alexander and the First Days of Nicholas.
       London: Richard Bentley, 1854, 83-210.
       Excerpts from the 1826 diary of an English acquaintance of
       Count Vorontsov of the Imperial Council of State. Lee com-
       ments on Nicholas I's quelling of the Decembrist Revolt and de-
       sire to improve Russia's administrative system. The author
       speculates that Nicholas' lack of able advisers and his unwill-
       ingness to tap public opinion for assistance in reforming Rus-
       sia would render effective change impossible. In an 1854
       postscript, Lee describes the cruelties perpetrated by Nicho-
       las during his reign, and presents a characterization of the
       tsar as "the scourge of the human race." DK191.L4

1360   Leibert, Karen A. "Reform and Reaction: Nicholas I and the
       Russian Nobility." University of Maryland, 1984. (disserta-
       tion)

1361   *Lentsyk, Wasyl. The Eastern Catholic Church and Czar
       Nicholas I. Rome: n.p., 1960, 148pp.
       An examination of the origins and implementation of Nicholas
       I's 1839 abolition of the Eastern Catholic Church. Lentsyk
       links the destruction of the Uniat Church to Nicholas' desire
       to Russify his empire in line with the ideals contained within
       the doctine of Official Nationality. Lentsyk denies that the
       church's abolition was an act of revenge on Nicholas' part
       against those members of the Uniat clergy who participated in
       the Polish insurrection of 1830-31. However, he adds that
       the government of Nicholas I successfully misled Western
       analysts into believing that the Uniats willingly accepted as-
       similation into the Russian Orthodox Church, when, in fact,
       "violence, perfidy, and treachery" were used to coerce them
       into abandoning their religion. BX4711.622.L43

1362   *Lincoln, W. Bruce. "The Composition of the Imperial Russian
       State Council Under Nicholas I. Can Am Slav S, 10, no. 3
       (1976): 369-81.
       A discussion of the State Council of Nicholas I as "a body to
       which men were appointed as a reward for past services rather
       than one from which serious advice, counsel, or administra-
       tive activity was expected...." Lincoln supports this thesis
       with a statistical analysis of Nicholas' appointments to the
       Council. He concludes that the appointees were men loyal to

Nicholas and well satisfied with the order of things in Nicholas' Russia.

1363 *_____. "The Genesis of an 'Enlightened' Bureaucracy in Russia, 1825-1856." Jahr Ges Ost, 20, no. 3 (1972): 321-30.
An analysis of Nicholas I's attempt to improve government in Russia through the creation of "a personal machinery of government staffed by a select group of bureaucrats loyal to their ruler's, rather than their class' interests." Lincoln states that the "enlightened" bureaucracy, which emerged as a consequence of Nicholas' efforts, not only showed excellent insight into economic and political conditions of the empire but also developed a pronounced social conscience. These characteristics, in turn, enabled certain enlightened bureaucrats to play a crucial role in the work of the commissions responsible for the 1861 emancipation of the serfs.

1364 *_____. "The Last Years of the Nicholas 'System': The Unpublished Diaries and Memoirs of Baron Korf and General Tsimmerman." Ox Slavonic P, 6 (1973): 12-27.
An examination of the unpublished writings of two top servitors of Nicholas I for insight into "state affairs, the bureaucracy, St. Petersbrug society, and the state of the Russian army during the last years of Nicholas' reign." Lincoln states that Tsimmerman's memoirs show that even the crown's most loyal supporters were aware of deficiencies in the "Nicholas system," particularly in regard to the military. Tsimmerman believed (as did Nicholas) that changes had to be made without upsetting the traditional order of things in Russia. Korf's diary is a particularly detailed and interesting source of information on Nicholas himself. Most notably Korf's writings provide evidence that Nicholas would not tolerate any criticism of his policies when third parties were present but held frank discussions with individual ministers whose judgment he valued.

1365 *_____. "The Ministers of Nicholas I: A Brief Inquiry into Their Backgrounds and Service Careers." Rus R, 34, no. 3 (1975): 308-23.
An analysis of the military background, age, education, and ethnic origin of the 52 nonroyal ministers who served Nicholas I during his riegn. Lincoln concludes that, with few exceptions, Nicholas appointed men whose views, values, and shortcomings mirrored his own, and thus he rarely received advice contrary to that which he wanted to hear.

1366 *_____. "Myth Versus Reality: Nicholas I's Image of Russia." Aus J Pol Hist, 25, no. 2 (1970): 237-49.
An argument that the system created by Nicholas I to ensure that he would be well informed about the condition of his realm had such serious deficiencies that the true state of Russia's economic and military strength eluded him. Lincoln maintains that the slowness of the bureaucracy combined with

the reluctance of bureaucratic underlings to report shortcomings which might reflect poorly on them resulted in Nicholas being given an incomplete and inaccurate image of the
condition and strength of Russia. It took the Crimean War,
Lincoln concludes, to bring to the crown's attention the serious shortcomings which plagued the nation.

1367   *_____. "N. A. Miliutin and the St. Petersburg Municipal
Act of 1846: A Study in Reform Under Nicholas I." Slav R,
33, no. 1 (1974): 55-68.
Nicholas I is not discussed in this article, but as a study of
the efforts of one of his enlightened bureaucrats to bring order
to the government of Russia's cities it sheds light on the process of reform during Nicholas' reign. Miliutin, who was appointed as director of the Provisional Section for the Reorganization of Municipal Government and Economy, created by
Nicholas on 27 March 1842, conducted a detailed investigation
of the condition of Russia's principal cities. He identified
class monopolies, corruption, administrative chaos, and
financial instability as the main abuses in urban government.
Through the 1846 St. Petersburg Municipal Act, Miliutin attempted to counter these various deficiencies without altering
the class principle upon which was founded the control of the
city's economic affairs. Lincoln sees the sense of dedication
and integrity shown by Miliutin's circle of enlightened bureaucrats as being consistent with that which characterized the
progressive elements in the Editing Commission of 1859 to
1860.

1368   _____. "Nicholas Alekseevich Milyutin and Problems of State
Reform in Nicholaevan Russia." University of Chicago, 1967.
(dissertation)

1369   *_____. "Nicholas I: Russia's Last Absolute Monarch."
Hist Today, 21, no. 2 (1971): 79-88.
A useful overview of the origin, operation, and decline of
Nicholas I's system of government. Lincoln states that following the Decembrist Revolt of 1825, Nicholas distrusted Russia's
intelligentsia and nobility, as well as his own bureaucracy,
and consequently attempted to rule the nation without involving these groups in the decision-making process. The narrow
basis of this conservative, paternalistic system of government
established by Nicholas made it difficult for the crown to deal
effectively with the major problems which it identified, most
notably the reorganization of state finances, quelling of peasant discontent, and the codification of Russian law. Lincoln
concludes that Nichoals' overreaction to the revolutions of
1848 led him to take an even more restrictive approach to
ruling Russia, and consequently the "Nicholas system" degenerated and, ultimately, collapsed amidst the humiliating
defeat suffered by Russia during the Crimean War.

1370 *_____. "Reform in Action: The Implementation of the
Municipal Reform Act of 1846 in St. Petersburg." Slavonic
E Eur R, 53, no. 131 (1975): 202-09.
An account of the remarkable persistence shown by N. Miliutin
in supervising the successful implementation of urban reform.
Lincoln maintains that the insight gained by Miliutin into the
workings of the Russian bureaucracy influenced the approach
to reform taken by enlightened bureaucrats in the 1860s.

1371 *_____. "Russia's Enlightened Bureaucrats and Problems
of State Reform, 1846-1856." Cahiers du monde, 12, no. 4
(1971): 410-21.
A reassessment of the thesis that as a reaction to the 1848
revolutions "all discussion of reform and change ceased in
Russia and the Empire was plunged into one of the darkest
periods of her modern history." Lincoln maintains that problems of reform continued to be discussed in concrete and
practical terms among the enlightened bureaucrats of St.
Petersburg who were relatively unknown at the time but later
gained prominence in planning the major reforms of the 1860s.
Most notable among these bureaucrats are N. A. Miliutin, A. K.
Giers, I. P. Arapetov, A. V. Golovin, and D. A. Oblensky.

1372 *McCormick, D. "Nicholas I Creates the Third Section."
HRSS (gen. study), 51-62.
An account of Nicholas I's motives for reorganizing the Russian secret service by creating the Third Section of His Majesty's Private Imperial Chancery. McCormick also discusses
the Third Section's investigation of the death of Alexander I
and its watchful eye on the activities of religious sects and
a variety of individuals including A. Herzen, P. Chaadaev,
and A. Pushkin.

1373 McGrew, Roderick Erle. "Nicholas I and the Genesis of Russian
Officialism." University of Minnesota, 1955. (dissertation)

1374 Malcom, N. R. "Ideology and Intrigue in Russian Journalism
Under Nicholas I: 'Moskovskii Telegraf' and 'Severnaya
Pchlea.'" Oxford University, 1974. (dissertation)

1375 *Mazour, Anatole G. "The Trial." The First Russian Revolution, 1825. Stanford: Stanford University Press, 1964, 203-
21.
An examination of Nicholas I's investigation of the Decembrist
conspiracy. Mazour presents Nicholas as a skilled prosecutor
committed to extracting the maximum of information from each
person detained in the aftermath of the Decembrist Revolt.
Of particular interest in Mazour's description of Nicholas'
clever adaptation of the tone and direction of his interrogations
to allow him to exploit the vulnerabilities of the accused.
Mazour concludes that the sentences eventually meted out

"were not only harsh, but in most instances appallingly un-
just," and thus certainly were more the product of a grimly
revengeful emperor than any reasonable legal procedure.
DK212.M3

1376   *Mirsky, D. S. "The Decembrists." Slavonic R, 4, no. 11
       (1925): 400-04.
       The centenary of the Decembrist Revolution prompted this
       discussion of Nicholas I's gross misinterpretation of the signif-
       icance of this event and mishandling of the Decembrists' trial.
       Mirsky states that Nicholas "exaggerated the actual and under-
       valued the latent importance of the revolt and of the rebels."
       Referring to the trial as "the first act of a reign whose mean-
       ness and moral smallness is unparalleled in history," Mirsky as-
       serts that by over-reacting to the revolt and focusing nation-
       al attention on the Decembrists' trial Nicholas inadvertently
       gave martyrdom to a group of inept conspirators.

1377   Monas, Sidney. "Bureaucracy in Russia Under Nicholas I."
       SRH (anthology), 269-81.
       This scholarly examination of the activities of the prominent
       bureaucrat Pavel Kiselev (1788-1872) does not focus on
       Nicholas I, but it provides some insight into his politics and,
       particularly, the rapid growth of the imperial bureaucracy
       which occurred during his reign.

1378   * _____ . "The Political Police: The Dream of a Beautiful
       Autocracy." The Transformation of Russian Society. Aspects
       of Social Change Since 1861. Cyril E. Black, ed. Cambridge:
       Harvard University Press, 1960, 164-90.
       In part, a discussion of Nicholas I's creation and use of the
       Third Section. In reviewing the Third Section's role during
       Nicholas I's reign, Monas provides most information on its
       propaganda, censorship, and surveillance activities.
       HN523.J6

1379   * _____ . The Third Section. Police and Society in Russia
       Under Nicholas I. Cambridge: Harvard University Press,
       1961, 352pp., bib. 297-314. Excerpt in IEH, Vol. II (an-
       thology), 140-46.
       A scholarly examination of Nicholas I's creation of the Third
       Section and use of it as an agency both to protect and en-
       hance autocracy. Monas links the Third Section's creation to
       Nicholas' desire to establish in Russia a well-ordered autocrat-
       ic state (Rechsstaat) and to protect the crown from the dan-
       ger of revolution. Because Nicholas wanted the political po-
       lice to be a direct extension of his personal will rather than
       to have an institutional existence of its own, he attached the
       newly created security force to the Imperial Chancery as its
       Third Section. However, Nicholas entrusted it with "two
       irreconcilable tasks: on the one hand, to create a broader

basis for the regime in public opinion; on the other, to maintain all initiative in political action in the hands of the autocrat." Monas shows that the Third Section gradually became
more conservative and its "activity shifted form the first task
to the second." But, despite its efficiency, honesty, and
devotion to duty, its approach to dissent (real and perceived)
only served to make the revolutionary movement more of a
threat to the monarchy. Monas concludes that "it was the
reign of Nicholas finally that gave birth to the revolutionary
intelligentsia.... This small group was hemmed about and
restricted, muffled by censorship, surrounded by gendarmes
and spies, its access to further education and to publicity
severely limited.... Young intellectuals retreated into Schiller's
realm of the 'beautiful soul,' and passed on from there to
Schelling and Hegel. When they returned to politics, it was
a visionary kind ... first, utopian socialism, later, revolutionary nihilism-apocalyptic and extreme." HV8224.M6
Reviewed in:
Am Hist R, 67, no. 2 (1962): 414
Ann Am Acad, 338 (1961): 171
History, 47 (1962): 203
Rus R, 20, no. 4 (1961): 363
Slav R, 20, no. 4 (1961): 705

1380 _____. "The Third Section. A Study of Political Police
Activity in Russia During the Reign of Nicholas I." Harvard
University, 1955. (dissertation)

1381 "Nicholas, Emperor of Russia." New Mo M, 16 (1826): 287-95.
An account of the difficulties and dangers encountered by
Nicholas I in his first year as tsar. The author commends
Nicholas for the courage which he displayed in dealing with
the Decembrist Revolt and conspiracies against his life.

1382 *Pintner, Walter McKenzie. Russian Economic Policy Under
Nicholas I. Ithaca, N.Y.: Cornell University Press, 1967,
291pp., bib. 265-81.
An examination of the conservative economic policy pursued
by Finance Minister Egor F. Kankrin and continued by Nicholas I after Kankrin's 1844 retirement. Pintner states that
"despite the well-established precedents in Russia for active
government involvement in the economy, the reign of Nicholas
was marked by unusual passivity, both toward the state's
needs for individual products ... and toward the economic
development of the country as a whole," largely because both
"the Tsar and the Minister of Finance usually felt they could
not risk temporary strain, either social or fiscal, for the sake
of eventual economic improvement." The major developments
in economic policy that did occur (currency reform, improvement of state peasant agriculture, construction of railroads)
did not emanate from any cohesive economic ideology but

rather were products of "a short-range, essentially hand-to-mouth view" of how to treat Russia's economic problems. Although Nicholas I did not always agree with Kankrin's economic conservatism and overruled him on some questions, he shared Kankrin's pessimistic outlook on the government's ability to effect fundamental economic change. Pintner concludes that the absence of external pressures gave Nicholas the latitude to pursue such undynamic economic policies, but with the Crimean War's exposure of the depth of seriousness of Russia's economic backwardness the state was compelled to "resume its role as the driving force in the economy." HC334.P5

Reviewed in:
Am Hist R, 73 (1967):   1580-81
Can Slav S, 2 (1968):   603-04
J Eco Hist, 28 (1968):   496-97
J Mod Hist, 41 (1969):   411-12
J Soc Hist, 4 (1971):   180
Jahr Ges Ost, 15 (1967):   576-77
Rus R, 27, no. 4 (1968):   472-74
Slav R, 28 (1969):   132-33

1383   *Raeff, Marc. "The Regime of Nicholas I." UIR (gen. study), 147-71.

A cogent discussion of the impact of Nicholas I's attempt to rationalize the imperial bureaucracy and improve the economic condition of his realm without allowing the nation's educated elite to play an open role in this transformation. Raeff contends that while Nicholas' administrative reforms and progressive economic policies were relatively effective, his efforts to prevent all but authorized personnel from involvement in the transformation process were far from successful. In reality, his reign witnessed not only a dynamic growth of both the cultural and governmental elites but also the advent of salons and circles where the two elites met and shared views on fundamental political, social, and economic issues. Raeff concludes that these two groups, along with the class of professional bureaucrats which emerged during Nicholas' reign, shared in common a desire to play a directing role in the development of Russia's potential and a fear of the unchanneled, elemental power of the peasant masses from whom the elites were isolated.

1384   *Rhinelander, L. Hamilton. "The Creation of the Caucasian Viceregency." Slavonic E Eur R, 59, no. 1 (1981):   15-40.

A study of the creation of the Caucasian Viceregency as an exception to Nicholas I's policy of non-delegation of authority. Rhinelander shows that because of Nicholas' complete trust in Count M. S. Vorontsov, he gave the count as viceregent "extraordinary governing authority." In so doing Nicholas

was not acting on the advice of his advisers nor was he ad-
mitting failure for tsarist policy in Transcaucasia but merely
was giving extraordinary power to a trusted and able administrator as a means of improving imperial control over a
difficult province.

1385   *Riasanovsky, Nicholas V.   "'Nationality' Policy in the State
       Ideology During the Reign of Nicholas I."   Rus R, 19, no. 1
       (1960):   38-46.
       An examination of the conflicting interpretations of "nation-
       ality" as one of the three pillars of the theory of Official
       Nationality advanced during the reign of Nicholas I. Riasa-
       novsky establishes that although the supporters of the theory
       shared in common certain ideals on "nationality," there was
       enough disagreement to speak of two separate camps: the
       dynastic and romantic. The former and dominant group saw
       "nationality" as a buttress for the existing order, while the
       romantics' definition of "nationality" was tinged with panslav-
       ism and called for a revision of the political order in Eastern
       Europe.

1386   *_____. Nicholas I and Official Nationality in Russia, 1825-
       1855. Berkeley: University of California Press, 1959, 296pp.,
       bib. 273-92.
       This study of the ideology of Official Nationality and its pro-
       ponents contains an opening chapter on Nicholas I's char-
       acter, intellect, and political philosophy. Riasanovsky de-
       scribes Nicholas as a remarkably conscientious autocrat whose
       profound emotional commitment to his work led him to be ener-
       getic and aggressive to a fault when performing his duties.
       Riasanovsky sees this same nervous energy, attention to de-
       tail, and striving for perfection as a type of defense mechan-
       ism developed by Nicholas to enable him to cope with a life
       "full of strife and frustration." To a large degree, Nicholas'
       overdeveloped sense of duty and patriotism were incorporated
       into the state doctrine of Official Nationality, and consequent-
       ly the monarchy during his reign "became incarnated in his
       personality." DK210.R5
          Reviewed in:
          Am Hist R, 65, no. 4 (1960):   901
          Ann Am Acad, 330 (1960):   175
          Historian, 22 (1960):   429
          History, 46 (1961):   265
          J Cent Eur Aff, 20 (1960-61):   453-54
          Rus R, 19, no. 2 (1960):   209
          Slav R, 19, no. 3 (1960):   442
          Slavonic E Eur R, 39 (1960-61):   259

1387   *_____. "Some Comments on the Role of the Intelligentsia
       in the Reign of Nicholas I."   Slav E Eur J, 15 (Fall 1957):
       163-76.

A discussion of the arguments advanced by nineteenth-century
Russians who attempted to provide an intellectual justification
for Nicholas I's autocratic rule. Citing such individuals as
Pushkin, Gogol, Tyutchev, Pogodin, and Uvarov, Riasanovsky
isolates four fundamental rationales for the then existing order:
religion, the base nature of man, the historical record of
autocracy, and the unique administrative needs of Russia as
a multinational realm. He sees all four arguments as being
permeated with romanticism and concludes that it was this
"romantic Weltanschauung that made it possible for many
Russian intellectuals to support their despotic government."

1388   *Schnitzler, J. H.   Secret History of Court and Government
       of Russia Under Emperors Alexander and Nicholas, 2 Vols.
       London: Richard Bently, 1847, 511pp.
       The focus of this work is the origins and impact of the
       Decembrist Revolution, including the various trials of the
       Decembrists. As part of this study, Schnitzler (who was an
       eyewitness to the Decembrist Revolt) describes carefully the
       effect had upon Nicholas I by the Decembrists' attempt to
       deny him the throne and the response of Russian society to
       both the abortive revolt and Nicholas' countermeasures.
       Schnitzler also reviews the first two decades of Nicholas' rule
       praising the tsar for his attempt to advance legality and jus-
       tice, counter bureaucratic inefficiency and corruption, and
       ameliorate the harsh conditions under which Russia's serfs
       suffered. Schnitzler notes that although Nicholas' reform ef-
       forts had not always met with success as of the mid-1840s,
       the portrayal of him as an insensitive tyrant, by authors
       such as N. Golovine, is unwarranted. DK189.S36

1389   Shahan, Thomas J.   "Czar Nicholas I and the Holy See (1825-
       1855)."   Am Cath Q, 30 (Oct. 1905): 720-45.
       A highly critical account of Nicholas I's policies toward Rus-
       sian and Polish Catholics and the Holy See. Shahan attacks
       Nicholas for his ruthless attempt to Russify Uniat Catholics,
       persecution of Uniat clergy, and failure to honor the 1848
       Concordat signed with Pope Gregory XVI in regard to the
       rights of Polish Catholics.

1390   *Squire, P. S.   "Nicholas I and the Problem of Internal Secur-
       ity in Russia in 1826."   RRH, Vol. I (anthology), 325-43.
       Originally in Slavonic E Eur R, 38 (1960): 431-58.
       A scholarly discussion of the genesis and operation of the Third
       Department of his Imperial Majesty's Own Chancery, created by
       Nicholas I on 3 July 1826. Squire states that "the legacy
       which Nicholas I inherited in the sphere of 'internal espionage'
       was a poor one," and that this fact combined with the urgent
       need to re-establish law and order in the wake of the Decem-
       brist Revolt led him to create a new secret police organization.
       Nicholas intended the Third Department to be omnipotent and

to serve "as the essential link between himself and his people, observing all that went on, righting wrongs and averting evil."

1391 *_____. The Third Department: The Establishment and Practices of the Political Police in the Russia of Nicholas I. Cambridge: Cambridge University Press, 1968, 272pp. A scholarly investigation of the origins, practices, and leadership of the Third Department, Nicholas I's political police. Squire states that while the Decembrist Revolt provided the immediate impetus for the Third Department's creation, Nicholas intended this agency to be far more than a means of ensuring the internal security of Russia against any further attempt at revolution. He envisioned the Third Department to be a beneficial institution which would root out bureaucratic corruption and abuses and "act as the supreme intermediary between himself and those he governed." However, "despite the apparent excellence both of Nicholas' motives and of the character of his Higher Police officials, it is impossible to regard the Third Department as anything but a pernicious organization." Squire supports this judgment with a discussion of the arbitrary nature of the Third Department's power, the inaccuracy of much of the information it gathered from spies and informers, and the arrest, imprisonment, and exile of thousands of citizens for minor indiscretions unearthed by prying police. In essence, the Third Department's few successes and benefits were far outweighed by the atmosphere of fear, suspicion, and oppression which emerged during Nicholas I's reign as a consequence of its activities and practices. HV8224.S59
   Reviewed in:
   Am Hist R, 75 (1969): 172
   Rocky Mt Soc Sci J, 6 (1969): 190-91
   Slav R, 28 (1969): 646-67

1392 *Stanislawski, Michael. Tsar Nicholas and the Jews. The Transformation of Jewish Society in Russia: 1825-1855. Philadelphia: Jewish Publication Society of America, 1983, 246pp., bib. 219-37. An examination of Nicholas I's various efforts to effect fundamental change in Jewish institutions and society in hope of shaping Russia's Jews in ways consistent with his conservative and nationalistic ideology. Stanislawski discusses the methods and agencies employed by Nicholas to secure his goal, most notably the Statute on the Recruitment of Jews, abolition of the kahal, and attempt to destabilize and fragment Jewish unity by pursuing an educational and cultural policy designed to undermine the forces of traditionalism within the Jewish community. Stanislawski does not see the "unprecedented obtrusion of Russian politics into Jewish society" that characterized the 1825 to 1855 period as being a product of any deep-seated anti-Semitism on the part of Nicholas and his advisers but rather as an expression of Nicholas' militantly conservative approach to governing all of his subjects. While Nicholas' Jewish policies "were both ill-conceived and unsuccessful..., they did transform the context and much of the content of the lives of the Russian Jews. From their insular existence on the margins of Russian society, in Nicholas' time the Jews were thrust into the maelstrom of Russian life and politics." DK135.R9S77

1393 *Strakhovsky, Leonid I. "Three Leaders of Conservatism: Guizot, Metternich, Nicholas I." Am R, 3 (Sept. 1934): 472-94.
In part, a discussion of Nicholas I as a mid-nineteenth-century conservative who hoped to preserve the best of Russia's traditions while adapting to the demands of modernity wherever necessary and countering the pernicious influence of radicalism and liberalism. Strakhovsky contends that Nicholas was not a blind reactionary but was simply relentless in his "resistance to revolutionary demagogy and mob rule."

1394 Strickland, Jane. "Revolutions of Russia. The Accession of Nicholas I, 1825." Sharpe's Lon M, 14 (1851): 217-22. Also in Liv Age, 55 (1851): 449+ and Eclectic M, 24 (1851): 401+.
A brief review of the circumstances surrounding the Decembrist Revolt of 1825; based upon the writings of Alexandre Dumas.

1395 *Tompkins, S. R. "The Press Under Nicholas." RM (gen. study), 171-86.
This chapter, as well as part of the previous one, contains a discussion of the development of the Russian press during the reign of Nicholas I despite the censorship of various government agencies and the emperor himself. Tompkins contends that "in spite of the gloom and despair in which his reign closed, the time of Nicholas I was one of the most remarkable in the history of Russian thought. It could perhaps be said that the minds of Russians began to attain something like maturity and to move freely in the intellectual atmosphere of Western Europe."

1396 *Vucinich, Alexander. "Official Nationalism and Counteravailing Thought." Science and Russian Culture. A History to 1860. Stanford: Stanford University Press, 1963, 247-94.
An examination of the negative impact on Russian scientific thought and writing had by the reactionary policies of Nicholas I. In highlighting the harm done by Nicholas' oppressive rule, Vucinich discusses the tsar's imposition of extensive censorship, restriction of academic freedom, curtailment of educational opportunity, and redirection of the curricula of Russia's schools towards didactic formalism and classicism. Q127.R9V8

1397 *Wortman, Richard S. "Bureaucratization, Specialization and
      Education." DRLC (gen. study), 34-50.
      In part, a discussion of Nicholas I's role in advancing the
      quality of the Russian judiciary by improving the education of
      members of the legal profession, particularly by way of the
      1835 establishment of the School of Jurisprudence. KR91.W6

1398 Zenkiewicz, Wincenty O. Lord Aberdeen, the Nuns of Minsk,
      Nicholas and the Russian State Church. London, 1846.
      Unavailable for annotation.

                FOREIGN POLICY AND MILITARY AFFAIRS

1399 *Anderson, M. S. "Anglo-Russian Relations and the Crimean
      War 1841-56." The Eastern Question, 1774-1923. A Study in
      International Relations. New York: St. Martin's Press, 1966,
      110-48.
      A discussion of Nicholas I's attempt to provide a peaceful,
      Anglo-Russian solution to what he saw as the inevitable dis-
      integration of the Ottoman Empire. Anderson asserts that be-
      cause Nicholas overestimated the importance of the 1844 agree-
      ment reached with British Foreign Secretary Lord Aberdeen,
      Nicholas misjudged seriously the 1853 attitude of the British
      government and disregarded the significance of the "increas-
      ingly anti-Russian public opinion in Britain." Although Nich-
      olas only made a bad situation worse by way of his January
      1853 conversation with British Ambassador to Russia Sir
      George Hamilton Seymour, Anderson agrees with Henderson's
      assertion that "a study of these negotiations does not reveal
      the Tsar as a plotter; it reveals him as a blunderer, whose
      blunders were equalled by those of British ministers." The
      miscalculations committed by Nicholas, British representatives,
      and the leaders of the other nations involved in the Eastern
      Question lead Anderson to conclude that the Crimean War
      "more than any great war of modern times, took place by
      accident." D371.A43

1400 Baddeley, John F. The Russian Conquest of the Caucasus.
      London: Longmans, Green and Company, 1908, 518pp.
      This detailed account of the Russian annexation of the
      Caucasus does not contain a separate chapter on Nicholas I
      but includes numerous references to his role in directing
      Russia's diplomatic and military efforts to gain control of the
      Caucasus region. DK511.C1B24

1401 Berlin, I. "Russia and 1848." Slavonic E Eur R, 26 (Apr.
      1948): 341-60.
      In part, a discussion of Nicholas I's militant response to the
      revolutions of 1848 in Europe and the consequent disillusion-
      ment which developed among Russian liberal and radical circles

over the triumph of his reactionary policies. Berlin maintains
that the failure of Western liberalism in 1848 prompted Russian
radicals to conclude that "ideas and agitation wholly unsupported
by material force were necessarily doomed to impotence."

1402   *Bolsover, G. H.   "Nicholas I and the Partition of Turkey."
       Slavonic E Eur R, 27, no. 68 (1949):   115-45.
       An examination of Nicholas I's efforts to guarantee that the
       eventual demise of the Turkish Empire would not take place
       without Russia playing a major role in the re-drawing of the
       Near Eastern map. Bolsover points to Nicholas' various nego-
       tiations with Austria and Britain in regard to the fate of the
       Ottoman Empire as evidence that the emperor never intended
       to impose on Europe a unilateral resolution of this problem.
       Bolsover concludes that "it was one of the major tragedies of
       Nicholas I that his reign ended in war over the Turkish
       problem which he had worked for so long to solve by peace-
       ful and negotiated agreement."

1403   *Brooks, E. Willis.   "Nicholas I as Reformer: Russian At-
       tempts to Conquer the Caucasus, 1825-1855." Nation and
       Ideology. Essays in Honor of Wayne S. Vucinich. Ivo Banac,
       John G. Ackerman and Roman Szporluk, eds. Boulder, Colo.:
       East European Monographs, 1981, 227-63.
       An examination of the military and administrative policies pur-
       sued by Nicholas I in regard to the Caucasus for insights into
       the nature of the Russian bureaucracy and the character of
       his reign as a whole. Brooks states that the tactics pur-
       sued by Nicholas in his attempt to integrate the Caucasus
       region into the Russian Empire, reveal "a kind of flexibility--
       a greater responsiveness to changing conditions and particu-
       lar situations than most accounts of the reign attribute to
       Nicholas." Far from being the "consistent" ruler described in
       Schiemann's classic German language study of Nicholas' reign,
       "in the Caucasus ... 'unsystematic,' 'ever-changing,' 'com-
       promising,' as well as 'persistent' seem apt characterizations
       of Nicholas' activity--as does the term 'reformist.'" Brooks
       maintains that this is particularly true in regard to Nicholas'
       "delegation of power" and "encouragement of local initiative
       within the Caucasus by Viceroy M. Vorontsov who Nicholas
       established as a 'superbureaucrat.'" Brooks concludes that
       although Nicholas was unable to achieve his main goal in the
       Caucasus, his administrative and military efforts in this area
       "helped to lay the groundwork for future combat successes
       in the Caucasus, and for military reform throughout the em-
       pire." DJK40.N37

1404   Cole, J. W. Russia and the Russians, Comprising an Account
       of the Czar Nicholas and the House of Romanoff. London:
       Rischard Bentley, 1854, 199pp.
       A highly critical survey of the foreign and military policies

of Nicholas I's Romanov predecessors, and a sharp attack on
Nicholas as a devious and brutal tyrant obsessed with the acquisition of Constantinople. DK211.C68

1405 Cowles, Virginia. "Philosophers at Court." RD (gen. study),
      13-40.
      A discussion of Nicholas I's Near Eastern policy, and an argu-
      ment that the imperialist policies of the Soviet government are
      consistent with the foreign policies of Russia's last four tsars.

1406 *Crawley, C. W. "Anglo-Russian Relations, 1815-40." Camb
      Hist J, 3, no. 1 (1929): 47-73.
      An examination of the deterioration of Anglo-Russian relations
      during the decades following the Congress of Vienna. Craw-
      ley contends that "the treatment of Poland, the decay of Tur-
      key, the conquest of the Caucasus with all that it portended,
      and finally ... the Russian commercial system" all combined
      to create a fear of the "Russian menace," a fear which the
      British press and conservative politicians publicized widely.

1407 *Curtiss, John Shelton. "Nicholas I As a Military Man."
      The Russian Army Under Nicholas I, 1825-1855. Durham:
      Duke University Press, 1965, 46-73.
      An examination of Nicholas I's abilities as a military com-
      mander and his efforts to make the Russian army more effi-
      cient and effective. Curtiss devotes most of his attention to
      Nicholas' personal leadership of the 1828 campaign against
      Turkey, the failure of which Curtiss attributes to Nicholas'
      misuse of the forces and materials at his disposal. Separate
      from Nicholas' poor leadership, Curtiss notes that the Russian
      army of 1828-29 suffered from the same shortcomings in logis-
      tics and medical care that plagued it during the Crimean War.
      The remainder of this work does not focus on Nicholas per
      se but contains references to virtually every aspect of his
      military policy including his use of the army for civilian
      purposes, penchant for discipline and trivia, and role in the
      military operations carried out during his reign. DK53.C85
          Reviewed in:
          Eng Hist R, 82 (1967): 410
          Mil Aff, 30, no. 2 (1966): 109
          Rus R, 25, no. 3 (1966): 307-08
          Slavonic E Eur R, 44, no. 103 (1966): 512-13

1408 _____. Russia's Crimean War. Durham: Duke University
      Press, 1979, 597pp., bib. 569-81.
      This study of the origins, course, and settlement of the Cri-
      mean War does not focus specifically on the roles played by
      either Nicholas I and Alexander II, but as a comprehensive,
      scholarly analysis of the war it merits consultation. Of
      particular interest is Curtiss' argument that the Western powers
      bear more responsibility for the outbreak and continuation

of the war than does Nicholas.   DK214.C86

1409   "The Czar and the Sultan."   Putnam's Mo M, 3 (1854):   502-
       05.
       A contrasting of Nicholas I's passion for military life and
       concern for the efficiency and fairness of his government
       with the decadence and disregard for effective rule demon-
       strated by the Turkish Sultan.   The author also defends
       Nicholas' decision to go to war with the Ottoman Empire in
       1853.

1410   "The Effects of the Czar's Death."   Liv Age, 45 (28 Apr.
       1855):   253-55.
       A brief discussion of the likelihood of the Crimean War's
       termination following the death of Nicholas I.

1411   "The Emperor Nicholas."   Eclectic M, 43 (Mar. 1858):   417-19.
       A presentation of Nicholas I as a ruler obsessed by the goal
       of extending Russia's military power and territorial boundaries.

1412   "The Emperor Nicholas."   Fraser's M, 30 (July 1844):   301-16.
       A glowing account of Nicholas I's personal qualities, family
       life, and domestic and foreign policies; occasioned by the
       tsar's 1844 visit to England.   The author concludes by pro-
       posing that Britain and Russia ally to maintain peace in
       Europe and the Near East.

1413   *Gooch, Brison D.   "A Century of Historiography on the Ori-
       gins of the Crimean War."   Am Hist R, 62, no. 1 (1956):
       33-58.
       A useful survey of 100 years of historical writing on the roots
       of the Crimean conflict.   Among the works discussed are those
       by Kinglake, Puryear, Temperley, Rambaud, Marx, and Hen-
       derson.

1414   Goryainov, Sergey M.   "The Secret Agreement of 1844 Between
       Russia and Great Britain."   Rus R (Liverpool), 1, no. 3
       (1912):   97-115; 1, no. 4 (1912):   76-91.
       Unavailable for annotation.

1415   *Hamlin, Cyrus.   "The Political Duel Between Nicholas, the
       Czar of Russia, and Lord Stratford de Redcliffe, the Great
       English Ambassador."   Proc Am Antiq S, 9 (Oct. 1894):   451-
       60.
       A discussion of the encounters between Nicholas I and the
       British statesman Lord Stratford Canning over various affairs
       related to the Eastern Question.   Hamlin depicts Stratford
       Canning as a brilliant statesman who, as ambassador to Tur-
       key, outmaneuvered Nicholas during each of their "diplomatic
       duels."

1416 Henderson, Gavin Burns. "The Diplomatic Revolution of 1854."
      Crimean War Diplomacy and Other Historical Essays. Glasgow:
      Jackson, Smith and Company, 1947, 153-89. Reprint from
      Am Hist R, 43, no. 1 (1937): 22-50.
      In part, a discussion of Russian reaction to the 2 December
      1854 treaty between France, Britain, and Austria, particularly
      in regard to its effects on relations between Russia and Aus-
      tria. Henderson states that the popular opinion in Russia
      was that "Austrian ingratitude" for the Russian aid given
      during the Hungarian Revolution and the treachery of Emperor
      Franz Josef, who Nicholas had regarded with "almost paternal
      affection," had "driven Nicholas to the grave." DK215.H49

1417 *_____. "The Seymour Conversations, 1853." Ibid., 1-14.
      An examination of Nicholas I's conversations with British
      Ambassador to Russia Sir Hamilton Seymour for insight into
      the tsar's responsibility for the outbreak of the Crimean War.
      Henderson contends that a study of the conversations reveals
      that Nicholas was not guilty of plotting war but was grossly
      in error when he assumed that a binding agreement had been
      reached in regard to the British cabinet's acceptance of his
      interpretation of Russia's rights in the Ottoman Empire as
      established in the Treaty of Kuchuk-Kainardji. Nicholas did
      not, however, believe that the Seymour conversations were
      merely a reaffirmation of the arrangement that he had worked
      out in regard to the Eastern Question while in Britain in 1844
      nor did he pursue a policy in the years between 1844 and
      1853 based on the assumption that the understanding
      worked out in 1844 was binding on future British cabinets.
      Henderson concludes that the connection of the 1844 and
      1853 "accords" and Nicholas' alleged nine-year pursuit of a
      policy of dismemberment in respect to the Turkish Empire was
      the work of Lord Aberdeen who was responsible for having
      Parliamentary papers pertinent to the talks published together
      so as to suggest the existence of a continuous policy of calcu-
      lated Near Eastern aggression on Nicholas' part.   DK215.H49

1418 Henningsen, Charles F. Eastern Europe and the Emperor
      Nicholas, Vol. III. London: T. C. Newby, 1846, 381pp.
      A contemporaneous critical estimate of Nicholas I, his govern-
      ment, and the policies which he pursued in his first two
      decades as emperor. Henningsen describes Nicholas as a
      cruel and vindictive tyrant presiding over a "hideous and
      repressive system in which vice and corruption are rampant
      and the interests and rights of the majority are meaningless."
      The author maintains that in spite of the popular opinion that
      the Russian monarchy was a secure one, Nicholas' rule had
      prompted, by the mid-1840s, a growing discontent likely to
      result in dramatic changes in the political make-up of Eastern
      Europe. DK211.H51

1419   Hepple, Edmond. <u>Satan, Balaam, and Nicholas, the Destiny</u>
       <u>of Russia; and the Mission of England.</u> To Which Is Added,
       <u>the Greek Church Versus the Roman Church; with a Letter</u>
       <u>to Lord Stratford de Redcliffe.</u> Newcastle-upon-Tyne, 1854,
       39pp.
       Unavailable for annotation.

1420   Horvath, Eugene. "Russia and the Hungarian Revolution
       (1848-49)." <u>Slavonic R</u>, 12, no. 36 (1934):   628-43.
       An examination of the diplomatic complexities associated with
       Austria's request for Russian aid in the suppression of the
       1848 Hungarian Revolution. Horvath also discusses Lord
       Palmerston's highly negative reaction to Russian intervention
       as a foreshadowing of the outbreak of war between Russia
       and Britain in 1853.

1421   Ingle, Harold N. <u>Nesselrode and the Russian Rapprochement</u>
       <u>with Britain, 1836-44.</u> Berkeley: University of California
       Press, 1976, 196pp., bib. 173-90.
       This scholarly analysis of Anglo-Russian relations during the
       tenure of Foreign Minister Count Karl Nesselrode does not
       include a separate chapter devoted to Nicholas I's part in
       Russia's rapprochement with Britain but does contain a num-
       ber of references to his role in this important diplomatic
       development. DK188.6.N4I53

1422   *Jelavich, Barbara. "Nicholas I." <u>CRFP</u> (gen. study), 71-124.
       A generally positive review of Nicholas I's foreign policy.
       Jelavich maintains that Russia's humiliating defeat in the Cri-
       mean War and Nicholas' pursuit of reactionary domestic policies
       have obscured the many successes that he had in his dealings
       with Russia's neighbors. Specifically, under Nicholas' lead-
       ership, "the Russo-Turkish War had ended in a Russian vic-
       tory, ... cooperation with Britain in the Greek and Egyptian
       questions had led to solutions satisfactory to Russia, ... (and)
       he also kept Germany divided and Poland in political bondage."

1423   *Kinglake, A. W. <u>The Invasion of the Crimea</u>, Vol. I. Lon-
       don: William Blackwood and Sons, 1885 (reprint of 1856 edi-
       tion), 428pp.
       Nicholas I is not the focus of any one chapter in this volume,
       but as part of a classic, eight volume study of the Crimean
       War, this work can be consulted with profit for a contemporary
       English perspective on Nicholas' foreign policy and the specific
       events and transactions which led up to the war's outbreak.
       Kinglake advances the argument that the machinations of
       Napoleon III were far more responsible for the outbreak of the
       conflict than the policies pursued by Nicholas I. DK214.K545

1424   Kipp, Jacob W. "A Few Comments Regarding Historical Sources
       on the Tsarist Navy During the Reigns of Nicholas I and Alex-
       ander II, 1825-1881." <u>Mil Aff</u>, 36, no. 4 (1972):   127-29.

A brief survey of the Russian language materials available
for the study of naval policy and deployment under Nicholas I
and Alexander II.

1425   *Lincoln, W. Bruce. "The Emperor Nicholas I in England."
       Hist Today, 25, no. 1 (1975):   24-30.
       A discussion of the origin and nature of Nicholas I's visit to
       England in June of 1844. Lincoln sees the exceptionally brief
       advance notice given to the British government in regard to
       the tsar's arrival as being a product of Nicholas' habit of
       making unannounced inspection tours of his realm and his re-
       luctance to publicize foreign journeys for fear of being assas-
       sinated by Polish nationalists. While Nicholas "engaged in a
       continual flurry of visits, state dinners, military reviews,
       and other entertainments" during his stay, his prime goal was
       to reach "a straightforward and honest understanding on the
       Eastern Question." Unfortunately for Nicholas, he regarded
       his conversations on this matter as "a formal statement of
       policy while the British regarded them simply as an exchange
       of views on a question of mutual interest."

1426   *_____. "Russia and the European Revolutions of 1848."
       Hist Today, 23, no. 1 (1973):   53-59.
       An account of the reaction of Nicholas I and St. Petersburg
       aristocratic society to the outbreak and spread of revolution
       in Europe in 1848. Lincoln establishes that when revolution
       first broke out in France, Nicholas showed restraint and Peters-
       burg aristocrats "displayed a certain romantic interest," but
       once the revolution began to spread to Central Europe and
       near Russia's western borders, many educated Russians became
       alarmed and Nicholas issued, on March 14th, a manifesto pledg-
       ing to wage a holy war against revolutionary madness.

1427   *Marriott, Sir J. A. R. "Nicholas I and Lord Palmerston--The
       Crimean War." Anglo-Russian Relations. 1689-1943. Lon-
       don: Methuen, 1944, 87-100.
       A discussion of the degree of responsibility shared by the
       principal powers involved in the outbreak of the Crimean War.
       Marriott maintains that while Napoleon III undoubtedly fanned
       the flames of war and various British leaders led Nicholas I
       to believe that "under no circumstances would England draw
       the sword against him," the ultimate responsibility for the war's
       outbreak rests with Nicholas for attempting to force a solution
       to the Eastern Question in advance of the collapse of the
       Ottoman Empire.   DA47.65.M35

1428   Murray, Charles. "Ten Days at Court. The Emperor Nicholas'
       Visit." Cornhill, 75 (Mar. 1897):   341-53.
       The Master to the Household of the Queen of England recollects
       the fanfare associated with the ten day visit of Nicholas I to
       the royal court in 1844.

1429   "Nicholas I and the War in the East." Bentley Misc, 35 (1854):
       213-22.
       A discussion of Nicholas I's responsibility for the outbreak of
       the Crimean War with much reference to the panslav and re-
       ligious motives which allegedly prompted his actions. The
       author makes an impassioned plea for England to thwart Rus-
       sia's drive on Constantinople so that "the peace of the world
       will not again be interrupted by the caprices of ambition or
       insanity."

1430   "Nicholas I's Visit to England." Blackwood's M, 56 (1842):
       127.
       Unavailable for annotation.

1431   "A Passage in the Life of the Late Czar." Bentley's Misc, 38
       (1855): 182-85.
       A brief discussion of Nicholas I's visit to Italy and the Vatican
       as the only time during his life that he actually saw the
       Mediterranean Sea to which he so badly wanted Russia to
       have open access. The author attributes Nicholas' death to
       the collapse of his health once he realized, amidst the defeats
       suffered by Russia in the Crimean War, that his ambitions
       were misguided.

1432   *Puryear, Vernon John. England, Russia, and the Straits
       Question 1844-1856. Berkeley: University of California
       Press, 1931, 481pp., bib. 450-68.
       A detailed and scholarly analysis of the complex origins of the
       Crimean War. Puryear states that "the general causes of the
       Crimean War may be viewed from two principal angles: the
       imperial rivalries of Great Britain and Russia in Asia, in
       which the commercial and strategic potentialities of the Near
       East played a dominant role, and the failure, in a time of
       crisis, of the diplomatic arrangements embodied in the Anglo-
       Russian secret agreement of 1844." In regard to the latter
       cause, Puryear stresses the role played by Nicholas I's view
       of the 1844 agreement as one rigidly binding on subsequent
       British governments, the lack of continuity in British policy
       toward the Eastern Question, and in particular, the inflam-
       matory reports sent to London from Constantinople by British
       diplomat Stratford Canning. Puryear concludes that "in jus-
       tice to historical accuracy the principal responsibility for the
       actual outbreak of the Crimean War should be assessed to
       Stratford Canning." DK215.P98

1433   *_____. "New Light on the Origins of the Crimean War."
       J Mod Hist, 3, no. 2 (1931): 219-34.
       An argument that documentary evidence for the years 1844-54
       proves that the secret understanding arranged by Nicholas I
       in the summer of 1844 in regard to Anglo-Russian cooperation
       in the peaceful settlement of all issues associated with the

dissolution of the Ottoman Empire "was continued in force in the nine years which preceded the Crimean War" and formed the basis for the 1853 conversations in St. Petersburg between Nicholas and Sir Hamilton Seymour regarding the partition of Turkey. Puryear also discusses the factors which led Britain to insist that the dissolution of Turkey was not at hand in 1853.

1434 *"Revelations of Russia." New Quar R, 4, no. 2 (1844): 357-91.

The two-volume work Revelations of Russia; or, The Emperor Nicholas and His Empire in 1844 (London: Colburn) serves as the basis for a sharp attack on the British press for serving as a "fawning courtier" of Nicholas I during his visit to England. The author draws from the Revelations a series of negative conclusions in regard to Nicholas' character and the corrupt and venal nature of his administration.

1435 Rock, Kenneth Willet. "Reaction Triumphant: The Diplomacy of Felix Schwarzenberg and Nicholas I in Mastering the Hungarian Insurrection, 1848-1850. A Study in Dynastic Power, Principles, and Politics in Revolutionary Times." Stanford University, 1969. (dissertation)

1436 *_____. "Schwarzenberg Versus Nicholas I, Round One: The Negotiation of the Habsburg-Romanov Alliance Against Hungary in 1849." Aust Hist Y, 6-7, (1970-71): 109-41; Reply, 160-63; Rejoinder, 164-65.

An examination of the 1849 emergence in Austria of the belief that Austria was not "to remain Russia's protégé but rather was to "carry its own weight as a European Great Power." Rock establishes that at the forefront of this attempt to rejuvenate Austria's image was Felix Schwarzenberg, who initially tried to present Russia's assistance in the crushing of the Hungarian rebels in such a way that Austria's international prestige would not suffer. Reluctantly, Schwarzenberg abandoned such an approach as he saw the urgent need for Russian military aid once the success of the rebels put him in a panicky frame of mind. However, Schwarzenberg remained determined to disavow "a subservient attitude toward the Romanov colossus" and as soon as victory was assured actively worked to downplay the significance of Russia's role in the Austrian victory.

1437 Rodkey, Frederick S. The Turco-Egyptian Question in the Relations of England, France and Russia, 1832-41. New York: Russell and Russell, 1972 (reprint of 1924 edition), 274pp., bib. 253-63.

This work does not contain a separate chapter devoted to Nicholas I, but as a scholarly study of the early stages of the Eastern Question, particularly in regard to England's response to Nicholas I's designs on Constantinople, it warrants consultation. D375.R7

1438 *Schmitt, Bernadette E. "The Diplomatic Preliminaries of the Crimean War." Am Hist R, 25, no. 1 (1919): 36-67.
A discussion of the degree of responsibility shared by the principal powers for the outbreak of the Crimean War. Schmitt concludes that Nicholas I "knew from the beginning what he wanted, and observing that Europe would not unite to oppose him, yielded none of his demands.... Napoleon probably desired war, but made a parade of pacific intentions. Great Britain at the outset unquestionably desired peace, but did not make clear that the designs of Russia would be resisted, by force if necessary, thereby encouraging the tsar to stand his ground. Austria's attitude, until too late, was equally uncertain.... In the face of such confusion war could not have been avoided only by a miracle."

1439 Tarsaidzé, Alexandre. "Always Poland." CP (gen. study), 94-104.
A discussion of the difficulties associated with America's attempt to negotiate a commercial treaty with the government of Nicholas I. Tarsaidzé maintains that Nicholas' fear of alienating England by concluding a treaty with America guaranteeing the rights of neutrals to trade in time of war and the negative press reaction caused by Nicholas' crushing of the Polish Revolt in 1831 were the principal obstacles to the conclusion of the treaty.

1440 _____. "Crimean War." Ibid., 149-67.
Although Nicholas I is not the focus of this chapter, it contains some interesting insights into Russian-American relations during the Crimean War, particularly in regard to his attempt to capitalize on pro-Russian feeling in America.

1441 *Tatischeff, Serge. "A Forgotten Chapter in Anglo-Russian Relations. Emperor Nicholas I in England." Nat R, 39 (June 1902): 564-80.
An account of Nicholas I's June 1844 visit to England. Tatischeff states that the purpose of Nicholas' visit was "to dissipate those anti-Russian prejudices which had taken root in the English court, government, and public opinion, to inspire confidence in himself and his personal character, and by a frank exchange of views on the chief questions of European politics to try to establish a sincere and lasting understanding with the British government." While Nicholas' visit was an outward success, Tatischeff concludes, it failed to win English support for Russia's position in regard to the settlement of the Eastern Question.

1442 *Temperley, Harold. "How Czar Nicholas Negotiated (1840-

1854)." England and the Near East. The Crimea. New York:
Archon Books, 1964 (reprint of 1936 edition), 251-79.
An analysis of Nicholas I's attempt to arrive at a mutually
beneficial understanding with Britain in regard to what he
perceived to be the imminent collapse of the Ottoman Empire.
Temperley contends that Nicholas, in his dealings with Palmerston, Seymour, and other British leaders, was inspired by
"sincere and even noble concerns" rather than the "dark ambitions" often attributed to him by Western analysts. If
Nicholas is to be criticized, Temperley concludes, it should
be for his use of poor judgment in discussing "potentialities
with parliamentarians" and believing that "the word or friendship of Queen Victoria was all-important." The remainder of
this scholarly study of British Near Eastern policy in the mid-
nineteenth century warrants consultation by students of the
events and developments which led Russia into the ill-fated
Crimean War. D376.G7T4

1443 Walker, F. A. "The Rejection of Stratford Canning by Nicholas I." Inst Hist Res B, 40 (May 1967): 50-64.
Unavailable for annotation.

1444 Webster, Sir Charles. "Tsar and Sultan: The Development
of the Eastern Question, 1835-1839." The Foreign Policy of
Palmerston 1830-1841, Vol. II. New York: Humanities Press,
1969, 523-618.
An examination of the Near Eastern policy pursued by Nicholas I in the late 1830s. Webster devotes most of his attention
to reviewing Britain's attempt to modernize the Ottoman Empire and to block, through diplomacy, and military means if
necessary, Russian expansion at Turkey's expense.
DA535.W4

GENERAL STUDIES AND ASSESSMENTS/
PERSONAL AFFAIRS AND CHARACTER

1445 Abrash, Merritt. "A Curious Royal Romance: The Queen's
      Son and the Tsar's Daughter." Slavonic E Eur R, 47 (1969):
      389-400.
      A discussion of the 1874 marriage of Queen Victoria's second
      son, Alfred, to Alexander II's only daughter, Marie, against
      the background of Anglo-Russian relations of the 1870s.

1446 Alexander, Grand Duke of Russia. Once a Grand Duke. New
      York: Farrar and Rinehart, 1932, 348pp.
      Recollections of various incidents in the life of Alexander II,
      most notably his relationship with Princess Catherine Yuriev-
      sky and family reaction to his 1881 assassination.
      DK219.6.A4A3 1932

1447 "Alexander II." Liv Age, 46 (1855): 501-06.
      Speculation on how Alexander II's reign might differ from that
      of Nicholas I.

1448 Almedingen, E. M. The Emperor Alexander II. London: Bod-
      ley Head, 1962, 367pp.
      A popular and favorable discussion of Alexander II's character
      and accomplishments. Almedingen notes the shortcomings of
      Alexander's reforms and his turn to more conservative rule in
      the second half of his reign but maintains that his achieve-
      ments nonetheless place him on the same general level as his
      most illustrious predecessors. She concludes that even though
      Russia was still in need of major reform upon the death of
      Alexander, he should not be faulted for this circumstance
      since "it would have demanded the united energies of several
      titans wholly to transform the Empire within one generation."
      DK241.B3

1449 Baddeley, John F. Russia in the 'Eighties.' Sport and Politics.
      London: Longmans, Green and Company, 1921, 466pp.

The memoirs of a British correspondent for the Standard who
was stationed in St. Petersburg during the 1880s. Baddeley
does not devote any one chapter of his work to Alexander II
but does present a number of observations and anecdotes in
regard to him and his successor. Of particular interest are
Baddeley's comments on Alexander's relationship with Princess
Yurievsky, the various attempts on the tsar's life, and public reaction to his assassination. DK241.B3

1450 Blanch, Lesley. "The Winter Palace." Pavilions of the Heart.
London: Weidenfeld and Nicolson, 1974, 178-88.
An emotional account of the love of Alexander II for his mistress and second (morganatic) wife Princess Catherine Yurievsky. Blanch discusses Alexander's initial contacts with Catherine, his fascination with her, and the difficulties he had
carrying on his affair with her under the eyes of the royal
family and imperial court. CT105.B584

1451 Burford, Robert. Description of a View of the City of Moscow,
with the Gorgeous Entry of His Imperial Majesty, The Emperor Alexander II, into the Kremlin. London: W. J. Gol-
burn, 1857, 20pp. DK601.B8
Unavailable for annotation.

1452 Crankshaw, Edward. "Chapters 9-16." The Shadow of the
Winter Palace. New York: Viking Press, 1976, 152-271.
An assessment of Alexander II's reign in terms of its place
on Russia's road to revolution. Crankshaw maintains that the
provocative influence of Alexander's inadequate reforms and
the disastrous consequences of his German and Near Eastern
policies were major factors in the growth of revolutionary
discontent within Russia and, more importantly, the deterioration of Russia's international position. DK189.C66

1453 Fülöp-Miller, René, ed. Under Three Tsars. The Memoirs
of the Lady-in-Waiting Elizabeth Narishkin-Kurakin. Julia E.
Loesser, trans. New York: E. P. Dutton, 1931, 231pp.
Recollections of the Russian court under the last three Romanovs. Narishkin-Kurakin, who was on intimate terms with various members of the royal family, comments most typically on
court reaction to Alexander's domestic policies, his relationship
with Princess Yurievsky, and his 1881 assassination.
DK188.6.N25A32

1454 Graham, Stephen. Tsar of Freedom. The Life and Reign of
Alexander II. Hamden: Archon Books, 1968 (reprint of 1935
edition), 324pp., bib. 315-17.
A discussion of Alexander II's principal policies as an expression of his attempt to cope with Russia's domestic needs as a
developing nation, and at the same time, advance Russia's
international position. Graham states that Alexander sincerely

wished to implement reforms that would bring Russia into
line with the mainstream of European development but lost his
enthusiasm for this demanding task because of conservative
opposition and the hostile response of radicals dissatisfied
with the extent of his changes. By the 1877 outbreak of
hostilities with Turkey, Alexander had become indolent, and
was content to withdraw into his personal life and delegate
authority for governmental affairs to trusted advisers. Despite becoming a victim of the tide of opinion which most
immediately surrounded him, Graham concludes, Alexander
still deserves credit for "the inauguration of freedom in Russia" and for sowing the seeds for the modernization of his
realm by way of the reforms of the 1860s. DK220.G7 1968

1455   Hodgetts, E. A. Brayley. "Alexander II." The Court of
       Russia in the Nineteenth Century, Vol. II. New York:
       Charles Scribner's Sons, 1908, 1-203.
       A readable and balanced narrative on Alexander II's life and
       reign. Hodgetts provides most depth on the emancipation of
       the serfs, the growth of the revolutionary movement, and
       Alexander's conduct of diplomacy, personal life, and 1881
       assassination. DK189.H75

1456   "Imperial Coronation at Moscow." Eclectic M, 68 (Jan. 1867):
       128-30.
       A brief, firsthand account of the coronation of Alexander II
       and the elaborate festivities associated with this event.

1457   Kelen, Betty. "Romance and Counter-Romance." The Mis-
       tresses. The Domestic Scandals of Nineteenth Century Mon-
       archs. London: W. H. Allen, 1966, 118-49.
       A dramatic portrayal of Alexander II's relationship with his
       wife, Elizabeth, and mistress, Princess Catherine Yurievsky.
       Kelen describes Alexander's attraction to the youthful princess,
       seduction of her, and close relationship which they came to
       share during the 1865-1881 period. Kelen gives special at-
       tention to the lengths to which Alexander went to maintain
       this relationship amidst the reproach of high society and
       the dangers posed by assassins. DK352.1.K4 1966

1458   Konovalov, S. "The Emperor Alexander II and Princess
       Ekaterina Dolgorukaya (Yurievskaya): Nine Letters." Ox
       Slavonic P, 11 (1964): 94-100.
       A brief introduction to nine letters exchanged between Alex-
       ander II and his morganatic wife which cast light on his
       character, personality, and private life. Six of the letters
       were written by Alexander, three by Catherine.

1459   Krasinski, Henryk. Private Anecdotes of the Late and Present
       Emperors of Russia, the King of Prussia, and the Sultan.
       London: Wells, 1858.
       Unavailable for annotation.

1460 *Kropotkin, Peter. Memoirs of a Revolutionist. New York:
      Horizon Press, 1968 (reprint of 1899 edition), 502pp.
      These memoirs of a noted Russian anarchist contain a char-
      acter sketch of Alexander II and an account of liberal disap-
      pointment with the reforms of the 1860s. Kropotkin, who was
      in the Corps of Pages in the early 1860s, describes how his
      youthful admiration for Alexander as the liberator of the serfs
      gave way to disdain as tsarist policy took a reactionary turn
      in the mid-1860s. Kropotkin also comments on court security,
      the 1866 Karakazov attempt on Alexander's life, and the public
      impact of the 1881 assassination of Alexander. HX915.K92

1461 Murphy, John. Russia at the Time of the Coronation of Alex-
      ander II. London: Bradbury and Evans, 1856, 171pp.
      A series of letters written by a correspondent to the Daily
      News describing the coronation of Alexander II. Murphy
      presents an account of the coronation ceremony and the vari-
      ous public functions which accompanied it and includes a copy
      of the official coronation program. DK26.M97

1462 Murray, Eustace C. The Russians Today. London: Smith,
      Elder and Company, 1878, 304pp.
      As part of a discussion of the basic characteristics of post-
      emancipation Russia, this work includes an assessment of
      Alexander II's failure to continue along the liberal path on
      which he placed the monarchy in the early 1860s. Murray
      maintains that Alexander was sincere in his desire to modern-
      ize Russia but his plans to implement enlightened reforms were
      thwarted by a shortsighted, conservative aristocracy.
      DK26.M98

1463 Oxley, T. Louis. A Glance at the Character and Reign of
      Alexander the Second, Late Emperor of Russia. London:
      Kerby and Endean, 1881, 25pp.
      Unavailable for annotation.

1464 Paléologue, Maurice. The Tragic Romance of Alexander II of
      Russia. Arthur Chambers, trans. London: Hutchinson and
      Company, 1927, 216pp.
      A dramatic and sympathetic account of Alexander II's romantic
      relationship with Princess Yurievsky. Paléologue, who was
      assigned to the French embassy in St. Petersburg during
      Alexander's reign, describes the origins and development of
      Alexander's relationship with Yurievsky, the scandal which
      the affair prompted within the royal court, and Alexander's
      eventual morganatic marriage to her upon the 1880 death of
      his wife, Empress Marie. DK220.P33 1927

1465 Pfeil-Burghausz, R. F. A. Graf Von. "An Explosion at the
      Winter Palace." RR, 10 (Dec. 1894): 677-79.
      A vivid description of the explosion at the Winter Palace on
      2 February 1880 during the festivities connected with the

silver jubilee of the coronation of Alexander II.

1466   Rhea, Hortense. "Acquaintance with Alexander II." Century,
        63 (Apr. 1902): 835-36.
        A positive recollection of a meeting with Alexander II following
        an acting performance by the author. Rhea also relates her
        feelings upon hearing that Alexander had been assassinated.

1467   *Rieber, Alfred J. "Alexander II: A Revisionist View."
        J Mod Hist, 43, no. 1 (1971): 43-58.
        An argument that historians who attempt to evaluate the motives
        and goals behind Alexander II's domestic policies by using
        "artificial criteria lifted from the experience of western Eu-
        rope" obscure the fundamental continuity of his reign and en-
        courage the erroneous conclusion that Alexander was a weak
        and inconsistent ruler. Rieber maintains that if one keeps in
        mind Alexander's habit of "balancing off the contending groups
        and personalities who sought his favor" so that he could ex-
        ploit rather than reconcile "the conflicting interests within the
        government and throughout the country," then one can see
        that, far from a liberal-conservative dichotomy, his reign was
        characterized by the consistent pursuit of a policy designed
        "to preserve both the power of the state and the loyalty of
        his subjects." Within this context, Rieber discusses Alex-
        ander's concerted effort to improve the fiscal and military
        condition of Russia.

1468   Robertson, James R. "The Assassination of Lincoln and the
        Attempt on the Life of Emperor Alexander." A Kentuckian
        at the Court of the Tsars. The Ministry of Cassius Marcellus
        Clay to Russia, 1861-1862 and 1863-1869. Berea, Ky.:
        Berea College Press, 1935, 191-97.
        An account of the Russian government's response to Lincoln's
        assassination and American official reaction to the 1866 at-
        tempt on Alexander II's life. Robertson devotes most of
        his attention to a description of the festivities which sur-
        rounded the St. Petersburg reception of the American dele-
        gation, headed by Assistant Secretary of the Navy Gustavus
        Fox, which conveyed a Congressional message to Alexander
        congratulating him for his "providential escape from danger."
        E415.9.C55R6

1469   Tarsaidzé, Alexandre. Katia. Wife Before God. New York:
        Macmillan, 1970, 348pp., bib. 327-36.
        An account of Alexander II's romantic relationship with
        Princess Catherine Yurievsky. In describing the genesis of
        this relationship, its tenderness, and the stir it created
        within the Russian court, Tarsaidzé sheds some light on
        Alexander's personality, daily habits, and family life. Based
        primarily on the correspondence between Alexander and
        Yurievsky. DK219.6.I8T37

1470 Towle, George Makepeace. "Three Emperors." Certain Men
      of Mark. Studies of Living Celebrities. Boston: Roberts
      Brothers, 1880, 213-42.
      A favorable sketch of the characters, abilities, and policies
      of Alexander II, William I of Germany, and Francis Joseph of
      Austria-Hungary. Towle sees Alexander as a humane and
      energetic monarch whose sincere desire to improve the general
      condition of Russia was dampened by conservative advisers,
      radical critics, and the enormity of the tasks which confronted
      him if he were to act upon his desires. CT119.T7

1471 "Vanished Splendor of Russia." Life, 38 (31 Jan. 1955): 60-
      67.
      A heavily illustrated commemoration of the centennial of Alex-
      ander II's coronation.

1472 Vassili, Count Paul. Behind the Veil at the Russian Court.
      New York: John Lane, 1914, 408pp.
      The diaries of Princess Catherine Radziwill who spent six
      decades immersed in Russian court life. In a gossipy, anec-
      dotal fashion, Radziwill comments on Alexander II's accession
      to the throne, principal reforms, relationship with key ad-
      visers, personal life, and his 1881 assassination. She char-
      acterizes Alexander as an individual easily influenced as a
      consequence of his accommodating personality and lack of
      firm commitment to any one set of ideals. DK189.R3

1473 Wellesley, Colonel F. A. "Alexander." With the Russians in
      Peace and War. London: Eveleigh Nash, 1905, 227-40.
      A portrayal of Alexander II as a compassionate, composed,
      and highly intelligent sovereign. Wellesley, a British military
      attaché stationed in St. Petersburg from 1871 to 1878, supports
      his generous character assessment with anecdotes based on
      conversations with and observation of Alexander at the royal
      court and while on military campaign in Bulgaria during the
      Russo-Turkish War. Wellesley also includes an account of
      Alexander's assassination as described by eyewitness Prince
      Michael Dolgoruky, the brother of Alexander's morganatic
      wife Catherine. DK221.W3

1474 Wortman, Richard. "The Russian Empress as Mother." FIR
      (anthology), 60-74.
      This essay contains a number of references to Alexander II
      as part of a discussion of the influence of nineteenth century
      Russian empresses on "the characters, personal style, and
      tastes of their sons, the heirs."

                  DOMESTIC POLICY AND AFFAIRS/
                  POLITICAL THOUGHT AND PRACTICE

1475 Appleton, Nathan. "Alexander II and Emancipation." Russian

Life and Society. Boston: Murray and Emery, 1904, 184-206.
A general account of the genesis, preparation, and implementation of the 1861 Emancipation Act, and a personal recollection
of public response to the assassination of Alexander II; written by an American army captain who met Alexander on several
occasions. DK 26.A 65

1476 "Assassination of Alexander II. And Its Effect upon the Future
of Russia." Am Cath Q, 6, no. 22 (Apr. 1881): 279-87.
An attack upon the Russian radicals responsible for the death
of Alexander II, and a warning that the "nihilism" which
threatened the existence of the Russian monarchy would soon
be a danger for all of Europe.

1477 Ayling, S. E. "Tsar Alexander II: Reform and Frustration
in Russia." Nineteenth Century Gallery. New York: Barnes
and Noble, 1970, 332-68.
A discussion of the initial reforms implemented by Alexander
II, his turn to more conservative policies in the mid-1860s, and
the hostile reaction of liberals and radicals who were both disappointed and angered by his failure to reform Russia to the
extent which they believed necessary. Ayling states that although Alexander's principal reforms "added up to a considerable revolution," their effectiveness was compromised from the
very beginning by the tsar's own ambivalent feelings toward
them and by the staunch opposition of conservatives who
feared that Alexander was "opening the floodgates to liberalism
and revolution." D 352.5.A 9

1478 *Balmuth, Daniel. "Bibliographical Note on the Russian Censorship Under Alexander II." Can Slav S, 3, no. 2 (1969):
377-82.
A brief review of Russian language sources available for the
study of Alexander II's censorship policy. Balmuth maintains
that "the study of press policy offers a prime example of
that delicate balance of change and stability that marked
Alexander II's reign."

1479 *_____. Censorship in Russia, 1865-1905. Washington,
D.C.: University Press of America, 1979, 249pp., bib.
225-39.
The first six chapters of this scholarly study focus upon the
censorship policy pursued by Alexander II during the last
fifteen years of his reign. Balmuth establishes that the government's initial easing of pre-publication controls on the
press was prompted by Alexander's desire to win support for
impending reforms. His liberal stance on censorship, however, was replaced in the mid-1860s by one of stern paternal-
ism as his inherent distrust of journalists surfaced in response to "irresponsible" behavior by some writers and because he felt less need for public support after the emancipation question had been settled. While censorship policy

became increasingly conservative during the last decade of
Alexander's rule, censorship itself was not as rigid or all
encompassing as official policy would indicate primarily because many censors were willing to cooperate with writers "in
softening the harsh phrase or eliminating the culpable sentence" so that works critical of the government might still be
published.

1480 * _____. "Origins of the Russian Press Reform of 1865."
Slavonic E Eur R, 47 (1969): 369-88.
An examination of the 1865 press reform from the perspective
of the conflict between the liberal position of A. V. Golovin,
the Minister of Education, and the conservative position of
P. A. Valuyev, the Minister of the Interior, supported by
Alexander II. Balmuth contends that the "long debate ended
in a compromise (which) reflected more of the 'conservative'
than the 'liberal' position," largely because of the government's increased fear of revolution and subversion.

1481 Baron, Salo W. "Under Nicholas I and Alexander II." RJTS
(gen. study), 31-50.
A discussion of the limited nature of Alexander II's progressive policy toward Russia's Jews. Baron maintains that Alexander was willing to abandon the ineffective and repressive
policies of Nicholas I but did not believe the Jews had any
innate right to equality with Russia's other citizens. Alexander subscribed to the conservative view that the Jews had
to "earn" emancipation even though he realized that their
ability to do so was severely restricted by the inequalities
under which they suffered.

1482 Broido, Vera. "Alexander II and Reform." Apostles into
Terrorists. Women and the Revolutionary Movement in Russia
of Alexander II. New York: Viking Press, 1977, 33-44.
A discussion of the intellectual climate in Russia during the
first decade of Alexander II's reign, and an account of radical
disappointment with the substance of the tsar's educational,
legal, and peasant reforms. DK221.B76 1977

1483 _____. "Regicide." Ibid., 191-205.
A review of the various plots devised by members of the
People's Will (Narodnaya Volya) to assassinate Alexander II.
Broida also describes Alexander's assassination, public reac-
tion to it, and the destruction of the People's Will by the
tsarist secret police in the aftermath of the tsar's death.
DK221.B76 1977

1484 *Brooks, E. Willis. "Reform in the Russian Army, 1856-1861."
Slav R, 43, no. 1, (1984): 63-82.
An argument that, contrary to prevailing historical opinion,
the period between 1856 and 1861 witnessed important reforms
in the Russian army which foreshadowed the more celebrated

reforms of the 1860s. Brooks concedes that General N. O.
Sukhozanet was, as Minister of War during this time period,
a pedantic dawdler who held his position solely because the
newly crowned Alexander II initially preferred to appoint
pliant ministers rather than ones with fixed and dynamic ideas
of their own. However, exclusive of the war ministry, important and far-reaching reforms were approved by Alexander
during the major military campaign he ordered to complete the
pacification of the Caucasian tribes. Under the direction of
Prince A. I. Bariatinsky, with the assistance of D. A. Miliutin, the army in the Caucasus region underwent a series of
reforms that radically improved the training of officers and
men, the system of promotions, and the chain of command.
Brooks concludes that while Alexander may not have understood from the outset that the changes introduced during the
Caucasian campaign might serve as models for a general reform of the army, he certainly demonstrated an eagerness to
improve the army and willingness to test reform ideas, and,
by so doing, paved the way for the fundamental reforms
authored by Miliutin in the 1860s.

1485   Chambers, Ross. "Orthodoxy and Reform in the Reign of Alex-
       ander II." J Relig Hist, 12, no. 3 (1983): 233-49.
       An examination of the response to Alexander II's reforms by
       the prominent ecclesiastics grouped around the Moscow journal
       Pravoslavnoe obozrenie (The Orthodox Review). Chambers
       establishes that the loosening of state regulation of church
       affairs and the weakening of control within the church during
       Alexander's first decade as tsar were welcomed by the contri-
       butors to Pravoslavnoe obozrenie as an opportunity to "re-
       define the church's role in society." More specifically, the
       journal's contributors believed that Orthodoxy, in the more
       open conditions of Alexander's reign, could play a major role
       in leading the nation along the path of progress, a path
       which they hoped might lead to the restoration of the church
       to "its proper place in Russian life" and, ultimately, to an
       end to social injustice. While these views proved to be too
       optimistic, Chambers concludes, they reveal "a continuing
       vitality within the church, a desire to find an independent
       Orthodox standpoint from which to evaluate state and society
       in Russia, and a willingness to respond to the modern world
       and issues of social change."

1486   "Emperor Alexander." Lippin M, 6 (Aug. 1870): 149-52.
       A recreation of a discussion with an anonymous Russian aristo-
       crat concerning Alexander II's reasons for emancipating the
       serfs. The author also comments on Alexander's interest in
       maintaining good relations with America.

1487   *Field, Daniel. The End of Serfdom. Nobility and Bureau-
       cracy in Russia, 1855-1861. Cambridge: Harvard University

Press, 1976, 471pp., bib. 449-64.
A scholarly examination of the immediate origins of the Emancipation Act. In discussing Alexander II's role in the formulation of the act, Field states that the complexities that marked the official deliberations on the abolition question were beyond Alexander but he had sufficient intelligence to delegate broad authority to the capable Count Rostovtsev. Alexander stood firmly behind Rostovtsev and, in this capacity, played a crucial role in the emancipation debates. Field sees considerable ambiguity and uncertainty in the reform process but does not believe these qualities indicate that there was a concerted opposition to emancipation which Alexander, through Rostovtsev, was called upon to counter. Emancipation was associated with the will of the sovereign and therefore the nobility did not question it but merely argued over its form since "the shibboleths of autocratic authority and unswerving will were powerful weapons in the political culture of Russia."
HD715.F47

1488 * _____. Rebels in the Name of the Tsar. Boston: Houghton Mifflin, 1976, 220pp.
An interesting investigation into the phenomenom of "naive monarchism," meaning the devotion of the common people to the tsar. As concrete illustrations of this abstracton, Field presents accounts of an 1861 incident in the village of Bezdna, which sprang from a rumor that the local gentry had misrepresented Alexander II's Emancipation Act, and the Chigrin affair of the late 1870s, which involved a conflict between the government and the peasants of the Chigrin district (near Kiev) over the institutional forms of land tenure. DK221.F48

1489 Footman, David. The Alexander Conspiracy. A Life of A. I. Zhelyabov. LaSalle, Ill.: Open Court, 1974, 354pp.
An account of the assassination of Alexander II from the perspective of one of the leading participants in the conspiracy from which the fatal deed sprang. DK219.6.Z5F6

1490 Freeze, Gregory L. "P. A. Valuyev and the Politics of Church Reform (1861-1862)." Slavonic E Eur R, 56, no. 1 (1979): 68-87.
The focus of this study is P. A. Valuyev's role in the creation of the Special Commission on the Affairs of the Orthodox Clergy, but it also includes some discussion of Alexander II's views on the composition of the Commission as well as on the broader issue of the reform of the Orthodox Church's structure.

1491 Greenberg, Louis. "Jewish Emancipation in the Reign of Alexander II of Russia." Yale University, 1941. (dissertation)

1492 *_____. "The New Era of Alexander II" and "The Jewish
Policies of Alexander II." JR, Vol. I (gen. study), 73-100.
A critical review of Alexander II's Jewish policies. Greenberg states that Alexander's liberalization of the laws on
Jewish educational, occupational, and settlement rights and
his abolition of juvenile conscription inspired Jewish confidence in his government. However, Greenberg adds, the
Jews' hope for the continued improvement of their status
and, eventually, for full emancipation was a naive one since
the tsar's reforms were due only to his need to make some concessions to the demands for social and political change which
surfaced after the Crimean War. Alexander, in fact, shared
the conservative views of his father, Nicholas I, in regard
to "the Jewish problem," and thus he believed that "only
through their 'moral' improvement, which, in his opinion,
could be achieved only through Russification and productive
activities, would the Jews earn their civic rights." Greenberg goes on to discuss the anti-Semitic sentiments and
policies which dominated upper governmental spheres in the
1870s as proof of Alexander's deep-rooted anti-Semitism.

1493 *Hans, N. "The Period of Liberal Reforms (1856-1866)" and
"The Administration of Count D. A. Tolstoy." HREP (gen.
study), 92-139.
An argument that Alexander II's general policy toward education was a "liberal and progressive" one despite "the severe
censorship and other reactionary policies that marred the
period." In support of this contention, Hans asserts that
during Alexander's reign "the number of schools of all kinds
and of scholars in them increased tremendously" as did "the
percentage of scholars of lower origin in general and of
peasants in particular." Thus while the division of Alexander's reign into liberal and conservative halves may be an
apt one when considering his domestic policies as a whole,
it is unwarranted when evaluating his educational reforms
since "the period of 1856-1881 witnessed the greatest evolution of Russian education, the Duma period excepted."

1494 Herbst, Clarence A. "The Assassination of Alexander II."
Hist Bull, 24, no. 2 (1946): 29-30, 40-42.
A review of the various attempts on Alexander II's life, and
an account of the decline of "nihilism" in Russia amidst the
police crackdown on radicalism which followed the tsar's
death.

1495 *Johanson, Christine. "Autocratic Politics, Public Opinion,
and Women's Medical Education During the Reign of Alexander
II, 1855-1881." Slav R, 38, no. 3 (1979): 426-43.
A discussion of the impact of public debate and interministeri-
al disputes on the direction taken by women's medical education under Alexander II. Johanson maintains that "the

simultaneous development of competing policies on women's
medical education not only testifies to the lack of coordina-
tion in the tsarist administration, but incidates that favored
statesmen enjoyed a relative degree of autonomy in matters
that were peripheral to the interests of the tsar."

1496 Kamen, Henry. "Women and Revolution Under Alexander II."
Hist Today, 15, no. 6 (1965): 400-08.
An account of the role played by such women revolutionaries
as V. Figner, S. Perovsky, and V. Zasulich in the radical
populist organization responsible for the assassination of
Alexander II.

1497 Knutson, Gordon D. "Peter Valuev: A Conservative's Approach and Reactions to the Reforms of Alexander II."
University of Kansas, 1970. (dissertation)

1498 Kohls, Winfried A. "The State-Sponsored Russian Secondary
School in the Reign of Alexander II. The First Phase:
Search for a New Formula, 1855-1864." University of Cali-
fornia, Berkeley, 1967. (dissertation)

1499 *Kucherov, Samuel. "The Judicial Reform of November 20,
1864." Courts, Lawyers and Trials Under the Last Three
Tsars. New York: Frederick A. Praeger, 1953, 21-106.
In part, an examination of the role played by Alexander II
in the deliberations which preceded the enactment of the
1864 reform of Russia's judicial system. Kucherov commends
Alexander for his January 1862 ordering of the State Chancellery to reform the nation's juridical institutions on the
basis of progressive European practices and for his soliciting
from the Russian public suggestions on the proposed reforms.
Kucherov also reviews Russian and European contemporary
reaction to the reform as well as the more recent views of
Soviet and Western analysts. KR397.K8

1500 Laugel, A. "Alexander II in European Politics." Nation, 32
(1881): 275-76.
A favorable review of Alexander II's domestic accomplishments,
and an attack on the Russian radicals responsible for the
premature termination of his reign.

1501 *Leary, D. B. "Alexander II, 1855-1881." EAR (gen. study),
67-81.
An evaluation of Alexander II's educational reforms within the
context of the division of his reign into progressive and reactionary stages. Leary concludes that Alexander's initial
reforms constituted an impressive foundation upon which a
modern system might have developed were it not for the conservative turn taken by tsarist policy in the mid-1860s.

1502 Lincoln, E. Bruce. "The Editing Commissions of 1859-1860:
      Some Notes on Their Members' Backgrounds and Service
      Careers." Slavonic E Eur R, 56, no. 3 (1979): 346-59.
      A study of the social and service backgrounds of the 38
      active members appointed by Alexander II to the Editing
      Commission which drafted the 1861 Emancipation Act. Lin-
      coln states that the Commission's members were relatively
      young and "were extremely well-educated and, on the whole,
      possessed a degree of specialization that was unusual for a
      commission of the time." He contends that the emperor
      "drew upon those segments of the nobility and intelligentsia
      which he regarded as least threatening to his autocratic
      power, and then made an effort to ensure their reliability by
      co-opting them into an essentially bureaucratic body."

1503 *_____. "The Ministers of Alexander II: A Survey of
      Their Backgrounds and Service Careers." Cahiers du monde,
      17, no. 4 (1976): 476-83.
      An argument that while Alexander II's ministers were better
      educated and had more technical and administrative expertise
      than those of Nicholas I, they still were "far from being able
      to deal effectively with the pressing problems which faced
      them." Lincoln identifies as the roots of their ineffectiveness
      the stifling of efficiency and creativity by the ministerial
      system itself and the insecurity felt by ministers due to Alex-
      ander's attempt to "maintain the fullness of his own power by
      fostering divergent outlooks at the highest level of govern-
      ment."

1504 _____. "Murder Near the Cathedral." Hist Today, 25, no.
      3 (1975): 175-84.
      A dramatic account of the conspiracy which led to the assas-
      sination of Alexander II by members of the People's Will.

1505 *_____. "The Problem of Glastnost' in Mid-Nineteenth Cen-
      tury Russian Politics." Eur St R, 11, no. 2 (1981): 171-88.
      A discussion of Alexander II's attempt to encourage the devel-
      opment of a body of public opinion which could be relied upon
      for "advice in planning change and assistance in carrying out
      any programme of reform." Lincoln maintains that Alexander's
      efforts in this direction were stifled by his unwillingness to
      risk establishing a voice that might, in some way, challenge
      his powers and prerogatives as an autocrat.

1506 _____. "Russian on the Eve of Reform: A Chinovnik's
      View." Slavonic E Eur R, 59 (Apr. 1981): 264-71.
      Alexander II is not central to the theme of this article, but
      as a case study of the bureaucratic reaction to his liberal
      reforms of the early 1860s it sheds some light on the political
      mood of official Russia during the emancipation period.

1507 *McCormick, D. "War on Secret Societies." HRSS (gen. study),
      63-70.
      A discussion of Alexander II's abolition of the dreaded Third
      Section, not as a liberal measure, but as an act which led to
      the absorption of the Third Section's duties by the Ministry
      of Interior and the perpetuation of the secret police in "a less
      dignified and less disciplined form." McCormick provides a
      number of examples of the activities of this agency during
      Alexander's reign, particularly in regard to its investigation
      of Russian radicalism both at home and abroad.

1508 *McCoubrey, H. "The Reform of the Russian Legal System
      Under Alexander II." Renais Mod S, 24 (1980): 115-30.
      An examination of the origin, nature, and effectiveness of
      Alexander II's reform of the Russian legal system. McCoubrey
      establishes that the emancipation of the serfs, which gave
      new status and rights to the majority of the population, neces-
      sitated a fundamental revision of the nation's legal structure.
      The reforms which followed were based upon contemporary
      European legal practice and led to the establishment of an in-
      dependent judiciary, trial by jury in criminal cases, and a
      simplified trial procedure. However, the ultimate effective-
      ness of the reforms was greatly lessened by retrogressions
      which occurred in the 1870s and 1880s and, more importantly,
      by Alexander's failure to supplement reform of the administra-
      tion of justice with an overhaul of the Russian code of laws:
      "In a sense the ultimate weakness of the Alexandrine reforms
      neatly reflected the conflict between the 'eastern' and 'western'
      elements in Russian cultural tradition. The substantive law
      remained essentially 'Muscovite' in outlook whereas the courts
      and their staff were very much 'western' in nature."

1509 Mathes, William L. "The Struggle for University Autonomy in
      the Russian Empire During the First Decade of the Reign of
      Alexander II (1855-1866)." Columbia University, 1966.
      (dissertation)

1510 Miller, Forrestt A. Dmitri Miliutin and the Reform Era in
      Russia. Nashville: Vanderbilt University Press, 1968,
      246pp., bib. 231-42.
      This work does not contain a separate chapter on Alexander
      II, but as a scholarly study of the ideals and actions of one
      of his principal ministers it is a useful source on the tsar's
      role in launching the reforms of the 1861-1874 period. Of
      particular interest is Miller's discussion of the deliberations
      of the various committees which shaped the reforms imple-
      mented during this thirteen-year period. DK219.6.M5M5

1511 *Mosse, W. E. Alexander II and the Modernization of Russia.
      New York: Collier Books, 1962, 159pp., bib. 154-55.

A balanced analysis of the reforms of Alexander II and their place in Russia's emergence as a modern European nation. Mosse maintains that Alexander's retreat from the progressive policies of the early 1860s, failure to liberalize the Russian government, and his violent death at the hands of an assassin certainly point toward the conclusion that his reign was an unsuccessful one. However, because Alexander's reforms applied to almost every sphere of Russian life, were directed at the nation's entire population, and resulted in the Russian Empire passing from "the semi-feudal to the early capitalist stage of its development," Mosse concludes, the results of his reign "challenge comparison with the more spectacular achievements of Peter the Great and Lenin. DK220.M6
Reviewed in:
Hist Today, 9 (1959): 437
History, 44 (1959): 284
Slav R, 18, no. 4 (1959): 591

1512 Muddock, J. E. "The Story of the Assassination of Alexander II." Gent M, 254 (1888): 19-29. Also in Liv Age, 176 (1888): 301+.
A discussion of the frustration of the various attempts on Alexander II's life as a "testament to the vigilance with which he was guarded." Muddock provides details on each of the assassination attempts, their failure, and the factors which account for the assassins' ultimate success.

1513 *Oliva, L. Jay, ed. "Reform and Revolution: 1855-1881." RW (anthology), 118-43.
A collection of brief excerpts from the writings of modern historians and nineteenth century Russian commentators on Alexander II's reforms. Included are selections from the works of P. Kropotkin, N. Chernyshevsky, F. Dostoevsky, J. Blum, T. von Laue, and M. Malia.

1514 Panin, I. "Assassination of the Tsar." Int R, 10 (June 1881): 594-99.
A discussion of the impetus given to the radical movement in Russia by the half-hearted reforms of Alexander II.

1515 *Pereira, N. G. "Alexander II and the Decision to Emancipate the Serfs, 1855-1861." Can Slavonic P, 22, no. 1 (1980): 99-115.
An argument that Alexander II played a more important role in formulating the decision to emancipate the serfs than is generally believed. Pereira asserts that Alexander's impartiality in the proceedings associated with the reform's preparation was but a political tactic: "From Alexander's point of view it was surely better to have everyone competing for his favor, each with some expectation of ultimate success, than to have a more clear cut assertion of his authority which might have

destroyed the monarchist illusions of large segments of Russian society." Pereira identifies four crucial occasions in the reform's preparation when Alexander either "personally turned things around or used one of his lieutenants to do so" as evidence that the leading role assigned to Rostovtsev by some historians was, in fact, played by Alexander through Rostovtsev who merely did the tsar's bidding.

1516 Poliakoff, V. "An Emperor Plays at Death." The Empress Marie and Her Times. New York: D. Appleton and Company, 1926, 116-35.
An account of the security precautions taken to protect Alexander II from assassination at the hands of Russian radicals. In addition to describing each of the attempts on Alexander's life, Poliakoff discusses the reaction of Alexander's immediate family to the ever-present threat of assassination, particularly their dismay over his refusal to alter his daily habits so as to make himself less accessible to his enemies. DK236.A2P6

1517 Pomper, Philip. "Nechaev and Tsaricide: The Conspiracy Within the Conspiracy." Rus R, 33, no. 2 (1973): 123-38.
In part, a discussion of Nechaev's involvement in a plot to assassinate Alexander II as a reflection of Nechaev's obsession with tyrannicide and martyrdom.

1518 Raeff, Marc. "The Peasant Commune in the Political Thinking of Russian Publicists. Laissez-faire Liberalism in the Reign of Alexander II." Harvard University, 1950. (dissertation)

1519 Rand, Larry A. "America Views Russian Serf Emancipation, 1861." Mid-Am, 50, no. 1 (1968): 42-51.
An account of the diverse and often contradictory American reactions to Alexander II's emancipation of Russia's serfs. Rand establishes that Northern liberals generally applauded the spirit but not the substance of the Emancipation Act because it failed to provide for the livelihood of the freed serfs, while Southern writers were quick to see distinctions between Russian serfdom and American slavery. Rand also discusses Lincoln's assessment of the Emancipation Act and Alexander's views on the liberation of America's slaves.

1520 *Rieber, Alfred J. "The Politics of Emancipation" and "The Politics of Imperialism." The Politics of Autocracy. Letters of Alexander II to Prince A. I. Bariatinskii 1857-1864. The Hague: Mouton, 1966, 15-93. Excerpt in Emancipation of the Russian Serfs. Terence Emmons, ed. New York: Holt, Rinehart and Winston, 1970, 72-80.
An analysis of Alexander II's 42 letters to his long-standing confidant A. I. Bariatinsky for insights into "the origins and aims of the great reforms and their relation to Alexander's

foreign policy." Rieber discounts the influence of public
pressure and fear of peasant revolt and argues instead that
Alexander's decisions "to free the serfs and to carry out a
policy of watchful waiting in Europe while supporting a cautious advance in Asia were based on the firm conviction that
only a strong army could preserve the Russian empire from
the dangers which threatened its continued existence as a
great European power." Rieber sees the paternalistic and
militaristic elements of Alexander's policies as being consistent
with the autocratic traditions established by Peter the Great
but outdated in a society as complex and fast changing as
mid-nineteenth-century Russia. DK129.A6A43
Reviewed in:
Am Hist R, 73, no. 1 (1967): 182-83
Can Slav S, 3 (1969): 431
Rus R, 26, no. 3 (1967): 313
Slav R, 26, no. 3 (1967): 481
Slavonic E Eur R, 46, no. 106 (1968): 245-46

1521 Rudnyckyj, J. B. "The Ems Ukase of 1876 and the Problems
of Linguicide." Ukr R, 22, no. 2 (1976): 6-8.
A critical examination of Alexander II's 18 May 1876 edict
which forbade the printing in Ukrainian of all but historical
works as well as the importation of any works in the Ukrainian
language.

1522 "Russia Under Alexander II." No Brit R, 41 (Aug. 1864):
134-69.
An examination of the policies and accomplishments of Alexander II during the first decade of his reign. The author devotes most of his attention to a discussion of public reaction
to the Emancipation Act of 1861 and the suppression of the
Polish insurrection of 1863.

1523 *Russo, Paul A. "Golos and the Censorship, 1879-1883."
Slavonic E Eur R, 61, no. 2 (1983): 226-37.
An analysis of "the experience of St. Petersburg's leading
daily newspaper at the end of the reign of Alexander II,
Golos," for insight into "the evolution of Imperial press policy."
Russo discusses the Golos articles which prompted temporary
suspension penalties from the censors, the relaxation of censorship under the brief tenure of Loris-Melikov, and the
government's turn to an oppressive censorship policy following the assassination of Alexander II. Given this turn and
Alexander III's personal dislike of Golos, Russo concludes, it
is no wonder that a newspaper as incorrigible as Golos failed
to survive.

1524 *Ruud, Charles A. "Censorship and the Peasant Question:
The Contingencies of Reform Under Alexander II (1855-1859)."
Calif Slav S, 5 (1970): 137-67.

An analysis of Alexander II's attempt to use the press as a
means of exerting public pressure on the conservative gentry
opposed to the emancipation of the serfs. Ruud asserts that
Alexander loosened the bonds of censorship, while the emancipation issue was being studied by various committees, on
the assumption that the press would endorse, out of grati-
tude, the government's position on peasant reform. Once the
principles of emancipation had been worked out however, Alexander "abruptly withdrew discussion privileges from the press
in regard to policies in the process of formation." Ruud
notes that, in addition to no longer needing to pressure conservatives, Alexander's return to censorship was motivated by
his belief that elements of the press had failed to behave in a
responsible fashion.

1525 *_____. "The Russian Empire's New Censorship Law of
1865." Can Slav S, 3, no. 2 (1969): 234-45.
An argument that the Censorship Law of 1865 is best understood as an expression of "the changing political requirements
of autocracy" rather than as a reflection of a struggle between
liberals and conservatives within the imperial bureaucracy.
Ruud contends that Alexander's belief that too many objection-
able publications were working their way past the censors led
him to replace preventative censorship with a more repressive
policy based upon strict accountability on the part of journals
publishing unacceptable material.

1526 *Schapiro, Leonard. "Chapters IV and V." Rationalism and
Nationalism in Russian Nineteenth Century Political Thought.
New Haven: Yale University Press, 1967, 85-142.
Alexander II is not central to the theme of these chapters,
but they contain an interesting discussion of the place of his
reforms and related proposals within the confines of the mid-
nineteenth-century clash between rationalist and nationalist
modes of Russian political thought.

1527 Seth, Ronald. "1st March 1881." The Russian Terrorists.
The Story of the Narodniki. London: Barrie and Rockliff,
1966, 96-101.
A brief account of the assassination of Alexander II. Other
chapters in this study may be consulted for information on
the motives and methods of the populist organization responsible for Alexander's death. DK189.S4

1528 Skerpan, Alfred A. "The Russian National Economy and Emancipation." Essays in Russian History: A Collection Dedicated
to George Vernadsky. Alan D. Ferguson, ed. Hamden, Conn.:
Archon Books, 1964, 161-229.
This scholarly discussion of the 1861 Emancipation Act as an
economic necessity does not contain a titled section on Alexander II but does address the question of his role in the

deliberations which preceded the act's issuance. Skerpan
maintains that Alexander's views on emancipation were quite
similar to those of mid-nineteenth-century economic liberals
who saw the state, not the individual or any social group,
as the most effective instrument of social and economic reform.

1529   Taylor, A. J. P. "Men of the 1860s. Alexander II, Tsar of
       Russia." Listener, 69 (27 June 1963): 1069-71.
       A brief, sympathetic review of Alexander II's attempt to cope
       with the overwhelming domestic problems which he inherited
       from his father, Nicholas I.

1530   Tcharykow, N. V. "The Assassination of Emperor Alexander
       II." Glimpses of High Politics Through War and Peace 1855-
       1929. London: George Allen and Unwin, 1931, 151-56.
       A brief, eyewitness account of court reaction to the assassina-
       tion of Alexander II. DK219.6.C4A3

1531   Vagts, Alfred. "Mark Twain at the Courts of Emperors."
       Jahr Amer, 9 (1964): 149-51.
       In part, a discussion of the censorship of the Russian trans-
       lation of Mark Twain's The Innocents which contained a light-
       hearted account of Twain's meeting with Alexander II and his
       family at Yalta in 1867.

1532   Venturi, Franco. "1st March 1881." Roots of Revolution. New
       York: Grosset and Dunlop, 1966, 709-20.
       A discussion of the assassination of Alexander II and the
       reaction to this event in both revolutionary and governmental
       circles. Venturi establishes that, while some groups and in-
       dividuals rejoiced over the death of a tyrant, public opinion,
       for the most part, was hostile toward the revolutionaries re-
       sponsible for Alexander's death. DK189.V413

1533   Volin, Lazar. "Emancipation." A Century of Russian Agri-
       culture. From Alexander II to Khrushchev. Cambridge:
       Harvard University Press, 1970, 40-56.
       This examination of the drafting of the Emancipation Act and
       the difficulties had by the Russian peasants following their
       liberation contains a brief discussion of the support given to
       emancipation by Alexander II, Grand Duchess Elena Pavlovna,
       and Grand Duke Konstantin Nikolaevich. S469.R9V57

1534   *Wagner, William G. "Tsarist Legal Policies at the End of the
       Nineteenth Century: A Study in Inconsistencies." Slavonic
       E Eur R, 54, no. 3 (1976): 371-94.
       A study of the fate of the 20 November 1864 Judicial Reform
       Act. Wagner contends that "the judicial system introduced by
       Alexander II was an anomaly, given Russian traditions and
       conditions prevailing in the mid-nineteenth century," and that
       this fact, along with the government's concern for the harm-
       ful social and political consequences of its policy of economic

development, led to the circumvention of the judiciary created
in 1864.

1535 *Wortman, Richard. "Judicial Personnel and the Court Reform
      of 1864." Can Slav S, 3, no. 2 (1969): 224-34.
      Alexander II is not the focus of this article, but it includes
      a discussion of his willingness to utilize legal experts to shape
      judicial reform in the early 1860s. Wortman establishes that
      Alexander relied on legal experts because he was under con-
      siderable pressure to reform the nation's legal system, but
      important decisions on judicial reform were still made by Alex-
      ander and the leading bureaucrats who shared his political
      views. Consequently, the influence of this dynamic group of
      specialists was short-lived since "once the moment had passed,
      their energy and initiative became irritants" which encouraged
      Alexander to return to dependence upon "the grey mediocri-
      ties" who traditionally had dominated the Russian bureaucracy.

1536 *_____. "The Politics of Court Reform." RSH (anthology),
      10-25.
      An examination of the circumstances which led Alexander II
      to approve the creation of an independent judiciary. Wortman
      maintains that the influence of two groups shaped Alexander's
      thought on the judiciary: the new legal cadres in the Ministry
      of Justice, who argued for "thoroughgoing reform on the basis
      of their own expertise," and members of the nobility, who
      believed that "the interests of property and stability demanded
      a judiciary that could instill a respect for law and a sense of
      personal responsibility in the citizenry."

1537 *_____. "Reform." DRLC (gen. study), 235-90.
      Although not centered upon Alexander II, this chapter con-
      tains considerable discussion of his positive role in the delib-
      erations which preceded and shaped the 1864 reform which
      created a modern judicial system in Russia. KR91.W6

1538 Wright, Patricia. "Loris-Melikov: Russia, 1880-1881." Hist
      Today, 24, no. 6 (1974): 413-19.
      A review of the actions taken by Loris-Melikov as he sought
      to combat the revolutionary ferment developing in Russia by
      improving, with Alexander II's support, police efficiency while
      making concessions to the forces of political moderation.

1539 Yarmolinsky, Avrahm. "Sic Temper Tyrannis." Road to Revo-
      lution. A Century of Russian Radicalism. New York: Collier
      Books, 1962, 259-79.
      An account of the various attempts against Alexander II's life
      by the radical organization the People's Will. Yarmolinsky
      gives a particularly dramatic description of Alexander's 1
      March 1881 assassination at the hands of I. Grinevitsky.

1540 *Zaionchkovsky, Peter A. The Abolition of Serfdom in Russia.

Susan Wobst, ed./trans. Gulf Breeze, Fla.: Academic International Press, 1978, 250pp.
The focus of this highly regarded Soviet study is the implementation of the 1861 Emancipation Act, but it contains considerable discussion of Alexander II's role in the promotion of peasant reform. Zaionchkovsky maintains that Alexander's support for emancipation was prompted by the need to address the problems associated with the economic backwardness revealed by the Crimean War and, more importantly, by his fear that a major peasant rebellion would soon sweep over Russia. Despite this sentiment, Zaionchkovsky adds, the reform sanctioned by Alexander defrauded the peasants by depriving them of the means of production to sustain themselves as farmers, a deprivation which led to an increase in rural wage labor and a bountiful supply of desperate workers willing to labor in Russia's newly developed factories for meager wages. HT807.Z313

1541   *Zenkovsky, Serge A. "The Emancipation of the Serfs in Retrospect." Rus R, 20, no. 4 (1961): 280-93.
A review of the struggle between liberals and conservatives in the secret committee that debated the form to be taken by the Emancipation Act, and an argument that the land settlement which was eventually legislated was not as detrimental to the interests of the ex-serfs as maintained by radical journalists of the nineteenth century and some contemporary historians. Zenkovsky contends that the peasants did not lose landholdings nor overpay for the land they received to the extent critics of the act have asserted. Moreover, despite its shortcomings, the act "did not perpetuate the domination of rural Russia by the nobility nor did it deprive the peasants of the opportunity for growth and development." He concludes that the impoverished condition of the peasantry in the decades after emancipation was due primarily to the peasants' "primitive methods of cultivation, lack of means for land reclamation, the absence of machinery, and unimproved seeds and stock."

FOREIGN POLICY AND MILITARY AFFAIRS

1542   *Abrash, Merritt. "Alexander II, Gorchakov and Great Britain, 1875-1878: A Study in Motivation." Can Slav S, 3, no. 2 (1969): 312-25.
An examination of the motives which shaped the diplomacy of Alexander II and Foreign Minister Gorchakov during the Eastern crisis of 1875-78. Abrash asserts that Alexander's actions cannot be understood solely from a political/territorial perspective but must also be considered in terms of his personal sentiments toward Queen Victoria and genuine concern for the Christian population of the Ottoman Empire. Abrash sees

Gorchakov as a rational, professional diplomat unmoved by the
type of emotions which swayed Alexander but very much influenced by his own vanity.

1543 *Adamov, E. A. "Russia and the United States at the Time
of the Civil War." J Mod Hist, 2, no. 4 (1930): 586-602.
An analysis of Russian motives for sending warships to American ports in 1863. Adamov disagrees with those who contend
that Alexander II sought safe harbors for the Russian fleet
because he feared that war with England and France would
lead to a British blockade of the fleet's home ports, and instead he maintains that "the purpose was to put the fleet in
the most favorable position for the opening of warlike activities with the maximum energy and productivity" against the
French and British navies. Adamov appends a series of
previously unpublished Russian archival documents which illustrate the motivation to which he refers and the complex
European circumstances which prompted Alexander to consider
such a strategy.

1544 "Alexander II: Emperor of Russia." Eclectic M, 72 (June
1869): 752-54.
A brief review of the main events which marked the first
fourteen years of Alexander II's reign with most emphasis on
Alexander's motives for disengaging Russia from the Crimean
War and for emancipating the serfs.

1545 "Alexander II on the Throne of Poland." Once a Week, 8
(1962): 415, 428, 469.
Unavailable for annotation.

1546 *Bailey, Thomas A. "The Russian Fleet Myth Re-Examined."
M Valley Hist R, 38 (June 1951): 81-90.
A refutation of the thesis, developed by William Nagengast,
that the American press and public were well aware of Alexander II's true reasons for ordering the Russian fleet to American waters in the autumn of 1863. Bailey states that Nagengast based his thesis on only twenty contemporaneous newspapers and magazines and presented it as the reigning opinion
in editorials and reports which, in fact, discussed various
reasons for the fleet's arrival. Bailey adds that his own
survey of 74 newspapers revealed the most popular theory
to have been that the fleet's presence signified Alexander II's
desire to publicize his friendship for America and his intention
to ally with the North in case of British intervention on the
side of the South.

1547 Cowles, Virginia. "Chapters II-VI." RD (gen. study), 41-
149.
A discussion of Alexander II's foreign policy in terms of its
similarity, in methodology and goals, to the imperialist policy
of the Soviet government.

1548   "The Emperor Alexander and the Policy of Russia." Brit Q R,
       57 (Jan. 1873): 125-51.
       A review of various writings published between 1868 and
       1872 which dealt with the foreign policy of Alexander II.
       Although the author discusses Alexander's Balkan and Black
       Sea policies, his central concern is "the advance of Russia
       into Central Asia," the importance of which, he believes, the
       English press of the time failed to recognize.

1549   *Golder, Frank A. "The Russian Fleet and the Civil War."
       Am Hist R, 20, no. 4 (1915): 801-12.
       A discussion of Alexander II's motives for sending in 1863 the
       Russian fleet to American ports. Golder stresses the impor-
       tance of Alexander's concern for the safety of the fleet in the
       face of an impending conflict with England and France over
       Poland and his belief that the tiny Russian navy could effec-
       tively prey on British and French commerical vessels in
       American waters, America being the only conceivable safe
       (blockade free) port for the fleet to wait for the outbreak of
       the hostilities. Golder also describes the warm reception given
       the fleet in New York, though he stresses that the fleet was
       not sent to benefit America, a fact overlooked at the time.

1550   *Jelavich, Barbara. "Alexander II." CRFP (gen. study), 125-
       88.
       An examination of Alexander II's foreign policy and its rela-
       tionship to the domestic condition of his realm. Jelavich
       states that "the Crimean disaster and the subsequent con-
       centration of Russia on internal development removed her from
       an active, aggressive role in European affairs for almost twenty
       years." While Alexander addressed the domestic needs of the
       nation, he pursued a vigorous and relatively successful foreign
       policy with respect to the lands to Russia's south and east
       and wisely avoided conflicts with the European powers of the
       time. However, he committed a colossal blunder by allowing
       the unification of Germany to take place and, therein, the
       emergence of a dynamic and powerful state on Russia's western
       border.

1551   *_____. "Russia and the Reacquisition of Southern Bessara-
       bia 1875-78." Südost-Forsch, 28 (1969): 199-237.
       A critical examination of Alexander II's decision to reclaim the
       south Bessarabian territory which Russia had lost as a conse-
       quence of the Crimean War. Jelavich contends that the dip-
       lomatic, military, and strategic costs of this decision were
       ignored by Alexander because of his fervent desire to erase
       the humiliation suffered by the Romanov dynasty with the
       signing of the Treaty of Paris which concluded the Crimean
       War. Jelavich demonstrates that the reacquisition of Bessara-
       bia alienated Rumania and was secured at the expense of
       territorial concessions to Austria-Hungary far more valuable
       than the land Russia gained.

1552   Medlicott, William N. The Congress of Berlin and After. Lon-
       don: Metheun, 1938, 442pp., bib. 420-27.
       This study does not contain a separate chapter on Alexander
       II, but as a comprehensive examination of Russian Near East-
       ern diplomacy of the late 1870s it includes numerous references
       to his role in the diplomatic settlements of 1878-1880.

1553   *Mosse, Werner E. The European Powers and the German
       Question, 1848-1871. Cambridge: Cambridge University
       Press, 1958, 409pp., bib. 395-97.
       Alexander II is not the focus of any one chapter in this
       scholarly study of the role of the European powers in the
       unification of Germany, but it contains considerable discus-
       sion of his views, policies, and influence on the emergence
       of a united Germany. Mosse sees the roles played by Eng-
       land and Russia as being pivotal since, unlike France and
       Austria, they were "less bound by traditional influences"
       and thus had a freedom of action to tip the scales in one
       direction or another. Close study of Alexander's actions
       during each phase of the unification process, Mosse concludes,
       reveals that the tsar was responding to Russia's basic foreign
       policy needs rather than to Bismarck's clever diplomacy.
       DK204.M6

1554   *_____. "How Russia Made Peace, September 1855-April
       1856." Camb Hist J, 11, no. 3 (1955): 297-316.
       An argument that the humanitarian motives which Alexander
       II cited as the official rationale for the acceptance of the
       harsh terms contained in the Treaty of Paris were reinforced
       by his concern over rumors that rural Russia was on the
       verge of a major revolt. Mosse also asserts that Alexander
       never viewed the peace terms as being binding but rather
       believed that they had to be repudiated at the first opportune
       moment.

1555   *_____. The Rise and Fall of the Crimean System. London:
       Macmillan, 1964, 213pp.
       This scholarly study does not contain a separate chapter
       devoted to Alexander II but includes a number of references
       to his influence on the negotiations leading up to the signing
       of the Treaty of Paris (30 March 1856) and his efforts to re-
       vise the treaty in Russia's favor in the decades which followed.
       Mosse links the collapse of the "Crimean system" to the fact
       that the Treaty of Paris was a Draconian peace and as such
       was based on the transient preponderance of the allied force
       represented by the victors. The persistent efforts of Alex-
       ander II and Foreign Minister Gorchakov to modify the treaty,
       Mosse concludes, thus met with success more because of the
       changing international situation in the years following the
       Crimean War than as a consequence of the cleverness of
       Russian diplomacy. DK215.M75 1964

1556 *Nagengast, William E. "The Visit of the Russian Fleet: Were
the Americans Deceived?" Rus R, 8 (1949): 46-55.
An argument that the American press did not view the Russian
fleet's 1863 arrival in American waters as a show of support
for the Union cause but rather displayed in its reports "an
understanding of European diplomacy and the motives behind
this Russian naval maneuver." Nagengast states that Frank
Golder's 1915 unearthing of Alexander II's secret orders to
the Russian fleet only served to confirm that which the American press and public of 1863 believed to be true in regard
to the motivation behind the fleet's visit. Golder failed to
realize this as he contended that Alexander successfully deceived a naive American public into believing that he had
dispatched the fleet for unselfish and altruistic reasons.

1557 *Pidhainy, Alexander. "Miliutin as War Minister: Reforms
and Foreign Policy." J. G. Purves and D. A. West, eds.
War and Society in Nineteenth Century Russia. Toronto:
New Review Books, 1972, 144-49.
A discussion of D. A. Miliutin's military reforms and influence
upon the Near Eastern and Asiatic policies pursued by Alexander II. According to Pidhainy, Miliutin believed that the
reformed Russian army was more than a match for the armies
of Russia's neighbors to the south but still inferior to those
of the major European powers. Miliutin thus encouraged Alexander to pursue an active policy of imperialism in Central
Asia but not in the Near East where Miliutin feared that a
conflict between Russia and the Ottoman Empire would provoke
an anti-Russian coalition of European powers with which the
revamped Russian army could not cope successfully. Pidhainy
shows that the cautious Miliutin tempered Alexander's militant
position during the early stages of the 1876 diplomatic crisis
with Turkey, but once Miliutin was certain that neither Britain nor Austria-Hungary would intervene in a Russo-Turkish
conflict, he encouraged the tsar to settle the crisis by military means.

1558 Ritchie, Galen B. "The Asiatic Department During the Reign
of Alexander II, 1855-1881." Columbia University, 1970.
(dissertation)

1559 *Rupp, George Hoover. "Ignatyev, Gorchakov and Alexander
II." A Wavering Friendship: Russia and Austria, 1876-1878.
Philadelphia: Porcupine Press, 1976 (reprint of 1941 edition),
49-60.
A discussion of Ignatyev's opposition to the plan advanced
by Gorchakov, and supported by Alexander II, "to buy
Austrian assent for Russian expansion south of the Danube
by the cession of Bosnia and Herzegovina." Other sections
in this study can be consulted with profit for information on
Alexander II's leading role in Russian diplomacy of the mid-

1870s, particularly his commitment to an aggressive Balkan policy. DK223.R78 1976

1560   Tarsaidzé, Alexandre. "Russian-American 'Entente.'" <u>CP</u>
       (gen. study), 181-222.
       An account of the sensation created by the arrival of the
       Russian fleet in the ports of New York and San Francisco
       with some reference to the European diplomatic circumstances
       which prompted Alexander II to order the fleet to America.

1561   _____. "Va-et-vient." <u>Ibid.</u>, 243-57.
       In part, a discussion of the American reaction to the 1866 at-
       tempt on the life of Alexander II. Tarsaidzé sees the formal
       letter sent by President Johnson to Alexander congratulating
       him on his miraculous escape as a unique act in the history
       of American diplomacy: "never before had the American re-
       public sent any message to a foreign nation that indicated
       personal feeling for the sovereign." Tarsaidzé also describes
       the warm reception given to Gustavus Fox who delivered John-
       son's message to Alexander.

1562   United States Department of State. <u>The Russian Account of</u>
       <u>the Official Mission to Russia of the Honorable Gustavus V.</u>
       <u>Fox in 1866.</u> S. N. Buynitzky, trans. Washington, D.C.:
       Government Printing Office, 1867, 38pp. DK26.C88
       Unavailable for annotation.

1563   Zornow, William F. "When the Czar and Grant Were Friends."
       <u>Mid-Am</u>, 43, no. 3 (1961): 164-81.
       A colorful account of the 1871-72 travels in America by Alex-
       ander II's son, Grand Duke Alexis, an event which further
       advanced the positive diplomatic relations which existed at
       that time between America and Russia.

1564   Zyzniewski, Stanley J. "The Futile Compromise Reconsidered:
       Wielopolski and Russian Policy in the Congress Kingdom,
       1861-1863." <u>Am Hist R</u>, 70, no. 1 (1965): 395-412.
       A reassessment of the various factors which determined the
       unsuccessful outcome of Polish aristocrat Alexander Wielopol-
       ski's attempt to establish a mutually beneficial relationship
       between Congress Poland and the Russian Empire. Zyzniew-
       ski contends that the slow and uncertain response of Alexander
       II to Wielopolski's proposals was crucial to the latter's failure
       to secure the desired compromise: "the single most glaring
       danger to his program was his inability to command a rapid
       and coordinated execution of his plan." Zyzniewski sees
       Alexander's dilatory response as being due to his suspicion
       over Wielopolski's motivaton for advancing such proposals.

GENERAL STUDIES AND ASSESSMENTS/
PERSONAL AFFAIRS AND CHARACTER

1565 Alexander, Grand Duke. Once a Grand Duke. New York:
Farrar and Rinehart, 1932, 348pp.
A series of disconnected recollections regarding, for the most
part, Alexander III's reaction to the assassination of his
father, the coronation of 1881, his relationship with various
advisers and ministers, and a number of incidents in his
private life. DK219.6.A4A3 1932

1566 "Alexander III." Spectator, 70 (June 1893): 5-6.
A brief statement on the disparate nature of the assessments
of Alexander III and his reign which appeared in European
newspapers and periodicals in the early 1890s.

1567 "Alexander III and Nicholas II." Pub Opin, 17 (8 Nov. 1894):
765-67.
A collection of newspaper articles on Alexander III's death
and legacy, and a brief commentary on the personal and political qualities of his successor.

1568 "Attempt to Kill the Czar." Spectator, 60 (19 March 1887):
376.
A brief account of the March 1887 attempt on Alexander III's
life, and speculation on how Russia might have changed had
he been killed.

1569 "Coronation of the Czar." Sat R, 55 (2 June 1883): 679-80.
A brief description of Alexander III's coronation and the
problems which confronted him in his first two years as tsar.

1570 "Coronation of the Tsar." Spectator, 56 (31 March 1883):
411-13; (26 May 1883): 669-70; (2 June 1883): 701-02.
A three part discussion of various facets of Alexander III's
coronation ceremony. Part I questions the wisdom behind
staging such an elaborate affair amidst the criticisms being

voiced against monarchy as a form of government. Part II
focuses on the "Asiatic" quality of Russia as reflected in the
Oriental splendor of the ceremony. Part III deals with the
unique aspects of the coronation ritual, especially its place-
ment of the tsar above the church, his people, and wife during the ceremony.

1571 Crankshaw, Edward. "Chapters 16-17." The Shadow of the
Winter Palace. New York: Viking Press, 1976, 272-302.
A critical assessment of Alexander III's reign in terms of its
place on Russia's road to revolution. Crankshaw asserts that
"with the accession of Alexander III Imperial Russia entered
a new phase in her history. It was not simply that all effective revolutionary activity was ended for many years to
come; more importantly, it was the end of serious reform from
above." This fact combined with Alexander's "institutionali-
sation of police rule" served to widen the gap between the
monarchy and its critics to such an extent, Crankshaw concludes, that his reign constituted a new stage in Russia's
progress toward revolution. DK189.C66

1572 Creelman, James. "The Czar on His Knees." On the Great
Highway. The Wanderings of a Special Correspondent. Boston: Lothrop, 1901, 256-67.
An account of Alexander III's tender relationship with his
childhood English nurse, Kitty, and his tearful response to
her death and funeral. Creelman maintains that Kitty was
"one of the hidden forces" that helped to shape Alexander's
character and political philosophy. D355.C92

1573 Curtis, William Elroy. Russia. Its People, Its Palaces, Its
Politics. Chicago: Belford, Carle and Company, 1888, 323pp.
Recollections of the condition of Alexander III's realm as observed by a correspondent for the Chicago Daily News during
the summer of 1887. Curtis also describes the daily habits
and family life of Alexander, the police precautions to secure
the royal family's safety, and the keen interest shown by
Alexander in the Maxim gun during a two-hour conversation
with the weapon's inventor.

1574 "Czar's Deathbed." Spectator, 73 (27 Oct. 1894): 548.
A brief statement on the people in attendance at Alexander
III's deathbed, and speculation on the response of the young
heir to the weighty problems which plagued Russia.

1575 "Czar's Departure for Kieff." Spectator, 72 (17 Feb. 1894):
224-25.
A commentary on a report that Alexander III's journey to
Kiev to escape the harsh St. Petersburg climate might lead
to the relocation of the Russian capital not only for the benefits the move would have for the tsar's health but for political

considerations as well.

1576 "Czar's Illness." Spectator, 72 (3 Feb. 1894): 151.
A report on Alexander III's bout with pneumonia during
which his life was believed to be in danger. The author also
comments on the differences in temperament between Alexander
and Tsarevich Nicholas.

1577 "Czar's Mood." Spectator, 60 (1 Jan. 1887): 9.
A discussion of Alexander III's moodiness as a reflection of his
loneliness and the lack of limitations on his behavior as an
autocrat.

1578 "Death of the Czar." Spectator, 73 (3 Nov. 1894): 597, 600-
01.
A brief report on public and family reaction to Alexander III's
death. The author also presents a balanced review of Alexander's accomplishments and speculates on the future of Russia under Nicholas II.

1579 *Dillon, E. J. "Tsar Alexander III." Contemp R, 63 (Jan.
1893): 1-24. Also in Liv Age, 196 (11 Feb. 1893): 387-403.
A sympathetic appraisal of Alexander III's character, and an
examination of the sources of the harshness of his rule. Dillon contends that the severity that marked Alexander's rule
was not due to the tsar's character and personality but rather
was a reflection of tsarist political traditions, the political
climate of the era, and the influence of conservative advisers.

1580 "Emperor of Russia." Harper's W, 38 (10 Nov. 1894): 1060.
A brief and balanced review of Alexander III's character, life,
and reign.

1581 Fischer, Henry W. "Truth About the Czar and the Royal
Guests at Fredensborg." Harper's W, 38 (17 Nov. 1894):
1095-96.
A sympathetic portrayal of Alexander III's personality and
character; based upon personal observations of him while
vacationing in Fredensborg.

1582 Forbes, Archibald. "The Military Courage of Royalty."
Contemp R, 63 (Feb. 1893): 189-95.
A refutation of E. B. Lanin's charge that Alexander III was
a coward.

1583 Fülöp-Miller, René, ed. Under Three Tsars. The Memoirs
of the Lady-in-Waiting Elizabeth Narishkin-Kurakin. Julia
E. Lesser, trans. New York: E. P. Dutton, 1931, 231pp.
Recollections of the Russian court under the last three
Romanovs, written by a confidante of various members of
the royal family. Narishkin-Kurakin provides most detail on

court reaction to Alexander III's accession to the throne, the
sources of his political conservatism, various incidents in his
family life, and his illness, death, and funeral.
DK188.6.N2A32

1584 "Funeral of the Czar." Spectator, 73 (24 Nov. 1894): 713,
      723-24.
      A description of the incredible splendor that accompanied
      Alexander III's funeral, and an enumeration of the foreign
      dignitaries in attendance.

1585 Hapgood, I. F. "Dead Czar's Journey Home." Harper's W,
      38 (17 Nov. 1894): 1096.
      A favorable commentary on Alexander III's personal qualities
      and accomplishments as ruler of a backward nation.

1586 _____. "The Dead Tsar." Nation, 60 (1895): 150-51.
      A critical review of C. Lowe's Alexander III of Russia. Hap-
      good asserts that Lowe's book is plagued by inaccuracies,
      omissions, and poor writing.

1587 Humphrey, Frances A. "The Imperial Family of Russia."
      Kings and Queens at Home. Boston: D. Lothrop and Company,
      1886, 26-30.
      A brief recreation of the coronation of Alexander III.
      D352.1.H8

1588 "Illness of Alexander III." Spectator, 73 (6 Oct.-27 Oct.
      1894): 426, 477, 509, 545.
      A series of short reports on Alexander III's condition during
      his fatal illness.

1589 "Imperial Tragedy." Outlook, 50 (10 Nov. 1894): 745-46.
      A brief review of Alexander III's difficult life as ruler of a
      vast and troubled realm, and a discussion of the problems
      which he created for himself by adopting a shortsighted ap-
      proach to dealing with these troubles.

1590 Is the Czar Mad? Revelations of His Private Life, by One Who
      Knows. London: H. Gugenheim, 1891, 15pp.
      Unavailable for annotation.

1591 Lincoln, W. Bruce. "Alexander III of Russia." Hist Today,
      26, no. 10 (1976): 644-52.
      A general survey of Alexander III's reign with most attention
      given to his persecution of Russia's Jews, repression of dis-
      sent, and efforts to advance the nation's economy.

1592 Lothrop, Almira S. The Court of Alexander III. Philadelphia:
      John C. Winston Company, 1910, 208pp.
      The letters of Mrs. Almira Lothrop, wife of George Van Ness
      Lothrop, the American ambassador to Russia from 1885 to 1888.

In addition to describing various court affairs, Mrs. Lothrop
presents a sympathetic account of Alexander III's personality,
public behavior, and family relations. She also comments favorably on his efforts to rule Russia in an efficient and fair
manner and to improve the general condition of his domain.

1593 Lowe, Charles. Alexander III of Russia. New York: Macmillan, 1895, 370pp.
A highly negative, undocumented assessment of Alexander III's
character, policies, and accomplishments. Lowe maintains that
Alexander's personality consisted of such a strange blend of
contradictory traits that he remained an enigma to even his
closest advisers. Lowe sees Alexander's domestic policies as
being completely without merit but reserves special criticism
for the Russian government's brutal treatment of minority
groups. While Alexander's tender relationship with the members of his family is admirable, Lowe concludes, such tender-
ness in no way alters the fact that Alexander was a brutal,
narrow-minded, and uncaring ruler. DK240.L9

1594 *Medlin, Virgil D. "Alexander III: His Modernizing Autocracy
and Authority." Red R Val Hist J, 3, no. 4 (1979): 328-41.
An argument that under the rule of Alexander III Russia was
"a modernizing autocracy which enjoyed external peace and used
limited internal coercion, which allowed the promotion of the
instrumental state goal of national 'survival' among nation-
states while maintaining the autocracy." Drawing upon recent
archival findings, Medlin cites, in support of this thesis, statistics which show rapid industrialization and urbanization and
a drastic reduction of political arrests and industrial and
agrarian disorders during the years between 1881 and 1894.

1595 Palmer, H. M. "Great Bear: A Royal Russian Love Story."
Ladies H J, 22 (June 1905): 6.
An account of Alexander III's marriage to Princess Dagmar of
Denmark, the fiancée of Alexander's older brother Nicholas
who died of tuberculosis in 1865.

1596 "Peasant Emperor." RR, 9 (Mar. 1894): 269.
A note on the recovery of Alexander III from an illness so
grave that it prompted discussion of a suitable epithet for
him upon his death. Apparently Alexander wished to be
known as "the peasant emperor" to commemorate his efforts
on the peasants' behalf.

1597 Peddie, James A. The Dead Czar. His Life and Doings. London: Boot, Son and Carpenter, 1894, 16pp.
Unavailable for annotation.

1598 Poliakoff, V. Mother Dear. The Empress Marie and Her Times.
New York: D. Appleton and Company, 1926, 324pp.

A sympathetic and popular account of the lengthy and event-
ful life of Empress Marie Feodorovna, wife of Alexander III
from 1866 to 1894, which sheds some light on Alexander's
court and family life. DK236.A2P6

1599 "Reported Illness of the Czar." Spectator, 73 (29 Sept. 1894):
      394-95.
      An argument that despite the disgusting nature of the Russian
      political system the world should pray for the recovery of the
      gravely ill Alexander III because of his fervent support for
      peace in Europe.

1600 Ritchie, D. G. "The Logic of a Despot's Advocate." Westmin
      R, 137 (Mar. 1892): 268-76.
      A critique of W. T. Stead's positive portrayal of the person-
      ality, character, and family life of Alexander III. Ritchie
      contends that Stead deliberately misrepresented Alexander as
      a kindly, compassionate individual so as to cloak the tsar's
      brutal and repressive domestic policies.

1601 Samson-Himmelstierna, H. von. Russia Under Alexander III
      and in the Preceding Period. J. Morrison, trans. New York:
      Macmillan, 1893, 306pp. Excerpt in RFR (anthology), 167-69.
      Only the beginning of this work deals with Alexander III,
      the remainder consists of a series of character sketches on
      prominent Russians of the time and a commentary on the
      backward condition of the Russian empire. Samson-
      Himmelstierna, a Prussian conservative and Russophobe,
      characterizes Alexander as a willful and ambitious monarch
      of limited intelligence wholly committed to a policy of expan-
      sionism. He warns his readers to be alert to the danger
      posed by Alexander's support of panslavism, a movement which
      could "unleash the half-tamed savagery of the Russian nation"
      upon the Western world. DK241.S211

1602 Schwartz, Theodore. "The Great White Czar." Munsey, 8
      (Nov. 1892): 137-41.
      A brief character sketch of Alexander III, and a description
      of the opulence of his court and the closeness of his family
      relations.

1603 Smith, Charles E. "The Young Czar and His Advisers."
      No Am R, 160 (Jan. 1895): 21-28.
      A brief commentary on Alexander III's qualities as tsar and
      the nature of the realm that he bequeathed to his son. Smith
      states that the youthfulness of Nicholas II and the seriousness
      of the problems confronting him make the role to be played by
      top advisers a particularly important one.

1604 "Sovereigns of Europe: The Emperor of Russia." Leisure H,
      39 (1890): 172-81.
      A rambling narrative on Alexander III's private life.

1605   Stead, W. T.   "The Czar and Russia of Today."   RR, 4 (Jan.
       1892):   667-80.
       An argument that conditions in Russia must not be evaluated
       from a strictly Western perspective but rather should be meas-
       ured in view of the nation's unique history and problems.
       Stead draws upon material presented in his book The Truth
       About Russia as he portrays Alexander III as a wise monarch
       well aware of Russia's shortcomings and determined to ad-
       vance the welfare of his subjects.

1606   *_____.   "Alexander III."   The M. P. for Russia.   Reminis-
       cences and Correspondence of Madame Olga Novikoff, Vol. II.
       London: Andrew Melrose, 1909, 236-56.
       An account of the assistance rendered by Olga Novikoff, a
       panslav enthusiast and apologist for Russian autocracy, in
       arranging an 1888 interview between the author and Alexander
       III.   Stead, a British journalist and Russophil, states that
       his purpose in requesting the interview was to acquire the
       means "to ascertain at first hand what manner of man Alex-
       ander III was and what was the policy he intended to pursue."
       Stead recollects the various questions that he put to Alexan-
       der in regard to Russia's foreign policy and how the tsar's
       responses convinced him that Russia was pursuing, and would
       continue to do so, an "essentially pacific policy."   Upon his
       return to London, Stead wrote his book The Truth About
       Russia which, despite its criticism of Pobedonostsev and the
       government's repressive policy toward minority groups, won
       the favor of Alexander and was widely circulated throughout
       Russia.   DK219.6.N8S8

1607   *_____.   The Truth About Russia.   London: Cassell and
       Company, 1888, 464pp.
       A highly favorable description of the character of Alexander
       III and the nature of the Russian state and people, written
       to counter the negative image of Russia prevalent in Britain
       since the Crimean War era and to advance the likelihood of
       the Anglo-Russian rapprochement which the author so fervent-
       ly desired.   While Stead's judgments on Alexander's intellect,
       values, and domestic policies are more than generous, it is
       Alexander's statesmanship which he singles out for particular
       praise.   Alexander's sincere abhorrence of war, efforts to
       preserve the European status quo, and desire to establish
       a "hearty working agreement" with both Britain and Germany,
       Stead concludes, make the tsar worthy of the title, "the
       peace-keeper of Europe."   DK241.S8

1608   Thornton, Mary C.   "Crowning Alexander III."   Century M,
       52, no. 1 (May 1896):   8-27.
       An eyewitness commentary on Alexander III's coronation cere-
       mony and the festivities which surrounded it, written by the
       daughter of the British ambassador to Russia.   Includes illus-
       trations from the official record of the ceremony released by

the Russian government.

1609   Tisdall, E. E. P.   The Dowager Empress.   London: Stanley
       Paul, 1957, 271pp., bib. 263.   Published in America under
       the title Marie Feodorovna.
       A popular biography of Marie Feodorovna, wife of Alexander
       III, with some mention of Alexander's principal policies, char-
       acter, and relationship with his wife and children.
       DK236.A2T5

1610   Vassili, Count Paul.   Behind the Veil at the Russian Court.
       New York: John Lane, 1914, 408pp.
       The diaries of Princess Catherine Radziwill, who spent six
       decades immersed in Russian court life.   Collectively the many
       scattered references to Alexander III provide a sketchy, anec-
       dotal account of his personal affairs, relationship with minis-
       ters and advisers, and his leading policies.   Throughout,
       Radziwill portrays Alexander as an intelligent, highly princi-
       pled, dedicated, and beloved monarch.   DK189.R3

1611   Waddington, Mary K.   "At the Coronation of the Czar Alex-
       ander III."   Scrib M, 33 (Mar. 1903):   293-316.
       A firsthand account of the coronation of Alexander III and
       the festivities staged for those dignitaries invited to the
       ceremony.

1612   *Witte, Sergei.   "Memories of Alexander III."   The Memoirs
       of Count Witte.   A. Yarmolinsky, ed./trans.   Garden City,
       N.Y.:   Doubleday Page and Company, 1921, 37-47.
       A highly favorable account of Alexander III's character,
       family life, and principal policies.   Witte, who served as Alex-
       ander's Director of Railways and Minister of Finance, describes
       the tsar as an intelligent ruler "who led an unimpeachable
       life" and was "a splendid example of the old-fashioned, god-
       fearing Russian type."   Witte asserts that as tsar, Alexander
       made vital contributions to the welfare and prosperity of his
       subjects and the international prestige of the empire particu-
       larly through his support for an extensive program of rail-
       road construction, the implementaiton of protective tariffs,
       and the maintenance of peace in Europe.   DK254.W5A5

1613   *Zaionchkovsky, Peter A.   The Russian Autocracy Under
       Alexander III.   Gulf Breeze, Fla.:   Academic International
       Press, 1976, 308pp.
       A comprehensive examination of the internal policies pursued
       by Alexander III and the political process which shaped them.
       Drawing upon an impressive body of primary sources,
       Zaionchkovsky, a Soviet specialist on late nineteenth-century
       tsarist Russia, develops an argument that reactionary policies
       did not emanate from any cohesive plan smoothly implemented
       from the very start of Alexander's reign but rather took
       shape as the tsar and his advisers responded to the specific

circumstances which confronted them in the early 1880s.
Specifically, the weakness of the liberal and radical movements
encouraged Alexander to launch, and later intensify, counter-
reforms of various types, while necessities of state dictated
that he pursue progressive economic policies at odds with the
remainder of his domestic program. Consequently, his counter-
reforms were far from successful, and, in the last years of
his reign, under pressure from the upsurge of public activity
which followed the 1891-1892 famine, he was "forced to retreat somewhat from policies of open reaction." Zaionchkovsky
concludes that not only did Alexander's policies fail to "divert
the general course of social and economic development" in
Russia, but they served to lay bare to all "the crisis of the
autocratic system and the decadence of its leadership, beginning with the imperial family and culminating with individual
local authorities." JN6515.Z5913 1976
Reviewed in:
Slav R, 37, no. 1 (1978): 127

DOMESTIC POLICY AND AFFAIRS/
POLITICAL THOUGHT AND PRACTICE

1614 *Adams, Arthur E. "Pobedonostsev and the Rule of Firmness."
      Slavonic E Eur R, 32, no. 78 (1952): 132-38.
      Alexander III is not central to the theme of this article, but
      the roots of his political philosophy receive some attention
      as part of a discussion of the conservatism of his most trusted
      adviser.

1615 *Aronson, I. M. "The Prospects for the Emancipation of Rus-
      sian Jewry During the 1880s." Slavonic E Eur R, 55, no. 3
      (1977): 348-69.
      An argument that Alexander III and his main advisers were
      not as close-minded on the "Jewish question" during the first
      half of his reign as historians have traditionally maintained.
      Aronson contends that in light of the divisions which existed
      within the top government circles in regard to Jewish affairs
      and the openness displayed by Alexander III and D. A. Tolstoy
      (Minister of the Interior, May 1882-April 1889) on the matter
      of Jewish emancipation, there existed, during the early years
      of Alexander's reign, "a genuine opportunity to change the
      government's course" in a more liberal direction. However,
      Aronson concludes, any hope of such a policy shift disappeared
      with the Borki incident of 1888 and Tolstoy's death the follow-
      ing year.

1616 *Balmuth, Daniel. "Censorship in the Reign of Alexander III,
      1881-1894" Censorship in Russia, 1865-1905. Washington,
      D.C.: University Press of America, 1979, 89-107.
      An argument that despite extensive censorship by the monarchy

the printing industry grew rapidly during Alexander III's
reign and writers were often able to address important political
and social questions in a manner contrary to the government's
wishes. Balmuth establishes Alexander's "special dislike for
the 'mangy' Russian press" and then enumerates the ingenious
ways that the government tried to restrict the growth of the
press and control its contents. Citing a 60 percent increase
in the number of works printed during the 1880s, Balmuth
refers to a "publishing revolution" which included a substantial number of publications that dealt with, in veiled form,
the pressing issues of the decade.

1617 *Baron, Salo W. "Under Alexander III and Nicholas II."
      RJTS (gen. study), 51-75.
      A sharp attack on Alexander III for pursuing policies respon-
      sible for the terrorization and death of thousands of Russia's
      Jews. Baron criticizes Alexander's government for promoting
      an image of the Jew as an exploiter of the Christian population,
      promulgating laws further restricting Jewish rights, and en-
      couraging, through direct and indirect means, vicious pogroms
      against an innocent Jewish population.

1618 Bennett, Helju Aulik. "The Chin System and the Raznochintsy
      in the Government of Alexander III." University of California,
      Berkeley, 1972. (dissertation)

1619 Brodhead, J. "Alexander III and a Polish Priest." Cath W,
      78 (Oct. 1903): 88-91.
      An account of Alexander III's relationship with Father Zud-
      mowski, a Polish priest who resided near a western Russian
      estate used by Alexander as a retreat from the demands of
      court life. Brodhead also discusses Alexander's concern for
      the welfare of Russia's subjects and interest in the reunifica-
      tion of the Roman Catholic and Russian Orthodox Churches.

1620 *Byrnes, Robert F. Pobedonostsev. His Life and Thought.
      Bloomington: Indiana University Press, 1968, 495pp.
      This scholarly study of Pobedonostsev's thought and career
      in the service of Alexander III and Nicholas II does not con-
      tain a titled section devoted to Pobedonostsev's relationship
      with either of the last two Romanov rulers but is nonetheless
      a useful source of information on the origin and nature of
      their political conservatism. DK236.P6B8

1621 "Conspiracy to Assassinate the Czar." Spectator, 72 (26 May
      1894): 705.
      A report on the uncovering of a nihilist plan to assassinate
      Alexander III while he was near Smolensk presiding over
      military maneuvers being conducted by the Russian army.

1622 Dubnow, S. "The Accession of Alexander III and the

Inauguration of Pogroms." <u>HJRP</u>, Vol. II (gen. study), 243-58.
A discussion of the onset of Judaeophobia as part of a broad
conservative reaction that developed in Russia after the
assassination of Alexander II. Dubnow examines the charges
and rumors advanced by various conservative journals and
newspapers that linked the Jews to some terrible revolutionary sect and portrayed them as an unproductive class exploit-
ive of the Christian population of Russia. He sees the plight
of the Jews who fell victim to the pogroms prompted by these
accusations as being made far worse by the government's unofficial support of anti-Semitic violence and its refusal to
provide aid for injured, wronged, and displaced Jews.

1623 *Duin, Egar C. "Alexander III and Pobedonostsev." <u>LUTS</u>
      (gen. study), 585-606.
      A discussion of the policy of Russification pursued by Alex-
      ander III in regard to Lutherans residing in the Baltic region
      of Russia. Duin establishes that the conversion to Orthodoxy
      by thousands of Baltic Lutherans was primarily a response to
      a 14 May 1886 decree that exempted non-Lutheran peasants
      from paying taxes levied in this region for the support of
      Lutheran churches and schools. He sees Pobedonostsev rather
      than Alexander as being the source of this decree and the
      restrictive measures taken against the Lutheran Church
      during the 1880s.

1624 Geffcken. "Russia Under Alexander III." <u>New R</u>, 5 (Sept.
      1891): 234-43.
      A critique of the Jewish policy pursued by the Russian govern-
      ment during Alexander III's reign. Geffcken blames Pobe-
      donostsev for the ruthless persecution of the Jews, and he
      questions whether Alexander III was fully aware of the extent
      of the atrocities being committed in his name.

1625 *Giffin, Frederick C. "The Prohibition of Night Work for
      Women and Young Persons: The Russian Factory Laws of
      June 3, 1885." <u>Can Slav S</u>, 2, no. 2 (1968): 208-18.
      A discussion of the 1885 Factory Laws as evidence that the
      conservative government of Alexander III "was willing, even
      eager, to move further along the path of factory legislation
      whenever there seemed valid reason to do so," especially if
      the conditions to be reformed threatened in any way the na-
      tion's economic or social stability.

1626 *Greenberg, Louis. "Anti-Semitism. 1881-1905." <u>JR</u>, Vol. II
      (gen. study), 19-47.
      A discussion of Alexander III's Jewish policy within the con-
      text of the aggressive nationalism that characterized his reign
      and the intensive efforts made to Russify "foreign groups."
      Of particular interest is Greenberg's description of the terror

that gripped the Jewish community in response to the government's encouragement of anti-Semitic violence. He sees these
unofficially sanctioned pogroms as but "a pretext to impose
new disabilities on the Jews and further limit their civil status
and economic opportunities."

1627 Hamburg, G. M. The Politics of the Russian Nobility 1881-
1905. New Brunswick, N.J.: Rutgers University Press,
1984, 296pp., bib. 273-87.
This scholarly examination of the Russian nobility's "unsuccessful economic and political competition with other social
groups" does not contain a separate section on Alexander III
but is a useful source for the study of the destructive and
divisive impact that his domestic policies had upon the nobility.
DK240.H35 1984

1628 Hans, N. "Alexander III." HREP (gen. study), 140-64.
A discussion of the educational policies of Alexander III as an
attempt to return to the reactionary approach to education
which so marked the reign of Nicholas I. Hans states that
Alexander was responsible for the decisions to reduce the
number of schools and scholars, curtail the influx into the
schools by students from the lower classes, tighten the
discipline and supervision in the school system, and increase
the attention given to vocational and religious education.
Hans views Alexander's reign as "the last attempt of the Russian autocracy to turn the wheel of history backwards," the
full significance of which "was only revealed ten years later
when the first Russian revolution broke out."

1629 *Heilbronner, Hans. "Alexander III and the Reform Plan of
Loris-Melikov." J Mod Hist, 33, no. 4 (1961): 384-97.
An argument that Alexander III's decision to reject the political reform plan of Loris-Melikov was not based upon any inherent dislike of the proposal nor was it connected to his
reaction to the assassination of Alexander II but rather was
prompted by a 6 March 1881 speech given by Pobedonostsev.
Heilbronner contends that prior to the speech Alexander was
still considering the proposal, and "only when he was sharply
reminded by Pobedonostsev that the obligations of an autocratic monarch had precedence over those to a dead father,
did he listen with unfeigned respect to the intrasigent ad-
jurations of Pobedonostsev and his allies."

1630 "Imperial Ukase." Spectator, 72 (2 June 1894): 739.
A commentary on Alexander III's decree which deprived "all
officials, from the Ministers downwards, of their power of
giving appointments and promotions in the civil service" and
gave this power to a special committee under the tsar's personal control. The author commends Alexander for attempting
to counter governmental corruption but sees the decree as

being doomed to failure because of its impracticability.

1631   Jayawardane, Sri Suddha. "Court Politics and the Fate of
       Bureaucratic Constitutionalism in Russia, 1879-1882." Uni-
       versity of Washington, Seattle, 1982. (dissertation)

1632   Katz, Martin. Mikail N. Katkov. A Political Biography, 1818-
       1887. The Hague: Mouton, 1966, 195pp., bib. 184-91.
       This scholarly work on the Russian conservative journalist
       M. N. Katkov does not contain a titled section on Katkov's
       relationship with Alexander III, but as a study of the dilemma
       faced by those conservatives who sought to modernize Russia
       while preserving its unique national identity it sheds consider-
       able light on Alexander III's domestic policies, particularly
       in the field of education. JA98.K3K3

1633   *Kipp, Jacob W. "Tsarist Politics and the Naval Ministry, 1876-
       1881: Balanced Fleet or Cruiser Navy?" Can Am Slav S,
       17, no. 2 (1983): 151-79.
       A discussion of the 1876-1881 "conflicts over naval strategy
       and warship procurement" as an aspect of "the political strug-
       gle between Grand Dukes Konstantin and Alexander." Kipp
       establishes that Konstantin's abrasive character, pronounced
       commitment to liberal reforms, and alleged support for the
       liason between Alexander II and Princess Yurievsky led
       Grand Duke Alexander to harbor a "pathological hatred" for
       Konstantin. In the realm of naval policy, the two grand dukes
       led opposing factions in the debate over the merits of a cruiser
       navy versus those of a navy composed of capital ships. As
       long as Alexander II was tsar, Grand Duke Alexander was
       unable to undermine Konstantin's position, and even with
       Grand Duke Alexander's assumption to the throne of Russia
       he refrained from dismissing Konstantin immediately for fear
       that such a move would be interpreted as an abrupt break
       with the policies of Alexander II. However, once Alexander
       III decided, under the influence of Pobedonostsev, to turn
       the government in a reactionary direction, Konstantin was
       dismissed from all his offices. Ironically, following Konstan-
       tin's removal from the political scene, Alexander "confirmed
       a twenty-year program of naval modernization that reflected
       the assumptions for which the Naval Ministry under the
       grand duke had been condemned."

1634   Laugel, A. "Alexander III." Nation, 59 (22 Nov. 1894):
       379-80.
       A brief commentary on the unlimited nature of the authority
       which Alexander III possessed as an autocrat and the ways in
       which he used this power to govern his realm.

1635   Leary, D. B. "Alexander III: 1881-1894." EAR (gen. study),
       82-91.

A broad review of the reactionary educational policies pursued
by Alexander III under the influence of D. Tolstoy and K.
Pobedonostsev.

1636   MacKenzie, David. The Lion of Tashkent: The Career of
General M. G. Cherniaev. Athens: University of Georgia
Press, 1974, 267pp.
Includes a short, untitled section on General Cherniaev's return to favor during the reign of Alexander III because his
conservative political views paralleled those of Alexander and
his advisers. DK219.6.C425M3

1637   Mosse, W. E. "Imperial Favourite: V. P. Meshchersky and
the Grazhdanin." Slavonic E Eur R, 59, no. 4 (1981): 529-
47.
An examination of the influence exerted on the last two
Romanov rulers by V. P. Meshchersky, editor of the journal
Grazhdanin (The Citizen) and conservative spokesman. Mosse
discusses Meshchersky's use of Grazhdanin, which was finan-
cially subsidized and personally supported by Alexander III
and Nicholas II, to counter "nihilism" and advance the cause
of conservatism. Mosse concludes the Meshchersky was more
of an adventurer than a serious political theorist whose influence was largely restricted to administrative appointments.

1638   Nabokoff, C. "Tolstoy's Power of Darkness and Alexander III."
Spectator, 138 (14 May 1927): 841-42.
A brief commentary on Alexander III's banning of the staging
of Tolstoy's play Power of Darkness as a consequence of
Pobedonostsev's charge that the play might have a harmful
moral influence on the audience because it dwelled upon
"degradation, crime, and savage behavior."

1639   *Naimark, Norman N. "The Government and the Revolutionaries." Terrorists and Social Democrats. The Russian Revolutionary Movement Under Alexander III. Cambridge: Harvard
University Press, 1983, 14-43.
A discussion of the "nihilist phobia" which gripped Alexander
III and his top advisers and ministers. Naimark maintains that
Alexander's attempt to buttress the old order through conservative legislation and repressive, police-state tactics was interpreted by some to have been successful because of the absence of overt revolutionary activity during his reign. However, the transformation of Russian society which began with
the reforms of the 1860s and was accelerated by the economic
policy pursued by Alexander III's own government was far too
elemental a process to be checked by the government's counter-
reforms. In reality, Naimark concludes, "the fundamental
instability of Russian society in the 1880s was only magnified
by the government's erratic and ultimately unsuccessful attempts to destroy the revolutionary movement."

1640   "Open Letter of the Revolutionary Executive Committee to the
       New Sovereign, Alexander III." <u>RFR</u> (anthology), 164-66.
       Excerpt from George F. Kennan, <u>Siberia and the Exile System</u>,
       Vol. II. London: 1891, 499-503.
       An appeal to the newly crowned Alexander III to convene a
       national constitutional assembly "to examine the existing frame-
       work of social and governmental life, and to remodel it in ac-
       cord with the people's wishes."

1641   *Pearson, T. S. "Origins of Alexander III's Land Captains:
       A Reinterpretation." <u>Slav R</u>, 40, no. 3 (1981): 384-403.
       A discussion of the Land Captain Statute of 1889 as the prod-
       uct of "practical statist considerations, rather than gentry
       interests or mere ideologies of reaction as argued by pre-
       revolutionary liberal historians, Soviet analysts, and many
       Western studies." Pearson maintains that the "mismanagement
       and abuses of power by elected officials" and, more generally,
       "the government's ineffectiveness at controlling economic and
       social change in the provinces ... necessitated the establish-
       ment of new officials to supervise the peasantry in order to
       maintain the autocracy itself."

1642   *Pobedonostsev and Alexander III." <u>Slavonic E Eur R</u>, 7
       (June 1928): 30-54.
       An examination of Pobedonostsev's 1863-1881 correspondence
       with the Tyutchev sisters for insight into the origin and
       evolution of his relationship with Grand Duke Alexander.
       The author maintains that Alexander was drawn to Pobedo-
       nostsev because of the latter's political conservatism, piety,
       and panslav sentiments. Following Alexander II's scandalous
       affair with Catherine Yurievsky, Pobedonostsev strengthened
       his ties with the grand duke through criticism of the tsar's
       immorality and by pointing out the virtues of firm autocratic
       rule as opposed to the vacillations of Alexander II. Through
       his association with the Russian Volunteer Fleet, in the late
       1870s, Pobedonostsev further impressed the grand duke with
       his energy, administrative skill, and powerful sense of com-
       mitment. Quite naturally, the author concludes, with the 1881
       death of Alexander II, the new tsar selected as his chief
       adviser and confidant the man who had reared him politically
       and philosophically over the previous fifteen years.

1644   "Rumor of Change in Succession." <u>Spectator</u>, 72 (28 Apr.
       1894): 569.
       A report of a rumor that Alexander III was planning to name
       as his heir Grand Duke Michael rather than Grand Duke
       Nicholas because of doubts over the latter's capabilities.

1645   Shklovsky, Victor. "Sofia Andreyevna Is Received by Alex-
       ander III." <u>Lev Tolstoy</u>. Moscow: Progress Publishers,
       1978, 602-10.

An account of the 13 April 1891 meeting between Alexander
III and the wife of Leo Tolstoy. Shklovsky examines Alexander's reasons for granting the audience and imposing a ban
on Tolstoy's The Kreutzer Sonata. Also receiving attention
is Tolstoy's negative reaction to his wife's efforts to soften
Alexander's critical opinion of his most recent writings.
PG3385.S4913

1646 Taranovski, Theodore. "The Politics of Counter-reform:
Autocracy and Bureaucracy in the Reign of Alexander III,
1881-1894." Harvard University, 1976. (dissertation)

1647 Tolstoi, Leo. "Letter to Emperor Alexander III." Independent,
61 (8 Nov. 1906): 1107-10.
A copy of the letter written by Tolstoy to Alexander III beg-
ging him to pardon the condemned prisoners who assassinated
Alexander II. Tolstoy suggests that Alexander would have
more success countering revolution if he replaced his policy
of oppression with one based upon the ideals of Christianity.

1648 *Vinogradoff, Igor. "Further Russian Imperial Correspondence
with Prince V. P. Meshchersky." Ox Slavonic P, 11 (1964):
101-11.
A series of letters exchanged between Grand Duke Alexander
and Prince Meshchersky, and a brief commentary on the nature
of the latter's relationship with the youthful Alexander. The
letters primarily pertain to famine relief, railway construction,
and the tariff question.

1649 *Whelan, Heide W. Alexander III and the State Council:
Bureaucracy and Counter-reform in Late Imperial Russia.
New Brunswick, N.J.: Rutgers University Press, 1982,
258pp., bib. 239-52.
An examination of the question, "How is it that the men who
ran the higher centers of government were so successfully
able to force Alexander III and the reactionary party around
him to a stalemate in the battle over counter-reforms, but
were unable, nonetheless, to press forward with any positive
program of their own or fill the power vacuum that seems to
have existed in the government?" Whelan contends that the
counter-reforms were dependent, to a large degree, on the
rationalized and autonomous bureaucracy which emerged as a
consequence of the reforms of the 1860s. However, although
this bureaucracy had the power "to thwart the autocrat and
his most powerful ministers on matters of legislation to which
they were firmly committed," it was unable to assume more
affirmative powers because "it neither represented nor was
tied to any group in society apart from the bureaucracy from
which it had sprung, there existed no power base on which
it could construct its own authority." Whelan thus concludes
that while "the tsar could not govern alone, ... neither could

any part of his administration govern without him."
JN6540.W47 1982

1650   *Zaionchkovsky, Peter A.   Russian Autocracy in Crisis, 1878–
       1882. Gulf Breeze, Fla.: Academic International Press, 1979,
       375pp.
       A scholarly analysis of the genesis and evolution of the mon-
       archy's general policy during the years surrounding the as-
       sassination of Alexander II.   Zaionchkovsky, a Soviet special-
       ist on late nineteenth-century tsarist history, contends that
       the economic and political concessions under consideration at
       the time of Alexander II's death were not abruptly abandoned
       by Alexander III upon assuming the throne. Liberal and
       conservative factions within the government struggled for
       nearly two months while the newly crowned tsar remained
       undecided in regard to the wisest line of policy to follow.
       The consequent confusion and disorientation within the gov-
       ernment might have been exploited for liberal purposes if
       there were demonstrations in favor of reform, but Russian
       society at this time did not contain any group of sufficient
       size and cohesion to launch such a protest. With the emer-
       gence of Pobedonostsev and Ignatiev as Alexander III's prime
       advisers, Zaionchkovsky concludes, the opportunity to shape
       the tsar's mentality in a liberal fashion passed and repressive
       policies became the order of the day. DK221.Z313
          Reviewed in:
          Slav R, 39, no. 4 (1980):   680–81

                  FOREIGN POLICY AND MILITARY AFFAIRS

1651   *Baylen, Joseph O.   "The Tsar and the British Press: Alex-
       ander III and the Pall Mall Gazette, 1888." East Eur Q, 15,
       no. 4 (1981):   425–39.
       An account of a 24 May 1888 interview between Alexander III
       and W. T. Stead, editor of the Pall Mall Gazette, in which the
       latter questioned the tsar in regard to Russian policy towards
       Bulgaria, Afghanistan, and the Straits. Stead, a proponent
       of Anglo-Russian friendship, left the interview convinced that
       Alexander's intentions in these areas were honorable and
       that he was a devout supporter of peace in Europe.

1652   Cowles, Virginia.   "Chapters VII–VIII." The Russian Dagger.
       Cold War in the Days of the Czars. London: Collins, 1969,
       189–216.
       A discussion of Alexander III's foreign policy within the con-
       fines of the argument that Soviet imperialism in Eastern Europe
       is but a successful application of techniques and goals devised
       by Russia's nineteenth-century rulers. DK189.C63

1653   Dodge, Theodore A.   "Death of the Czar and the Peace of
       Europe." Forum, 18 (Dec. 1894):   396–405.

A favorable review of Alexander III's efforts to promote peace
in Europe, and a discussion of the likelihood that peace would
not persist with the removal of Alexander from the international scene.

1654 *Dorpalen, Andreas. "Tsar Alexander III and the Boulanger
      Crisis." J Mod Hist, 23, no. 2 (1951): 122-36.
      An investigation of the source of Alexander III's resistance
      to pressure from Russian conservatives to forge an alliance
      with France which was then under the leadership of General
      Boulanger. Dorpalen sees Alexander's opposition as being
      due to a personal dislike of Boulanger and republican France
      as well as to his sentimental ties to Germany, France's most
      powerful enemy.

1655 *Jelavich, Barbara. "Alexander III." CRFP (gen. study),
      189-221.
      A generally favorable review of Alexander III's conduct of
      foreign affairs. Jelavich states that Alexander wisely chose
      not to take an aggressive stance in his relations with the
      Ottoman Empire and European powers but instead opted to
      concentrate on "internal development and the remaking of
      the alliance with the conservative powers." The collapse
      of Russia's alliance with Germany is not seen by Jelavich
      as being Alexander's fault but rather a consequence of de-
      cisions reached in Berlin which left him with no choice but
      to seek an accord with France. Since such an alignment could
      not have been avoided in the early 1890s and, in any case,
      was "a strictly defensive alliance," Jelavich concludes, it
      is difficult to accept as valid the charge that the Franco-
      Russian accord was responsible for "the creation of the alli-
      ance system that eventually brought the European states into
      a major war over a minor Balkan incident."

1656 Katkov, George, and Michael Futrell. "Russian Foreign Policy,
      1880-1914." Russia Enters the Twentieth Century, 1894-1917.
      Erwin Oberlander et al., eds. New York: Schocken Books,
      1971, 9-33.
      In part, a discussion of the factors which led to the collapse
      of the Three Emperors' League and the signing of the Franco-
      Russian alliance of 1894. DK262.R8813 1971

1657 *Kennan, Geoge F. The Decline of Bismarck's European Order.
      Franco-Russian Relations, 1875-1890. Princeton, N.J.: Prince-
      ton University Press, 1979, 466pp., bib. 439-50.
      In part, an analysis of the circumstances which led Alexander
      III to abandon Russia's alliance with Germany in favor of one
      with France. Kennan states that during the period under
      study, France consistently looked to Russia for an alliance as
      a means of escape from the diplomatic isolation under which
      she suffered in Bismarck's "European order." Alexander III

came to accept such an alliance as a desirable one, however, not because of the cleverness of French diplomacy or any failure on Bismarck's part but rather because Russia's relations with Austria-Hungary and Germany deteriorated drastically due to the aggressive Near Eastern policy pursued by Russia. Given Russia's pressing domestic problems, Kennan concludes, such a policy was ill-advised, but Alexander's less than clear understanding of his country's basic needs combined with the emergence of a virulent form of nationalism in Russia so clouded his vision that the self-destructive nature of his diplomacy eluded him. DK76.5.F8K36

1658 *_____. "The Mystery of the Ferdinand Documents." Jahr Ges Ost, 26, no. 3 (1978): 321-52.
An investigation of the origins of four documents which allegedly prove that Bismarck deceived Alexander III by secretly encouraging Prince Ferdinand of Saxe-Coburg-Gotha to accept the Bulgarian throne and thereby deny Russia influence in that state. Kennan traces the forged documents to General Boulanger of France who hoped that they would lead to the termination of the Three Emperors' League and thus clear the way for a rapprochement between France and Russia.

1659 *Langer, William L. The Franco-Russian Alliance. New York: Octagon Books, 1967, 455pp., bib. 421-42.
This scholarly study includes considerable discussion of Alexander III's reasons for concluding an alliance with France despite his intense dislike of the political philosophy upon which the French Third Republic was founded. Langer establishes that Russia's need to escape the diplomatic isolation it encountered as a result of Germany's support of Austria's Balkan policy and the failure of Kaiser William II to renew the Reinsurance Treaty with Russia led Alexander to the conclusion that an accord with France, however distasteful on a personal level, was essential diplomatically. D397.L3 1967

1660 *Maxwell, Margaret. "A Re-examination of the Role of N. K. Giers as Russian Foreign Minister Under Alexander III." Eur St R, 1, no. 4 (1971): 351-78.
An argument that N. K. Giers deserves more credit than he has received as a source for the successfulness of Alexander III's foreign policy. Maxwell contends that the emphasis placed upon preserving the European status quo which characterized Russian foreign policy under Alexander was, to a significant degree, the result of Giers' ability to convince Alexander that the survival of the monarchy depended on avoiding war and, consequently, rejecting the advice of conservative advisers who urged him to pursue a more aggressive policy in the Near East.

1661 Medlicott, W. N. "Bismarck and the Three Emperors' Alliance, 1881-87." Trans Roy Hist S, 27 (1945): 61-83.

In part, a discussion of Alexander III's distrust of Bismarck's motives for promoting the Three Emperors' Alliance.

1662 Rollins, Patrick J. "Imperial Russia's African Colony." Rus R, 27, no. 4 (1968): 432-51.
An examination of "imperial Russia's attempt to join in the European scramble for Africa" by way of an 1889 cossack expedition to Ethiopia. Rollins discusses how the attempts of Foreign Minister Giers to scuttle the expedition were checked, and he traces the fate of this farcical mission which was widely believed to have had the personal support of Alexander III.

1663 Stead, W. T. "Alexander III, Peace-keeper of Europe." RR, 10 (Dec. 1894): 630-33.
A positive sketch of Alexander III's character and reign with most attention devoted to his efforts to promote peaceful relations among the leading nations of Europe.

1664 Stepniak, Sergius. "How the Czar's Death Affects Europe." No Am R, 159 (Dec. 1894): 735-41.
An assessment of Alexander III as a man and a ruler, and speculation about the leadership capabilities of the new tsar, Nicholas II. Stepniak expresses concern over Nicholas' ability to promote the cause of European peace as successfully as Alexander III had been able to do.

1665 Tarsaidzé, Alexandre. "A Friendship Cools." CP (gen. study), 319-28.
A discussion of Alexander III's repressive measures against Russia's Jewish population as a source of strain on the long-standing friendly relations that existed between America and Russia. Tarsaidzé states that America's leaders "put pressure on the Russian government to pursue a liberal policy with regard to the Jewish people" in the name of humanitarianism but were also motivated by the desire to prevent "hordes of Jews" from emigrating to the United States.

1666 *Walsh, Warren B. "Pobedonostsev and Panslavism." Rus R, 8, no. 4 (1949): 316-21.
A review of the bond between Count Pobedonostsev and Alexander III in terms of their common support of slavophilism and panslavism. Walsh also presents an account of the spring 1883 diplomatic rift that developed between St. Petersburg and Vienna due to Austro-Hungarian concern over Russian support for panslav sentiments within Austria-Hungary.

1667 *Whyte, Frederic. "Stead and Tsar Alexander III." LWTS, Vol. II (gen. study), 259-64.
Extracts from W. T. Stead's May 1888 interview with Alexander III, the substance of which Stead was sworn to keep confidential. In the interview, Stead stressed his disdain for those

British journalists who propagated a negative image of Alex-
ander III and Russia, and he discussed frankly with the tsar
Russian and British policy in regard to Bulgaria, the Straits,
Afghanistan, and Germany.

GENERAL STUDIES AND ASSESSMENTS/
PERSONAL AFFAIRS AND CHARACTER

1668 "Accident at Moscow." Spectator, 76 (6 June 1896): 792-93.
A vivid account of the death of thousands of commoners as
a consequence of the human stampede which occurred when a
huge crowd pressed forward to obtain keepsakes handed out
by government officials at Nicholas II's coronation. While
the author does not blame Nicholas for the disaster, he does
criticize him for allowing the fetes and gaities to continue as
if nothing had happened.

1669 Alberg, Victor L. "Nicholas II, 1868-1918." Soc S, 47 (Apr.
1956): 140-48.
A biographical sketch of Nicholas II as a weak-willed and politically myopic ruler who excelled only as a loving husand and
devoted parent.

1670 Alexander, Grand Duke. "Millions That Were." Fortune,
4 (Sept. 1931): 108.
An account of the family and court expenditures of Nicholas
II. Grand Duke Alexander states that Nicholas' generosity
and extravagant life style so depleted the royal treasury,
including foreign bank accounts, that if the royal family had
emigrated from Russia in 1918 its members would have been
forced to assume a bourgeois existence.

1671 * _____. Once a Grand Duke, Vol. I. New York: Farrar
and Rinehart, 1932, 348pp.
Recollections of incidents in the life of Nicholas II, the most
noteworthy concerning his warm family relations, reactions to
the 1905 Revolution, dislike of Rasputin, conduct during
World War I, and abdication in February of 1917. In general,
Grand Duke Alexander portrays Nicholas as an emotional,
weak-willed individual overly susceptible to the influence of
Empress Alexandra and others close to him and, consequently,
wholly unsuited for the demands of his exalted position.
DK219.6.A4A3

1672 Almedingen, E. M. The Empress Alexandra 1872-1918. A
      Study. London: Hutchinson, 1961, 244pp., bib. 299-31.
      A popular, somewhat sympathetic biography of Empress Alex-
      andra. Almedingen concentrates on Alexandra's relationship
      with Nicholas and their children, involvement in politics,
      and her contacts with Rasputin. Alexandra emerges from
      this study as a woman of limited vision and poor political
      judgment but dedicated to her husband and possessing remark-
      able integrity and grace. Almedingen does not feel that Alex-
      andra's poor political advice was responsible for the monarchy's
      collapse nor does she believe that Alexandra was ever motivated
      by anything but her desire to provide support for Nicholas
      during the trying years of World War I. DK254.A5A6

1673 "The Betrothal of the Cesarewitch." Spectator, 72 (28 Apr.
      1894): 574-75.
      A brief discussion of the genesis and political implications of
      the betrothal of Nicholas II to Princess Alix.

1674 Biddle, Winthrop. "The Czar and His Family." Munsey, 51
      (Feb. 1914): 3-9.
      A sympathetic portrayal of Nicholas II as a loving father and
      devoted husband.

1675 *Bing, Edward J., ed. The Letters of Tsar Nicholas and Em-
      press Marie. R. H. Bruce-Lockhart, pref. London: Nichol-
      son and Watson, 1937, 311pp.
      Also published under the title The Secret Letters of the Last
      Tsar. A representative sampling of the more than 500 letters
      exchanged between Nicholas II and his mother, Dowager Em-
      press Maria Feodorovna. Bing has edited the letters to re-
      move trivial information and has added explanatory notes
      where necessary. The correspondence sheds considerable
      light on Nicholas' character, family affairs, and politics, es-
      pecially in regard to the 1905 Revolution. In a preface, R.
      H. Bruce-Lockhart provides an interesting assessment of the
      correspondence and its historical significance. DK254.A4M27
            Reviewed in:
            Am Hist R, 44 (1939): 623
            Commonweal, 27 (15 Apr. 1915): 698
            Sat R Lit, (19 Mar. 1938): 6

1676 Bird, Anthony. Empress Alexandra of Russia. Geneva: Edito-
      Service, 1970, 319pp.
      A popular and sympathetic biography of Empress Alexandra.
      Although Bird refrains from passing judgment on Alexandra's
      role in the downfall of the Russian dynasty, he does state that
      her inability to function well in formal society led her to
      create "a world of family make-believe" in which her subjec-
      tivity and narrow-mindedness held sway over her weak-willed
      husband. In an appendix, titled "Nicholas II and the Roman-
      ovs," Bird discusses Nicholas' upbringing and education as

the twin sources of his ineptness as an autocrat.
DK254.A4B37

1677 Bishop of Peterborough.   "The Imperial Coronation at Moscow."
Cornhill, 74 (Sept. 1896):   305-25.
A detailed, eyewitness account of Nicholas II's coronation,
and a brief discussion of the historical significance of the
coronation ceremony.

1678 Borges, E.   "New Czar, and What We May Expect from Him."
Harper's M, 91 (June 1895):   129-38.   Reply, I. F. Hapgood.
Nation, 61 (5 Sept. 1895):   161-78.
A favorable account of Nicholas II's character and capabilities.
Borges reviews Nicholas' genealogy, youth, and accession to
the throne and suggests that Nicholas will be a kind, just,
and progressive leader.

1679 Bovey, Kate Koon.   Russian Coronation 1894.   Minneapolis:
Privately Printed, 1942, 50pp.
A series of letters depicting in a dramatic style the festivities
surrounding Nicholas II's coronation.   Includes photographs of
various coronation related events.   DK258.4.B6

1680 Buchanan, Meriel.   The Dissolution of an Empire.   London:
J. Murray, 1932, 312pp.
An account of the Russian court during the years just prior
to the February Revolution of 1917.   Buchanan, the daughter
of the British ambassador to Russia, describes Nicholas, his
family life, and court intrigues, and provides some information on the circumstances leading to his overthrow.
DK265.B86

1681 Butler, Maynard.   "The Coronation Days of His Imperial Majesty
Nicholas Alexandrovitch."   Harper's W, 40 (20 June 1896):
618.
A description of Nicholas II's coronation, the dignitaries in
attendance, and the festivities associated with the event.

1682 "Camera Bug to Czar Nicholas; Photograph Album of G. N.
Taube."   Life, 72 (9 June 1972):   69-70+.
A series of photographs of the royal family taken by George
Taube, an officer on the imperial yacht.

1683 "The Character of the Czarewich."   Spectator, 73 (13 Oct.
1894):   477.
Speculation in regard to the character of Nicholas II (about
which little was known at the time) and the possibility of an
attempt on his life by Russian radicals.

1684 *Chernavin, T.   "The Home of the Last Tsar as Material for a
Study of Character."   Slavonic R, 17, no. 51 (1939):   659-
67.

An interesting account of the furnishings and character of
Nicholas II's residence, the Alexander Palace in Tsarskoe Selo.
Chernavin states that Nicholas and Alexandra had none of the
good taste for art or furnishings which their Romanov predecessors possessed. The decoration of the rooms in which
they lived "clashed badly with the basic style of the palace,"
and their artistic ignorance led them to adorn their walls with
discordant pictures painted by second-rate artists. Rooms
were cluttered with photographs and albums depicting family
members and with hundred of mystical pictures and icons
which Alexandra considered to have magical and protective
powers.

1685   A Collection of Material Relating to the Coronation of Czar
       Nicholas II Including Invitations, Lists of Distinguished Guests,
       Programs, the Order of Ceremonies, Photographs.   London:
       From the Illustrated London News, 1896.   DK258.4.C6
       Unavailable for annotation.

1686   Coudert, Amalie Kussner.   "The Human Side of the Czar."
       Century, 50 (Oct. 1906):   845-55.
       A sympathetic character portrait of Nicholas II by an Ameri-
       can artist who was commissioned to paint miniatures of the
       royal family.

1687   Cowles, Virginia.   The Last Tsar and Tsarina.   New York:
       Putnam Press, 1977, 232pp.
       A popular, illustrated account of the lives of Nicholas II
       and Alexandra.   Cowles includes nearly 100 photographs and
       illustrations in support of her text as she presents an objec-
       tive narrative on the character of the Romanovs, their family
       relations, and the circumstances which led to the 1917 Revolu-
       tion.   DK258.C68

1688   "Czar and Admiral Alexiev."   Outlook, 76 (30 April 1904):
       1017-14.
       A discussion of Nicholas II's reactionary political views and
       general incompetence as a ruler; prompted by the retirement
       of Admiral Alexiev form his position as viceroy of Russia's
       Far Eastern territories.

1689   "The Czar at Home."   Harper's W, 48 (17 Sept. 1904):   1435.
       A brief account of the family life of Nicholas II; based on a
       German language book by Bresnitz von Sydaroff.

1690   "Czar Nicholas II of Russia."   Cassell's M, 38 (July 1904):
       115-22.
       A discussion of Nicholas II's extravagant and relatively care-
       free existence despite the pressing political, social, and
       economic problems in early twentieth-century Russia.

1691 "Czar's Flight to Finland." Cur Lit, 41 (Nov. 1906): 500-02.
A discussion of the royal family's November 1906 trip to Finland as a reaction to an attempt on Nicholas II's life.

1692 Davis, Richard H. "The Coronation." A Year from a Correspondent's Yearbook. London: Harper and Brothers, 1898,
3-68. Originally in Harper's M, 94 (Feb. 1897): 335-52.
A detailed eyewitness description of Nicholas II's coronation
and the incredible pageantry which surrounded this event.
Of particular interest is Davis' account of the police precautions taken to protect the tsar and the difficulties encountered by journalists attempting to cover the royal ceremony. PS1522.Y4

1693 Dehn, Madame Lili. The Real Tsaritsa. London: Thornton
Butterworth, Limited, 1922, 253pp.
A sympathetic assessment of Alexandra written to dispel the
many negative accounts of her behavior as empress. Dehn
portrays Alexandra as a sensitive, deeply religious, and
loving person who, far from being the bigoted, hysterical,
pro-German political meddler described by her critics, was a
Russian patriot concerned only with the welfare of the nation
entrusted to the care of Nicholas II. DK254.A5D4

1694 Deriabin, P. "Götterdämmerung Russian Style." WT, (gen.
study), 90-101.
A discussion of Nicholas II as "a little man, not only in
stature, but also in character and intelligence" whose ill-
founded policies had a disastrous effect on the growth of
unrest during his reign.

1695 Diagram Group. "Princess Dagmar: Maria Fyodorovna."
Mothers: 100 Mothers of the Famous and the Infamous. New
York: Paddington Press, 1976, 184pp.
A brief biographical sketch of Nicholas II's mother with some
reference to the conditions of his youth which shaped his
personality and character.

1696 Dillon, E. J. "The Tsar." Good Words, 41 (July 1900):
446-53.
A review of the conflicting popular images of Nicholas II's
character, intelligence, and ability to rule. Dillon commends
Nicholas for his demeanor, insightfulness, and astounding
memory.

1697 Dudko, Dimitry. "Father Dimitry Dudko on the Last Russian
Tsar." Orth Life, 28, no. 4 (1978): 46-48.
An argument that the pronounced Christian qualities of
Nicholas II's character and behavior and the suffering that
he and his family endured warrant his being considered a
martyr and a saint. Dudko, a Russian Orthodox priest,

draws heavily upon Gilliard's biography for examples of
Nicholas' piety and heroism in the face of adversity.

1698   Durland, Kellog. "The Empress Alexandra Feodorovna of
        Russia." Real Romances of To-day. New York: Duffield
        and Company, 1911, 107-216.
        A favorable biography of Alexandra with considerable atten-
        tion devoted to her courtship with Grand Duke Nicholas,
        their tender marital relationship, and the warm family life
        they enjoyed. D413.7.D6

1699   *E. T. "Diary of Nicholas II." Liv Age, 318 (4 Aug. 1923):
        225-27. From Sovremennya Zapiski, (Jan.-Feb. 1923).
        An examination of Nicholas II's 1905 diary as an illustration
        of his inability to distinguish important events from petty
        ones.

1700   Eagar, M. Six Years at the Russian Court. London: Hurst
        and Blackett, 1906, 283pp.
        Uncritical reminiscences of court life and Romanov family
        relations by the English tutor of Grand Duchess Olga. Eagar,
        who served the Romanovs from 1898 to 1904, describes anec-
        dotally the royal family's daily routine, personal tastes, per-
        sonalities, and a number of incidents in their lives, including
        two attempts to assassinate Nicholas II. DK258.E23

1701   Edgar, William C. "Personal Impressions of the New Czar."
        Harper's W, 38 (24 Nov. 1894): 1118.
        A brief portrayal of Nicholas II as a humane individual deeply
        concerned with the internal problems which plagued Russia.

1702   Elchaninov, Major-General A. The Tsar and His People. A.
        P. W., trans. London: Hodder and Stoughton, 1914, 149pp.
        A hagiographic, undocumented account of Nicholas II's char-
        acter and the policies which he pursued in his first eighteen
        years as tsar. In glowing patriotic language, Elchaninov
        portrays Nicholas as an indefatigable "imperial worker" in
        the service of Russia's best interests and the "sovereign
        father" beloved by the Russian people. DK258.E58

1703   Essad-Bey, Mohammed. Nicholas II. Prisoner of the Purple.
        Paul and Elsa Branden, trans. London: Hutchinson and
        Company, 1936, 292pp., bib. 283-86.
        A highly favorable and somewhat fanciful account of the life of
        Nicholas II. Essad-Bey states that his book is more "an his-
        torical biography ... than a biographical novel" but admits
        that he has presented as direct quotations "certain indirect
        statements gleaned from memoirs and documents" and has
        rearranged certain occurrences so that the reader might better
        understand and sympathize with Nicholas as "the most unfor-
        tunate figure of his time." DK258.E8

1704 Eulalia, Infanta. "Cabbages and Kings; Czar and His People
      Recollections of Great Rulers and Their Courts." Century,
      90 (May 1915): 87-94.
      A portrayal of Nicholas II as a ruler with the best of inten-
      tions but unable to cope with the staggering domestic and
      war-related problems that confronted him.

1705 Field, Margaret. "A Future Emperor and Empress." Munsey,
      11 (Sept. 1894): 629-32.
      A flowery commentary on the significance of Nicholas and
      Alexandra's marriage. Field predicts that "the royal love
      match may change the destiny of Russia and Europe."

1706 Fitzlyon, Kyril and Tatiana Browning. Before the Revolution.
      A View of Russia Under the Last Tsar. Woodstock, N.Y.:
      Overlook Press, 1979, 233pp.
      A general survey of Nicholas II's reign and the conditions of
      turn of the century Russia precedes 135 pages of photographs
      of the royal family and various aspects of Russian society and
      culture. DK260.B43

1707 Fletcher, R. "Royal Mothers and Their Children." Good H,
      54 (April 1912): 450-59.
      A portrayal of Alexandra as a simple-minded, superstitious
      woman unsuited for her role and an overprotective mother
      responsible for Tsarevich Alexis being a spoiled brat.

1708 Forsyth, Alastair. "Sovereigns and Steam Yachts: The Tsar
      at Cowes." Country Life, 176 (2 Aug. 1984): 310-12.
      Unavailable for annotation.

1709 *Fülöp-Miller, René, ed. Under Three Tsars. The Memoirs
      of the Lady-in-Waiting Elizabeth Narishkin-Kurakin. Julia
      E. Loesser, trans. New York: E. P. Dutton and Company,
      1931, 231pp.
      Recollections of the Russian court by a confidante of various
      members of the royal family during the reigns of the last
      three tsars. Most noteworthy are Narishkin-Kurakin's recol-
      lections of Nicholas II's coronation, the catastrophe on the
      Khodinsky Field, the assistance which Nicholas rendered to
      her in her efforts to improve conditions in Russia's prisons,
      Nicholas' relations with various advisers, the influence of
      Rasputin, and the circumstances surrounding Nicholas' abdica-
      tion. In addition, Narishkin-Kurakin relates many incidents
      in the life of the royal family and provides an interesting
      sketch of Nicholas II in which she portrays him as indecisive
      and lacking in self-confidence. DK186.6.N25132

1710 Geraschinevsky, Michael Z. "The Ill-Fated Children of the
      Czar." Scrib M, 65 (Feb. 1919): 58-76.
      An illustrated, sympathetic portrayal of the wartime life and
      character of Nicholas II's children.

1711 Gibbon, Perceval. "What Ails Russia. Glimpses of the Inef-
      ficiency and Dissoluteness of the Royal Family." McClure's M,
      24 (April 1905): 609-15.
      A description of Nicholas II as a "puppet Czar, lacking in
      personality and personal conviction."

1712 *Grabbe, Paul and Beatrice, eds. The Private World of the
      Last Tsar. Boston and Toronto: Little, Brown and Com-
      pany, 1984, 191pp., bib. 189-91.
      A collection of more than 200 photographs of Nicholas II and
      his family taken by General Alexander Grabbe who served as
      a military aide to the tsar from 1911 until the February Revolu-
      tion of 1917. The majority of the photographs are of the
      royal family in various informal settings but a significant per-
      centage are of Nicholas while he was at the front and army
      headquarters at Mogilev during World War I. The editors
      draw upon General Grabbe's diary and journal to provide his-
      torical background and captions for the photographs.
      DK259.4.G73 1984

1713 Grenfell, Francis W. Three Weeks in Moscow. London: Harri-
      son and Sons, 1896, 152pp.
      A series of letters in which the author presents a vivid por-
      trayal of the extravaganza which accompanied the coronation
      of Nicholas II. DK601.G83

1714 Guild, Curtis. "Russia and Her Emperor." Yale R, 4 (July
      1915): 712-22.
      A favorable review of Nicholas II's domestic and foreign pol-
      icies, and a portrayal of his critics as narrow-minded, self-
      serving agitators.

1715 *Gurko, V. I. "The Death of Alexander III and the Accession
      of Nicholas II." Features and Figures of the Past. Govern-
      ment and Opinion in the Reign of Nicholas II. Laura Matveev,
      trans. Stanford: Stanford University Press, 1939, 13-21.
      A perceptive discussion of the differences between the char-
      acter and policies of Alexander III and Nicholas II. Gurko,
      who held positions in the Imperial Chancellery, Ministry of
      Interior, and the State Council during Nicholas's reign, states
      that Alexander III's reign "exemplifies in a striking manner
      the great value of a clearly defined and constant course of
      political conduct. Because Alexander III followed such a
      course, even though it ran counter to the hopes of society's
      progressive circles, his reign experienced neither sharp pro-
      testations nor open uprisings" and contributed to the growth
      of Russia's economy and the maintenance of international
      peace. Upon accession to the throne, the inexperienced
      Nicholas II attempted to continue those policies in the same
      manner as had Alexander III without understanding the com-
      plexities associated with them or possessing the personal

qualities upon which they were dependent. Nicholas' deficiencies became apparent at the very beginning of his reign
when he tactlessly dismissed as "senseless dreams" those
pleas made by several public institutions (especially the Tver
Zemstvo Assembly) for a political course more liberal than that
pursued by Alexander III. Gurko concludes that as Nicholas'
reign progressed, Nicholas' shortsightedness and political
immaturity resulted in policies which continued to widen the
gap between government and public, a fateful development
accelerated by his susceptibility to the disjointed advice of
his closest ministers. This work is also of considerable value
as a source of information on the principal ministers of the
government of Nicholas II, their political views, and relationships with the tsar. DK260.G82

1716 Hanbury-Williams, Sir John. The Emperor Nicholas II As I
      Knew Him. New York: E. P. Dutton, 1924, 270pp.
      Recollections of Nicholas II and his immediate entourage by
      a British major-general attached to the general headquarters
      of the Russian army in the October 1914 to April 1917 period.
      In diary fashion, Hanbury-Williams presents a series of ob-
      servations and commentaries in regard to Nicholas' behavior
      in both relaxed and stressful situations which collectively
      yield an image of the emperor as a poised, compassionate,
      and pensive sovereign dedicated to his people and the Allied
      cause.

1717 Hapgood, I. F. "Russia's Czarina." Harper's B, 40 (Feb.
      1906): 103-09.
      A sympathetic description of Alexandra's childhood and char-
      acter.

1718 Hersh, J. J. "Cup of Blood: Commemoration of the Corona-
      tion of Czar Nicholas II." Antiq J, 33 (Jan. 1978): 38.
      A description of the ceremonial cups created for Nicholas II's
      coronation which were used during the three days of festivities
      and then thrown to the crowds. The ensuing rush to obtain
      the cups resulted in hundreds of people being crushed to
      death.

1719 Johnston, Charles. "Czar Nicholas II." Harper's W, 48 (5
      Nov. 1904): 1706.
      A discussion of Nicholas II's unpopularity as a consequence
      of his attempting to rule like his father without possessing
      the character and temperament to do so successfully.

1720 Joubert, Carl. The Truth About the Tsar and the Present
      State of Russia. London: Eveleigh Nash, 1905, 265pp.
      An exposé on the miserable condition of the common people
      in Russia at the turn of the century, and a scathing attack
      on the character and policies of Nicholas II. Joubert presents

1905 Russia as an impoverished and oppressed nation seething
with a discontent unheeded by Nicholas and the corrupt bureaucratic apparatus which buttressed the monarchy. He characterizes Nicholas as a weakling "surrounded by sycophants
who constantly pander to his vanity and encourage him to
think well of himself" and to see as traitors all who dared to
speak the truth about Russia's plight. Joubert is also highly
critical of those Western newspapers and journals which presented Nicholas and his policies in too favorable a light.
DK262.J87

1721 Kaun, Alexander. "The Twilight of the Romanov Dynasty."
      Am R, 3, no. 2 (1925): 129-41.
      A negative account of the character and political behavior of
      Nicholas II and Alexandra; based upon the "Nicky-Sunny"
      correspondence.

1722 Knupffer, George. Nicholas II and His Successor. London:
      Monarchist Press Associates, 1958, 16pp.
      A monarchist tribute to Nicholas II on the 40th anniversary
      of the execution of the Romanovs. Knupffer asserts that
      Nicholas was "betrayed by immoral, degenerate and subverted
      men at the top ... but the mass of the people were as they
      still are, true to the Monarchy." Knupffer concludes with a
      statement of support for the claim to the Romanov throne ad-
      vanced by Prince Vladimir, the only son of Grand Duke
      Cyril, first cousin of Nicholas II. DK258.K57

1723 Kochan, Miriam. "The Imperial Family." The Last Days of
      Imperial Russia. London: Weidenfeld and Nicolson, 1976,
      160-87.
      A heavily illustrated review of the personal life and character
      of Nicholas II and his family in the years just prior to the
      1917 revolution. Kochan provides most information on Nicho-
      las' relationship with Alexandra. DK262.K63

1724 Kshessinska, M. Dancing in Petersburg. Garden City, N.Y.:
      Doubleday Press, 1961, 28-56.
      Reminiscences of the author's romantic relationship, as a young
      ballerina in the early 1890s, with Tsarevich Nicholas. Kshes-
      sinska characterizes Nicholas as an intelligent, erudite, sensi-
      tive, and remarkably poised young man with a highly developed
      sense of duty. However, she states that "the Tsarevitch did
      not have the qualities needed to be a ruler. Not that he lacked
      character and will-power, but he did not have the gift of mak-
      ing his opinion prevail, and he often gave in to others though
      his first impulse had been right." Kshessinska also discusses
      her sad separation from Nicholas with the arrival in St. Peters-
      burg of Princess Alice, Nicholas' fiancée. GV1785.K75A33

1725 "Last Czar Canonized." Christ Cent, 98 (18 Nov. 1981): 1185.

An account of the canonization of Nicholas II and his family
by an anti-Soviet, Russian Orthodox group in New York City.

1726 Logan, John A., Jr. In Joyful Russia. New York: D. Appleton and Company, 1897, 275pp.
An eyewitness account of the coronation of Nicholas II. Logan
describes vividly the pageantry and festivities associated with
the coronation, the ceremony itself, and the joyous mood in
Russia at that time. Although Logan was quite impressed by
the majesty of the coronation fete and the seriousness with
which the affair was taken by the Russian people, he reminds
his readers that he saw the country "in holiday attire" and
therefore his account of conditions and the popular mood
should not be considered as an accurate portrayal of Russian
life. DK26.L83

1727 Low, A. M. "Foreign Affairs: Character Study of Nicholas
II." Forum, 36 (Apr. 1905): 499-500.
Speculation on the likelihood of the monarchy's collapse as a
consequence of Nicholas II's political ineptness and lack of
resolve.

1728 *Lyons, Marvin. Nicholas II. The Last Tsar. Andrew Wheat-
croft, ed. London: Routledge and Kegan Paul Limited,
1974, 224pp.
The stated aim of this illustrated biography of Nicholas II is
"to cut the text to a minimum, and to allow the photographs
to create their own impression." To this end Lyons presents
over 100 photographs of Nicholas II in attendance at various
state functions and family affairs. Most obvious in the photographs is the warmth of Nicholas' family relationship.
DK259.4.L93

1729 "Man of Destiny." No Am R, 186 (Nov. 1907): 459-61.
An account of Nicholas II's brush with tragedy when the Imperial yacht Standat struck rocks while the royal family was
cruising near Finland.

1730 Mano, D. K. "Russian Martyrs." Nat R, 33 (25 Dec. 1981):
1560-61.
A report on the impending canonization of the royal family
and their portrayal in an icon made for the event.

1731 Marie, Queen of Rumania. "Some Memories of the Russian
Court." Liv Age, 303 (4 Oct. 1919): 16-18 and 303 (18 Oct.
1919): 157-60.
A favorable commentary on Nicholas II's character and interest
in improving the condition of the Russian people. Queen Marie
suggests that Nicholas' unpopularity with his subjects was due
more to the harmful influence of Alexandra (Marie's cousin)
rather than to his own shortcomings.

1732   "Marriage of Nicholas II." Spectator, 73 (1 Dec. 1894):   A
       brief commentary on Nicholas II's marriage and the critical
       response to this event by Russian radicals.

1733   Martin, William. "Nicholas II." Statesmen of the War in Retro-
       spect, 1918-1928. New York: Minton, Blach and Company,
       1928, 28-42.
       A critical character sketch of Nicholas II as a man and leader.
       Martin states that although Nicholas was a model son and an
       excellent husband and father he was completely unsuited to
       the demands of his exalted station and had as his prime politi-
       cal goal the blind maintenance of Russia's "tsarist heritage."
       Martin notes that Nicholas did not want Russia to become in-
       volved in a major war yet remained for three years a faithful
       ally of England and France despite the disintegration of his
       realm under the burdens which accompanied the conflict.
       D507.M35

1734   Massie, Robert. Nicholas and Alexandra. New York: Atheneum,
       1967, 613pp., bib. 589-94.
       A popular, sympathetic account of the life and reign of Nicho-
       las II.   Drawing on a wide range of English language primary
       and secondary sources, Massie portrays Nicholas as a well-
       intentioned, compassionate ruler caught up in a web of ex-
       plosive historical circumstances beyond his control.   Massie
       states that the political, social, and economic conditions of
       Russia required a concerted, dynamic, and progressive plan
       of action, but Nicholas, by training, temperament and family
       circumstances, could not provide sufficient leadership to de-
       vise and implement needed reforms.   In particular, Nicholas'
       concern over the hemophiliac condition of his only son, Alexis,
       not only consumed much of his time and energy, but, indirect-
       ly resulted in the monarchy's prestige, honor, and credibility
       being compromised through the activities of Gregory Rasputin.
       Massie concludes that "to the end, Nicholas did his best,
       and for his wife and family that was a very great deal.   For
       Russia it was not enough." DK258.M3

1735   Maude, Aylmer. "After the Tsar's Coronation." Tolstoy and
       His Problems. London: Richards, 1901, 161-84.
       In part, a restatement of Leo Tolstoy's protest against the
       waste and extravagance which characterized Nicholas II's
       coronation. PG3410.M3

1736   _____. "The Czar." Independent, 62 (21 Mar. 1907):
       655-68.
       A portrayal of Nicholas II as a narrow-minded autocrat cling-
       ing to his royal prerogatives with "Byzantine cunning" and
       blocking the improvement of the condition of Russia's huge
       lower class.

1737 _____. The Tsar's Coronation. London: Brotherhood Publishing Company, 1896, 128pp.
Unavailable for annotation.

1738 Merindol, Comte Gaston de. "Russian Peasant and the Czar."
Cur Hist, 9, no. 2 (1919): 343-44.
A brief sketch of Nicholas II as a kind and paternalistic lead-
er beloved by the common people and undeserving of the harsh
treatment he and his family received after his abdication.
Written one month before the Romanovs' execution.

1739 Morris, F. "The Czar's Simple Life." Cosmopol, 33 (Sept.
1902): 483-90.
A contrast of Nicholas II's simple and quiet family life with
the vast power and wealth at his disposal.

1740 "Moscow Coronation." Spectator, 76 (30 May 1896): 761-62.
Reply, 76 (6 June 1896): 805.
An argument that the most impressive feature of Nicholas II's
coronation is not the opulence and ritual of the coronation
ceremony itself, but rather the awesome, uncontrolled power
that the rite conveys to a man whose intentions and capabilities were, at that time, unknown.

1741 Mossolov, A. A. At the Court of the Last Tsar. Being the
Memoirs of A. A. Mossolov. E. W. Dickes, trans. A. A.
Pilenco, ed. London: Methuen and Company, 1935, 273pp.
Recollections of Nicholas II, his family, immediate relatives,
and personal entourage. Mossolov, who served as head of
the court chancellery from 1900 to 1916, is at his best when
describing the inner workings of the imperial court and the
personal habits of Nicholas II. DK258.M62

1742 "Most Beautiful Woman on Any Throne." Cur Lit, 41 (Nov.
1906): 514-16.
A sympathetic appraisal of Alexandra with particular attention
to her physical beauty and noble character.

1743 Mouchanou, Madame Marfa. My Empress. New York: John
Lane Company, 1928, 256pp. Excerpts in Ladies H J, 35
(Jan.-Mar. 1918): 9-10; 13+; 25-26+.
The memoirs of a lady-in-waiting who attended Alexandra from
the time of her marriage to Nicholas up to the Romanovs' exile
to Siberia. Mouchanou discusses Alexandra's loving relationship with Nicholas and their children, difficulties in dealing
with Nicholas' mother, her circle of friends (including Rasputin),
role in the events and decisions which led to the dynasty's downfall, and her life as a prisoner prior to Siberian exile. Throughout, the author writes of Alexandra with compassion and supports her sympathetic portrayal of the empress with numerous

anecdotes illustrating Alexander's intelligence, grace, and
concern for her family and the Russian nation.   DK254.A5M7

1744   "A New St. Nicholas for Russia."   Time, 118 (16 Nov. 1981):
       63.
       A brief statement on the canonization of Nicholas II and other
       Russians who died at the hands of the Bolsheviks during the
       revolutionary era.

1745   "Nicholas II: Russian Czar with the Artistic Temperament."
       Cur Opin, 57 (Sept. 1914): 170-71.
       A sympathetic biographical sketch of Nicholas II asserting
       that he is often incorrectly portrayed because observers
       dwell on Russia's shortcomings and remain insensitive to his
       thoughtfulness and artistic temperament.

1746   Nomad, Max. "Tsars and Kaisers Were Liberals. Am Merc,
       50 (June 1940): 155-61.
       A portrayal of Nicholas II and William II of Germany as liberals
       in comparison to Stalin and Hitler.

1747   *Oldenburg, S. S. Nicholas II, His Reign and His Russia,
       4 Vols. Leonid I. Mihalap and Patrick J. Rollins, trans.
       Patrick J. Rollins, ed. Gulf Breeze, Fla.: Academic Inter-
       national Press, 1975.
       A comprehensive, favorable reassessment of Nicholas II's char-
       acter, personality, and policies. Oldenburg, a conservative
       Russian historian, contends that the image of Nicholas as a
       weak and indecisive ruler stems from historians' confusion of
       the tsar's kind and gentle nature with lack of resolve and
       consistency. Citing examples of Nicholas' courage, energy,
       and willpower, Oldenburg develops in detail an argument that
       Nicholas wisely attempted to steer Russia along a path of con-
       servative reform, in the tradition of Alexander II, but his
       efforts in this direciton were thwarted, in the long run, be-
       cause of the opposition of a contentious and seditious intel-
       ligentsia.   DK262.0413
          Reviewed in:
          Rus R, 1, no. 2 (1942): 97
          Slav R, 1 (1941): 381
          Slavonic E Eur R, 19/20 (1939-40): 381

1748   *Paléologue, Maurice. An Ambassador's Memoirs, 3 Vols. F.
       A. Holt, trans. New York: Octagon Books, 1972 (reprint
       of 1923 edition).
       The July 1914 to May 1917 memoirs of the French ambassador
       to the Russian court. The memoirs are chronologically ar-
       ranged as diary entries in which Paléologue comments, in anec-
       dotal fashion, on a wide range of court events and personali-
       ties as well as on the domestic, diplomatic, and military pol-
       icies pursued by Nicholas II. Of special interest are Paléo-
       logue's observations on Nicholas' blindness and impotence in

the face of the deterioration of the monarchy's popularity with
virtually every segment of Russian society. Paléologue's
memoirs are also considered to be one of the best sources of
information on the character of Nicholas and, especially,
Alexandra as well as on the influence of Rasputin on the de-
cline of the Romanovs' prestige. DK265.P255
Reviewed in:
Am Pol Sci R, 18 (1924): 827
Rus R, 32 (1973): 454
Slav R, 32, no. 2 (1973): 388

1749 "Personality of the Tsar." World's W, 8 (Oct. 1940): 5414-
30.
An extremely negative analysis of Nicholas II's character and
political judgment, allegedly written by a "Russian official of
high authority."

1750 Pisney, Raymond F., ed. "The Czar's Reception at Tsarskoe
Selo: A Graphic First Hand Account by U. S. Ambassador,
David Rowland Francis." Gateway H, 1, no. 3 (1980): 34-39.
A reprint of a letter written by D. R. Francis, American am-
bassador to St. Petersburg, describing a formal reception for
a number of Western diplomats held by Nicholas II at Tsarskoe
Selo in 1917.

1751 Poliakoff, V. Mother Dear. The Empress Marie and Her Times.
New York: D. Appleton and Company, 1976, 324pp.
The focus of this popular biography is the life of Empress
Marie Feodorovna, wife of Alexander III and mother of Nicholas
II. As such, it is a useful, though undocumented, source of
information on Nicholas' upbringing and youth and his family
relations as emperor. Of particular interest are the sections
dealing with Marie's attempts to discredit Rasputin as a means
of persuading Nicholas to terminate the former's influence
over Empress Alexandra. DK236.A3P6

1752 _____. The Tragic Bride. The Story of Empress Alexandra
of Russia. New York: D. Appleton and Company, 1927,
300pp.
A sympathetic portrayal of Alexandra as a woman victimized
by her deep love for Nicholas II. Poliakoff denies that Alexandra's involvement in Russian politics was motivated by ma-
liciousness or lust for power and maintains instead that she
advised Nicholas because she wanted him to be recorded in
history as a great monarch but realized that he lacked the
qualities needed to rule decisively. To the misfortune of
Alexandra and Russia, Poliakoff concludes, her counsel to
Nicholas, under the influence of Rasputin, served only to
damage his popularity and undermine his political position.
DK254.A5P6

1753 *Poliakov-Litovtzev, S. "Nicholas II Through Russian Eyes."

New Eur, 8, no. 94 (1918):   53-55.
An outline of two popular views on Nicholas II's character,
one being that he was kind and magnanimous but cursed with
a weak character and bad advisers, the other that he was
evil, cunning, and the source of the reactionary policies of
the Russian government. The author contends that neither
judgment is correct but rather that Nicholas' political naiveté
and inability to make decisions caused him to accept the reactionary advice of those who supported him as an autocrat.

1754   Pollack, J. H.   "Old Stereographs, Saved from Oblivion, Stir
       Our Memories." Smithsonian, 9 (Feb. 1979):   90-95.
       A brief account of conditions in Russia during Nicholas II's
       reign; stimulated by the unveiling of the Keystone Mast
       collection of stereographs. The article contains pictures of
       the stereographs and a description of Nicholas II as a weak
       ruler dominated by his wife and conservative political advisers.

1755   Preston, Thomas B.   "How Will the Czar Wear His Crown?"
       Chaut, 22, no. 5 (1896):   569-77.
       Speculation that Nicholas II's "gentle rule" will lead Russia
       to better times.

1756   Radziwill, Princess Catherine.   "The Empress Alexandra and
       Her Sister."   Secrets of Dethroned Royalty. New York:
       John Lane Company, 1920, 75-84.
       A portrayal of Alexandra as an impersonable, cold, and un-
       popular woman who had a high opinion of her own judgment
       and intellectual capacity. Radziwill maintains that Alexandra's
       negative personal attributes were compounded under the ma-
       licious influence of her sister Grand Duchess Elizabeth, who
       introduced Alexandra to Rasputin and later denounced her as a
       German agent when Rasputin replaced Elizabeth as the em-
       press' confidant. D412.7.R33

1757   _____. Nicholas II. The Last of the Tsars. London:
       Cassell and Company, 1931, 306pp.
       An account of Nicholas II's life with little attention given to
       his political behavior and leadership. Radziwill draws primari-
       ly upon Nicholas' diaries and letters as she strives to present
       him "with all his qualities and his defects, leaving readers to
       form their own judgment unbiased by any inferences or opin-
       ions." Nicholas emerges from this study as a sensitive, com-
       passionate, and well-intentioned individual immersed in family
       life, withdrawn, and overly susceptible to the harmful influ-
       ence of his wife and advisers of dubious character.
       DK258.R3

1758   Reginin, Simon.   "The Czar." Independent, 63 (11 July 1907):
       85-89.
       A portrayal of Nicholas II as a weak-willed, insecure individual

manipulated by shortsighted, reactionary advisers into pursuing the very policies guaranteed to promote revolution.

1759 "Richest Man in the World." Lit D, 52 (13 May 1916): 1377.
A brief description of the phenomenal wealth at Nicholas II's disposal despite the backwardness of his realm.

1760 "The Rights of Man Even for Princesses." Spectator, 73
(1 Sept. 1894): 265–66.
A statement in support of Alexandra's alleged resistance to being forced to convert to the Russian Orthodox faith.

1761 Rodzianko, Paul. "The Chevalier Guards and the Emperor Nicholas II." Tattered Banners: An Autobiography. London: Seeley Service and Company, 1939, 81–96.
Reminiscences of Nicholas II's kindness and consideration for the soldiers who served him directly; written by a colonel of the guards at the Winter Palace. DK254.R6A3

1762 Rousillon, J. E. "Emperor of the Knout." Bookman, 25
(Mar. 1907): 34–39.
A review of M. Jean Grand Carteret's book of cartoons on Nicholas II. Rousillon contends that, unlike Carteret's portrayals of other rulers which make light fun of minor personality quirks and physical characteristics, the cartoons of Nicholas are colored by the "sombre tragedy of his reign, and the poignant sufferings of his people."

1763 "Russian Coronation." Spectator, 76 (23 May 1896): 729–30.
A discussion of the coronation ceremony as an elaborate Eastern ritual the object of which is "to deepen the Russian impression that the position of the Czar is in some way supranatural and that his resources are as limitless as his power."

1764 Sava, George. "Coronation Tragedy." One Russian's Story.
London: Robert Hale, 1970, 79–96.
An account of the tragedy that occurred at the coronation of Nicholas II when the planking in part of the viewing area collapsed under the spectators' weight causing thousands of casualties. The author's father, an officer in the Russian army who took part in the preparation of Khodinsky Field for the coronation ceremony, describes the panic that accompanied the disaster and the public's discontent with Nicholas II's callous reaction to this event. Other sections in this work contain references to the gradual collapse of Nicholas' popularity and authority within the Russian army as a consequence of the harmful influence exerted on imperial policy by Rasputin through Empress Alexandra. CT1218.S354B3

1765 Sherrington, M. "Queens of Europe: The Czarina." Can M,
19 (Aug. 1902): 332–35.

A sympathetic account of Alexandra's reaction to the demands
placed upon her following her betrothal to Nicholas II. Sherrington discusses Alexandra's conversion to the Orthodox
faith, study of the Russian language, and careful attention
to the needs of her husband and their children.

1766   Smith, W. H. C. The Last Czar. London: Wayland Pub-
       lishers, 1973, 96pp.
       A general review of Nicholas II's life and reign; intended for
       young readers.

1767   Start, Edwin A. "Nicholas II and the Russian Empire."
       Chaut, 37, no. 4 (1903): 361-66.
       An overview of Nicholas II's role as tsar with emphasis on
       the vastness and complexity of his empire and the historical
       precedents which affected his rule.

1768   Stead, W. T. "The Real Nicholas II." World T, 10 (Jan.
       1906): 56-60.
       A portrayal of Nicholas II as the innocent victim of the poor
       counsel of his ministers. As an example of such counsel,
       Stead points to Nicholas' 1894 decision to dismiss as "senseless
       dreams" the Russian moderates' hope for political reform.

1769   _____. "The Tsar Nicholas II. A True Caricature."
       RR, 30 (Aug. 1904): 158-59.
       A defense of Nicholas II against the criticisms levied against
       him in a July 1904 article in the Quarterly Review (200: 180-
       209) titled "The Tsar."

1770   Swezey, M. P. "Fabergé and the Coronation of Nicholas and
       Alexandra." Antiq J, 123 (June 1983): 1210-13.
       A description of the decorative egg given by Nicholas II to
       Alexandra on Easter of 1897 to commemorate their coronation.
       Swezey also describes the eggs presented to Alexandra by
       Nicholas in 1904 and 1911.

1771   Tames, Richard. Last of the Tsars. The Life and Death of
       Nicholas and Alexandra. London: Pan Books, 1972, 65pp.
       As part of the Panorama of History series, this brief work
       presents a vividly illustrated outline of Nicholas II's life
       and reign. Receiving most attention is Nicholas' relationship
       with his wife and children. DK262.T27

1772   Tcharykow, N. V. "Reminiscences of Nicholas II." Contemp
       R, 134 (Oct. 1928): 445-53.
       A positive description of Nicholas II's character and political
       intentions; written by an official in Russia's pre-war diplomatic
       service. Tcharykow recollects incidents in Nicholas II's politi-
       cal and private life as a means of demonstrating that Nicholas
       was "the best-intentioned, gentle, patriotic, unselfish, and
       most unfortunate of Russian monarchs."

1773   Tisdall, E. E. P. The Dowager Empress. London: Stanley
       Paul, 1957, 271pp., bib. 263.
       This study does not contain a separate chapter on Nicholas II,
       but as a biography of Marie Feodorovna, Nicholas' mother, it
       does shed considerable light on his childhood, personality,
       and character as well as on a number of his policies as tsar.
       DK236.A2T5

1774   Tolstoy, L. N. "Czar Nicholas II." Comtemp R, 125 (Apr.
       1924): 474-84. Also in Liv Age, 321 (Apr. 1924): 692-98.
       Russia's foremost novelist gives a relatively positive appraisal
       of Nicholas II as a man genuinely concerned with world peace
       and the welfare of his people; based upon a personal recollec-
       tion of the author's meeting with the tsar.

1775   Treue, Wilhelm. "The Empress Alexandra of Russia." DAC
       (gen. study), 155-58.
       A court physician gives a brief description of Alexandra's
       leading personality traits and her loving relationship with
       Nicholas II.

1776   *Trotsky, Leon. "The Tzar and the Tzarina." The Russian
       Revolution. Garden City, N.Y.: Doubleday Press, 1959
       (reprint of 1932 edition), 49-60. Also in Trotsky's Portraits.
       New York: Pathfinder Press, 1977, 81-92.
       A portrayal of Nicholas II as a shallow-minded, irresolute in-
       dividual incapable of perceiving even the most obvious signs
       that all was not well within his realm. Trotsky, a renowned
       Marxist intellectual, revolutionary and prominent figure in
       early Soviet h istory, draws upon Nicholas' diary to demon-
       strate that even amidst the most catastrophic of events Nich-
       olas' mind was occupied by the trivial happenings that marked
       his daily routine: to the impending revolution, "the last
       Romanov opposed only a dumb indifference. It seemed as
       though between his consciousness and his epoch there stood
       some transparent but absolutely impenetrable medium." Nich-
       olas' shortcomings, Trotsky adds, made him uneasy in the
       company of men of ability, eager to surround himself with
       fools and flunkies, and prone to seek counsel from his wife
       who possessed even less good judgment than he did.
       DK265.T774

1777   Troyat, Henri. "The Tsar and His Entourage." Daily Life
       in Russia Under the Last Tsar. Malcom Barnes, trans.
       Stanford: Stanford University Press, 1979, 174-94.
       A colorful and dramatic description of the glamour of the im-
       perial court and the striking appearance of the royal family
       in attendance at official court functions. DK260.T7613

1778   "The Tsar." Quar R, 200 (July 1904): 180-209. Also in
       Liv Age, 242 (27 Aug. 1904): 513-32.
       A scathing attack on Nicholas II's personality, character, and

rule; written by an anonymous "Russian official of high rank."
The author sees Nicholas as a shortsighted and indecisive
ruler unable to take the initiative necessary to address effectively Russia's pressing domestic problems.

1779   "The Tsar: A Character Sketch." Fortn R, 81 (Mar. 1904):
       363-70.
       A review of the various factors that account for the widely
       disparate judgments of Nicholas II as a man and ruler.

1780   The Tsar's Coronation As Seen by "De Monte Alto" Resident
       in Moscow. London: Brotherhood Publishing Company, 1896,
       128pp.
       Unavailable for annotation.

1781   Ukhtomski, Esper E. Travels in the East of Nicholas II, Em-
       peror of Russia, Cesarewitch, 1890-91. Written by Order of
       H.I.M..., 2 Vols. Sir G. Birdwood, ed. R. Goodlet, trans.
       London: A. Constable and Company, 1896-1900. DS8.V34
       Unavailable for annotation.

1782   Vacaresco, Helene. "The Czar and the Czarina." Kings and
       Queens I Have Known. New York: Harper and Brothers,
       1904, 143-63.
       A favorable comparison of Nicholas II to his immediate prede-
       cessors, and a description of the personal qualities of the
       youthful Nicholas and Alexandra whom the author met sep-
       arately in 1890. D399.7.V2

1783   Vassili, Count Paul. Behind the Veil at the Russian Court.
       New York: John Lane Company, 1914, 408pp.
       A highly critical account of the personality, character, and
       policies pursued by Nicholas II. Vassili (Princess Catherine
       Radziwill), who was immersed in Russian court life throughout
       Nicholas' reign, draws upon her personal recollections and
       those of others prominent in court circles to construct an
       image of Nicholas as a poorly educated and indecisive political
       weakling who, under the disastrous influence of Empress Alex-
       andra, pursued policies insensitive to the needs of his sub-
       jects and the general welfare of the monarchy. In an anec-
       dotal fashion, Radziwill touches upon, among many subjects,
       Nicholas' coronation, family life, advisers, and relationship
       with the Duma, the war with Japan, and the 1905 Revolution.
       DK189.R3

1784   _____. Confessions of the Czarina. New York: Harper
       and Brothers, 1918, 298pp.
       A continuation of the attack launched upon the Romanovs in
       the author's Behind the Veil at the Russian Court (see pre-
       vious entry). Drawing upon information gleaned, allegedly,
       from various members of the Russian court, Radziwill portrays

Empress Alexandra as "a superstitious, intriguing, and half-demented woman" whose political meddling contributed substantially to the destruction of the dynasty and the imperial family. DK254.A5R3

1785 *Vinogradoff, I. "Some Russian Imperial Letters to Prince V. P. Meshchersky." Ox Slavonic P, 10 (1962): 105-58.
A translation of a series of letters written by Alexander III and Nicholas II to Prince V. P. Meshchersky, a courtier-journalist whose writings Alexander had subsidized. In an introduction, Vinogradoff discusses the nature of Meshchersky's relationship with both monarchs and the significance of the correspondence.

1786 Vyrubova, Anna A. Memories of the Russian Court. Vladimir M. Roudneff, appendix. New York: Macmillan, 1923, 399pp.
A hagiographic recollection of the life and character of Empress Alexandra and, to a lesser extent, Nicholas II. Vryubov, an intimate of Alexandra for over twenty years, describes a diverse array of incidents in the life of the royal family which collectively attest to the sincere and loving nature of the empress. In a lengthy appendix, V. M. Roudneff reviews Vryubov's relationship with Alexandra and Rasputin. DK254.V2A5

1787 *_____, comp. The Romanov Family Album. Robert K. Massie, intro. New York: Vendone Press, 1982, 127pp.
A collection of over 170 photographs of Nicholas II, his family, friends, and advisers covering the entire span of his reign as well as his months in exile. DK259.4.V97

1788 *Walsh, Warren B. "Romanov Papers; a Bibliographic Note." Historian, 31, no. 2 (1969): 163-72.
A review of the published versions of Nicholas II's diaries and correspondences, especially with Empress Alexandra and Kaiser William II of Germany. Walsh discusses the general content of the Romanov papers and the views expressed by various historians in regard to these documents as a source of information on Nicholas II's personality and policies.

1789 *Warth, Robert D. "Before Rasputin. Piety and the Occult at the Court of Nicholas II." Historian, 47, no. 3 (1985): 323-37.

1790 Washburn, Kitsos. Nicholas II, Last Tsar of All the Russias. Washington, D.C.: Stinehour Press, 1971, 6pp.
A reproduction of a 1971 narrative on the life of Nicholas II written by a seventh grade student at the Maret School, Washington, D.C.; based upon Massie's Nicholas and Alexandra. DK258.W36

1791   Washburn, Mary S. "Monarchs at Home: The Tsar and the
       Tsaritsa of Russia." Eng Ill M, 19 (July 1898): 304-14.
       A description of the ornate residences of the Romanovs, and
       an account of the royal couple's daily routine, likes, and
       dislikes.

1792   White, Arnold. "The Tsar: A Study in Personality." Every-
       body's M, 10, no. 3 (1904): 293-303.
       A description of Nicholas II as an extraordinarily gentle and
       kindly man whose indecisiveness and susceptibility to the ad-
       vice of scheming favorites made him unfit to rule Russia
       effectively.

1793   Williams, Harold. "Nicholas II Through English Eyes." New
       Eur, 8, no. 94 (1918): 49-52.
       A discussion of Nicholas II's demise as a consequence of the
       immense difficulties which confronted him as the ruler of a
       vast and diverse realm plagued with staggering domestic prob-
       lems. Williams also notes that the nightmarish condition of
       Russia would have challenged the sanity of even the most
       dynamic of autocrats and thus overwhelmed the fragile and
       indecisive Nicholas II long before his forced abdication in
       February of 1917.

1794   Wilmer, Aubrey. "The Little Father: A Peep into the Life of
       the Tsar." Lond M, (Jan. 1916): 579-85.
       Unavailable for annotation.

1795   *Witte, Sergius. "Czar and the Czarina and Occultism at the
       Russian Court." World's W, 41 (Nov. 1920): 39-63.
       Excerpts from the diary of Nicholas II's former minister of
       finance and premier dealing with the royal couple's fascination
       with occultism. Of particular interest is Witte's discussion of
       the harmful political consequences of their susceptibility to
       the advice of occultist charlatans such as Dr. Phillipe.

1796   *Wolfe, Bertram D. "Autocracy Without an Autocrat." Revolu-
       tion and Reality: Essays on the Origin of the Soviet System.
       Chapel Hill: University of North Carolina Press, 1981, 60-78.
       A discussion of Nicholas II as an individual completely unsuited
       for the political station which he inherited. Wolfe asserts that
       "one of the difficulties of monarchial legitimacy ... is that
       autocracy does not automatically engender autocrats. This is
       likely to be particularly true if the previous head of state was
       an autocrat also in his household." Alexander III was just
       such an autocrat, and consequently Nicholas was "trained to
       be an obedient son, ... but he was not brought up to be the
       ruler of a great nation. In him had been planted the habit
       of obedience, not those of decision and command. He had been
       trained to stoic courage but not to initiative or audacity."
       Wolfe adds that an autocracy can survive such weak leadership

only if it is attended by, fortuitously, an era of peace and
stability, "but woe to the kingdom and its internal peace if
the interregnum be a time of invasion by a powerful foreign
foe or rapid economic and social transformation." Within
this context Wolfe examines the character, ability, policies,
and fate of Nicholas II. HX313.W64

1797 "The Womanly Qualities of the Czar." Cur Lit, 39 (Aug. 1905):
201-03.
Drawing upon various anonymous writings that appeared in
the Quarterly Review and National Review, this article asserts
that Nicholas II developed pronounced feminine characteristics
because of his close relationship with his mother and constant contact with his wife and daughters.

1798 Wortman, Richard. "The Russian Empress as Mother." FIR
(anthology), 60-74.
In part, a discussion of the influence of Nicholas II's mother
on his character, tastes, and style of rule.

1799 Wright, C. Hagberg. "Nicholas II of Russia." Quar R, 248
(Apr. 1927): 225-41.
A review of the various assessments of Nicholas II's character
and personality, most of which portray him as a kindly soul
and a devout family man but politically shortsighted.

INTERNAL AFFAIRS

Domestic Policy/Political Thought and Practice

1800 *Allshouse, Robert H., ed. Photographs for the Tsar: The
Pioneering Color Photography of Sergei Mikhailovich Prokudin-
Gorskii, Commissioned by Tsar Nicholas II. New York:
Dial Press, 1980, 216pp.
An impressive collection of color photos of pre-World War I
imperial Russia. Allshouse states that Prokudin-Gorsky
"traveled the vast reaches of the Russian Empire photograph-
ing 'things of interest and significance' in what he called
natural color." Allshouse also provides an account of Nicholas II's conversation with Prokudin-Gorsky and enthusiastic
support for the entire project. TR140.P76A34

1801 Askew, W. C. "An American View of Bloody Sunday." Rus R,
11, no. 1 (1952): 35-43.
A commentary on the confidential report of Robert S. McCormick, United States ambassador to St. Petersburg, on the 22
January 1905 massacre of petitioning workers in front of the
Winter Palace. The report discusses why the disaster occurred
and concludes that, as a consequence of the massacre, Nicholas
II had lost forever the affection and support of the Russian
people.

1802 *Balmuth, Daniel. "Censorship in the Reign of Nicholas II."
      Censorship in Russia, 1865-1905. Washington, D.C.: Uni-
      versity Press of America, 1979, 109-38.
      An examination of Nicholas II's efforts to maintain censorship
      amidst the rapid growth of the publishing industry which
      marked his reign. Balmuth establishes that prior to the 1905
      Revolution Nicholas tried to cope with the anti-censorship
      pressure exerted by an increasingly powerful press by re-
      laxing some restrictions while preserving the government's
      right to censor publications it deemed unpatriotic or irre-
      sponsible. However, writers and publishers were unwilling
      to respond favorably to "partial concessions which did not
      concede the principle of freedom of the press." Consequent-
      ly, Nicholas created a commission on 23 January 1905 to place
      the press under rule of law, but amidst the conservative
      reaction which set in following the 1905 Revolution, reform
      was put aside and repressive measures against the press in-
      creased dramatically. Despite these measures, Balmuth con-
      cludes, the repressiveness of post-1905 censorship was limited
      because of the monarchy's reluctance to attempt to force upon
      society uniformity of opinion.

1803 "Baron, Salo W. "Under Alexander III and Nicholas II."
      RJTS (gen. study), 51-75.
      A discussion of Nicholas II's policies toward Russia's Jews as
      an extension and, in some cases, an intensification of the
      restrictive and punitive policies pursued by Alexander III.
      Baron states that, in addition to issuing harsh anti-Semitic
      legislation, Nicholas supported 'blood accusations' and funded
      the scurrilous Protocols of the Elders of Zion as a means of
      "blackening the Jewish name," endeavors which were prompted
      by the government's desire to counter the growth of "Jewish
      self-assertiveness and political consciousness."

1804 *Baylen, Joseph O.   The Tsar's "Lecturer-General"; W. T.
      Stead and the Russian Revolution of 1905, with Two Unpub-
      lished Memoranda of Audiences with the Dowager Empress
      Maria Feodorovna and Nicholas II. Atlanta: Atlanta School
      of Arts and Sciences, Georgia State College, 1969, 93pp.,
      bib. 79-86.
      An account of the 1905 mission to Russia by W. T. Stead,
      a British journalist and Russophil. Stead hoped to establish
      a working relationship between Nicholas II and Russia's lib-
      erals as a means of restoring Nicholas' popularity with his
      subjects and improving the image of the Russian monarchy in
      England in the aftermath of the 1905 Revolution. To this end,
      Stead wrote articles for liberal and conservative Russian
      journals urging the acceptance of the Bulygin Duma as a first
      step toward the establishment of a constitutional monarchy.
      He also arranged separate and lengthy audiences with the
      Dowager Empress Marie Feodorovna and Nicholas II in which

he recommended that the tsar make political concessions in
order to preserve the monarchy. Baylen establishes that
Nicholas' lack of resolve and the resentment which developed
against Stead among the influential Russians who viewed him
as a presumptuous meddler led to the failure of Stead's mission. The last 50 pages of Baylen's book consist of Stead's
previously unpublished record of his interviews with Nicholas
and Marie Feodorovna. AS36.G378A3 no. 23
    For a condensed version of Stead's mission see Baylen's
    "W. T. Stead and the Russian Revolution of 1905." Can J
    Hist, 2, no. 1 (1967): 45-66.

1805 Bestor, A. E. "Nicholas II, and Autocracy in the 20th Cen-
     tury." Chaut, 69 (Feb. 1913): 265-81.
     A review of the first two decades of Nicholas II's reign, and
     an argument that autocracy's shortcomings as a modern political
     system make inevitable the establishment of a constitutional
     regime in Russia.

1806 Blind, Karl. "Czarism at Bay." No Am R, 179 (Oct. 1904):
     481-93.
     A negative assessment of popular life in Russia under the
     autocratic rule of Nicholas II.

1807 Brounoff, Platon. Czar Nicholas Becomes a Jew; or Jesus
     Demands His Christianity Back. New York: Liberal Art
     Society, 1906, 24pp.
     Unavailable for annotation.

1808 Conolly, Violet. "The 'Nationalities Question' in the Last Phase
     of Tsardom." Russia Enters the Twentieth Century. Erwin
     Oberländer et al., eds. New York: Schocken Books, 1971,
     152-81.
     An examination of Russification policy in Poland, the Ukraine,
     and Finland as case studies of the monarchy's disastrous
     treatment of the "nationalities question" began in the nine-
     teenth century and continued by Nicholas II. DK262.R8813

1809 Conroy, Mary Schaeffer. Peter Arkad'evich Stolypin. Practi-
     cal Politics in Late Tsarist Russia. Boulder, Colo.: Westview
     Press, 1976, 235pp., bib. 195-208.
     This work does not contain a separate chapter on Nicholas II,
     but as a scholarly study of P. A. Stolypin, who served as
     Nicholas II's Minister of Internal Affairs and Chairman of the
     Council of Ministers from 1906 to 1911, it may be consulted with
     profit for insight into tsarist politics and Nicholas' relations
     with his ministers. DK254.S595C66

1810 "A Correspondent of the Paris Journal Sees Blood Flow on the
     Hardened Snow of St. Petersburg. Swindburne Advises the
     Tsar to Make a Cowardly Escape." A Treasury of Great

Reporting. Louis L. Snyder and Richard B. Morris, eds.
New York: Simon and Schuster, 1949, 263-67.
A 29 January 1905 article from the London Weekly Times and
Echo which describes the bloody Sunday massacre and criticizes Nicholas II's handling of the affair. Appended is a brief
critical statement by the French Socialist Juares and a sonnet
by Swindburne in which Nicholas II is advised to flee before
he suffers the same fate which befell Louis XVI of France.
PN4726.S6

1811   Cunliffe-Owen, F. "Succession to the Russian Throne."
       Munsey's M, 49 (Apr. 1913): 49-57.
       A discussion of the complexities associated with Romanov dy-
       nastic succession in light of the hemophiliac condition of
       Nicholas II's only son.

1812   "Czar and Duma." Fortn R, 88 (July 1907): 149-54.
       A report on the dissolution of the Second Duma with some
       assessment of the negative impact this action had upon Nicho-
       las II's popularity.

1813   "The Czar and the Duma." Outlook, 83 (19 May 1906): 104-
       06.
       An account of Nicholas II's address to the First Duma, and
       a portrayal of the Duma's opening as the climax of the demo-
       cratic movement in Russia during the first decade of Nicholas'
       reign.

1814   "The Czar and the Duma." Outlook, 112 (8 Mar. 1916): 540-
       41.
       A discussion of Nicholas II's troubled relationship with the
       Fourth Duma as a consequence of his unwillingness to tolerate
       any criticism of royal policy.

1815   "Czar and His Manifesto." Munsey's M, 29 (July 1903): 561.
       A brief discussion of Nicholas II's 3 March 1903 imperial edict
       as a first step toward reducing the social and economic ills
       which plagued Russian society.

1816   "Czar and His Premier." Cur Lit, 50 (May 1911): 486-87.
       A review of the domestic and diplomatic problems which
       prompted Peter Stolypin to resign as Chairman of the Council
       of Ministers.

1817   "The Czar Refuses." Independent, 60 (31 May 1906): 1246-
       48.
       An outline of Nicholas II's negative response to the First
       Duma's discussion of the need for major social and economic
       reforms. The author also discusses the reaction of the Duma
       to Nicholas' statement as a veritable "declaration of war"
       against the monarchy.

1818   "The Czar's Answer." Outlook, 79 (7 Jan. 1905):   15-16.
       A review of Nicholas II's response to the Chernigov zemstvo
       on the question of its jurisdiction, and a restatement of his
       views on land and legal reform.

1819   "Czar's coup d'etat." Outlook, 86 (29 Jan. 1907):   450-51.
       A sharp attack on Nicholas II for his dissolution of the Duma
       and flagrant violation of its constitution. The author asserts
       that Nicholas' arbitrary and illegal action cost the monarchy
       the faith, trust, and loyalty of the Russian people.

1820   "Czar's Crusade Against Vodka." Cur Opin, 56 (Apr. 1914):
       264-65.
       A review of Nicholas II's political behavior in the spring of
       1914. The author discusses Nicholas' impending visit to
       Paris, replacement of Goremykin as head of the Council of
       Ministers, attempt to control the consumption of vodka, and
       pursuit of a broad reactionary policy.

1821   "The Czar's Decree." Nation, 76 (19 Mar. 1903):   223-24.
       A favorable assessment of Nicholas II's 2 March 1903 "exten-
       sion of religious toleration, increase in the powers of provin-
       cial and local assemblies and relaxation of some of the old
       and tyrannous practices of the village community."

1822   "The Czar's Decree." Outlook, 73 (21 Mar. 1903):   660-62.
       A negative assessment of Nicholas II's 3 March 1903 edict.
       The author asserts that platitudes and limited reforms could
       not possibly "furnish any real relief for the evils from which
       the Russian people are suffering."

1823   "Czar's Decree of Liberality." World's W, 6 (May 1903):   3376-
       79.
       A restatement of the liberal aspects of Nicholas II's 3 March
       1903 decree on personal freedoms, and a sympathetic discus-
       sion of his attempt to cope with the difficult and perplexing
       domestic situation in Russia at that time.

1824   "Czar's Limited Power." RR, 29 (June 1904):   720-22.
       A portrayal of Nicholas II as a ruler who cares for the good
       of his people but who is unable to rule effectively because of
       the vastness of his empire and the intrigues of his ministers.

1825   "Czar's Manifesto: Its Genesis and Meaning." RR, 27 (May
       1903):   595-97.
       A discussion of Nicholas II's manifesto of 3 March 1903 as a
       sign of his desire to change some of Russia's old ways but
       not a declaration of his intention to effect basic reforms or
       establish civil liberties.

1826   "Czar's New and Respectful Attitude Toward the Duma."

Cur Opin, 60 (June 1916): 394-95.
A discussion of Nicholas II's appearance before the Duma as
a political maneuver designed to improve his image and lessen
the pressure being exerted on him to liberalize Russia's political system.

1827 "The Czar's Problem." Liv Age, 237 (2 May 1903): 312-14.
      A discussion of Nicholas' March 1903 decree as a reflection of
      his genuine concern for the condition of the peasantry.

1828 "The Czar's Reform Proclamation." Gunton's M, 24 (Apr. 1903):
      295-301.
      A highly favorable review of Nicholas II's March 1903 procla-
      mation in favor of freedom of religion and the improvement of
      the condition of farm laborers. The author attacks Nicholas'
      liberal critics in Russia and the West for their failure to
      realize that such reform was necessary before any major al-
      teration in Russia's political system could be considered.

1829 Dillon, E. J. "The First Day of Year One in Russia." Contemp
      R, 89 (June 1906): 876-98.
      An account of the opening of the Duma and popular skepticism
      over Nicholas II's willingness to cooperate with its leaders in
      addressing Russia's principal domestic problems.

1830 *_____. "The Tsar's Manifesto." Contemp R, 83 (Apr.
      1903): 590-98. Also in Liv Age, 237 (16 May 1903): 394-
      401; Eclectic M, 141 (July 1903): 52-59.
      A sympathetic examination of Nicholas II's March 1903 decree
      and his motives for issuing it. Dillon asserts that the decree
      should not be compared to Western documents that promoted
      or founded constitutional regimes but rather should be con-
      sidered merely as the expression of Nicholas II's intention
      "to have old-world forms ... in Russia ... readjusted to
      latter-day requirements" as a means of placing the monarchy
      in direct contact with its subjects to discern their needs and
      improve the general condition of the nation. The author sees
      the decree as an expression of Nicholas' desire "to be just to
      the needs of the present without being untrue to the best
      traditions of the past."

1831 *Doctorow, Gilbert. "The Fundamental State Laws of 23 April
      1906." Rus R, 35, no. 1 (1976): 33-52.
      An examination of the events, circumstances, and personalities
      which determined the nature of the Russian Fundamental State
      Laws of 23 April 1906. Doctorow focuses on the five months
      which preceded the promulgation of the laws as he discusses
      the roles played by Sergei Witte, D. M. Solsky of the State
      Council, and Nicholas II in working out a compromise to accom-
      modate conservatives, moderates, and liberals.

1832 _____. "The Government Program of 17 October 1905."
     Rus R, 34, no. 2 (1975): 123-36.
     A discussion of the October Manifesto in terms of the two
     months of deliberations which preceded its issuance, the mod-
     ifications in Witte's first drafts, and the understanding of
     the manifesto in court circles. Doctorow provides some in-
     sight into Nicholas II's negative reaction to the act as an un-
     desirable and irreversible concession to the forces of liberal-
     ism.

1833 Dubnow, S. "The Accession of Nicholas II." HJRP, Vol. III
     (gen. study), 3-39.
     A sharp critique of the Jewish policy pursued by Nicholas II.
     In support of the statement that, for Russia's Jews "the reign
     of Nicholas II proved the most gloomy and reactionary of all,"
     Dubnow discusses Nicholas' further restriction of the Jews'
     occupational and residential rights, intensification of anti-
     Semitic propaganda, and support for pogroms and ritualistic
     murder trials. Dubnow concludes that Nicholas' Jewish policy
     achieved results far different from those intended since it was
     responsible for the rise of Zionism and an influx of Jews into
     the revolutionary movement. For a discussion of the imple-
     mentation of Nicholas' harsh policies and a lurid description
     of the pogroms which took place during his reign, see Vol.
     III, pp. 40-164 of Dubnow's work.

1834 Edgar, William C. "The Last of the Romanoffs." Bellman,
     22 (28 Apr. 1917): 457-68.
     A recollection of the favorable impression made by Tsarevich
     Nicholas during an audience with the author, a member of the
     American Relief Commission to Russia during the 1891-92 fam-
     ine. Nicholas questioned Edgar in regard to the progress be-
     ing made in combating the famine and thanked him for the
     brotherly assistance of the American Relief Commission. There
     follows a survey of Nicholas' reign and an argument that he
     should have come to terms with the zemstvo organizations
     whose dedication and efficiency during the famine were so
     impressive.

1835 Farlow, L. S. "Czar's Body-Guard of Spies." Harper's W,
     49 (2 Dec. 1905): 1740.
     A brief examination of the network of body-guards and spies
     which surrounded Nicholas II to protect him from revolution-
     aries.

1836 Florinsky, M. "Twilight of Absolutism: 1905." Rus R, 8
     (Oct. 1949): 322-33.
     A discussion of the events associated with the 1905 Revolution
     with some reference to Nicholas II's reluctant acceptance of
     Count Witte's liberal program as a means of quelling the dis-
     turbance.

1837 "Four Good Deeds of the Czar." Independent, 90 (2 Apr.
      1917): 7-8.
      A brief review of Nicholas II's "four greatest deeds": his
      promotion of the Hague Conference, formation of the Duma,
      banishment of vodka at financial loss to the crown, and his
      resignation as tsar.

1838 Gottschling, Andrew. Tsar and Tolstoi Played Out. London:
      Published by the author, 1899, 35pp.
      Unavailable for annotation.

1839 Greenberg, Louis. "Anti-Semitism, 1881-1905." JR, Vol. II
      (gen. study), 47-54.
      A discussion of Nicholas II's reign as one in which the cam-
      paign launched by Alexander III against Russia's Jews reached
      new heights. Greenberg states that Nicholas II's "deep-seated
      hatred" of Jews (largely due to the influence of Pobedonostsev)
      led him to reject all arguments for the reduction of Jewish
      disabilities, while his belief that Jewish workers and students
      were inciting rebellion caused him to intensify efforts to
      destroy, force into emigration, or assimilate Russia's Jewish
      population. Nicholas was also directly responsible for legis-
      lation which reduced even further the travel, educational,
      and occupational rights of Jews and for the increase in "ritu-
      alistic murder" trials and anti-Semitic propaganda which incited
      the public to commit, or at least view dispassionately, acts of
      violence against Jews.

1840 *Hans, N. "The Last Years of Autocracy (1894-1904)" and
      "Between Two Revolutions." HREP (gen. study), 165-221.
      A discussion of Nicholas II's educational policy as a reflection
      of the hesitations, contradictions, and lack of foresight which
      marked his entire reign. Hans states that during the first
      decade of Nicholas' rule a tremendous increase in the number
      of schools and the size of the student population occurred
      despite the monarchy's opposition to the establishment of uni-
      versal education. When Nicholas did approve the introduction
      of universal elementary education and the democratization of
      secondary and higher instruction, he did so in the form of a
      reluctant concession granted after open revolution in 1905
      rather than as a progressive reform willingly legislated by a
      farsighted monarch.

1841 *Harcave, Sidney. First Blood. The Russian Revolution of
      1905. New York: Macmillan Company, 1964, 316pp., bib.
      301-05.
      This scholarly study of the origin, development, and settle-
      ment of the 1905 Revolution does not contain a separate chap-
      ter on Nicholas II but includes numerous references to and
      short sections on his autocratic mentality, the policies which
      he pursued that prompted the revolt, and the countermeasures
      which he took in response to the rebellion. DK263.H3

1842 Healy, Ann Erickson. The Russian Autocracy in Crisis 1905-
      1907. Hamden: Archon Books, 1976, 328pp., bib. 305-21.
      Nicholas II is not the focus of this work, but as a detailed
      examination of the struggle between the monarchy and the
      opposition in the First Duma it warrants consultation.
      DK262.H36

1843 Howe, M. A. De Wolfe, ed. "Talks with Four Monarchs;
      Passages from the Diary of George von Lengerke Meyer."
      Scrib M, 66 (Sept. 1919): 287-96.
      Passages from the diary of George von Lengerke Meyer,
      American ambassador to Russia from 1905-07. Most notably,
      Meyer comments on the 1905 Revolution, the events leading
      to the Portsmouth Peace Conference, and the first meeting
      of the Duma.

1844 James, A. "The Russian Ruler and His Dreams." World's W,
      25 (May 1915): 520-28.
      Unavailable for annotation.

1845 Kennan, George. "Czar and the Jews." Outlook, 109 (27
      Jan. 1915): 171-75.
      A critical review of Nicholas II's maintenance of a repressive
      Jewish policy despite the Jews' show of patriotism during the
      first year of World War I.

1846 *_____. "Reaction in Russia: A Review of Events Since
      the 'Bloody Sunday' of January 1905. First Paper: Revolu-
      tion and Counter-Revolution." Century M, 80 (June 1910):
      163-76.
      An account of the events leading up to and following the
      Bloody Sunday massacre. Of particular interest is Kennan's
      description of the diverse public reaction to Nicholas II's
      October Manifesto and the tsar's launching of a successful
      counter-revolution after the immediate danger of open revolu-
      tion had subsided.

1847 *_____. "The Reaction in Russia, A Review of Events since
      the 'Bloody Sunday' of January 1905. Second Paper: The
      Dumas, the Czar and the 'True Russians.'" Century M, 80
      (July 1910): 403-14.
      A critical review of Nicholas II's relationship with Russia's
      first three Dumas. Kennan maintains that political shortsight-
      edness led Nicholas to condone the murderous activities of
      right wing fanatics and to devise a scheme for emasculating
      the Duma, the very institution whose existence was essential
      to the monarchy's popularity and stability.

1848 *Kokovtsov, Count Vladimir N. Out of My Past. The Memoirs
      of Count Kokovtsov. H. H. Fisher, ed. Laura Matveev,
      trans. Stanford: Stanford University Press, 1935, 615pp.

These memoirs of Russia's Minister of Finance (1904-14) and
Chairman of the Council of Ministers (1911-14) are a rich
store of information on Nicholas' character, leadership, and
government. Kokovtsov provides particularly insightful and
detailed accounts of Nicholas II's relationship with his principal ministers and the Duma, his preoccupation with family
affairs, the harmful influence exerted by Empress Alexandra,
and the domination of the empress by Rasputin. The editor's
provision of a detailed subject index makes for ready access
to the subjects listed above as well as to Kokovtsov's other
references to Nicholas and his policies. DK254.K63A3

1849   Law, E. F. "Change of Tsars." Blackwood's M, 157 (Feb.
       1895): 306-34. Also in Liv Age, 204 (9 Mar. 1895): 579-603.
       Speculation on the likelihood of Nicholas II pursuing a political
       course less reactionary than that followed by Alexander III.

1850   *Leary, D. B. "Nicholas II, 1894-1917." EAR (gen. study),
       92-107.
       A discussion of the policies pursued by Nicholas II in the field
       of education as an extension of 'the great reaction' which be-
       gan during the reign of Alexander III. Stressing the leading
       role played by Konstantin Pobedonostsev in determining the
       conservative characteristics of the educational program of the
       last two Romanov tsars, Leary states that even with the signif-
       icant increase of public pressure to improve the scope and
       quality of education in Russia, Nicholas failed to adopt any-
       thing but compromise measures to benefit public education,
       and, consequently, his reign ended with the main problems of
       education unsolved.

1851   Levin, Alfred. "June 3, 1907: Action and Reaction." Essays
       in Russian History. A Collection Dedicated to George Vernad-
       sky. Alan D. Ferguson and Alfred Levin, eds. Hamden:
       Archon Books, 1964, 231-73.
       An examination of the origin and impact of the manifesto,
       penned by P. A. Stolypin and issued in Nicholas II's name,
       which dissolved the Second Duma and established further re-
       strictions on popular suffrage and representation. Levin does
       not focus upon Nicholas' part in this decision, but he does
       discuss the tsar's outrage over the "rebellious" and "seditious"
       speeches made by various Duma members as the source of his
       support for the punitive measures taken against the Duma.
       DK42.F4

1852   Lieven, Dominic C. B. "Bureaucratic Liberalism in Late Im-
       perial Russia: The Personality, Career and Opinions of A.
       N. Kulomzin." Slavonic E Eur R, 60, no. 3 (1982): 413-32.
       A study of the activities of a leading liberal in Russia's
       bureaucratic elite which sheds some light on the relationship
       between Nicholas II and the enlightened senior officials who
       sought to win his support for their plans and policies.

1853 _____ . "The Russian Civil Services Under Nicholas II;
Some Variations on the Bureaucratic Theme." Jahr Ges Ost,
29, no. 3 (1981): 336-403.
Although this article does not focus on Nicholas II, it provides an interesting statistical analysis of the diverse ethnic,
social, and educational backgrounds of the 215 appointed
members of the State Council.

1854 _____ . "The Russian Establishment in the Reign of Nicholas
II: The Appointed Members of the Council of State, 1894-
1914." University of London, 1979. (dissertation)

1855 _____ . "Russian Senior Officialdom Under Nicholas II.
Careers and Mentalities." Jahr Ges Ost, 32 (1984): 199-225.
The focal points of this scholarly study are the sources of
career success in the imperial bureaucracy and the nature of
the influences which shaped the mentality of top bureaucrats,
but it includes some discussion of the decline of Nicholas II's
effective power as the growth of the complexity of government
in Russia furthered his dependence on an ever expanding
corps of professional civil servants.

1856 "The 'Little Father' and His Children." Liv Age, 244 (18 Feb.
1905): 443-45.
A discussion of Nicholas II's lack of sympathy for the plight
of St. Petersburg's factory workers.

1857 Long, R. E. C. "The Tsar, His Ministers and His Manifesto."
Fortn R, 79 (June 1903): 971-90.
A portrayal of Nicholas II's 3 March 1903 manifesto as an obvious attempt by the tsar and his conservative advisers to
appease the monarchy's critics by issuing hollow statements on
reform rather than by addressing the real needs of the nation.

1858 McKean, R. B. The Russian Constitutional Monarchy, 1907-
1917. London: The Historical Association, 1977, 47pp.,
bib. 14-47.
A short analysis of the dilemma which Nicholas II faced as he
sought to modernize the Russian economy without making political concessions to the industrial and professional classes or
upsetting the traditional social order of the nation. DK260.M3

1859 *McNeal, Robert H., ed. Russia in Transition 1905-1914.
Evolution or Revolution? New York: Holt, Rinehart and Winston, 115pp., bib. 110-15.
Nicholas II is not central to the theme of any one of the
fourteen essays included in this anthology, but collectively
they illuminate the main domestic trends, developments, and
issues that marked his reign. DK255.M25

1860 *Mehlinger, Howard D. and John M. Thompson. Count Witte

and the Tsarist Government in the 1905 Revolution. Bloomington: Indiana University Press, 1972, 434pp., bib. 399-419.
This scholarly study of Prime Minister Sergei Witte's policies
and leadership during the 1905 Revolution does not contain a
separate chapter on Nicholas II but includes a number of references to and brief sections on his political views and relationship with Witte and other high officials in the imperial
government.   DK254.M5W44

1861   *Mosse, W. E.   "Aspects of Tsarist Bureaucracy: Recruitment
       to the Imperial State Council 1855-1914."   Slavonic E Eur R,
       57, no. 2 (1979):   240-54.
       This study of the appointments to the Imperial State Council
       in the 1855-1914 period provides interesting insights into the
       personnel policies of the last three Romanovs.   Drawing upon
       an impressive body of statistical evidence, Mosse demonstrates
       that there was a marked decrease in the number of councillors
       with military backgrounds and with elite education, while there
       was an increase in the proportion of landless councillors.
       Mosse adds that this trend toward the bureaucratization of the
       State Council was somewhat cyclical and strongest under Alex-
       ander III and during the second half of Nicholas II's reign
       while the first half of Nicholas' reign shows an "aristocratic
       reaction" in imperial appointments.

1862   "Nicholas II and the Duma."   No Am R, 183 (July 1906):   143-
       50.
       A review of the sources of conflict between Nicholas II and
       the Duma with particular attention given to their disagreements
       over the need for agrarian and legal reforms.

1863   "Nicholas II on the Eve of Another Russian Cataclysm."   Cur
       Opin, 55 (Dec. 1913):   398-99.
       A report on Nicholas II's inability to establish a working re-
       lationship with the Duma.   The article also deals with his in-
       volvement in the Beilis trial as an indication of the depth and
       intensity of his anti-Semitism.

1864   "Nicholas II's Attitude to the Liberal Elements in Russia."   Cur
       Opin, 59 (Oct. 1915):   230-32.
       A discussion of the likelihood of Nicholas II agreeing to the
       formation of a cabinet that enjoyed the confidence of Russian
       liberals and moderates.   The author also refers to the possi-
       bility of Russia concluding a separate peace with Germany.

1865   "Oath of Allegiance to Nicholas."   Spectator, 73 (3 Nov. 1894):
       597.
       A brief report on the oath of allegiance taken by the imperial
       family to Nicholas II, with some speculation on the direction of
       S. Witte's political future as a close adviser to the newly
       crowned Nicholas.

1866 "Open Letter to the Czar of Russia." Independent, 75 (11 Sept.
      1913): 607-10.
      An anonymous plea to Nicholas II to "open his eyes" to the
      atrocities being committed against Russia's Jews.

1867 "The Opening of the Duma." Independent, 60 (17 May 1906):
      1125-26.
      A report on the opening of Russia' first national legislative
      assembly on 10 May 1906. This article includes the text of
      Nicholas II's speech and some unfavorable comments regarding
      its "colorlessness" and failure to mention the question of
      amnesty for political prisoners.

1868 *Pearson, Raymond. "The Last Crisis of Russian Octobrism."
      Durham Univ J, 70, no. 1 (1977): 41-51.
      A historical review of Octobrism from 1905, when Nicholas II
      tried "to unite various sections of Russian society to promote
      conservative reform," to 1913, by which time he had so moved
      to the right and popular opinion to the left that the remaining
      Octobrists found themselves without a political audience to
      which to appeal.

1869 Pobedonosteff, C. "The Czar's Manifesto." Independent, 55
      (16 Apr. 1903): 894.
      A response to Prince Kropotkin's letter, printed in the London
      Daily News, suggesting that Nicholas II's 3 March 1903 mani-
      festo was a reactionary measure inspired by Pobedonostsev.
      Pobedonostsev claims that he was not involved in the drafting
      of the manifesto and adds that the manifesto has been viewed
      in Russia not as a reactionary measure but as a "precursor
      of reform looking toward parliamentary institutions."

1870 "The Responsibilities of the Tsar." Liv Age, 240 (6 Feb.
      1904): 381-83.
      An argument that Nicholas II's natural disposition toward
      peace, compassion, and philanthropy failed to yield positive
      results because his advisers were able to take advantage of
      his irresolute character to turn imperial policy in aggressive
      and reactionary directions.

1871 *Rigberg, Benjamin. "Tsarist Censorship Performance, 1894-
      1905." Jahr Ges Ost, 18, no. 1 (1969): 59-76.
      An analysis of the degree of success had by tsarist censor-
      ship authorities during the first decade of Nicholas II's reign.
      Rigberg maintains that "the administration of censorship
      functioned badly and was riddled with inconsistencies," so
      much so that "patterns of enforcement deny formulation."
      Consequently, "the system of absolutism failed to achieve
      its goal of a regulated press."

1872 *Rogger, Hans. "The Beilis Case: Anti-Semitism and Politics

in the Reign of Nicholas II." Slav R, 25, no. 4 (1966): 615-
29.
A portrayal of the 1911 trial of an obscure Jewish clerk wrongly charged with ritual murder as a test case designed to
measure the malleability of public sentiment in the direction
of Judeophobia and anti-Semitism.

1873 "The Rumored Abdication of the Czar." Spectator, 83 (12
Aug. 1899): 209.
A discussion of the foundation of the rumor that Nicholas II
was, in August of 1899, on the verge of abdicating the throne
in favor of Grand Duke Michael. The author speculates that
the immense burden of ruling a realm as large and troubled
as the Russian Empire was too difficult a task given Nicholas'
temperament and intellectual ability.

1874 *Samuel, Maurice. "The Angel." Blood Accusation. The
Strange History of The Beiliss Case. New York: Alfred A.
Knopf, 1966, 97-118.
A critical assessment of Nicholas II's character and the nature
of his anti-Semitism serves as the foundation for the author's
explanation of Nicholas' support for the 1911 trial of Mendel
Beilis, a Russian Jew accused of the murder of a young
Christian to secure the latter's blood for use in a Jewish
ceremony. Samuel dismisses the widely accepted notion that
the tsar was a kindly soul and maintains instead that Nicholas
could be, and often was, obstinate and merciless when "called
upon to make a personal sacrifice or to suffer an intrusion
into his dream life of all-autocracy." This character trait,
his belief that 'the Jews' were responsible for the 1905 Revolution, and the inflammatory influence of Empress Alexandra's
reactionary political views led him to support enthusiastically
the prosecution of Beilis for the fabricated charge of ritual-
istic murder. A last factor which dramatically reinforced
Nicholas' patronage of the case was his witnessing of the
September 1911 assassination of Premier Peter Stolypin by a
young Jew, D. Bogrov: "If the profoundly anti-Semitic Czar
had until then been deeply interested in the development of a
ritual murder case, the assassination of his premier by a
Jew ... must have turned his interest into something of a
mania." KM343.S26

1875 Semenoff, Eugene. "Czar's Decree." Independent, 55 (30
Apr. 1903): 1021-24.
A condemnation of Nicholas II's March 1903 manifesto as a
desperate and futile attempt to save the government from collapse. The author sees the vague language of the manifesto
as a reflection of Nicholas' irresolute character.

1876 "The Silence in Russia." Spectator, 73 (1 December 1894):
772-73.

Speculation on the policies of young Nicholas II regarding personal liberty and freedom of the press.

1877   Simkhovitch, Vladimir G. "Russia's Struggle with Autocracy."
        Pol Sci Q, 20 (Mar. 1905): 111-39.
        In part, a discussion of Nicholas II's unwillingness to accept
        any limitation of his autocratic powers and prerogatives.

1878   *Stavrou, Theofanis George, ed. Russia Under the Last Tsar.
        Minneapolis: University of Minnesota Press, 1969, 265pp.,
        bib. 233-46.
        A collection of eight scholarly writings on the political, social,
        economic, and cultural characteristics of turn-of-the-century
        Russia. DK255.R8

1879   Stead, W. T. "Nicholas II, the New Tsar." RR, 10 (18 Dec.
        1894): 633-34.
        An optimistic statement on the direction most likely to be taken
        by Russia under the leadership of Nicholas II.

1880   Stone, N. I. "Manifesto of the Czar." Independent, 55 (26
        Mar. 1903): 733-35.
        A discussion of Nicholas II's March 1903 manifesto concerning
        governmental reforms and expansion of the sphere of activity
        for the zemstvos as a cunning move orchestrated by V. Plehve
        and designed to dupe the public into thinking reform was at
        hand.

1881   "Strong Personalities in the Duma." Cur Lit, 41 (July 1906):
        24-29.
        A discussion of Nicholas II's inability to form a working rela-
        tionship with the most prominent members of the Duma.

1882   *Szeftel, Marc. "Nicholas II's Constitutional Decisions of Octo-
        ber 17-19, 1905 and Sergius Witte's Role." Album J. Balon.
        Namur, Belgium: Les Anciens Establissements Gordenne, 1968,
        463-493.
        An account of the events and steps leading up to the October
        Manifesto which reformed the institutional structure of the
        Russian Empire. Szeftel maintains that S. Witte's proposals
        to and meetings with Nicholas II illustrate that Witte was moti-
        vated by a genuine concern for the fate of the monarchy, and
        did not, as contemporary critics claimed, manipulate the tsar
        into constitutional limitations of autocracy so as "to concentrate
        public power in his own hands."

1883   _____ . "The Parliamentary Reforms of the Witte Administra-
        tion (October 19, 1905-April 23, 1906)." Parl Est Rep, 1,
        no. 1 (1981): 71-94.
        Unavailable for annotation.

1884 *_____. The Russian Constitution of April 23, 1906. Political
      Institutions of the Duma Monarchy. Bruxelles: Les Editions
      de la Librairie Encyclopédique, 1976, 517pp., bib. 485-516.
      This work does not contain a separate chapter on Nicholas II,
      but as a scholarly and comprehensive analysis of the 1906
      constitution (including its sources, drafting, and principles)
      it is a valuable source of information on the most important
      document of Nicholas II's reign. Of special interest is Szeftel's
      discussion of Nicholas' reluctant acceptance of the need for a
      constitution and intense dislike of the Duma and its leaders.
      KR9.S9

1885 Tager, Alexander B. The Decay of Czarism. The Beiliss
      Trial. Philadelphia: Jewish Publication Society of America,
      1935, 297pp.
      An account of the 1913 Beilis trial, and an argument that
      Nicholas II was well aware that the entire Beilis affair was an
      elaborate hoax designed to foster public enmity towards Rus-
      sian Jews. DS135.R9T253

1886 *Tokmakoff, George. P. A. Stolypin and the Third Duma:
      An Appraisal of the Three Major Issues. Washington, D.C.:
      University Press of America, 1982, 246pp., bib. 209-42.
      An examination of P. A. Stolypin's political philosophy and
      action as premier in regard to the three major legislative issues
      that he initiated in the Third Duma and were promulgated into
      law: the agrarian, Finnish, and Western zemstvo issues.
      Although this study does not contain a separate section on
      Stolypin's relationship with Nicholas II, it sheds considerable
      light on Nicholas as an obstacle to the very reforms which
      Stolypin believed to be essential if the monarchy were to be
      preserved in a modernized form. Tokmakoff contends that
      Nicholas' resistance to any reform that he perceived as a
      threat to his royal prerogatives, his moodiness, and suscepti-
      bility to influence on a short term basis led Stolypin, even as
      a monarchist, to lose all trust in Nicholas. DK262.T59

1887 "Tolstoi, the Statesman." Independent, 53 (13 July 1901):
      1390-91.
      A short note on the encouragement given to Nicholas II by
      Leo Tolstoy in regard to the monarchy's support for major
      land reforms.

1888 "Tolstoi to the Tsar." Harper's W, 50 (3 Feb. 1906): 172-73.
      A reprint of Leo Tolstoy's letter to Nicholas II appealing for
      reforms and assistance to the needy.

1889 "Tolstoy's Reply to the Tsar." Chaut, 50 (May 1908): 438-89.
      The text of Tolstoy's response to Nicholas II's request that he
      reconcile with the Russian Orthodox Church.

1890   Treadgold, Donald W.   "The Constitutional Democrats and
       the Russian Liberal Tradition."   <u>ASEER</u>, 10, no. 1 (1951):
       85-94.
       A discussion of Nicholas II's October Manifesto, liberal and
       radical reaction to it, and the inability of the Constitutional
       Democrats (Kadets) to capitalize on the opportunities which
       the manifesto presented.

1891   *_____.   "Tsarism Is Too Late."   <u>Lenin and His Rivals</u>.
       New York: Frederick A. Praeger, 1955, 17-30.
       A portrayal of Nicholas II as a politically myopic ruler com-
       pletely out of touch with the condition of his realm and con-
       sequently unable even to recognize the course to chart to
       preserve the monarchy.   Treadgold maintains that Nicholas
       was so "at sea" politically that he never even formulated a
       policy to follow as tsar but simply took "what his father had
       bequeathed to him, including the institutions of autocracy,
       and assumed their suitability and permanence."   He naively
       assumed that the normal condition for Russia was one in
       which "a tranquil people were loyal to an absolute monarch,
       and any temporary abnormality was ... the work of 'trouble-
       makers.'"   The only positive step taken by Nicholas during
       his entire reign was the promulgation of the October Mani-
       festo but this document was neither conceived nor supported
       by him.   More importantly, Treadgold concludes, Nicholas
       failed to realize that concessions like those made in the October
       Manifesto, and not police repression, were the only possible
       means of saving the monarchy from complete and violent de-
       struction.   DK263.T74

1892   "Triumph of Reaction at the Court of Czar Nicholas II."
       <u>Cur Opin</u>, 55 (Oct. 1913):   238.
       An attack on Nicholas II's turn toward more conservative
       policies, particularly in regard to religious toleration and
       freedom of the press.

1893   "The Tsar and Reform."   <u>Chaut</u>, 37 (May 1903):   120-21.
       A discussion of Nicholas II's March 1903 manifesto as a mere
       declaration of principles rather than a broad program of re-
       form.

1894   "The Tsar's Rescript: The Russian Official View."   <u>Sat R</u>,
       95 (25 Apr.; 2 May 1903):   511-12; 543-44.
       A defense of Nicholas II's March 1903 manifesto against critics
       who saw it as an attempt to deflate the popular movement
       toward reform by making vague statements on the monarchy's
       'progressive' political and economic intentions.   The author
       states that the critics are ignorant of Russian conditions and
       fail to realize that the principles of liberty must be associated
       with those of authority and order for Russia to evolve peace-
       fully into a modern, prosperous nation.

1895   "Vacillating Czar." Nation, 83 (30 Aug. 1906): 176-77.
       A portrayal of Nicholas II's decision to make available for
       peasant settlement 20,000,000 acres of public land as a political
       move designed to reduce popular unrest. The author concludes
       that like Nicholas' other reforms this measure came too late to
       be seen as anything but a concession forced upon Nicholas by
       historical circumstances.

1896   "Vacillation of the Czar." RR (Apr. 1905): 411.
       Criticism of Nicholas II as an irresolute ruler whose vacillations
       served to complicate further the chaotic situation in St. Peters-
       burg in March of 1905.

1897   Volkhovsky, Felix. "Hopes and Fears of Russia." Forum, 31
       (Mar. 1901): 69-84.
       A commentary on the political hopefulness of lower and middle
       class Russians despite the reactionary tone of Nicholas II's
       policies.

1898   *Von Laue, Theodore H. Sergei Witte and the Industrializa-
       tion of Russia. New York: Atheneum, 1969, 360pp., bib.
       311-49.
       This scholarly study of the program for the industrialization
       of Russia proposed by Minister of Finance Sergei Witte does
       not contain a separate chapter on Nicholas II but includes a
       number of references to the tsar's perception of Russia's
       economic condition and his response to Witte's progressive
       proposals. HC334.5.V58

1899   Von Schierbrand, Wolf. "The Advisers of the Czar." World
       T, 8 (Apr. 1905): 376-80.
       A discussion of the reform opportunities open to Nicholas II's
       principal advisers as a consequence of his complete lack of
       resolve and political acumen. Von Schierbrand speculates that
       because of the advisers' lack of courage and foresight they
       most likely will prove unable to address the plethora of inter-
       nal problems evident in turn of the century Russia.

1900   Walling, William English. "The Power Behind the Czar."
       Independent, 664 (1908): 610-20.
       A discussion of the reactionary political, social, and economic
       views of the Russian aristocracy as expressed at the Monarch-
       ists' Congress held in Moscow in July 1907. Walling sees Nich-
       olas' power as being firmly founded upon an identity of inter-
       ests between the crown and the 100,000 members of the aris-
       tocracy that the state drew upon to govern the country and
       staff the top positions in the military.

1901   Walz, John D. "State Defense and Russian Politics Under the
       Last Tsar." Syracuse University, 1967. (dissertation)

1902 "Why the Czar Dislikes Witte." Cur Lit, 39 (Sept. 1905): 334.
      A brief statement on Nicholas II's hatred of Count Witte be-
      cause of the latter's support for reforms that changed the
      fabric of autocratic rule in Russia.

1903 Whyte, Frederic. "Stead's Russian Adventure of 1905." LWTS,
      Vol. II (gen. study), 271-78.
      An account of W. T. Stead's defense of the Russian monarchy
      against its English critics and his efforts to convince Russian
      progressives and reactionaries to cooperate in supporting the
      gradual establishment of a constitutional monarchy. Whyte
      credits Stead with good intentions and some initial successes
      but sees the failure of Stead's intervention to be an inevita-
      bility given the conditions that existed in Russia in 1905.

1904 *Witte, Sergei. The Memoirs of Count Witte. A. Yarmolinsky,
      ed./trans. Garden City, N.Y.: Doubleday, Page and Com-
      pany, 1921, 445pp.
      A revealing set of memoirs on the pre-war policies pursued by
      Nicholas II. Witte served as Minister of Finance, 1892-1903,
      headed the Russian delegation to the peace conference at
      Portsmouth, authored the October Manifesto, and was Presi-
      dent of the Council of Ministers, 1905-1906, and thus had a
      unique opportunity to observe closely the inner workings of
      the imperial bureaucracy and the policies and leadership qual-
      ities of Nicholas II. While Witte's discussion of Nicholas' fit-
      ful attempts at reform, the Russo-Japanese War, and the 1905
      Revolution is both revealing and insightful, it is his critical
      commentary on Nicholas' turn to conservative policies only
      months after issuing the October Manifesto that illuminates
      best the tsar's indecisiveness, susceptibility to influence by
      reactionaries, and shortsighted views on the political course
      required for the preservation of the monarchy. DK254.W5A5

Influence of Rasputin

1905 "Czarina and Rasputin." Cur Hist M, 13, no. 1 (Oct. 1920):
      153-57.
      An account of Alexandra's conservative political views and ad-
      vice to Nicholas II, and an analysis of the decline of her
      reputation within the Russian court and the Holy Synod as a
      consequence of her relationship with Rasputin.

1906 DeJonge, Alex. The Life and Times of Grigorii Rasputin.
      New York: Coward, McCann and Geoghegan, 1982, 368pp.,
      bib. 357-61.
      A popular recreation of Rasputin's rise to prominence and
      exercise of political power as a confidant of Empress Alexandra.
      DeJonge portrays Rasputin as a simple man of God who "lacked
      the conceptual intelligence and self-discipline" to handle the

immense power that he acquired as a consequence of his relationship with Nicholas II and Alexandra: "power corrupted him, turning him from a quest for the spiritual to a quest for pleasure, position, and consideration." While DeJonge treats Rasputin sympathetically in a number of respects, he agrees with the popular judgment that "Rasputin made a substantial contribution to the fall of the dynasty, by alienating persons who could have advised the tsar and tsarina better, by encouraging the disastrous influence of Alexandra, and by advocating the most injudicious ministerial appointments--Khvostov and Protopopov." DK254.R3D4

1907 The Fall of the Romanoffs. How the Ex-Empress and Rasputine Caused the Russian Revolution. By the Author of Russian Court Memoirs. London: Herbert Jenkins, 1918, 312pp.
An argument that "the responsibility for the wreck of the Russian monarchy lies entirely with the Empress Alexandra Feodorovna." The author presents an image of Nicholas II as an individual whose temperament and training made him unsuited for the high office which he held and whose character flaws rendered him vulnerable to the harmful influence of Alexandra. The empress appears in this work as a narrow-minded, ignorant, and scheming "German princess" whose political meddling, combined with that of Rasputin, amounted to state treason. DK265.F3 1917

1908 Fülöp-Miller, René. Rasputin. The Holy Devil. New York: Frederick Ungar Publishing Company, 1975 (reprint of 1928 edition), 386pp., bib. 375-80.
An argument that Rasputin was far from being the demonic force primarily responsible for the downfall of the Romanov dynasty. Fülöp-Miller states that "Rasputin was neither entirely bad nor entirely good, he was neither altogether a libertine nor a saint. He was a man of rich nature and exuberant vitality, endowed with many good qualities and cursed with many weaknesses." Drawing upon "official documents, police records, diaries, letters, depositions of witnesses, and other adequately documented and authentic sources," Fülöp-Miller presents a picture of Rasputin as a man with saintly aspirations and pronounced earthly tastes whose personal life and public behavior gave those who resented and/or envied the favor he enjoyed with Nicholas and Alexandra sufficient grounds to develop the myth that he was a profligate and a charlatan wielding a destructive influence on the Romanovs. DK254.R3F85

1909 Halliday, E. M. "Rasputin Reconsidered." Horizon, 9, no. 4 (1967): 80-87.
A portrayal of Rasputin as a well meaning and legitimate faith healer whose 'sexploits' have been exaggerated and whose

advice to Nicholas on World War I should have been heeded.

1910 Heath, L. T. "Rasputin and the Russian Revolution." <u>Mankind</u>, 1, no. 1, (1967): 5-12, 70-73.
A straightforward account of how Rasputin came to the attention of the Romanovs and then gained favor with and influence over them. Heath also discusses the decline of the Romanovs' popularity as a consequence of Rasputin's meddling with imperial appointments and policies.

1911 Hirsch, Richard. "Sanctity and Sex: Rasputin." <u>Crimes that Shook the World</u>. New York: Dull, Sloan and Pearce, 1949, 78-102.
An account of Rasputin's shift in interest, during World War I, from sex to politics and military affairs, and a discussion of the plot which led to his assassination. D412.H56

1912 Hook, Donald. "Rasputin." <u>Madmen of History</u>. Middle Village, New York: Jonathan David, 1976, 177-89.
A portrayal of Rasputin as a mentally unbalanced intriguer who, having gained the confidence of the royal family through his "miraculous" healing of Tsarevich Alexis, abused his privileged position particularly by interfering in political affairs about which he was ignorant. Hook provides most detail on Rasputin's gory death. D110.H6

1913 Judas, Elizabeth. <u>Rasputin, Neither Devil nor Saint</u>. Los Angeles: Wetzel Publishing Company, 1942, 283pp.
A discussion of Rasputin as a man of character and principle whose true relationship with the Romanovs and political influence have been obscured by the slanderous accusations leveled against him by the "enemies of Russia" within the royal court. Judas maintains that Rasputin was a genuine faith healer who was without interest in state affairs and, therefore, in no way should be portrayed as a political schemer responsible for the monarchy's collapse. DK254.R3J8

1914 Kantacuzene, Princess Julia Grant. <u>Revolutionary Days: Recollections of Romanouffs and Bolsheviki, 1914-1917</u>. Boston: Small, Maynard and Company, 1919, 411pp.
Personal recollections of the character of the Romanovs and their family relations, court life, and the royal favorites who swayed imperial policy, especially Vryubov and Rasputin. Of particular interest is Kantacuzene's account of Alexandra's reaction to Nicholas II's abdication, an event for which the author blames the empress. DK265.K3

1915 Kulikowski, Mark. "Rasputin and the Fall of the Romanovs." State University of New York, Binghamton, 1982. (dissertation)

1916   Le Queux, William. The Secret Life of the Ex-Tsaritza. Lon-
        don: Odhams Limited, 1918, 190pp.
        A portrayal of Alexandra as a Germanophil with a haughty
        disregard for Russia, its traditions, and people. Le Queux
        draws upon the disclosures of Baroness Kamensky, a member
        of Alexandra's entourage, to develop an argument that the
        empress, along with Rasputin, so promoted the interests of
        Germany at the expense of her adopted country that she must
        be considered to have been an agent of the German govern-
        ment. DK254.A5L4

1917   Liepmann, Heinz. Rasputin and the Fall of Imperial Russia.
        Edward Fitzgerald, trans. New York: Robert M. McBride,
        1959, 264pp. Also titled: Rasputin: A New Judgment.
        An argument that Rasputin's scandalous personal life, arro-
        gant behavior, and influence on imperial appointments were
        less important in arousing opposition against him than were
        his abhorrence of war and his various efforts to end World
        War I. Leipman maintains that prominent members of the
        "war party" were so outraged over Rasputin's promotion of
        peace with Germany that they felt compelled to assassinate
        him for the good of the Russian nation.

1918   Mackenzie, Frederick A. "The Fakir Who Wrecked a Throne."
        Twentieth Century Crimes. Boston: Little, Brown and
        Company, 1927, 67-102.
        A discussion of the origin and nature of Rasputin's influence
        over Empress Alexandra, and a lurid account of his death.
        HV6241.M3

1919   *Maklakov, B. "On the Fall of Tsardom." Slavonic R, 18
        (July 1939): 73-92.
        A review of B. Pares' The Fall of the Russian Monarchy.
        Makalov agrees with Pares' assertion that Rasputin and Empress
        Alexandra had a destructive effect upon Nicholas II's political
        fortunes but adds that the revolutions of 1917 might have been
        avoided if prominent Russian liberals had the foresight to
        realize that support of the monarchy throughout the nation's
        wartime crisis could be a means of advancing the authority of
        the Duma and, eventually, establishing a constitutional mon-
        archy in Russia.

1920   "Murder of Rasputin--the Power Behind the Russian Throne."
        Lit D, 56 (2 Feb. 1918): 38-50.
        An account of Rasputin's influence over Empress Alexandra
        and his gruesome death at the hands of assassins.

1921   Omessa, Charles. "Lecherous Fraud Who Wrecked a Dynasty."
        Great Hoaxes of All Time. Robert M. McBride and N. Pritchie,
        eds. New York: McBride, 1956, 25-52.
        A portrayal of Rasputin as an ambitious, unprincipled individual

whose greed blinded him to the destructive consequences of his actions.

1922 _____ . Rasputin and the Russian Court. London: George Newnes, 1918.
Unavailable for annotation.

1923 *Pares, Bernard. "Rasputin and the Empress; Authors of Russian Collapse." For Aff, 6 (Oct. 1927): 140-54.
An argument that Empress Alexandra, under the influence of Rasputin, bears prime responsibility for the collapse of the monarchy. Pares blames Alexandra for a series of devastating royal decisions, especially Nicholas' dismissal of Duma leaders critical of Rasputin, an act which cost the monarchy the last of its popular support. Based primarily upon Rodzianko's The Reign of Rasputin, Paléologue's La Russie des Tsar, Gilliard's Thirteen Years at the Russian Court, and The Letters of the Tsar to the Tsaritsa, 1912-1916.

1924 Rasputin, Marie. The Real Rasputin. Arthur Chambers, trans. London: John Long, 1929, 223pp.
A portrayal of Rasputin as a generous, compassionate, and sincere individual who, though led astray by enemies and sycophants alike, in no way resembled the scheming and lecherous religious charlatan that many have made him out to be. The author, the daughter of Rasputin, also maintains that the political influence of Rasputin was limited by his own lack of interest in governmental affairs and in no way could have been responsible for the 1917 fall of the dynasty. For a similar argument see the author's My Father. London: Cassel and Company, 1934, 157pp.

1925 "Rasputin, Nemesis of the Tsar." Cur Hist M, 6, no. 2 (1917): 288-92.
A negative account of Rasputin's character and influence on the Romanovs. The author maintains that Rasputin's saving of Tsarevich Alexis' life was contrived. When Rasputin left the capital Alexis fell ill because of small doses of poison administered by Alexandra's favorite lady-in-waiting at Rasputin's request thereby giving the appearance that the tsarevich's good health required Rasputin's presence.

1926 *Rodzianko, M. V. The Reign of Rasputin. An Empire's Collapse. Catherine Zvegintzoff, trans. Bernard Press, intro. David R. Jones, new intro. Gulf Breeze, Fla.: Academic International Press, 1973 (reprint of 1927 edition), 270pp.
A portrayal of Rasputin as an omnipotent and thoroughly evil political force in wartime Russia. Rodzianko, the last president of the Imperial State Duma, presents a detailed and exceptionally unflattering portrait of Rasputin's character and behavior as he argues that through Empress Alexandra,

Rasputin was able to serve the interests of the scoundrels, intriguers, and pro-German elements that surrounded him and therein exert a fatal influence on appointments made and policies followed by Nicholas II. In an interesting and insightful introduction, David Jones discusses "the intellectual and human climate" which shaped Rodzianko's views and the limitations of the thesis that Rasputin exerted any significant influence over the political course and fate of Nicholas II. DK262.R6313

1927   Steffens, Lincoln. "Rasputin--the Real Story." Everybody's M, 37 (Sept.-Oct. 1917): 276-85; 385-94.
A popularized account of Rasputin's relationship with Alexandra, harmful influence on imperial policy and appointments, and his consequent assassination.

1928   Vinogradoff, Igor. "The Emperor Nicholas II, Stolypin and Rasputin: A Letter of 16th October 1906." Ox Slavonic P, 12 (1965): 114-16.
A brief introduction to a 1906 letter by Nicholas II which contains the first recorded mention of Rasputin. The letter was sent by Nicholas to P. Stolypin, Chairman of the Council of Ministers, and mentions a lengthy meeting between Rasputin and the royal couple. Nicholas suggested that arrangements be made for Rasputin to bless Stolypin's daughter who was seriously ill.

1929   Vogel-Jørgensen, Torkild. Rasputin: Prophet, Libertine, Plotter. W. F. Harvey, trans. New Hyde Park, N.Y.: University Books, 1970 (reprint of 1917 edition), 143pp.
An argument that Rasputin unwittingly caused the monarchy's overthrow because his absorption in sexual affairs and his "sense of a historic mission" blinded him to the damage being done to the royal family's reputation as a consequence of "the intrigues, blackmail, and swindling" conducted by his companions and political appointees. DK254.R3V513

1930   *Wilson, Colin. Rasputin and the Fall of the Romanovs. New York: Farrar, Straus, 1964, 240pp., bib. 218-20.
A reassessment of Rasputin's character, personality, and role in the collapse of the Romanov dynasty. Wilson contends that Rasputin was a deeply religious individual whose "messianic self-belief was his mainspring, not sexual voracity or a will to power." Wilson discounts the views of historians and observers who maintain that Rasputin was responsible for Nicholas II's political demise and argues instead that long-standing domestic problems exacerbated by the demands placed upon the nation during World War I caused the February Revolution: "The old order was a rotten tree, asking to be struck by lightning, it is astonishing that it did not collapse under its own weight long before the turn of the century." DK254.R3W5

1931 *Wolfe, Bertram D. "The Reign of Alexandra and Rasputin."
      Revolution and Reality: Essays on the Origin and Fate of
      the Soviet System. Chapel Hill: University of North Carolina
      Press, 1981, 31-40.
      An argument that the hemophilia of Tsarevich Alexis created
      in Empress Alexandra a fanatical devotion to "delivering the
      autocratic power, undiminished, to the royal heir toward
      whom she felt such love and such unconscious guilt." Con-
      sequently "whenever some minister was about to succeed in
      persuading Nicholas to make some sensible concession to
      public opinion, always her hysterial voice or unceasing pen
      would reach him with the admonitory words, "Remember Baby!
      You have not the right...." Because of Baby's hopeless ill-
      ness she surrounded herself with quacks and charlatans and
      hearkened to their advice on affairs of state. More and more
      they lived in a world apart, a world created by her fantasy
      and fanaticism, her ministerings to the needs of the boy and
      their hangers-on." Within such an environment, Wolfe con-
      cludes, Rasputin's influence proved to be disastrous, partic-
      ularly since Russia so badly needed responsible, progressive,
      and insightful leadership during the trying years of World
      War I. HX313.W64

1932 Youssoupoff, Prince Felix. Rasputin. New York: Dial Press,
      1927, 256pp.
      A scathing attack on Rasputin as a "criminal upstart" whose
      pernicious influence at the royal court was responsible for
      Nicholas II's selection of advisers and pursuit of policies
      harmful to Russia's best interests. Youssoupoff, who played a
      leading role in the 1916 assassination of Rasputin, maintains
      that the inherent shyness of Nicholas II and the failure of
      Alexandra to win acceptance in Russian court circles resulted
      in the Romanovs' fatal tendency toward isolation from the pub-
      lic and neglect of official state duties. With the advent of
      Rasputin, largely through the influence of Alexandra's confi-
      dante, Anna Vryubov, this tendency became so pronounced as
      to be self-destructive. As World War I broke out, Youssoupoff
      states, a "morbid mysticism" settled over the Russian court,
      and "the Emperor and Empress, cut off from the world, out
      of touch with their subjects, surrounded by the Rasputin clan,
      were deciding questions of world-wide importance."
      DK254.R3I8

Responsibility for Monarchy's Collapse

1933 *Alexandra, Consort of Nicholas II, Emperor of Russia. Letters
      of the Tsaritsa to the Tsar, 1914-1916. B. Pares, intro.
      Westport: Hyperion Press, 1979 (reprint of 1924 edition),
      478pp.
      The wartime letters of Empress Alexandra constitute a valuable

source of information on the royal couple's tender relationship,
the counsel which Alexandra gave to Nicholas, and the mentality of the tsar during the stressful years of the war.
As Bernard Pares states, in his introduction to the correspondence, Alexandra's letters illustrate well, "the growing
and finally almost complete isolation of the Imperial family
circle from the Russian nation," the ignorance of the royal
couple in regard to the problems which plagued their realm,
and the misguided advice which Alexandra gave to Nicholas
in regard to his relations with the Duma and conduct of the
war.   DK254.A5A45
Reviewed in:
Lit R, (22 Mar. 1924): 608
Nation, 34 (19 Jan. 1924): 575
TLS, (22 Nov. 1923): 779

1934   *Bennigsen, G. "The Twilight of Autocracy." Dublin R,
206 (Jan. 1940): 85-101.
An analysis of Nicholas II's character and perception of his
duties and position as Russia's monarch. Bennigsen agrees
with B. Pares' portrayal of Nicholas as a weak-willed individual who, under the catastrophic influence of Empress Alexandra and Rasputin, pursued a political course that doomed
the monarchy to destruction.

1935   Buchanan, Sir George. My Mission to Russia and Other Diplomatic Memories, 2 Vols. Boston: Little, Brown and Company,
1923.
The 1910-1917 memoirs of the British ambassador to Russia
which, in scattered sections, contain comments and observations on Nicholas II's character, relations with various ministers, and inability to counter, or even perceive, the wartime
decline of the monarchy's public image. DK258.B8

1936   *Charques, Richard. The Twilight of Imperial Russia. London:
Oxford University Press, 1965, 256pp., bib. 251-52.
Nicholas II is not the focus of this study, but as a perceptive
analysis of the forces, events, and personalities which led
to the 1917 revolution it warrants consultation for insight into
Nicholas' character and policies. Charques presents Nicholas
as an indecisive, narrow-minded autocrat, easily swayed by
the insidious opinions of flatterers but so jealous of his autocratic prerogatives that he refused to take direct counsel from
even the most capable of his advisers. Charques maintains
that the 1917 Revolution was not inevitable; in fact, Nicholas
missed a variety of opportunities which, as late as 1915,
might have enabled him to save the monarchy if he had taken
advantage of them. DK260.C37

1937   Crankshaw, Edward. "Chapters 18-22." The Shadow of the
Winter Palace. New York: Viking Press, 1976, 303-93.

An assessment of the place of Nicholas II's reign along Russia's path to revolution. Crankshaw maintains that the fundamental contribution made by Nicholas to the outbreak of revolution in 1917 was his inability to recognize from the onset of his reign that major reform was an urgent necessity. Even as discontent mounted and the condition of his realm deteriorated, Nicholas failed to respond to the obvious challenges which confronted the monarchy. Crankshaw concludes that while Nicholas certainly did not cause the problems from which sprang the revolution, his inability to address them in a dynamic and positive fashion makes him the last and most important link in the chain of royal leaders responsible for the collapse of the Romanov dynasty. DK139.C66

1938 *Durnovo, Peter. "Memorandum to Nicholas I." RRC, Vol. II (anthology), 465-78. Also in DRH (anthology), 3-23.
A February 1914 memorandum, written by a conservative who held a number of high positions in the imperial government under the last two Romanov rulers, warning Nicholas II of the disastrous consequences which most certainly would befall the monarchy if Russia were to become embroiled in a major European war. While Nicholas II chose to ignore Durnovo's warning, the memorandum is nonetheless of interest and value as a cogent statement of conservative concern over the impetus that would be given to the forces of revolution if Russia were to become involved in a protracted struggle against the Triple Alliance nations.

1939 *Golder, Frank A. "Government by the Empress." DRH (anthology), 227-38.
Excerpts from the 11 September 1915 to 15 March 1916 letters of Alexandra to Nicholas II which illustrate how she used her influence with him to secure the appointment of the unpopular and scheming A. N. Khvostov as Minister of the Interior.

1940 *_____. "Imperial Family." Ibid., 239-53.
Excerpts from the 6 September 1915 to 17 February 1917 diaries and letters of Grand Dukes Andrei Vladimirovich, Nikolai Mikhailovich, Georgi Mikhailovich, and Alexander Mikhailovich in which the quarrelsome Romanovs express a common concern over the harmful influence of Empress Alexandra. Collectively these documents illustrate well the grand dukes' awareness that the political appointments and policies of Nicholas II were leading to such a decrease in the crown's popularity that disaster loomed on the horizon.

1941 *Gurko, V. I. "The Growth of Opposition to the Emperor and His Advisers." Features and Figures of the Past. Government and Opinion in the Reign of Nicholas II. Laura Matveev, trans. Stanford: Stanford University Press, 1939, 549-85.
A discussion of the deterioration of Nicholas II's political

position as a consequence of his failure to deal effectively,
either in person or through his ministers and advisers, with
the military and domestic problems which plagued Russia in
1915. Of particular interest is Gurko's account of the August-
September 1915 attempt by the Council of Ministers to convince
Nicholas of the need for the dismissal of Goremykin and for
the formation of a ministry in which the public could place its
confidence. Goremykin's selfish desire to keep his position at
any cost and the letters of Empress Alexandra urging Nicholas
to stand firmly behind him led Nicholas not only to retain
Goremykin as head of government but to dismiss those ministers who had criticized him. Gurko concludes that Nicholas'
actions at this vital point in Russia's history drastically increased the split between the government and the public and
therefore directly contributed to the 1917 demise of the monarchy. DK260.G82

1942 "How the Czarina's Superstitions Helped to Bring on the Russian
Revolution." Cur Opin, 69 (Sept. 1920): 358-60.
A summary of Arthur Ransome's Manchester Guardian review
of Alexandra's letters to Nicholas II. According to Ransome,
the letters reveal that Alexandra was shortsighted, superstitious, and meddlesome, and was gripped by hysteria bordering on madness.

1943 *Kennan, George F. "The Breakdown of the Tsarist Autocracy."
Revolutionary Russia. Richard Pipes, ed. Cambridge: Harvard University Press, 1968, 1-15. Also in The Fall of the
Russian Empire. Edward Chmielewski, ed. New York: John
Wiley and Sons, 1973, 191-208.
An argument that Nicholas II's overthrow in 1917 was more a
result of the monarchy's own ill-chosen policies than any historically inevitable revolution. Along with the government's
"irresponsible policy of Great Russian Nationalism" and failure
to establish a parliamentary supplement to its authority, Kennan points to Nicholas' personal inadequacies as being instrumental in the breakdown of autocracy in the years immediately
preceding 1917. DK265.A135

1944 Kerensky, Alexander. "Russia on the Eve of World War I."
Rus R, 5, no. 1 (1945): 10-30.
A discussion of Russia's political and economic condition in the
decade preceding World War I. Kerensky, a critic of the
tsarist government and later head of the Provisional Government of 1917, states that Nicholas II's pre-war policies so
alienated enlightened members of the state apparatus that
they became convinced that "an early end to the monarchy
was inevitable." Kerensky is particularly critical of Empress
Alexandra because she pushed the tsar towards autocratic
politics and away from reconciliation with the Russian people.

1945 _____. "Why the Russian Monarchy Fell." Slavonic R, 8
     (1929–30): 496–513.
     A discussion of the harmful consequences of the political
     meddling of Alexandra and Rasputin as a major factor in the
     monarchy's inability to rally support amidst the February
     Revolution.

1946 Marye, George Thomas. Nearing the End in Imperial Russia.
     New York: Arno Press, 1971 (reprint of 1929 edition), 479pp.
     The American ambassador to Russia gives an inside view of
     the problems faced by Nicholas II in the years just prior to
     the February Revolution.

1947 *Miliukov, Paul. Political Memoirs. Arthur P. Mendel, ed.
     Carl Goldberg, trans. Ann Arbor: University of Michigan
     Press, 1967, 508pp.
     Selections from the memoirs of the foremost spokesman of Rus-
     sian liberals during the reign of Nicholas II. Miliukov does
     not focus on Nicholas in any one section of his memoirs,
     but the editor's provision of a detailed subject index makes
     for easy access to Miliukov's frequent reference to the tsar
     and imperial policy, notably in regard to the Duma, the Bal-
     kans, and World War I. Of special interest is Miliukov's dis-
     cussion of the efforts which he and other liberals made to
     convince Nicholas that concessions to the forces of political
     modernization were essential to the monarchy's survival.
     DK254.M52A313

1948 "Nicholas Romanoff." Lit D, 54 (31 Mar. 1917): 934–38.
     A chronological review of the mistakes made by Nicholas II
     that contributed to the overthrow of the monarchy.

1949 *Pares, Bernard. The Fall of the Russian Monarchy. A Study
     of the Evidence. New York: Random House, 1939, 510pp.
     Excerpt in "Rasputin and the Empress Alexandra." The Rus-
     sian Revolution and Bolshevik Victory. Why and How?
     Arthur E. Adams, ed. Boston: D. C. Heath, 1966, 8–14.
     An argument that the Romanov dynasty collapsed in 1917
     not because of the forces of dissolution at work within Russian
     society but rather as a result of the mistakes and miscalcula-
     tions of those at the very top of the tsarist political edifice,
     namely Rasputin, Empress Alexandra, and Nicholas II. Pares
     asserts that "the Tsar had many opportunities of putting
     things right," particularly in the summer of 1915 when he
     could have formed a national coalition ministry to unite the
     country behind the war effort. However, through the cata-
     strophic influence of the empress and Rasputin, Nicholas re-
     coiled from this opportunity and therein converted the war
     into an instrument of revolution. Pares concludes that the
     disastrous consequences of the political meddling of Alexandra
     and Rasputin make them "the prime authors of the collapse

of the Empire and of Russia." DK260.P3
Reviewed in:
Am Hist R, 46 (1940): 148
Dublin R, 206 (Jan. 1940): 85-101
History, 24 (1940): 361
Int Aff, 18 (1939): 708
Slavonic E Eur R, 18 (July 1939): 73092

1950 _____. "Sir George Buchanan in Russia." Slavonic R, 3,
no. 9 (1925): 576-86.
An account of the wartime observations of British Ambassador
to Russia Sir George Buchanan with most attention given to
the last five months of the monarchy when Buchanan repeatedly urged Nicholas II and his ministers to adopt a more liberal
governmental policy.

1951 Pearson, Raymond. The Russian Moderates and the Crisis of
Tsarism, 1914-1917. London: Macmillan, 1977, 208pp., bib.
197-202.
This scholarly study of the personalities and views of the
wartime political moderates does not contain a separate chapter
on Nicholas II but includes a cogent discussion of the moderates' perception of and reaction to Nicholas' policies and the
deterioration of popular support for the war and monarchy.
DK260.P35

1952 Rivet, Charles. The Last of the Romanofs. New York: E.
P. Dutton, 1918, 309pp.
An account of Nicholas II's role in the collapse of the Romanov
dynasty; written by the St. Petersburg correspondent for
the Paris Temps, 1901-1917. Rivet counters the often repeated
charge that Nicholas II's indecisiveness was primarily responsible for his political misfortunes with the assertion that Nicholas
pursued consistently one goal, the bequeathal to his descen-
dants "a patrimony not less than that which he had inherited."
Nicholas' demise, Rivet contends, was prompted by his failure
to devise a viable plan to realize this goal and to select advisers more perceptive than himself, a failure which stemmed
from his belief that Russia was stable and all claims to the
contrary were seditious. Rivet is particularly critical of Empress Alexandra for contributing to Nicholas' misfounded confidence and for undermining wartime public confidence in the
monarchy by her pro-German behavior. DK262.R5

1953 *Rollins, Patrick J. "Searching for the Last Tsar." S. S.
Oldenburg. Last Tsar. Nicholas II, His Reign and His
Russia, 4 Vols. Leonid I. Mihalap and Patrick J. Rollins,
trans. Patrick J. Rollins, ed. Gulf Breeze, Fla.: Academic
International Press, 1975, xiv-xxxi.
An investigation of two questions: was Nicholas II really
"the blind, spineless, ineffective monarch perceived by his

contemporaries and subsequently by historians": and "what
impact did his reign have on the fate of monarchy in Russia
and the direction taken by the nation in the early twentieth
century?" Rollins maintains that the absence of reliable information on Nicholas II's character and rule makes it difficult
to answer conclusively either of these questions and, at the
same time, contributes to widely disparate assessments of the
place of his reign in Russia's history. In analyzing the various interpretations of Nicholas and his rule, Rollins devotes
most of his attention to a critical review of Oldenburg's thesis
that Nicholas was a conservative reformer of conviction and
vision who was betrayed by the Russian intelligentsia during
the national crisis spawned by World War I. DK262.0413

1954 Schapiro, Leonard B. "The Lessons of the Liberal Failure."
      Rationalism and Nationalism in Russian Nineteenth Century
      Political Thought. New Haven: Yale University Press, 1967,
      143-70.
      In part, a discussion of Nicholas II's blind resistance to the
      political changes necessary for the preservation of the mon-
      archy. JA84.R9S353

1955 Shirley, Ralph. "Warnings for the Czar." Fate, 29 (Mar.
      1976): 75-77. Adapted from the Occult Review, (July-Dec.
      1922).
      A recreation of occultist Madame O'Sullivan van Beare's warn-
      ing to Empress Alexandra that unless the monarchy discon-
      tinued its persecution of Jews and aggressive foreign policy
      the Romanovs faced certain dethronement and execution.

1956 *Taylor, Edmund. "Chapters 9-16." The Fall of Dynasties.
      The Collapse of the Old Order, 1905-1922. Garden City, N.Y.:
      Doubleday Press, 1963, 161-317.
      An interesting discussion of the collapse of the Romanov dy-
      nasty as a consequence of Nicholas II's personal shortcomings,
      the political meddling of Rasputin, and the premature death
      of P. Stolypin. Taylor asserts that "just as Stolypin was
      simultaneously a symbol of residual vitality in a wasting au-
      tocracy and the main instrument of its potential recovery,
      Rasputin was both an ominous symptom of its decay and the
      ultimate agent of its collapse." Following the 1911 assassina-
      tion of Stolypin, Nicholas, deprived of wise political counsel,
      became the victim of his own lack of intelligence and his con-
      sequent preoccupation with trivia and family affairs. Taylor
      sees the immediate circumstances which surrounded Nicholas'
      abdication and execution as being consistent with the tsar's
      lackluster rule: without glory or martyrdom the Romanovs
      were slaughtered "in circumstances of prosaic squalor that
      recall the gas ovens of Hitler's Germany rather than the tum-
      brils of 18th century France." D412.7.T3

1957   *Trotsky, Leon. "The Death Agony of the Monarchy." The
        Russian Revolution. Garden City, N.Y.: Doubleday Press,
        1959, 75-96.
        A critical examination of Nicholas II's response to the immediate
        events and developments associated with the February Revolu-
        tion. Trotsky, a prominent figure in the October Revolution
        and early history of the Soviet state, establishes that amid
        the strikes, demonstrations, and mutinies in wartime Petro-
        grad, Nicholas still failed to realize that the situation was a
        most critical one. Even when he learned from close advisers
        that the army no longer supported him and Empress Alexandra
        telegraphed that major concessions had to be made at once
        if the monarchy were to be saved, Nicholas adhered to the
        belief that loyal soldiers would soon restore law and order
        and all would be well again. By the time Nicholas could be
        persuaded to make concessions the moment for compromise
        had passed and the fate of the monarchy was sealed. Trotsky
        concludes with a penetrating overview of the personal and his-
        torical factors responsible for Nicholas' fate. DK265.T774

1958   *_____. "The Idea of a Palace Revolution." Ibid., 61-74.
        A discussion of the growing awareness among various circles
        during the wartime years that something had to be done in
        regard to the startling deterioration of the monarchy's politi-
        cal fortunes if a violent revolution were to be averted. Trot-
        sky establishes clearly that prominent conservatives and
        moderates, members of the royal family, and various Allied
        diplomats independently arrived at the conclusion, by late
        1916, that Nicholas had to be removed from power if the mon-
        archy were to be preserved in some form, but none of these
        groups could muster the courage to formulate a plot to depose
        the tsar. Since "the determination was lacking for a 'big'
        palace revolution," the best that anyone among the ruling
        class could do was to assassinate Rasputin as a means of
        removing one of the prime sources of the monarchy's unpopu-
        larity.

1959   Walsh, Edmund A. "The Fall of the Russian Empire." Atlan
        M, 141 (Jan.-Mar. 1928): 46-59, 228-40, 339-54.
        A discussion of the collapse of the monarchy as a consequence
        of a series of long standing domestic problems aggravated by
        the wartime political course pursued by Nicholas II under the
        harmful influence of his wife. Walsh also examines Nicholas'
        abdication and imprisonment, and speculates that German mili-
        tary leaders nearly succeeded in arranging for the Romanovs'
        release just prior to their execution at the hands of the Bol-
        sheviks.

1960   _____. The Fall of the Russian Empire. The Story of the
        Last Romanovs and the Coming of the Bolsheviki. Boston:
        Little, Brown and Company, 1928, 357pp.

An analysis of the causes of the collapse of the Romanov
dynasty with emphasis placed upon the personal responsibility
shared by Nicholas II, Alexandra, and Rasputin. Walsh maintains that Nicholas tended to make hasty and poor political
decisions primarily because his time, thoughts, and energy
were consumed by devotion to family concerns, especially the
hemophiliac condition of the tsarevich. This latter concern
provided the opportunity for Rasputin to exert a powerful
and eventually fatal influence over Alexandra and, through
her, the tsar, an influence to which Walsh constantly refers
as he chronicles the disastrous decisions made by Nicholas in
the last few years of the monarchy's existence. Walsh concludes with a dramatic account of the arrest, exile, and execution of the Romanov family. DK26.W335

1961 *Washburn, Stanley. On the Russian Front in World War I:
Memoirs of an American War Correspondent. New York:
Robert Speller and Sons, 1982, 332pp.
The memoirs of a reporter for The Times of London from 1914
to 1917 whose accounts of the Russian front shaped world
opinion about Nicholas II's military forces. Washburn, who
was attached to the imperial staff of Nicholas II, sheds considerable light on the military policy pursued by the tsar,
Nicholas' character, and his abdication, an act which the
author witnessed. Washburn maintains that Nicholas was not
the political weakling that many of his contemporaries believed
him to be but rather simply possessed an overly considerate
nature which often served to render him ineffective as an
autocratic ruler. By being a compassionate and understanding
individual, Nicholas unwittingly allowed himself to be manipulated by those around him, particularly Empress Alexandra,
and consequently pursued policies, political and military, harmful to his own and Russia's best interests. D550.W28

1962 Waters, W. H-H. "Secret and Confidential." The Experiences
of a Military Attaché. New York: Frederick A. Stokes Company, 1926, 388pp.
The memoirs of a British military attaché stationed in the capital during the early part of Nicholas II's reign and with him
at Imperial Army Headquarters, 1916-17. Waters portrays
Nicholas as an intelligent and caring ruler who was victimized
by poor counsel from advisers, especially Minister of Interior
Protopopov. DA46.W3A3

1963 Wrangell-Rokassowski, Baron Carl. "The Reign of Czar
Nicholas II." Before the Storm. Vetimiglia, Italy: Tipo-
Litografia Ligure, 1972, 251pp., bib. 249-51.
A discussion of Nicholas II's policies toward Russia's minorities
and peasant population as a prime cause of the 1917 revolu-
tion. Wrangell-Rokassowsky also comments briefly on Nicholas'
support for the ill-advised 1905 war with Japan.
CT1218.W72W72

1964 *Wright, C. Hagberg. "Introduction." The Letters of the
      Tsar to the Tsaritsa, 1914-1917. C. E. Vulliamy, ed. New
      York: Dodd, Mead and Company, 1929, v-xii.
      A discussion of Nicholas II's wartime letters to Alexandra as
      the most revealing documents bearing on the last years of
      the Russian monarchy. Wright comments on the insights
      which the letters provide in regard to Nicholas' character,
      perception of his station, relationship with his ministers,
      and reaction to the principal events of the time. DK268.A4A6

Abdication, Exile, and Death

1965 Ackerman, Carl W. "How the Czar Was Doomed to Death. An
      Authentic Document Written by His Major-Domo, Describes His
      Last Known Hours of Life. Cur Hist M, 9, no. 2 (1919):
      338-43.
      A sympathetic, eyewitness account of Nicholas II's behavior
      and conversations with his wife and children just prior to the
      family's execution.

1966 Alexandrov, Victor. The End of the Romanovs. Boston:
      Little, Brown and Company, 1966, 256pp.
      An account of the events leading up to Nicholas II's abdica-
      tion, the arrest and confinement of the royal family, and their
      death at the hands of the Bolsheviks. Alexandrov asserts
      that careful study of all available evidence leads to the con-
      clusion that the entire royal family was executed in July
      1918. Includes a collection of family photographs, taken by
      Nicholas II, and the major evidence gathered by N. Sokolov
      when he investigated the Romanovs' execution. DK258.A5613

1967 "Arrest and Exile of the Romanoffs." Lit D, 56 (9 Mar. 1918):
      47-52.
      An account of the circumstances which led to the arrest of
      the Romanovs, and a description of their lifestyle in exile.

1968 *Bark, Sir Peter. "The Last Days of the Russian Monarchy-
      Nicholas II at Army Headquarters." Rus R, 16, no. 3 (1957):
      35-44.
      A review of the events of 14-15 March 1917 which prompted
      Nicholas II to abdicate. Bark reproduces the appeals to
      Nicholas II to surrender the throne made by Grand Duke
      Nicholas and Generals Brusilov, Evert, and Alexeev, and then
      summarizes the reaction of the royal family and military lead-
      ers to Nicholas' formal statement of abdication.

1969 *Basily, Nicholas de. "The Abdication of Nicholas II." Nicolas
      de Basily. Memoirs. Diplomat of Imperial Russia 1903-1917.
      Stanford: Hoover Institute Press, 1973, 103-48.
      A recollection of the circumstances which prompted Nicholas II

to abdicate; written by a diplomat who served as a liason officer between the Ministry of Foreign Affairs and the tsar.
Basily, who had access to the reports received by Nicholas
in regard to the political situation in February of 1917, re-
calls the stance taken by the Duma spokesmen and military
leaders at Imperial Army Headquarters in respect to the tsar's
abdication, Nicholas' response to the request that he step
down from the throne, and the intricacies associated with the
contents of the abdication statement, a document which General Alexeev commissioned Basily to draft.   DK254.B37A33
Reviewed in:
Am Hist R, 80, no. 2 (1975):   441-42
Slav R, 34, no. 1 (1975):   149

1970   *Benckendorff, Count Paul.   Last Days at Tsarskoe Selo.
Maurice Baring, trans.   London: William Heinemann Limited,
1927, 165pp.
A recollection of the 1 March to 1 August 1917 stay of the
Romanovs at Tsarskoe Selo.   Benckendorff, who was the Grand
Marshal of the Imperial Court and shared the captivity of the
Romanovs at Tsarskoe Selo, provides a detailed account of
Nicholas II's abdication, transfer to Tsarskoe Selo, and
daily life during his six months there under house arrest.
Throughout, Benckendorff characterizes Nicholas and Alex-
andra as courageous, gracious, and poised despite their ob-
vious concern over the safety of their family.   DK258.B4

1971   Bessell, Peter.   "The Escape of Czar Nicholas and Alexandra."
E Eur, 20, no. 6 (1971):   7-9.
Speculation on the existence of evidence that Nicholas II and
his family secretly escaped from Russia and assumed new
identities abroad through a scheme formulated by Russia's
wartime allies and accepted by the Bolshevik government.
Bessell admits that conclusive proof is presently lacking to
substantiate this hypothesis but believes that irrefutable evidence will soon be released by the governments which were
involved in the conspiracy.

1972   Botkin, Gleb.   The Real Romanovs.   New York: Fleming H.
Revell Company, 1931, 335pp.
A highly favorable portrayal of Nicholas II and his relationship with his family, and a detailed discussion of the arrest,
incarceration, and execution of the Romanovs.   Botkin, the
son of Nicholas' personal physician, gives special attention
to the theory that Nicholas' daughter Anastasia was not among
the Romanovs executed.   DK258.B6

1973   *Bulygin, P.   "In Prison at Ekaterinburg: An Account of an
Attempt to Rescue the Imperial Family."   Slavonic R, 7, no.
19 (1928):   55-66.
Details on the conception, execution, and failure of an attempt,

by the author and other Russian officers, to free the Romanovs from their Ekaterinburg captivity.

1974 *_____. The Murder of the Romanovs. The Authentic
Account, Gleb Kerensky, trans. Sir Bernard Pares, intro.
London: Hutchinson, 1935, 286pp. Includes a foreword,
The Road to Tragedy, by Alexander Kerensky.
A firsthand account of the last months and death of the
Romanov family. Bulygin, who was a member of the Imperial
Guard, reconstructs his role in both an attempt to rescue
the royal family from their Bolshevik captivity and in the
detailed Sokolov investigaiton of the circumstances surrounding the family's death. He describes the Romanovs, and
especially Nicholas II, as being remarkably calm and courageous in the face of death and accepts as fact Sokolov's conclusion that the entire royal family was executed on 18 July
1918. DK258.B83

1975 Buxhoeveden, Baroness Sophie. Left Behind. Fourteen Months
in Siberia During the Revolution. December 1917-February
1919. London: Longmans, Green and Company, 1929, 182pp.
An account of the royal family's exile to and life in the
Siberian town of Tobolsk. Buxhoeveden, a member of Empress
Alexandra's entourage who was with the Romanovs during their
imprisonment at Tsarskoe Selo and Tobolsk, gives a detailed
description of the conditions under which the Romanovs lived,
their relations with the soldiers who guarded them, and their
transfer to Ekaterinburg at which point the Baroness was sep-
arated from them by Bolshevik order. DK254.A5B8

1976 _____. The Life and Tragedy of Alexandra Feodorovna.
Empress of Russia. J. C. Squire, intro. London: Longmans, Green and Company, 1928, 360pp.
A sympathetic and dramatic account of Alexandra's life while
both empress of Russia and political prisoner in Siberia. As
Buxhoeveden chronicles Alexandra's daily actions, words and
thoughts, she notes the empress' shortcomings and failures,
but it is very much Alexandra's positive attributes which shine
throughout the narrative. DK265.R8

1977 *Bykov, P. M. The Last Days of Tsar Nicholas. Andrew
Rothstein, trans./pref. New York: International Publishers,
1934, 86pp.
A Soviet account of the arrest, exile, and execution of the
royal family. Bykov, who was in charge of the Romanovs
while in Ekaterinburg, devotes most of his attention to the
plans and efforts of counter-revolutionaries who hoped to free
the Romanovs, the consequent security measures taken to prevent such an escape, and the circumstances which led to the
decision to execute the entire family. In a provocative preface,
A. Rothstein questions the accuracy of the interpretation

which characterizes Nicholas II as a kind, caring ruler victimized by circumstances beyond his control.

1978 "Carefree Gaiety of a Captive Czar." Lit D, 98 (18 Aug.
      1928): 37-38.
      A description of the royal family's daily routine while in
      Ekaterinburg; written by an officer assigned to guard the
      Romanovs.

1979 Danilov, Goury. "How the Tsar Abdicated." Liv Age, 336
      (Apr. 1929): 99-104.
      An eyewitness recreation of events aboard Nicholas II's private
      train just prior to his abdication.

1980 De Wissen, H. "Mystery of the Czarina." Forum, 62 (Aug.
      1919): 169-81.
      A sympathetic account of Alexandra's life during the revolu-
      tionary period, and a review of the evidence that she escaped
      execution at the hands of the Bolsheviks.

1981 Enel, Sacrafice. An Attempt to Explain Certain Signs Which
      Are Stated in Robert Wilton's "Last Days of the Romanovs"
      Which Have Been Inscribed on the Wall of the Room Where
      Nicholas II Was Killed. Brussels, 1923, 19pp.
      Unavailable for annotation.

1982 Ernst, Otto. "The Romanovs." Kings in Exile. London:
      Jarrolds Publishers, 1933, 197-210.
      A brief review of Nicholas II's abdication, arrest, exile, and
      execution. Ernst sees the Romanovs' overthrow as being
      directly due to the evil influence of Rasputin. D412.7.E72

1983 "Fall of Nicholas II." Newsweek, 69 (20 Mar. 1967): 46+.
      A popular recreation of the events which led to Nicholas II's
      abdication.

1984 *Francq, Henri G. The Knout and the Scythe and the Story
      of the Hyenas. New York: Vantage Press, 1980, 299pp.,
      bib. 297-99.
      The first half of this work is devoted to a general account
      of the conditions which led to the February 1917 abdication
      of Nicholas II and to the circumstances which surrounded the
      Romanovs' Siberian exile and execution. Franq discusses the
      various plots to free the royal family, provides a lurid account
      of the Romanovs' execution, and reviews the conflicting inter-
      pretations of the Romanovs' fate advanced by Guy Richards
      and John O'Conor. In an appendix, Francq describes the
      efforts of King George V of England to gain the release of
      the royal family. DK265.F66

1985 *Frankland, Noble. Imperial Tragedy. Nicholas II, Last of the

Tsars. New York: Coward-McCann, 1961, 193pp., bib.
184-87. Also published under the title, Crown of Tragedy.
A balanced, readable account of Nicholas II's abdication and
the Romanovs' arrest, exile, death, and burial. Franklin
asserts that Nicholas lacked the ability to recognize the decisive challenges which confronted the monarchy and therefore
was helpless to prevent its demise: "by nature he was the
slave of characters and of circumstances stronger than his
own." Adding to this pathos and tragedy is the loving relationship Nicholas had with his family whose members became
victims of Nicholas' shortcomings. Drawing primarily on the
works of Gilliard and Wilton, Frankland concludes with a
compassionate description of the Romanovs' daily existence as
political exiles. DK258.F7
     Reviewed in:
     Rus R, 20, no. 3 (1961): 266
     Slav R, 21, no. 1 (1962): 161

1986   *Gilliard, Pierre. Thirteen Years at the Russian Court. F.
       Appleby Holt, trans. New York: George H. Doran and
       Company, 1923, 304pp.
       A recollection of the last few years of the Romanov family;
       written by the tutor of Tsarevich Alexis. Gilliard describes
       sympathetically a wide range of incidents in the lives of the
       Romanovs and comments upon their reaction to such major
       historical developments as the outbreak of World War I, the
       strains placed upon the nation as the war progressed, and
       the disintegration of popular support for the monarchy to
       the point where Nicholas II's abdication became imperative.
       Of particular interest is Gilliard's account of the Romanovs'
       period of captivity. The author concludes with a review of
       the findings of the Sokolov Commission's investigation of the
       royal family's execution. DK258.G45

1987   *Golder, Frank A. "Abdication of the Romanovs." DRH
       (anthology), 294-302.
       A series of documents which collectively illustrate the circum-
       stances which prompted Nicholas II to abdicate. Golder in-
       cludes records of various meetings held to discuss the abdica-
       tion question, the abdication manifesto itself, and the minutes
       of the 16 March 1917 meeting of the Petrograd Soviet in which
       the matter of the Romanovs' arrest was resolved.

1988   Hamilton, Gerald. "Holy Russia." Blood Royal. London:
       Anthony Gibbs and Phillips, 1964, 125-38.
       A brief, favorable account of the life and character of Nicho-
       las and Alexandra, and a sharp attack on the Bolshevik gov-
       ernment for its "butchering" of the royal family. D352.1.H3

1989   Hirsch, Ronald. "Nothing but Ashes: The End of the Roman-
       ovs." Crimes that Shook the World. New York: Duell,

Sloan and Pearce, 1949, 139-62.
A standard account of the arrest and exile of the Romanovs, and a graphic description of their execution and the destruction of their physical remains. Hirsch also summarizes the findings of the Sokolov Commission which investigated the Romanovs' execution. D412.H56

1990 "His Last Day as Czar." Lit D, 54 (7 Apr. 1917): 996-997, 1,000.
A brief account of Nicholas II's thoughts and behavior on the day that he abdicated.

1991 *Kerensky, Alexander. "The Road to Tragedy." Paul Bulygin. The Murder of the Romanovs. London: Hutchinson, 1935, 25-160.
A discussion of the events and circumstances which led to Nicholas II's overthrow, imprisonment, and eventual execution. Kerensky, a socialist critic of the monarchy in the years before the February Revolution, was, as Minister of Justice in the Provisional Government, entrusted with the custody of the deposed Romanovs. He sees the monarchy's demise as being prompted by a series of fateful decisions made by Nicholas II, the political meddling of Alexandra, and the destructive influence of Rasputin. DK258.B83

1992 Lange, Christian L. "Story of the Russian Upheaval." Cur Hist M, 6, no. 1 (1917): 105-16.
A contemporaneous American perspective on the immediate sources of Nicholas II's abdication, and an eyewitness account of the abdication ceremony.

1993 "Light on the Murder of Tsar Nikolas." Liv Age, 311 (10 Dec. 1921): 638-45.
Excerpts from various articles dealing with the question of the Provisional Government's responsibility for Nicholas II's execution through its failure to secure asylum for him in England.

1994 *McCullagh, Francis. "The Murder of the Tsar" and "The Burial of the Tsar." A Prisoner of the Reds. The Story of a British Officer Captured in Siberia. London: John Murray, 1921, 124-85.
An account of the murder and disposal of the remains of the Romanovs; based primarily on information gathered in a March 1920 interview with Yurovsky who was in charge of the Romanovs' execution. McCullagh also reviews various sources of information which both corroborate and contradict the official Bolshevik account of the treatment and eventual execution of the royal family. DK265.M26

1995 *_____. "Yurovsky; and the Murder of the Tsar." Nineteenth C, 88 (Sept. 1920): 377-427. Excerpts in Cur Opin,

69 (Nov. 1920):   674-78 and <u>Lit D</u>, 67 (23 Oct. 1920):   50-57.
A dramatic and detailed account of the execution of the Romanovs. McCullagh bases his report on interviews with the
Romanovs' jailers, especially Yurovsky who was in charge of
the royal family's execution.

1996 Mackenzie, Frederick A.   "The Murder of the Czar." <u>Twentieth</u>
      <u>Century Crimes</u>. Boston: Little, Brown and Company, 1927,
      103-20.
      A portrayal of the execution of the Romanovs as one of the
      "greatest crimes of the century, not merely on account of the
      high place of the victims and the vast political issues involved,
      but because of the circumstances of horror and brutality
      which surrounded it." Mackenzie labels the Bolshevik govern-
      ment as a criminal one because the Romanovs were cruelly
      maltreated in captivity, were denied a trial, and "were taken
      to a cellar and slain like pigs in a pen." HV6241.M3

1997 Magnifico, Meda. <u>The Human Saint. A True Biography of</u>
      <u>the Empress of All the Russias</u>. Boston: Boston House
      Publishers, 1962, 195pp.
      An argument that Empress Alexandra escaped from Russia,
      on 12 October 1919, by way of a submarine which took her
      to a lighthouse off the Florida coast where she died on 4 July
      1920. Magnifico claims that details of the escape plan had
      been worked out in 1915 by Rasputin, in cooperation with
      both the German and American governments, and that just
      prior to her death Alexandra gave birth to a daughter who
      was still living in America as of 1962. DK254.A5M3

1998 Markov, Sergei V. <u>How We Tried to Save the Tsaritsa</u>. F. S.
      Flint and D. F. Tait, trans. London: G. P. Putnam's Sons,
      1929, 288pp.
      An account of how the author, a lieutenant in the Empress'
      Own Crimean Cavalry Regiment, organized and led a group of
      twelve officers ("the club of the dark powers") to rescue the
      imperial family. Markov asserts that his initial plan to rescue
      the Romanovs from Tsarskoe Selo by a bomb-diversion was
      thwarted when the royal family was suddenly moved to Tobolsk.
      While the Romanovs were imprisoned in Ekaterinburg, Markov
      began to work on another escape plan but was so hampered by
      the lack of funds and reliable supporters and by his inability
      to contact the Romanovs that he was forced to abandon the
      project. He concludes with an account of his attempt to enlist
      in the Romanovs' cause Empress Alexandra's brother, the Duke
      of Hess of Germany, an endeavor frustrated by the royal
      family's execution. DK265.M34

1999 "Mr. and Mrs. Romanoff at Home." <u>Lit D</u>, 55, no. 2 (1917):
      43-46.
      An account of the austere life of the Romanovs while in

confinement under the supervision of the Provisional Government.

2000   *Murder of the Czar's Family." Cur Hist M, 13, no. 2 (1920):
       177-94.
       A restatement of the London Times' account of the Romanovs'
       incarceration and execution; based on a number of eyewitness
       reports.

2001   Null, Gary. The Conspirators Who Saved the Romanovs. Engle-
       wood Cliffs, N.J.: Prentice-Hall, 1971, 177pp., bib. 169-70.
       An argument that Aaron Simanovitsch not only constructed and
       led an elaborate machine which saved thousands of Russian
       Jews from persecution but also was instrumental in the 1918
       secret escape of the Romanovs from Siberian imprisonment.
       Null contends that Simanovitsch was responsible for William II's
       pressuring the Bolshevik government into accepting a secret
       clause in the 3 March 1918 Treaty of Brest-Litovsk by which
       the Bolsheviks agreed to allow the Romanovs to be "rescued."
       When the Bolsheviks reneged on their promise, Simanovitsch,
       with the aid of Charles Fox, an American agent, allegedly was
       able to bribe the Romanovs' captors to stage the royal family's
       death (complete with fake bodies and buckets of animal blood)
       and allow them to escape. DK258.N83

2002   *O'Conor, John F., ed./trans. The Sokolov Investigation of
       the Alleged Murder of the Russian Imperial Family. New
       York: Robert Speller and Sons, 1971, 257pp., bib. 251-52.
       A reassessment of the conclusion reached by the Sokolov Com-
       mission, and supported by Bulygin, Bykov, and Wilton, that
       Nicholas II and all of the members of his immediate family
       were executed in Ekaterinburg on 18 July 1918. O'Conor
       contends that Sokolov's investigation was flawed by various
       irregularities and that the investigators were deceived by
       the Bolsheviks who 'planted' false evidence and arranged for
       fallacious eyewitness testimony. He also maintains that there
       is a considerable body of evidence that the German govern-
       ment made serious efforts to secure the release of the Roman-
       ovs. Included is a translation of the main parts of Nicholas
       Sokolov's report on the death of the imperial family.
       DK258.S63330282
          Reviewed in:
          Choice, 9 (June 1972):   569
          Libr J, 97 (Mar. 1972) 874
          Rus R, 31, no. 2 (1972):   418

2003   Pollock, John. "Why the Tsar Was Murdered." Fortn R, (19
       Nov. 1920): 715-23.
       An argument that the Romanovs failed to avoid execution be-
       cause Nicholas II refused to agree to a complex German plan
       to secure his release from the Bolsheviks. Nicholas allegedly

rejected the plan because it called for the restoration of the
monarchy in Russia under the rule of his son Alexis who
would be controlled by a German regent.

2004 Pridham, Vice-Admiral Francis. "The Captivity and Murder
      of the Imperial Family." Close of a Dynasty. London:
      Allan Wingate, 1956, 99-115.
      A straightforward account of the arrest, exile, and execution
      of the royal family, and an examination of the possibility that
      one of the many plans conceived to rescue the Romanovs
      actually succeeded. Reluctantly, Pridham comes to the con-
      clusion that Nicholas II and his entire immediate family were
      executed on 18 July 1918, an act for which he vigorously
      condemns the Bolsheviks. DK258.P74

2005 "Prisoners of Tsarskoe Selo." Liv Age, 293 (19 May 1917):
      427-29.
      A straightforward, eyewitness description of the Romanovs'
      routine and condition while at Tsarskoe Selo under house
      arrest; written by the Assistant Director of Ordnance Stores
      who was received by the Romanovs during their imprisonment.

2006 "Private Diary of the Late Czar; His Own Record of His Down-
      fall." Cur Hist M, 9, no. 2 (1919): 344-47.
      Excerpts from Nicholas II's diary during the period of his im-
      prisonment along with some brief negative comments on his
      reign published by the Berlin Vorwärts.

2007 "Proof of the Murder of the Czar." Cur Hist M, 10, no. 3
      (1919): 395-400.
      The text of the Omsk government's report on the Romanovs'
      execution.

2008 Rasputin, Marie. "To Rescue the Tsar." The Real Rasputin.
      Arthur Chambers, trans. London: John Long, 1929, 182-94.
      An account of a plan devised by Anna Vryubov, Rasputin's
      son and daughter, and Bishop Hermogenes to rescue the royal
      family from their Tobolsk imprisonment by diverting the at-
      tention of the soldiers guarding them and then spiriting the
      Romanovs' by carriage to nearby White supporters. The
      author states that while Nicholas II pondered the plan the
      Bolsheviks uncovered the plot and tightened security around
      the Romanovs' place of captivity thus making their rescue
      impossible.

2009 Richards, Guy. Hunt for the Czar. Garden City, N.Y.:
      Doubleday Press, 1970, 265pp., bib. 255-59.
      A review of various studies conducted in regard to the royal
      family's fate, and an argument in favor of the theory that a
      group led by Charles Fox, an American agent, was able to
      rescue the Romanovs from their Bolshevik captors. Richards

claims that Fox's account, published anonymously in 1920 under the title Rescuing the Czar, is a dubious one when taken
verbatim, but, in fact, was written in code ("a Rosetta Stone
of the Revolution") and when unscrambled makes a great deal
of sense. DK258.A45

2010 _____. Imperial Agent. The Goleniewski-Romanov Case.
New York: Devin-Adair Company, 1966, 284pp.
An argument that not only is the Soviet account of the death
of Nicholas II a "colossal hoax" but in reality "all seven members of the Imperial Family survived." Richards maintains that
the five Romanov children were still alive as of 1966 and were
living under cover names in different parts of the world. He
also asserts that Nicholas' son Alexis, under the name of
Lieutenant-Colonel Michael Goleniewski, became "one of the
most effective secret agents who ever served the West."
DK258.R46

2011 _____. The Rescue of the Romanovs. Newly Discovered
Documents Reveal How Czar Nicholas II and the Russian
Imperial Family Escaped. Old Greenwich: Devin-Adair Company, 1975, 215pp., bib. 204-07.
An argument that the Romanovs escaped from their Bolshevik
captors and were smuggled out of Russia by way of Odessa in
1918, a fact covered up by Soviet authorities and a host of
international collaborators including American and British
secret service agents. Richards presents a number of documents in support of his hypothesis but relies primarily upon a
series of coded messages (the "Chivers Papers") sent to President Wilson by American intelligence officers in Russia.
DK258.R47

2012 Roberts, C. E. Bechofer. "Tsar's Murder and the Soviet
Government's Guilt." Nineteenth C, 96 (July 1924): 116-22.
An attack on the Bolshevik government of Lenin for directly
ordering the execution of Nicholas II and his family.

2013 Rodzianko, Paul. "The Siberian Expedition and the Murder
of the Royal Family." Tattered Banners: An Autobiography.
London: Seely Service and Company, 1939, 243-56.
A description of the conditions under which the royal family
spent its last weeks, and a recollection of the author's interviews with various townfolk in Ekaterinburg in pursuit of
details on the murder as part of an investigation conducted
for a British military mission under General Knox.
DK257.R6A3

2014 Russky, Nicholas V. "Account of the Czar's Abdication."
Cur Hist M, 7, no. 2 (1917): 262-64.
A translation of a firsthand account of Nicholas II's abdication;
written for the Russkaya Volya by a representative of the

Russian army. Russky describes the abdication scene, Nicholas' mood, and the reaction of those in attendance.

2015   Semenoff, E. "How Nicholas Abdicated." Liv Age, 310 (24
        Sept. 1921): 781-84.
        A composite of the eyewitness accounts of several Russian
        generals in attendance at Nicholas II's abdication.

2016   Smythe, James P. Rescuing the Czar. Two Authentic Diaries
        Arranged and Translated by James P. Smythe. San Francisco:
        California Printing Company, 1920, 269pp. PZ3.S6683
        Unavailable for annotation.

2017   *Summers, Anthony and Tom Mangold. The File on the Tsar.
        New York: Harper and Row, 1976, 416pp., bib. 395-402.
        A BBC sponsored documentary investigation of the assassina-
        tion of the Romanovs. Summers and Mangold state that early
        in their investigation the work of forensic scientists, cipher
        experts, and hand-writing specialists from Scotland Yard
        began to reveal flaws in "significant pieces of old evidence."
        This revelation moved the authors "to travel worldwide, track-
        ing down the handful of people still alive who might yet be
        able to explain the growing discrepancies." Summers and
        Mangold state that they uncovered the original dossier of the
        White Russian investigation, lost for decades, which "shows
        that most of the Romanov family were alive for many months
        after their historical 'deaths.'" The authors conclude that
        Nicholas II was executed on 18 July 1918 but the women of
        the family were transferred to Perm where they were seen as
        late as March of 1919, after which time their fate is unknown.
        DK258.S86
            Reviewed in:
            Economist, 260 (11 Sept. 1976): 107
            Libr J, 101 (Nov. 1976): 2371
            New Yorker, 52 (31 Jan. 1977): 82
            TLS, (15 Oct. 1976): 1303

2018   *Sworakowski, W. S. "Authorship of the Abdication Document
        of Nicholas II." Rus R, 30, no. 3 (1971): 277-86.
        An argument that the au thor of the 15 March 1917 abdication
        statement was Nicholas A. de Basily (Vice Director of the
        Chancellery of the Ministry of Foreign Affairs) and not
        Nicholas II as most historians have erroneously claimed.

2019   "Tragic End of Nicholas II, Czar of All the Russias." Lit D,
        58 (31 Aug. 1918): 66-74.
        A portrayal of Nicholas II as a political weakling and a coward
        even in the last days of his life.

2020   Trewin, J. C. Tutor to the Tsarevich. An Intimate Portrait
        of the Last Days of the Russian Imperial Family Compiled from

the Papers of Charles Sydney Gibbes. London: Macmillan,
1975, 148pp.
The notes kept and photographs taken by Charles Sydney
Gibbes, the tutor of the grand duchesses and the tsarevich,
serve as the foundation for this intimate chronicle of the
daily lives of the members of the exiled royal family.
DK251.T7

2021 *Trotsky, L. "April 9th." Diary in Exile. Cambridge:
Harvard University Press, 1958, 80-82. Excerpt in RFR
(anthology), 181-83.
A 9 April 1935 diary entry on the circumstances which led
Lenin to order the Ural Executive Committee to execute the
Romanovs. Trotsky stresses that while a public trial was
considered to be the best way to deal with Nicholas, Lenin
felt that there was insufficient time for legal formalities and
that a summary execution would not only show the world the
Bolsheviks' determination to succeed at all costs but would
also eliminate the living symbol of the Whites' cause in the
civil war. DK254.T6A43

2022 Warwick, Francis E. "Ex-Czarina; Some Memories and Impressions." Bookman, 46 (Jan. 1918): 561-62.
A description of the exiled Empress Alexandra as "a greatly
suffering and distraught woman whose case calls for the pity
of all and the hatred of none."

2023 *Wilton, Robert. The Last Days of the Romanovs. London:
Thornton Butterworth Limited, 1920, 320pp.
A detailed account of the Romanovs' arrest, exile, and
death. Wilton, a correspondent for The Times of London,
states that he was in constant touch with the course of the
Sokolov inquiry into the Romanovs' death and "personally
took part in the search for the remains of the victims."
He states that Sokolov's investigation constitutes "an over-
whelming mass of evidence," the veracity of which is beyond
dispute. Wilton appends to his study a translation of the
minutes of the Sokolov investigation (published separately in
America by M. G. Telberg, ex-Minister of Justice in the Omsk
government of Admiral Kolchak) which contains depositions by
Colonel Kobylinsky (the officer in charge of the Romanovs
from March 1917 to May 1918), M. Gilliard (the Romanovs'
physician), S. Gibbes (tutor to the tsarevich), P. Medvedev
(one of the Romanovs' executioners), and P. Proskuriakov
(one of the Romanovs' guards). DK258.L3

2024 "Yurovsky and the Murder of the Czar." Cur Hist M, 13 (Nov.
1920): 195-98.
An argument that the Romanovs were executed because their
Bolshevik guards panicked when counter-revolutionary forces
began to near Ekaterinburg. The author suggests that the

guards feared that they would be put to death if they allowed
the Romanovs to be rescued.

FOREIGN POLICY AND MILITARY AFFAIRS

2025 *Bernstein, Herman, ed. The Willy-Nicky Correspondence.
Theodore Roosevelt, foreword. Herman Bernstein, intro.
New York: Knopf, 1918, 158pp.
A reproduction of the 65 telegrams exchanged secretly between
Kaiser William II of Germany and Nicholas II from 1904 to 1907.
In a lengthy introduction, Bernstein reviews the contents of
the exchanges which he believes show the Kaiser to be "a
master of intrigues and Mephistophelian plotter for German
domination of the world," and Nicholas to be "a capricious
weakling, a characterless, colourless nonentity" easily manipulated by William. DD228.7.R8B5

2026 Bigelow, Poultney. "The Czar and the French People." Independent, 53 (17 Oct. 1901): 2464-66.
A firsthand account of Nicholas II's 1901 visit to France.
The report is somewhat uncomplimentary of Nicholas as it
suggests that he is haughty and aloof, and it questions the
need for the extensive security set up on his behalf.

2027 _____. "When Nicholas Answered Wilhelm in French."
Independent, 80 (26 Oct. 1914): 132-33.
An account of an official ceremony attended by Nicholas II in
Germany when he apparently insulted his host, William II, by
responding to William's toast in the French language.

2028 Clarke, G. S. "The Tsar's Proposed Conference and Our
Foreign Affairs." Nineteenth C, 44 (Nov. 1898): 697-706.
An argument that irrespective of the motives which may have
prompted Nicholas II to issue his peace rescript, his proposal
to limit arms must be applauded since it resulted in international discussion of the most pressing problem in turn-of-the-
century European international affairs.

2029 *Clemens, Walter C., Jr. "Nicholas II to Salt II: Continuity
and Change in East-West Diplomacy." Int Aff, 49, no. 3
(1973): 385-401.
An argument that contemporary disarmament negotiation behavior bears "striking resemblances to the approach of Tsarist
Russia to the Hague Conference on the Limitation of Arma-
ments in 1899." Clemens asserts that the support for disarmament by both Nicholas II and Leonid Brezhnev can be
traced to the leaders' awareness of "Russia's technical and
material disadvantages vis-à-vis the west."

2030 Cowles, Virginia. "Chapters IX-X." RD (gen. study), 217-320.

A critical assessment of Nicholas II's foreign policy in light
of the larger thesis that Soviet imperialism is but a logical
extension of the diplomatic techniques and goals pursued by
Russia's last four tsars.

2031   "The Czar." Spectator, 74 (22 June 1895): 841-42.
A brief review of Nicholas II's initial diplomatic relations with
France, Japan, and Great Britain.

2032   "The Czar." Spectator, 81 (3 Dec. 1898): 823-24.
A review of the mechanics of the arbitration process proposed
by Nicholas II as a means of settling international disputes
peacefully. The author questions the practicality of Nicholas'
proposal but credits him with having good intentions and for
pointing Europe's leaders in a fruitful direction.

2033   "The Czar and His Concerns." RR, 20 (Sept. 1899): 276.
A brief commentary on the concerns facing Nicholas II upon
the turn of the century including his alliance with France,
the Hague Peace Conference, and the death of his brother.

2034   "The Czar and Universal Peace." Outlook, 60 (10 Sept. 1898):
116-17.
A restatement of Nicholas II's peace rescript, and a favorable
commentary on its noble intent.

2035   "The Czar in Paris." Spectator, 77 (10 Oct. 1896): 473-74.
A critical review of the French reception of Nicholas II upon
his visit to Paris. The author ridicules French officials for
casting aside their democratic values to fawn upon a man who
rules as a brutal autocrat over millions of impoverished subjects. The Frenchman's love of glitter, pomp, and parades
accounts for some of this spectacle, the author concludes, but
the desire to flaunt before the world the newly formed alliance
between France and Russia was the most pressing reason for the
fanfare with which Nicholas was greeted in Paris.

2036   "The Czar on Tour." RR, 14 (Dec. 1896): 724-25.
Nicholas II's 1896 visit to France prompted this article which
portrays his call for world peace as being hypocritical given
Russia's imperialistic record in the Near East.

2037   "Czar's Visit." Spectator, 44 (26 Sept. 1896): 389-90.
A call for British statesmen to press Nicholas II, who was then
visiting London, to assume the responsibility of protecting Armenia from the intense persecution that it was suffering at
the hands of the Turkish sultan. The author points out that
as an autocrat, Nicholas may choose, perhaps whimsically,
either to tolerate or counter Turkish policy in Armenia without any concern over the reaction of his subjects.

2038   "Dedication of the Monument to Alexander II."   Harper's W,
       42 (1 Oct. 1893):   974.
       A favorable commentary on Nicholas II as a humanitarian;
       prompted by his proposal for universal disarmament.

2039   Deniken, Anton I.   The Career of a Tsarist Officer.   Memoirs,
       1872-1916.   Margaret Patoski, trans.   Minneapolis: University
       of Minnesota Press, 1975, 333pp.
       These memoirs do not contain a titled section dealing with
       Nicholas II but are nonetheless of interest for the light they
       shed on the military establishment's reaction to his conduct of
       foreign and military affairs.   Of particular interest is General
       Deniken's criticism of a number of wartime decisions reached
       by Nicholas in response to the advice given by Rasputin
       through Empress Alexandra.   DK254.D45A313

2040   "Discord Between Czar Nicholas II and His Allies."   Cur Opin,
       59 (Sept. 1915):   156-57.
       A brief commentary on the concern shown by Russia's wartime
       allies for the impact that Nicholas' poor relations with the
       Duma might have upon the war effort and the monarchy's
       popularity.

2041   Dittmer, Helen R.   "The Russian Foreign Ministry Under
       Nicholas II: 1894-1914."   Universtiy of Chicago, 1977.
       (dissertation)

2042   Dod, Karl C.   "The Friendship of William II and Nicholas II
       and Its International Implications."   University of Illinois,
       1934.   (dissertation)

2043   Dubensky, Major-General.   "With the Tsar and the Tsarevich
       at the Front."   Twent Cent Rus, 2, no. 1 (1916):   31-33.
       A sympathetic description of the daily life of Nicholas II and
       his son while at the Russian front.   Dubensky stresses Nich-
       olas' concern for the welfare of the common soldier and dedica-
       tion to Russia's victory in a just war.

2044   *Esthus, R. A.   "Nicholas II and the Russo-Japanese War."
       Rus R, 40 (Oct. 1981):   396-411.
       An examination of Nicholas II's leadership during the Russo-
       Japanese War for insight into his character and personality.
       Esthus maintains that the popular assessment of Nicholas as
       an indecisive and weak ruler must be questioned in view of
       "the tenacity and resolution" which he demonstrated during
       the war and the peace making process.

2045   *Fay, Sidney B.   "Kaiser's Secret Negotiations with the Tsar;
       1904-1905."   Am Hist R, 24, no. 1 (1918):   48-72.
       An account of William II's clever manipulation of Nicholas II
       during the year's correspondence that preceded the 24 July

1905 signing of the secret Treaty of Bjorko. Fay also discusses the successful efforts of Nicholas' advisers in securing
an annulment of the treaty on the grounds that a defensive
military alliance with Germany was in direct conflict with Russia's existing alliance with France.

2046   *Florinsky, Michael T. "The Russian Mobilization of 1914."
Pol Sci Q, 52, no. 2 (1927): 203-27. Also in Sidney Harcave,
ed. Readings in Russian History, Vol. II. New York:
Thomas Y. Crowell, 1968, 134-50.
A reassessment of the motivation for and significance of Nicholas II's order of 31 July 1914 to mobilize the Russian army
in response to Austria's declaration of war on Serbia. Florinsky argues that Nicholas and Foreign Minister Sazonov did
everything in their power to settle the Balkan crisis peacefully. They yielded to the view of Russia's military leaders
that general mobilization was essential only after all other options had been ruled out by the force of circumstances. Florinsky also maintains that Nicholas, as well as the leaders of
Germany and Austria, did not believe that Russian mobilization
was tantamount to a declaration of war.

2047   *Ford, Thomas K. "The Genesis of the First Hague Peace
Conference." Pol Sci Q, 51, no. 3 (1936): 354-82.
An analysis of the origins of the 12 August 1898 "peace
rescript" of Nicholas II. Ford argues that despite statements
made by various Russian officials that the document "originated
in the Tsar's own initiative," the role played by Nicholas and
altruism in the genesis of the proposal was a negligible one.
Ford agrees that there were political and military advantages
to be gained by Russia through a moratorium on arms production and warfare but concludes that "the move was primarily the result of economic necessity."

2048   *Godwin, Robert K. "Russia and the Portsmouth Peace Conference." ASEER, 9, no. 4 (1950): 279-91.
An account of the steps which led Nicholas II to accept Theodore Roosevelt's offer to mediate the 1905 dispute between
Russia and Japan. Godwin focuses on the role played by
Roosevelt, Nicholas, and Sergei Witte in the resolution of the
deadlock that gripped the conference over Russia's refusal to
accept Japan's demands for payment of an indemnity and
possession of Sakhalin Island.

2049   *Golder, Frank A., ed. "The Empress and Rasputin as Military
Advisers." DRH (anthology), 213-19.
A series of 23 June 1915 to 17 December 1916 letters from
Alexandra to Nicholas II which illustrate how Rasputin's views
on both the war and military strategy were presented to Nicholas II as wise counsel that should be heeded for the good of
the nation.

2050 *_____. "Peace Preparation." Ibid., 63-81.
      A series of 5 May to 4 October 1916 letters from Grand Duke
      Nikolai Mikhailovich to Nicholas II in which the former expresses
      his opinion on the diplomatic and military situation in Europe
      and urges Nicholas to form, with great care, a special com-
      mission to prepare Russia for the peace conference which,
      eventually, would end World War I.

2051 Graham, Stephen. "Great White Tsar." Harper's W, 60 (6 Feb.
      1915): 124-25.
      A discussion of Nicholas II's recapturing of his image as "the
      Tsar of Peace" as a consequence of the favorable press he
      received as an ally of the Western nations fighting against
      German and Austrian imperialism.

2052 Grant, N. F., ed. The Kaiser's Letters to the Tsar. London,
      n.p., 1920, 281pp.
      Unavailable for annotation.

2053 Hale, Edward E. "Out of the Mouth of Czars." New Eng M,
      n.s. 19 (Jan. 1899): 580-85.
      A favorable commentary on Nicholas II's promotion of world
      peace by attempting to arrange a world disarmament confer-
      ence.

2054 Harden, Maximillan. "The Tsar of Russia (Nicolai Alexandro-
      vitsch)." Monarchs and Men. Philadelphia: John C. Win-
      ston Company, 1913, 167-208.
      An attack on Nicholas II for pursuit of an aggressive Far
      Eastern policy responsible for the outbreak of war with Japan.
      Harden also presents a lengthy apology, written in Nicholas'
      name, to the Russian people for prompting such a disaster
      and concludes with a plea to Nicholas to abdicate in favor of
      Grand Duke Michael.   CT106.H34

2055 Hargreaves, J. D. "Imperial Visit, 1901." Hist Today, 2,
      no. 3 (1952): 206-09.
      A discussion of French motivation for the proposal that
      Nicholas II visit France. Hargreaves believes that French
      leaders were moved by their desire to bolster France's inter-
      national status by parading before the world the tsar in Paris
      as the symbol of Franco-Russian solidarity.

2056 Jefferson, Margaret M., ed. "Lord Salisbury's Conversations
      with the Tsar at Balmoral, 27 and 29 September 1896." Slavonic
      E Eur R, 39, no. 92 (1960): 216-22.
      A reproduction of Lord Salisbury's memorandum of September
      1896 on his discussion with Nicholas II of "possible courses of
      action which the European powers might take in the Near East"
      to stabilize the political situation in that region.

2057 *Jelavich, Barbara. "Nicholas II." CRFP (gen. study), 222-
      86.
      A critical review of the foreign policy pursued by Nicholas II.
      Jelavich asserts that "the great period of Russian diplomacy
      in the nineteenth century" came to an end under Nicholas as
      a consequence of his pursuit of a policy far too aggressive in
      light of Russia's domestic condition and lack of military prow-
      ess. Jelavich sees Nicholas' personal limitations and those of
      the seven foreign ministers who served him before the 1917
      revolution as being the immediate source of Russia's disastrous
      foreign policy but adds that Nicholas' position as tsar was
      gravely complicated by his having to deal with the conse-
      quences of the alliance which he inherited and the patronage
      of Balkan nationalism by his Romanov predecessors.

2058 "Kaiser's Letters to the Czar." Cur Hist, 11, no. 3 (1920):
      525-31.
      A discussion of William II's letters to Nicholas II as an at-
      tempt by the kaiser to drive a wedge between Russia and
      her Western allies.

2059 *Katkov, George and Michael Futrell. "Russian Foreign Policy
      1880-1914." Russia Enters the Twentieth Century 1894-1917.
      Erwin Oberländer et al., eds. New York: Schocken Books,
      1971, 9-33.
      An examination of the forces which shaped the foreign policy
      pursued by Nicholas II prior to World War I. Katkov and
      Futrell identify three key factors which made Russian foreign
      policy extremely complex: the rapid development of railway
      communications, the marked increase in the destructive power
      of the instruments of war, and the emergence of an aggres-
      sive, Europeanized Japan on Russia's eastern border. The
      authors assert that Nicholas' awareness of these factors made
      him alert to the need for Russia, as a nation in its industrial
      infancy, to avoid war, and prompted him to issue his famous
      12 August 1898 note to the great powers in which he proposed
      a conference for the purpose of limiting the production of arms.
      DK262.R8813

2060 Langer, William. "Peace Dreams and Political Realities."
      The Diplomacy of Imperialism 1890-1902. New York: Alfred
      A. Knopf, 1968, 581-604.
      An analysis of the motivation behind Nicholas II's peace re-
      script. Langer maintains that Russia's inability to compete in
      an arms race and desire to maintain the military status quo in
      the Far East formed the foundation for the rescript, the gene-
      sis and contents of which were heavily influenced by Minister
      of War Kuropatkin, Minister of Finance Witte, and M. Basily,
      an official in the Foreign Office. Langer also notes that while
      Nicholas' motives certainly are questionable and the Hague

Conference itself failed to yield any practical results, the
tsar nonetheless was responsible for "the first step ... in
the direction of an international organization." D397.L82

2061   Laugel, A. "Nicholas II in Paris." Nation, 63 (5 Nov. 1896):
       261.
       A short note on Nicholas II's reception by French officials
       upon his visit to Paris. Laugel discusses the enthusiastic
       nature of the French response to Nicholas' arrival as a re-
       flection of France's need of Russia as an ally and not as a
       sign of any genuine respect or feeling for Nicholas.

2062   Lensen, George A. "The Attempt on the Life of Nicholas II
       in Japan." Rus R, 20, no. 3 (1961): 232-53.
       A recreation of the attempt on Tsarevich Nicholas' life on
       11 May 1891 in Otsu, Japan, and an account of the incident's
       aftermath, particularly Nicholas' decision to abort the remain-
       der of his trip.

2063   *Morrill, Dan L. "Nicholas II and the Call for the First Hague
       Conference." J Mod Hist, 46, no. 2 (1974): 296-313.
       An argument that the 12 August 1898 circular to members of
       the diplomatic corps of St. Petersburg which called for the
       convening of an international conference to limit the arms
       race was motivated by a mixture of genuine idealism and
       practical political and economic concerns. Morrill admits how-
       ever that while "neither pragmatism nor idealism monopolized
       the scene, ... the relative weight of the latter lost ground
       ... from the beginning," especially because of Nicholas' grow-
       ing realization that "the circular would further the interests
       of Russian foreign policy particularly in the Far East."

2064   "Nicholas II Prepares for a Long War." Cur Opin, 60 (Feb.
       1916): 87-88.
       A brief discussion of Nicholas II's realization that World War
       I would be a protracted conflict for which Russia was not pre-
       pared.

2065   Novikoff, Olga. "Another League of Nations." Asiatic R, 15,
       no. 42 (1919): 243-48.
       A sympathetic review of Nicholas II's 1898 proposal for the
       creation of a "league of nations," and a sharp attack on
       Kaiser William II of Germany for "the shipwrecking of that
       scheme."

2066   _____. "The Tsar and the Slavonic World." Asiatic R,
       no. 43 (1919): 425-30.
       A favorable commentary on Nicholas II's 1914 declaration that
       Russia had entered World War I as the leader of the entire
       Slavic world. Novikoff voices strong panslav views as she
       defends Nicholas as the champion of oppressed Balkan Slavs
       and a united Poland.

2067   Paoli, Xavier. "The Tsar Nicholas II and the Tsaritsa Alex-
       andra Feodorovna." Their Majesties As I Knew Them. A. T.
       Mattos, trans. New York: Sturgis and Walton, 1911, 127-61.
       Excerpt in McClure, 35 (May 1910): 3-17.
       Memoirs of the "Grand Chamberlain" of the Third Republic
       who served as liason between the French government and vis-
       iting foreign dignitaries. Paoli, who was in charge of security
       during the Romanovs' September 1901 visit to Paris, discusses
       the elaborate precautions taken to guarantee that there were
       no incidents destructive to Franco-Russian relations in any
       way. He also presents a very generous character sketch of
       both Nicholas and Alexandra and gives a few anecdotes to
       support his favorable statements on the royal couple's poise,
       charm, and affability. D352.1.P2

2068   *Renzi, William A. "Who Composed 'Sazonov's Thirteen Points?'
       A Re-Examination of Russia's War Aims of 1914." Am Hist R,
       88, no. 2 (1983): 347-57.
       An argument that the thirteen-point program of war aims sup-
       posedly composed by Russian Foreign Minister Sergei Sazonov
       in mid-September of 1914 and ratified, in a slightly different
       form, by Nicholas II later that year, did not constitute a docu-
       mentary statement of official Russian policy. Renzi maintains
       that the program was, in fact, the creation of the French
       Ambassador to St. Petersburg, Maurice Paléologue, who, on
       the basis of conversations with Sazonov and Nicholas II, pro-
       jected the war aims of Russia into a thirteen-point program
       of his own design and then forwarded this list to the French
       Foreign Minister Declassé as the official position of Nicholas
       II.

2069   Rodionoff, Count S. "What the Czar Thinks of King George
       of England." World T, 21 (Oct. 1911): 1230-33.
       A chamber attendant to Nicholas II reports that the tsar ex-
       pressed dislike for George V as a person and asserted that
       Russia had no need for its English ally.

2070   *Rogers, J. Guinness. "The Tsar's Proposed Conference and
       Our Foreign Affairs." Nineteenth C, 44 (Nov. 1898): 707-17.
       A critical account of public reaction to Nicholas II's peace
       rescript, and an assessment of the rescript's significance.
       Rogers states that the emotional idealism of those who accept
       the rescript at face value serves to encourage cynics who see
       no merit at all in the proposal. He contends that between
       such sentimentalism and contemptuous scorn there is a sane
       public posture which correctly judges Nicholas' proposal as
       an important opportunity to establish some method of settling
       international disputes of war.

2071   Schelking, Eugene de. Recollections of a Russian Diplomat.
       The Suicide of Monarchies. New York: Macmillan, 1918,
       255pp. Published in London as The Game of Diplomacy.

of the eleven letters which Stead sent to Nicholas II, while
the peace conference was in session, in which Stead advised
the tsar on world reaction to the conference and encouraged
him to support vigorously the cause of world peace.

2082 Wolfe, Bertram. "War Comes to Russia." <u>Rus R</u>, 22, no. 2
      (1963): 123-38.
      A discussion of the reaction in Russia to the outbreak of
      World War I with most attention given to the response by the
      various factions in the Duma to Nicholas II's manifesto of 2
      August 1914 which called for national unity.